J. H. (Joseph Henry) Shorthouse

John Inglesant

A Romance

J. H. (Joseph Henry) Shorthouse

John Inglesant
A Romance

ISBN/EAN: 9783744692267

Printed in Europe, USA, Canada, Australia, Japan

Cover: Foto ©Thomas Meinert / pixelio.de

More available books at **www.hansebooks.com**

JOHN INGLESANT

A Romance

Ἀγαπητοί, νῦν τέκνα Θεοῦ ἐσμεν, καὶ
οὔπω ἐφανερώθη τί ἐσόμεθα.

London
MACMILLAN AND CO.
1883

Dedication to the First Edition

TO

RAWDON LEVETT, Esq.

MY DEAR LEVETT

I dedicate the volume to you that I may have an opportunity of calling myself your friend.

J. HENRY SHORTHOUSE.

LANSDOWNE, EDGBASTON,
June 17, 1880.

PREFACE TO THE NEW EDITION.

EMBOLDENED by the kindness with which this book has been received, I venture to risk a few words of introduction to this new edition. The generous reception by the Press of a somewhat hazardous venture cannot be too specially or too warmly acknowledged by me.

The book is an attempt at a species of literature which I think has not hitherto had justice done to it, but which I believe to be capable of great things,—I mean Philosophical Romance. There will at once occur to the reader's mind numerous works of fiction of the highest talent, where philosophical ideas have been introduced with surpassing effect. By Nathaniel Hawthorne this art was carried to such perfection that it is only with difficulty that we perceive how absolutely every character, nay, every word and line, is subordinated to the philosophical idea of the book. There is another kind of philosophical romance, however, which allows the introduction of much which cannot find place in such a work of pure art. William Smith's *Thorndale* may be taken as in some sense indicating what I mean—books where fiction is used expressly for the purpose of introducing Philosophy. In such books, where philosophy is put first and fiction only second, it is evidently permissible to introduce much, and to introduce it in a way, which could not be tolerated in pure fiction. There have been works of the same character, where a small amount of fiction has been introduced, simply for the purpose of relating History. The reason, I conceive, of the comparative failure of these books has been that the philosophy has so far outweighed the romance, just as in historical fiction, as a rule, the opposite error has prevailed, romance so far outweighing history. As in the latter case I believe that all that is wanted to constitute an historical romance of the highest interest is the recovery of the detailed incidents of everyday life, and the awakening of the individual need and striving, long since quiet in the grave; so, in books where fiction is only used to introduce philosophy, I believe that it is not to be expected that human life is to be described simply as such. The characters are, so to speak, sublimated: they are only introduced for a set purpose, and having fulfilled this purpose—were it only to speak a dozen words—they vanish from the stage. Nor is this so unlike real life as may at first appear. Human life, as revealed to most of us, does not group itself in stage effect, does not arrange itself in elaborate plot; and brilliant dialogue declares the glory of the author more frequently than it increases reality of effect. If Fiction, therefore, is allowed to select and to condense from life, surely Philosophy may do so too. If we may view life from an artistic, or dramatic, or picturesque standpoint, using such incidents and characters only as meet one or other of these requirements, surely we may select incidents and characters with a philosophic intent. If we fail in combining real life and philosophy with sufficient *vraisemblance*, the failure be upon our own head: the attempt is not on that account declared impossible or undesirable. To compare such a book with the most successful efforts of the greatest masters of modern fiction, where everything is sacrificed to sparkling dialogue, to picturesque effect, to startling plot, is to aim beside the mark. Everything which these great masters have so successfully accomplished, it was, fortunately for me, my business carefully to avoid.

I have spoken of Romance as subordinate, but I should be sorry to be so misunderstood as to be supposed to undervalue this wonderful exertion of the imaginative faculty. In this prosaic age the patient toilers among the obscure details of scientific research need no apology. They and their followers preen and plume themselves, amid general applause, on their aristocratic standpoint, amid a general plebeian throng, thirsting for something of human interest, and colour, and life. This democratic rabble know by their own experience that it is only when these dry details are touched by the enchanter's wand that they strike them with any sense of reality, any likeness to beings of their own lineage—that these dry bones assume any appearance of life, any attribute of love, or pity, or even of hate. It will be the same with Philosophy. For centuries the people have utterly refused to recognize metaphysic as anything but a worthless jargon. Let us condescend to this simple, touching art taught us by the Provençal singers. Let us try to catch something of the skill of the great masters of Romance, of Cervantes and Le Sage, of Goethe and Jean Paul, and let us unite to it the most serious thoughts and speculations which have stirred mankind. If James Hinton had thrown the *Mystery of Pain* into the form of story, do you not think that for one sorrowful home which has been lightened by his singular genius, there would have been hundreds?—that in place of one sorrowing heart to which his message has brought peace and salvation, he might have reckoned thousands?

"But," you say, "it is only a Romance."

True. It is only human life in the "highways and hedges," and in "the streets and lanes of the city," with the ceaseless throbbing of its quivering heart; it is only daily life from the workshop, from the court, from the market, and from the stage; it is only kindliness and neighbourhood and child-life, and the fresh wind of heaven, and the waste of sea and forest, and the sunbreak upon the stainless peaks, and contempt of wrong and pain and death, and the passionate yearning for the face of God, and woman's tears, and woman's self-sacrifice and devotion, and woman's love. Yes, it is only a Romance. It is only the ivory gates falling back at the fairy touch. It is only the leaden sky breaking for a moment above the bowed and weary head, revealing the fathomless Infinite through the gloom. It is only a Romance.

It is a sad fall, doubtless, from such heights as these—heights, however, which none who remember a long roll of names, some of them most happily still with us, can think of as unapproachable—to the book which lies before us. Nevertheless this may be said for it, that it is an attempt, and an honest one, to blend together these three in one philosophy—the memory of the dead—the life of thought—the life of each one of us alone. Amid the tangled web of a life's story I have endeavoured to trace some distinct threads—the conflict between Culture and Fanaticism—the analysis and character of Sin—the subjective influence of the Christian Mythos.[1] I have ventured to depict the Cavalier as not invariably a drunken brute, and spiritual life and growth as not exclusively the possession of Puritans and Ascetics. I feel the responsibility of introducing real historical characters and orders of men into a work of this kind. My general defence must be that I have written nothing which I should not equally have set down in an historical or a controversial work.

J. H. S.

LANSDOWNE, EDGBASTON,
  October 18, 1881.

---

[1] Mythos. Eternal Truth manifested in Phenomena.

Memoirs of the Life
OF
MR. JOHN INGLESANT
SOMETIME SERVANT TO KING CHARLES I.

WITH

AN ACCOUNT OF HIS BIRTH, EDUCATION, AND TRAINING BY

THE JESUITS

AND

A PARTICULAR RELATION OF THE SECRET SERVICES

IN WHICH HE WAS ENGAGED

ESPECIALLY IN CONNECTION WITH THE LATE
IRISH REBELLION

WITH

SEVERAL OTHER REMARKABLE PASSAGES AND OCCURRENCES,

ALSO

A HISTORY OF HIS RELIGIOUS DOUBTS AND EXPERIENCES

AND OF THE MOLINISTS OR QUIETISTS IN ITALY

IN WHICH COUNTRY HE RESIDED FOR MANY YEARS

WITH AN ACCOUNT OF

THE ELECTION OF THE LATE POPE

AND

MANY OTHER EVENTS AND AFFAIRS.

JOHN INGLESANT.

INTRODUCTORY CHAPTER.

DURING my second year at Oxford I became acquainted with a Roman Catholic gentleman, the eldest son of a family long resident on the borders of Shropshire towards Wales. My friend, whose name was Fisher, invited me to his home, and early in my last long vacation I accepted his invitation. The picturesque country was seen to great advantage in the lovely summer weather. That part of Shropshire partakes somewhat of the mountain characteristics of Wales, combined with the more cultivated beauties of English rural scenery. The ranges of hills, some of which are lofty and precipitous, which intersect the country, form wide and fertile valleys which are watered by pleasant streams. The wide pastures are bordered by extensive plantations covering the more gradual ascents, and forming long lines along the level summits. We had some miles to drive even from the small station on the diminutive branch line of railway which had slowly conveyed us the last dozen miles or so of our journey. At last, just at the foot of one of the long straight hills, called Edges in that country, we came upon my friend's house, seen over a flat champaign of pasture land, surrounded by rows of lofty trees, and backed by fir and other wood, reaching to the summit of the hill behind it. It was an old and very picturesque house, jumbled together with the additions of many centuries, from the round tower-like staircase with an extinguisher turret, to a handsome addition of two or three years ago. Close by was the mutilated tower of a ruined priory, the chancel of which is used as the parish church. A handsome stone wing of one story, built in the early Gothic style, and not long completed, formed the entrance hall and dining-room, with a wide staircase at the back. The hall was profusely hung with old landscapes and family portraits. After a short introduction to my friend's family, we were soon assembled in the newly finished dining-room, with its stone walls and magnificent overhanging Gothic fireplace. The dinner party consisted of my friend's father and mother, his two sisters, and a Roman Catholic clergyman, the family chaplain and priest of a neighbouring chapel which Mr. Fisher had erected and endowed. The room was hung entirely with portraits, several of them being ecclesiastics in different religious costumes, contrasting, to my eyes, strangely with the gay cavaliers and the beautiful ladies of the Stuarts' Court, and the not less elaborately dressed portraits of the last century, and with those of my host and hostess in the costume of the Regency. I was struck with the portrait which happened to be opposite me, of a young man with a tonsured head, in what appeared to me to be a very simple monk's dress, and I asked the Priest, a beautiful and mild-looking old man, whom it was intended to represent.

"A singular story is attached to that portrait," he said, "which, it may surprise you to learn, is not that of a—a member of our communion. It is the portrait of a young Englishman named Inglesant, a servant of King Charles the First, who was very closely connected with the Roman Catholics of that day, especially abroad, and was employed in some secret negotiations between the King and the Catholic gentry; but the chief interest connected with his story consists in some very remarkable incidents which took place abroad, connected with the murderer of his only brother—incidents which exhibit this young man's character in a noble and attractive light. He is connected with Mr. Fisher's family solely through the relations of his brother's wife, but, singularly, he is buried not far from here, across the meadows. In the latter years of his life he purchased an estate in this neighbourhood, though it was not his native country, and founded an almshouse, or rather hospital for lunatics, in the chapel in which his tomb is still standing. That portrait, in which he appears in the dress of a novice," he continued, turning to the one before me, "was taken in Rome, when he was residing at the English college, where he certainly was received, as he appears to have been generally when abroad, into full communion with us. As a contrast to it, I will show you another in the drawing-room, by Vandyke,

which, though it really was intended for his brother, yet may equally well represent himself, as, at that period, the two brothers are said to have been so exactly alike that they could not be known apart. On his tomb at Monk's Lydiard, as you may see if you incline to take the trouble to walk so far—and it is a pleasing walk—he is represented in his gown of bachelor of civil law, a degree which he received at Oxford during the civil war, and he is there also represented with tonsured head. I have often thought," continued the Priest, musingly, "of arranging a considerable collection of papers referring to this gentleman's story, which is at present in the library; or at least of writing out a plain statement of the facts; but it would be better done, perhaps, by a layman. I have the authority of these young ladies," he continued, with a smile, turning to the Miss Fishers, "that the story is a more entertaining and even exciting one than the sensational novels of the day, of which, I need not say, I am not a judge."

The young ladies confirmed this as far as their knowledge went; but they had heard only fragments of the story, and were urgent with the clergyman to set about the task. He, however, replied to their entreaties only by a shake of the head; and the ladies soon after left the room.

When we went into the drawing-room, I was eager to see the Vandyke, and was shown a magnificent picture at one end of the room, representing a singularly handsome young man, in a gorgeous satin court dress of the reign of Charles the First, whose long hair and profusion of lace and ornament would probably, in the work of another artist, have produced an unpleasing impression, but, softened by the peculiar genius of Vandyke, the picture possessed that combination of splendour and pathos which we are in the habit of associating only with his paintings. His satin shoes and silk stockings contrasted curiously with the grass on which the cavalier stood, and the sylvan scene around him; and still more so with his dogs and two horses, which were held at some little distance by a page. His face was high and noble, but on closely comparing it—as I did several times—with that of the Monk in the dining-room, I arrived at the conclusion that either the likeness between the brothers was exaggerated, or the expression of the survivor must have altered greatly in after years; for no difference in dress, great as was the contrast between the coarse serge of the novice and the satin of the cavalier, and between the close-cropped tonsured head and the flowing love locks, would account for the greater strength and resolve of the portrait in the dining-room, combined, strangely, as this expression was, with a slightly wild and abstracted look, indicating either religious enthusiasm, or perhaps unsettlement of the reason within; this latter expression being totally wanting in the face of the cavalier.

The next day was Sunday, and I opened my window on a lovely prospect of lawn and water, with the fir woods sweeping up the hill-sides beyond. Walking out in the avenue when I was dressed, I met the family returning from low mass at the Chapel. I attended high mass with them at eleven o'clock. The Chapel was picturesquely built higher up in the wood than the house. It had a light and graceful interior, and the coverings of the altar were delicate and white. The exquisite, plaintive music, the pale glimmer of the tapers in the morning sunlight, the soothing perfume of the incense, the sense of pathetic pleading and of mysterious awe, as if of the possibility of a Divine Presence, produced its effect on me, as it does, I imagine, on most educated Churchmen; but this effect failed in convincing me (then, as at other times) that there was more under that gorgeous ceremonial than may be found under the simpler Anglican ritual of the Blessed Sacrament. After church, my friend, who had some engagement with the Priest, accepted my assurance that I was fond of solitary walks; and I set off alone on my quest of the tomb of John Inglesant.

I followed a footpath which led direct from the ruined Church near the house, across the small park-like enclosure, into the flat meadows beyond. The shadows of the great trees lay on the grass, the wild roses and honeysuckle covered the hedges, a thousand butterflies fluttered over the fields. That Sunday stillness which is, possibly, but the echo of our own hearts, but which we fancy marks the day, especially in the country, soothed the sense. The service in the morning had not supplied the sacrament to me, but it had been far from being without the sense of worship; and the quiet country in the lovely summer weather, in connection with it, seemed to me then, as often, the nearest foretaste we can gain of what the blissful life will be. As I went on, the distant murmur of Church bells came across the meadows, and following a footpath for a couple of miles, I came to the Hospital or Almshouse, standing amid rows of elms, and having a small village attached to it, built probably since its erection. The bells which I had heard, and which ceased a little before I reached the place, were in a curious turret or cupola attached to the Chapel, which formed one side of the court. The buildings were of red brick, faced with stone, in the latest style of the Stuart architecture. The door of the Chapel was wide open, and I entered and dropped into a seat just as the Psalms began. The room was fitted in a style exactly corresponding to the outside; a circular recess at the upper end took the place of chancel, lighted with three windows, which were filled with innumerable small panes of glass. The altar was richly draped; and on it, besides vases of flowers, were two massive candlesticks of an antique pattern, and an old painting, apparently of the Virgin and Child. The lower walls of the chancel and of the whole Chapel were panelled, and the whole had a flat ceiling of panelled oak, painted in the centre with a sun with rays. Partly in the chancel, and partly in the Chapel, the surpliced choir was accommodated in stalls or pews, and the organ and pulpit, in elaborate carved mahogany, completed the interior. There was a good congregation: and from this, and from many tablets on the walls, I gathered that the Chapel was used by the neighbourhood as probably being nearer than the Parish Churches. The soft afternoon light filled the place, gilding the old brasswork, and lighting up the dark carving and the sombre narrow pews. The music was of a very high class, deliciously sung, and I found afterwards that there was an endowment especially for the choir, and that the chaplains were required to be musical. The service bore comparison favourably with the morning's mass, and a short sermon followed. When all was over, and the people were gone out into the sunshine, I began to look for the tomb I had come to see, and the chaplain, having come out of the vestry, and seeming to expect it, I went up and spoke to him. I told him I had walked from Lydiard —my friend's house—to see the tomb of the founder, to which I had been directed by the Roman Catholic gentleman who resided there. He was well acquainted with Father Arnold, he told me, and took me at once to the tomb, which was in a recess by the altar, screened from view by the choir seats. There he lay, sure enough, just as the Priest had told me, carved from head to foot in alabaster, in his gown of bachelor of civil law, and his tonsured head. The sculptor had understood his work; the face was life-like, and the likeness to the portrait was quite perceptible. The inscription was curious—"sub marmore isto Johannes Inglesant, Peccator, usque ad judicium latet, expectans revelationem filiorum Dei."

I told the Chaplain what Father Arnold had told me of this man's story, and of the materials that existed for writing it. He had heard of them too, and even examined them.

"The Priest will never write it," he said.

"Why do not you ?" I asked.

He laughed. "I am a musician," he said, "not an author. You seem more interested in it than most people; you had better do it."

As I came back across the fields I pondered over this advice; and after dinner I asked the Priest the story. He told me the outline, and the next morning took me into the library, and showed me the papers.

The library at Lydiard is a very curious room below the level of the ground, and in the oldest part of the house. It adjoins the tower with the extinguisher turret, by which there is communication with the bed chambers, and with the leads and garrets at the top of the house. The room was large, and had several closets besides a smaller room beyond, which had no visible communication except into the library, but the Priest showed me a secret doorway and staircase, which, he said, descended into the cellars. Both these rooms and the closets were crammed with books, the accumulation of four hundred years—most of them first editions, and clean as when they came from the binder, but browned and mellowed with age. Early works of the German press, a Caxton, the scarce literature of the sixteenth century—all the books which had once been fashionable—Cornelius Agrippa, and Cardan, two or three editions of the Euphues, folios of Shakespeare and the dramatists, and choice editions of the literature of the seventeenth and eighteenth centuries, down to our own day. Besides this general literature, there was a large collection of Roman Catholic works and pamphlets, many privately printed at home or published abroad; biographies of Seminary Priests who had suffered death in England, reports of trials, private instructions, and even volumes of private letters, for Lydiard had always been a secure hiding-place for the hunted priests, and more than one had died there, leaving all his papers in the library. No fitter place could exist in which to attempt the task I had already determined to undertake, and I obtained leave of the Priest, promising to make nothing public without his approval. I had the whole vacation before me; too idle and desultory to read for honours, I had always been fond of literature and the classics, and was safe for my degree, and I gave myself up unreservedly to my task. I have endeavoured, as Father Arnold said, to tell a plain story. I have no pretensions to dramatic talent, and I deprecate the reader's criticism. If I have caught anything of the religious and social tone of the seventeenth century, I am more than content.

GEOFFREY MONK, M.A.

CHAPTER I.

WHEN Cromwell, Earl of Essex, was in the zenith of his power, and was engaged in completing the suppression of the smaller monasteries before commencing on the greater,—he had in his service a young gentleman named Richard Inglesant, the son of a knight, and descended from a knightly family, originally of Flanders, who had come into England with the Princess of Hainault. This young man was of an attractive person, a scholar, active and useful in many ways, and therefore a favourite with his master. One evening in the end of June 1537, he was sent for by Cromwell into the great gallery of his magnificent house in Throgmorton Street, where he found his master walking up and down in thought.

"You must be ready to depart at once, Richard," he said, "into Wiltshire. I have in this commission appointed you Visitor of the Priory of Westacre, six miles south of Malmsbury, on the way into Somerset, which they call the Priory in the Wood. The King's Grace is resolved on the suppression of this house, as a priory; but note very carefully what I tell you;—it will be for your guidance. Great interest has been made to his Grace's Highness on behalf of this house, both by many of the gentry dwelling thereabout, and also by the common people by the mouth of the Mayor of Malmsbury. They say the house is without any slander or evil fame; that it stands in a waste ground, very solitary, keeping such hospitality, that except with singular good management it could not be maintained though it had half as much land again as it has, such a number of the poor inhabitants nigh thereunto are daily relieved. The Prior is a right honest man, and well beloved of all the inhabitants therewith adjoining, having with him, in the house, eight religious persons, being priests of right good conversation, and living religiously. They spend their time in writing books with a very fair hand, in making garments for the poor people, in printing or graving. Now the prayer of these people is that the King's Highness shall translate this priory into a college, and so continue as many of the priests as the lands will maintain for the benefit of the neighbours; and the King is much inclined to do this. Now, on the other hand, this house has a proper lodging, where the Prior lay, with a fair garden and an orchard, very meet to be bestowed on some friend of mine, and some faithful servant of the King's Grace. There is no small number of acres ready sown with wheat, the tilth ordered for barley; the house and grounds are well furnished with plate, stuff, corn, cattle; the woods well saved, and the hedgerows full of timber, as though the Prior had looked for no alteration of his house. I had set mine hand on this house for a friend of mine, but the King's Grace is determined upon this:—if the Prior will surrender the house in a discreet and frank manner, and will moreover, on Sunday next, which is the Feast of the most Precious Blood, after mass, to which all the neighbouring people shall have been called, in his sermon, make mention of the King's title of Supreme Head, and submit himself wholly, in all matters spiritual, to the King's Grace, under Christ, the house shall be continued as a college, and no man therein disturbed, and not so much as an ounce of plate taken, that they may pray God Almighty to preserve the King's Grace with His blessed pleasure. Now I send you on this mission because, if things go as I think they may, I mean this house for you; and there is so much clamour about this business that I will have no more hands in it than I can help. Take two or three of the men with you whom you can trust; but see you fail not in one jot in the course you take with the Prior, for should it come to the King's ears that you had deceived the Prior—and it surely would so come to his Grace—your head would not be your own for an hour, and I should doubt, even, of my own favour with the King."

Richard Inglesant was on horseback before daylight the next morning; and riding by easy stages, arrived at Malmsbury at last, and slept a night there, making inquiries about the way to Westacre. At Malmsbury, and at all the villages where he stopped, he heard nothing but what agreed with what Cromwell had told him; and what he heard seemed to make him loiter still more, for he slept at Malmsbury a second night, and then did not go forward to Westacre till noonday. In the middle of the summer afternoon he crossed the brow of the hilly common, and saw the roofs of the Priory beneath him surrounded by its woods. The country all about lay peaceful in the soft, mellow sunlight; wide slopes of wood, intermixed with shining water, and the quiet russet downs stretching beyond. Richard had sent on a man the day before to warn the Prior, who had been expecting his coming all day. The house stood with a little walled court in front of it, and a gate-house; and consisted of three buildings—a chapel, a large hall, and another building containing the Prior's parlour and other rooms on the ground floor, and a long gallery or dormitory above, out of which opened other chambers; the kitchens and stables were near the latter building, on the right side of the court. The Prior received Inglesant with deference, and took him over the house and gardens, pointing out the well-stocked fish-ponds and other conveniences, with no apparent wish of concealing anything. Richard was astonished at the number of books, not only in the book-room, but also in the Prior's own chamber; these latter the Prior seemed anxious he should not examine. As far as Richard could see, they were, many of them, chemical and magical books. He supped with the Prior in hall, with the rest of the household, and retired with him to the parlour afterwards, where cakes and spiced wine were served to them, and they remained long together. Inglesant delivered his commission fairly to his host, dwelling, again and again, on every particular, while the Prior sat silent or made but short or inconclusive replies. At last Inglesant betook himself to rest in the guest-chamber, a room hung with arras, opening from the gallery where the monks slept, towards the west; one of his servants slept also in the dormitory near his door. The Prior's care had ordered a fire of wood on the great hearth that lighted up the carved bed and the hunting scene upon the walls. He lay long and could not sleep. All night long, at intervals, came the sound of chanting along the great hall and up the stairs into the dormitory, as the monks sung the service of matins, lauds, and prime. His mind was ill at ease. A scholar, and brought up from boyhood at the Court, he had little sympathy with the new doctrines, and held the simple and illiterate people who mostly followed them in small esteem. He was strongly influenced by that mysterious awe which the Romish system inspires in the most careless, even when it is not strong enough to influence their lives. The mission he had undertaken, and the probable destruction of this religious house, and the expulsion of its inmates for his benefit, frightened him, and threatened him with unknown penalties and terrors hereafter which he dared not face. He lay listlessly on his bed listening to the summer wind, and when at last he fell asleep, it was but a light fitful slumber, out of which he woke ever and anon to hear the distant chanting of the monks, and see by the flickering fire-light the great hounds coursing each other over the walls of his room.

In the morning he heard mass in the Chapel, after which the Prior sent a message to explain his absence, informing him that he was gone to Malmsbury to consult with his friends there how he might best serve the King's Grace. All that morning Richard Inglesant sat in the hall receiving the evidence of all who came before him (of whom there was no lack)—of the neighbours, gentry and country people. He evidently examined them with great care and acuteness, noting down every answer in a fair clerkly hand, exactly as he received it, neither extenuating anything nor adding the least word. He also in the same report kept an exact account of how he passed his time while at Westacre. There appears—as Cromwell had said—not to have been the least breath of scandal against the Prior or any of the priests in the house. The only report at all injurious to the character of the Prior seems to have been an opinion—oftentimes hinted at by the witnesses—that he was addicted to the study of chemistry and magic; that, besides his occult books, he had in his closet in his chamber a complete chemical apparatus with which he practised alchemy, and was even said to be in possession of the Elixir of Life. These reports Inglesant does not appear to have paid much attention to, probably regarding them as not necessarily coming within the limits of his commission; and, indeed, there is evidence of his having acted with the most exact fairness throughout the investigation, more than once putting questions to the witness, evidently for the purpose of correcting misapprehensions which told against the Prior. After dinner he rode out to the downs to a gentleman who had courteously sent him word that he was coursing with greyhounds: he, however, was not absent from the Priory long, declining the gentleman's invitation to supper. After he had supped he spent the rest of the evening in his own chamber, reading what he calls

"Ovidii Nasonis metamorphoseos libri moralizati," an edition of which, printed at Leipsic in 1510, he had found in the Prior's room.

The next forenoon he spent in the same manner as the last, the people flocking in voluntarily to give their evidence in favour of the house. A little after noon the Prior came back, travelling on foot and alone. As he came along he was thinking of the words of the gospel which promise great things to him who gives up houses and land for the Lord's sake.

When he reached the brow of the hill from which he could see the three red-tiled roofs of the Priory peeping out from among the trees, with the gardens and the green meadows, and the cattle seen here and there, he stood long to gaze. The air was soft and yet fresh, and the woods stretching up the rising-grounds about the Priory were wavering and shimmering all over with their myriad rustling leaves, instinct with life and beauty both to the ear and eye; a perpetual change from light to shadow, from the flight of the fleecy clouds, would have made the landscape dazzling but for the green on which the eye dwelt with a sense of rest to the wearied and excited brain. A gentle sound and murmur, as of happy and contented beings, made itself softly felt rather than heard, through the noontide air. "Omnes qui relinquunt patrem, domos, uxorem," said the Prior; but his eyes were so dim that he stumbled as he went on down the hill.

Richard Inglesant and he were some time alone together that evening. Whether the Prior prepared him at all for the course he had determined to pursue, does not appear, but certainly he did not, to any great extent.

The next day was Sunday, being the "Feast of the most Precious Blood"—a Sunday long remembered in that country side. The people, for a score of miles round, thronged to hear the Prior's sermon. The Mayor of Malmsbury was there; but the clergy of the Abbey, it was noticed, were not present. The little Chapel would not hold a tithe of the people—indeed few more than the gentry and their ladies, who came in great numbers, were allowed admission. Richard Inglesant and the Sheriff had Fald-stools in front of the altar, where they remained kneeling the whole of mass. The doors and windows of the Chapel were opened, that the people outside might assist at the celebration. They stood as thick as they could be packed in the little courtyard, and up the sloping fields around the Priory, listening in silence to the music of the mass; and at the sound of the bell the whole multitude fell on their knees as one man, remaining so for several minutes. Mass being over, the Prior came in procession from the Chapel to where a small wooden pulpit had been set up just outside the gate-house, in front of which seats were placed for the Sheriff and Inglesant, and the chief gentry. The silence was greater than ever, when the Prior, who had changed the gorgeous vestments in which he had celebrated mass, and appeared only as a simple monk, ascended the pulpit and began to preach. The Prior was a great preacher; a small and quiet man enough to look at, when he entered the pulpit he was transfigured. His form grew dignified, his face lighted up with enthusiasm, and his voice, even in the open air, was full and clear, and possessed that magical property of reaching the hearts of all who heard him, now melted into tenderness, and now raised to firm resolve. He began with the text that had haunted his memory the day before, and the first part of his sermon was simply an earnest and eloquent exhortation to follow Christ in preference to anything beside on earth. Then, warming in his subject, he answered the question (speaking that magnificent English tongue that even now rings in the pages of Foxe), Where was Christ? and urging the people to follow Him as He manifested Himself in the Church, and especially in the sacrament of the altar. Then suddenly throwing aside all reserve, and with a rapidity of utterance and a torrent of eloquence that carried his hearers with him, he rushed into the question of the day, brought face to face the opposing powers of the State and Christ, hurled defiance at the former, and while not absolutely naming the King or his Council, denounced his policy in the plainest words. Then, amid the swaying of the excited crowd, and a half-stifled cry and murmur, he suddenly dropped his voice, pronounced the formal benediction, and shrank back, to all appearance, into the quiet, timid monk.

It is needless to describe the excitement and astonishment of the crowd. The Prior and his procession with difficulty returned to the Chapel through the press. The Sheriff and Richard Inglesant, who with the other leading gentry had affected perfect unconsciousness that anything unusual was taking place, entered the hall of the Priory, and the Prior had a message sent into the sacristy that the King's commissioner desired to see him immediately in the parlour.

When the Prior entered, Inglesant was standing upon the hearth; he was pale, and his manner was excited and even fierce.

"You are a bold man, master Prior," he said almost before the other was in the room; "do you know that you have this day banished yourself and all your fellowship into the world without shelter and without help? Nay, I know not but the King's Grace may have you up to answer for this day with your life! Do you know this?"

The Prior looked him steadily in the face, but he was deadly pale, and his manner was humble and cowed.

"Yes, I know it," he said.

"Well," continued the other still more excitedly, "I call you to witness, master Prior, as I shall before the throne of God Almighty, that I have neither hand nor part in this day's work; that you have brought this evil upon yourself by your own deed and choice, by no want of warning and no suddenness on my part, but by your own madness alone."

"It is very true," said the Prior.

"I must to horse," said Inglesant, scarcely heeding him, "and ride post to my lord. It is as much as my head is worth should any rumour of this day's business reach the King's Grace by any other tongue than mine. You will stay here under the Sheriff's guard; but I fear you will too soon hear what a tragedy this day's play has been for you! God have you in His keeping, Prior! for you have put yourself out of all hope of mercy from the King's Grace."

He might have said more, but an alarming noise made him hasten into the hall. The most lawless and poorest of the people—of whom numbers had mingled in the crowd in the hope of spoil, taking for granted that the house was dissolved —had made an attack upon the Chapel and the Prior's lodging, and it was some time before the Sheriff, assisted by Inglesant and the other gentlemen and their servants, all of whom were armed, could restore order. When this was done, and the peaceable people and women reassured, Inglesant's horses were brought out, and he mounted and rode off through the dispersing but still excited and lawless crowds, leaving the Priory to a strong guard of the Sheriff's men. As he rode up the hill —the people shrinking back to let him pass—he muttered, bitterly:

"A fine piece of work we have set our hands to, with all

the rascal people of the country to aid. And why should not the Poverty get some of the droppings, when the Gentry cuts the purse?"

Travelling at a very different pace from that at which he had ridden from London, he reached the city the next night, and went at once to the Lord Cromwell, who, the next morning, took him to the King, to whom he gave a full account of what had occurred. Henry—who appears to have been induced to form his previous intention by the influence of a gentleman at Court who probably had his private expectations with regard to the future possession of the Priory—seems to have really cared little about the matter. He was, however, highly incensed at the Prior's sermon, and made no difficulty of immediately granting the Priory to Richard Inglesant. A pursuivant was sent down to bring the Prior up to London to be examined before the Council, but it does not appear that he ever was examined. Probably Inglesant exerted his influence with Cromwell in his behalf, for Cromwell examined him himself, and appears to have informed the King that he was harmless and mad. At any rate, he was set at liberty; and his troubles appear to have actually affected his reason, for he is said to have returned to the neighbourhood of Malmsbury, and to have wandered about the Priory at nights. The other inmates of the Priory had been dispersed, and the house taken possession of by Inglesant's servants; but he himself seems to have taken but little pleasure in his new possession, for it was more than a year before he visited it; and when he did so, events occurred which increased his dislike to the place.

It was late in October when his visit took place, and the weather was wild and stormy. He slept in the Prior's guest-chamber, which was in the same state as when he had occupied it before. The wind moaned in the trees, and swept over the roofs and among the chimneys of the old house. In the early part of the night he had a terrible dream, or what was rather partly a dream and partly a feverish sense of the objects around him. He thought he was lying in the bed in the room where he really was, and could not sleep; a fierce contention of the elements and of some powers more fearful than the elements seemed going on outside. The room became hateful to him, with its dark, hearse-like bed and the strange figures on the tapestry, which seemed to his bewildered fancy to course each other over the walls with a rapidity and a fantastic motion which made his senses reel. He thought that, unable to remain where he was, he rose and went out into the old dormitory, now silent and deserted, from one end of which he could look into the courtyard, while from the other he could see a dark mass of woodland, and a lurid distant sky. On this side all was quiet; but the courtyard seemed astir. The moon shone with the brightness of day on the mouldering, ivy-grown walls, and on the round pebble stones between which the long grass was growing all over the court. The wind swept fiercely across it, and splashes of rain, every now and then, made streaks in the moonlight like fire; strange voices cried to him in an unknown language, and undistinguished forms seemed passing to and fro. The Chapel was all alight, and low and mournful music proceeded from it, as for the dead. Fascinated with terror, he left the gallery and descended into the court. An irresistible impulse led him to the Chapel, which was open, and he went in. As he did so, voices and strange forms seemed to rush forward to enter with him, and an overwhelming horror took possession of him. Inside, the Chapel was hung with black; cowled forms filled the stalls, and chanted, with hollow, shadowy voices, a dirge for the departed. A hooded and black form stood before the altar, celebrating the mass. · The altar was alight with tapers, and torches were borne by sable attendants on either side of the choir. The ghostly forms that entered with him now thronged about him in the form and habit of living men. Voices called from without, and were answered from within the Chapel; rushing sounds filled the air as though the trees were being torn up, and the Chapel and house rocked. There was no coffin nor pall, nor any sign of mourning; and it seemed to Inglesant that he was present at the celebration of some obyte, or anniversary of the death of one long departed, over whom a wild and ghostly lamentation was made by beings no longer of the earth. An inexpressible dread and sorrow lay upon him—an overwhelming dread, as if the final Reckoning were near at hand, and all hope taken away—sorrow, as though all whom he had ever loved and known lay before him in death, with the solemn dirge and placebo said over them by the ghostly choir. The strain was too intense and painful to be borne, and with a cry, he awoke.

Utterly incapable of remaining where he was, he dressed,

and went out into the gallery, and down into the courtyard. The court was lighted by the moonlight as brightly as in his dream for one moment, and then was totally dark from the passing clouds flitting over the moon. All was calm and still. A small door in the corner of the court near the Chapel was open, and, surprised at this, Inglesant crossed over and passed through it. It led into the graveyard of the Priory outside the Chapel, where the monks and some of the country people had been used to bury their dead. It was walled round, but the wall at the farther side was old and ruinous, and had partly fallen down. As Inglesant reached the postern door, the moon shone out brightly, and he saw, between himself and the ruined wall, a wasted and cowled figure slowly traversing the rows of graves. For a moment he felt a terror equal to that of his dream, but the next the thought of the Prior flashed upon his mind, and he crossed the graveyard and followed silently in the track of the figure. The ghostly form reached the opposite wall, and commenced, with some substance that shone like fire, to draw magic figures upon the stones of one of its most perfect parts. Placing himself in a position evidently indicated by these geometrical figures, he carefully observed the precise spot where his shadow was projected on the wall before him by the moonlight, and going to this spot, he carefully loosened and removed a stone. By this time Inglesant was close upon him, and saw him take from within the wall an antique glass or vial, of a singular and occult shape. As he raised it, some slight motion the other made caused him to turn round, and at the sight of Inglesant he dropped the magic glass upon the stone he had removed, and shattered it to pieces. When he saw what had happened, the strange and weird creature threw his arms above his head, and with a piercing cry that rang again and again through the chill night air, fell backwards senseless, and lay in the pale moonlight white and still among the graves. Inglesant removed him into the house, and he was restored to sense, but scarcely to reason. He lived for more than five years, never leaving the Priory, where Inglesant directed that all his wants should be attended to, wandering about the gardens, and sometimes poring over his old books, which still remained upon his shelves. Inglesant never saw him again; but when he died the old man sent him his blessing, and was buried before the altar in the Chapel, where all

c

the Priors of the house had lain before him; he on whom the evil days, which they perhaps had merited but had escaped, had fallen, and had crushed.

CHAPTER II.

RICHARD INGLESANT never, till the last few years of his life, lived at Westacre, and visited it very seldom. He was a successful courtier; and at Cromwell's fall became a servant of the King. He married, and lived entirely at the Court. He was all his life a Catholic at heart, but conformed outwardly to the religion of the hour. He had one son, named after him, who was educated at Oxford, and intended for the bar, but his father left him so considerable a fortune that he was independent of any profession. That Richard Inglesant left no more than he did, shows that he adhered through life to the line of conduct we have seen him pursue at Westacre—conduct which probably satisfied his conscience as being rigidly exact and honest. On Henry's death he still retained one of his places about the Court; but on King Edward's death, being a partisan of Queen Mary's and a hearty conformer, he became a great favourite, and held a lucrative post. He visited Westacre more frequently, and built a stately range of buildings on one side of the court, where formerly the old stables and kitchen were, no doubt for his son's sake, enlarging the garden on that side to form a terrace in front of the new rooms. At Queen Mary's accession service was recommenced in the Prior's Chapel, which was repaired and fitted up afresh, and a regular priest appointed to serve it. Inglesant's name does not appear in the trials of the Protestants, a circumstance which makes it appear probable that he was true to the temporizing policy of his youth, and kept his zeal under good control. When Elizabeth came to the throne, the service in the Chapel underwent some modification, King Edward's Service Book being used. The service then had been found so useful to the neighbours that the parish petitioned for its continuance, and it was legally settled as a chapelry. The priest conformed to the new order of things, and Richard Inglesant—who at that time resided constantly at Westacre—attended the service regularly. He remained a

Catholic, but during the first seven years of Queen Elizabeth's reign, which were all he lived to see, the Catholics generally came to their Parish Churches until forbidden by the Pope's Bull. It remained, therefore, for his son, who was eighteen years of age at his father's death, to declare himself; and he conformed to the usage of the English Church. He resided entirely at Westacre, with an occasional visit to Court, keeping open-handed hospitality, and slightly embarrassing the estate, though, like his father, he had only one child. He was a favourer of the Papists, and once or twice was in trouble on that account; but being perfectly loyal, and a very popular man, he was rather a favourite with the Queen, who always noticed him when he came to Court, and was wont to say that "the dry crust Dick Inglesant gave a Papist should never choke him while she lived." He lived beyond the term of years usual in his family, and died in 1629, at the age of eighty-two, having been for the last twenty years of his life, since the death of the Queen, entirely under the guidance of his son, very much to his own advantage, as during those black years for the Papists, he would most probably have committed imprudences which might have been his ruin. His son, whose name was Eustace, was a shrewd lawyer and courtier. He was—much more than his father—a Papist at heart, but he conformed strictly to the English Church, and possessed considerable indirect influence at Court. He was thought much of by the Catholics, who regarded him as one of their most powerful friends. He married young, in 1593, but he had no children by his first wife, who died in 1610; and in 1620 he married again, a Catholic lady who was his ward. With this lady he came to reside at Westacre; but two years after, his wife died in giving birth to two boys; and, disgusted with the country, he left the two infants to their grandfather's care and returned to London, visiting Westacre, however, regularly at intervals; where, with a small number of servants, the old gentleman, totally forgetful of his old hospitality, and of his friends the Papists, spent his last days with the greatest delight, in anxiously watching over his little grandchildren. They were beautiful boys, so exactly alike that it was impossible to tell them apart, and from their earliest infancy so united in love to each other that they became a proverb in the neighbourhood. The eldest was named Eustace, after his father; but the youngest, at the entreaty of his young mother—uttered in her faint and dying voice, as the children lay before her during the few moments that were given her in mercy to look at them before her eyes were closed on these dearly purchased treasures and all other earthly things—was named John, after her brother, a Seminary priest of Douay, executed in England for saying mass, and refusing the oath of supremacy.

Little need be told of the infancy of these boys: traditions remain, as in other cases, of their likeness to each other, needing different coloured ribbons to distinguish them; and of the old man's anxious doting care over them. Many a pretty group, doubtless, they made, on warm summer afternoons, on the shady terrace; but the old grandfather died when they were seven years old, and slept with his father beneath the Chapel floor. After the funeral, Eustace Inglesant had intended taking both the children back with him to London, but he had discovered— or fancied he had discovered—that the youngest was sickly, and would be better for the country air; and therefore kept him at Westacre, when he returned to the city with his brother. The truth appears to be that he was a worldly, selfish man, and while fully conscious of the advantage of an heir, he was by no means desirous of giving himself more trouble than was necessary about either of his children. The old Priory, however, was, at this time, not a bad place to bring up a child in, though it had been neglected during the last ten or eleven years; though the woods were overgrown, and the oaks came up, in places, close to the house; though the Prior's fish-ponds had transformed themselves into a large pool or lake; though the garden was a tangled wilderness, and centaury, woodsorrel, and sour herbs covered the ground; though the old courtyard and the Chapel itself were mouldering and ruinous, yet the air of the rich vales in the north of Wiltshire is more healthy than that of the higher downs, which are often covered with fogs when the vales are clear, and the sky is bright and serene. It was remarked that people lived longer in the valleys than at places that would be supposed peculiarly healthy on the hills; that they sang better in the churches; and that books and rooms were not so damp and mouldy in the low situations as they were in those which stood very high, with no river or marsh near them. The fogs at times, indeed, came down into the valleys; and in the courtyard of the Priory dim forms had been seen flitting through the mist, in reality the shadows of the spectators thrown upon the mist itself, from the light of a lanthorn. Such sights as those in such a place, so haunted by the memories of the past, gave rise to many strange stories—to which young Inglesant listened with wonder, as he did, also, to others of the *ignis fatuus*, which, called by the people "Kit of the Candlestick," used, about Michaelmas, to be very common on the downs, and to wander down to the valleys across the low boggy grounds—stories of its leading travellers astray, and fascinating them. The boy grew up among such strange stories, and lived, indeed, in the old world that was gone for ever. His grandfather's dimly remembered anecdotes were again and again recalled by others, all of the same kind, which he heard every day. Stories of the rood in the Chapel, of the mass wafer with its mysterious awfulness and power; of the processions and midnight singing at the Priory. The country was full of the scattered spoil of the monasteries; old and precious manuscripts were used everywhere by the schoolboys for covering their books, and for the covers of music; and the glovers of Malmsbury wrapped their goods in them. In the churchyards the yew-trees stood thick and undecayed, scarcely grown again from the last lopping to supply boughs for the archers of the King's army. The story was common of the Becket's path, along which he had been used to pass when curé priest at Winterbourn, and which could be seen through the deepest snow, or if ploughed up and sown with corn. Indeed the path itself could be seen within a pleasant ride across the downs from Westacre.

The boy's first instructor was the old curate of the Chapel, who taught him his Church Catechism and his Latin grammar. This man appears to have been one of those ministers so despised by the Puritans as "mere grammar scholars," who knew better how to read a homily than to make a sermon; yet John Inglesant learnt of him more good lessons than he did, as he himself owned, afterwards from many popular sermons; and in his old age he acknowledged that he believed the only thing that had kept him back in after years and under great temptations, from formally joining the communion of the Church of Rome, was some faint prejudice, some lingering dislike, grounded on the old man's teaching. Other teachers, of a different kind, the child had in plenty. The old servants who still remained in the house; the woodsmen and charcoal burners; the village girls whom the housekeeper hired from year to year at Malmsbury fair; the old housekeeper who had been his mother's maid, and whom the boy looked on as his mother, and who could coax him to her lap when he was quite a tall boy, by telling him stories of his mother; one or two falconers or huntsmen who lingered about the place, or watched the woods for game for the gentry around. When he was ten years old, in 1632, the curate of the Chapel died; and Mr. Inglesant did not at once replace him, for reasons which will appear presently. John led a broken scholastic life for a year, going to school when it was fine enough to make a pleasant walk attractive to ——; where the Vicar taught some boys their grammar and Latin Terence in the Church itself; and where there was a tradition that the great antiquary, Master Camden, Clarencieux King of Arms, coming on his survey to examine the Church, found him, and spoke to him and his scholars. At the end of a year, however, his father coming into the country, arranged for him to go to school at Ashley, where he was to stay in the house with the Vicar, a famous schoolmaster in the West country. This gentleman, who was a delicate and little person, and had an easy and attractive way of teaching, was a Greek scholar and a Platonist, a Rosicrucian and a believer in alchemy and astrology. He found in little Inglesant an apt pupil, an apprehensive and inquisitive boy, mild of spirit, and very susceptible of fascination, strongly given to superstition and romance; of an inventive imagination though not a retentive memory; given to day-dreaming, and,—what is more often found in children than some may think, though perhaps they could not name it,—metaphysical speculation. The Vicar taught his boys in the hall of his Vicarage—a large room with a porch, and armorial bearings in the stained glass in the windows. Out of this opened a closet or parlour where he kept his books, and in this he would sit after school was over, writing his learned treatises, most of which he would read to John Inglesant, some of them in Latin. This, with his readings in Plato, assisted by his eager interest, gave John, as he grew older, a considerable acquaintance with both languages, so that he could read most books in either of them, and turn over the remnants of the old world learning that still remained in the Prior's library, with that lazy facility which always gives a meaning, though often an incorrect one—not always a matter of regret to an imaginative reader, as adding a charm, and, where his own thought is happy, a beauty. Here he imbibed that mysterious Platonic philosophy, which—seen through the reflected rays of Christianity—becomes, as his master taught him, in some sort a foreshadowing of it, as the innocent and heroic life of Socrates, commended and admired by Christians as well as heathens, together with his august death, may be thought, in some measure, to have borne the image of Christ; and, indeed, not without some mystery of purpose, and preparation of men for Christianity, has been so magnified among men. Here, too, he eagerly drank in his master's Rosicrucian theories of spiritual existences : of the vital congruity and three several vehicles of the soul; the terrestrial, in which the soul should be so trained that she may stay as short [a time as possible in the second or aerial, but proceed at once to the third, the ethereal, or celestial; "that heavenly chariot, carrying us, in triumph, to the great happiness of the soul of man." Of the aerial genii, and souls separate, and of their converse with one another, and with mankind. Of their dress, beauty, and outward form; of their pleasures and entertainments, from the Divinest harmony of the higher orders, who, with voices perfectly imitating the passionate utterance of their devout minds, melt their souls into Divine love, and lose themselves in joy in God; while all nature is transformed by them to a quintessence of crystalline beauty by the chemical power of the spirit of nature, acting on pure essences. Of the feastings and wild dances of the lower and deeply lapsed, in whom some sad and fantastic imitation of the higher orders is to be traced; and of those aerial wanderers to whom poetical philosophers or philosophical poets have given the rivers and springs—the mountains and groves; with the Dii Tutelares of cities and countries; and the Lares familiares, who love the warmth of families and the homely converse of men. These studies are but a part of the course of which occult chemistry and the lore of the stars form a part; and that mysterious Platonism which teaches that Pindar's story of the Argo is only a secret recipe for the philosopher's stone; and which pretends that at this distance of time the life of Priam can be read more surely in the stars than in history.

More than three years passed in these pursuits, when Inglesant,—now a tall, handsome, dreamy-looking boy of fourteen, was suddenly recalled to Westacre by his father, who had unexpectedly arrived from London. His master, who was very fond of him, gave him many words of learned advice; for he expected, as proved to be the case, that his school-days—at least as far as he was concerned—were ended. He concluded with these words:—

"I have done my best to show you those hidden truths which the heathen divines knew as well as we; how much more, then, ought we to follow them, who have the light of Christ! Do not talk of these things, but keep them in your heart; hear what all men say, but follow no man: there is nothing in the world of any value but the Divine Light,—follow it. What it is no man can tell you; but I have told you many times, and you know very well, it is not here nor there, as men shall tell you, for all men say they have it who are ignorant of its very nature. It will reveal itself when the time shall come. If you go to the Court, as I think you will, attach yourself wholly to the King and the Church party, the foundations of whose power are in the Divine will. I foresee dark clouds overhanging the Church, but let not these affright you; behind, the Divine Light shineth—the Light that shineth from the hill of God. I have taught you to clear your soul from the mists of carnal error, but I have never told you to act freely in this world: you are not placed here to reason (as the sectaries and precisians do), but to obey. Remember it is the very seal of a gentleman—to obey; remember the Divine words of Plato, in the Crito, when Socrates was about to suffer: how he refused, when urged, to break those laws under which he was falsely condemned. Let those words ring in your ears as they did in his; so that, like the worshippers of Cybele, who heard only the flutes, you shall hear nothing but the voice of God, speaking to you in that rank in which He has placed you, through those captains whom he has ordained to the command. Whenever—and in whatever place—the Divine Light shall appear to you, be assured it will never teach you anything contrary to this."

There was no horse sent for John, but he was obliged to ride in an uncomfortable manner before the serving man who was sent to fetch him; children, and especially younger sons, being treated as little better than servants, and they were indeed often tyrannized over by the latter. When he reached Westacre, he was told his father was in one of the rooms in the new wing of the house, and on entering, he found him in company with three other persons. One of these was the newly appointed curate of the Church, whom Johnny had never yet seen; the other was a fine, handsomely dressed man, with a lofty high-bred look, and in the window was a beautiful boy of about John's own age in the costly dress of a page. Inglesant knew that this must be his brother Eustace; and after humbly receiving his father's rather cold greeting, he hastened to embrace him, and he returned the greeting with warmth. But his father immediately presented him to the gentleman who stood by him; telling him that this gentleman would probably spend some time at Westacre, and that it was chiefly that he should attend him, that he had sent for him home; charging him, at the same time, to serve and obey him implicitly, as he would his father or the King.

"He is a mere country lad," he said, "very different from his brother; but he is young, and may be useful in after days."

The gentleman looked at Johnny kindly, with a peculiar expression which the boy had never before seen, penetrating and alluring at the same time.

"He is, as you say, Esquire, a country lad, and wants the fine clothes of my friend the page, nevertheless he is a gallant and gentle boy, and were he attired as finely, would not shame you, Mr. Inglesant, more than he does. And I warrant," he continued, "this one is good at his books."

And sitting down, he drew Johnny on his knee, and taking from his pocket a small book, he said: "Here, my friend, let us see how you can read in this."

It was the Phaedo of Plato, which Johnny knew nearly by heart, and he immediately began, with almost breathless rapidity, to construe with, here and there, considerable freedom, till the gentleman stopped him with a laugh. "Gently, gently, my friend. I saw you were a scholar, but not that you were a complete Platonist! I fear your master is one who looks more to the Divine sense than to the grammar! But never mind, you and I shall be much together, and as you are so fond of Plato, you shall read him with me. You shall go to your brother, who, if he cannot read 'In Phaedone,' can tell you many wonderful things of the Court and the city that no doubt you will hear very gladly;" and letting Johnny go, he turned to his father, saying, in an undertone, which, however, the boy heard, "The lad is apt, indeed! more so than any of us could have dreamt; no fitter soil, I could wager, we could have found in England!"

Johnny went to his brother, and they left the room together. The two boys,—as the two children had been,—were remarkably alike; the more so as this likeness of form and feature, which to a casual observer appeared exact, was consistent with a very remarkable difference of expression and manner—the difference being, as it were, contained in the likeness without destroying it. Their affection for each other, which continued through life, was something of the same character, arising apparently from instinct and nature, apart from inclination. Their tastes and habits being altogether different, they pursued their several courses quite contentedly, without an effort to be more united, but once united, or once recalled to each other's presence or recollection even in the most accidental manner, they manifested a violent and overpowering attachment to each other. On the present occasion they wandered through the gardens and neighbourhood of the Priory; and as the strange gentleman had foretold, Johnny took the greatest interest in the conversation of his brother, whom, indeed, he both now and afterwards most unfeignedly admired, and to whose patronage he invariably submitted with perfect satisfaction. Eustace, who had lately been admitted one of the junior supernumerary pages to the King, talked incessantly of the King's state and presence chamber, of the yeomen of the guard, of the pageants and masques, and of banquets, triumphs, interviews, nuptials, tilts, and tournaments, the innumerable delights of the city; of the stage players, tumblers, fiddlers, inn-keepers, fencers, jugglers, dancers, mountebanks, bear-wardens; of sweet odours and perfumes, generous wines, the most gallant young men, the fairest ladies, the rarest beauties the world could afford, the costly and curious attire, exquisite music, all delights and pleasures which, to please the senses, could possibly be devised; galleries and terraces, rowing on the Thames, with music, on a pleasant evening, with the goodly palaces, and the birds singing on the banks.

All this Johnny listened to with admiration, and made little reply to his brother's disparaging remarks on the miserable life he had led in the country, or to his sage advice to endeavour, by some means, to come to London to the Court.

Johnny remembered his master's counsel, and was silent on

his own pleasures and pursuits. His pleasant walks by the brook side, pleasant shade by the sweet silver streams, good air, and sweet smell of fine, fresh meadow flowers, his walks among orchards, gardens, green thickets, and such-like places, in some solitary groves between wood and water, meditating on some delightful and pleasant subject—he thought his brother would only ridicule these things. It is true the next day when they went to the Avon to see an otter hunted, Johnny occupied the foremost place for a time; he was known to the keepers, and to two or three gentlemen who were at the sport, and was familiar with the terms in tracing the mark of the otter, and following through all the craft of the hunting, tracing the marks in the soft and moist places to see which way the head of the chase was turned. He carried his otter spear as well as any of the company, while the hounds came trailing and chanting along by the river-side, venting every tree root, every osier bed and tuft of bulrushes, and sometimes taking to the water, and beating it like spaniels. But as soon as the otter, escaping from the spears, was killed by the dogs, or, having by its wonderful sagacity and craft avoided the dogs, was killed by the spears, Eustace assumed his superior place, coming forward to talk to the gentlemen, who were delighted with him, while Johnny fell back into the quiet, dreamy boy again.

The two brothers were left together for several days, their father, with the strange gentleman—whose name Eustace told Johnny was Hall—having departed on horseback, on a visit to a gentleman in Gloucestershire. Eustace observed great caution in speaking of Mr. Hall, telling Johnny he would know all about him soon from himself. The boys passed the time happily enough. Johnny's affection for his brother increased every day, and withstood not only Eustace's patronage, but—what must have been much more hard to bear—the different way in which the servants treated the two boys. Eustace, who, though only a few minutes older than his brother, was the heir, was treated with great deference and respect; which might possibly also be owing to his being a stranger and to his Court breeding. Johnny, on the contrary, though he was quite as tall as his brother, they treated like a child: the housekeeper took him up to bed when it pleased her; the old butler would have caned him without hesitation had he thought he deserved it; and the maids alternately petted and scolded him, the first of which was more disagreeable to him than the last. The hard condition of children, and especially of younger brothers, is a common theme of the writers of the period, and Johnny's experience was not different from that of others. His disposition, however, was not injured by it, though it may have made him still fonder of retirement and of day-dreaming than he would have been. This hard discipline made him resolve to be silent on those wonderful secrets and the learning that his master had taught him, and to meditate increasingly upon them in his heart. He delighted more and more in wandering by the river-side, building castles in the air, and acting an infinite variety of parts. When his brother left him, this became still more delightful to him, and but for other influences he might have gone on in this fascinating habit till he realised Burton's terrible description, and from finding these contemplations and fantastical conceits so delightful at first, might have become the slave of vain and unreal fancies, which may be as terrible and dismal as pleasing and delightful.

After about a fortnight's absence, Mr. Inglesant and Mr. Hall returned from their visit, or visits, for they appeared to have stayed at several places; and the next day Eustace and his father departed for London. His father displayed more affection than usual on leaving Johnny behind him, assuring him of his love, and that if he heard a good account of him from Mr. Hall, he should come up to London and see the Court. Eustace's grief at losing his brother again was much lessened by his joy at returning to his congenial life in London; but Johnny watched him from the old gate-house in front of the Priory with a sad heart.

While he is standing looking after his father and brother, as they ride up the hill by the same path which the Prior came down that fine summer morning long years before, we will take a moment's time to explain certain events of which he was perfectly ignorant, but which were soon to close about him and involve him in a labyrinth from which he may have been said never to have issued during his life. We call ourselves free agents;—was this slight, delicate boy a free agent, with a mind and spirit so susceptible, that the least breath affected them: around whom the throng of national contention was about to close; on whom the intrigue of a great religious party was about to seize, involving him in a whirlpool and rapid current of party strife and religious rancour? Must not the utmost that can be hoped,—that can be even rationally wished for—be, that by the blessing of the Divine guidance, he may be able to direct his path a little towards the Light?

The laws oppressing the Roman Catholics, which had been stringently enforced during the greater part of James's reign, had been considerably relaxed when he was negotiating with the Spaniards for the marriage of his son, and again on King Charles's marriage with Henrietta Maria of France. From that time greater and greater leniency was shown them, not only by the exertion of Catholic influence at Court, but also through Puritan jealousy; the juries refusing to punish popish recusants, because Puritan separatists were included in the lists. Spasmodic exertions of severity were made from time to time by the King and the Church party; but, on the whole, the Papists enjoyed more and more liberty, especially between 1630 and 1640. Advantage was taken by the party of this freedom to the fullest extent; money was amassed abroad, an army of missionary priests poured into England, agents were sent from the Pope, and every effort made in every part of England to gain converts, and confirm uncertain members. Many Papists who had conformed to the authority of the English Church beginning to entertain hopes of the ultimate success of the old religion, fell away and became recusants—that is, ceased to attend their Parish Church. Mr. Inglesant, who—through all his life—had watched the progress of affairs with a careful and far-reaching penetration, had, from the first, been in communication with chiefs of the popish party; but he was far too important a friend where he was to allow of any change in his behaviour, and he still rigidly conformed to the Established Church. The Roman Catholics were divided into two parties, holding two opinions, which, under different aspects, actuate all religious parties at the present day. The one viewed the English Church and its leader Archbishop Laud with hatred, regarding him, and doubtless with great truth, as their most formidable opponent, as occupying a place in the country and in the allegiance of the majority of Englishmen which otherwise could only have been filled by the older Church: the other, looking more at the resemblances between the two Churches, held the opinion that little was needed to bring the Established Church into communion and submission to the Papal See, and by that means, at once, and without trouble, restore the papal authority in England. The efforts of this party were of a more political nature than those of the other; they endeavoured to win over Archbishop Laud to a conference, and a Cardinal's hat was offered to him more than once. To this party Mr. Inglesant belonged. Occupying a neutral position himself, and possessed of the confidence of members of both Churches, he was peculiarly fitted for such negotiations, and was in constant communication with those Churchmen, very numerous at Court, and among the clergy and the country gentry, who were favourably disposed to the Papists, though at the same time sincere members of their own Church. The value of emissaries possessing in this way the confidence of Church people and Papists alike was so obvious, that Mr. Inglesant and his friends did all they could to add to their number, especially as they were not very easy to procure, great jealousy existing, among nearly all Church people, of any foreign or armed interference in England on the part of the Romanists, who were always suspected of such intentions. Mr. Inglesant, therefore, whom nothing escaped, had marked out his younger son's temperament as one peculiarly fitted to be trained for such a purpose, and had communicated this idea to his intimate associate among the Papists, Father Sancta Clara, as he was called, of an English family named St. Clare, a Jesuit missionary priest who travelled in England under the name of Mr. Hall. The latter was a man of great influence, unbounded devotion to his order, and unflinching courage; a profound scholar, and, according to the knowledge of that day, a man of science, trained, indeed, in every variety of human learning, and taking advantage of every scrap of knowledge and information for the advancement of his purpose. Of elegant and fascinating manners, and accustomed to courtly life abroad, he was, perhaps, the most influential agent among the thousand mission priests at that time scattered through England. His time, of course, was fully taken up with his difficult embassy, but he was interested in the account Inglesant gave of his son; and the idea of training him to such usefulness in three or four years' time, when their plans might be expected to be ripe, commended itself exceedingly to his peculiar genius and habit of mind. He was at this time Superior over part of the south-west of England, and was much engaged among the gentry in those parts—a position of peculiar difficulty, as the people of the greater part of that district were strongly Puritan, and the gentry hostile to

Rome. So secluded and convenient a position as Westacre Priory was exactly adapted to aid him in his mission, and he resolved to take up his quarters there, from whence he could, with great hopes of escaping observation, continue his work in the adjoining country. Mr. Inglesant, with an eye to such a contingency, had purposely omitted to appoint a chaplain at the Priory for some time, and now nominated a Mr. ——, a graduate of Oxford, a man who was "ex animo" a Papist, and who only waited a suitable time to declare himself one. The number of such men was very great, and they were kept in the English Church only by the High Church doctrines and ceremonies introduced by Archbishop Laud; affording one out of numberless parallels between that age and the present. It is perhaps not necessary to say more in this place to explain the presence of Mr. Hall (otherwise Father Sancta Clara) at Westacre, nor the future that lay before Johnny Inglesant as he stood by the gatehouse of the old Priory looking after his father and Eustace as they rode up the hill.

CHAPTER III.

FATHER SANCTA CLARA was obliged to remain quiet at Westacre for some time, and devoted himself entirely to gaining an influence over Johnny. Of course in this he was entirely successful. There was a good library, for that day, at the Priory; the Prior's old books were still on the shelves, and Richard Inglesant, who we have seen was a scholar, added largely to them, bringing all his books into the country when he came to live at Westacre. The difference between Johnny's former master and his present one was that between a theorist and dreamer and a statesman and man of the world and critical student of human nature. The Father made Johnny read with him every day, and by his wealth of learning and acquaintance with men and foreign countries, made the reading interesting in the highest degree. In this way he read the classics, making them not dead school books, but the most human utterances that living men ever spoke; and while from these he drew illustrations of human life when reading Plato—which he did every day—he led his pupil to perceive, as he did more fully when he grew older, that wonderful insight into the spiritual life and spiritual distinctions which even Christianity has failed to surpass. He led him, step by step, through that noble resolve by which Socrates—at frightful odds, and with all ordinary experience against him—maintains the advantage to be derived from truth; he pointed out to him the three different elements to be found in Plato: the Socratic or negative argument, simply overthrowing received opinion; the pseudo-scientific, to which Plato was liable from the condition of knowledge in his day; and, finally, the exalted flight of the transcendental reason, which, leaving alike the scepticism of the negative argument and the dreams of false science, flies aloft into the pure ether of the heavenly life. He read to him Aristophanes, pointing out in him the opposing powers which were at work in the Hellenic life as in the life of every civilized age. He did not conceal from him the amount of right there is on the popular side of plain common sense, nor the soundness of that fear which hesitates to overthrow the popular forms of truth, time-honoured and revealed, which have become in the eyes of the majority, however imperfect they may really be, the truth itself. Nor did he fail to show him the unsuitability of the Socratic argument to the masses of the people, who will stop at the negative part, and fail of the ethereal flight beyond; and he showed him how it might be possible, and even the best thing for mankind, that Socrates should die, though Socrates at that moment was the noblest of mankind: as, afterwards, though for a different reason, it was expedient that a nobler than Socrates should die for the people,—nobler, that is, in that he did what Socrates failed in doing, and carried the lowest of the people with him to the ethereal gates. And in this entering into sympathy with the struggle of humanity, he prepared his pupil to receive in after years (for it is a lesson that cannot be fully learned until middle life is approached) that kindly love of humanity; that sympathy with its smallest interests; that toleration of its errors, and of its conflicting opinions; that interest in local and familiar affairs, in which the highest culture is at one with the unlearned rustic mind.

The boy drank in all this with the greatest aptitude, and would have listened all day, but his tutor insisted on his taking his full amount of exercise, and himself commanded his admiration as much by skill in the sports of the field as by learning.

He made no effort to draw his mind away from the English Church, farther than by giving him a crucifix and rosary, and teaching him the use of them, and pointing out the beauties of the Roman use; he even took pains to prevent his becoming attached to Popery, telling him that his father would not wish him to leave the Church of England; and though that Church was at present in schism, it would probably soon be reunited, and that meanwhile the difference was unimportant and slight. He knew, indeed, that from the excitable and enthusiastic nature of his pupil, if he once became attached strongly to Roman theology, all his use as a mediator between the two parties would at once be lost; and he therefore contented himself with securing his own influence over Johnny; which he accomplished to the most unlimited extent.

After certain preparations had been made, and some needful precautions taken, a great change took place in the life at Westacre Priory. Strangers were constantly arriving, stayed a few hours, and departed, mostly coming in the night, and leaving, also, after sunset. Several, however, remained a longer time, and took great pains to conceal themselves. They all had long interviews with the Father. Services were also performed in the Chapel, frequently in Latin. It was death to say mass in England, except in the Queen's Chapels at St James's, at Somerset House, and at Woodstock, nevertheless mass was said in all parts of England, and it was said at Westacre. One night, after Johnny had been asleep for some hours, he was awakened by Father St. Clare, who told him to dress himself and come with him, and, at the same time, charged him never to tell any one what he might be about to see—an injunction which the boy would have died rather than disobey. The long streaks of the summer dawn stretched across the sky before them as they crossed the courtyard towards the Chapel, and the roofs stood out sharp and distinct in the dim, chill air. The Chapel was lighted, and on the white cloth of the altar were tapers and flowers. Half awake in the sweet fresh morning air, Johnny knelt on the cold flag-stones of the Chapel and saw the mass. Strangers who had come to the Priory on purpose were present, and some gentlemen of the neighbourhood whom Johnny knew. It is strange that the Jesuit should have placed so much trust in the prudence and fidelity of a boy; but he probably knew his pupil, and certainly had no cause to repent. This was not the

D

only time mass was said; for one winter night—or rather morning—an old peasant, known in the neighbourhood as Father Wade, had been to Marlborough wake, and being benighted, bethought himself of asking a lodging at the Priory, and approached it by a pathway from the east, which, crossing the meadows beyond the Chapel, came round to the gate-house at the front. He, however, never reached the gate, and being found at home the next day, and questioned as to where he passed the night, he was at first evasive in his replies, but on being pressed, told a mysterious story of strange lights and shapes of men he had seen about the Priory; and approaching—he said—fearfully along the path, there, sure enough! were the old monks passing up in procession from the graveyard through the wall into the Chapel, as through a door; and he heard the long-remembered chanting of the mass, and saw the tapers shining through the east window, as he had seen them when a little boy.

This manner of life went on for about a year, at the end of which time Father St. Clare's absences became more frequent, and Johnny was left much alone. The Father's mission in the west of England was not prospering, for the very simple reason that he was too good for the work. As far as the duties of a Superior went, everything was satisfactory. The country was mapped out in districts, and emissaries were appointed to each; but for the peculiar mission of Father St. Clare—that of personal influence—there was no scope. It was the habit of the Jesuits, by the charms of their conversation and learning, by their philosophical theories, and in some cases by their original systems of science, to gain the confidence and intimacy of the highest both in station and intellect, and for this seed to spring up, there must be first a suitable soil for it to be sown in, and this soil was particularly scarce in Wiltshire. All the refinement and learning of Father St. Clare was thrown away upon the country squires; any boon companion would have influenced them quite as well. Becoming conscious of this, the Jesuit rode frequently to London, where work which required the highest skill and talent was going on; and in his absence Johnny was left very much to his own devices. During one of these absences a priest who had remained concealed several days at the Priory, and who had taken a fancy to the boy, gave him, at parting, a little book, telling him to read it carefully, and it would be of use to him through life. It was entitled "The Flaming Heart, or the Life of

St. Theresa," of which a later edition, printed in 1642, was dedicated to Henrietta Maria. It opened a new world of thought to Johnny, who was now sixteen years of age, and he read it many times from beginning to end. A great deal of it was so strange to Inglesant, that he was repelled by it. The exaggeration of the duty of self-denial, the grotesque humility, the self-denunciation for the most trifling faults, most of the details indeed appeared to him either absurd or untrue; but, running through all the book, the great doctrine of Divine Illumination fascinated him. The sublime but mysterious way of devotion pointed out in it, while quite different from anything he had previously heard of, was still sufficiently in accordance with the romantic habit of his mind, and with the mystic philosophy in which his old master had trained him, to cause him to follow it with an eager sympathy. The natural and inspired writings of the great mystics, indeed, breathe a celestial purity, entirely distinct from those of their inferior disciples, who brought down their spiritual system to earth and earthly purposes. The rest from individual effort, the calm after long striving, the secret joy in God, the acquiescing in His will, in which the true elevation of devotion lies, and which is not the effect of lively imaginations or of fruitful inventions—of these, all men are not capable, but all may reach the silent and humble adoration of God which arises out of a pure and quiet mind; just as when a man enters into an entire friendship with another, then the single thought of his friend affects him more tenderly than all that variety of reflections which may arise in his mind where this union is not felt. This inward calm and quiet in which men may in silence form acts of faith and feel those inward motions and directions which, as this book taught, follow all those who rise up to this elevation, and which lead them onward through the devious paths of this life, what must this be but the Divine Light of which his old master had so often told him he was ignorant, but whose certain coming he had led him constantly to expect? Enticed by such thoughts as these, he passed the days, hardly knowing what he did; and wandered in this perplexed labyrinth without a guide. Without a guide! but this book of his told him of a guide—a spiritual guide—nay, even recommended obedience and entire submission to this director; and dissuaded from self-confidence. Where, then, was this guide, to whom, in the midst of such spiritual light and life, and after such ecstatic visions, he should turn? The book said it was the priest—any priest would do—but still it was the priest. This seemed to John Inglesant, whose perceptions the Jesuit had sharpened, but whose unrestrained romance he had not crushed, to be very different from that Divine Light of which his master spoke, from that transcendental voice of the Platonic Reason speaking in the silence of the soul; nay, it seemed to him to be a fall even from the teaching of the book itself. Meditating on these things, Johnny thought he would visit his old master, to see what he had to say about this new doctrine.

It was a fine summer morning when he made the visit; he had a horse of his own now, and a servant if he chose, but he preferred to-day to go alone. He found Mr. ——— had discontinued his school, and was entirely buried in his books; only reading morning and evening prayers, and a homily or one of his old sermons in the Church on Sundays. He never left his study on other days, except for a turn in his little garden. His house was by the wayside, with a small paved court before the hall; and by the side of this court, the garden, into which the window of the study, in a gabled wing adjoining the hall, looked towards the road. He was pleased to see Inglesant, though he very dimly remembered him, and questioned him of his studies. Johnny read him some Plato with the Jesuit's comments, of which the old gentleman took notes eagerly, and afterwards incorporated them in his book. The book he was writing was upon Talismanic figures, but he was not particular what he put into it, anything of an occult and romantic character being welcome, and introduced with not a little ingenuity. He had no sense nor understanding of anything else in the world but such subjects and his books; and being exceedingly infirm, he could scarcely lift some of the larger folios which lay heaped about him within reach. He blessed God that his eyesight was so good, and that he could still read Greek—the contracted Greek type of that day. After some conversation, Inglesant opened his mind to him, told him what he had been reading, and asked his opinion. The old scholar pricked up his ears, and set to work with great delight, taking notes all the time; and Johnny found, years afterwards, when he happened to read his book in London, that all he told him was introduced into it.

"I find nothing, my dear pupil," he said, "in the Christian

Church, very old, concerning this doctrine — for that author who goes by the name of Dionysius the Areopagite is of far later date—But I will discover to you some mysteries concerning it, which, so far as I know, have never been brought to light by any man. I find the germ of this doctrine in those fragments of metaphysics which go under Theophrastus his name; who was a disciple of Aristotle, and succeeded him in his school; and was an excellent philosopher certainly, by the works by him which remain to this day. Here he says that the understanding joined to the body, can do nothing without the senses, which help it as far as they can to distinguish sensible things from their first causes, but that all knowledge and contemplation of the first causes, must be by very touching and feeling of the mind and soul; which knowledge, thus gained, is not liable to error. Synesius, a man well known amongst scholars, being vexed that this new divinity began in his day to be in request amongst Christians; and some illiterate monks and others taking advantage of it to magnify ignorance, to bring themselves into repute;—Synesius, I say, wrote that exquisite treatise which he inscribed 'Dio,' to prove the necessity of human learning and philosophy to all who will contemplate high things with sobriety and good success. 'God forbid,' he says, 'that we should think that if God dwell in us, He should dwell in any other part of us than that which is rational, which is His own proper temple.'

"Now whether the writings of some ancient and later Platonists, Greeks and Arabs, Heathens and Mahometans, be a sufficient ground and warrant for them that profess to ascribe more to the Scriptures, by which sobriety of sense is so much commended unto us, than to the opinions of heathen philosophers, I leave you to consider."

Then Inglesant left him, for he seemed more desirous to put ideas into his book than to impart them, and rode home across the downs. As he went, he overtook a gentleman riding an easy-going palfrey, whom he found to be one whom he knew; one, indeed, of those who had attended the early morning mass in the Chapel. This gentleman, who was one of those called Church Papists, that is, Papists who saved themselves from the charge of recusancy by sometimes attending their Parish Church, knowing Johnny, and placing faith in him, began at once to relate his troubles. He dwelt sadly on the fines he had to pay and his difficulties in avoiding the communion at Easter; but his greatest troubles were caused by his wife, who was much more zealous than he was, and refused to go to Church once a month to keep off the Churchwardens. Her religion, indeed, was so costly to him, that he had rather have had a city lady with her extravagant dress. He was very particular in inquiring after Father St. Clare, and whether Inglesant knew of anything he was engaged in; but John could give him no information, not knowing anything of the Jesuit's plans. They were hard times, he said, for a good quiet subject who wished to live at peace with his King and with his clergyman; but what with the fear of the apparitor on one hand, and of his wife and her advisers among the Catholics on the other—he had a hard time of it. He was a cheerful man naturally, however, and leaving this discourse, which he thought would tire his companion, he entertained him for some time with the news of the country, of which he gathered great abundance in his rides. Among other things, he told him of a clergyman at a parish not far off, who, he said, must be a Catholic in his heart, for his piety was so great and his punctuality in reading common prayer, morning and evening, in the Church alone in his surplice so regular, that—so the common report ran—he had brought down an angel from heaven, who appeared to him in the Church one evening in the glow of the setting sun, and told him many wonderful and heavenly things. When the gentleman had related this, they came to the point where their roads parted, and he invited Johnny—for he was very courteous—to come on to his house, and sup with him. To this Inglesant consented, visits being a rare pleasure to him, and they rode together to the gentleman's house, which stood on the edge of the downs, with a courtyard and gate-house before it, and at the back a fair hall and parlour, having a wide prospect over the valley and the distant view. Johnny was courteously received by the popish lady and her sister, who was devout and very pretty. The supper would have been very plain—the day being a fast—but the gentleman insisted on waiting while a rabbit was cooked for his friend; and when it came, he partook of it himself, in spite of his wife's remonstrances—out of courtesy to his guest, he said, and also to enable him to get over his next fine, which, he said, it ought to do. The ladies asked John Inglesant many questions about the Father, and what took place at the Priory; also about his brother the Page. This made him leave early, for though he knew nothing of any plots or treason, he was constantly afraid of saying something he ought not to do; nothing was said, however, about the morning mass, which was too serious a matter to be lightly spoken of.

As he rode away through the soft evening light, he thought so much of the story the gentleman had told him, that he made up his mind to ride to the village and see the clergyman whose goodness was so manifest and so rewarded. He, surely—if no one else could—would show him the true path of Devotion.

Two or three days afterwards he took the ride, and arrived at the small old Church at a very opportune moment, for the clergyman in his surplice was just going into it to read the evening prayers. Inglesant attended devoutly, being the only person present; for the sexton's wife, who rang the bell, did not consider that her duty extended farther. Prayers being over, the parson invited Johnny to supper—a much better one than he had had at the Papist's—and Inglesant stated his difficulties to him, and asked his advice. The Parson showed him several small books which he had written; one on bowing and taking off the hat at the name of Jesus; another on the cross in baptism, and kneeling at the communion; a third on turning to the east, which last appeared to be mostly quotations and enlargements from Dr. Donne; a fourth on the use of the surplice. He repudiated being popishly inclined; having disproved, he said, that any of these practices were popish, in all his books, all of which, as far as Johnny could see, displayed considerable ingenuity; and while he inserted many trivial and weak passages, he seemed to have been well read in the Fathers and other old authors, and to have been a loyal, honest, and zealous advocate, according to his capacity, of the Church of England. He evidently looked on forms and ceremonies with the greatest reverence, and was totally incapable of telling his visitor anything of that mystical life he was so anxious to realize. Johnny inquired about the angel, but his host, while not appearing displeased at the reports being spread abroad, professed to deny all knowledge of it, but in such a way as to make Inglesant think he would like to have acknowledged it, had he dared. He rode away disappointed, and began to think he must consult Father St. Clare; which, for some reason or other, he had felt a disinclination to do.

While he was in this perplexity, he bethought himself of his first schoolmaster, the man who taught in the Church where Camden visited him. He had forgotten all about this man, except that he was of a mild and kind nature; but he was so anxious for direction that he went to him at once. This man had been very poor, and brought up a large family, all of whom, however, he had put forward in life, some at the University and the Church, and some among the clothiers and glove-makers at Malmsbury and the other towns of Wiltshire. Johnny found him living alone—for his wife was dead—in a small cottage no better than a countryman's, with a few books, which with his garden were all the wealth he possessed. He was a great herbalist, and famous in the country for his cures and for his sermons, though no two people could agree why they admired the latter: all uniting in considering him a simple and rather poor preacher. This Inglesant learnt from a countryman who walked at his horse's side as he came near the village; but when he found the old gentleman sitting on a bench before his study window, and he rose and met his look, Inglesant saw at once—thanks to the cultivation of his perception by the Jesuit's teaching—what it was that gained him the people's love. He had large and melting eyes that looked straight into the hearts of those who met him, as though eager to help them and do them good. He received Johnny with great kindness, though he had quite forgotten him, and did not even remember when he told him who he was. But when Inglesant, who found it very easy to speak to him of what had brought him there, told him of his difficulties, he listened with the greatest interest and sympathy. When he had finished speaking, he remained some minutes silent, looking across the garden where the hot midday air was playing above the flowers.

"You have been speaking," he said at length, "of very high and wonderful things, into which, it would seem, even the angels dare not look; for we are, as would appear, taught in Scripture that it is in man's history that they see the workings of Divine Glory. And indeed, worthy Mr. Inglesant, when you have lived to the limit of my many years, you will not stumble at this; nor think this life a low and poor place in which to seek the Divine Master walking to and fro. These high matters of which you speak, and this heavenly life, is not to be disbelieved, only it seems to me—more and more—that the soul or spirit of every man in passing through life among familiar things is among supernatural things always, and many things seem to me miraculous which men think nothing of, such as memory, by which we live again in place and time—and of which, if I remember rightly, for I am a very poor scholar, you doubtless know, St. Augustine says many pertinent things—and the love of one another, by which we are led out of ourselves, and made to act against our own nature by that of another, or, rather, by a higher nature than that of any of us; and a thousand fancies and feelings which have no adequate cause among outward things. Here, in this book which I was reading when you so kindly came to see me, are withered flowers, which I have gathered in my rambles, and keep as friends and companions of pleasant places, streams and meadows, and of some who have been with me, and now are not. There is one, this single yellow flower—it is a tormentilla, which is good against the plague— what is it, that, as I hold it, makes me think of it as I do? Faded flowers have something, to me, miraculous and supernatural about them: though, in fact, it is nothing wonderful that the texture of a flower being dried survives. It is not in the flower, but in our immortal spirit that the miracle is. All these delightful thoughts that come into my mind when I look at this flower—thoughts, and fancies, and memories—what are they but the result of the alchemy of the immortal spirit, which takes all the pleasant, fragile things of life, and transmutes them into immortality in our own nature! And if the poor spirit and intellect of man can do this, how much more may the supreme creative intellect mould and form all things, and bring the presence of the supernatural face to face with us in our daily walk. Earth becomes to us, if we thus think, nothing but the garden of the Lord, and every fellow-being we meet and see in it, a beautiful and invited guest; and, as I think I remember, many of the heathen poets, after their manner, have said very fine things about this; that we should rise cheerfully from this life, as a grateful guest rises from an abundant feast; and though doubtless they were very dark and mistaken, yet I confess they always seemed to me to have something of a close and entire fellowship with the wants of men, which I think the Saviour would have approved. If you, sir, can receive this mystery, and go through the honourable path of life which lies before you, looking upon yourself as an immortal spirit walking among supernatural things—for the natural things of this life would be nothing were they not moved and animated by the efficacy of that which is above nature—I think you may find this doctrine a light which will guide your feet in dark places; and it would seem, unless I am mistaken, that this habit of mind is very likely to lead to the blessedness of the Beatific Vision of God, on the quest of which you have happily entered so young; for surely it should lead to that state to which this vision is promised—the state of those who are Pure in Heart. For if it be true, that the reason we see not God is the grossness of this tabernacle wherein the soul is incased, then the more and the oftener we recognize the supernatural in our ordinary life, and not only expect and find it in those rare and short moments of devotion and prayer, the more, surely, the rays of the Divine Light will shine through the dark glass of this outward form of life, and the more our own spirit will be enlightened and purified by it, until we come to that likeness to the Divine Nature, and that purity of heart to which a share of the Beatific Vision is promised, and which, as some teach, can be attained by being abstract from the body and the bodily life. As we see every day that the supernatural in some men gives a particular brightness of air to the countenance, and makes the face to shine with an inimitable lustre, and if it be true that in the life to come we shall have to see through a body and a glass however transparent, we may well practise our eyes by making this life spiritual, as we shall have also to strive to do in that to which we go. My predecessor in this living, doubtless a very worthy man (for I knew him not), has left it recorded on his tombstone —as I will show you if you will come into the Church—that he was 'full of cares and full of years, of neither weary, but full of hope and of heaven.' I should desire that it may be faithfully recorded of me that I was the same!"

John went with him into the Church, and read the old vicar's epitaph and several more—for he was very much taken with the old gentleman's talk, and indeed stayed with him the whole day: his host adding a dish of eggs and a glass of small beer to his daily very frugal meal. Johnny invited him to come to the Priory, and so left him, more pleased and satisfied with this than with any of his other visits. As he rode back through the darkening valley, and through the oak wood before the Priory gate, he little thought that not only should he not see the old Parson again, but that his quiet contemplative life was come to an end, and his speculations would now be chased away by a life of action; and for the future the decision, often to be made at once, as to what he ought to do, would appear of more consequence than that other decision, which had seemed to him, sometimes, the only important one, as to what it was right to think.

When he reached the Priory, he found the Jesuit had returned, and when at supper he inquired of Johnny if his ride had been a pleasant one, as the servant had told him he had been out since the morning, Johnny began at once and told him all that had been passing in his mind since the priest had given him the book, and of all the directors he had sought for his guidance. Father St. Clare listened (though it may be doubted whether the recital was altogether agreeable to him) with great attention, and seemed pleased and amused at the boy's descriptions, which showed his pupil's fine perception of character.

"You have taken a wise course," he said, "which has led you to see much of the workings of the minds of men: this is the most useful study you can follow, and the most harmless to yourself, if you keep your own counsel, and gain knowledge without imparting it. I am glad you have told me all this, because it shows me I have not been deceived in you, but that the time is fully ripe for you to play the part your father and I have destined for you, and to play it—to great extent—alone. The day after to-morrow we shall go up to London; on the way, I will open to you the position of parties, the crisis of affairs—a position and a crisis such as never was before in this or any other country! You are very young, but you are years older in mind than most of your age, and your youth renders you all the more fit for the work I have for you to do. I trust you without reserve; I shall commit to your keeping secrets which would, if revealed, bring the highest heads in England, not to speak of my own, to the block. I have no fear of you."

Inglesant listened breathlessly and with open eyes to this address. It made his heart beat high with delight and excitement. Death—nay, the bitterest torture—would be nothing to him, if only he could win this man's approval, and be not only true but successful in his trust. His entire devotion to the Jesuit cannot be looked upon as anything wonderful, for the whole mental power of the latter, directed by the nicest art

—a power and an art at that time not surpassed in Europe—had been directed to this end upon the boy's susceptible nature, and the result could not be doubtful.

The Jesuit might well say that the crisis was imminent, and the position of affairs peculiar. Plotters were at work in all directions, and for different ends; but the schemes of all miscarried, and the expectations of all proved to be miscalculations: those of the Roman Catholics—with whom St. Clare was associated—more than all. Their expectations were at the highest pitch. The Court influence was with them to a large extent. The Church of England was at its highest summit of glory and power, and its standing-point was almost their own. Laud was partly gained. He had refused a Cardinal's hat; but in such a way that the offer was immediately renewed, and remained open. It seemed, indeed, as though little more remained to do when this goodly edifice began to crumble, slowly, indeed, but surely, and with accelerating speed. A new power appeared in the country; hostile, indeed, to Catholicism, but, what was much worse, also slightly contemptuous of it, directing its full force against the Church and the Crown. The Church collapsed with wonderful suddenness; and the Crown was compelled to seek its own preservation, extending what little aid it might be able to render to the Church; neither had the least power or time to give to the assistance of their former allies. All this had not happened when the Jesuit and Johnny rode up to London, but it was foreshadowed clearly in the immediate future.

CHAPTER IV.

FATHER ST. CLARE and Johnny set out the next day, accompanied by two servants on horseback. The road was quite new to Inglesant after they left Malmsbury; and he was greatly delighted and amused with all he saw. The fair landscapes, the prospects of goodly cities with the towers and spires of their Churches rising into the clear smokeless air; the stately houses and gardens, the life of the country villages, the fairs and markets, strolling players, the morris dancing, the drinking and smoking parties, the conjurors and mountebanks, peasants quarrelling "together by the ears," and buying and selling; wandering beggars, and half-witted people called "Tom o' Bedlams" who were a recognized order of mendicants—everything amused and delighted him, especially with his companion's witty and penetrating comments upon all they met with.

At Windsor they walked on the terrace, from which Johnny saw the view, which was then considered only second to that of Greenwich, of the river and many pleasant hills and valleys, villages and fair houses, far and near. As they rode along, at every suitable opportunity, and at night after supper at the inns, the Jesuit explained to Johnny the position of public affairs. He told him that though the power of the King and the Archbishop was apparently at its greatest height, as the trial and condemnation of Laud's traducers, Prynne, Baswick, and Burton, had just been decided, and the trial of Hampden for refusal to pay ship-money was about to commence, yet nevertheless, the impossibility of governing without a Parliament was becoming so evident, and the violent and aggressive temper of the people was so marked, that he, and those like him, who possessed the best information of what was passing throughout all classes, and among all parties, however secret, considered that changes of a very remarkable character were imminent. The temper of the people, he said, was the more remarkable, because in the one case, libellers like Prynne would have been put to death without mercy in either of the preceding reigns, and no notice taken by the people; and the tax, called ship's money, was so light and so fairly levied, as to be scarcely felt. The Archbishop, he said, was determined to force the service book upon the Scots; a most unwise and perilous proceeding at the present moment, and he was informed by the emissary priests then in the north of England and Scotland, that the resistance to it would be determined, and that the Scottish malcontents were supported by the Puritan party in the English Parliament. Under these circumstances, he explained to Johnny that a change had taken place in the policy of some of the Roman Catholic party, who had formerly acted with Mr. Inglesant and Father St. Clare, and they had arrived at the conclusion that the Church of England was no longer worth the pains of humouring and conciliating. The Queen had been advised to attempt the perversion of the Parliamentary leaders, and several of the Catholic plotters had undertaken a similar enterprise. Father St. Clare told Johnny candidly that he had neither sympathized entirely with these views nor altogether with those of the party to which he had hitherto belonged. On the one hand, he had arrived at the conclusion that Laud was a true servant of the Church of England, and would never consent to submission to Rome, except on terms which could not be granted, but on the other, he had so long regarded the Church as the natural ally of Rome, and the uselessness of attempting to win over the Puritans was so apparent, that he had not entered warmly into these new schemes. He, however, was inclined to think that were a change to take place, and the Puritan party to gain the supreme power in the State, the reaction among the upper classes would be so great, that the Romish faith would gain numberless converts. He finally pressed upon Johnny the necessity of great prudence, telling him that he should be immediately placed about the person of the Queen as one of her pages; and, as soon as possible, transferred to the King's service in as high a post as the influence to be exerted could command, in order that he should possess as much influence as possible: that in the meantime his business would be simply to become acquainted with as many of all parties as he possibly could, and to gain their confidence, opportunities for doing which should be given him both in the assemblies he would meet at his father's house, and in other company into which he should be introduced. He warned him against crediting anything he heard, unless assured of its truth by himself—the most exaggerated reports upon every subject, he said, prevailing in the Court and city. The conversions to Romanism, he told him, though numerous, were nothing like so many as were reported, as might be supposed when the reputed ones included such men as Mr. Endymion Porter, the most faithful servant of the King and a firm Church of England man, though, like many others, entertaining very friendly opinions of the Papists.

Conversing in this way, they entered London one afternoon at the beginning of August 1637. Johnny, as may be supposed, was all eyes as they entered London, which they did by Kensington and St. James's Park. The beautiful buildings at Kensington, and the throng of gentry and carriages in the park astonished him beyond measure. As they passed through the park many persons recognized Father St. Clare, but they passed on without stopping, through the gateway by the side of the beautiful banqueting-house into the narrow street that led by Charing Cross and the Strand. The crowds were now of a different kind from those they had passed in the park. They passed several groups assembled round quack doctors and itinerant speakers, one of whom was relating how the congregation of a Parish Church the Sunday before had been alarmed by an insurrection of armed Papists—stories of this kind being then a common invention to excite and stir up the people. At one of these groups they were startled by hearing a man who was selling books, announce the name as "Jesus' Worship Confuted;" as the thing was new to the Jesuit, he stopped and ordered one of his men to dismount and bring him one, when it was found to be a tract against ceremonies, and especially against bowing at the name of Jesus. They resumed their passage down the Strand, Father St. Clare remarking on the strange ideas a stranger would attach to the state of religion in England if he listened only to the opposing cries. All down the Strand the Jesuit pointed out the beautiful houses of the nobility, and the glimpses of the river between them. They stopped at last at Somerset House, then a large rambling series of buildings extending round several courts with gardens and walks on the river banks, and a handsome water-gate leading to the river. They went to the lodgings of Father Cory, the Queen's confessor, who was at home, and received them hospitably. Johnny was so taken up with all the astonishing sights around him, especially with the wonderful view up and down the river, with the innumerable boats and barges, the palaces and gardens, and churches and steeples on the banks, that it was a day or two before he could talk or think calmly of anything. The next morning the Jesuit took him to his father's house on the north side of the Strand, where he saw both his father and brother, it not being the latter's turn in waiting at the Court. Mr. Inglesant was not more affectionate to his son than usual; he appeared anxious and worn, but he told him he was pleased at his arrival, that he must obey Father St. Clare in all things, and that he would become a useful and successful man. Father St. Clare had sent for a Court tailor, and ordered a proper dress and accoutrements for Johnny, who was astonished at his own appearance when attired in lace and satin, and his long hair combed and dressed. The Jesuit regarded him with satisfaction, and told him they were going at once to the Queen. Mr. Inglesant's coach was sent for them, and was waiting in one of the courts; and entering, they were driven through the Strand to Whitehall.

It was the third of August, and the Archbishop was marrying the Duke of Lennox to the Lady Mary Villiers, the daughter of the great Duke of Buckingham, in his Chapel at Lambeth. The King was expected to go to Lambeth to be present at the ceremony, but this was of no consequence to the Jesuit, who wished to introduce his protégé to the Queen alone. When they reached Whitehall, however, they found that both their Majesties had gone to the wedding, and the day being very rainy, news had been sent from Lambeth immediately after the ceremony that the Queen was returning, and she was then on the water. The Jesuit and Johnny left their carriage and went down to the water-gate. The Jesuit was evidently well known at the Court, and way was made for him everywhere. At that time the greatest laxity was allowed to the Catholics, and other priests besides the Queen's confessors were tolerated openly in London. As they reached the water-gate, the rain had ceased for a time, and a gleam of sunlight shone upon the river, and rested on the Queen's barge as it approached. Johnny's heart beat with excitement, as it reached the steps amid a flourish of trumpets, and the guard presented arms. The Queen, splendidly dressed, came from under the awning and up the steps, accompanied by her gentlemen and the ladies of her Court. Johnny never forgot the sight to his dying day, and it was doubtless one to be long remembered by those who saw it for the first time. When the Queen was near the top of the stairs and saw St. Clare, she stopped, and extending her hand she welcomed him to the Court. She seemed to remember something, and spoke to him rapidly in French, to which he replied with the utmost deference, in the same language. Then falling back, he indicated Johnny to the Queen, saying—"This is young John Inglesant, your Majesty, of whom I spoke to your Grace concerning the business you wot of."

The Queen looked kindly at the boy, who indeed was handsome enough to incline any woman in his favour.

"They are a handsome race," she said, still speaking French; "this one, I think, still more so than his brother."

"This is a refined spirit, your Majesty," said the Jesuit, in a low voice, "of whom I hope great things, if your Majesty will aid."

"You wish to be one of my servants, my pretty boy," said the Queen, extending her hand to Johnny, who kissed it on one knee; "Father Hall will tell you what to do."

And she passed on, followed by her train, who looked at St. Clare and the boy with curiosity, several nodding and speaking to the Jesuit as they proceeded.

Johnny was duly entered the next day as one of the supernumerary pages without salary, and entered upon his duties at once, which consisted simply of waiting in anterooms and following the Queen at a distance in her walks. This life, however, was beyond measure interesting to Johnny: the beautiful rooms and galleries in the palace, with their wonderful contents, were an inexhaustible source of delight to him; especially the King's collection of paintings which was kept in a single apartment, and was admired over Europe. Father Hall took him also to many gentlemen's virtuoso collections of paintings and curiosities, where his intelligence and delight attracted the interest and kindness of all his hosts. Father St. Clare also gave him, from time to time, small editions of the classics and other books which he could keep in his pocket, and read in the anterooms and galleries when he was in waiting. He would have been astonished, if the Jesuit had not told him it would be so, at the number of persons of all ranks and opinions in the Court, who spoke to him and endeavoured to make his acquaintance that they might remember him at a future time, evidently at the request of the priest.

Shortly after he came to London, he was present at the Chapel Royal, at Whitehall, when the King took the sacrament and presented the gold pieces coined especially for this purpose. The sight impressed Johnny very much. The beautiful Chapel, the high altar on which candles were burning, the Bishops and the Dean of the Chapel in their copes, the brilliant crowd of courtiers, the King—devout and stately—alone before the altar, the exquisite music, and the singing of the King's choir, which was not surpassed in Rome itself. As the sunlight from the stained windows fell on this wonderful scene, it is not surprising that young Inglesant was affected by it, nor that this young spirit looking out for the first time on the world and its surprising scenes, and pageants, and symbols, realized the truth of what the old Parson had told him, and converted all these sights into spiritual visions; this one in particular, which led back his thoughts, as it was meant, to the three kings of old, who knelt and offered gifts before the mysterious Child.

Johnny saw his brother frequently, as the latter had grown out of his page-hood, and held another post about the Court, which gave him much leisure. The two young courtiers were at this time more alike than ever, and were much admired at Court as a pair. At one of the Queen's Masques, about this time, they acted parts somewhat similar to the brothers in Comus, but requiring greater resemblance, as in Shakespeare's Comedy of Errors, and both their acting and appearance was applauded by the King himself, who began to take notice of Johnny. Mr. Inglesant, the elder, had never been a favourite with the King, who was aware of his leaning to Popery, and indeed, at this time, both he and his friend the Jesuit were very much discouraged at the aspect of affairs. The position of the Papists had never been so good as at present, but this very circumstance was the ruin of their party. All restraints and reproaches of former times seemed forgotten; a public agent from Rome resided openly at the Court, and was magnificently fêted and caressed; the priests, though to avow popish orders was by law punishable with death, went about and preached openly without fear; and it was related as a sign of the times, that a Jesuit at Paris who was coming into England, coolly called on the English ambassador there, who knew his profession, offering his services in London, as though there were no penal law to condemn him the moment he landed! High Mass at Somerset House was attended at noon-day by great numbers of the Papists, who returned together from it through the streets as openly as the congregation of the Savoy, and the neighbouring churches. Their priests succeeded in converting several ladies of some of the greatest families, thereby provoking the anger of their relations, and causing them to long for their suppression. They held large political conferences openly, and ostentatiously subscribed a large sum of money to assist the King against the Scots. Clarendon, indeed, says that they acted as though they had been suborned by these latter to root out their own religion.

It would seem, indeed, that the English mind is not habituated to plotting, and that the majority of any party are not equal to a sustained and concealed effort. The Jesuit, Mr.

Inglesant, and the other astute members of their party, perceived with sorrow the course things were taking without being able to remedy it. The former desisted from all active efforts, contenting himself with assisting the Queen in her attempts to win over members of the Parliament to her interest, and in opposing and counteracting the intrigues of a small and fanatical section of the Papists who were attempting a wild and insane plot against the King and the Archbishop, which was said to extend to even the attempting their death. As neither of these occupations was very arduous, he had little need of Johnny's assistance, and left him very much to himself. Inglesant, therefore, continued the cultivation of his acquaintance with both parties pretty much in his own way. He had several friends whose society he much valued among the Papists, and he frequently attended mass when not obliged to by his attendance upon the Queen; but he was rather more inclined to attach himself to the members of the Laudian and High Church party, who presented many qualities which interested and attracted him. He read with delight the books of this party, Dr. Donne's and Herbert's Poems, and the writings of Andrews and Bishop Cosin's Devotions, which last was much disliked by the Puritans, and, indeed, the course he took could not have been more in accordance with the Jesuit's plan of preparing him for future service, should the time ever arrive when such usefulness should be required. In his mind he was still devoted, though in a halting and imperfect manner, to that pursuit of the spiritual life and purity which had attracted him when so young, and he lost no opportunity of consulting any on these mysterious subjects who he thought would sympathize with his ideas. In this he had no assistance from his brother, who was devoted to the pursuit of pleasure—of worldly pleasure, it is true, in its most refined aspect—but still of such pleasures as are entirely apart from those of the soul.

One of his friends had presented Inglesant with a little book, "Divine Considerations of those things most profitable in our Christian profession," written in Spanish by John Valdesso, a Papist, and translated by a gentleman of whom Johnny heard a great deal, and was exceedingly interested in what he heard. In this book the author says several very high and beautiful things concerning the Spiritual life, and of the gradual illumination of the Divine Light shed upon the mind, as the sun breaks by degrees upon the eyes of a traveller in the dark. But though Johnny was attracted to the book itself, he was principally interested in it by what he heard of the translator. This was Mr. Nicholas Ferrar, who had founded a religious house at Little Gidding, in Huntingdonshire, or, as it was called in the world, the "Protestant Nunnery," in which he lived with his mother and several nephews and nieces, in the practice of good works and the worship of God. Extraordinary attention had been attracted to this establishment by the accounts of the strange and holy life of its inmates; and still more by the notice which the King had condescended to take of it, not only visiting it on his journey to Scotland, in 1633, but also requesting and accepting presents of devotional books, which it was part of the occupation of the family to prepare.

The accounts of this religious house, and of the family within it, so excited Johnny's imagination that he became exceedingly desirous to see it, especially as it was said that Mr. Ferrar was very infirm, and was not expected to survive very long.

It was late in the autumn when he made this visit, about two months before Mr. Ferrar's death. The rich autumn foliage was lighted by the low sun as he rode through the woods and meadows, and across the sluggish streams of Bedford and Huntingdon. He slept at a village a few miles south of Little Gidding, and reached that place early in the day. It was a solitary, wooded place, with a large manor house, and a little Church close by. It had been for some time depopulated, and there were no cottages nor houses near. The manor house and Church had been restored to perfect order by Mr. Ferrar, and Inglesant reached it through a grove of trees planted in walks, with latticed paths and gardens on both sides. A brook crossed the road at the foot of the gentle ascent on which the house was built. He asked to see Mr. Ferrar, and was shown by a man-servant into a fair spacious parlour, where Mr. Ferrar presently came to him. Inglesant was disappointed at his appearance, which was plain and not striking in any way, but his speech was able and attractive. Johnny apologized for his bold visit, telling him how much taken he had been by his book, and by what he had heard of him and his family; and that what he had heard did not interest him merely out of curiosity, as he feared it might have done many, but out of sincere desire to learn something of the holy life which doubtless that family led. To this Mr. Ferrar replied that he was thankful to see any one who came in such a spirit, and that several, not only of his own friends, as Mr. Crashaw the poet, but many young students from the University at Cambridge came to see him in a like spirit, to the benefit, he hoped, of both themselves and of him. He said with great humility, that although on the one hand very much evil had been spoken of him which was not true, he had no doubt that, on the other, many things had been said about their holiness and the good that they did which went far beyond the truth. For his own part, he said he had adopted that manner of life through having long seen enough of the manners and vanities of the world; and holding them in low esteem, was resolved to spend the best of his life in mortifications and devotion, in charity, and in constant preparation for death. That his mother, his elder brother, his sisters, his nephews and nieces, being content to lead this mortified life, they spent their time in acts of devotion and by doing such good works as were within their power, such as keeping a school for the children of the next parishes, for teaching of whom he provided three masters who lived constantly in the house. That for ten years they had lived this harmless life, under the care of his mother, who had trained her daughters and grand-daughters to every good work; but two years ago they had lost her by death, and as his health was very feeble he did not expect long to be separated from her, but looked forward to his departure with joy, being afraid of the evil times he saw approaching.

When he had said this, he led Inglesant into a large handsome room upstairs, where he introduced him to his sister, Mrs. Collet, and her daughters, who were engaged in making those curious books of Scripture Harmonies which had so pleased King Charles. These seven young ladies, who formed the junior part of the Society of the house, and were called by the names of the chief virtues, the Patient, the Cheerful, the Affectionate, the Submiss, the Obedient, the Moderate, the Charitable, were engaged at that moment in cutting out passages from two Testaments, which they pasted together so neatly as to seem one book, and in such a manner as to enable the reader to follow the narrative in all its particulars from beginning to end without a break, and also to see which of the sacred authors had contributed any particular part.

Inglesant told the ladies what fame reported of the nuns of

Gidding, of two watching and praying all night, of their canonical hours, of their crosses on the outside and inside of their Chapel, of an altar there richly decked with plate, tapestry, and tapers, of their adoration and genuflexions at their entering. He told Mr. Ferrar that his object in visiting him was chiefly to know his opinion of the Papists and their religion, as, having been bred among them himself and being very nearly one of them, he was anxious to know the opinions of one who was said to hold many of their doctrines without joining them or approving them. Mr. Ferrar appeared at first shy of speaking, but being apparently convinced of the young man's sincerity, and that he was not an enemy in disguise, he conversed very freely with him for some time, speaking much of the love of God, and of the vanity of worldly things; of his dear friend Mr. George Herbert, and of his saintly life; of the confused and troublesome life he had formerly led, and of the great peace and satisfaction which he had found since he had left the world and betaken himself to that retired and religious life. That, as regards the Papists, his translating Valdessa's book was a proof that he knew that among them, as among all people, there were many true worshippers of Jesus, being drawn by the blessed Sacrament to follow him in the spiritual and divine life, and that there were many things in that book similar to the mystical religion of which Inglesant spoke, which his dear friend Mr. George Herbert had disapproved, as exalting the inward spiritual life above the foundation of holy Scripture: that it was not for him, who was only a deacon in the Church, to pronounce any opinion on so difficult a point, and that he had printed all Mr. Herbert's notes in his book, without comment of his own: that though he was thus unwilling to give his own judgment, he certainly believed that this inward spiritual life was open to all men, and recommended Inglesant to continue his endeavours after it, seeking it chiefly in the holy Sacrament accompanied with mortification and confession.

While they were thus talking, the hour of evening prayer arrived, and Mr. Ferrar invited Johnny to accompany him to the Church; which he gladly did, being very much attracted by the evident holiness which pervaded Mr. Ferrar's talk and manner. The family proceeded to Church in procession, Mr. Ferrar and Inglesant walking first. The Church was kept in great order, the altar being placed upon a raised platform at the east end, and covered with tapestry stretching over the floor all round it, and adorned with plate and tapers. Mr. Ferrar bowed with great reverence several times on approaching the altar, and directed Inglesant to sit in a stalled seat opposite the reading pew, from which he said the evening prayer. The men of the family knelt on the raised step before the altar, the ladies and servants sitting in the body of the Church. The Church was very sweet, being decked with flowers and herbs; and the soft autumn light rested over it. From the seat where Inglesant knelt, he could see the faces of the girls as they bent over their books at prayers. They were all in black, except one, who wore a friar's grey gown; this was the one who was called the Patient, as Inglesant had been told in the house, and the singularity of her dress attracted his eye towards her during the prayers. The whole scene, strange and romantic as it appeared to him, the devout and serious manner of the worshippers—very different from much that was common in churches at that day—and the abstracted and devout look upon the faces of the girls struck his fancy, so liable to such influences, and so long trained to welcome them; and he could not keep his eyes from this one face from which the grey hood was partly thrown back. It was a passive face, with well-cut delicate features, and large and quiet eyes.

Prayers being over, the ladies saluted Inglesant from a distance, and left the Church with the rest, in the same order as they had come, leaving Mr. Ferrar and Johnny alone. They remained some time discoursing on worship and Church ceremonies, and then returned to the house. It was now late, and Mr. Ferrar, who was evidently much pleased with his guest, invited him to stay the night, and even extended his hospitality by asking him to stay over the next, which was Saturday, and the Sunday, upon which, as it was the first Sunday in the month, the holy Sacrament would be administered, and several of Mr. Ferrar's friends from Cambridge would come over and partake of it, and to pass the night and day in prayer and acts of devotion. To this proposition Inglesant gladly consented, the whole proceeding appearing to him full of interest and attraction. Soon after they returned to the house supper was served, all the family sitting down together at a long table in the hall. During supper some portion of Foxe's Book of Martyrs was read aloud. Afterwards two hours were permitted for diversion, during which all were allowed to do as they pleased.

The young ladies having found out that Inglesant was a Queen's page, were very curious to hear of the Court and royal family from him, which innocent request Mr. Ferrar encouraged, and joined in himself. One reason of the success with which his mother and he had ruled this household appears to have been his skill in interesting and attracting all its inmates by the variety and pleasant character of their occupations. He was also much interested himself in what Johnny told him, for in this secluded family, themselves accustomed to prudence, Inglesant felt he might safely speak of many things upon which he was generally silent; and after prayers, when the family were retired to their several rooms, Mr. Ferrar remained with him some time, while Johnny related to him the aspect of religious parties at the moment, and particularly all that he could tell, without violating confidence, of the Papists and of his friend the Jesuit.

The next morning they rose at four, though two of the family had been at prayer all night, and did not go to rest till the others rose. They went into the oratory in the house itself to prayers, for they kept six times of prayer during the day. At six they said the psalms of the hour, for every hour had its appropriate psalms, and at half-past six went to Church for matins. When they returned at seven o'clock, they said the psalms of the hour, sang a short hymn, and went to breakfast. After breakfast, when the younger members of the family were at their studies, Mr. Ferrar took Inglesant to the school, where all the children in the neighbourhood were permitted to come. At eleven they went to dinner, and after dinner there was no settled occupation till one, every one being allowed to amuse himself as he chose. The young ladies had been trained not only to superintend the house, but to wait on any sick persons in the neighbourhood who came to the house at certain times for assistance, and to dress the wounds of those who were hurt, in order to give them readiness and skill in this employment, and to habituate them to the virtues of humility and tenderness of heart. A large room was set apart for this purpose, where Mr. Ferrar had instructed them in the necessary skill, having been himself Physic Fellow at Clare Hall, in Cambridge, and under the celebrated Professors at Padua, in

Italy. This room Inglesant requested to see, thinking that he should in this way also see something of and be able to speak to the young ladies, whose acquaintance he had hitherto not had much opportunity of cultivating. Mr. Ferrar told his nephew to show it him—young Nicholas Ferrar, a young man of extraordinary skill in languages, who was afterwards introduced to the King and Prince Charles, some time before his early death. When they entered the room Inglesant was delighted to find that the only member of the family there was the young lady in the Grey Friar's habit, whose face had attracted him so much in Church. She was listening to the long tiresome tale of an old woman, following the example of George Herbert, who thought on a similar occasion, that "it was some relief to a poor body to be heard with patience."

Johnny, who in spite of his Jesuitical and Court training was naturally modest, and whose sense of religion made him perfectly well-bred, accosted the young lady very seriously, and expressed his gratitude at having been permitted to stay and see so many excellent and improving things as that family had to show. The liking which the head of the house had evidently taken for Inglesant disposed the younger members in his favour, and the young lady answered him simply and unaffectedly, but with manifest pleasure.

Inglesant inquired concerning the assumed names of the sisters and how they sustained their respective qualities, and what exercises suited to these qualities they had to perform. She replied that they had exercises, or discourses, which they performed at the great festivals of the year, Christmas and Easter; and which were composed with reference to their several qualities. All of these, except her own, were enlivened by hymns and odes composed by Mr. Ferrar, and set to music by the music master of the family, who accompanied the voices with the viol or the lute. But her own, she said, had never any music or poetry connected with it; it was always of a very serious turn, and much longer than any other, and had not any historical anecdote or fable interwoven with it, the contrivance being to exercise that virtue to which she was devoted. Inglesant asked her with pity if this was not very hard treatment, and she only replied, with a smile, that she had the enjoyment of all the lively performances of the others. He asked her whether they looked forward to passing all their lives in this manner, or whether they allowed the possibility of any change, and if she had entirely lost her own name in her assumed one, or whether he might presume to ask it, that he might have wherewithal to remember her by, as he surely should as long as he had life. She said her name was Mary Collet; and that as to his former question, two of her sisters had had, at one time, a great desire to become veiled virgins, to take upon them a vow of perpetual chastity, with the solemnity of a Bishop's blessing and ratification, but on going to Bishop Williams he had discouraged, and at last dissuaded them from it.

Inglesant and the young lady remained talking in this way for some time, young Nicholas Ferrar having left them; but at last she excused herself from staying any longer, and he was obliged to let her go. He ventured to say that he hoped they would remember him, that he was utterly ignorant of the future that lay before him, but that whatever fate awaited him, he should never forget the "Nuns of Gidding" and their religious life. She replied that they would certainly remember him, as they did all their acquaintances, in their daily prayer, especially as she had seldom seen her uncle so pleased with a stranger as he had been with him. With these compliments they parted, and Inglesant returned to the drawing-room, where more visitors had arrived.

In the afternoon there came from Cambridge Mr. Crashaw the poet, of Peterhouse, who afterwards went over to the Papists, and died Canon of Loretto, and several gentlemen, undergraduates of Cambridge, to spend the Sunday at Gidding, being the first Sunday of the month. Mr. Crashaw, when Inglesant was introduced to him as one of the Queen's pages, finding that he was acquainted with many Roman Catholics, was very friendly, and conversed with him apart. He said he conceived a great admiration for the devout lives of the Catholic saints, and of the government and discipline of the Catholic Church, and that he feared that the English Church had not sufficient authority to resist the spread of Presbyterianism, in which case he saw no safety except in returning to the communion of Rome. Walking up and down the garden paths, after evening prayers in Church, he spoke a great deal on this subject, and on the beauty of a retired religious life, saying that here at Little Gidding and at Little St. Marie's Church, near to Peterhouse, he had passed the most blissful moments of his life, watching at midnight in prayer and meditation.

That night Mr. Crashaw, Inglesant, and one or two others, remained in the Church from nine till twelve, during which time they said over the whole Book of Psalms in the way of antiphony, one repeating one verse and the rest the other. The time of their watch being ended they returned to the house, went to Mr. Ferrar's door and bade him good-morrow, leaving a lighted candle for him. They then went to bed, but Mr. Ferrar arose according to the passage of Scripture "at midnight I will arise and give thanks," and went into the Church, where he betook himself to religious meditation.

Early on the Sunday morning the family were astir and said prayers in the oratory. After breakfast many people from the country around and more than a hundred children came in. These children were called the Psalm children, and were regularly trained to repeat the Psalter, and the best voices among them to assist in the service on Sundays. They came in every Sunday, and according to the proficiency of each were presented with a small piece of money, and the whole number entertained with a dinner after Church. The Church was crowded at the morning service before the Sacrament. The service was beautifully sung, the whole family taking the greatest delight in Church music, and many of the gentlemen from Cambridge being amateurs. The Sacrament was administered with the greatest devotion and solemnity. Impressed as he had been with the occupation of the preceding day and night, and his mind excited with watching and want of sleep and with the exquisite strains of the music, the effect upon Inglesant's imaginative nature was excessive. Above the altar, which was profusely bedecked with flowers, the antique glass of the east window, which had been carefully repaired, contained a figure of the Saviour of an early and severe type. The form was gracious and yet commanding, having a brilliant halo round the head, and being clothed in a long and apparently seamless coat; the two fore-fingers of the right hand were held up to bless. Kneeling upon the half-pace, as he received the sacred bread and tasted the holy wine, this gracious figure entered into Inglesant's soul, and stillness and peace unspeakable, and life, and light, and sweetness, filled his mind. He was lost in a sense of rapture, and earth and all that surrounded him faded away. When he returned a little to himself, kneeling in his seat in the Church, he thought that at no period of his life, however extended, should he ever forget that morning or lose the sense and feeling of that touching scene, of that gracious figure over the altar, of the bowed and kneeling figures, of the misty autumn sunlight and the sweeping autumn wind. Heaven itself seemed to have opened to him, and one fairer than the fairest of the angelic hosts to have come down to earth.

After the service, the family and all the visitors returned to the mansion house in the order in which they had come, and the Psalm children were entertained with a dinner in the great hall; all the family and visitors came in to see them served, and Mrs. Collet, as her mother had always done, placed the first dish on the table herself to give an example of humility. Grace having been said, the bell rang for the dinner of the family, who, together with the visitors, repaired to the great dining-room, and stood in order round the table. While the dinner was being served they sang a hymn accompanied by the organ at the upper end of the room. Then grace was said by the Priest who had celebrated the communion, and they sat down. All the servants who had received the Sacrament that day sat at table with the rest. During dinner one of the young people whose turn it was, read a chapter from the Bible, and when that was finished conversation was allowed; Mr. Ferrar and some of the other gentlemen endeavouring to make it of a character suitable to the day, and to the service they had just taken part in. After dinner they went to Church again for evening prayer; between which service and supper Inglesant had some talk with Mr. Ferrar concerning the Papists and Mr. Crashaw's opinion of them.

"I ought to be a fit person to advise you," said Mr. Ferrar with a melancholy smile, "for I am myself, as it were, crushed between the upper and nether millstone of contrary reports, for I suffer equal obloquy—and no martyrdom is worse than that of continual obloquy—both for being a Papist and a Puritan. You will suppose there must be some strong reason why I, who value so many things among the Papists so much, have not joined them myself. I should probably have escaped much violent invective if I had done so. You are very young, and are placed where you can see and judge of both parties. You possess sufficient insight to try the spirits whether they be of God. Be not hasty to decide, and before you decide to join the Romish communion, make a tour abroad, and if you can, go to Rome itself. When I was in Italy and Spain, I made all the inquiries and researches I could. I bought many scarce and valuable books in the languages of those countries, in collecting which I had a principal eye to those which treated on the subjects of spiritual life, devotion, and religious retirement, but the result of all was that I am now, and I shall die, as I believe and hope shortly, in the Communion of the English Church. This day, as I believe, the blessed Sacrament has been in the Church before our eyes, and what can you or I desire more?"

The next morning before Inglesant left, Mr. Ferrar showed him his foreign collections, his great treasure of rarities and of prints of the best masters of that time, mostly relative to historical passages of the Old and New Testaments. Inglesant dined with the family, of whom he took leave with a full heart, saluting the ladies with the pleasant familiarity which the manners of the time permitted. Mr. Ferrar went with him to the borders of the parish, and gave him his blessing. They never saw each other again, for two months afterwards Nicholas Ferrar was in his grave.

CHAPTER V.

The next year of Inglesant's life contained several incidents which had very important results. The first of these was the illness and death of his father, which occurred shortly after Johnny's return to London. His end was doubtless hastened by the perplexity and disappointment of many of his political projects, for his life in many respects was a failure. Though a rich man he had spent large sums in his political intrigues, and the property he left was not large. His lands and all his money he left to his eldest son, but he left Johnny some houses in the city, which Inglesant was advised to sell. He therefore disposed of them to a Parliament man, and deposited the money with a goldsmith to be ready in case of need. The possession of this money made him an important person, and he was advised to purchase a place about the Court, which, with his interest with the Queen's advisers, would secure his success in life. He endeavoured to act on this advice, but it was some time before he was successful.

After his return to London Inglesant saw Mr. Crashaw

two or three times, when that gentleman was in London, and his conversation led him to think more of the Roman Catholics than he had hitherto done, and inclined him more and more to join them. Nothing would have recommended him so much to the Queen as such a step, and his feelings and sympathies all led him the same way. He was exceedingly disgusted with the conduct and conversation of the Puritans, and the extreme lengths to which it was evident they were endeavouring to drive the people. Most of his friends, even those who were themselves sound Churchmen, looked favourably on the Papists, and it was thought the height of ill breeding to speak against them at Court. It is probable, therefore, that Inglesant would have joined them openly but for two very opposite causes. The one was his remembrance of the Sacrament at Little Gidding, the other was the influence of his friend the Jesuit. The first of these prevented that craving after the sacrifice of the Mass, which doubtless is the strongest of all the motives which lead men to Rome; the other was exerted several ways.

It was one of the political maxims of this man that he never, if possible, allowed anything he had gained or any mode of influence he had acquired to be lost or neglected, even though circumstances had rendered it useless for the particular purpose for which he had at first intended it. In the present case he had no intention of permitting all the care and pains he had been at in Inglesant's education to be thrown away. It is true the exact use to which he had intended to devote the talents he had thus trained no longer existed, but this did not prevent his appreciating the exquisite fitness of the instrument he had prepared for such or similar use. Circumstances had occurred which in his far-seeing policy made the Church of England scarcely worth gaining to the Catholic side, but in proportion as the Church might cease to be one of the great powers in the country, the Papists would step into its place : and in the confused political struggles which he foresaw, the Jesuit anticipated ample occupation for the peculiar properties of his pupil. In the event of a struggle, the termination of which none could foresee, a qualified agent would be required as much between the Papists and the popular leaders as between the Catholics and the Royal and Church party. Acting on these principles, therefore, the Jesuit was far from losing sight of Inglesant, or even neglecting him. So far indeed was he from doing so, that he was acquainted with most that passed through his mind, and was well aware of his increased attraction towards the Church to which he himself belonged. Now for Inglesant to have become actively and enthusiastically a Papist would at once have defeated all his plans for him, and rendered him useless for the peculiar needs for which he had been prepared. He would doubtless have gone abroad, and even if he had not remained buried in some college on the Continent, he would have returned merely as one of those mission priests (for doubtless he would have taken orders) of whom the Jesuit had already more than he required. It was even not desirable that he should associate exclusively with Papists. He was already sufficiently known and his position understood among them for the purposes of any future mission on which he might be engaged; and it would be more to the purpose for him to extend his acquaintance among Church of England people, and gain their confidence. To this end the Jesuit thought proper to remove him from the immediate attendance on the Queen, where he saw few except Papists, and to assist in his endeavours to purchase a place about the King's person. In this he was successful, and about the end of 1639 Inglesant purchased the place of one of the Esquires of the Body who relinquished his place on account of ill health. This post, which followed immediately after that of the gentlemen of the Privy Chamber, was looked upon as a very important and influential one, and cost Inglesant a large sum of money before he obtained it. He was, as we have seen, rather a favourite with the King, who had noticed him more than once, and he began to be regarded as a rising courtier whose friendship it would be well to keep.

When the Jesuit had seen him settled in his new post, he put in motion another and still more powerful engine which he had prepared for preventing his pupil from joining the Romish Church. He had himself inculcated as much as possible a broad and philosophical method of thought upon his pupil, but he was necessarily confined and obstructed in this direction by his own position and supposed orthodoxy, and he was therefore anxious to infuse into Inglesant's mind a larger element of rational inquiry than in his sacred character it was possible for him to accomplish without shocking his pupil's moral sense. If I have not failed altogether in representing that pupil's character, it will have been noticed that it was one of those which combine activity of thought with great faculty of reverence and of submission to those powers to which its fancy and taste are subordinated. These natures are enthusiastic, though generally not supposed to be so, and though little sign of it appears in their outward conduct; for the objects of their enthusiasm being generally different from those which attract most men, they are conscious that they have little sympathy to expect in their pursuit of them, and this gives their enthusiasm a reserved and cautious demeanour. They are not, however, blindly enthusiastic, but are never satisfied till they have found some theory by which they are able to reconcile in their own minds the widest results to which their activity of thought has led them, with the submission and service which it is their delight and choice to pay to such outward systems and authorities as have pleased and attracted their taste. This theory consists generally in some, at times half-formed, conception of the imperfect dispensation in which men live, which makes obedience to authority, with which the most exalted reason cannot entirely sympathize, becoming and even necessary. This feeling more than anything else, gives to persons of this nature a demeanour quite different from that of the ordinary religious or political enthusiast, a demeanour seemingly cold and indifferent, though courteous and even to some extent sympathetic, and which causes the true fanatic to esteem them as little better than the mere man of the world, or the minion of courtly power. The enthusiastic part of his character had been fully cultivated in Inglesant, the reasoning and philosophic part had been wakened and trained to some extent by his readings in Plato under the direction of the Jesuit; it remained now to be still more developed, whether to the ultimate improvement of his character it would be hard to say.

The Jesuit took him one day into the city to Devonshire House, where, inquiring for Mr. Hobbes, they were shown into a large handsome room full of books, where a gentleman was sitting whose appearance struck Inglesant very much. He was tall and very erect, with a square mallet-shaped head and ample forehead. He wore a small red moustache, that curled upward, and a small tuft of hair upon his chin. His eyes were hazel and full of life and spirit, and when he spoke they shone with lively light; when he was witty and laughed the lids closed over them so that they could scarcely be seen, but when he was serious and in earnest they expanded to their full orb, and penetrated, as it seemed, to the farthest limit of thought. He was dressed in a coat of black velvet lined with fur, and wore long boots of Spanish leather laced with ribbon.

When the first compliments were over, the Jesuit introduced Inglesant to him as a young gentleman of promise, who would derive great benefit from his acquaintance, and whose friendship he hoped might not prove unacceptable to Mr. Hobbes.

Inglesant came often to Mr. Hobbes, whose conversation delighted him. It frequently referred to the occurrences of the day, in which Mr. Hobbes sided with the Government, having a great regard for the King personally, as had Harrington afterwards, and most of the philosophers—all their sympathies and theories being on the side of law and strong government; but their discourse frequently went beyond this, and embraced those questions of human existence which interest thinking men. He soon found out Inglesant's tendency towards Catholicism, and strongly dissuaded him from it.

"Your idea of the Catholic system," he said, "is a dream, and has no real existence among the Papists. Your ideal is an exalted Platonic manifestation of the divine existence diffused among men: the reality is a system of mean trivial details, wearisome and disgusting to such men as you are. Instead of the perfect communion with the Divine Light, such as you seek, you will have before you and above you nothing but the narrow conceptions of some ignorant priest to whom you must submit your intellect. What freedom of thought or existence will remain to you when you have fully accepted the article of transubstantiation, and truly believe that the priest is able of a piece of bread to make absolutely and unconditionally our Saviour's body, and thereby at the hour of death to save your soul? Will it not have an effect upon you to make you think him a god, and to stand in awe of him as of God Himself if he were visibly present?"

"I suppose it would," said Inglesant.

"One of our divines of the English Church, writing much above their wont—for they are much stronger in their lives than in their writings—puts this very plainly in the matter of the judgment of the priest in confession. 'Yet this extorted confession on Pain of Damnation is not the stripping a man to his naked body, but the stripping him of his body, that they may see his naked heart, and so, by the force of this superstition, break into those secrets, which it is the only due privilege of Almighty God to be acquainted with, who is the only rightful Searcher of hearts.' These men may well pretend to be followers of Aristotle, who reason only from the names of things, according to the scale of the Categories; but of those of the better sort, as you and I take ourselves to be, who follow Plato, and found our doctrine on the conceptions and ideas of things, we must ever submit to be called heretics by them as a reproach, though we, doubtless, and not they, are the true sacramentalists, that is, the seekers for the hidden and the divine truth. It is for this reason that I take the Sacrament in the English Church, which I call in England the Holy Church, and believe that its statutes are the true Christian Faith."

"There seems to me," he went on after a pause, "something frightfully grotesque about the Romish Church as a reality. Showing us on the one side a mass of fooleries and ridiculous conceits and practices, at which, but for the use of them, all men must needs stand amazed; such rabble of impossible relics, —the hay that was in the manger, and more than one tail of the ass on which Christ rode into Jerusalem, besides hundreds which for common decency no man in any other case would so much as name. To look on these, I say, on one side, and on the other to see those frightful and intolerable cruelties, so detestable that they cannot be named, by which thousands have been tormented by this holy and pure Church, has something about it so grotesque and fantastic that it seems to me sometimes more like some masque or dance of satyrs or devils than the followers of our Saviour Christ."

"All this," said Inglesant, "I partly believe, yet I imagine that something may be said upon the other side of the argument, and I should suppose that there is not one of these doctrines and practices but what has some shadow of truth in it, and sprang at first from the wellspring of truth."

"Doubtless," said the philosopher, "there is nothing but has had its origin in some conception of the truth, but are we 'for this cause,' as that same divine says, 'also to forsake the Truth itself, and devotionally prostrate ourselves to every evanescent and far-cast show of Him—shadows of shadows —in infinite myriads of degenerations from Him?' Surely not."

"What is truth?" said Inglesant; "who shall show us any good?"

"Truth," said the philosopher, "is that which we have been taught, that which the civil government under which we live instructs us in and directs us to believe. Our Saviour Christ came as the Messiah to establish His kingdom on earth, and after Him the Apostles and Christian Princes and Commonwealths have handed down His truth to us. This is our only safe method of belief."

"But should we believe nothing of Christianity," said Inglesant, "unless the civil government had taught it us?"

"How can you believe anything," said Hobbes, "unless you have first been taught it? and in a Christian Commonwealth the civil government is the vicar of Christ. I know the Jesuits," said Hobbes, "and they me; when I was in France, some of them came to trouble me about something I had said. I quieted them by promising to write a book upon them if they did not let me be: what they seek is influence over the minds of men; to gain this they will allow every vice of which man is capable. I could prove it from their books. It is not for me, whom you scarcely know, to say anything against a friend whom you have known so long; but, as I understand you, your friend does not advise you to become a Papist. I do not suppose, though possibly you may do so, that he has no other object in view than your welfare. He has doubtless far-reaching reasons of which we know nothing; nevertheless, be not distrustful of him, but in this especially follow his advice. Shakespeare, the play-writer, says 'there's a divinity that shapes our ends,' or, I should say, the ends that others work out for us, to His higher purpose. Let us have faith in this beneficent Artist, and let Him accomplish His will on us."

"But this," said Inglesant, "is very different from what my reading and experience in mystical religion has taught me. Is there then no medium between the Divine Life and ourselves than that of the civil government? This would seem to me most repulsive and contrary to experience."

"If you pretend to a direct revelation," said Hobbes with a smile, "I have nothing to allege against it, but, to the rest of us, Christian Sovereigns are the supreme pastors and the only persons we now hear speak from God. But because God giveth faith by means of teachers, therefore I call hearing the immediate cause of faith. In a school where many are taught, some profit, others profit not; the cause of learning in them that profit is the Master, yet it cannot be thence inferred that learning is not the gift of God. All good things proceed from God, yet cannot all that have them say that they are inspired, for that implies a gift supernatural and the immediate hand of God, which he that pretends to, pretends to be a prophet."

"I am loath to believe what you say," said Inglesant; "I am no prophet, yet I would willingly believe that God is speaking to me with an immediate voice, nay, more, that I may enter into the very life that God is leading, and partake of His nature. Also, what you now say seems to me to contradict what you said before, that we should endeavour to found our doctrine on the conceptions and ideas of things, which I take to mean a following after divine truth: nor do I see why you take the sacrament, as you say you do, except you expect some immediate communication from God in it."

The philosopher smiled. "One may see you have been taught in the Jesuits' college," he said, "and are a forward pupil and a close reasoner. But what I have said concerning faith coming by hearing need not prevent that afterwards God may convey other gifts to men by other means. Yet I confess I am not a proficient in this divine knowledge or life of which you speak; nor do I follow your master Plato very far into the same conclusions which many profess to find in him. One disputant grounds his knowledge upon the infallibility of the Church, and the other on the testimony of the private spirit. The first we need not discuss, but how do you know that your private spirit, that this divine life within you, is any other than a belief grounded on the authority and arguments of your teachers?"

Inglesant made no reply, which the philosopher perceiving, began to talk of something else, and the other soon after took his leave. Hobbes's doctrine was new to him, as it was to every one in that day, indeed, the particular form it took was peculiar to Hobbes, and perished with him; but the underlying materialism which in some form or other has presented itself to the thinkers of every age, and which now for the first time came before Inglesant's mind, was not without its effect. "How do I know indeed," he said, "that this divine life within me is anything but an opinion formed by what I have heard and read ? How do I know that there is any such thing as a divine life at all ?"

Such thoughts as these, if they produced no other effect, yet gradually lessened that eagerness in his mind towards divine things which had been so strong since his visit to Little Gidding, and quite satisfied him to defer at any rate any thoughts of joining the Church of Rome. But his thoughts were turned into other channels by the events which were occurring in the political world, and which began now to assume a very exciting character.

CHAPTER VI.

ON the 20th of August 1640 the King set out for York on his way to Scotland, in some haste, and Inglesant accompanied or rather preceded him, his duty being to provide apartments for the King. The King advanced no farther than North Allerton, Lord Strafford being at Darlington, and a large part of the army at Newburn-upon-Tyne, from whence they retreated before the Scots almost without fighting. It was at this time that Inglesant began to see more of the real state of affairs among the leaders of the royal party, and became aware of the real weakness of their position. He appears to have formed the opinion that Lord Strafford, in spite of his great qualities, had failed altogether in establishing himself on a firm and lasting footing of power, and was deficient in those qualities of a statesman that ensure success, and incapable of realizing the necessities of the times. His army, on which he relied, was disorganized, and totally without devotion or enthusiasm. It melted away before the Scots, or fraternized with them, and the trained bands and gentry who came into the King's standard and to the Earl, prefaced all their offers of service with petitions for the redress of grievances and the calling together a Parliament. Inglesant had already formed the opinion that the Archbishop, who was now left at the head of affairs in London with the Privy Council, and was vainly endeavouring to prevent the citizens from sending up monster petitions to the King, was even more at variance with the inevitable course of events, and more powerless to withstand them, than the Earl; and he appears to have written to his friend the Jesuit, for his guidance, careful explanations of his own views on these subjects. Father Hall, however, was not a man hastily to change his course. He had belonged from the beginning to that section of the popish party whose policy had been to support the High Church party rather than to oppose it, and this policy was strengthened now that the royal power itself began to be attacked. Whatever others of the popish party might think, those with whom the Jesuit acted, and the party at Rome which directed their conduct, were undeviating supporters of the King, and were convinced that all advantage which the Papists might in future achieve was dependent upon him. It is not apparent what action the Jesuit was taking at this moment, probably he was contented to watch the course of events; but this much is certain, that his efforts to induce Churchmen to work with him were increased rather than diminished.

While the King was at York, the Marquis of Montrose, who was in the Covenanters' army, carried on a correspondence with him, and copies of his letters were believed to be stolen from the King's pockets at night by one of the gentlemen of the bedchamber, and sent to the leader of the Scots' army. Montrose retired into Scotland, and as the King was desirous of continuing a correspondence which promised so much, he decided upon sending a special messenger to the Marquis. Inglesant was fixed upon for this mission, as being known by the Royalists as a confidential agent of the Court, but at the same time almost entirely unknown to the opposite party. He found Montrose at Edinburgh, at a time when the Marquis was endeavouring to form a party among the nobility of Scotland, in opposition to the Covenant. Inglesant was probably little more in this negotiation than an accredited letter-carrier; but a circumstance occurred in connection with his stay in Scotland which is not without interest with reference to his future character. Among the gentlemen with whom Montrose was in connection, were some of the Highland chiefs, and to one of these the Marquis sent Inglesant as a safe agent, being perfectly unknown in Scotland. This gentleman, understanding that the messenger of Montrose was coming to meet him, travelled down from the Highlands with a great retinue of servants, and sent on one of his gentlemen, with a few attendants, to meet the young Englishman on the borders of Perthshire. Inglesant had ridden from Stirling, and the night being stormy and dark, he had stopped at a gentleman's house in a lonely situation at the foot of the Badenoch Hills. Here, late in the evening, his entertainers met him, and they passed the night in company. After supper, as they were sitting in front of the fire with the master of the house and several more, the conversation turned upon the faculty of second sight and the numberless instances of its certainty with which the Highland gentlemen were acquainted. While they were thus discoursing, the attention of the gentleman who had come to meet Inglesant was attracted by an old Highlander who sat in the large chimney, and he inquired whether he saw anything unusual in the Englishman, that made him regard him with such attention. He said no, he saw nothing in him fatal or remarkable more than this, that he was much mistaken if that young man was not a seer himself, or, at any rate, would be able before many months were over to see apparitions and spirits. Inglesant thought little of this at the time, but he remembered it afterwards when an event occurred on his return to London which recalled it to his recollection.

The treaty having been settled with the Scots, and the writs issued for a new Parliament, the King returned to London.

One day in September, Inglesant received a visit from one of the servants of the Archbishop of Canterbury, who brought a message from Laud expressing a wish to see Mr. Inglesant at his dinner at Lambeth Palace on any day that would suit his convenience. He went the next day by water at the proper hour, and was ushered into the great hall of the palace, where dinner was laid, and many gentlemen and clergymen standing about in the windows and round the tables, waiting the Archbishop. Inglesant's entrance was remarked at once, his dress and appearance rendering him conspicuous, and his person being well known, and occasioned some surprise; for the Archbishop had not been latterly on friendly terms with the Queen, whom he had opposed on some questions relating to Papists, to whose party, even since his being in the King's household, Inglesant was considered to belong. The servants had evidently received orders concerning him, for he was placed very high at table, and waited upon with great attention. On the Archbishop's entrance he noticed Inglesant particularly, and expressed his pleasure at seeing him there. The conversation at dinner turned entirely on the Scotch rebellion, and the failure of the Earl of Strafford to repress it; and on the King's return to London, which had not long taken place. Several gentlemen present had been with the army, and spoke of the insubordination among the officers, especially such as had been Parliament men. The elections for the new Parliament were expected shortly to take place, and many of the officers were deserting from the army, and coming up to London and other places to secure their return. The utmost dissatisfaction and insubordination prevailed over the whole country, for Laud and Strafford, after exciting the animosity of the people, had proved themselves weak, and the people began to despise as well as hate them—not perceiving that this probably proved that they were not the finished tyrants they were supposed to be. Strafford's army, raised by himself, having proved powerless against the Scots and insubordinate against its master, the popular party was encouraged to attack him, whom they hated as much as ever, though they began to fear him less. The violent excitement of the popular party against the High Churchmen and against ceremonies was also a subject of conversation. The wildest rumours were prevalent as to the probable conduct of the new Parliament, but all agreed that the Lord Lieutenant and the Archbishop, and probably the Lord Keeper, would be impeached. After dinner the Archbishop rose from table, and retired into one of the windows, at the upper end of the hall, overlooking the river, requesting Inglesant, to whom he pointed out the beauties of the view, to follow him. Having done this, he said a few words to him in a low voice, explaining his regret at the difference which had arisen between himself and the Queen, whose most faithful servant he protested he had ever been, and whom he was most desirous to please. He then went on to say that he both could and intended to inform Her Majesty of this through other channels than Mr. Inglesant, though he bespoke his good offices therein; but he wished principally to speak to him of another matter, which would require privacy to explain fully to him; but thus far he would say, that although he had always been a true servant of the Church of England, and had never entertained any thoughts inconsistent with such fidelity, yet he believed the Roman Catholics were aware that he had always behaved with great toleration to them, and had always entertained a great respect for their religion, refusing to allow it to be abused or described as Antichrist in the English pulpits; that it was notorious that he had excited the enmity of the popular party by this conduct; and that whatever he might suffer under the new Parliament would be in consequence of it. He was aware that Mr. Inglesant was in the confidence of that party, and especially the particular friend of Father Hall, the leader of the most powerful section of it; and he entreated his services to bring the Jesuit and himself to some understanding and concerted action, whereby, at least, they might ward off some of the blows that would be aimed at them. The Archbishop said that many of the wisest politicians considered that the two parties who would divide the stage between them would be the popular party and the Papists; and if this were really the case (though he himself thought that the loyal Church party would prove stronger than was thought) it was evident that Mr. Inglesant's friend would be well able to return any kindness that the Archbishop had shown the Romanists.

Inglesant went to the Jesuit as soon as possible, and related his interview with the Archbishop. Father Hall listened to it with great interest.

"He has been like a true ecclesiastic," he said, "blind to facts while he was in the course of his power, astonished and confounded when the natural results arrive. Nevertheless, I fancy he will make a good fight, or at least a good ending. The people know not what they want, and might have been led easily, but it is too late. What was the real amount of tyranny and persecution the people suffered? The Church officers were blamed on the one hand for not putting the laws in force against the Papists, and on the other, for putting them in force against the Puritans. However, he has a right view of the power of the Church party, in which I join him. We shall see the good fight they will make for the King yet. The gentry and chivalry of England are rather rusty for want of use, but we shall see the metal they are made of before long. However, the Catholics will be ready first, are ready in fact now, and I have great hopes of the use that we shall make of these opportunities. I am much mistaken if such a chance as we shall have before many months are over will not be greater than we have had for a century. I shall count on you. We have been long delayed, and you must have thought all our pains would come to nothing: but we must have long patience if we enter on the road of politics.

"You are now," said the Jesuit, "embracing the cause full of enthusiasm and zeal, and this is very well; how else could we run out the race, unless we began with some little fire? But this will not last, and unless you are warned, you may be offended and fall away. When you have lived longer in this world and outlived the enthusiastic and pleasing illusions of youth, you will find your love and pity for the race increase tenfold, your admiration and attachment to any particular party or opinion fall away altogether. You will not find the royal cause perfect any more than any other, nor those embarked in it free from mean and sordid motives, though you think now that all of them act from the noblest. This is the most important lesson that a man can learn—that all men are really alike; that all creeds and opinions are nothing but the mere result of chance and temperament; that no party is on the whole better than another; that no creed does more than shadow imperfectly forth some one side of truth; and it is only when you begin to see this that you can feel that pity for mankind, that sympathy with its disappointments and follies, and its natural human hopes, which have such a little time of growth, and such a sure season of decay.

"I have seen nothing more pathetic than touches in the life of some of these Puritans—men who have, as they thought in obedience to the will of the Deity, denied themselves pleasure —human pleasure—through their lives, and now and then some old song, some pleasant natural tale of love flashes across their path, and the true human instinct of the sons of Adam lights up within them.

"Nothing but the Infinite pity is sufficient for the infinite pathos of human life.

"As you know, we have many parties in our Church, nay, in our own order: different members may be sent on opposing missions; but it is no matter, they are all alike. Hereafter it will be of little importance which of these new names, Cavalier or Roundhead, you are called by, whether you turn Papist or Puritan, Jesuit or Jansenist, but it will matter very much whether you acted as became a man, and did not flinch ignobly at the moment of trial. Choose your part from the instinct of your order, from your birth, or from habit or what not; but having chosen it, follow it to the end. Stand by your party or your order, and especially in the hour of trial or danger be sure you never falter; for, be certain of this, that no misery can be equal to that which a man feels who is conscious that he has proved unequal to his part, who has deserted the post his captain set him, and who, when men said 'such and such a one is there on guard, there is no need to take further heed,' has left his watch or quailed before the foeman, to the loss, perhaps the total ruin, of the cause he had made his choice. I pray God that such misery as this may never be yours."

The elections being over, London became very full. The new members hastened up. The nobility and country gentry came crowding in, and all the new houses in the Strand and Charing Cross were occupied, and a throng of young Cavaliers filled the courts and precincts of the palace. As soon as the King arrived, Inglesant went into waiting in his new post, in which great responsibility in the keeping of the royal household, especially at night, devolved upon him. His post came immediately after that of the gentlemen of the privy chamber, with whom the immediate attendance on the person of the King stopped, but the charge of the King's rooms brought him continually into the royal presence.

As soon as the Parliament met, the impeachment of Strafford began; and as it proceeded, the excitement grew more and more intense. It was not safe for the courtiers to go into the city, except in numbers together, and a court of guard was kept by the Cavaliers before Whitehall towards Charing Cross.

One day Inglesant received a letter from the Jesuit, whom he seldom saw, as follows:—

"Jack, tell your friend the Archbishop, that Lambeth House will be attacked two nights from this, by a rabble of the populace. The Parliament leaders will not be seen in this, but they can be felt. Burn this, but let the Archbishop know the hand from which it comes."

On receiving this warning the Archbishop fortified his house, and crossed the water to his chamber in Whitehall, where he slept that night and two others following. His house was attacked by a mob of five hundred men; one of them was wounded and afterwards executed; not much damage was done.

History can furnish few events so startling and remarkable as the trial and death of Lord Strafford—events which, the more they are studied the more wonderful they appear. It is not easy to find words to express the miserable weakness and want of statesmanship which led to, and made possible, such an event; and one is almost equally surprised at the comparatively few traces of the sensation and consternation that such an event must have produced. I am not speaking of the justice or the injustice of the sentence, nor of the crime or innocence of the accused,—I speak only of a great minister and servant of the Crown, in whose policy and support the whole of the royal power, the whole strength of the national establishment, was involved and pledged. That such a man, by the simple clamour of popular opinion, should have been arrested, tried, and executed in a few days, with no effort but the most degrading and puny one made on his behalf by his royal master and friend, certainly must have produced a terror and excitement, one would think, unequalled in history. That the King never recovered from it is not surprising; one would have thought he would never have held up his head again. That the royal party was amazed and confounded is not wonderful; one would have thought it would have been impossible ever to have formed a royal party afterwards. That there was no power in the country able to protect either the Lords or the Monarch in the discharge of their conscience seems too strange to be believed.

It was two nights after the execution. The guard was set at Whitehall and the "all night" served up. The word for the night was given, and the whole palace was considered as under the sole command of Inglesant, as the esquire in waiting. He had been round to the several gates and seen that the courts and anterooms were quiet and clear of idlers, and then came up into the anteroom outside the privy chamber, and sat down alone before the fire. In the room beyond him were two gentlemen of the privy chamber, who slept in small beds drawn across the door opening into the royal bedchamber beyond. The King was in his room, in bed, but not asleep; Lord Abergavenny, the gentleman of the bedchamber in waiting, was reading Shakespeare to him before he slept. Inglesant took out a little volume of the classics, of the series printed in Holland, which it was the custom of the gentlemen of the Court, and those attached to great nobles, to carry with them to read in antechambers while in waiting. The night was perfectly still, and the whole palace wrapped in a profound quiet that was almost oppressive to one who happened to be awake. Inglesant could not read; the event that had just occurred, the popular tumults, the shock of feeling which the royal party had sustained, the fear and uncertainty of the future, filled his thoughts. The responsibility of his post sat on him to-night like a nightmare, and with very unusual force: a sense of approaching terror in the midst of the intense silence fascinated him and became almost insupportable. His fancy filled his mind with images of some possible oversight and of some unseen danger which might be lurking even then in the precincts of the vast rambling palace. Gradually, however, all these images became confused and the sense of terror dulled, and he was on the point of falling asleep when he was startled by the ringing sound of arms and the challenge of the yeoman of the guard, on the landing outside the door. The next instant a voice, calm and haughty, which sent a tremor through every nerve, gave back the word, "Christ." Inglesant started up and grasped the back of his chair in terror.

Gracious Heaven! who was this that knew the word? In another moment the hangings across the door were drawn sharply back, and with a quick step, as one who went straight to where he was expected and had a right to be, the intruder entered the antechamber. It wore the form and appearance of Strafford—it was Strafford—in dress, and mien, and step. Taking no heed of Inglesant, crouched back in terror against the carved chimney-piece, the apparition crossed the room with a quick step, drew the hangings that screened the door of the privy chamber, and disappeared. Inglesant recovered in a moment, sprang across the room, and followed the figure through the door. He saw nothing; but the two gentlemen raised themselves from their couches, startled by his sudden appearance and white, scared look, and said, "What is it, Mr. Esquire?"

Before Inglesant, who stood with eyes and mouth open, the picture of terror, could recover himself, the curtain of the bed-chamber was drawn hastily back, and the Lord Abergavenny suddenly appeared, saying in a hurried, startled voice:—

"Send for Mayern; send for Dr. Mayern, the King is taken very ill!"

Inglesant, who by this time was recovered sufficiently to act, seized the opportunity to escape, and, hurrying through the antechamber and down the staircase to the guard-room, he found one of the pages, and despatched him for the Court physician. He then returned to the guard at the top of the staircase.

"Has any one passed?" he asked.

"No," the man said; "he had seen no one."

"Did you challenge no one a moment ago?"

The man looked scared, but finally acknowledged what he feared at first to confess, lest it should be thought he had been sleeping at his post, that he had become suddenly conscious of, as it seemed to him, some presence in the room, and found himself the next moment, to his confusion, challenging the empty space.

Failing to make anything of the man, Inglesant returned to the privy chamber, where Lord Abergavenny was relating what had occurred.

"I was reading to the King," he repeated, "and His Majesty was very still, and I began to think he was falling asleep, when he suddenly started upright in bed, grasped the book on my knee with one hand, and with the other pointed across the chamber to some object upon which his gaze was fixed with a wild and horror-stricken look, while he faintly tried to cry out. In a second the terror of the sight, whatever it was, overcame him, and he fell back on the bed with a sharp cry."

"Mr. Inglesant saw something," said both the gentlemen at once; "he came in here as you gave the alarm."

"I saw nothing," said Inglesant; "whatever frightened me I must tell the King."

Dr. Mayern, who lodged in the palace, soon arrived; and as the King was sensible when he came, he merely prescribed some soothing drink, and soon left. The moment he was gone the King called Abergavenny into the room alone to him, and questioned him as to what had occurred. Abergavenny told him all he knew, adding that the esquire in waiting, Mr. Inglesant, was believed to have seen something by the gentlemen of the privy chamber, whom he had aroused. Inglesant was sent for, and found the King and Abergavenny alone. He declined to speak before the latter, until the King positively commanded him to do so. Deadly pale, with his eyes on the ground, and speaking with the greatest difficulty, he then told his story; of the deep silence, his restlessness, the sentry's challenge, and the apparition that appeared. Here he stopped.

"And this figure," said Abergavenny in a startled whisper, "did you know who it was?"

"Yes, I knew him," said the young man; "would to God I had not."

"Who was it?"

Paler, if possible, than before, and with a violent effort, Inglesant forced himself to look at the King.

A contortion of pain, short but terrible to see, passed over the King's face, but he rose from the chair in which he sat (for he had risen from the bed and even dressed himself), and, with that commanding dignity which none ever assumed better than he, he said,—

"Who was it, Mr. Esquire?"

"My Lord Strafford."

Abergavenny stepped back several paces, and covered his face with his hands. No one spoke. Inglesant dared not stir, but remained opposite to the King, trembling in every limb, and his eyes upon the ground like a culprit. The King continued to stand with his commanding air, but stiff and rigid as a statue; it seemed as though he had strength to command his outward demeanour, but no power besides.

The silence grew terrible. At last the King was able to make a slight motion with his hand. Inglesant seized the opportunity, and, bowing to the ground, retired backward to the door. As he closed the door the King turned towards Abergavenny, but the room was empty. The King was left alone.

CHAPTER VII.

In the beginning of 1642 the King left Whitehall finally, and retired with the Queen to Hampton Court, from which he went to the south to see Her Majesty embark, and without returning to London proceeded to the north. Very few attendants accompanied him, and Inglesant was left at liberty to go where he pleased. His brother was in France, and he was at the moment ignorant where the Jesuit was. Several motives led him to go to Gidding, where he felt sure of a welcome, though Mr. Ferrar was dead, and he accordingly rode there in the end of March. Mr. Nicholas Ferrar jun. had been dead nearly a year, having not long survived his uncle, and the household was governed by Mr. John Ferrar, Mr. Nicholas Ferrar's brother. Their usual quiet and holy life seemed quieter and more holy; a placid melancholy and a sort of contented sorrow seemed to fill the place, which was not disturbed even by those expectations of approaching trouble and danger which all felt. They received Inglesant with kindness and even affection, and begged him to remain as long as he pleased. Mary Collet, who, secretly he acknowledged to himself, was the principal reason of his coming down, met him frankly, and seemed more attractive and beautiful than before. He felt awed and quieted in her presence, yet nothing was so delightful to him as to be in the room or garden with her, and hear her speak. He endeavoured to assist her in her work of attending to the poor and sick, and in tending the garden, and became like a brother to her, without saying or desiring to say one word of gallantry or of love. The Puritans of the neighbouring towns, who had always disliked the Ferrars, came more frequently into their neighbourhood, and endeavoured to set the country people against them, and even to stir them up to acts of violence; but the Ferrars remarked that these annoyances were lessened by the efforts of a Puritan gentleman, who was possessed of considerable property in Peterborough, and who had latterly taken advantage of several excuses to come to Little Gidding.

Inglesant saw this gentleman once or twice, and became rather attracted towards him in a strange way. He appeared to him to be a man in whom a perpetual struggle was going on between his real nature and the system of religion which he had adopted, but in whom the original nature had been subdued and nearly extinguished, until some event, apparently of recent occurrence, had renewed this conflict, and excited the conquered human nature once more to rebellion. This alone would have afforded sufficient interest and attraction to a man of Inglesant's temperament; but this interest was increased tenfold when he perceived, as he did very soon, that this disturbing event and the reason which brought Mr. Thorne to Gidding were in fact one and the same, the same indeed which brought himself there—attraction to Mary Collet. The peaceful halfreligious devotion with which he regarded his friend prevented him from being incited to any feeling of jealousy by this discovery, and indeed would have made the idea of such a sentiment and opposition almost ridiculous. He treated Mr. Thorne, when they met at table or elsewhere, with the most marked courtesy—a courtesy which the other very imperfectly returned, at first ignoring Inglesant altogether, and when this was no longer possible, taking every opportunity to reprove and lecture him in the way the Puritans took upon them to do, all of which Inglesant bore good-humouredly. Things had gone on this way for several weeks, and Mr. Thorne's visits had grown less frequent, when one summer afternoon he rode over, and after seeing Mr. John Ferrar, came to seek Mary Collet. He found her and Inglesant alone in one of the small reading parlours looking on the garden. Inglesant had been reading aloud in Mr. Crashaw's poems; but on the other's entering the room, he rose and stood behind Mary Collet's chair, his hand resting on the high back. His attitude probably annoyed Mr. Thorne, whose manner was more severe and stern than usual. He made the lady a formal greeting, and took slight heed of Inglesant, who wished him Good-day.

"The days are far from good, sir," he said severely, "and the night of the soul is dark; nevertheless, there is a path open to the saints of God, which will lead to a brighter time."

He looked hard at Mary Collet as he spoke.

"I should hope, sir," said Inglesant, with a conciliatory smile, "that you and I may one day stand together in a brighter dawn."

The other's face slightly softened, for indeed the indescribable charm of Inglesant's manner few could resist, but he hardened himself instantly, and replied,—

"It is a fond hope, sir. How can two walk together unless they are agreed? What fellowship is there between the saints (however unworthy) and the followers of the pleasures of this world? And how may you, on whom the Prince of this world has bestowed every brilliant gift and power, stand at the resurrection amongst the poor and despised saints of God?"

Mary Collet moved slightly, and put her hand back upon the chair elbow, so that it partly and slightly touched Inglesant's hand, at which movement, a spasm, as of pain, passed over Mr. Thorne's features, and he drew himself up more sternly than before.

"But I am idling my time vainly and sinfully here," he said, "in chambering and wantonness, when I should be buckling on my armour. Mistress Collet, I came here to wish you farewell. I am going to London in the good cause, and I shall in all human probability never see you more. I entreat you to listen to the bridegroom's voice, and from my heart I wish you God-speed."

G

As she rose, he pressed her hand lightly, and raised his eyes to heaven, as the Puritans were ridiculed for doing; then he bowed stiffly to Inglesant, and was gone.

Inglesant followed him to the courtyard, where his horses were standing, but he took no further notice of him, and rode off through the gate. Johnny stood looking after him down the alley, between the latticed walks of the garden. At last he stopped and looked back. When he saw Inglesant still there, he seemed to hesitate, but finally dismounted and led his horse back. Inglesant hastened to meet him, with his plumed hat in his hand.

"Mr. Inglesant," said the Puritan, speaking slowly and with evident hesitation, "I am going to say something which will probably make you regard with increased contempt not only myself, which you may well do, but the religion which I profess to serve, but which I betray, in which last you will commit a fatal sin. But before I say it, I beg of you, if a few moments ago I said anything that was unnecessarily severe and more than my Master would warrant, that you will forgive it. Woe be to us if we falter in the truth, and speak pleasant things when we should set our face as a flint; nevertheless, there is no need for us to go beyond the letter of the Spirit, and I almost feel that the Lord has disowned my speech, seeing that so soon after I fear I myself am fallen from grace."

He stopped, and Inglesant wondered what this long preamble might mean.

He assured him that he bore no ill-feeling, but very much the contrary; but the Puritan scarcely allowed him to finish before he began again to speak, with still greater difficulty and hesitation.

"I came here to-day, sir, with the intention at which I have arrived, not without long wrestling in prayer, of proposing in the Lord's name a treaty of marriage with Mrs. Mary Collet. In this I have sought direction, as I say, for a long time before addressing her. At length, yesterday, sitting all alone, I felt a word sweetly arise in me as if I heard a voice, which said, 'Go and prevail!' and faith springing in my heart with the word, I immediately arose and went, nothing doubting. But when I came into her presence, and found her with you, upon whom I have ofttimes apprehended that her affections were fixed; when I thought of the disadvantage at which doubtless, in the world's eye at least, I should be thought to stand with regard to you; when I considered her breeding and education in every sort of prelatical and papistical superstition—which latter has all through been a great stumbling-block to me, and to some others of the godly to whom I have opened this matter;—when I thought of these things, I, wretched man that I am! I mistrusted the Lord's power. I was deaf to the voice that spoke within me, and I left my message unsaid. What my sin is in this cannot be told. It may be that I have frustrated the Lord's will and purpose with regard to her, not only as regards calling her out of that empty show and profession in which she is, but, which doubtless will seem of more force to you, of providing her with some refuge from the storm which assuredly is not far from this household. I have already, if you will believe me, done something in warding off the first advances of that storm, and think I do not deceive myself that I have power sufficient to continue to do so. I entreat you, Mr. Inglesant, to think of this, if you have not yet done so, for her sake, and not for mine." He spoke these last words in a different manner, and with an altered voice, as though they were not part of what he had originally intended to say, but had been forced from him by the spectacle his mind presented of danger to her whom it was evident he unselfishly loved. "I am not so ignorant in the world's ways," he went on, "as not to know how absurd such an appeal to you must seem; probably it will afford amusement to your friends in after days. Nevertheless I cannot refrain myself. I am distracted between two opinions, and as I rode away it came into my mind that I might after all be flying away from a shadow, and that there might be no such relation between you as that which I have supposed—no other than that of a free and fair friendship; in which case I entreat you, Mr. Inglesant, though I confess I have no right nor claim upon you even for the commonest courtesy, to let me know it."

Inglesant had listened to this singular confession at first with surprise, but as the man went on, he became profoundly touched. There was something extremely pathetic in the sight of the human nature in this man struggling within him beneath the force of his Puritanism, the one now urging him to conciliate, and the next moment the old habit breaking out in insult and denunciation; the one opening to him glimpses of human happiness which the other immediately closed. And what he said was doubtless very true, and pointed plainly to Inglesant what men would say was his duty. What ground had he to oppose himself to this man—he, with scarcely any formed purpose of his own? If the lofty Strafford had fallen, and the Archbishop had proved powerless to protect himself, how was he to protect any who might trust to him? Even if he had thought nothing of this, it would have been impossible to have been angry with the distracted man before him, untrained to conceal his thoughts, nay, taught by his religion that self-restraint or concealment is a sin, and that to keep back a word or a thought is a frustration of the will of God—a training that would lay him open at every point before the polished pupil of the Jesuit and the Court.

These reflections gave to his ordinary courtesy an additional charm, which plainly commanded the confidence of his rival, and he said,—

"What do you wish me to do, Mr. Thorne? I am willing to leave everything to Mrs. Collet's decision."

"I will take nothing on myself again," said the other; "I will leave everything in the Lord's hands. If it is His will that we be brought together, we shall be so brought. I will not stay now—indeed I am in no fit state of mind—but in a few days I will come again, and whatever the Lord shall do in the meanwhile, His will be done."

The inconsistency of this last resolution with the denunciation of the Ferrar family, and especially of Inglesant, which he had before expressed, struck Inglesant as so extraordinary that he began to doubt the sanity of his companion; but finding that Mr. Thorne was determined to go, he parted from him with mutual courtesy, and returned at once into the house.

As he entered the room where Mary Collet was still sitting alone, she looked up with a smile, and was about to speak, no doubt to palliate the rudeness of their guest; but seeing from his manner that something extraordinary had occurred, she stopped, and Inglesant, who had resolved to tell her all that the Puritan had said, began at once and related simply, and, as closely as he could, word for word, what had happened. As he went on, the sympathy which the strange conflict he had witnessed in the other's breast had excited in his own, and the feeling he had of the truth of the other's power to protect, inspired his manner so that he spoke well and eloquently of his rival's nature, and of the advantages that alliance with him would bestow; but honest as his purpose was, no course more fatal to his rival's chance could probably have been taken, while at the same time he seriously, if he had any cause himself, jeopardized that also.

Mary Collet listened with ever-increasing surprise, and the light in her eyes died away to coldness as she continued to look at Inglesant. Her calm look suffered no other change; but that acute perception which Inglesant's training had given him —perception which the purest love does not always give— showed him what was passing in his friend's mind; he stopped suddenly in his pleading, and knew that he had said too much not to say more. He sank on the ground before the chair, and rested his hands upon the carved elbow, with his face, to which excitement gave increased beauty, raised to Mary Collet's eyes.

"It is all true, Mary," he said. It was the first time he had called her by her name, and it sounded so sweetly that he said it again. "It is all true, Mary; I might have spoken to you of another, would many times have spoken, if all this had not been true. As he said to me, dark days are coming on, the State is shaken to its base, the highest in the realm are disgraced and ruined, and even harried to death; what will happen the wisest heads cannot think; the King is a fugitive; I am all but penniless, should be homeless but for you. This even is not all; if it had been I might have spoken, but there is more which must be told. I am not my own. I am but the agent of a mighty will, of a system which commands unhesitating obedience—obedience which is part of my very being. I cannot even form the thought of violating it. This is why, often, when I tried to speak, my tongue refused its office, my conscience roused itself to keep me still. But if, happily for me, I have been wrong; if, even for me, the gates of heaven may still open,—the gates that I have thought were inexorably closed,—I dare not face the radiance that even now issues through the opening space. Mary, you know me better than I know myself; I am ignorant and sinful and worldly; you are holy as a saint of God. Do with me what you will, if there is anything in me worthy of you, take me and make it more worthy; if not, let me go: either way I am yours—my life belongs to you—neither life nor death is anything to me except as it may advantage you."

The light shone full on Mary Collet's face, looking down on him as he spoke. The odour of the garden flowers filled the room. The stillness of the late afternoon was unbroken, save by the murmur of insect life. Her eyes—those wonderful eyes that had first attracted him in the Church—grew larger and more soft as they looked down on him with a love and tenderness which he had never seen before, and saw only once again. For some seconds she did not—perhaps could not—speak, for the great lustrous eyes were moist with tears. He would have lain there for ever with no thought but of those kindly eyes. At last she spoke, and her voice was tender, but low and calm; "Johnny,"—it was the first time she had called him so, and she said it twice,—"Johnny, you are right, I know you better than you know yourself. Your first instinct was right; but it was not your poverty, nor the distraction of the time, nor yet this mysterious fate that governs you, which kept you silent; poverty and the troubles of the times we might have suffered together; this mysterious fate we might have borne together or have broken through. No," she continued with a radiant smile, "cavalier and courtier as you are, you also, in spite of Mr. Thorne, have heard a voice behind you saying, 'This is the way, walk in it.' That way, Johnny, you will never leave for me. As this voice told you, this is not a time for us to spend our moments like two lovers in a play; we have both of us other work to do, work laid out for us, from which we may not shrink; a path to walk in where there is neither marrying nor giving in marriage. As for me, if I can follow in any degree in the holy path my uncle walked in, growing more into the life of Jesus as he grew into it, it is enough for me; as for you, you will go on through the dark days that are at hand, as your way shall lead you, and as the divine voice shall call; and when I hear your name, as I shall hear it, Johnny, following as the divine call shall lead, you may be sure that my heart will beat delightedly at the name of a very noble gentleman who loves me, and whom—I love."

The evening sun that lighted all the place went down suddenly behind the hedges of the garden, and the room grew dark.

CHAPTER VIII.

THE manner of life at Gidding went on after this without the least alteration, and Inglesant's position in the family remained the same. Two or three days after, Mr. Thorne returned, and had an interview with Mary Collet alone. She told him she had not thought of marriage with any one, but had dedicated her life to other work. He attempted a flowing discourse upon the evils of celibacy, and managed to destroy by his manner much of the kindly feeling which Mary had conceived for him. He met John Ferrar and Inglesant coming from the Church, and Inglesant tried to exchange some kindly words with him; but he avoided conversation with him, and soon left. Inglesant passed most of his time (for he was not quite so much with Mary Collet as before) in reading, especially in Greek, and in assisting some of the family in preparing that great book which was afterwards presented to Prince Charles. The influence of Mr. Hobbes's conversation wore off in the peaceful religious talk and way of life of this family. It was here that he had first obtained glimpses of what the divine life might be, and it was here alone that he felt any power of approach to it in his own heart. His love for Mary Collet, which was increased tenfold by the acknowledgment she had made to him, and which grew more and more every day that he spent at Gidding, associated as it was with all the teachings and incidents of these quiet holy days, made this life of devotion more delightful than can be told, and, indeed, made that life more like to heaven than any other that Inglesant ever lived. As he knelt in Church during the calm hours of prayer, and now and again looked up into Mary Collet's face from where he knelt, he often felt as though he had found the Beatific Vision already, and need seek no more, so closely was her beauty connected with all that was pure and holy in his heart. In these happy days all pride and trouble seemed to have left him, and he felt free in heart from all self-will and sin. It was a dream, and unreal, doubtless; but it was allowed him not altogether without design, perhaps, in the divine counsel, and it could not be without fruit in his spiritual life.

The long summer days that passed so quietly at Gidding

were days of disturbance all over England, the King's friends and those of the Parliament endeavouring to secure the counties for one or other of the contending parties. Nearly the whole of the eastern counties were so strong for the Parliament that the King's friends had little chance, and those gentlemen who attempted to raise men or provide arms for the King were crushed in the beginning. But Huntingdonshire was more loyal, and considerable preparation had been made by several gentlemen, among others, Sir Capel Beedel and Richard Stone, the High Sheriff, to repair to the King's quarters when the standard should be set up. Inglesant was waiting to hear from his brother, who had returned from France, and was in Wiltshire with the Lord Pembroke, who had set in force the commission of array in that county. Inglesant would have joined him but for the close neighbourhood of the King, who might be expected in those parts every day. Accordingly, one afternoon, the King, accompanied by the Prince, afterwards Charles the Second, and the Duke of Lennox, and by Prince Rupert, whom some called the Palsgrave after his father, came to Huntingdon. Inglesant rode into Huntingdon that evening, and found the King playing at cards with the Palsgrave. The King received him graciously, and spoke to him privately of Father St. Clare, who had latterly, he said, been very active among the Catholics of Shropshire and Staffordshire, from whom he soon expected to receive large sums of money. He said the Jesuit had told him where Inglesant was, and that he intended on the next day to come by Little Gidding on his way, and should spend some hours there, as he was very desirous again to see a place which had so pleased him, and of whose inmates he had formed so high an opinion from what he had seen of them. Inglesant slept that night in Huntingdon, but very early on the fine summer morning he rode out to Little Gidding to warn the family of the honour that was intended them. Accordingly, about noon, they saw from the windows of the house the royal party approaching at the bottom of the hill. The whole family went out to meet them to the boundary of the lordship, at a little bridge that spans the brook.

When the King approached foremost of all, they went to meet him, and kneeling down, prayed God to bless and preserve His Majesty, and keep him safe from his enemies' malice. The King rode up the hill at a foot pace, and alighted at the Chapel, which he examined carefully, and was then shown over the whole house, being particularly pleased with the almshouses, for whose inmates he left five pieces of gold, saying it was all he had. He had won them from the Palsgrave the night before at cards.

When he was come into the house, the great book that was being prepared for the Prince was brought him, and he spent some time in examining it and admiring the prints of which it was full, pointing out to the Palsgrave, who appeared to understand such things, the different style of each engraver. When he had sufficiently admired the book, and walked about the house, admiring the pleasant situation upon a little hill, the sun beginning to go down, the horses were brought to the door, and the King and the rest mounted. The whole family, men and women, knelt down as the King mounted, and prayed God to bless and defend him from his enemies, and give him a long and happy reign. "Ah!" said the King, raising his hat, "pray for my safe and speedy return again," and so rode away, not knowing that he should return there again once more, in the very dead of night, a fugitive, and almost alone.

*   *   *   *   *

When John Inglesant had said to Mary Collet that he was almost penniless, he had used rather a strong hyperbole, for at that time the sum of money his father had left him was almost untouched. Upon leaving London, he had managed to get it transferred from the goldsmith with whom he had deposited it to another at Oxford, by a bill of exchange on the latter, as was the custom in transmitting sums of money in those days. This bill being now due, Inglesant decided on going to Oxford to secure possession of the money. He lodged at first at Mr. Martin Lippiard's, a famous apothecary; but after a few days he entered himself at Wadham College, where he got rooms which were of great use to him afterwards, when the Court came to Oxford.

No place could have been found which offered more to interest and delight a man of Inglesant's temperament than Oxford did at this time. It was still at the height of that prosperity which it had enjoyed under the King and Laud for so many years, but which was soon to be so sadly overcast. The colleges were full of men versed and intelligent in all branches of learning and science, as they were then taught.

The halls and chapels were full of pictures and of rich plate soon to be melted down; the gardens and groves were in beautiful order, and the bowling greens well kept. The utmost loyalty to Church and State existed. Many old customs of the Papists' times, soon to be discontinued, still survived. One of the scholars sang the Gospel for the day in Hall at the latter end of dinner. The musical services in the Chapels on Sundays, Holy Days, and Holy Day Eves, were much admired, and the subject of great care. Music was studied deeply as a science, antiquity and every foreign country being ransacked for good music, and every gentleman pretending to some knowledge of it. The High Church party, which reigned supreme, were on excellent terms with the Papists, and indeed they were so much alike that they mixed together without restraint. No people in England were more loyal, orthodox, and observant of the ceremonies of the Church of England than the scholars and generality of the inhabitants.

Every kind of curious knowledge was eagerly pursued; many of the Fellows' rooms were curious museums of antiquities and relics, and scarce books and manuscripts. Alchemy and astrology were openly practised, and more than one Fellow had the reputation of being able to raise Spirits. The niceties of algebra and the depths of metaphysics were inquired into and conversed upon with eagerness, and strange inquiries upon religion welcomed. Dr. Cressy, of Merton, was the first who read Socinus's books in England, and is said to have converted Lord Falkland, who saw them in his rooms. A violent controversy was going on among the physicians, and new schools had risen up who practised in chemical remedies instead of the old-fashioned vegetable medicines.

The members of the university had put themselves into array and a posture of defence, for as yet there was no garrison at Oxford, and divers parties of soldiers were passing through the country, sent by the Parliament to secure Banbury and Warwick. The deputy Vice-Chancellor called before him in the public schools every one who had arms, and the recruits were trained in the quadrangles of the colleges and other places. Matters being in this state, late in October, in the middle of the week, news reached Oxford that the King had left Shrewsbury with his army, and was marching through Warwickshire on his way to London. The Parliamentary army was following from Worcester, and, as was thought, the two armies would soon engage. Numbers of volunteers immediately started to meet the King's army; many of the undergraduates stealing out of Oxford secretly, and setting forth on foot. Inglesant joined himself to a company of gentlemen who had horses, and who, with their servants, made quite a troop.

Some way out of Oxford he overtook a young undergraduate, the elder brother of Anthony Wood, afterwards the famous antiquary (who had stolen out of Oxford as above), and made one of his servants take him up behind him. They went by Woodstock and Chipping Norton, and slept the Friday night at Shipston-upon-Stour, and early the next morning obtained news of the royal army, which arrived under the Wormleighton Hills in the evening of Saturday. The King lodged that night at Sir William Chauncy's, at Ratoll Bridge, some distance from the army, where Inglesant went late in the evening. These quiet woodland places, some of the most secluded in England, both then and now—so much so, that it was said in those days that wolves even were found there—were disturbed by unwonted bustle these dark October nights, parties marching and counter-marching, recruits and provisions arriving. It was not known where Lord Essex's army was, but after it was dark it was discovered by the Prince of Wales's regiment, which had been quartered in two or three villages under Wormleighton Hills. The whole regiment was drawn out into the fields, and remained there all night, provisions being brought to them from the villages, and news was sent to the King and Prince Rupert.

At Sir William Chauncy's Inglesant found the Jesuit and some other Catholic gentlemen whom he knew, for the number of Papists in the royal army was very great. Father Hall was dissatisfied at seeing Inglesant, and tried hard to persuade him to keep out of the battle, saying he had different and more useful work for him to do; but Inglesant would not consent, though he agreed not to expose himself unnecessarily. The Jesuit told him that his brother was with the Prince's regiment, but counselled him not to join him, but stay in the King's bodyguard, which his place at Court might well account for his doing. He enlarged so much upon the coming danger, that Inglesant, who had never seen a battle, became quite timid, and was glad when the Jesuit was sent for to the King. Inglesant slept in a farm-house, not far from Sir William's, with several other gentlemen,—for those were fortunate who had half a bed, —and on the morning rode with the King's pensioners to the top of Edgehill. The church-bells were ringing for morning service as they rode along. The King was that day in a black velvet coat lined with ermine, and a steel cap covered with velvet. He rode to every brigade of horse and to all the tertias of foot, and spoke to them with great courage and cheerfulness, to which the army responded with loud huzzahs. An intense feeling of excitement prevailed as this battle—the first fought in England for more than a century—was joined. Numbers of country people crowded the heights, and the army was full of volunteers who had only just joined, and had no idea of war. The King was persuaded with difficulty to remain on a rising-ground at some little distance, with his guard of pensioners on horseback; but Inglesant did not remain with him, but joined his brother in the Prince's regiment, under the Palsgrave, and rode in the charge against the enemy's horse, whom the Prince completely routed and chased off the field. Inglesant, however, did not share in the glory of this victory, for his horse was killed under him at the first shock of the encounter, and he went down with him, and received more than one kick from the horses' hoofs as they passed over him, rendering him for some time senseless. On recovering himself he managed to get on his feet, and crossed the field to the royal foot, but unfortunately joined the foot guards at the moment they were attacked and routed by the Parliamentary horse and foot. The Earl of Lindsay and his son were taken prisoners, and the royal Standard was taken. At this moment the King was in great danger, being with fewer than a hundred horse within half a musket shot of the enemy. The two regiments of his reserve, however, came up, and Charles was desirous of charging the enemy himself. Inglesant remained with the broken regiment of the guard who retreated up the road over the hill, along which the enemy's horse advanced, but, the early October evening setting in, the enemy desisted and fell back upon their reserves. It was a hard frost that night, and very cold. The King's army marched up the hills which they had come down so gallantly in the morning. Inglesant remained with the broken foot guards and the rest of the foot, which were confusedly mixed together, all night. The men made fires all along the hill top to warm themselves, and gathered round them in strange and motley groups. Many of the foot were very badly armed, the Welshmen, especially, having only pitchforks, and many only clubs; but Prince Rupert the next day made a descent upon Keinton, and carried off several waggon-loads of arms, which were very useful. The officers and men were mixed up together round the fires without distinction. As Inglesant was standing by one of them stiff and stunned with the blows he had received, and weak from a sabre cut he had received on the arm, he heard some one who had come up to the fire inquiring for him by name. It was the Jesuit, who had given him up for dead, as he had met his brother who had returned with Prince Rupert when he rejoined the King, and had learnt from him that Inglesant had fallen in the first charge. He told him that Eustace had gone down into the plain to endeavour to find him, which surprised and touched Inglesant very much, as he suspected his brother of caring very little for him. Father St. Clare stayed with Inglesant at the fire all night, for the latter was too stiff to move, and made himself quite at home with the soldiers, as he could with people of every sort, telling them stories and encouraging them with hopes of high pay and rewards when the King had once marched to London and turned out the Parliament. Inglesant dozed off to sleep and woke up again several times during this strange night, with a confused consciousness of the flaring fire lighting up the wild figures, and the Jesuit still talking and still unwearied all through the night.

One of the first men he saw in the morning was Edward Wood, whom he had helped on his way from Oxford. This young man had been much more fortunate than Inglesant, for he had come on foot without arms, and he had succeeded in getting a good horse and accoutrements.

"You are much more lucky than I am," said Inglesant; "I have lost my horses and servants and all my arms, and am beaten and wounded, as you see, till I can scarcely stand, while you seem to have made your fortune."

"I shall certainly get a commission," said the young man, who was only eighteen, and certainly was very much pleased with himself; "but never mind, Mr. Inglesant," he continued, patronizingly, "it is your first battle, as it is mine, and you have no doubt learnt much from it that will be useful to you."

It had been one of the principal parts of Inglesant's training to avoid assumption himself, and to be amused with it in others, so he took his patronage meekly, and wished him success on his return to Oxford, where he really was made an officer in the King's service soon after.

Soon after he was gone Inglesant found his brother, and with him his own servants, with an additional horse they had managed to secure, with which he replaced the one he had lost; and the next morning he rode with the Palsgrave into Keinton, where they surprised the rear of the Parliamentary army, and took much spoil of the arms and ammunition, and many wounded officers and other prisoners; but his wound being very painful, and being sick and weary of the sight of fighting, and especially of plundering, he left the Prince in Keinton and returned to Oxford, where he was very glad to get back to his pleasant rooms in Wadham. After the King had wasted his time in taking Banbury and Broughton Castle, he marched to Oxford with his army, where he was received with demonstrations of joy, and stayed some days.

After the King had rested a short time at Oxford, he proceeded to march to London; but Inglesant did not accompany him. The blows he had received about the head, together with his wound and the excitement he had gone through, brought on a fever which kept him in his rooms for some time. The Jesuit stayed with him as long as he could, but many other of Inglesant's friends at Oxford showed him great kindness. When he recovered, he found himself, to his great surprise, something of a hero. Though, as we have seen, few men could have done less at Edgehill than Inglesant did, or have had less influence on the event of the day, yet, as he had been in the charge of the Prince's horse, and also in the rout of the foot guards, and had been wounded in both, and above all was, especially with the ladies, something of a favourite, of whom no one objected to say a good word, he gained a decided reputation as a soldier. It was indeed reported and believed at Little Gidding that he had performed prodigies of valour, had saved the King's life several times, and retrieved the fortunes of the day when they were desperate. In some respects this reputation was decidedly inconvenient to him; he was looked upon as a likely man to be in all foraging parties and in expeditions of observation sent out to trace the marchings and countermarchings of the enemy. Now, as he was pledged to the Jesuit not to expose himself to unnecessary danger, these expeditions were very troublesome to him, besides taking him away from the studies to which he was anxious to apply himself, and from the company of the leaders of both the Churchmen and Papists, to obtain the acquaintance and confidence of whom he still applied himself, both from inclination and in accordance with the Jesuit's wish. It is true, however, that in these expeditions about the country he formed several friendships of this kind, which might afterwards be useful.

CHAPTER IX.

THE King returned to Oxford in December, and the Court was established at Christ Church College. There has perhaps never existed so curious a spectacle as Oxford presented during the residence of the King at the time of the civil war. A city unique in itself became the resort of a Court under unique circumstances, and of an innumerable throng of people of every rank, disposition, and taste, under circumstances the most extraordinary and romantic. The ancient colleges and halls were thronged with ladies and courtiers; noblemen lodged in small attics over bakers' shops in the streets; soldiers were quartered in the college gates and in the kitchens; yet, with all this confusion, there was maintained both something of a courtly pomp, and something of a learned and religious society. The King dined and supped in public, and walked in state in Christ Church meadow and Merton Gardens and the Grove of Trinity, which the wits called Daphne. A Parliament sat from day to day; service was sung daily in all the Chapels; books both of learning and poetry were printed in the city; and the distinctions which the colleges had to offer were conferred with pomp on the royal followers, as almost the only rewards the King had to bestow. Men of every opinion flocked to Oxford, and many foreigners came to visit the King. There existed in the country a large and highly intelligent body of moderate men, who hovered between the two parties, and numbers of these were constantly in Oxford,—Harrington the philosopher the King's friend, Hobbes, Lord Falkland, Lord Paget, the Lord Keeper, and many others.

Mixed up with these grave and studious persons, gay courtiers and gayer ladies jostled old and severe divines and college heads, and crusty tutors used the sarcasms they had been wont to hurl at their pupils to reprove ladies whose conduct appeared to them at least far from decorous. Christmas interludes were enacted in Hall, and Shakespeare's plays performed by the King's players, assisted by amateur performers; and it would have been difficult to say whether the play was performed before the curtain or behind it, or whether the actors left their parts behind them when the performance was over, or then in fact resumed them. The groves and walks of the colleges, and especially Christ Church meadow and the Grove at Trinity, were the resort of this gay and brilliant throng; the woods were vocal with song and music, and love and gallantry sported themselves along the pleasant river banks. The poets and wits vied with each other in classic conceits and parodies, wherein the events of the day and every individual incident were portrayed and satirized. Wit, learning, and religion joined hand in hand, as in some grotesque and brilliant masque. The most admired poets and players and the most profound mathematicians became "Romancists" and monks, and exhausted all their wit and poetry and learning in furthering their divine mission, and finally, as the last scenes of this strange drama came on, fell fighting on some hardly-contested grassy slope, and were buried on the spot, or in the next village churchyard, in the dress in which they played Philaster, or the Court garb in which they wooed their mistress, or the doctor's gown in which they preached before the King, or read Greek in the schools.

This gaiety was much increased the next year, when the Queen came to Oxford, and the last happy days of the ill-fated monarch glided by. It was really no inapt hyberbole of the classic wits which compared this motley scene to the marriage of Jupiter and Juno of old, when all the Gods were invited to the feast, and many noble personages besides, but to which also came a motley company of mummers, maskers, fantastic phantoms, whifflers, thieves, rufflers, gulls, wizards, and monsters, and among the rest Crysalus, a Persian Prince, bravely attended, clad in rich and gay attire, and of majestic presence, but otherwise an ass; whom the Gods at first, seeing him enter in such pomp, rose and saluted, taking him for one worthy of honour and high place; and whom Jupiter, perceiving what he was, turned with his retinue into butterflies, who continued in pied coats roving about among the Gods and the wiser sort of men.

Something of this kind here happened, when wisdom and folly, vice and piety, learning and gaiety, terrible earnest even to death and light frivolity, jostled each other in the stately precincts of Parnassus and Olympus.

With every variety and shade of this strange life Inglesant had some acquaintance; the philosophers knew him, the Papists confided in him; Cave, the writer of news-letters for the Papists, sought him for information; the Church party, who knew his connection with the Archbishop, and the services he had rendered him, sought his company; the ladies made use of his handsome person and talents for acting, as they did also that of his brother. He had the entrée to the King at all times, and was supposed to be a favourite with Charles, though in reality the King's feelings towards him were of a mixed nature. No man certainly was better known at Oxford, and no man certainly knew more of what was going on in England than Inglesant did.

Among the chief beauties of the Court the Lady Isabella Thynne was the most conspicuous and the most enterprising: the poet Waller sang her praise, music was played before her as she walked, and she affected the garb and manner of an angel. She was most beautiful, courteous, and charitable; but she allowed her gaiety and love of intrigue to lead her into very equivocal positions. She was intimately acquainted with Eustace Inglesant, who was one of her devoted servants, and assisted her in many of her gaieties and gallant festivals and sports; but she was shy of Johnny, and told Eustace that his brother was too much of a monk for her taste. She had a bevy of ladies, who were her intimate friends, and were generally with her, some of whom she did not improve by her friendship.

There was in Oxford a gentleman, a Mr. Richard Fentham, who was afterwards knighted, a member of the Prince's Council, and a person of great trust with the King. This gentleman had been at school with Eustace Inglesant at that famous schoolmaster's Mr. Farnabie, in Cripplegate Parish in London,—a school at one time frequented by more than three hundred young noblemen and gentlemen, for whose accommodation he had handsome houses and large gardens. One day Fentham took Eustace Inglesant to call on two young ladies, the daughters of Sir John Harris, who had lately come to Oxford to join their father, who had suffered heavy losses in the royal cause, and had been made a baronet. They found these two young ladies, to the eldest of whom Fentham was engaged, in a baker's house in an obscure street, ill-furnished and mean-looking. They were both, especially the eldest, extremely beautiful, and had been brought up in a way equal to any gentleman's daughters in England, so that the gentlemen could not help condoling with them on this lamentable change of fortune, to which they were reduced by their father's devotion to the royal cause.

The eldest young lady, Ann, a spirited lively girl, confessed it was "a great change from a large well-furnished house to a very bad bed in a garret, and from a plentiful table to one dish of meat—and that not the best ordered,—with no money, for they were as poor as Job, and had no clothes," she said, "but what a man or two had brought in the cloak bags." Eustace Inglesant pursued the acquaintance thus begun; and both he and his brother were at Wolvercot Church some time afterwards, when Richard Fentham and Mistress Ann were married in the presence of Sir Edward Hyde, afterwards the Lord Chancellor, and Geoffry Palmer, the King's attorney. Lady Fentham was much admired and sought after, and became one of Lady Isabella's intimate friends. She was a lively, active girl, and fond of all kinds of stirring exercise and excitement, and was peculiarly liable to be led into scrapes in such society. Besides Lady Isabella, she was also exposed to other temptations from political ladies, who endeavoured to persuade her that a woman of her talent and energy should take some active part in public affairs, and get her husband to trust to her the secrets of the Prince's Council. They succeeded so far as to cause her to press her husband on this matter, and to cause some unpleasant feeling on her part, which, but for his kind and forgiving conduct, might have led to a serious breach. This danger passed over, but those springing from the acquaintance with Lady Isabella were much more serious. Sir Richard was much away at Bristol with the Prince, and during his absence Lady Isabella promoted an intimacy between Lord H——, afterwards the Duke of P——, and her young friend. In this she was assisted by Eustace Inglesant, who appeared to be actuated by some very strange personal motive, which Johnny, who saw a great deal of what was going on, could not penetrate.

Matters were in this state when one day Shakespeare's play of "The Comedy of Errors," or an adaptation of it, was given by the gentlemen of the Court, assisted by the King's players, in the Hall at Christ Church. The parts of the brothers Antipholus were taken by the two Inglesants, who were still said to be so exactly alike that mistakes were continually being made between them. The play was over early, and the brilliant company streamed out into the long walk at Christ Church, which was already occupied by a motley throng. The players mingled with the crowd, and solicited compliments on their several performances. The long avenue presented a singular and lively scene—ladies, courtiers, soldiers in buff coats, clergymen in their gowns and bands, doctors of law and medicine in their hoods, heads of houses, beggars, mountebanks, jugglers and musicians, popish priests, college servants, country gentlemen, Parliament men, and townspeople, all confusedly intermixed; with the afternoon sun shining across the broad meadow, under the rustling leaves, and lighting up the windows of the Colleges, and the windings of the placid river beyond.

John Inglesant, in the modern Court dress in which, according to the fashion of the day, he had played Antipholus of Ephesus, was speaking to Lord Falkland, who had not been at the play, but who, grave and melancholy, with his dress neglected and in disorder, was speaking of the death of Hampden, which had just occurred, when a page spoke to Inglesant, telling him that Lady Isabella desired his presence instantly. Rather surprised, Inglesant followed him to where the lady was walking, a little apart from the crowd, in a path across the meadows leading from the main walk. She smiled as Inglesant came up.

"I see, Mr. Esquire Inglesant," she said, "that the play is not over. It was your brother I sent for, whom this stupid boy seemingly has sought in Ephesus and not in England."

"I am happy for once to have supplanted my brother, madam," said Johnny, adapting from his part. "I have run hither to your grace, whom only to see now gives me ample satisfaction for these deep shames and great indignities."

"I am afraid of you, Mr. Inglesant," said the lady; "you have so high a reputation with grave and religious people, and yet you are a better cavalier than your brother, when you condescend that way. That is how you please the Nuns of Gidding so well."

"Spare the poor Nuns of Gidding your raillery, madam,"

said Inglesant; "surely Venus Aphrodite is not jealous of the gentle dove."

"I will not talk with you, Mr. Inglesant," said the lady pettishly; "find your brother, I beseech you; his wit is duller than yours, but it is more to my taste."

Inglesant went to seek his brother; but before he found him his attention was arrested from behind, and turning round he found his scarf held by Lord H——, who said at once, "Is the day fixed, and the place? have you seen the lady?"

"My lord," said Inglesant, "the play really is over, though no one will believe it. 'I think you all have drunk of Circe's Cup.' I am afraid as many mishaps wait me here as at Ephesus."

Lord H—— saw his mistake. "I beg your pardon," he said; "I took you for your brother, who has some business of mine in hand. I wish you good day."

"I must get to the bottom of the mischief that is brewing," said Inglesant; "there is some mystery which I cannot fathom. The lady no doubt is pretty Lady Fentham, but Eustace surely can never mean to betray his friend in so foul a way as this."

That evening he sought his brother, and telling him all he had noticed, and what he had overheard, he begged him to tell him the plain facts of what was going on, lest he might add to the confusion in his ignorance. Eustace hesitated a little, but at last he told him all.

"There is no real harm intended, except by Lord H——," he said; "Lady Isabella simply wants to make mischief and confusion all around her. She has persuaded Ann Fentham to encourage Lord H—— a little, to lead him into a snare in which he is to be exposed to ridicule. There is a lady in Oxford, whom you no doubt know, Lady Cardiff, whom, if you know her, you know to be one of the most fantastic women now living, to bring whom into connection with Lord H—— Mrs. Fentham has conceived would be great sport; now, to tell you a secret, this lady, who entered into this affair merely for excitement and sport, is gradually becoming attached to me. I intend to marry her with Lady Isabella's help. She has an immense fortune and large parks and houses, and has connections on both sides in this war, so that her property is safe whatever befalls. This is a profound secret between me and the Lady Isabella, who is under obligations to me. Mrs. Fentham knows nothing of it, and is occupied solely with bringing Lord H—— and Lady Cardiff together. The ladies are going down to Nuneham to-morrow. I meet them there, and Lord H—— is to be allowed to come. I intend to press my suit to Lady Cardiff, and certainly by this I shall spoil Lady Fentham's plot; but this is all the harm I intend. What will happen besides I really cannot say, but nothing beyond a little honest gallantry doubtless."

"But is not such sport very dangerous?" said John. "Suppose this intimacy came to Richard Fentham's ears, what would he say to it? You told me there had already been some mischief made by some of the women between them."

"If he hears of it," said Eustace carelessly, "it can be explained to him easily enough; he is no fool, and is not the man to misunderstand an innocent joke."

Inglesant was not satisfied, but he had nothing more to say, and changed the subject by inquiring about Lady Cardiff, of whom he knew little.

This lady was a peeress in her own right, having inherited the title and estates from her father. She had been carefully educated, and was learned in many languages. She had acted all her life from principles laid down by herself, and different from those which governed the actions of other people. She had bad health, suffering excruciating pain at frequent intervals from headache, which it is supposed unsettled her reason. At her principal seat, Oulton, in Dorsetshire, she collected around her celebrities and uncommon persons, "Excentrics" as they were called, principally great physicians and quacks, and religious persons and mystic theologians. Van Helmont, the great alchemist, spent much time there, attempting to cure her disorder or allay her sufferings, and Dr. Henry More of Cambridge condescended to reside some time at Oulton. It was a great freestone house, surrounded by gardens, and by a park or rather chase of great extent, enclosing large pieces of water, and surrounded by wooded and uncultivated country for many miles. At the time at which we are arrived, however, her health was better than it afterwards became, and she was chiefly ambitious of occupying an important position in politics, and of seeing every species of life. She was connected with some of the principal persons on both sides in the civil contention, and passed much time both in London and in Oxford. In both these places, but especially in the royal quarters, where greater license was possible, she endeavoured to be included in anything of an exciting and entertaining character that was going on. Whatever it was, it afforded her an insight into human nature and the manners of the world. Such a character does not seem a likely one to be willing to submit to the restraints of the married life, and indeed Lady Cardiff had hitherto rejected the most tempting offers, and, as she had attained the mature age of thirty-two, most people imagined that she would not at that time of life exchange her condition. It appeared, however, that her fate had at last met her in the handsome person of Eustace Inglesant, and the secret which Eustace had told his brother was already beginning to be whispered in Oxford, and opinions were divided as to whether the boldness of the young man or his good fortune were the most to be admired.

When Inglesant left his brother and walked under the starry sky to his lodgings at Wadham, his mind was ill at ease. He had taken a great interest in Lady Fentham and her husband; indeed, his feelings towards the former were those of an attached friend, attracted by her lively innocence and good nature. He was, as the reader will remember, still very young, being only in his twenty-second year. He was sincerely and vitally religious, though his religion might appear to be kept in subordination to his taste, and he had formed for himself, from various sources, an ideal of purity, which in his mind connected earth to heaven, and which, at this period of his life at any rate, he may have been said faultlessly to have carried out. The circumstances of his youth and early training, which we have endeavoured to trace, acting upon a constitution in which the mental power dominated, rendered self-restraint natural to him, or rather rendered self-restraint needless. It was one of the glories of that age that it produced such men as he was, and that not a few; men who combined qualities such as, perhaps, no after age ever saw united; men like George Herbert, Nicholas Ferrar, Falkland, the unusual combination of the courtier and the monk. Yet these men were naturally in the minority, and even while moulding their age, were still regarded by their age with wonder and a certain kind of awe. It is not meant that John Inglesant was altogether a good specimen of this high class of men, for he was more of a courtier than he was of a saint. He was a sincere believer in a holy life, and strongly desirous of pursuing it: he endeavoured conscientiously to listen for the utterances of the Divine Voice; and provided that Voice pointed out the path which his tastes and training had prepared him to expect, he would follow it even at a sacrifice to himself; but he was not capable of a sacrifice of his tastes or of his training. On the other hand, as a courtier and man of the world, he was profoundly tolerant of error and even of vice (provided the latter did not entail suffering on any innocent victim), looking upon it as a natural incident in human affairs. This quality had its good side, in making him equally tolerant of religious differences, so that, as has been seen, it was not difficult to him to recognize the Divine prompting in a Puritan and an opponent. He was acutely sensitive to ridicule, and would as soon have thought of going to Court in an improper dress as of speaking of religion in a mixed company, or of offering any advice or reproof to any one. In the case which was now disturbing his mind, his chief fear was of making himself ridiculous by interfering where no interference was necessary.

He passed a restless night, and the next morning went to Trinity Chapel, then much frequented for the high style of the music. He was scarcely here before Lady Isabella and young Lady Fentham, who lodged in that college, came in, as was their habit, dressed to resemble angels in loose and very inadequate attire. At another time he might not have thought much of it, but, his suspicions being aroused, he could not help, courtier as he was, contrasting the boldness of this behaviour with the chaste and holy life of the ladies at Little Gidding; and it made him still more restless and uncertain what to do. He avoided the ladies after Chapel, and returned to his own rooms quite uncertain how to act. It came at last into his mind to inquire of the Secretary Falkland whether Sir Richard Fentham was expected shortly in Oxford, as his journeys were very irregular, and generally kept a profound secret. He went to Lord Falkland and asked the question, telling him that he did so from private reasons unconnected with the State. Falkland declined at first to answer him; but on Inglesant's taking him a little more into his confidence, he confided to him, as a great secret, that Sir Richard was expected that very night, and further, that he would pass through Nuncham in the afternoon, where he would meet a messenger with despatches. Upon learning this startling piece of news, Inglesant hastened to his brother's rooms, but found he was too late, Eustace having been gone more than two hours, and as he started considerably after the ladies' coach, there could be no doubt but that the party was already in Nuneham. Inglesant went to the stables where his horses were kept, and having found one of his servants, he ordered his own horse to be saddled, as he was going to ride alone. While it was being prepared he attempted to form some plan upon which to act when he arrived at Nuneham, but his ingenuity completely failed him. Merely to walk into a room where some ladies and gentlemen were at dinner, to which he was not invited, and inform one of the ladies that her husband was in the neighbourhood, appeared an action so absurd that he discarded the intention at once. When his horse was brought out and he mounted and rode out of Oxford towards the south, telling his servant he should be back at night, he probably did not know why he went. He rode quickly, and arrived in about an hour. The Plough at Nuneham (it has long disappeared) stood upon the banks of the river, in a picturesque and retired situation, and was much frequented by parties of pleasure from Oxford. The gardens and bowling-greens lay upon the river bank, and the paths extended from them through the fields both up and down the river. It was apparent to Inglesant that a distinguished party was in the house, from the servants loitering about the doors, and coming in and out. More than one of these he recognized as belonging to Lord H——. The absurdity of suspecting any mischief from so public a rendezvous struck Inglesant as so great, that he was on the point of passing the house. He however alighted and inquired of one of the men whether any of his brother's servants were about. The man, who knew him, replied that Mr. Eustace Inglesant had dined there with his lordship and the ladies, but was then, he believed, either in the garden or the fields with Lady Cardiff; he had brought no servants with him. Having got thus into conversation with the man, Inglesant ventured to inquire, with as careless a manner as he could assume, if Lady Isabella were there.

Lady Isabella, the man said, had dined there, but after dinner had gone on a little farther in her coach, and attended by her servants, he believed to make some call in the neighbourhood.

Then Inglesant knew that he had done right to come.

"I have a message to Lady Ann Fentham," he said to the

man, "but not being of the party, I would rather have sent it through my brother. As I suppose it is useless to attempt to find him, I shall be glad if you will tell me in which room the lady is, for I suppose his lordship is with her."

"His lordship left orders that he was not to be disturbed," said the man insolently; "you had better try and find your brother."

"Nevertheless, I must give her my message," said Inglesant quietly: "therefore, pray show me upstairs."

"I don't know the room," said the man still more rudely, "and you cannot go upstairs; his lordship has engaged the house."

During the conversation the other men had gathered round, and it seemed to Inglesant that his lordship must have brought all his servants with him, for the house appeared full of them. None of the ordinary servants of the place were to be seen.

Inglesant had no arms but his riding sword, and even if he had had, the use of them would have been absurd.

"You know who I am," he said, looking the man steadily in the face, "one of the King's gentlemen whom they call the Queen's favourite page. I bring a message to Lady Fentham from her husband, the Secretary to the Prince's Council: do you think your lord will wish you to stop me?"

As he spoke he made a step forward as though to enter, and the man, evidently in doubt, stepped slightly on one side, making it possible to enter the house. The rest took this movement to imply surrender, and one of the youngest, probably to gain favour, said, "The lady is in the room opposite the stairs, sir." Inglesant walked up the low oak staircase to the door, the men crowding together in silence at the bottom of the stairs.

Inglesant tried the latch of the door, though he did not intend to go in without knocking.

The door was fastened, and he knocked.

For a moment there was silence, and then a voice said, angrily, "Who is there?"

"A message from Sir Richard Fentham," said Inglesant.

There was another and a longer pause, and then the same voice said,—

"Is Sir Richard without?"

"No," replied Inglesant; "but he may be here any moment; he is on the road."

The door was immediately opened by his lordship, and Inglesant walked in.

The moment he did, Lady Fentham, who was in the further part of the room, started up from the seat in which she was lying, and throwing herself on Johnny's shoulder said,—

"Help me, Mr. Inglesant, I have been cruelly deceived."

Inglesant took no notice of her, but turning to Lord H—— he said with marked politeness,—

"I have to beg your lordship's pardon for intruding upon your company, but I am charged to let Lady Fentham know that Sir Richard is expected in Oxford to-night, and may pass this house at any time, probably in a few minutes. I thought Lady Fentham would wish to know this so much that I ventured to knock, though your servants told me you wished to be private."

His words were so chosen and his manner so faultless and devoid of suspicion, that Lord H—— could find nothing in either to quarrel with, though he was plainly in a violent passion, and with difficulty controlled himself. It had also the effect of calming Lady Fentham, who remained silent; indeed, she appeared too agitated to speak. It was an awkward pause, but less so to Inglesant than to the other two.

"I wished," he continued, still speaking to Lord H——, "to have sent my message by my brother, but I find he is walking in the fields, and Lady Isabella appears to have gone in her carriage to make a call in the neighbourhood. I presume she will call for you, Lady Fentham, on her way back."

Lady Fentham made a movement of anger, and Lord H—— roused himself at last to say,—

"I am much obliged to you, Mr. Inglesant, for the great trouble you have taken. I assure you I shall not forget it. Lady Fentham, as Sir Richard will so soon be here"—he stopped suddenly as an idea struck him, and looking full at Inglesant, said slowly and with marked emphasis, "Supposing Mr. Inglesant to"—to have spoken the truth he would have said, but Johnny's perfectly courteous attitude of calm politeness, the utter absence of any tangible ground of offence, and his own instincts as a gentleman, checked him, and he continued,—"has not been misinformed, you will not need my protection any further. I will leave you with Mr. Inglesant; probably Lady Cardiff will be back before long."

He took his leave with equal courtesy both to the lady and Inglesant, and went down to his men.

Ann Fentham sank into her chair, and began to sob bitterly, saying,—

"What shall I say to my husband, Mr. Inglesant? He will be here directly, and will find me alone. What would have happened to me if you had not come?"

"If I may offer any advice, madam, I should say, Tell your husband everything exactly as it happened. Nothing has happened of which you have need to be ashamed. Sir Richard will doubtless see that you have been shamefully deceived by your friends, as far as I understand the matter. You can trust to his sympathy and kindness."

She did not reply, and Inglesant, who found his situation far more awkward than before, said, "Shall I seek for Lady Cardiff, madam, and bring her to you?"

"No, don't leave me, Mr. Inglesant," she said, springing up and coming to him; "I shall bless your name for ever for what you have done for me this day."

Inglesant stayed with the lady until it was plain Lord H—— had left the house with his servants, and he then left her and went into the garden to endeavour to find his brother and Lady Cardiff; but in this he was not successful, and returned to the house, where he ordered some dinner—for he had eaten nothing since the morning—and seated himself at the window to wait for Sir Richard. He had sat there about an hour when the latter arrived, and drew his rein before the house before dismounting. Inglesant greeted him and went out to him in the porch. Fentham returned his greeting warmly.

"Your wife is upstairs, Sir Richard," Inglesant said; "she came down with Lady Isabella Thynne, and is waiting for her to take her back."

Fentham left his horse with the servant and ran upstairs straight to his wife, and as Inglesant followed him into the house he met Lady Cardiff and his brother, who came in from the garden. Eustace Inglesant was radiant, and introduced Lady Cardiff to his brother as his future wife. He took them into a private room, and called for wine and cakes. Johnny thought it best not to tell them what had occurred, but merely said that Sir Richard and his wife were upstairs; upon which Eustace sent a servant up with his compliments, asking them to come and join them. Both Lady Cardiff and Eustace appeared conscious, however, that some blame attached to them, for they expressed great surprise at the absence of Lady Isabella, and took pains to inform Johnny that they had left Lady Fentham with her, and had no idea she was going away. Sir Richard and Lady Fentham joined the party, and appeared composed and happy, and they had not sat long before Lady Isabella's coach appeared before the door, and her ladyship came in. The ladies returned to Oxford in the coach, and the gentlemen on horseback. Nothing was said by the latter as to what had occurred until after they had left Eustace at his lodgings, and Johnny was parting with Fentham at the door of Lord Falkland, to whom he was going. Then Sir Richard said,—

"Mr. Inglesant, my wife has told me all, and has told me that she owes everything to you, even to this last blessing, that there is no secret between us. I beg you to believe two things, —first, that nothing I can do or say can ever repay the obligation that I owe to you; secondly, that the blame of this matter rests mostly with me, in that I have left my wife too much."

Inglesant waited for several days in expectation of hearing from Lord H——, but no message came. They met several times and passed each other with the usual courtesies. At last Eustace Inglesant heard from one of his lordship's friends that the latter had been very anxious to meet Johnny, but had been dissuaded.

"You have not the slightest tangible ground of offence against young Inglesant," they told him, "and you have every cause to keep this affair quiet, out of which you have not emerged with any great triumph. Inglesant has shown by the line of conduct he adopted that he desires to keep it close. None of the rest of the party will speak of it for their own sakes. Were it known, it would ruin you at once with the King, and damage you very much in the estimation of all the principal men here, who are Sir Richard's friends, and such as are not would resent such conduct towards a man engaged on his master's business. Besides this, you are not a remarkably good fencer, whereas John Inglesant is a pupil of the Jesuits, and master of all their arts and tricks of stabbing. That he could kill you in five minutes if he chose, there can be no doubt."

These and other similar arguments finally persuaded Lord H—— to restrain his desire of revenge, which was the easier for him to do as Inglesant always treated him when they met with marked deference and courtesy.

The marriage of Lady Cardiff and Eustace Inglesant was hurried forward, and took place at Oxford some weeks after the foregoing events; the King and Queen being present at the ceremony. It was indeed very important to attach this wealthy couple unmistakably to the royal party, and no efforts were spared for the purpose. Lady Cardiff and her husband, however, did not manifest any great enthusiasm in the royal cause.

The music of the wedding festival was interrupted by the cannon of Newbury, where Lord Falkland was killed, together with a sad roll of gentlemen of honour and repute. Lord Clarendon says,—"Such was always the unequal fate that attended this melancholy war, that while some obscure, unheard-of colonel or officer was missing on the enemy's side, and some citizen's wife bewailed the loss of her husband, there were on the other above twenty officers of the field and persons of honour and public name slain upon the place, and more of the same quality hurt." In this battle Inglesant was more fortunate than in his first, for he was not hurt, though he rode in the Lord Biron's regiment, the same in which Lord Falkland was also a volunteer.

The King returned to Oxford, where Inglesant found every one in great dejection of mind; the conduct of the war was severely criticised, the army discontented, and the chief commanders engaged in reproaches and recriminations.

One afternoon Inglesant was sent for to Merton College, where the Queen lay, and where the King spent much of his time; where he found the Jesuit standing with the King in one of the windows, and Mr. Jermyn, who had just been made a baron, talking to the Queen. The King motioned Inglesant to approach him, and the Jesuit explained the reason he had been sent for.

The trial of Archbishop Laud was commencing, and in order to incite the people against him Mr. Prynne had published the particulars of a popish plot in a pamphlet which contained the names of many gentlemen, both Protestant and Catholic, the publication of which at such a moment excited considerable uneasiness among their relations and friends.

"I wish you, Mr. Inglesant," said the King, "to ride to London. Mr. Hall has provided passes for you, and letters to several of his friends. The new French Ambassador is landing; I wish to know how far the French Court is true to me. Prynne's wit has overreached himself. His charges have frightened so many that a reaction is setting in in favour of the Archbishop, and many are willing to testify in his favour in order to exonerate themselves. You will be of great use in finding out these people. Seek every one who is mentioned in Prynne's libel; many of them are men of influence. Your familiar converse with Papists, in other respects unfortunate, may be of use here."

Inglesant spent some time in London, and was in constant communication with Mr. Dell, the Archbishop's secretary. He was successful in procuring evidence from among the Papists of their antipathy to Laud, and in various other ways in providing Dell with materials for defence. Laud was informed of these acts of friendship, and being in a very low and broken state, was deeply touched that a comparative stranger, and one who had been under no obligation to him, should show so much attachment, and exert himself so much in his service, at a time when the greatest danger attended any one so doing, and when he seemed deserted both by his royal master and by those on whom he had showered benefits in the time of his prosperity. He sent his blessing and grateful thanks, the thanks of an old and dying man, which would be all the more valuable as they never could be accompanied by any earthly favour. Inglesant's name was associated with that of the Archbishop, and the Jesuit's aim in sending him to London was accomplished.

CHAPTER X.

INGLESANT was of so much use in gaining information, and managed to live on such confidential terms with many in London in the confidence of members of the Parliament, that he remained there during all the early part of the year, and would have stayed longer; but the enemies of the Archbishop, who pursued him with a malignant and remorseless activity, set their eyes at last upon the young envoy, and he was advised to leave London, at any rate till the trial was over. He was very unwilling to leave the Archbishop, but dared not run the risk of being imprisoned, and thwarting the Jesuit's schemes, and therefore left London about the end of May, and returned straight to Oxford.

He left London only a few days before the allied armies of Sir W. Waller and the Earl of Essex, and had no sooner arrived in Oxford than the news of the advance of the Parliamentary forces caused the greatest alarm. The next day Abingdon was vacated by some mistake, and the rebels took possession of the whole of the country to the east and south of Oxford; Sir William Waller being on the south, and the Earl of Essex on the east. It was reported in London that the King intended to surrender to the Earl's army, and such a proposition was seriously made to the King by his own friends a few days afterwards in Oxford. The royal army was massed about the city, most of the foot being on the north side; Inglesant served with the foot in Colonel Lake's regiment of musketeers and pikes, taking a pike in the front rank. It was a weapon which the gentlemen of that day frequently practised, and of which he was a master. Several other gentlemen volunteers were in the front rank with him. The Earl's army was drawn up at Islip, on the other side of the river Cherwell, having marched by Oxford the day before, in open file, drums beating and colours flying, so that the King had a full view of them on the bright fine day. The Earl himself, with a party of horse, came within cannon shot of the city, and the King's horse charged him several times without any great hurt on either side. It was a gay and brilliant scene to any one who could look upon it with careless and indifferent eyes.

The next morning a strong party of the Earl's army endeavoured to pass the Cherwell at Gosford bridge, where Sir Jacob Astley commanded, and where the regiment in which Inglesant served was stationed. The bridge was barricaded with breast-works and a bastion, but the Parliamentarian army attempted to cross the stream both above and below. They succeeded in crossing opposite to Colonel Lake's regiment, under a heavy fire from the musketeers, who advanced rank by rank between the troops of pikes and a little in advance of them, and after giving their fire, wheeled off to the right and left, and took their places again in the rear. The rebels reserved their fire, their men falling at every step; but they still advanced, supported by troops of horse, till they reached the Royalists, when they delivered their fire, closed their ranks, and charged, their horse charging the pikes at the same time. The ranks of the royal musketeers halted and closed up, and the pikes drew close together shoulder to shoulder, till the rapiers of their officers met across the front. The shock was very severe, and the struggle for a moment undecided; but the pikes standing perfectly firm, owing in a great measure to the number of gentlemen in the front ranks, and the musketeers fighting with great courage, the enemy began to give way, and having been much broken before they came to the charge, fell into disorder, and were driven back across the stream, the Royalists following them to the opposite bank, and even pursuing them up the slope. Inglesant had noticed an officer on the opposite side who was fighting with great courage, and as they crossed the river he saw him stumble and nearly fall, though he appeared to struggle forward on the opposite slope to where an old thorn tree broke the rank of the pikes. Johnny came close to him and recognized him as the Mr. Thorne whom he had known at Gidding. As he knew the regiment would be halted immediately he fell out of his rank, leaving his file to the bringer-up or lieutenant behind him, and stooped over his old rival, who evidently was desperately hurt. He raised his head, and gave him some *aqua vitæ* from his flask. The other knew him at once, and tried to speak; but his strength was too far gone, and his utterance failed him. He seemed to give over the effort, and lay back in Inglesant's arms, staining his friend with his blood. Inglesant asked him if he had any mission he would wish performed, but the other shook his head, and seemed to give himself to prayer. After a minute or two he seemed to rally, and his face became very calm. Opening his eyes, he looked at Johnny steadily and with affection, and said, slowly and with difficulty, but still with a look of rest and peace,—

"Mr. Inglesant, you spoke to me once of standing together in a brighter dawn; I did not believe you, but it was true; the dawn is breaking—and it is bright."

As he spoke a volley of musketry shook the hill-side, and the regiment came down the slope at a run, and carrying Inglesant with them, crossed the river, and, halting on the other side, wheeled about and faced the passage in the same order in which they had stood at first. This dangerous manœuvre was executed only just in time, for the enemy advanced in great force to the river-side; but the Royalists being also very strong, they did not attempt to pass. After facing each other for some time, the fighting having ceased all along the line, Inglesant spoke to his officer, and got leave to cross the river with a flag of truce to seek his friend. An officer from the other side met him, most of the enemy's troops having fallen back some distance from the river. He was an old soldier, evidently a Low-country officer, and not much of a Puritan, and he greeted Inglesant politely as a fellow-soldier.

Inglesant told him his errand, and that he was anxious to find out his friend's body, if, as he feared, he would be found to have breathed his last. They went to the old thorn, where, indeed, they found Mr. Thorne quite dead. Several of the rebel officers gathered round. Mr. Thorne was evidently well known, and they spoke of him with respect and regard. Inglesant stopped, looking down on him for a few minutes, and then turned to go.

"Gentlemen," he said, raising his hat, "I leave him in your care. He was, as you have well said, a brave and a good man. I crossed his path twice—once in love and once in war—and at both times he acted as a gallant gentleman and a man of God. I wish you good day."

He turned away, and went down to the river, from which his regiment had by this time also fallen back, the others looking after him as he went.

"Who is that?" said a stern and grim-looking Puritan officer. "He does not speak as the graceless Cavaliers mostly do."

"His name is Inglesant," said a quiet, pale man, in dark and plain clothes; "he is one of the King's servants, a concealed Papist, and, they say, a Jesuit. I have seen him often at Whitehall."

"Thou wilt not see him much longer, brother," said the other grimly, "either at Whitehall or elsewhere. It were a good deed to prevent his further deceiving the poor and ignorant folk," and he raised his piece to fire.

"Scarcely," said the other quietly, "since he came to do us service and courtesy." But he made no effort to restrain the Puritan, looking on, indeed, with a sort of quiet interest as to what would happen.

"Thou art enslaved over much to the customs of this world, brother," said the other, still with his grave smile;

"knowest thou not that it is the part of the saints militant to root out iniquity from the earth?"

He arranged his piece to fire, and would no doubt have done so; but the Low-country officer, who had been looking on in silence, suddenly threw himself upon the weapon, and wrested it out of his hand.

"By my soul, Master Fight-the-fight," he said, "that passes a joke. The good cause is well enough, and the saints militant and triumphant, and all the rest of it; but to shoot a man under a flag of truce was never yet required of any saint, whether militant or triumphant."

The other looked at him severely as he took back his weapon.

"Thou art in the bonds of iniquity thyself," he said, "and in the land of darkness and the shadow of death. The Lord's cause will never prosper while it puts trust in such as thou." But he made no further attempt against Inglesant, who, indeed, by this time had crossed the river, and was out of musket shot on the opposite bank.

A few days afterwards the King left Oxford and went into the West. Inglesant remained in garrison, and took his share in all the expeditions of any kind that were undertaken. The Roman Catholics were at this time very strong in Oxford; they celebrated mass every day, and had frequent sermons at which many of the Protestants attended; but it was thought among the Church people to be an extreme thing to do, and any of the commanders who did it excited suspicion thereby. The Church of England people were by this time growing jealous of the power and unrestrained license of the Catholics, and the Jesuit warned Inglesant to attach himself more to the English Church party, and avoid being much seen with extreme Papists. Colonel Gage, a Papist, was appointed governor by the King; but being a very prudent man and a general favourite, as well as an excellent officer, the appointment did not give much offence. Inglesant was present at Cropredy Bridge, which battle or skirmish was fought after the King returned to Oxford from his hasty march through Worcestershire, and was wounded severely in the head by a sword cut—a wound which he thought little of at the time, but which long afterwards made itself felt. Notwithstanding this wound he intended following the King into the West, for His Majesty had latterly shown a greater kindness to him, and a wish to keep him near his person; but Father St. Clare, after an interview with the King, told Inglesant that he had a mission for him to perform in London, and so kept him in Oxford.

The trial of the Archbishop was dragging slowly on through the year, and the Jesuit procured Inglesant another pass and directed him to endeavour in every way to assist the Archbishop in his trial, without fear of his prosecutors, telling him that he could procure his liberation even if he were put in prison, which he did not believe he would be. Inglesant, therefore, on his return to London, gave himself heartily to assisting the counsel and secretary of the Archbishop, and found himself perfectly unmolested in so doing. He lodged at a druggist's over against the Goat Tavern, near Toy Bridge in the Strand, and frequented the ordinary at Haycock's, near the Palsgrave's Head Tavern, where the Parliament men much resorted. Here he met among others Sir Henry Blount, who had been a gentleman pensioner of the King's, and had waited on him in his turn to York and Edgehill fight, but then, returning to London, walked into Westminster Hall, with his sword by his side, so coolly as to astonish the Parliamentarians. He was summoned before the Parliament, but pleading that he only did his duty as a servant, was acquitted. This man, who was a man of judgment and experience, was of great use to Inglesant in many ways, and put him in the way of finding much that might assist the Archbishop; but it occurred to Inglesant more than once to doubt whether the latter would benefit much by his advocacy, a known pupil of the Papists as he was. This caused him to keep more quiet than he otherwise would have done; but what was doubtless the Jesuit's chief aim was completely answered; for the Church people, both in London and the country, who regarded the Archbishop as a martyr, becoming aware of the sincere and really useful exertions that Inglesant had made with such untiring energy, attached themselves entirely to him, and took him completely into their confidence, so that he could at this time have depended on any of them for assistance and support. The different parties were at this time so confused and intermixed—the Papists playing in many cases a double game—that it would have been difficult for Inglesant, who was partly in the confidence of all, to know which way to act, had he stood alone. He saw now, more than he had ever done, the intrigues of that party among the Papists who favoured the Parliament, and was astonished at their skill and duplicity. At last the Commons, failing to find the Archbishop guilty of anything worthy of death, passed a Bill of Attainder, as they had done with Lord Strafford, and condemned him with no precedence of law. The Lords hesitated to pass the Bill, and on Christmas Eve, 1644, demanded a conference with the Commons. The next day was the strangest Christmas Day Inglesant had ever spent. The whole city was ordered to fast in the most solemn way by a special ordinance of Parliament, and strict inquisition was made to see that this ordinance was carried out by the people. Inglesant was well acquainted with Mr. Hale, afterwards Chief Justice Hale, one of the Archbishop's counsel, then a young lawyer in Lincoln's Inn, who, it was said, had composed the defence which Mr. Hern, the senior counsel, had spoken before the Lords. Johnny spent part of the morning with this gentleman, and in the afternoon walked down to the Tower from Lincoln's Inn. The streets were very quiet, the shops closed, and a feeling of sadness and dread hung over all—at any rate in Inglesant's mind. At the turnstile at Holborn he went into a bookseller's shop kept by a man named Turner, a Papist, who sold popish books and pamphlets. Here he found an apothecary, who also was useful to the Catholics, making "Hosts" for them. These both immediately began to speak to Inglesant about the Archbishop and the Papists, expressing their surprise that he should exert himself so much in his favour, telling him that the Papists, to a man, hated him and desired his death, and that a gentleman lately returned from Italy had that very day informed the bookseller that the news of the Archbishop's execution was eagerly expected in Rome. The Lords were certain to give way, they said, and the Archbishop was as good as dead already. They were evidently very anxious to extract from Inglesant whether he acted on his own responsibility or from the directions of the Jesuit; but Inglesant was much too prudent to commit himself in any way. When he had left them he went straight to the Tower, where he was admitted to the Archbishop, whom he found expecting him. He gave him all the intelligence he could, and all the gossip of the day which he had picked up, including the sayings of the wits at the taverns and ordinaries respecting the trial and the Archbishop, of whom all men's minds were full.

Laud was inclined to trust somewhat to the Lords' resistance, and Inglesant had scarcely the heart to refute his opinion. He told him the feeling of the Papists, and his fear that even the Catholics at Oxford were not acting sincerely with him. After the failure of the King's pardon, Laud entertained little hope from any other efforts Charles might be disposed to make; but Inglesant promised him to ride to Oxford, and see the Jesuit again. This he did the next day, before the Committee of the Commons met the Lords, which they did not do till the 2d of January. He had a long interview with the Jesuit, and urged as strongly as he could the cruelty and impolicy of letting the Archbishop die without an effort to save him.

"What can be done?" said the Jesuit; "the King can do nothing. All that he can do in the way of pardon he has done: besides, I never see the King; the feeling against the Catholics is now so strong that His Majesty dare not hold any communications with me."

Inglesant inquired what the policy of the Roman Catholic Church really was; was it favourable to the King and the English Church, or against it?

The Jesuit hesitated, but then, with that appearance of frankness which always won upon his pupil, he confessed that the policy of the Papal Court had latterly gone very much more in favour of the party who wished to destroy the English Church than it had formerly done; and that at present the Pope and the Catholic powers abroad were only disposed to help the King on such terms as he could not accept, and at the same time retain the favour of the Church and Protestant party; and he acknowledged that he had himself under-estimated the opposition of the bulk of English people to Popery. He then requested Inglesant to return to London, and continue to show himself openly in support of the Archbishop, assuring him that in this way alone could he fit himself for performing a most important service to the King, which, he said, he should be soon able to point out to him. The old familiar charm, which had lost none of its power over Johnny, would, of itself, have been sufficient to make him perfectly pliant to the Jesuit's will. He returned to London, but was refused admission to the Archbishop until after the Committee of the Commons had met the Lords, and on the 3d of January the Lords passed the Bill of Attainder. When the news of this reached the Archbishop, he broke off his history, which he had written from day to day, and prepared himself for death. He petitioned that he might be beheaded instead of hanged, and the Commons at last, after much difficulty, granted this request. On the 6th of January it was ordered by both Houses that he should suffer on the 10th. On the same day Inglesant received a special message from the Jesuit in these words, in cypher:—"Apply for admission to the scaffold; it will be granted you."

Very much surprised, Inglesant went to Alderman Pennington, and requested admission to attend the Archbishop to the scaffold, pleading that he was one of the King's household, and attached to the Archbishop from a boy.

Pennington examined him concerning his being in London, his pass, and place of abode, but Inglesant thought more from curiosity than from any other motive; for it was evident that he knew all about him, and his behaviour in London. He asked him many questions about Oxford and the Catholics, and seemed to enjoy any embarrassment that Inglesant was put to in replying. Finally he gave him the warrant of admission, and dismissed him. But as he left the room he called him back, and said with great emphasis,—

"I would warn you, young man, to look very well to your steps. You are treading a path full of pitfalls, few of which you see yourself. All your steps are known, and those are known who are leading you. They think they hold the wires in their own hands, and do not know that they are but the puppets themselves. If you are not altogether in the snare of the destroyer come out from them, and escape both destruction in this world and the wrath that is to come."

Inglesant thanked him and took his leave. He could not help thinking that there was much truth in the alderman's description of his position.

The next three days the Archbishop spent in preparing for death and composing his speech; and on the day on which he was to die, Inglesant found when he reached the Tower, that he was at his private prayers, at which he continued until Pennington arrived to conduct him to the scaffold. When he came out and found Inglesant there, he seemed pleased, as well he might, for, excepting Stern, his chaplain, the only one who was allowed to attend him, he was alone amongst his enemies. He ascended the scaffold with a brave and cheerful courage, some few of the vast crowd assembled reviling him, but the greater part preserving a decent and respectful silence. The chaplain and Inglesant followed him close, and it was well they did so, for a crowd of people, whether by permission or not is not known, pressed up upon the scaffold, as Dr. Heylyn said, "upon the theatre to see the tragedy," so that they pressed upon the Archbishop, and scarcely gave him room to die. Inglesant had never seen such a wonderful sight before—once afterwards he saw one like it, more terrible by far. The little island of the scaffold, surrounded by a surging, pressing sea of heads and struggling men, covering the whole extent of Tower Hill: the houses and windows round full of people, the walls and towers behind covered too. People pressed underneath the scaffold; people climbed up the posts and hung suspended by the rails that fenced it round; people pressed up the steps till there was scarcely room within the rails to stand. The soldiers on guard seemed careless what was done, probably feeling certain that there was no fear of any attempt to rescue the hated priest.

Inglesant recognized many Churchmen and friends of the Archbishop among the crowd, and saw that they recognized him, and that his name was passed about among both friends and enemies. The Archbishop read his speech with great calmness and distinctness, the opening moving many to tears, and when he had finished, gave the papers to Stern to give to his other chaplains, praying God to bestow His mercies and blessings upon them. He spoke to a man named Hind, who sat taking down his speech, begging him not to do him wrong by mistaking him. Then begging the crowd to stand back and give him room, he knelt down to the block; but seeing through the chinks of the boards the people underneath, he begged that they might be removed, as he did not wish that his blood should fall upon the heads of the people. Surely no man was ever so crowded upon and badgered to his death. Then he took off his doublet, and would have addressed himself to prayer, but was not allowed to do so in peace; one Sir John Clotworthy, an Irishman, pestering him with religious questions. After he had answered one or two meekly, he turned to the executioner and forgave him, and kneeling down, after a very short prayer, to which Hind listened with his head down and wrote word for word, the axe with a single blow cut off his head. He was buried in All Hallows Barking, a great crowd of people attending him to the grave in silence and great respect,—the Church of England service read over him without interruption, though it had long been discontinued in all the Churches in London.

News of his death spread rapidly over England, and was received by all Church people with religious fervour as the news of a martyrdom; and wherever it was told, it was added that Mr. John Inglesant, the King's servant, who had used every effort to aid the Archbishop on his trial, was with him on the scaffold to the last. Inglesant returned to Oxford, where the Jesuit received him cordially. He had, it would have seemed, failed in his mission, for the Archbishop was dead; nevertheless, the Jesuit's aim was fully won.

On the King's leaving Oxford, before the advance of General Fairfax, Inglesant accompanied him, and was present at the battle of Naseby, so fatal to the royal cause. No mention of this battle, however, is to be found among the papers from which these memoirs are compiled; and the fact that Inglesant was present at it is known only by an incidental reference to it at a later period. Amid the confusion of the flight, and the subsequent wanderings of the King before he returned to Oxford, it is impossible to follow less important events closely, and it does not seem clear whether Inglesant met with the Jesuit immediately after the battle or not. Acting, however, there can be no doubt, with his approval, if not by his direction, he appears very soon after to have found his way to Gidding, where he remained during several weeks.

CHAPTER XI.

THE autumn days passed quickly over, and with them the last peaceful hours that Inglesant would know for a long time, and that youthful freshness and bloom and peace which he would never know again. Such a haven as this, such purity and holiness, such rest and repose, lovely as the autumn sunshine resting on the foliage and the grass, would never be open to him again. It was long before rest and peace came to him at all, and when they did come, under different skies and an altered life, it was a rest after a stern battle that left its scars deep in his very life; it was apart from every one of his early friends; it was unblest by first love and early glimpse of heaven.

It was about the end of October that he received a message from the Jesuit, which was the summons to leave this paradise sanctified to him by the holiest moments of his life. The family were at evening prayers in the Church when the messenger arrived, and Inglesant, as usual, was kneeling where he could see Mary Collet, and probably was thinking more of her than of the prayers. Nevertheless he remembered afterwards, when he thought during the long lonely hours of every moment spent at Gidding, that the third collect was being read, and that at the words "Lighten our darkness" he looked up at some noise, and saw the sunlight from the west window shining into the Church upon Mary Collet and the kneeling women, and, beyond them, standing in the dark shadow under the window, the messenger of the Jesuit whom he knew. He got up quietly and went out. From his marriage feast, nay, from the table of the Lord, he would have got up all the same had that summons come to him.

His whole life from his boyhood had been so formed upon the idea of some day proving himself worthy of the confidence reposed in him (that perfect unexpressed confidence which won his very nature to a passionate devotion capable of the supreme action, whatever it might be, to which all his training had tended), that to have faltered at any moment would have been more impossible to him than suicide, than any self-contradictory action could have been—as impossible as for a proud man to become suddenly naturally humble, or a merciful man cruel. That there might have been found in the universe a power capable of overmastering this master passion is possible; hitherto, however, it had not been found.

Outside the Church the messenger gave him a letter from the Jesuit, which, as usual, was very short.

"Jack, come to me at Oxford as soon as you can. The time for which we have waited is come. The service which you and none other can perform, and which I have always foreseen for you, is waiting to be accomplished. I depend on you."

Inglesant ordered some refreshment to be given to the messenger, and his own horses to be got out. Then he went back into the Church, and waited till the prayers were over.

The family expressed great regret at parting with him; they

were in a continual state of apprehension from their Puritan neighbours; but Inglesant's presence was no defence but rather the contrary, and it is possible that some of them may have been glad that he was going.

Mary Collet looked sadly and wistfully at him as they stood before the porch of the house in the setting sunlight, the long shadows resting on the grass, the evening wind murmuring in the tall trees and shaking down the falling leaves.

"Do you know what this service is?" she said at last.

"I cannot make the slightest guess," he answered.

"Whatever it is you will do it?" she asked again.

"Certainly; to do otherwise would be to contradict the tenor of my life."

"It may be something that your conscience cannot approve," she said.

"It is too late to think of that," he said, smiling; "I should have thought of that years ago, when I was a boy at Westacre, and this man came to me as an angel of light—to me, a weak, ignorant, country lad—to me, who owe him everything that I am, everything that I know, everything—even the power that enables me to act for him."

Did she remember how he had once offered himself without reserve to her, then at least without any reservation in favour of this man? Did she regret that she had not encouraged this other attraction, or did she see that the same thing would have happened whether she had accepted him or no? She gave no indication of either of these thoughts.

"I think you owe something to another," she said, softly; "to One who knew you before this Jesuit; to One who was leading you onward before he came across your path; to One who gave you high and noble qualities, without which the Jesuit could have given you nothing; to One whom you have professed to love; to One for whose Divine Voice you have desired to listen. Johnny, will you listen no longer for it?"

He never forgot her, standing before him with her hands clasped and her eyes raised to his,—the flush of eager speaking on her face,—those great eyes, moistened again with tears, that pierced through him to his very soul,—her trembling lip,—the irresistible nobleness of her whole figure,—her winning manner, through which the love she had confessed for him spoke in every part. He never saw her again but once—then in how different a posture and scene; and the beauty of this sight never went out of his life, but it produced no effect upon his purpose; indeed, how could it, when his purpose was not so much a part of him as he was a part of it? He looked at her in silence, and his love and admiration spoke out so unmistakably in his look that Mary never afterwards doubted that he had loved her. He had not power to explain his conduct; he could not have told himself why he acted as he did. Amid the distracting purposes which tore his heart in twain he could say nothing but,—

"It may not be so bad as you think."

Mary gave him her hand, turned from him, and went into the house; and he let her go—her of whom the sight must have been to him as that of an angel—he let her go without an effort to stay her, even to prolong the sight. His horses were waiting, and one of his servants would follow with his mails; he mounted and rode away. The sun had set in a cloud, and the autumn evening was dark and gloomy, yet he rode along without any appearance of depression, steadily and quietly, like a man going about some business he has long expected to perform. I cannot even say he was sad: that moment had come to him which from his boyhood he had looked forward to. Now at last he could prove, at any rate to himself, that he was equal to that effort which it had been his ideal to attempt.

When Inglesant reached Oxford he sought out the Jesuit, and found him alone. The royal affairs were at the lowest ebb. Since the battle of Naseby the King had done little but wander about like a fugitive. He was now at Oxford; but it was doubtful whether he could stay there in safety through the winter, and certainly he would not be able to do so after the campaign began, unless some change in his fortunes meanwhile occurred. All this Inglesant knew only too well. The ruin of the royal cause, entailing his own ruin and that of all his friends, was too palpable to need description. The Jesuit therefore at once proceeded to the means which were prepared to remedy this disastrous state of things. The Lord Lieutenant of Ireland, the Duke of Ormond, had, with the consent of the King, concluded a truce with the Irish, who, after long years of oppression, spoliation, and misery, had, a few years before, broken out suddenly in rebellion, and massacred hundreds of the unprepared Protestants, men, women, and children, under circumstances, as is admitted by Catholics, and is perhaps scarcely to be wondered at, of frightful cruelty. A feeling of intense hatred and dread of these rebels had consequently filled the minds of the English Protestants, both Royalists and Parliamentarians; a feeling in which horror at murderous savages—for as such they not unnaturally regarded the Irish—was united with the old hatred and fear of popish massacres and cruelties. The Parliament had remonstrated with the King for his supineness in not concluding the war by the extirpation of these monsters, and when at last a truce was concluded with them, the anger of the Parliament knew no bounds, and even loyal Churchmen, although they acknowledged the hard necessity which obliged the King to such a step, yet lamented it as one of the severest misfortunes which had befallen them. The King hoped by this peace not only to be able to recall the soldiers who had been engaged against the rebels to his own assistance, but also to procure a detachment of Irish soldiers for the same purpose from the popish leaders. But the popish demands being very excessive, Ormond had not been able to advance far towards a settled peace, when, in the previous spring, the Lord Herbert (afterwards Earl of Glamorgan), the son of the Marquis of Worcester, of a devoted Catholic family, and of great influence, announced his intention of going to Ireland on private business, and offered to assist the King with his influence among the Catholics. He had married a daughter of the great Irish house of Thomond, and undoubtedly possessed more influence in that island among the Papists than any other of the royal party.

The King eagerly accepted his assistance, and Glamorgan afterwards produced a commission, undeniably signed by the King, in which he gives him ample powers to treat with the Papists, and to grant them any terms whatever which he should find necessary, consistent with the royal supremacy and the safety of the Protestants. In this extraordinary commission he creates him Earl of Glamorgan, bestows on him the Garter and George, promises him the Princess Elizabeth as a wife for his son, gives him blank patents of nobility to fill up at his pleasure, and promises him on the word of a King to endorse all his actions. The only limit which appears to have been set to the Earl was an obligation to inform the Lord Lieutenant of all his proceedings; and the only doubt respecting this commission appears to be whether it was filled up before the King signed it, or written on a blank signed by the King, in accordance with conclusions previously agreed upon between him and the Earl.

The Earl left Oxford for Ireland, where the Nuncio from the Pope had arrived, and proceeded in his negotiations with this dignitary and the Supreme Council of the rebel Papists and Irish —negotiations in which he found endless difficulties and delays, owing chiefly to a mutual distrust of all parties towards each other;—a distrust of the King not unnatural on the part of the Irish, who knew that nothing but the utmost distress induced the King to treat with them at all, and that to treat with them, or at least to make any important concessions to them, was to alienate the whole of the English Protestants—both Royalists and Parliamentarians—to an implacable degree. The Irish demanded perfect freedom of religion; the possession of all Cathedrals and Churches; and that all the strong places in Ireland, including Dublin, should be in the hands at any rate of English Roman Catholics; that the English Papists should be relieved from all disabilities; and that the King in the first Parliament, or settlement of the nation, should ratify and secure all these advantages to them. In return for this the Pope offered a large present of money, and the Earl was promised 10,000 men from the rebel forces—3000 immediately for the relief of Chester, and 7000 to follow before the end of March.

In order to realize how repulsive such a proceeding as this would appear to the whole English nation, it is necessary to recollect the repeated professions of attachment to Protestantism on the part of the King, and of his determination to repress Popery; the intense hatred of Popery on the part of the Puritan party, and of most of the Church people; and the horror caused in all classes by the barbarities of the Irish massacre—something similar to the feeling in England during the Sepoy rebellion. No Irish ever came into England, and the English knew them only by report as ferocious, half-naked savages, to which state, indeed, centuries of oppression had reduced them. So universal was this feeling, that the King dared only proceed in the most secret manner; and in a letter to Glamorgan he acknowledges that the circumstances are such that he cannot do more than hint at his wishes, promising him again, on the word of a King, to ratify all his actions, and to regard his proceedings with additional gratitude if they were conducted without insisting nicely on positive written orders, which it was impossible to give.

Communications between the Earl and the Court continued to be kept up, and the former represented the progress of the negotiations as satisfactory; but the state of the King's affairs became so pressing, especially with regard to the relief of Chester, which was reduced to great distress, that it was absolutely necessary that some envoy should be sent to Ireland to hasten the treaty, and if possible assist the Earl to convince the Supreme Council of the good faith of the King; and it was also as important that an equally qualified agent should go to Chester to prepare the leaders there to receive the Irish contingent, and to encourage them to hold out longer in expectation of it.

"There is no man so suited to both these missions as yourself," said the Jesuit. "You are a King's servant and a Protestant, and you will therefore have weight with the rebel Council in Ireland. Still more, as you are a Churchman and a favourite with the Church people—especially since the death of the Archbishop—you will be able to prepare the mind of the Lord Biron and the commanders at Chester to receive the Irish troops favourably; they will believe that you act by the King's direction, and will not know anything of the concessions which have been made in Ireland. You are ready to undertake it?"

Inglesant hesitated for a moment, but then he said simply and without effort,—

"I am ready; I will do my best; but there are some things I should like to ask."

"Ask what you will," said the Jesuit, quickly; "everything I know I will tell you."

"As a Churchman," said Inglesant, "if I lend myself to this plan I shall be considered by all Churchmen to have betrayed my religion, and to have done my best to ruin my country as a Protestant country. Is not this the case?"

"Probably," said the Jesuit, after a moment's hesitation.

"Shall I have any authority direct from the King for what I do?"

"I have advised not," said the Jesuit; "but His Majesty thinks that you will need some other warrant, both in Ireland and at Chester, than the mere fact of your belonging to the Household. He therefore intends to give you an interview, and also a written commission signed by himself."

"And in case the whole scheme miscarries and becomes public?" said Inglesant.

"I cannot answer," said the Jesuit, "for what course His Majesty may be advised to take; but in your case it will, of course, be your duty to preserve the strictest silence as to what has passed between the King and yourself."

"Then if I fall into the hands of the Parliament," Inglesant said, "my connection with the King will be repudiated?"

"His Majesty pledges his word as a King"—began the Jesuit.

Inglesant made a slight impatient motion with his head, which the other saw, and instantly stopped.

He raised his eyes to Inglesant, and looked fully in his face for a moment; then, with that supreme instinct which taught him at once how to deal with men, he said:—

"If the necessities of the State demand it, all knowledge of this affair will be denied by the King."

"That is all I have to say," said Inglesant; "I am ready to go."

The next day Inglesant saw the King. The interview was very short. The King referred him to Father St. Clare for all instructions, telling him distinctly that all the instructions he would receive from him would have his approval, urging him to use all his efforts to assist Lord Glamorgan, but at all events to lose no time, after seeing his Lordship, in getting to Chester, and, when there, to use every exertion to induce the Cavaliers to receive the Irish troops, as they, no doubt, would be glad in their extremity to do. He received a few lines written by the King in his presence and signed, requiring all to whom he might show them to give credit to what he might tell them as if it came direct from the King. The King gave him his hand to kiss, and dismissed him.

Inglesant lost no time in reaching Bristol, taking with him all that remained of his money, considerable sums of which he had from time to time lent to the King. He found a vessel sailing for Waterford, and was fortunate enough to reach that harbour without loss of time. He did not stay by the ship while she went up to the city, but landed at Dunmore, and immediately took horses to Kilkenny. There he found the Earl and the Papal Nuncio engaged in negotiations with each other, and with the Supreme Council, the principal difficulty being an intense distrust of the King. The Nuncio, John Baptista Rinuccini, Archbishop of Fermo, was of a noble family of Florence, and of long experience at the Court of Rome. He appeared pleased to see Inglesant, and came to visit him privately at his lodgings, where he entered into a long discourse with him, endeavouring to find out the real standing and authority of the Earl, and whether the King could be trusted or not. Inglesant, who spoke both French and Italian as well as Latin, was able to enter very fully and freely into the state of affairs with him. He told him that the only way to gain any advantages which the Catholics might have in view was to assist the King promptly and effectively at once; that the King could only be enabled to fulfil his promises by being placed in a strong and independent position; and that if, by delays and half measures, the help was postponed till it was too late, or the negotiations became publicly known, the King would be powerless to fulfil his promises, and would be compelled to repudiate them altogether. He submitted to the Nuncio that, even supposing the King's good faith was doubtful, he was much more likely to be favourable to the Catholics, when restored to power, than the Parliament and the Puritan faction would ever be; he reminded the Nuncio of the great favour and leniency which had ever been shown to the Romanists during the King's reign, and he spoke warmly of the base ingratitude which had been shown to the King by that party among the Catholics who had intrigued with the Parliament against a King, very many of whose troubles had arisen from his leniency towards their religion.

The Nuncio was evidently much impressed with Inglesant's arguments, and was very courteous in his expressions of regard, assuring Inglesant that he should not forget to mention so excellent and intelligent a friend of the Romish Church in Rome itself, and that he hoped he might some time see him there, and receive him into closer relations to that glorious and tender mother.

Inglesant saw the Earl immediately after this interview; he found him perplexed and discouraged with the difficulties of his position. He introduced Inglesant to several of the Supreme Council, and many days were taken up in argument and negotiations. At last both Inglesant and the Earl agreed that the most important thing for him to do was to get to Chester without loss of time, as the delays and negotiations were so great that there was imminent danger that the city would be surrendered before the treaty could be completed. Inglesant therefore left Kilkenny immediately, and, posting to Dublin without loss of time, embarked for Anglesea, and arrived there on the 29th of December. Here he procured horses, and, crossing the island, he passed over into Flintshire and proceeded towards Chester. It was exceedingly unfortunate that he had not arrived a few days before, as the Parliamentary army, having lately received a reinforcement of Colonel Booth and the Lancashire forces who had just reduced Latham House, had now entirely surrounded the city, guarding with sufficient force every gate and avenue, causing a great scarcity of provisions, and rendering it almost impossible for any one to gain admission to the garrison.

CHAPTER XII.

LORD BIRON and some of the Commissioners who were associated with him in the defence of the city were at supper in a long, low room in the Castle on the evening of the 12th of January. Lord Biron and more than one of the noblemen and gentlemen then in Chester had their ladies with them, but they lived apart, mostly at Sir Francis Gammul's house in the Lower Bridge Street, opposite to St. Olave's Church, and were provided for rather better than the rest; but the commanders partook of exactly the same food as the rest of the besieged, and their supper that night consisted of nothing but boiled wheat, with water to drink. The conversation was very flat, for the condition of the besieged was becoming utterly hopeless; and although they had rejected several offers of capitulation, they foresaw that it could not be long before they should be obliged to submit. The town had been singularly free from discontent and mutiny, and Lord Biron's high position and renown made him particularly fitted for the post he filled; but he felt that the task before him was well-nigh hopeless. He sat buried in thought, few of the other gentlemen present spoke, and they were on the point of separating, Lord Biron to make the round of the walls, when a servant came up from the court below, saying that there was a man below in the dress of a miner, who said he was Mr. Inglesant, the King's gentleman, and wished to see his lordship.

"Who did you say?" exclaimed Lord Biron, and the others crowded round in excitement, "Inglesant, the King's Esquire?"

"John Inglesant."

"The Esquire of the body?"

"No doubt from Oxford and the King.'

"How could he have have got in?"

"In the dress of a miner, he says."

"Perhaps the King is near at hand?"

"At any rate he has not forgotten us."

"He has used his Jesuit's teaching to some purpose."

These and many other exclamations were uttered while Lord Biron told the servant to send Inglesant up at once. He entered the room in his miner's dress, his hands and face stained with dust, his hair matted and hanging over his eyes. He carried a large kind of bag, such as the miners used, and his first action was to place it on the table, and to remove from it five or six bottles of claret, a large ham, and a goose.

"I knew you were somewhat short here," he said, "and I ran the risk of bringing these things, though I do not know, if I had been caught, that it would have told much against me, for we miners live well, I can tell your lordship."

"But how on earth did you get in?" said Lord Biron, "and where have you come from?"

"I thought I never should have got in," he replied. "The leaguer is well kept, and there is scarcely a weak point. But I fear," he added sadly, "from the state I find you in, it really mattered little whether I got in or not."

"Oh, never say that," said Lord Biron cheerily; "the sight of you is a corps of relief in itself. Come in here and let me hear what you have to say. I will not keep the news a moment from you, gentlemen," he added courteously to the rest.

"If you will pardon me, my lord," said Inglesant, "and allow me a moment to wash this dirt off, and if some one will lend me a suit of clothes, it would be a courtesy. I had to leave my own in Flintshire, and these are none of the pleasantest. My news will keep a few minutes, and your lordship will be all the better for a glass or two of this claret, which is not the worst you ever drank."

Lord Biron took him into another room, and left him to

change his dress, lending him one of his own suits of clothes. Inglesant really wished to gain time, and also to say what he had to say with every advantage of appearance and manner, for he felt that his mission was a difficult one—how difficult he felt he did not know.

When he came back he found the gentlemen had opened one of the bottles, and were drinking the wine very frugally, but with infinite relish. They were warm in their thanks to Inglesant, and in congratulations on his improved appearance. Lord Biron took him on one side at once.

Inglesant had a letter for him from the Duke of Ormond, which the Duke had given him unsealed, telling him to read it. John Inglesant had done so several times during his journey, and did not altogether like its contents. The Duke alluded by name to Lord Glamorgan, and mentioned the number (10,000) of the troops intended to be sent to England. Neither fact would Inglesant have wished to communicate himself, at any rate at once, and he had resolved not to deliver the letter until he saw how Lord Biron took the rather vague information he intended to give him. But there is always this difficulty with negotiations of this kind, that while the first requisite is entire frankness, the least caution, even at the beginning, may convey a sense of suspicion which nothing afterwards can remove. Inglesant felt, therefore, that he should have to watch Lord Biron most closely, and decide instantly, and on the spur of the moment, when to trust him and to what extent.

He began, after Lord Biron had expressed his cordial admiration at his exploit and his sense of obligation, by telling him he came direct from Lord Ormond, in Dublin, and that his object in getting into Chester was to let them know that they might expect relief from Ireland, at most within a few days, and to urge them to hold out to the last moment and the last bag of wheat.

Without appearing to do so, he watched Lord Biron narrowly as he spoke, and saw that he expected to hear a great deal more than this vague account.

He went on telling him of his interview with Ormond, of the King's great anxiety for the relief of Chester, and the difficulties the Lord Lieutenant met with in treating with the Irish; but he saw that Lord Biron was manifestly getting impatient. At last the latter said,—

"But you have not told me, Mr. Inglesant, where this relief is to come from. Ormond has no troops to spare—he has told us so often; indeed, all the troops that could be spared passed through Chester years ago when the truce was first proclaimed. He must keep all his to keep those murderous villains, the Irish Papists, in check. They will respect no truce. We hear something of Lord Glamorgan; have you seen him in Ireland? Have you no letter from Ormond to me?"

Inglesant saw that he must trust him at once to a very great extent.

"I have a letter from the Duke to you," he said; "but I wish first to show you this warrant the King gave me at Oxford, that you may see I do not speak without his authority. When he gave me that, he told me all the negotiations which the Duke was engaged in, at his desire, with the Irish Papists; and all that I tell you has been done with his sanction. As to Lord Glamorgan, I saw him at Kilkenny; he is striving all he can to second the Lord Lieutenant's efforts with the Irish and the Papal Nuncio, and he has the fullest warrant from the King."

Lord Biron read the warrant from the King carefully more than once; then returned it, and took Lord Ormond's letter, which he also read once or twice.

Inglesant walked to the window and looked out.

"The letter is not sealed, Mr. Inglesant," Lord Biron said.

"No," said Inglesant, "the Duke insisted on my bringing it open, and on my reading it. I requested him to seal it, but he refused."

"And you have read it?"

"Certainly."

"I see he speaks of a very large contingent—10,000 men, and that Glamorgan is to get them entirely from the Irish Papists. Ten thousand Irish Papists and murderers in England, Mr. Inglesant, is not what I should like to see, and I do not like the negotiation being intrusted so much to Glamorgan, a determined Papist. We know not what concessions he may make unknown to the King. I beg your pardon for my plain speaking; they say you are half a Papist yourself."

"You will only have 3000 men sent here," said Inglesant, "and from what I saw in Ireland I fear it may be some time before the rest follow. Besides, surely, my lord, nothing can be worse than your present state here."

"It is sad enough, certainly, but there may be things much worse. I tell you, sir, I would rather die of hunger on these walls than see my country given over to murderous Irish rebels and savage Kerns. And bad as the King's affairs are at present, I am convinced that His Majesty would endure all gladly, rather than make any concessions to such as these,—much less expose England to their ravages."

"The troops who will be sent will be under the strictest orders, and commanded by gentlemen of honour and rank," said Inglesant; "and I assure your lordship, upon my sacred word of honour as a Christian, that nothing will be attempted but what has His Majesty's cordial consent."

Lord Biron was unsatisfied, but Inglesant considered he had achieved a success; his lordship had plainly not the least suspicious feeling towards him, all his dissatisfaction arising from his dislike to the means proposed for his relief. He would, moreover, hold out as long as possible, and this all the more as he saw help approaching, from whatever source it came.

They went back to the other officers, and communicated the news to them, rather to their disappointment; for Inglesant having spoken some words of encouragement to the soldiers of the guard below, the report had run through Chester that the King was at hand with 3000 horse. The effect, however, which Inglesant's news produced in Chester was altogether exhilarating. Officers, soldiers, and inhabitants set to work with redoubled vigour, and Inglesant became a hero wherever he went, and was introduced to Lady Biron and the ladies, who received him with gratitude, as though he had already raised the siege. He was himself, however, very far from being at ease, as day after day passed and no signs of help appeared. Lord Biron, though showing the greatest signs of confidence openly, had evidently become more and more hopeless, and continually sought opportunities of speaking to Inglesant privately: and Inglesant found it impossible to avoid letting him see more and more into the real facts of the case; so that the Duke and his share in the negotiations fell, day by day, deeper into the shade, and Lord Glamorgan and his share appeared every day in greater prominence. Lord Biron expressed himself increasingly dissatisfied, and suspicious that such negotiations did not originate with the King; but as no help or troops of any kind appeared, these imaginary dangers were not of much import. Sir William

Brereton, the Parliamentary commander, was continually sending letters summoning them to surrender. Nine of these they refused, but when there appeared no longer any hopes of succour, Lord Biron answered the tenth. To this Sir William answered, upbraiding Lord Biron with having delayed so long, "every day producing loss of blood and expense of treasure," but offering to appoint commissioners to treat on the terms of surrender. This letter was received on the 26th of January, and the same day Lord Biron replied. Sir William's answer came the next day, and the same morning, that is on the 27th of January, an event occurred which decided Lord Biron to surrender, and at the same time sealed Inglesant's fate.

Early in the forenoon a rumour spread through Chester, the source of which could not be discovered, but which no doubt arose from some soldiers' gossip between the outposts. It was said that some great Earl (Lord Glamorgan's name was immediately introduced into the report, but whether it was in the original rumour is doubtful) had been arrested in Ireland, for having concluded in the King's name, but without his sanction, a treaty with the Irish rebels and Papists, by which the latter were relieved from all disabilities and restored to the command of the island, in return for which they agreed to march a large army into England, to destroy the Parliament and the Protestant party, and restore the King and Popery. This report, garnished with great variety of additional horrors, spread rapidly through the city, and about ten o'clock reached Lord Biron's ears. Chiming in as it did with his worst suspicions, it excited and alarmed him not a little. His first thought was of Inglesant, and he sent at once to his lodgings to know if he was within. Inglesant had spent the whole of the night at one of the advanced bastions, where, having some reason to believe that the enemy were working a mine, the garrison made a sortie, and, wearied out, had come home to his room in the Bridge Street to rest. His wounds, and especially the one in his head, which had been supposed to be cured, began to affect him again, probably through exhaustion, excitement, and want of food, and for several days he had felt a giddiness and confusion of brain which at times was so great that he scarcely knew what he did. He had scarcely fallen asleep on the great bed in the small room, crowded with the valuables of the good people of the house in which he lodged, when the messenger from the governor entered the room and aroused him. Sending the man back before him he waited a few minutes to collect his faculties and arrange his dress, and then followed him to the Castle. He found Lord Biron in the state dining-room, a noble room, handsomely furnished, with large windows at the end overlooking the Dee estuary, and a great carved fireplace, before which Lord Biron was standing impatiently awaiting him.

"Mr. Inglesant," he said, as he entered the room, "you showed me once a commission from His Majesty; will you let me see it again?"

Inglesant, who had heard nothing of the rumour that had caused such dismay, and who suspected nothing, immediately produced the paper and handed it to Lord Biron, who took out another from his pocket, and compared the two carefully together, going to the window to do so.

Then, coming back to Inglesant, and holding the two papers fast in his hand, he said :—

"Mr. Inglesant, I have heard this morning, what I have reason to believe is true, that the Lord Glamorgan has been arrested in Dublin by the King's Council for granting the Papists terms in the King's name, and conspiring to bring over a Papist army into England. Have you any knowledge of such matters as these?"

Inglesant's astonishment and dismay were so unfeigned that Lord Biron saw at once that such news was most unexpected by him. He had indeed, among all the dangers he was on his guard against, never calculated upon such as this. Distasteful as he supposed the negotiations with the Papists would be to numbers of the Church party, the idea never entered his mind that any loyal authorities would take upon them, without communicating with the King, the responsibility of arresting the negotiations or making them public, and this with a high hand, presupposing that they were without the King's sanction. But, supposing this extraordinary news to be true, he saw at once an end to his efforts,—he saw himself at once helpless and deserted, nothing before him but long imprisonment and perhaps death.

He stood for some moments looking at Lord Biron, the picture of astonishment and dismay. At last, he said,—

"I cannot think, my lord, that such news can be true. What possible motive could the Council have to take such a step? I give you my word of honour as a Christian, that Lord

Glamorgan has done nothing but what he had authority for from the King."

"You are much in his confidence evidently, sir," said Lord Biron severely; "but I am inclined to believe my information nevertheless."

"But he had commission and warrants signed by the King himself; and private letters from him, which would have removed all suspicion," said Inglesant.

"Yes, sir, no doubt he had commissions, professedly from the King, as you have," said Lord Biron still more severely. "Your commission names Lord Glamorgan, and you are evidently of one council with him. Will you pledge me your honour that this paper was written by the King?"

And he held out Inglesant's commission.

Johnny hesitated: the circumstances of the case were beginning to arrange themselves before him, racked and weary as his brain was. If this news were true, if the Lord Lieutenant and the Council had really disclaimed, in the King's name, the negotiations, and boldly before the world proclaimed them unauthorized, and the warrants a forgery, the game was evidently played out, and his course clear before him, dark and gloomy enough. Yet he thought he would make one effort to recover the paper, a matter, whatever might turn out, of the first importance to the King.

"If I swear to you, Lord Biron, that the King wrote it, will you give it me back?"

"I am sorry, sir, that I cannot," said Lord Biron. "I am grieved at my heart to do anything which would seem to doubt in the least the word of a gentleman such as I have always believed you to be; but in the post I hold, and in the crisis of an affair so terribly important as this, I must act as my poor judgment leads me. I cannot give this paper up to any one until I learn more of this distressing business."

"If I swear to you," said Inglesant, beaten at every point, but fighting to the last, "that it is the King's writing, will you give me your word of honour that you will burn it immediately?"

"No, sir," said the other loftily; "what the King has been pleased to write, it can be the duty of no man to conceal."

"Then it is not the King's," said Inglesant.

Lord Biron stared at him for a moment, then folded up the

papers carefully, and replaced them in his pocket-case. Then he went to the door of the dining-room at the top of the stairs and called down.

"Without! send up a guard."

Inglesant unhooked his sword from the scarf, and handed it to Lord Biron without a word. Then he said,—

"It can be of no advantage to me now, may probably tell against me, when I entreat your lordship to believe me when I tell you, as I hope for salvation before the throne of God, that if you burn that paper now you will be glad of it every day you live."

"I certainly shall not burn it, sir," said the other, speaking now with a cold disdain. And he turned his back upon Inglesant, and stood looking at the fire.

Johnny went to the window and looked out. The bright winter's sun was shining on the walls and roofs of the town, on the dancing waves of the estuary, and on the green oak banks of Flintshire beyond. He remembered the view long afterwards, as we remember that on which the eye rests almost unconsciously in any supreme moment of our lives.

Presently the guard came up.

"This gentleman is under arrest," said Lord Biron to the sergeant; "you will secure him in one of the strong rooms of the tower, and see that he has fire and his full share of provisions until the garrison is relieved; but no one must be admitted to see him, and you are responsible for his person to me. You can send word to your servant to bring you anything you may want from your lodgings, Mr. Inglesant," he said, "but he must not come to you, and all the things must pass through my hands."

Inglesant bowed. "I have to thank you for the courtesy, Lord Biron," he said; "I have nothing to complain of in your treatment of me."

The other turned away, half impatiently, and Inglesant followed the sergeant to his room, the guard following one by one, through the passages and up the narrow staircase of the tower.

It was a pleasant room enough, fitted with glass windows strongly barred. The sergeant caused a fire to be lighted, and left Inglesant to himself.

It was the first time he had ever been imprisoned, and as

the door locked upon him that terrible feeling crept over him which the first sense of incarceration always brings,—a nameless dread and a frantic desire of escape, of again mixing with fellow-men. But to Inglesant this sad feeling was increased immensely by the circumstances that surrounded him, and the peculiar nature of his position. The very nature of his position debarred him from all hope, cut him off from all help alike from friend and foe. Those who in any other case would be most forward to help him were now his jailers, nay, he was turned by this strange reverse into his own jailer and enemy; debarred from attempting anything to help himself, he must actually employ all his energies in riveting the chains more tightly on his limbs, in preparing the gallows himself. Exposed to the contempt and hatred of all his friends, of those dearer to him than friends, he could make no effort to clear himself, nay, every word he spoke must be nicely calculated to increase their aversion and contempt. He was worn and ill and half-starved, and his brain was full of confusion and strange noises, yet the idea of faltering in his course never so much as presented itself to him. The Jesuit's work was fully done.

The next day the Commissioners for the surrender of the city met, and the day after Sir William Brereton's Commissioners made a formal announcement of the news that had been received from Ireland. Lord Glamorgan, they said, had arrived in Dublin from Kilkenny. The 26th of December was fixed for him to appear before the Council, but in the meantime letters were received by several persons in Dublin giving an account of some papers found on the person of the titulary Archbishop of Tuam, who was slain in an encounter at Sligo in October. The papers contained the details of the treaty come to between Lord Glamorgan and the Papists, which details threw the Council into such dismay that they concluded that if such things were once published, and they could be believed to be done by His Majesty's authority, they could have no less fatal an effect than to make all men conclude all the former scandals cast upon His Majesty of the inciting the Irish Rebellion true; that the King was a Papist, and designed to introduce Popery even by ways the most unkingly and perfidious; and consequently, that there would be a general revolt of all good Protestants from him. Now, the Council, considering all this, and also hearing that the affair was already public through Dublin, and beginning to work such dangerous effects that they did not consider themselves safe, they concluded that the only course open to them was to arrest Lord Glamorgan in the Council, which was accordingly done on the 26th of December.

The Commissioners also informed Lord Biron that they were told that there were many Irish in Chester, born of Irish parents, who had formerly served in the rebel armies in Ireland, and that also there was even then in Chester an emissary from Lord Glamorgan. They therefore demanded that these Irish should be exempted from the general terms of surrender, and made over to them as prisoners of war, and that the emissary from Lord Glamorgan should also be given up to them as a traitor, seeing that he was condemned by the royal party as well as by themselves.

To this it was answered by Lord Biron's Commissioners that the Irish—such at least as were born of Irish parents and had served with the rebels—should be delivered as they requested, and that as to Mr. Inglesant, the emissary alluded to, he was already under arrest on the charge of treason, and should remain so until more of this affair could be known, when, if the truth appeared to be as was supposed, he should be given up also.

With this the Parliamentary Commissioners professed themselves satisfied, and the treaty was proceeded with, and on the 3d of February Chester was formally surrendered. On the same day Sir William Brereton informed Lord Biron that the King, in a message to the Parliament, dated from Oxford, January 29, utterly repudiated all knowledge of the Earl of Glamorgan's proceedings, and denied that he had given him any authority whatever to treat with the Irish Papists. Sir William added, he supposed Lord Biron would no longer have any scruple to surrender the person of Lord Glamorgan's emissary, as by so doing could he alone convince men of the sincerity of his belief in the King's freedom from complicity in his designs. Lord Biron answered that he had nothing to object to in this, and would give Mr. Inglesant up, and indeed it was not in his power to do anything else. On the 3d day of February the Parliamentary forces were marched into the town, and Lord Biron with his lady, and the rest of the noblemen and gentlemen and their ladies, prepared to leave. According to the articles of the treaty, carriages were provided for them and their goods, and a party of horse appointed to convey them to Conway. The ladies and gentlemen were assembled at Sir Francis Gammul's in the Lower Bridge Street. The street was blocked with carriages and horses, and carts full of goods; companies of foot were forcing their way through; the overhanging rows and houses were full of people, the Church bells were ringing, the Parliamentary officers passing to and fro. There was a certain amount of relief and gaiety in all hearts; the Royalists were relieved from the hardships of the siege, and were expecting to go to their homes; the Parliamentarians, of course, were jubilant. The principal inhabitants of Chester were the worst off, but even they looked forward to a time of quiet, and to the possibility of at last retrieving their losses and their position in the town. Amid all this confusion and bustle, a sergeant's guard entered the room where Inglesant was confined, and desired him to accompany them to the commander, that the transfer of his person might be arranged. He followed them out of the Castle, by St. Mary's Church, and up the short street into the Bridge Street, at the corner of which Sir Francis Gammul's house stood. Forcing his way through the crowd that gaped and pressed upon them, the sergeant conducted Inglesant into the house, and up into one of the principal rooms, where the commanders and the ladies and many others were assembled. A crowd of curious spectators pressed after them to the door as soon as it was known whom the sergeant had brought; a dead silence fell upon the whole company, and the two commanders, who were seated at a table, on which were the articles of surrender, rose and gazed at Inglesant. A confused murmur, the nature of which it would have been difficult to describe, ran through the room, and the ladies pressed together, with mingled timidity and curiosity, to look on. Inglesant was thin and pale, his clothes shabby and uncared for, his hair and moustache undressed, his whole demeanour cowed and dispirited—very different in appearance from the fine gentleman who had played Philaster before the Court. Doubtless, many among the Royalists pitied him; but at present no doubts were felt, or at any rate had time to circulate, of the King's sincerity, and the dislike to the Jesuits, even by the High Church Loyalists, closed their hearts against him. The Lord Biron asked him whether he had anything to say before he was delivered over to Sir William, to which he replied,—

"No."

He made no effort to speak to any one, or to salute Lady Biron or any of his acquaintances, but stood patiently, his eyes fixed on the ground.

Sir William asked whether he adhered to his statement that the commission he had exhibited was a forgery?

At which he looked up steadily, and said,—

"Yes; it was not written by the King."

As he made the avowal a murmur of indignation passed through the room, and Sir William ordered him to be removed, telling him he should be examined to-morrow, the account of his answers sent up to London, and the will of the Parliament communicated to him as soon as possible. Inglesant bowed in reply and turned to leave the room, making no effort to salute or take leave of any one; but Lord Biron stopped him with a gesture, and said, probably actuated by some feeling which he could not have explained,—

"I wish you good-day, Mr. Inglesant. I may never see you again."

Inglesant looked up, a slight flush passing over his features, and their eyes met.

"I wish you good-day, my lord," he said; "you have acted as a faithful servant of the King."

Lord Biron made no further effort to detain him, and he left the room.

The next day he was brought up before Sir William Brereton, and examined at great length. He stated that the plot had originated with the Roman Catholics, especially the Jesuits, whose envoy Lord Glamorgan was; that all the warrants and papers were forged by them, and that he had received his instructions and the King's commission from Father St. Clare himself. He stated that if the design failed, the King was to know nothing of it, and if it succeeded it was supposed that he would pardon the offenders on consideration of the benefits he would receive. A vast mass of evidence was taken by Sir William from Irish soldiers, inhabitants of Chester, and people of every description, relative to what had taken place in the city, and all was sent to London to the Parliament. In the course of a few days orders came down to bring Inglesant up to town, together with some of the most important witnesses, to be examined before a Committee of the House of Commons; and this was accordingly done at once, Sir William Brereton accompanying his prisoner and conveying him by easy stages to London, where he was confined in St. James's Palace till the will of the Parliament should be known.

CHAPTER XIII.

WHEN the news of the arrest of the Earl of Glamorgan reached Oxford, it caused the greatest consternation, and the King wrote letters in his own name and in that of the Chancellor, to the Parliament, and to all the principal politicians, denying all participation in or knowledge of his negotiations.

The most violent excitement prevailed on the subject all over England. All parties, except the Papists, joined in expressing the most lively horror and indignation at proposals which not only repudiated the policy of the last hundred years, and let loose the Papists to pursue their course unimpeded, but also placed England at the mercy of the most repulsive and lawless of the followers of the Roman Catholic faith. The barbarities of the Irish rebels, which were sufficiently horrible, were magnified by rumour on every side; and the horror which the English conceived at the thought of their homes being laid open to those monsters, was only equalled by their indignation against those who had conceived so treasonable and unnatural a plot. Besides this, the King having denied all knowledge of such negotiations, the indignation of all loyal Churchmen was excited against those who had so treasonably and miserably done all they could to compromise the King's name, and make him odious to all right-thinking Englishmen. The known actors in this affair being very few, consisting, indeed, only of the Earl and Inglesant, and of the Jesuits (which last was a vague and intangible designation, standing in the ordinary English mind merely as a synonym for all that was wicked, base, and dangerous), and the Earl being, moreover, out of reach, the public indignation concentrated on Inglesant, and his life would have been worth little had he fallen into the hands of the mob. When the news of the fall of Chester and of Inglesant's arrest and subsequent transference to the Parliamentary commander, reached Oxford, the King sent for the Jesuit privately, and received him in his cabinet at Christ Church.

The King appeared anxious and ill, and as though he did not know where to turn or what to do.

"You have heard the news, Father, I suppose," he said. "Lord Biron, as well as Digby, has taken upon himself to keep the King's conscience, and know the King's mind better than he does himself. How many Kings there are in England now, I do not know, but I have ever found my most faithful servants my most strict masters. You know Jack Inglesant has been given over to the rebels? What are we to do for him?"

"Your Majesty can do nothing," said the Jesuit. "All that could be done has been done, and as far as may be has been done well. All that your Majesty has to do now is to be silent."

"Then Inglesant must be given up," said the King.

"He must be given up. Your Majesty has no choice."

"Another!" said the King, bitterly. "Strafford, whose blood tinges every sight I see! Laud, Glamorgan, now another! What right have I to suppose my servants will be faithful to me, when I give them up, one by one, without a word?"

"Your Majesty does not discriminate," said the Jesuit; "your good heart overpowers your clearer reason. It is as much your duty for the good of the State, to be deaf to the voice of private feeling and friendship, as it is for your servants to be deaf to all but the call of duty to your Majesty; and this your servants know, and do not dream that they have any cause to complain. Strafford and the Archbishop both acknowledged this, and now it will be the same again. There is no fear of John Inglesant, your Majesty."

"No," said the King, rising and pacing the closet with unequal steps, "there is no fear of John Inglesant, I believe you. There is no fear that any man will betray his friends, and be false to his Order and his plighted word, except the King!—except the King!"

Apparently the Jesuit did not think it worth while to answer this outbreak, for he said, after a pause,—

"Your Majesty has written to Glamorgan?"

"Yes, I have told him to keep quiet," said the King, sitting down again; "he is in no danger—I am clear of him. But do you mean to say, Father, that Inglesant must be left to the gallows without a word?"

"No, I do not say that, your Majesty," said the other;

"the rebels will do nothing in a hurry, you may depend. They will do all they can to get something from him which may be useful against your Majesty, and it will be months before they have done with him. I have good friends among them, and shall know all that happens. When they are tired of him, and the thing is blown over a little, I shall do what I can."

"And you are sure of him," said the King; "any evidence signed by him would be fatal indeed."

"Your Majesty may be quite easy," said the other, "I am sure of him."

"They will threaten him with the gallows," said the King; "life is sweet to most men."

"I suppose it is," said the Jesuit, as if it were an assertion he had heard several times lately, and began to think he must believe; "I have no experience in such matters. But, however sweet it may be, its sweetness will not induce John Inglesant to utter a syllable against the cause in which he is engaged."

"You are very confident of your pupil," said the King. "I hope you will not be deceived."

The Jesuit smiled, but did not seem to think it necessary to make any further protestations, and soon after left the closet.

*   *   *   *   *

Inglesant remained some time in confinement at St. James's before he was summoned before the Parliamentary Committee, but at the beginning of March another of those extraordinary events occurred which seemed arranged by some providential hand to fight against the King. A packet boat put into Padstow, in Cornwall, supposing it to be a royal garrison; on discovering their mistake, and some slight resistance having been overpowered, the captain threw a packet of letters and some loose papers overboard. The papers were lost, but the packet was fished out of the sea, and proved to contain the most important of the correspondence from Lord Digby, describing the discovery of the plot, the articles of agreement with the Papists, the copy of the warrant from the King to the Earl of Glamorgan, and several letters from the Earl himself, all asserting his innocence of any actions but those directed and approved by the King. These letters were published *in extenso* by the Parliament in a pamphlet which appeared on the 17th of March. The information contained in these papers was of the greatest use to the Parliament, for, though there was nothing in them absolutely to inculpate the

King (indeed the letters of Lord Digby, as far as they went, were strong proofs to the contrary), yet it placed it in their power to make assertions and inquiries based upon fact, and it brought forward Lord Glamorgan as an evidence on their side. If they could now have produced a confession signed by Inglesant to the same effect, the case would have been almost complete—at any rate few would have hesitated to call the moral proof certain. A Committee of the Commons was appointed to examine Inglesant, and he was summoned to appear before them.

On the day appointed he was brought from St. James's across the Park in a sedan, guarded by soldiers, and not being recognized escaped without any notice from the passers-by.

The Committee sat in one of the rooms of the Parliament House, and began by asking Inglesant his name.

"I understand," said one of the members savagely, "that your name is Inglesant, of a family of courtiers and sycophants, who for generations have earned their wretched food by doing any kind of dirty work the Court set them; and that they never failed to do it so as to earn a reputation even among the mean reptiles of the Court precincts. This is true, is it not? And you have held some of those posts which an honest man would scorn."

Inglesant had recovered his health during his imprisonment, thanks to rest and sufficient food, and his manner was quiet and confident. To the attack of the Parliamentarian he answered simply,—

"My name is Inglesant; I have been Esquire of the Body to the King."

The Chairman checked the warmth of the Puritan, and began to question Inglesant concerning the plot, endeavouring to throw him off his guard by mentioning facts which had come to their knowledge through the recent discoveries. But Inglesant was prepared with his story. Though he was surprised at the amount of knowledge the Committee possessed, yet he stood to his assertion that he knew nothing of any instructions except those which he had himself received, and that the whole plot originated with the Jesuits, as far as he knew, and had every reason to believe. When he was asked how he, a Protestant and a Churchman, could lend himself to such a plot, he replied that he was very much inclined to the Romish Church, and that he thought the King's affairs so desperate that the plan of

L

obtaining help from the Irish rebels appeared to him and to Father St. Clare as almost the only resource left to them. The Committee, finding gentle means fail, adopted a sterner tone, telling him he was guilty of high treason, without benefit, and that he might certainly, on his own confession, be condemned to the gallows without further trial. They then offered him a statement to sign, which, they said, they had sure information contained nothing but the truth. Inglesant looked at it, and saw that in truth it did contain a very fair statement of what had really taken place.

He replied that it was impossible for him to sign anything so opposite to what he had himself confessed; and that even if he did, no one would believe so monstrous a statement, and one so contrary to the known opinions and professions of the King.

The Committee then asked him why, if the King's commission was forged, it was kept back, and where it was?

Inglesant said that "the Lord Biron had it, having forcibly taken it from him, and refused to return it, telling him plainly that he should keep it as evidence against him."

He observed that this impressed the Committee, and he was soon after dismissed. He returned to St. James's the same way that he came, but found a strong guard summoned to attend him; for, the news of his examination having got wind, the crowd assembled at the Parliament House, and accompanied him, with hootings and insults of every kind, across the Park.

As one result of his examination, Inglesant was removed from St. James's, and sent by water to the Tower, where a close confinement in a small cell, and insufficient diet, again affected his health. He formed the idea that the Parliament intended to weaken him with long imprisonment, and so cause him to confess what they wished; he feared that the state of his health, and especially the extent to which his brain was affected, would assist this purpose; and this fear preyed upon him, and made him nervous and miserable—dreading above everything that, his mind being clouded, he might say something inadvertently which might discover the truth. His health rapidly declined, and he became again thin and worn. The Parliament Committee now spread a report that the royal party, who pretended to indicate the offenders in this plot, did not really do so; and that in particular they kept back the originals of the King's warrants and commissions, which they asserted to be forgeries, and refused to bring them forward and submit them to proof, which would be the surest way of making the fact of the King's ignorance of them certain. They did this because they knew Lord Biron's character as a man of unstained and unsuspicious honour, and they calculated that such a taunt as this would be certain to bring him forward with the commission, which he had in his keeping, and which they trusted to be able to prove was a genuine document. Their policy had the desired effect. Lord Biron, who was at Newstead, without consulting any one, sent up a special messenger to the Speaker to say that, a safe-conduct being granted him, he would come up to London, and appear before the Committee of Parliament, bringing the commission, which he asserted was a palpable forgery, with him. The safe-conduct was immediately sent him, and he came up. The Committee were rejoiced at the success of their policy, and fixed a day for him to appear before them, and at the same time ordered Inglesant to be fetched up from the Tower to be confronted with his lordship. The affair caused the greatest interest, and the Committee Room was thronged with all who could command sufficient influence to obtain entrance, and crowds filled the corridors and the precincts of the House. Lord Biron was introduced, and gave his evidence with great clearness, describing the arrest of Inglesant, his suspicious conduct, and his attempt to induce Lord Biron to destroy the warrant; and finally produced the paper, and handed it to the clerk of the Committee. The Chairman then ordered Inglesant to be brought in through a side door, and he came up to the bar.

His appearance was so altered, and his manner so cowed and embarrassed, that a murmur ran through the room, and Lord Biron could not restrain an exclamation of pity. Inglesant started when he saw him, for he had been kept in complete ignorance of what had occurred, and his mind immediately recurred to the commission. He was evidently making the greatest efforts to collect himself and keep himself calm. Nothing could have told more against himself, or in favour of the part he was playing, than his whole demeanour.

He was examined minutely on the circumstances of his arrest, and related everything exactly as it occurred, which, indeed, he had done before—both his relations tallying exactly with Lord Biron's.

When asked what his business was in Chester, he said—to

prepare the Cavaliers to receive the Irish help; and added that he had been obliged to communicate a great deal more to Lord Biron than he had wished or intended, and that Lord Biron had always manifested the greatest suspicion of him and of his mission.

He gave his evidence steadily, but without looking at Lord Biron, or indeed at any one.

When asked why he wished to recover possession of the commission, or at least to induce Lord Biron to burn it, he replied,—

"Lest it should serve as evidence against myself."

This seemed to most present a very natural answer; yet it caused Lord Biron to start, and to fix a searching glance on Inglesant.

As a gentleman of high breeding and instinctive honour, it jarred upon his instinct, and conveyed a sudden suspicion that Inglesant was acting. That the latter might be so utterly perverted by his Jesuit teaching as to be lost to all sense of right and truth, he was prepared to believe; that he might have been led into treason knowingly or inadvertently, he was willing to think; but the low and pitiful motive that he gave was so opposed to his previous character, notorious for a fantastic elevation and refinement of sentiment, that it supposed him a monster, or that some miracle had been wrought upon him. A terrible doubt—a doubt which Biron had once or twice already seen faintly in the distance—approached nearer and looked him in the face.

The Committee had examined the commission one by one, comparing it with some of the King's writing which they had before them; finally it passed into the hands of a Mr. Greenway, a lawyer skilled in questions of evidence and of writing, who examined it attentively.

It was curious to see the behaviour of the two men under examination while this was going on; Lord Biron, as a noble gentleman, from whose mind the doubt of a few minutes ago had passed, standing erect and confident, looking haughtily and freely at the expert, secure in his own honour and in that of his King: Inglesant, cowed and anxious, leaning forward over the bar, his eyes fixed also on the lawyer—pale, his lips twitching,—the very picture of the guilty prisoner in the dock.

The expert looked at both the men curiously, then threw down the paper contemptuously.

"It is a palpable forgery," he said; "and not even a clever imitation of the King's hand."

And indeed, from some accident or other, the letters were, some of them, formed in a manner unusual to the King.

Inglesant, weakened with illness and anxiety, could not restrain a movement of intense relief. He drew a long breath and stood erect, as if relieved from an oppressive weight. He raised his eyes, and they caught those of Lord Biron, which had been attracted towards him, and were fixed full on his face.

Biron started again; there was not the least doubt that Inglesant rejoiced in the proof of the forgery of the warrant. That terrible doubt stood close now before his lordship, and grasped him by the throat.

Suppose, after all, this man whom he had imprisoned and despised, whose mission he had thwarted—this man whom all the royal party were calling by every contemptuous name, who stood there pale, cowed, beaten down;—suppose, after all, that this man, alone against these terrible odds, was all the time fighting a desperate battle for the King's honour, forsaken by God and men! But the consequences which would follow, if this view of the matter were the true one, were, in Lord Biron's estimation, too terrible to be thought of.

"I wish to say," said Inglesant, looking straight before him, "that the Lord Biron obtained possession of that paper when he was in possession of information of which I was ignorant. His lordship would probably have behaved differently, but he thought he was speaking to a thief."

There was something in this covert reproach, so worded, which so exactly accorded with what was passing in Lord Biron's mind that it cut him to the quick.

"I assure you, Mr. Inglesant," he said eagerly, "you are mistaken. Whatever I may think of the cause in which you are engaged, I have always wished to behave to you as to a gentleman. If you consider that you have cause of complaint against me, I shall be ready, when these unhappy complications are well over, as I trust they may be, to give you satisfaction and to beg your pardon afterwards."

He said these last words so pointedly that Inglesant started, and saw at once that his fear had been well founded, and that, thrown off his guard by the success of the examination of the warrant, he had made a mistake. He looked up quickly at Biron—a strange terror in his face—and their eyes met.

That they understood each other is probable; at any rate Inglesant's look was so full of warning that Biron understood *that* if nothing more, and restrained himself at once. All this had passed almost unnoticed by the Committee, who were consulting together.

Lord Biron left the room, and Inglesant was taken back to the Tower as he had come. Mr. Secretary Milton, who had been present as a spectator, left the Parliament House and proceeded at once to Clerkenwell Green to the house of General Cromwell, and related to him and to General Ireton, who was with him, what had occurred.

"They have gained nothing by getting this warrant," he said; "nay, you have lost, rather. You have brought up Lord Biron, who comes forward in the light of day and with the utmost confidence, and challenges this paper to be a forgery, and your own lawyers bear him out in it. I have not the least doubt it is the King's; but some of the letters, either purposely or more probably by accident, are not in his usual hand, and the best judges cannot agree on these matters. Out of Inglesant you will get nothing. He is a consummate actor, as I have known of old. He is prepared at every point, and carefully trained by his masters the Jesuits. I know these men, and have seen them both here and abroad. Acting on select natures the training is perfect. They will go to death more indifferently than to a Court ball. You may rack them to the extremity of anguish, and in the delirium of pain they will say what they have been trained to say, and not the truth. You may wear him out with fasting and anxiety until he makes some mistake; he made two to-day, besides one which was a necessity of the case,—for I do not see what else he could have said,—that was so slight that no one saw it but Biron. Weakened by anxiety, doubtless, he could not restrain a movement of relief when the expert declared the warrant a forgery; Biron saw that too, for I watched him. Last, which was the greatest mistake of all, and would show that his training is not entirely perfect, were we not to make allowance for his broken health, he forgot his part, and suffered his passion to get the better of him, and to taunt Lord Biron in such a way that Biron, who I think till then honestly believed the King's word, very nearly let out the truth in his astonishment. But what do you gain by all this? It rather adds to the apparent truth of the man's story, and gives life to his evidence. Nothing but his written testimony will be of any use, and this you will never get."

"He shall be tried for his life at any rate," said Cromwell.

"You have threatened him with that already."

"Threatening is one thing," replied the General, "to stand beneath the gallows condemned to death another."

* * * * *

News of the taking of Chester and of the arrest of John Inglesant on such a terrible charge—a charge at once of treason against the King, his country, and his religion—as it travelled at once over England, reached Gidding in due course. It caused the greatest dismay and distress in that quiet household. About the middle of April a gentleman of Huntingdon, a Parliament man, who had lately come from London, dined with the family. He told them during dinner that he had been present in the Committee Room when Mr. Inglesant had been examined. When dinner was over Mr. John Ferrar, who was now at the head of the family, remained at table with this gentleman, being anxious to hear more, and Mary Collet also stayed to hear what she could of her friend, watching every word with eager eyes. In that family, where there was nothing but love and kindliness and entire sympathy, it was thought only natural that she should do so, and no ill-natured thought occurred to any member of it. The Parliament man described more at full the examination before the Committee, and Inglesant's worn and guilty appearance,—sad news, indeed, to both his hearers. He described Lord Biron's examination, and the production of the forged warrant.

"And did John Inglesant admit that it was forged?" said Mr. Ferrar.

"Yes, he said from his own knowledge that it was prepared by Father St. Clare the Jesuit."

"It is a strange world," said Mr. Ferrar dreamily, "and the Divine call seems to lead some of us into slippery places—scarcely the heavenly places in Christ of which the Apostle dreamt."

The gentleman did not understand him, nor did Mary Collet altogether until afterwards.

Presently Mr. Ferrar said,—

"And what do you think of it all? Was the warrant forged or not?"

"I am somewhat at a loss what to think," said the other, "I am not, as you know, Mr. Ferrar, and without wishing to offend you, an admirer of the King, but I do not believe him to be a fool and mad. There is no doubt that he has tampered with the Papists throughout, yet I cannot think, unless he is in greater extremities than we suppose, that he would have practised so wild and mad a scheme as this one of the Irish rebels and murderers. On the other hand, I can conceive nothing too bad for the Jesuits to attempt; and it seems to me that I can discern something of their hand in this—an introduction of an armed Papist force into the country, to be joined, doubtless, by all the English Papists; only I should have thought they could have procured this without bringing in the King's name, but doubtless they had some reason for this also. The general opinion among the Parliament men is that the warrant is the King's, and that he has planned the whole thing. On the other hand, it is plain the Cavaliers do not believe it, or Lord Biron would never have come boldly up of his own accord, and brought up the warrant so confidently."

"But does not the warrant itself prove something one way or the other?" said Mr. Ferrar.

"These things are very difficult to judge upon," said the gentleman. "The expert to whom the Committee gave it pronounced it a forgery upon the spot, but he has been greatly blamed for precipitancy; and others to whom it has been shown pronounce it genuine. Some of the letters certainly are not like the King's, but the style of the hand is the King's they say, even in these unusual letters. By the way, if you had seen Inglesant's guilty look when the expert took the paper in his hand, you would say with me it was a forgery. You could not, to my mind, have a stronger proof."

"But if the King had ordered this, would not he help Mr. Inglesant?" Mary Collet ventured to say.

"Help? madam," said the gentleman warmly; "when did the King help any of his friends?"

"Whichever way it is," said Mr. Ferrar mildly, "he cannot help. To help would be to condemn himself in public opinion, which in these unhappy distractions he dare not do. Did Lord Biron speak to Mr. Inglesant, sir?"

"Very little. They taunted each other once, and seemed about to come to blows. All the evidence went to show that Lord Biron suspected him from the first."

The gentleman soon after left. Mr. Ferrar returned to the dining-room after seeing him to his horse, and found Mary Collet sitting where they had left her, lost in sad and humiliating thought.

He sat down near her and said kindly,—

"My dear Mrs. Mary, I hardly know which of the two alternatives is the best for your friend—for my friend; but it is better at least for you to know the truth, and I think I can now pretty much tell which is the true one. If this plot were altogether the Jesuits', John Inglesant would not say it. If the King had no hand in it, proof would be given a thousand ways without having recourse to this. There are other facts which to my mind are conclusive that this way of thinking is the right one, but I need not tell them all to you. What I have said I should say to none but you. You will see that it is of the utmost importance that you say nothing of it to any. I believe you may comfort yourself in thinking that, according to the light which is given him, John Inglesant is following what he believes to be his duty, and none can say at any rate that it is a smooth and easy path he has chosen to walk in."

Mary Collet thanked him, her beautiful eyes full of tears, and left the room.

A few days afterwards the news ran like wildfire over England that the King had left Oxford secretly, and that no one knew where he was; and a night or two afterwards Mr. John Ferrar was called up by a gentleman who said he was Dr. Hudson, the King's Chaplain, and that the King was alone, a few paces from the door, and that he would immediately fetch him in.

Mr. Ferrar received His Majesty with all possible respect. But fearing that Gidding, from the known loyalty of the family, might be a suspected place, for better concealment he conducted the King to a private house at Coppingford, an obscure village at a small distance from Gidding, and not far from Stilton. It was a very dark night, and but for the lantern Mr. Ferrar carried, they could not have known the way. As it was, they lost their way once, and wandered for some time in a ploughed field. Mr. Ferrar always spoke with the utmost passionate distress of this night, as of a night the incidents of which must have awakened the compassion of every feeling heart, however biassed against the King. As a proof of the most affecting distress, the King, he said, was serene and even cheerful, and said he was protected by the King of kings. His Majesty slept at Coppingford, but early in the May morning he was up, and parted from Mr. Ferrar, going towards Stamford. Mr. Ferrar returned to his house, and two days after it was known that the King had given himself up to the Scottish army.

CHAPTER XIV.

INGLESANT remained in prison, and would have thought that he had been forgotten, but that every few weeks he was sent for by the Committee and examined. The Committee got no new facts from him, and indeed probably did not expect to get any; but it was very useful to the Parliament party to keep him before the public gaze as a Royalist and a Jesuit. It was a common imputation upon the Cavaliers that they were Papists, and anything that strengthened this belief made the King's party odious to the nation. Here was a servant of the King's, an avowed Jesuit, and one self-condemned in the most terrible crimes. It is true he was disowned by the royal party, apparently sincerely; but the general impression conveyed by his case was favourable to the Parliament, and they therefore took care to keep it before the world. These examinations were looked forward to by Inglesant with great pleasure, the row up the river and the sight of fresh faces being such a delight to him. He was not confined to his room, being allowed to walk at certain hours in the court of the Tower, and he found a box containing a few books, a Lucretius and a few other Latin books, probably left by some former occupant of the cell. These were not taken from him, and he read and re-read them, especially the Lucretius, many times. They saved him from utter prostration and despair,—they and a secret help which he acknowledged afterwards,—a help, which to men of his nature certainly does come upon prayer to God, to whatever source it may be ascribed; a help which in terrible sleepless hours, in hours of dread weariness of life, in hours of nervous pain more terrible than all, calms the heart and soothes the brain, and leaves peace and cheerfulness and content in the place of restlessness and despair. Inglesant said that repeating the name of Jesus simply in the lonely nights kept his brain quiet when it was on the point of distraction, being of the same mind as Sir Charles Lucas, when, "many times calling upon the sacred name of Jesus," he was shot dead at Colchester.

More than a year passed over him. From the scraps of news he could gather from his jailer, and from the soldiers in the court during his walks, he learnt that the King had been given up by the Scots, had escaped from Hampton Court, had been retaken and sent to Carisbrook, and was soon to come to London, the man said, for his trial.

It was soon after he had learnt this last news that his jailer suddenly informed him that he was to be tried for his life.

Accordingly, soon after, a warrant arrived from Bradshaw, the President of the Council of State, to bring him before that body.

The Council sat in Essex House, and some gentlemen, who had surrendered Pembroke upon terms that they should depart the country in three days, but—accounting it base to desert their prince, and hoping that there might be farther occasion of service to His Majesty,—had remained in London, were upon their trial. When Inglesant arrived with his guard these gentlemen were under examination, and one of them, who had a wife and children, was fighting hard for his life, arguing the case step by step with the lawyers and the Council. Inglesant was left waiting in the anteroom several hours; from the conversation he overheard, the room being constantly full of all sorts of men coming and going—soldiers, lawyers, divines—he learnt that the King's trial was coming on very soon, and he fancied that his name was mentioned, as though the nearness of the King's trial had something to do with his own being hurried on. It was a cold day, and there was a large fire in the anteroom. Inglesant had had nothing to eat since morning, and felt weak and faint. He wished the other examinations over that his own might come on; his, he thought, would not take long. At last the gentlemen were referred to the Council of War, to be dealt with as spies, and came out of the Council chamber with their guards. The one was a plain country gentleman, and neither of them knew Inglesant, but, stopping a moment in the anteroom, while the guard prepared themselves, one of them asked his name, saying he was afraid they had kept him waiting a long time. This was Colonel Eustace Powell, and Inglesant met him again when he thought he had only a few minutes to live.

The Council debated whether they should hear Inglesant that day, as it was now late in the afternoon, and the candles were lighted, but finally he was sent for into the Council.

As soon as he came to the bar, Bradshaw asked him suddenly when he saw the King last, to which he replied that he had not seen the King since Naseby field.

"You were at Naseby, then?" said Bradshaw

"Yes," said Inglesant.

"And you ran away, I suppose?"

"Yes," said Johnny, "I ran away."

"Then you are a coward as well as a traitor," said Bradshaw.

"I am not braver than other men," said Inglesant.

Inglesant was then examined more in form, but very shortly; everything he said having been said so often before.

The President then told him that, by his own confession, he was guilty of death, and should be hanged at once if he persisted in it, but that the Council did not believe his confession—indeed, had evidence and confessions from others to prove the reverse; and therefore, if he persisted in his course, he was his own murderer, and could hope for no mercy from God. That if he would sign the declaration which they offered him, which they knew to be true, and which stated that he had only acted under the King's orders, he should not only have his life spared, but should very shortly be set at liberty.

To this he replied that if they had evidence to prove what they said, they did not want his; that he could not put his name to evidence so contrary to what he had always confessed, and was prepared to stand by to death; that, as to his fate before God, he left his soul in His hands, who was more merciful than man.

To this Bradshaw replied that they were most merciful to him, and desired to save him from himself; that, if he died, he died with a lie upon his lips, from his own obstinacy and suicide.

Making no answer to this, he was ordered back to the

Tower, and warned to prepare himself for death. He saw clearly that their object was to bring out evidence signed by him on the eve of the King's trial, which no doubt would have been a great help to their cause. As he went back in his barge to the Tower, he wondered why they did not publish something with his name attached, without troubling themselves about his consent. As they went down the river, the darkness became denser, and the boat passed close to many other wherries, nearly running them down; the lights on the boats and the barges glimmered indistinctly, and made the course more difficult and uncertain. They shot the bridge under the mass of dark houses and irregular lights, and proceeded across the pool towards the Tower stairs. The pool was somewhat clear of ships, and the lanterns upon the wharves and such vessels as were at anchor made a clearer light than that above the bridge. As they crossed the pool, a wherry, rowed by a single man, came towards them obliquely from the Surrey side, so as to approach near enough to discern their persons, and then, crossing their bows, suffered itself to be run down before the barge could be stopped. The waterman climbed in at the bows, as his own wherry filled and went down. He seemed a stupid, surly man, and might be supposed to be either deaf or drunk. To the abuse of the soldiers and watermen he made no answer but that he was an up-river waterman, and was confused by the lights and the current of the bridge. The officer called him forward into the stern, and as he came towards them Inglesant knew him in spite of his perfect disguise. It was the Jesuit. He answered as many of the officer's questions as he appeared to understand, and took no manner of notice of Inglesant, who of course appeared entirely indifferent and uninterested. When they landed at the stairs, the waterman, with a perfectly professional manner, swung himself over the side into the water, and steadied the boat for the gentlemen to land, which act the officer took as an awkward expression of respect and gratitude. As Inglesant passed him he put his hand up for his to rest on, and Johnny felt a folded note passed into it. Without the least pause, he followed the officer across the Tower wharf, and was conducted to his room. As soon as he was alone he examined the paper, which contained these words only:—

"You are not forgotten. Keep on a little longer. The end is very near."

It made little impression upon him, nor did it influence his after conduct, which had already been sufficiently determined upon. He expected very little help from any one, though he believed that Father St. Clare would do what he could. The Jesuit would have died himself at any moment had his purpose required it, and he could not think that he would regard as of much importance the fall of another soldier in the same rank. He was mistaken, but he did not know it; the Jesuit, beneath his placid exterior, retained for his favourite and cleverest pupil an almost passionate regard, and would have done for him far more than he would have thought worth the doing for himself. Meanwhile, Inglesant translated his words into a different language, and thought more than once that doubtless they were very true, and that, though in a sense not intended, the end was very near.

This took place at the beginning of December, and about a week afterwards the jailer advised Inglesant to prepare for death, for the warrant to behead him was signed, and would be put into execution that day week at Charing Cross. He immediately sent a petition to the Council of State, that a Priest, either of the Roman Catholic or the English Church, he was indifferent which, might be sent him. To this an answer was sent immediately that he was dying with a lie upon his lips, and that the presence of no priest or minister could be of any use to him, and would not be granted. The same day a Presbyterian minister was admitted to him, who used the same arguments for some time without effect, representing the fearful condition that Inglesant was in as an unrepentant sinner. Inglesant began to regret that he had made any application, and this regret was increased two days afterwards when a man, who offered him certain proofs that he was a Roman Catholic Priest, was admitted, and gave him the same advice, refusing him Absolution and the Sacrament unless he complied. Upon this Inglesant became desperate, and refused to speak again. The Priest waited some time and then left, telling him he was eternally lost.

This was the severest trial he had yet met with; but his knowledge of the different parties in the Romish Church, and the extent to which they subordinated their religion to their political intrigues, was too great to allow him to feel it so much as he otherwise would. He resigned himself to die unassisted.

He applied for an English Prayer Book, but this also was refused. He remembered the old monastic missals he had possessed at Westacre, and thought over all those days with the tenderest regret.

The fatal morning arrived at last. Inglesant had passed a sleepless night; he had not the slightest fear of death, but excitement made sleep impossible. He thought often of his brother, but he had learned that he was in Paris alone; and even had he been in England, he felt no especial desire to see him under circumstances which could only have been intensely painful. Mary Collet he thought of night and day, but he knew it was impossible to obtain permission to see her, and he was tired of fruitless requests. He was tired and wearied of life, and only wished the excitement and strain over, that he might be at rest. It struck him that the greatest harshness was used towards him; his food was very poor and of the smallest quantity, and no one was admitted to him; but he did not wonder at this, knowing that his case differed from any other Loyalist prisoner.

At about eight o'clock on the appointed morning, the same officer who had conducted him before entered his room with the lieutenant of the Tower, bringing the warrant for his death. The lieutenant parted from him in a careless and indifferent way. They went by water and landed by York Stairs, and proceeded by back ways to a house nearly adjoining Northumberland House, facing the wide street about Charing Cross. From one of the first floor windows a staircase had been contrived, leading up to a high scaffold or platform on which the block was fixed. Inglesant had not known till that morning whether he was to be hanged or beheaded; like every other thought, save one, it was indifferent to him—that one, how he should keep his secret to the last. In the room of this house opening on the scaffold, he found Colonel Eustace Powell, whom he had met at Essex House, who was to precede him to death. He greeted Inglesant with great kindness, but, as Johnny thought, with some reserve. He was a very pious man, strongly attached to the Protestant party in the Church of England, and he had passed the last three days entirely in the company of Dr. S——, who was then in the room with him, engaged in religious exercises, and his piety and resignation had attached the Doctor to him very much. The Doctor now proceeded to ask the Colonel, before Inglesant and the others, a series of questions, in order that he should give some account of his religion, and of his faith, charity, and repentance, to all of which he answered fully; that he acknowledged his death to be a just punishment of God for his former sins; that he acknowledged that his just due was eternal punishment, from which he only expected to escape through the satisfaction made by Christ, by which Mediator, and none other, he hoped to be saved. The Doctor then asking him if, by a miracle (not to put him in vain hope), God should save him that day, what life he would resolve to lead hereafter? he replied, "It is a question of great length, and requires a great time to answer. Men in such straits would promise great things, but a vow I would make, and by God's help endeavour to keep it, though I would first call some friend to limit how far I should make a vow, that I might not make a rash one, and offer the sacrifice of fools."

In answer to other questions he said,—" He wished well to all lawful governments; that he did not justify himself in having ventured against the existing one; he left God to judge it whether it be righteous, and if it be, it must stand. He desired to make reparation to any he had injured, and he forgave his enemies."

The Doctor then addressed him at length, saying,—

"Sir, I shall trouble you very little farther. I thank you for all those heavenly colloquies I have enjoyed by being in your company these three days, and truly I am sorry I must part with so heavenly an associate. We have known one another heretofore, but never so Christianlike before. I have rather been a scholar to learn from you than an instructor. I wish this stage, wherein you are made a spectacle to God, angels, and the world, may be a school to all about you; for though I will not diminish your sins, yet I think there are few here have a lighter load upon them than you have, and I only wish them your repentance, and that measure of faith that God hath given you, and that measure of courage you have attained from God."

The Colonel, having wished all who were present in the room farewell, went up on the scaffold accompanied by the Divine. The scaffold was so near that Inglesant and the officers and the guards, who stood at the window screened from the sight of the people, could hear every word that passed. They understood that the whole open place was densely crowded, but they could scarcely believe it, the silence was so profound.

Colonel Powell made a speech of some length, clearing himself of Popery in earnest language, not blaming his judges, but throwing the guilt on false witnesses, whom, however, he forgave. He bore no malice to the present Government, nor pretended to decide controversies, and spoke touchingly of the sadness and gloom of violent death, and how mercifully he was dealt with in being able to face it with a quiet mind. He finally thanked the authorities for their courtesy in granting him the death of the axe—a death somewhat worthy of his blood, answerable to his birth and qualification—which courtesy had much helped towards the pacification of his mind.

Inglesant supposed the end was now come, but to his surprise the Doctor again stepped forward, and before all the people repeated the whole former questions, to each of which the Colonel replied in nearly the same words.

Then stepping forward again to the front of the scaffold, the Colonel said, speaking to the people in a calm and tender voice,—

"There is not one face that looks upon me, though many faces, and perhaps different from me in opinion and practice, but methinks hath something of pity in it; and may that mercy which is in your hearts now be meted to you when you have need of it! I beseech you join with me in prayer."

The completest silence prevailed, broken only by a faint sobbing and whispering sound from the excited and pitying crowd. Colonel Powell prayed for a quarter of an hour with an audible voice; then taking leave again of his friends and directing the executioner when to strike, he knelt down to the block, and repeating the words, "Lord Jesus, receive me," his head was smitten off with a blow.

A long deep groan, followed by an intense silence, ran through the crowd. The officer who accompanied Inglesant looked at him with a peculiar expression; and, bowing in return, Inglesant passed through the window, and as he mounted the steps and his eyes came to the level of, and then rose higher than the interposing scaffold, he saw the dense crowd of heads stretching far away on every hand, the house windows and roofs crowded on every side. He scarcely saw it before he almost lost the sight again. A wild motion that shook the crowd, a roar that filled the air and stunned the sense, a yell of indignation, contempt, hatred, hands shook and clutched at him, wild faces leaping up and staring at him, cries of " Throw him over !" "Give over the Jesuit to us!" "Throw over the Irish murderer!" made his senses reel for a moment, and his heart stop. It was inconceivable that a crowd, the instant before placid, pitiful, silent, should in a moment become like that, deafening, mad, thirsting for blood. The amazing surprise and reaction produced the greatest shock. Hardening himself in a moment, he faced the people, his hat in his hand, his pale face hard set, his teeth closed. Once or twice he tried to speak; it would have been as easy to drown the Atlantic's roar. As he stood, apparently calm, this terrible ordeal had the worst possible effect upon his mind. Other men came to the scaffold calm in mind, prepared by holy thoughts, and the sacred, tender services of the Church of their Lord, feeling His hand indeed in theirs. They spoke, amid silence and solemn prayers, to a pitying people, the name of Jesus on their lips, the old familiar words whispered in their ears, good wishes, deference, respect all around, their path seemed smooth and upward to the heavenly gates. But with him—how different! Denied the aid of prayer and sacrament, alone, overwhelmed with contempt and hatred, deafened with the fiendish noise which racked his excited and overwrought brain. He was indifferent before; he became hardened, fierce, contemptuous now. Hated, he hated again. All the worst spirit of his party and of his age became uppermost. He felt as though engaged in a mad duel with a despised yet too powerful foe. He turned at last to the officer, and said, his voice scarcely heard amid the unceasing roar,—

"You see, sir, I cannot speak; do not let us delay any longer."

The officer hesitated, and glanced at another gentleman, evidently a Parliament man, who advanced to Inglesant, and offered him a paper, the purport of which he knew by this time too well.

He told him in his ear that even now he should be set at liberty if he would sign the true evidence, and not rush upon his fate and lose his soul. He repeated that the Parliament knew he was not guilty, and had no wish to put him to death.

Inglesant saw the natural rejoinder, but did not think it worth his while to make it. Only get this thing over, and escape from this maddening cry, tearing his brain with its terrible roar, to something quieter at any rate.

He rejected the paper, and turning to the officer he said, with a motion towards the people of inexpressible disdain,—

"These good people are impatient for the final act, sir; do not let us keep them any longer."

The officer still hesitated, and looked at the Parliament man, who shook his head, and immediately left the scaffold. The officer then leaned on the rail, and spoke to his lieutenant in the open space round the scaffold within the barriers. The latter gave a word of command, and the soldiers fell out of their rank so as to mingle with the crowd. As soon as the officer saw this manœuvre completed, he took Inglesant's arm, and said hurriedly,—"Come with me to the house, and be quick." Not knowing what he did, Inglesant followed him hastily into the room. They had need to be quick. A yell, to which the noise preceding it was as nothing—terrible as it had been, a shower of stones, smashing every pane of glass, and falling in heaps at their feet,—showed the fury of a maddened, injured people, robbed of their expected prey.

The officer looked at Inglesant, and laughed.

"I thought there would be a tumult," he said; "we are not safe here; the troops will not oppose them, and they will break down the doors. Come with me."

He led Inglesant, still almost unconscious, through the back entries and yards, the roar of the people still in their ears, till they reached a stair leading to the river, where was a wherry and two or three guards. The officer stepped in after Inglesant, crying, "Pull away! The Tower!" then, leaning back, and looking at Inglesant, he said,—

"You stood that very well. I would rather mount the deadliest breach than face such a sight as that."

Inglesant asked him if he knew what this extraordinary change of intention meant.

To which he replied,—

"No; I acted to orders. Probably you are of more use to the Parliament alive than dead; besides, I fancy you have friends. I should think you are safe now."

That afternoon, a report spread through London that Inglesant, the King's servant, had confessed all that was required of him upon the scaffold, and had his life given him in return.

This report was believed mostly by the lower orders, especially those who had been before the scaffold; but few of the upper classes credited it, and even these only did so for a day or two. The Parliament made no further effort; and Inglesant was left quietly in prison.

This happened on the 19th of December, and on the 20th of January the King's trial began. That could scarcely be called a trial which consisted entirely in a struggle between the King and the Court on a point of law. In the charge of high treason, read in Westminster Hall against the King, special mention was made of the commission which he "doth still continue to the Earl of Ormond, and to the Irish rebels and revolters associated with him, from whom further invasions upon the land are threatened." There appear to have been no witnesses examined on this point, all that were examined during three days, in the painted chamber, simply witnessing to having seen the King in arms. Indeed, all witnesses were unnecessary, the sentence having been already determined upon, and the King utterly refusing to plead or to acknowledge the Court. The King, indeed, never appeared to such advantage as on his trial; he was perfectly unmoved by any personal thought; no fear, hesitation, or wavering appeared in his behaviour. He took his stand simply on the indisputable point of law that neither that Court, nor indeed any Court had any authority to try him. To Bradshaw's assertion that he derived his authority from the people, he in vain requested a single precedent that the Monarchy of England was elective, or had been elective, for a thousand years. In his abandonment of self, and his unshaken constancy to a point of principle, he contrasted most favourably with his judges, whose sole motive was self. That none of the Parliamentary leaders were safe while the King lived is probable; but sound statesmanship does not acknowledge self-preservation as an excuse for mistaken policy, and the murder of the King was not more a crime than it was a blunder. Having been condemned by this unique Court, he was, with the most indecent haste, hurried to his end. A revolting coarseness marks every detail of the tragic story; the flower of England on either side was beneath the turf or beyond the sea, and the management of affairs was left in the hands of butchers and brewers. Ranting sermons, three in succession, before a brewer in Whitehall, are the medium to which the religious utterance of England is reduced, and Ireton and Harrison in bed together, with Cromwell and others in the room, signed the warrant for the fatal act. The horror and indignation which it impressed on the heart of the people may be understood a little by the fact, that in no country so much as in England the peculiar sacredness of Monarchy has since been carried so far. The impression caused by his death was so profound, that, forty years afterwards, when his son was arrested in his flight, the only thing that during the whole course of that revolution caused the least reaction in his favour was (according to the Whig Burnet) the fear that the people conceived that the same thing was going to be acted over again, and men remembered that saying of King Charles—"The prisons of princes are not far from their graves." He walked across the Park from the garden at St. James's that January morning with so firm and quick a pace that the guards could scarcely keep the step, and stepping from his own banqueting-house upon the scaffold, where the men who ruled England so little understood him as to provide ropes and pulleys to drag him down in case of need, he died with that calm and kingly bearing which none could assume so well as he, and by his death he cast a halo of religious sentiment round a cause which, without the final act, would have wanted much of its pathetic charm, and struck that key-note of religious devotion to his person and the Monarchy which has not yet ceased to reverberate in the hearts of men.

> " That thence the royal actor borne
> The tragic scaffold might adorn,
>   While round the armed bands
>   Did clap their bloody hands :
> He nothing common did, nor mean,
> Upon that memorable scene ;
>   But with his keener eye
>   The axe's edge did try ;
> Nor called the gods with vulgar spite
> To vindicate his helpless right,
>   But bowed his comely head
>   Down, as upon a bed."
>   *The Republican, Andrew Marvell.*

CHAPTER XV.

INGLESANT remained in the Tower for several months after the King's death. The Lords Hamilton, Holland, and Capel were the first who followed their royal master to the block, and many other names of equal honour and little inferior rank followed in the same list. In excuse for the murders of these men there is no other plea than, as in the case of their master—self-preservation. But the purpose was not less abortive than the means were criminal. The effect produced on the country was one of awe and hatred to the ruling powers. Thousands of copies of the King's Book, edged with black, were sold in London within the few days following his death, and Milton was obliged to remonstrate pitifully with the people for their unaccountable attachment to their King. The country, it is true, was for the moment cowed, and, although individual gentlemen took every opportunity to rise against the usurpers, and suffered death willingly in such a cause, the mass of the people remained quiet. The country gentlemen indeed were, as a body, ruined; the head of nearly every family was slain, and the widows and minors had enough to do to arrange, as best they might, with the Government agents who assessed the fines and compositions upon malignants' estates. It required a few years to elapse before England would recover itself, and declare its real mind unmistakably, which it very soon did; but during those years it never sank into silent acquiescence to the great wrong that had been perpetrated. It is the custom to regard the Commonwealth as a period of great national prosperity and peace. Nothing can be a greater mistake. There never was a moment's peace during the whole of Cromwell's reign of power. He began by destroying that Parliament utterly, for seeking the arrest of five members of which the King lost his crown and was put to death. The best of the Republican party were kept in prison or exiled, just as the King had been seized and executed by Cromwell, independently of the Parliament. But the oppressed sections of the Puritan party never ceased to hate the usurper as much as the Royalists did, and the want of their support insured the fall of the Republic the moment the master hand was withdrawn.

After a few months Inglesant's imprisonment was much lighter; he was allowed abundance of food, and liberty to walk in the courtyards of the Tower, and was allowed to purchase any books he chose. He had received a sum of money from an unknown hand, which he afterwards found to have been that of Lady Cardiff, his brother's wife, and this enabled him to purchase several books and other conveniences. He remained in prison under these altered circumstances until the end of January 1650, when, one morning, his door opened, and without any announcement his brother was admitted to see him. Eustace was much altered: he was richly dressed, entirely in the French mode, his manner and appearance were altogether those of a favourite of the French Court, and he spoke English with a foreign accent. He greeted his brother with great warmth, and it need not be said that Johnny was delighted to see him.

Eustace told his brother at once that he was free, and showed him the warrant for his liberation.

"I was in Paris," he said, "on the eve of starting for England on affairs which I will explain to you in a moment, when 'votre ami' the Jesuit came to see me. He told me he understood I was going to England on my private affairs, but he thought possible I might not object to do a little service for my brother;—you know his manner. He said if I would apply in certain quarters, which he named to me, I should find the way prepared, and no difficulties in obtaining your release. The words were true, and yesterday I received this warrant. As soon as it is convenient to you I shall be glad for you to leave this sombre place, as I want you to come with me to Oulton, to my wife,—my wife, who is indeed so perfectly English in all her manners, as I shall proceed to explain to you. Since you were at Oulton my wife has been growing worse and worse in health, and more and more eccentric and crotchety; every new remedy and every fresh religious notion she adopts at once. She has filled the house with quacks, of whom Van Helmont is chief, mountebanks, astrologers, and physicians,—a fine collection of beaux-esprits. The last time I was there I could not see her once, though I stayed a fortnight; she was in great misery, extremely ill, and said she was near her last. Since I have been in Paris I have been obliged to give up many of my suppers with the French King and Lords, from her letters saying she was at the point of death. She is ill at present, and no one has seen her these ten days; but I suppose it is much after the same sort; and she sends me word that Van Helmont has promised that she shall not be buried, but preserved by his art till I can come and see her. To crown all, she has lately become a Quaker, and in my family all the women about my wife, and most of the rest, are Quakers, and Mons. Van Helmont is governor of that flock,—an unpleasing sort of people, silent, sullen, and of reserved conversation, though I hear one of the maids is the prettiest girl in all the county. These and all that society have free access to my wife, but I believe Dr. More, the Platonist, who is a scholar and gentleman, if an enthusiast, though he was in the house all last summer, did not see her above once or twice. She has been urging me for months to search all over Europe for an eagle's stone, which she says is of great use in such diseases as hers; and when I, at great labour and expense, found her one, she sends back word that it is not one, but that some of her quacks were able to decipher it at once, and that it is a German stone, such as are commonly sold in London at five shillings apiece. I have grown learned in these stones, by which the fairies in our grandfather's time used to preserve the fruits from hail and storms. There is a salamander stone. This eagle stone is one made after a cabalistic art and under certain stars, and engraved with the sign of an eagle. I could prove their virtue to you," he continued, laughing, "throughout all arts and sciences, as Divinity, Philosophy, Physic, Astrology, Physiognomy, Divination of Dreams, Painting, Sculpture, Music, and what not. This affair of the stone, and these reports of sickness and death, however, and doleful stories of coffins prepared by art, and of open graves, would not have brought me over, but for another circumstance of much greater moment. When I was in Italy and staying some time at Venice, and was desirous of engaging in some of the intrigues and amusements of the city, I was recommended to an Italian, a young man, who made himself useful to several of the nobility, as a man who could introduce me to, and show me more of that kind of pleasure, than any one else. I found him all that had been represented to me, and a great deal more, for, not to tell you too long a story, he was an adept at every sort of intrigue, and was acquainted at any rate with every species of villany and vice that the Italians have conceived. The extent to which they carry these tastes of theirs cannot be described, and from them the wildest of the gallants of the rest of Europe start back amazed. To cut this short, I was very deeply engaged to him, and in return I held some secrets of his, which he would not even now have known. At last, upon some villainous proposal made by him, I drew upon him. We had been dining at one of the Casinos in St. Mark's Place, and I would have run him through the body, but the crowd of mountebanks, charlatans, and such stuff, interposed and saved him. I have often wished since I had. He threatened me highly, but as I was a foreigner and acquainted with most of the principal nobles, he could do me no harm. He endeavoured to have me assassinated more than once, and one Englishman was set upon and desperately wounded in mistake for me; but by advice I hired bravoes myself who baffled his plots, for I had the longest purse. I knew nothing of him afterwards until I heard that he had left Italy, a ruined and desperate man, whose life was sought by many; and the next thing I heard, not many weeks ago, was that he was at Oulton, having gained admission to my wife as a foreign physician who had some especial knowledge of her disease. She fancies herself much the better for his nostrums, and gives herself entirely to his directions, and I believe he professes Quakerism, or some sort of foreign mysticism allied to it, which has established him with the rest of her confidants. I no sooner heard this pleasing information than I resolved to come over to England at once, and at least drive away this villain from my family, even if I had no other way to do it than by running him through the body, as I might have done in Italy. I, however, sent a messenger to my wife to inform her that I was coming, and on my reaching London a few days ago, I found him waiting for me with a packet from Oulton. In a letter my wife desires me earnestly not to come to Oulton to see her, as she is assured by good hands that some imminent danger awaits me if I do, and she encloses this horoscope, which no doubt one of her astrologers has prepared for her. Now I have no doubt the Italian is at the bottom of all this, and that, at his instigation, the horoscope has been drawn out; yet I confess that it appears to me to have something about it that looks like the truth, something beyond what would be written at the instigation of an enemy. You can read it and judge for yourself. I have dabbled a little in astrology as in other arts."

John Inglesant took the paper from his brother and examined it carefully. At the top was an astrological scheme, or drawing of the heavens, taken at some moment when the intention of Eustace to come to Oulton had first become known to his wife. Beneath was the judgment of the adept, in the following words:—

"Saturn, the significator of the quesited, being in conjunction with Venus, I judge him to have gained by ladies to a considerable extent, to be much attached to them, greatly addicted to pleasure, and very fortunate where females are concerned, and to be a man of property. The significator being affected both by Mercury, lord of the eighth in the figure, and also by Mars, the lord of the quesited's eighth house, and the aspect of separation of the moon being bad,—namely, conjunction of Jupiter and square of Mercury, who is ill aspected to Jupiter, and is going to a square of the sun on the cusp of the mid-heaven,—I judge that the quesited is in imminent danger of death; and the lord of the third house being in the eighth, and the significator being combust, in conjunction with the lord of the eighth, and the hyleg afflicted by the evil planets, makes it more certain. His significator being in the eleventh house denotes that at the present time he is well situated and with some near friend (I should judge, as he is well aspected with the moon, the lady of the third house, a brother), and happy. Mars being in the ascendant, and the cusp of the first house wanting only three degrees of the place of the evil planet in a common sign, I judge the time of death to occur in three weeks' time, and that it will be caused by a sword or dagger wound, by which Mars kills. The danger lies to the south-west—south, because the quarter of the heaven where the lord of the ascendant is, is south—west, because the sign where he is, is west."

John Inglesant read this paper two or three times, and returned it to his brother with a smile. "I should not be greatly alarmed at it," said he: "that is not a true horoscope, or rather it is a true horoscope tampered with. The man who erected the scheme, I should say, was an honest man, though not a very clever astrologer. It has, however, as most schemes have, a glimmering of a truth not otherwise known (you and I being together, which no one at Oulton could have thought of, though you see he was wrong as to the time); but some other hand has been at work upon the judgment, and a very unskilful one. It contradicts itself. What is most important, however, is that the artist has no ground to take Saturn for your significator, which should be either the lord of the third house, the cusp of the third, or the planets therein, neither of which Saturn is. Besides, he takes the place of Fortune to be hyleg, for which he has no ground. He has taken Saturn as significator, as suiting what he knows of your character, and I think there is no doubt the Italian's hand is in this. Now I should rather say that Venus, the lady of the third, being significator, and applying to a friendly trine of Jupiter, lord of the ascendant, and Saturn being retrograde, and Venus also casting a sextile to the cusp of the ascendant is a very good argument that the querent should see the quesited speedily, and that in perfect health. I would have you think no more of this rubbish, with which a wicked man has tried to make the heavens themselves speak falsely."

"I did not know you were so good an astrologer, Johnny," said his brother.

"Father St. Clare taught it me among other things," said Inglesant; "and I have seen many strange answers that he has known himself; but it is shameful that the science should be made a tool of by designing men."

Eustace returned the papers to his pockets, and requested his brother again to prepare to leave the Tower at once. After taking leave of the Lieutenant, and feeing the warders, the two brothers departed in a coach in which Eustace had come to the Tower, and went to the lodgings of the latter in Holborn. Eustace furnished his brother with clothes until he could procure some for himself, and gave him money liberally, of which he seemed to have no stint. He wished his brother to come with him to all the places of resort in the city, but Johnny prudently declined. Indeed, the city was so quiet and dull, that few places of amusement remained. The theatres were entirely closed. Whitehall was sombre and nearly empty, and the public walks were filled only with the townspeople in staid and sober attire. The two brothers were therefore reduced to each other's society, and it seemed as though absence or a sense of danger united them with a warmth of affection which they had seldom before known.

To John Inglesant, who had always been devotedly attached to his brother, this display of affection was delightful, cut off as he had been so long from all sympathy and friendliness. Dressed in his brother's clothes, the likeness which had once been so striking returned again, and as they walked the streets people turned to look at them with surprise. The brothers felt in their hearts old feelings and thoughts returning, which had long been forgotten and had passed away; and to John Inglesant especially, always given to half melancholy musings and brooding over the past, all his happiest recollections seemed to concentrate themselves on his brother, the last human relation that seemed left to him, since he had, as he thought, lost the favour of all his friends, relations, and acquaintances in the world. Possibly a sense of a great misfortune made this sentiment more tender and acute, for, as we shall see, there were some things in his brother's position, and in the horoscope he had shown him, which Inglesant did not like. At present, however, his whole nature, so long crushed down and lacerated, seemed to expand and heal itself in the light of his brother's love and person, and to concentrate all its powers into one intense feeling, and to lose its own identity in this passion of brotherly regard.

This feeling might also be increased by his own state of health, which made him cling closer to any support. His long imprisonment, and the sudden change from his quiet cell to all the bustle of the city life, affected his mind and brain painfully. He was confused and excited among a crowd of persons and objects to which he had been so long unaccustomed; his brain and system had received a shock from which he never entirely recovered, and, for some time at any rate, he walked as one who is in a dream, rather than as a man engaged in the active pursuits of life.

After two or three days Eustace told his brother one morning that he was ready to go into the West, but before starting he said he wished Johnny to accompany him to a famous astrologer in Lambeth Marsh, to whom already he had shown the horoscope, and who had appointed a meeting that night to give his answer, and who had also promised to consult a crystal, as an additional means of obtaining information of the future.

Accordingly, late in the afternoon, they took a wherry at the Temple Stairs, and were ferried over to Lambeth Marsh, a wide extent of level ground between Southwark and the Bishop's Palace, on which only a few straggling houses had been built. The evening was dark and foggy, and a cold wind swept across the marsh, making them wrap their short cloaks closely about them. It was almost impossible to see more than a yard or two before them, and they would probably have found great difficulty in finding the wizard's house had not a boy with a lantern met them a few paces from the river, who inquired if they were seeking the astrologer. This was the wizard's own boy, whom, with considerable worldly prudence at any rate, he had despatched to find his clients and bring them to his house. The boy brought them into a long low room, with very little furniture in it, a small table at the upper end, with a large chair behind it, and three or four high-backed chairs placed along the wall. On the floor, in the middle of the room, was a large double circle, but there were no figures or signs of any kind about it. On the table was a long thin rod. A lamp which hung from the roof over the table cast a faint light about the room, and a brazier of lighted coals stood in the chimney.

The astrologer soon entered the room with the horoscope Eustace had left with him in his hand. He was a fine-looking man, with a serious and lofty expression of face, dressed in a black gown, with the square cap of a divine, and a fur hood or tippet. He bowed courteously to the gentlemen, who saluted him with great respect. His manner was coldest to John Inglesant, whom he probably regarded with suspicion as an amateur. He, however, acknowledged that Inglesant's criticisms on the horoscope were correct, but pointed out to him that in his own reading of it many of the aspects were very adverse. John Inglesant knew this, though he had chosen to conceal it from his brother. The astrologer then informed them that he had drawn out a scheme of the heavens himself at the moment when first consulted by Eustace, and that, in quite different ways, and by very different aspects, much the same result had been arrived at. "As, however," he went on to say, "the whole question is to some extent vitiated by the suspicion of foul play, and it will be impossible for any of us to free our minds entirely from these suspicions, I do not advise any farther inquiry; but I propose that you should consult a consecrated beryl or crystal—a mode of inquiry far more high and certain than astrology, so much so, indeed, that I will seriously confess to you that I use the latter but as the countenance and blind; but this search in the crystal is by the help of the blessed spirits, and is open only to the pure from sin, and to men of piety, humility, and charity."

As he said these words he produced from the folds of his gown a large crystal or polished stone, set in a circle of gold, supported by a silver stand. Round the circle were engraved the names of angels. He placed this upon the table, and continued,—

"We must pray to God that He will vouchsafe us some insight into this precious stone; for it is a solemn and serious matter upon which we are, second only to that of communication with the angelical creatures themselves, which, indeed, is vouchsafed to some, but only to those of the greatest piety, to which we may not aspire. Therefore let us kneel down and humbly pray to God."

They all knelt, and the adept, commencing with the Prayer-book collect for the festival of St. Michael, recited several other prayers, all for extreme and spotless purity of life.

He then rose, the two others continuing on their knees, and struck a small bell, upon which the boy whom they had before seen entered the room by a concealed door in the wainscot. He was a pretty boy, with a fair and clean skin, and was dressed in a surplice similar to those worn by choristers. He took up a position by the crystal, and waited his master's orders.

"I have said," continued the adept, "that these visions can be seen only by the pure, and by those who, by long and intense looking into the spiritual world, have at last penetrated somewhat into its gloom. I have found these mostly to be plain and simple people, of an earnest faith,—country people, grave-diggers, and those employed to shroud the dead, and who are accustomed to think much upon objects connected with death. This boy is the child of the sexton of Lambeth Church, who is himself a godly man. Let us pray to God."

Upon this he knelt down again and remained for some time engaged in silent prayer. He then rose and directed the boy to look into the crystal, saying, "One of these gentlemen desires news of his wife."

The boy looked intently into the crystal for some moments, and then said, speaking in a measured and low voice,—

"I see a great room, in which there is a bed with rich hangings; pendent from the ceiling is a silver lamp. A tall dark man, with long hair, and a dagger in his belt, is bending over the bed with a cup in his hand."

"It is my wife's room," said Eustace in a whisper, "and it is no doubt the Italian; he is tall and dark."

The boy continued to look for some time into the crystal,

but said nothing; then he turned to his master and said, "I can see nothing; some one more near to this gentleman must look; this other gentleman," he said suddenly, and turning to John Inglesant, "if he looks, will be able to see."

The astrologer started. "Ah!" he said, "why do you say that, boy?"

"I can tell who will see aught in the crystal, and who will not," replied the boy; "this gentleman will see."

The astrologer seemed surprised and sceptical, but he made a sign to Inglesant to rise from his knees, and to take his place by the crystal.

He did so, and looked steadily into it for some seconds, then he shook his head.

"I can see nothing," he said.

"Nothing!" said the boy; "can you see nothing?"

"No. I see clouds and mist."

"You have been engaged," said the boy, "in something that was not good—something that was not true; and it has dimmed the crystal sight. Look steadily, and if it is as I think, that your motive was not false, you will see more."

Inglesant looked again; and in a moment or two gave a start, saying,—"The mist is breaking! I see;—I see a large room, with a chimney of carved stone, and a high window at the end; in the window and on the carved stone is the same coat many times repeated—three running greyhounds proper, on a field vert."

"I know the room," said Eustace; "it is the inn parlour at Mintern, not six miles from Oulton. It was the manor of the Vinings before the wars, but is now an inn; that was their coat."

"Do you see aught else?" said the adept.

Inglesant gave a long look; then he stepped back, and gazed at the astrologer, and from him to his brother, with a faltering and ashy look.

"I see a man's figure lie before the hearth, and the hearthstone is stained, as if with blood. Eustace, it is either you or I!"

"Look again," said the adept eagerly, "look again!"

"I will look no more!" said Inglesant fiercely; "this is the work of a fiend, to lure men to madness or despair!"

As he spoke, a blast of wind—sudden and strong—swept

through the room; the lamp burnt dim; and the fire in the brazier went out. A deathly coldness filled the apartment, and the floor and the walls seemed to heave and shake. A loud whisper, or muffled cry, seemed to fill the air; and a terrible awe struck at the hearts of the young men. Seizing the rod from the table, the adept assumed a commanding attitude, and waved it to and fro in the air; gradually the wind ceased, the dread coldness abated, and the fire burned again of its own accord. The adept gazed at Inglesant with a stern and set look.

"You are of a strange spirit, young sir," he said; "pure in heart enough to see things which many holy men have desired in vain to see; and yet so wild and rebellious as to anger the blessed spirits with your self-will and perverse thoughts. You will suffer fatal loss, both here and hereafter, if you learn not to give up your own will, and your own fancies, before the heavenly will and call."

Inglesant stared at the man in silence. His words seemed to him to mean far more than perhaps he himself knew. They seemed to come into his mind, softened with anxiety for his brother, and shaken by these terrible events, with the light of a revelation. Surely this was the true secret of his wasted life, however strange might be the place and action which revealed it to him. Whatever he might think afterwards of this night, it might easily stand to him as an allegory of his own spirit, set down before him in a figure. Doubtless he was perverse and headstrong under the pressure of the Divine Hand; doubtless he had followed his own notions rather than the voice of the inward monitor he professed to hear; henceforth, surely, he would give himself up more entirely to the heavenly voice.

Eustace appeared to have seen enough of the future, and to be anxious to go. He left a purse of gold upon the wizard's table; and hurried his brother to take his leave.

Outside the air was perfectly still; a thick motionless fog hung over the marsh and the river; not a breath of wind stirred.

"That was a strange wind that swept by as you refused to look," said Eustace to his brother; "do you really think the spirits were near, and were incensed?"

Inglesant did not reply; he was thinking of another spirit than that the wizard had evoked.

They made their way through the fog to Lambeth, and took boat again to the Temple Stairs.

CHAPTER XVI.

THE next morning, when the brothers awoke and spoke to each other of the events of the night, Eustace did not seem to have been much impressed by them: he ridiculed the astrologer, and made light of the visions in the crystal; he, however, acknowledged to his brother that it might be better to avoid the inn parlour at Mintern, and said they might reach Oulton by another route.

"There is a road," he said, "after you leave Cern Abbas, which turns off five or six miles before you come to Mintern; it is not much farther, but it is not so good a road, and not much frequented. It will be quite good enough for us, however, and will not delay us above an hour. But I own I feel ashamed of taking it."

John Inglesant, however, encouraged him to do so; and towards middle day they left London on the Windsor Road. Inglesant noticed as they started, that his brother's favourite servant was absent, and asked his brother where he was. He replied that he had sent him forward early in the morning to inform his wife of their coming.

"I would not have let them know of your intentions," said Johnny.

Eustace shrugged his shoulders with a peculiar gesture, saying in French,—

"It is not convenient for me to come into my family unannounced. I do not know what I might find going forward."

Johnny thought that his brother had bought his fortune rather dear; but he said nothing more upon the subject.

They slept that night at Windsor, and hoped to have reached Andover the next day; but their servants' horses, and those with the mails, were not equal to so long a distance, and they slept at Basingstoke, not being able to get farther. The weather was pleasant for the season, and to Inglesant especially —so long confined within stone walls—the journey was very agreeable. It reminded him of his ride up to London with the Jesuit long ago when a boy, when everything was new and delightful to him, and the future open and promising. The way had then been enlivened and every interest doubled by the conversation of his friend, who had known how to extract interest and amusement from the most trivial incidents; but it was not less made pleasant now by the society of his brother. A great change seemed to be coming over Eustace. He was affectionate and serious. He spoke much of past years, of their grandfather, and of the old life at Westacre; of his early Court life, before Johnny came to London, and of the day when he came down to Westacre with his father and the Jesuit, and saw his brother again. He asked Johnny much about his own life, and listened attentively to all Inglesant thought proper to tell him of his religious inquiries. He asked about the Ferrars, and told Inglesant some of the things that had been said at Court about him and them. A sense of danger—even though it made little impression upon him—seemed to have called forth kindly feelings which had been latent before; or perhaps some foreboding sense hung over him, and—by a gracious Providence—fitted and tuned his mind for an approaching fate. Inglesant felt his heart drawn towards him with an intensity which he had never felt before. The whole world seemed for the time to be centred in this brother; and he looked forward to life associated with him.

They slept at Andover; and the next day made a shorter journey to Salisbury, where they slept again. The stately Cathedral was closed and melancholy-looking, and knowing no one in the town, they passed the long evening alone in the inn. The next morning early they set out. They halted at Cern Abbas about one o'clock, and dined. Eustace made some inquiries about the road he had mentioned to his brother, but seemed more and more unwilling to take it, and it required all Inglesant's persuasion to keep him to his promise. The people at the inn seemed surprised that any one should think of taking it, and made out that the delay would be very great, and the chance of missing the way altogether not a little. At this, however, Eustace laughed, saying that he knew the country very well. Indeed his desire to show the truth of this assertion rather assisted his brother's purpose, and they left Cern Abbas with the full intention of taking the unusual route. The country was thickly wooded, many parts of the ancient forest remaining, and here and there rather hilly. In descending one of these hills John Inglesant's horse cast a shoe, just as they reached the point where the two roads diverged, the right hand one of which they were to take. As it was impossible for them to proceed with the horse as it was, Johnny proposed sending it back with one of the servants to Cern Abbas, and taking the man's horse instead, who could easily follow them. As they were about to put in practice this scheme, however, one of the men said there was a forge about a mile beyond, on the road before them, where it would be easy to get the shoe put on. Eustace immediately approved of this plan, and Johnny was obliged at last reluctantly to yield. It seemed to him as though the impending fate came nearer and nearer at every step. The man proved himself to be an uncertain guide as to distance, and it was fully two miles before they reached the forge. When they reached it they found that a gentleman's coach, large and unwieldy, had broken some portion of its complicated machinery, and was taxing all the efforts of the smith and his assistants to repair it. The gentlemen dismounted and accosted the two ladies who had alighted from the coach, and whom Eustace remembered to have met before at Dorchester. The coach was soon mended, and the ladies drove off; but by this time Eustace had grown impatient, and, saying carelessly to his brother, "You will follow immediately," he mounted and turned his horse's head still along the main road, his men mounting also.

"You are not going on that way," said Johnny; "you said we should turn back to the other road."

"Oh, we cannot turn back now," said his brother; "we have come farther than I expected. We will not stop at Mintern," he added significantly.

And so saying he rode away after the carriage, followed by his men.

Inglesant looked after him anxiously, a heavy foreboding filling his mind. He saw his brother mount the little hill before the forge, between the bare branches of the trees on either side of the road; then a slight turn of the way concealed him, but, for a moment or two more, he could see glimpses of the figures as the leafless boughs permitted, then, when he could see even these no longer, he went back into the forge. It was some ten minutes before the horse was ready, and then Inglesant himself mounted, and rode off quickly after his brother. He had felt all the day, and during the one preceding it, a weariness and dulness of sense, the result, no doubt, of fatigue acting upon his only partially recovered health, and on a frame shattered by what he had gone through. As he rode on, his brain became more and more confused, so that for some moments together he was almost unconscious, and only by an effort regained his sense of passing events. The woods seemed to pass by him as in a dream, the thick winter air to hang about him like the heavy drapery of a pall, whether he was sleeping or waking he could scarcely tell. What added to his distress was an abiding sense of crisis and danger to his brother, which required him at that moment, above all others, to exert a strength and a prescience of which he felt himself becoming more and more incapable. He was continually making violent efforts to retain his recollection of what was passing and of what it behoved him to do,— efforts which each time became more and more painful, and of the futility of which he became more and more despairingly conscious. Words cannot describe the torture of such a condition as this.

At last he overtook some of his brother's servants with the led horses, whom he scarcely recognized, so far were his senses obscured. Their master had ridden on before with two servants, they told him; he would have to ride hard to overtake them. He seemed eager, they said, to be at home. Inglesant could scarcely sit his horse, much less expect to overtake his brother— who was well mounted and an impetuous rider—nevertheless he gave his horse the spur, and the animal, also a good roadster, soon left the servants far behind. The confusion of mind which he suffered increased more and more as he rode along, and the events of his past life came up before his eyes as clearly and palpably as the objects through which he was riding, so that he could not distinguish the real from the imaginary, the present from the past, which added extremely to his distress. He stood again amid the confusion and carnage of Naseby field; once more he saw the throng of heads, and heard that terrible cry that had welcomed him to the scaffold; again he looked into the fatal crystal, and strange visions and ghostly shapes of death and corruption came out from it, and walked to and fro along the hedgerows and across the road before him, making terrible the familiar English fields; a tolling of the passing bell rang continually in his ear, and his horse's footfalls sounded strange and funereal to his diseased sense. He knew nothing of the road, nor of what happened as he rode along, nor what people he passed; but he missed the direct turning, and reached Mintern at last by another lane which led him some distance round. The servants with the led horses were there before him, standing before the inn door, and other strange servants in his brother's liveries and several horses stood about.

The old manor that was now an inn stood close to the Church, at the opening of the village, with a little green before it and a wall, in the centre of which was a pair of gates flanked with pillars. The iron gates were closed, but the wall had been thrown down for some yards on either side, thus giving ample access to the house within. It was a handsome house with a large high window over the porch, in the upper panes of which Inglesant could see coats of arms. Amid the tracery of the iron gates running greyhounds were interlaced.

John Inglesant saw all this as in a dream, and he saw besides creatures that were not real, walking among the living men; haggard figures in long robes, and others beneath the grave shrouds, ghostly phantoms of his disordered brain. He made a desperate effort for the hundredth time to clear his sense of these terrible distracting sights, of this death of the brain that disabled all his faculties, and for the hundredth time in vain. It appeared to him—whether it was a vision or a reality, he did not know—that one of his brother's servants came to his horse's side, and told him something of a gentleman of his lady's, a foreign physician, having met his master purposely, and that they were within together. Inglesant dismounted mechanically and entered the hotel, telling the servant to come with him. He had some dim feeling of dragging his brother away from a great danger, and a desire of gathering about him, if he could but distinguish them, such as would assist him and were of human flesh and blood. Inside the porch, and in the narrow hall beyond, the place swarmed with these distracting visions walking to and fro; the staircase at the farther end was crowded with them going up and down. He saw, as he thought, his brother, attended by a dark, handsome man, in the gown of a physician, come down the stairs to meet him, but when they came nearer they dissolved themselves and vanished into air.

The host came to meet him, saying that his brother and the foreign gentleman were upstairs in the parlour; he had thought they were having some words a while ago, but they were quiet now. The whole house, Inglesant thought, was deadly quiet, though seemingly to him so full of life. To what terrible deed were all these strange witnesses and assistants summoned? He told the host to follow him as he had told the man before; and he did so, supposing he meant to order something. They went up the two flights of the oak stairs, and entered the room over the hall and porch. It was a large and narrow room, and was seemingly empty. Opposite them, in the high window, and on the great carved chimney to the right, running greyhounds coursed each other, as it seemed to Inglesant, round the room. A long table hid the hearth as they came in. With a fatal certainty, as if mechanically, Inglesant walked round it towards the fire, the others with him; there they stopped—sudden and still. On the white hearthstone—his hair and clothes steeped in blood—lay Eustace Inglesant, the Italian's stiletto in his heart.

CHAPTER XVII.

THE sight of his brother's corpse seemed to steady Inglesant's nerves, and clear his brain. He turned to the host, and said, "What way can the murderer have escaped?"

The host shook his head; he was incapable of speech, or even thought. The three men stood looking at each other without a word. Then Inglesant knelt down by the body, and raised the head; there was no doubt that life was extinct— indeed, the body must have been nearly drained of blood; the fine line of steel had done its work fully, and with no loss of time. Inglesant rose from the ground; his sight, his recollection, his senses were speedily failing him; nothing kept him conscious but the terrible shock acting with galvanic effect upon his frame. The back of the premises was searched, and mounted messengers were sent to the neighbouring towns and to the cross roads, and notice sent to the nearest Justice of the Peace. The country rose in great numbers, and came pouring in to Mintern before the early evening set in. The body was deposited on the long table in the parlour where the deed was committed; and more than one Justice examined the room that afternoon. Inglesant saw that the guard was set, and proper care taken; and then he mounted to ride to Oulton. He was not fit to ride; but to stay in the house all night was impossible—to lie down equally so. In the night air he rode to Oulton, through the long wild chase, by the pools of water—from which the flocks of birds rose startled as he passed, and by the herds of deer. The ride settled his nerves, and when he reached the house he was still master of himself. The news had preceded him; Lady Cardiff was said to be in a paroxysm of grief; but, as no one had seen her for days except her immediate servants, Inglesant did not attempt to obtain an interview with her. He was received by Dr. More and the superior servants, and sat down to supper. Not a word was spoken during that sombre meal except by the Doctor, who pressed Inglesant to eat and drink, and offered to introduce him to Van Helmont, who was not present. The Doctor said grace after supper; but when he had done, one of the female servants, a Quakeress, stood up and spoke some words recommending patience and a feeling after God, if perchance He might be found to be present, and a help in such a terrible need. The singularity of this proceeding roused Inglesant from the lethargy in which he was, and the words seemed to strike upon his heart with a familiar and not uncongenial sense. The mystical doctrine which he had studied was not unlike much that he would hear from Quaker lips. He went to his room after supper, intending to rise early next morning; but before daybreak he was delirious and in a high fever, and Van Helmont was sent for to his room, and bled him freely, and administered cordials and narcotic draughts. The skilful treatment caused him to sleep quietly for many hours; and when he awoke, though prostrate with weakness, he was free from fever, and his brain was calm and clear.

From inquiries which he made, it appeared that the Italian had been making preparations for leaving for several days, probably doubting the success of his attempt to win over Eustace to tolerate his continued stay at Oulton. Inglesant was told that it was supposed that he had not intended to murder his brother; but that Eustace had probably threatened him, and that in the heat of contention the blow was struck. The Italian had destroyed all his papers, and everything that could give any clue to his conduct or history; but he had left a very bad reputation behind him, independently of his last murderous act; and his influence with Lady Cardiff was attributed to witchcraft.

The funeral of Eustace Inglesant took place a few days

after, at the Church on the borders of the chase. Snow had fallen in the meanwhile; and the train of black mourners passed over the waste of white that covered the park. A multitude of people filled the churchyard, and crowded round the outside of the hall. Lady Cardiff, by lavish almsgiving and other vagaries, had always attracted a number of vagrant and masterless people to Oulton; and there were always some encampments of such people in the chase. She particularly favoured mountebanks and quacks of all kinds, and numbers of them were present at the funeral. Some few of the country gentry attended; but Eustace being almost unknown in the country, and his wife by no means popular, many who otherwise would have been present were not so. The Puritan authorities of the neighbourhood suspected Lady Cardiff's establishments as a haunt of recusants. Dr. More was a known royalist; Eustace had been only restrained from active exertion on the same side by his love of pleasure and his wife's prudence; and the Puritans regarded the Quakers with no favour. The herd of idle and vicious people, as the authorities considered them, who frequented Oulton, was an abomination in their eyes; and understanding that a number of them would be at the funeral, two or three Puritan magistrates, with armed servants and constables, assembled to keep order, as they said, but, as it proved, to provoke a riot. To make matters worse, Dr. More began to read the Prayer Book service, which was forbidden by law. The Justices interposed; the mob of mountebanks, and players, and idle people, sided with the Church party, which had always given them a friendly toleration, and commenced an assault upon the constables and Justices' servants, driving them from the grave side with a storm of snowballs. The funeral was completed with great haste, and the mourning party returned to the house, whither the mob also resorted, and were regaled with provisions of all kinds during the afternoon, being with difficulty induced to disperse at night.

Inglesant took no part in this riot, being indeed still too weak and ill to exert himself at all. He expected to be arrested and sent back to London; but the authorities did not take much notice of the riot, contenting themselves with dispersing the people, and seeing that most of them left the neighbourhood, which they were induced to do by being set in the village stocks, and otherwise imprisoned and intimidated.

Lady Cardiff had sent messages to Inglesant every day,

expressing her interest in him, and she now sent Van Helmont to him with the information that a large sum of money, which she had assigned to his brother, would now be his. This sum, which amounted to several thousand pounds, she was ready to pay over to Inglesant whenever he might desire it. She hoped he would remain at Oulton till his health was more established, but she hinted that she thought it was for his own interest that neither his stay there, nor indeed in England, should be unnecessarily prolonged. Meanwhile, she recommended him to Dr. More and to the Quakers; the teaching which he would derive from both sources, she assured him, would be much to his benefit. Inglesant returned a courteous message expressive of his obligation for her extraordinary generosity, and assuring her that he should endeavour to benefit by whatever her inmates might communicate to him. He informed her that he intended, as soon as his strength was sufficiently established, to go to Paris, where the only friend he had left was, and that any sum of money she was so generous as to afford him might be transmitted to the merchants there. He had some thoughts, he said, of going to Gidding, but had learnt that soon after the execution of the King, the house had been attacked by a mob of soldiers and others, and that the family, who had timely warning of their intention, had left the neighbourhood and were dispersed. He concluded by hoping that before he left he might be allowed to thank his benefactress in person.

Some weeks passed over at Oulton with great tranquillity, and Inglesant regained his strength and calmness of mind. There was a large and valuable library in the house, and the society of Dr. More was pleasant to Inglesant, though in many ways they were far from congenial; indeed, there was more in Van Helmont's character and tastes that suited his tone of mind. During these weeks, however, Inglesant began to adapt himself to a course of religious life from which he never altogether departed, and which, after some doubts and many attempts on the part of others to divert him from it, he followed to the end of his life. He was no doubt strengthened at the beginning of this course by the conversation of Dr. More, and also of the Quakers. These latter, whom Inglesant had been led to regard with aversion, he found harmless and sober people, whose blameless lives, and the elevated mysticism of their conversation, commended them to him.

The transient calm of this existence was, however, broken by one absorbing idea—the desire of being revenged upon his brother's murderer, of tracking the Italian's path, and bringing him to some terrible justice. It was this that induced him to seek the Jesuit, whom at one time he had been inclined to shun. No one, he considered, would have it in his power, from the innumerable agents in every country with whom he had connection, to assist him in his search so much as the Jesuit; and he believed that he had deserved as much at his master's hand. But it was not natural that, at any rate at once, he should suppose that such a motive as this would be any hindrance to him in a religious life, and for a long time he was unconscious of any such idea.

It will be as well here to endeavour to understand something of the peculiar form which Christianity had assumed in Inglesant's mind—a form which was not peculiar to himself, but which he possessed in common with most in that day whose training had been more or less similar to his own. It was similar in many respects to that which prevails in the present day in most Roman Catholic countries, and may be described as Christianity without the Bible. It is doubtful whether, except perhaps once or twice in College Chapel, he had ever read a chapter of the Bible himself in his life. Certainly he never possessed a Bible himself; of its contents, excepting those portions which are read in Church and those contained in the Prayer Book, he was profoundly ignorant. It was not included in the course of studies set him by the Jesuit. Of the Protestant doctrines of justification by faith and by the blood of Christ, and of the Calvinistic ones of predestination and assurance, he was only acquainted in a vague and general way, as he might have heard mention of them in idle talk, mostly in contempt and dislike. It is true the Laudian School in the Church, in which he had been brought up, held doctrines which, in outward terms, might seem to bear some affinity with some, if not all of these; but they were in reality very different. The Laudian School held, indeed, that the sacrifice of Christ's blood had removed the guilt of sin, and that by that, and that only, was salvation secured to men; but they held that this had been accomplished on the Cross, once for all, independently of anything that man could do or leave undone. The very slightest recognition, on the part of man, of this Divine sacrifice, the very least submission to the Church ordinances, combined with freedom from outward sin, was sufficient to secure salvation to the baptized; and indeed the Church regarded with leniency and hope even the wild and reprobate. It is true that the Laudian press teemed with holy works, setting the highest of pure standards before its readers, and exhorting to the following of a holy life; but this life was looked upon rather as a spiritual luxury and privilege, to which high and refined natures might well endeavour to attain, rather than as absolutely necessary to salvation. With this view the Church regarded human error with tolerance; and amusements and enjoyments with approbation, and as deserving the highest sanctions of religion. Inglesant's Christianity, therefore, was ignorant of doctrine and dogma of almost every kind, and concentrated itself altogether on what may be called the Idea of Christ, that is, a lively conception of and attraction to the person of the Saviour. This idea,—which comes to men in different ways, and which came to Inglesant for the first time in the sacrament at Gidding, being, I should suppose, a purely intellectual one,—would no doubt be inefficient and transitory, were it not for the unique and mysterious power of attraction which it undoubtedly possesses. In the pursuit of this idea he received little assistance from Dr. More. The school to which the Doctor belonged,— the Christian Platonists,—had no tendency to that exclusive worship of the person of Jesus, which, in some religious schools, has almost superseded the worship of God. This he had received from the Jesuits, and the mystical books of Catholic devotion which had had so great an influence over him. The Jesuits, with all their faults, held fast by the motive of their founder, and the worship of Jesus was by them carried to its fullest extent. Dr. More's theology was more that of a philosophical Deism, into which the person and attributes of Christ entered as a part of an universal scheme, in which the universe, mankind, the all-pervading Spirit of God, and the objects of thought and sense, played distinct and conspicuous parts.

One fine and warm day in the early spring, Inglesant and the Doctor were walking in the garden at the side of the house bordering on the chase and park. The wide expanse of grassy upland stretched before them; overhead the arch of heaven, chequered by the white clouds, was full of life and light and motion; across the water of the lakes the Church bells, rung for amusement by the village lads, came to the ear softened and yet enriched in tone; the spring air, fanned by a fresh breeze, refreshed the spirits and the sense. The Doctor began, as upon a favourite theme, to speak of his great sense of the power and benefit of the fresh air.

"I would always," he said, "be '*sub dio*,' if it were possible. Is there anything more delicious to the touch than the soft cool air playing on our heated temples, recruiting and refrigerating the spirits and the blood? I can read, discourse, or think nowhere as well as in some arbour, where the cool air rustles through the moving leaves; and what a rapture of mind does such a scene as this always inspire within me! To a free and divine spirit how lovely, how magnificent, is this state for the soul of man to be in, when, the life of God inactuating her, she travels through heaven and earth, and unites with, and after a sort feels herself the life and soul of this whole world, even as God! This indeed is to become Deiform—not by imagination, but by union of life. God doth not ride me whither I know not, but discourseth with me as a friend, and speaks to me in such a dialect as I can understand fully,— namely, the outward world of His creatures; so that I am in fact '*Incola cœli in terrâ*,' an inhabitant of paradise and heaven upon earth; and I may soberly confess that sometimes, walking abroad after my studies, I have been almost mad with pleasure, —the effect of nature upon my soul having been inexpressibly ravishing, and beyond what I can convey to you."

Inglesant said that such a state of mind was most blessed and much to be desired; but that few could hope to attain to it, and to many it would seem a fantastic enthusiasm.

"No," said the Doctor, "I am not out of my wits, as some may fondly interpret me, in this divine freedom; but the love of God compelleth me; and though you yourself know the extent of fancy, when phantoms seem real external objects, yet here the principle of my opponents, the Quakers (who, it may be, are nearer to the purity of Christianity—for the life and power of it—than many others), is the most safe and reasonable,—to keep close to the Light within a man."

"You agree with the Quakers, then, in some points?" said Inglesant.

"They have indeed many excellent points, and very nobly Christian, which I wish they would disencumber from such things as make them seem so uncouth and ridiculous; but the reason our lady has taken so to them as to change some of her servants for Quakers, and to design to change more, is that they prove lovers of quiet and retirement, and they fit the circumstances that she is in, that cannot endure any noise, better than others; for the weight of her affliction lies so heavy upon her, that it is incredible how very seldom she can endure any one in her chamber; and she finds them so still, quiet, and serious, that their company is very acceptable to her; and she is refreshed by the accounts of their trials and consolations, and their patience and support under great distress. Baron Van Helmont frequents their meetings."

"What do you think of the Baron?"

"I think he knows as little of himself, truly and really, as one who had never seen him in his life."

Inglesant did not try to penetrate into this oracular response; but said,—

"Have you seen Mr. Fox, the famous Quaker?"

"Yes; I saw him once," replied the Doctor; "and in conversation with him I felt myself, as it were, turned into brass, so much did his spirit and perversity oppress mine."

"There are some men," the Doctor went on, after a pause— but Inglesant did not know of whom he was thinking—"that by a divine sort of fate are virtuous and good, and this to a very great and heroical degree; and come into the world rather for the good of others, and by a divine force, than through their own proper fault, or any immediate or necessary congruity of their natures. All which is agreeable to that opinion of Plato, that some descend hither to declare the being and nature of the gods, and for the greater health, purity, and perfection of this lower world. I would fain believe, Mr. Inglesant," he continued, to the other's great surprise, "that you are one of those. Ever since I first saw you I have had some thought of this; and the more I see of you the more I hope and believe that some such work as this is reserved for you. You have, what is very happy for you, what I call an ethereal sort of body—to use the Pythagoric phrase—even in this life, a mighty purity and plenty of the animal spirits, which you may keep lucid by that conduct and piety by which you may govern yourself. And this makes it all the more incumbent on you to have a great care to keep in order this luciform vehicle of the soul, as the Platonists call it; for there is a sanctity of body which the sensually-minded do not so much as dream of. And this divine body should be cultivated as well as the divine life; for by how much any person partakes more of righteousness and virtue, he hath also a greater measure of this divine body or celestial matter within himself; he throws off the baser affections of the earthly body, and replenishes his inner man with so much larger draughts of ethereal or celestial matter; and to incite you still more to this effort, you have only to consider that the oracle of God is not to be heard but in His holy temple, that is to say, in a good and holy man, thoroughly sanctified in spirit, soul, and body."

CHAPTER XVIII.

SHORTLY after the conversation recorded in the previous chapter, Inglesant, who appeared completely restored to health,—thanks to the Baron Van Helmont and to rest of body,—left Oulton, and, without going to London, went to Rye, and sailed thence to France, where he arrived about the middle of May 1651. He had taken a passage in a vessel sailing to Dieppe, and from thence he posted to Paris, this route being thought much safer than the one through Calais, which was much infested by robbers,

He found Paris full of the fugitive Royalists in a state of distress and destitution, which was so great, that on the Queen of England's going to St. Germain's on one occasion, her creditors threatened to arrest her coach. The young King Charles was in Scotland, previous to his march into England, which terminated in the battle of Worcester. Inglesant was well received by the Royalists to whom he made himself known on his arrival. The Glamorgan negotiations were by this time pretty well understood among the Royalists, and Inglesant's conduct fairly well appreciated. He had the reputation of being a useful and trustworthy agent, and as such was well received by the heads of the party. He presented himself at the Louvre, where the Queen was, who received him graciously, and expressed a wish that he would remain in Paris, as she had been speaking not many days ago with Father St. Clare concerning him. Inglesant inquired where the Jesuit was, and was told, at St. Germain's with the French Court, and that he would be in Paris again shortly. After leaving the Queen, Inglesant applied to the merchants with whom his money was to have been lodged; but found that by some misunderstanding a much smaller sum had arrived than he had expected. Such as it was, however, he was able from it to make advances to the Royalist gentlemen, many of whom of the highest rank were in absolute distress; and he even advanced a considerable sum indirectly to the Queen, and, through the Duke of Ormond, to the young Duke of Gloucester.

It is not necessary to enter into any details with regard to the state of France or the French Court at that time. The Court had been obliged to leave Paris some time before, owing to the violence of the populace, and was at present much embarrassed from the same cause. It was therefore quite unable to afford any help to the distressed fugitives from England, had it wished to do so, and even the Queen Henrietta,—a daughter of France,—could scarcely obtain assistance, and was reduced to the greatest pecuniary distress. The Duke of Ormond parted with his last jewel to procure money for the use of the Duke of Gloucester, whose guardian he was, and the inferior Royalists were reduced to still greater necessities. No sooner, therefore, was it known that Inglesant had means at his disposal, than he became once more a person of the greatest consequence, and every one sought him out, or, if not before acquainted with him, desired an introduction. He frequented the Chapel of Sir Richard Browne, who had been ambassador from Charles the First, and still retained his privileges, his chapel, and his household, being accredited from the young fugitive King to the French Court. This was the only Anglican place of worship in Paris, or indeed at that time, perhaps, in the world. Ordinations were performed there, and it was frequented by the King and the two young Princes, the Duke of York and the Duke of Gloucester, and by all the Royalist fugitives then in Paris.

Inglesant was the more welcome, as many of the Royalist gentlemen who had any money at all, refused to stay in Paris, where there were so many claims upon them, but went on to other countries, especially Italy. He found many of these gentlemen in a very excited state, owing to the efforts of the Queen Mother to discourage the English Church, and to win over perverts to Romanism. The King and the Duke, it is true, received the sacrament in the Ambassador's Chapel, partaking of it together before the other communicants, Lord Biron, Inglesant's old friend, and Lord Wilmot, holding a white cloth before the two Princes; but the Queen Mother was making every effort to pervert the young Duke of Gloucester, and throwing all the weight of her influence and patronage on the side of the Papists. Several of the maids of honour had been discharged shortly before Inglesant's arrival in Paris, for refusing to conform to the Romish Mass. Dr. Cosin, the Dean of Peterborough, a profound Ritualist, but at the same time devoted to the Anglican Church, had preached a sermon in the Chapel comforting and supporting these ladies. Inglesant being with the Queen at the Palais Royal, one morning as she was going to her private mass, was commanded to accompany her; and upon his readily complying, the Queen afterwards spoke to him on the subject of religion, inquiring why he, who had so long been so closely connected with the Catholic Church, did not become one of its members. Inglesant pleaded that the Jesuit, Father.St. Clare, had discouraged him from joining the Papists as not convenient in the position in which he had been placed. The Queen said that the reasons which actuated the Father did not any longer exist, but that she would wait till she could take his advice; in the meantime requesting Inglesant to attend the Romish services as much as possible, which he promised to do. As a matter of choice, he preferred the English communion to the mass, but he regarded both as means of sacramental grace, and endeavoured at low mass to bring his mind into the same devout stillness and condition of adoration as at a communion. It would appear that about this time he must have been formally received into the Romish Church, for he confessed and received the sacrament at low mass; but no mention of the ceremony occurs, and it is possible that the priests received instructions respecting him, while there is clear proof that he attended the services at the Ambassador's Chapel, and once at any rate partook of the sacrament there.

Here he met with Mr. Hobbes, who expressed himself pleased to see him, and entered into long discourses with him respecting the Glamorgan negotiations and the late King's policy generally,—discourses which were very instructive to Inglesant, though he felt a greater repugnance to the man than when he formerly met him in London. The religious thoughts which had filled Inglesant's mind at Oulton were far from forgotten, and when he arrived in Paris, his first feeling had been one of dissatisfaction at finding himself at once involved again in political intrigue; but his affection for the Jesuit, apart from his desire to discover the Italian by his means, made him desire to meet him; and he continued in Paris, waiting with this intention, when an event occurred which altogether diverted his thoughts.

He spent his time in many ways,—partly in acts of religion, partly in studies, frequenting several lectures, both in letters and in science, such as Mons. Febus's course of chemistry. He also frequented the tennis court in the Rue Verdelet, where the King of England, and the princes and nobles, both of that country and of France, amused themselves. He had been at this latter place one morning, and something having happened to prevent the gentleman who had arranged to play the match from appearing, Inglesant, who was a good tennis player, had been requested to take his place against Mons. Saumeurs, the great French player. There was a large and brilliant attendance to watch the play, and Inglesant exerted himself to the utmost, so much so, that he earned the applause and thanks of the company for the brilliant match played before them. Having at last been beaten, which occurred probably when the great player considered he had afforded sufficient amusement to the spectators, Inglesant turned to leave the court, having resumed his dress and sword, when he was accosted by an English nobleman whom he very slightly knew; who, no doubt influenced by the applause and attention which Inglesant had excited, asked him to dine with him at a neighbouring place of entertainment. After dinner the gentleman told Inglesant that he was in the habit, together with many other English who wished to perfect their knowledge of French, of resorting to one or other of the convents of Paris, to talk with the ancient sisters, whose business it was to receive strangers, and had several such acquaintances with whom he might "chat at the grates, for the nuns speak a quaint dialect, and have besides most commonly all the news that passes, which they are ready to discourse upon as long as you choose to listen, whereby you gain a greater knowledge of the most correct and refined manner of speaking of all manner of common and trifling events

O

than you could otherwise gain." He said that he had received a parcel of English gloves and knives from England the day before, some of which he intended that afternoon taking to one of his "Devota" (as they call a friend in a convent, he said, in Spain), and would take Inglesant with him if the latter wished to come. Inglesant willingly consented, and they went to a convent of the —— in the Rue des Terres Fortes. They found the ancient nun—a little courtly old lady—as amusing and pleasant as they expected; and she was on her part apparently equally pleased with Lord Cheney's presents, and with Inglesant's courteous discourse and good French. She invited Inglesant to visit her again, but the next day he received a message which was brought by a servant of the convent, who had found his lodgings with some difficulty through Lord Cheney, requesting him to come to the convent at once. It lay in a retired and rather remote part of the city, and but for his friend's introduction he would never have visited it. Thinking the message somewhat strange, he complied with the request, and in the afternoon found himself again in the convent parlour. The nun came immediately to the grate.

"Ah, monsieur," she said, "I am glad that you are come. You think it strange, doubtless, that I should send for you so soon; but I spoke of you last night to an inmate of this house, who is a compatriot of yours, and who, I am sorry to say, is very ill,—nay, I fear at the point of death,—and she told me she had known you very well—ah, very well indeed—in times past; and she entreated me to send to you if I could find out your residence. I only knew of you through Milord Chene, but I sent to him."

"What is this lady's name, madame?" said Inglesant, who, even then, did not guess who it was.

"Ah, her name," said the nun; "her name is Collette—Mademoiselle Marie Collette."

She had the door in the grate opened for Inglesant, and took him through the house, and past a court planted with trees, to a small and quiet room overlooking the distant woodlands. There, upon a little bed—her face white, her hands and form wasted to a shadow, only her wonderful eyes the same as ever—lay Mary Collet, her face lighting up and her weak hands trembling as he came in. On his knees by the bedside, his face buried in his hands, her white fingers playing over his hair, Inglesant could not speak, dare not even look up. The old nun looked on kindly for some few minutes, and then left them.

Mary was the first to speak, and as she spoke, Inglesant raised his head and fixed his eyes on hers, keeping down the torrent of grief that all but mastered him as he might.

She spoke to him of her joy at seeing him—she so lonely and lost in a foreign land, separated from all her friends and family,—not knowing indeed where they were; of the sufferings and hardship she had passed through since they had left Gidding—hardships which had caused the fever of which she lay dying as she spoke. She had come to Paris after parting from her uncle in Brittany, where they had suffered much deprivation with the Lady Blount, and had been received into this convent, where she had meant to take the veil; but the fever grew upon her, and the physicians at last gave her no hope of recovery. There she had lain day after day, tended by the kind nuns with every care, yet growing weaker and more weary—longing for some voice or face of her own country or of former days. While she had been well enough to listen, the nuns had told her all the little scraps of news relating to her own countrymen and to the Queen which had reached them; but Inglesant's arrival was not likely to be among these, and Mary had heard nothing of his being in Paris till the night before, when the kindly old nun, finding her a little better than usual, had thought to amuse her by speaking of the pleasant young Englishman who spoke French so well, and whose half foreign name she could easily remember, and who, Lord Cheney had told her, had been one of the most faithful servants of the poor murdered King.

The start of the dying girl before her, her flushed face as she raised herself in bed and threw herself into her friend's arms, entreating her that this old friend, the dearest friend she had ever known—ah! dearer now than ever—might be sent for at once while she had life and strength to speak to him, showed the nun that this was yet again a reacting of that old story that never tires a woman's heart. The nuns were not strict—far from it—and, even had Mary already taken the veil, the sisters would have thought little blame of her even for remembering that, once she dreamt of another bridegroom than the heavenly Spouse. The nun had promised to send early in the morning to Lord Cheney, who, no doubt, knew the abode of his friend; and Mary, as she finished telling all this in her low and weak speech, lay still and quiet, looking upon her friend almost with as calm and peaceful a glance of her absorbing eyes as when she had looked at him in the garden parlour at Gidding years ago. He himself said little; it was not his words she wanted, could he have spoken them That he was there by her, looking up in her face, holding her hand, was quite enough. At last she said,—

"And that mission to the Papist murderers, Johnny, you did not wish to bring them into England of your own accord, or only as a plot of the Jesuits? Surely you were but the servant of one whom you could not discover."

"I had the King's own commission for all I did, for every word I said," said Inglesant eagerly—"a commission written by himself, and signed in my presence, which he gave me himself. That was the paper the Lord Biron would not burn."

"I knew it must be so, Johnny; my uncle told me it must be so. It seems to me you have served a hard master, though you do not complain. We heard about the scaffold at Charing Cross. Will you serve your heavenly Master as well as you have served your King?"

"I desire to serve Him, am seeking to serve Him even now, but I do not find the way. Tell me how I can serve Him, Mary, and I swear to you I will do whatever you shall say."

"He must teach you, Johnny, not I. I doubt not that you follow Him now, will serve Him hereafter much better than I could ever show you—could ever do myself. Whatever men may think of the path you have already chosen, no one can say you have not walked in it steadily to the end. Only walk in this way as steadily, Johnny,—only follow your heart as unflinchingly, when it points you to Him. I will do nothing night and day while I live, Johnny, but pray to Jesus that He may lead you to Himself."

The old familiar glamour that shed such a holy radiance on the woods and fields of Gidding, now, to Inglesant's senses, filled the little convent room. The light of heaven that entered the open window with the perfume of the hawthorn was lost in the diviner radiance that shone from this girl's face into the depths of his being, and bathed the place where she was in light. His heart ceased to beat, and he lay, as in a trance, to behold the glory of God.

CHAPTER XIX.

INGLESANT was present at the funeral in the cemetery of the convent, and caused a white marble cross to be set over the grave. He remained in his lodgings several days, melancholy and alone. His whole nature was shaken to the foundation, and life was made more holy and solemn to him than ever before. The burden of worldly matters became intolerable, and the coil that had been about his life so long grew more oppressive till it seemed to stifle his soul. He desired to listen to the Divine Voice, but the voice seemed silent, or to speak only the language of worldly plans and schemes. He desired to live a life of holiness, but the only life that seemed possible to him was one of business and intrigue. What was this life of holiness that men ought to lead? Could it be followed in the world? Or must he retire to some monastic solitude to cultivate it; and was it certain that it would flourish even there? It seemed more and more impossible for him to find it; he was repulsed and turned back upon his worldly life at every attempt he made. He almost resolved to give up the Jesuit, and to seek some more spiritual guide. He remembered Cressy, who had become a Romanist, and a Benedictine monk of the Monastery at Douay, and was at that moment in Paris.

When Inglesant had been last in Oxford, the secession of Hugh Paulin Cressy, as he had been named at the font in Wakefield Church,—Serenus de Cressy, as he called himself in religion,—had created a painful and disturbed impression. A Fellow of Merton, the chaplain and friend of Lord Strafford, and afterwards of Lord Falkland, a quick and accurate disputant, a fine and persuasive preacher, a man of sweet and attractive nature, and of natural and acquired refinement,—he was one of the leaders of the highest thought and culture of the University. When it was known, therefore, that this man, so admired and beloved, had seceded to Popery, the interest and excitement were very great, and one of Archbishop Usher's friends writes to him in pathetic words of the loss of this bright ornament of the Church, and of the danger to others which his example might cause.

He was at present in Paris, where the conjuncture of religious affairs was very exciting. There was much in the discussions which were going on singularly fitted to Inglesant's state of mind, and in some degree conducive to it. The Jesuits, both in Rome and Paris, were occupied as they had been for several years, in that great controversy with the followers of Jansenius, which, a few years afterwards, culminated in those discussions and that condemnation in the Sorbonne so graphically described by Pascal. We have only to do with it as it affected Inglesant, and it is therefore not necessary to inquire what were the real reasons which caused the Jesuits to oppose the Jansenists. The point at which the controversy had arrived, when Inglesant was in Paris, was one which touched closely upon the topics most interesting to his heart. This was the doctrine of sufficient grace. The Jesuits, on this as in all other matters, had taken that side which is undoubtedly most pleasing to the frailty of the human heart,—an invariable policy, to which they owed their supremacy over the popular mind.

When the faithful came to the theologians to inquire what was the true state of human nature since its corruption, they received St. Augustine's answer, confirmed by St. Bernard and St. Thomas Aquinas, and finally adopted by the Jansenists,— "That human nature has no more sufficient grace than God is pleased to bestow upon it, and that fresh efficacious grace must constantly be given by God, which grace God does not give to all, and without which no man can be saved." In opposition to this, the Jesuits, about the time of the Reformation, came forward with what was called a new doctrine,—that sufficient grace is given to all men, as men, but so far compliant with free-will that this latter makes the former efficacious or inefficacious at its choice, without any new supply from God. The Jansenists retorted that this doctrine rendered unnecessary the efficacious grace of Jesus Christ; but that this does not follow is plain, for this efficacious grace of God that is given to all men once for all, may be owing to the sacrifice of Christ. To many natures this universal gracious beneficent doctrine of all-pervading grace, which includes all mankind, was much more pleasing than the doctrine of the necessity of special grace, involving spiritual assumption in those who possess it, or say they do, and bitter uncertainty and depression in humble, self-doubting, and thoughtful minds. It resembled also the doctrines of the

Laudian School, in which Inglesant had been brought up. So attractive indeed was it, that the Benedictines were compelled to profess it, and to pretend to side with the Jesuits, while in reality hating their doctrine.

When Inglesant remembered Cressy, and remembered also that he belonged to the Benedictines, the polished and learned cultivators of the useful arts, and was told that Cressy had chosen this order that he might have leisure and books to prosecute his studies and his writings, he conceived great hope that from him he should learn the happy mean he was in search of, between the worldliness of the Jesuits on the one hand, and the narrow repulsiveness of the Mendicant orders and the Calvinists on the other. In this frame of mind he sought an interview with Cressy. The directions of the Jesuits and of the Laudian School seemed to Inglesant to have failed; to have associated himself with the Jansenists or Calvinists would have been distasteful to him, and almost impossible. He sought in the Benedictine monk that compromise which the heart of man is perpetually seeking between the things of this world and the things of God. But though for the time the influence of the training of his life was somewhat shaken, it was far from removed, and an event occurred which, even before he saw Cressy, reforged the chains upon him to some extent. One Sunday evening, the day before he was to meet Cressy, walking along the Rue St. Martin from the Boulevard where he had lodgings, he turned into the Jesuits' Church just as the sermon had begun. The dim light found its way into the vast Church from the stained windows; a lamp burning before some shrine shone partially on the preacher, as he stood in the stone pulpit by a great pillar, in his white surplice and rich embroidered stole. He was a young man, thin and sad-looking, and spoke slowly, and with long pauses and intervals, but with an intense eagerness and pathos that went to every heart. The first words that Inglesant heard, as he reached the nearest unoccupied place, were these:—

"Ah! if you adored a God crowned with roses and with pearls, it were a matter nothing strange; but to prostrate yourselves daily before a crucifix, charged with nails and thorns, —you living in such excess and superfluity in the flesh, dissolved in softness,—how can that be but cruel? Ah, think of that crucifix as you lie warm in silken curtains, perfumed with eau de naffe, as you sit at dainty feasts, as you ride forth in the sunshine in gallantry. He is cold and naked; He is alone; behind Him the sky is dreary and streaked with darkening clouds, for the night cometh—the night of God. His locks are wet with the driving rain; His hair is frozen with the sleet; His beauty is departed from Him; all men have left Him—all men, and God also, and the holy angels hide their faces. He is crowned with thorns, but you with garlands; He wears nothing in his hands but piercing nails; you have rubies and diamonds on yours. Ah! will you tell me you can still be faithful though in brave array? I give that answer which Tertullian gave,— 'I fear this neck snared with wreaths and ropes of pearls and emeralds. I fear the sword of persecution can find no entrance there.' No! hear you not the voice of the crucifix? Follow me. We are engaged to suffer by His sufferings as we look on Him. Suffering is our vow and profession. Love which cannot suffer is unworthy of the name of love."

* * * * *

The next day, at the appointed hour, he went to the Benedictine Monastery, in the Rue de Varrennes, and sent in his name to Father de Cressy. He was shown, not into the visitors' room, but into a private parlour, where Cressy came to him immediately. Dressed in the habit of his order, with a lofty and refined expression, he was a striking and attractive man; differing from the Jesuit in that, though both were equally persuasive, the latter united more power of controlling others than the appearance of Cressy implied. He had known Inglesant slightly at Oxford, and greeted him with great cordiality.

"I am not surprised that you are come to me, Mr. Inglesant," he said, with a most winning gesture and smile; "De Guevara, who was himself both a courtier and a recluse, says that the penance of religious men was sweeter than the pleasures of courtiers. Has your experience brought you to the same conclusion?"

Inglesant thanked him for granting him an interview: and sitting down, he told him shortly the story of his life, and his early partiality for the mystical theology; of his wishes and attempts; of his desire to follow the Divine Master; and of his failures and discouragements, his studies, his Pagan sympathies; and how life and reality of every kind, and inquiry, and the truth of history, and philosophy, even while it sided with or supported religion, still seemed to hinder and oppose the heavenly walk.

"I do not know, Mr. Inglesant," said De Cressy, "whether your case is easier or more difficult than that of those who usually come to me; I have many come to me; and they usually, one and all, come with the exact words of the blessed gospel on their lips, 'Sir, we would see Jesus.' And I look them in the face often, and wonder, and often find no words to speak. See Jesus, I often think, I do not doubt it! who would not wish to see Him who is the fulness of all perfection that the heart and intellect ever conceived, in whom all creation has its centre, all the troubles and sorrows of life have their cure, all the longings of carnal men their fruition? But why come to me? Is He not walking to and fro on the earth continually, in every act of charity and self-sacrifice that is done among men? Is He not offered daily on every altar, preached continually from every pulpit? Why come to me? Old men of sixty and seventy come to me with these very words, 'Sir, we would see Jesus.' If the course of sixty years, if the troubles and confusions of a long life, if He Himself has not revealed this Beatific Vision to them,—how can I? But with you it is very different. By your own story I know that you have seen Jesus; that you know Him as you know your dearest friend. This makes our discourse at first much the easier, for I need waste no words upon a matter to enlarge upon which to you would be an insult to your heart. But it makes it more difficult afterwards, when we come to ask how it is that, with this transcendental knowledge, you are still dissatisfied, and find life so difficult a path to tread. I make no apology for speaking plainly; such would be as much an insult to you as the other. You remind me of the rich oratories I have seen of some of our Court ladies, where everything is beautiful and costly, but where a classic statue of Apollo stands by the side of a crucifix, a Venus with our Lady, a Cupid near St. Michael, and a pair of beads hanging on Mercury's Caduceus.

"You are like the young man who came to Jesus, and whom Jesus loved, for you have great possessions. You have been taught all that men desire to know, and are accomplished in all that makes life delightful. You have the knowledge of the past, and know the reality of men's power, and wisdom, and beauty, which they possess of themselves, and did possess in the old classic times. You have culled of the tree of knowledge, and know good and evil: yea, the good that belongs to this world, and is part of it, and the strength and wisdom and beauty of the children of this world; yea, and the evil and ignorance and folly of the children of light. Let us grant—I am willing to grant—that Plato has a purer spiritual instinct than St. Paul. I will grant that Lucretius has the wisdom of this world with him; ay, and its alluring tongue. Paul did not desire spiritual insight; he wanted Jesus. You stand as a god free to choose. On the one hand, you have the delights of reason and of intellect, the beauty of that wonderful creation which God made, yet did not keep; the charms of Divine philosophy, and the enticements of the poet's art; on the other side, Jesus. You know Him, and have seen Him. I need say no more of His perfections.

"I do not speak to you, as I might speak to others, of penalties and sufferings hereafter, in which, probably, you do not believe. Nor do I speak to you, as I might to others, of evidences that our faith is true, of proofs that hereafter we shall walk with Christ and the saints in glory. I am willing to grant you that it may be that we are mistaken; that in the life to come we may find we have been deceived; nay, that Jesus Himself is in a different station and position to what we preach. This is nothing to your purpose. To those who know Him as you know Him, and have seen Him as you have, better Jesus, beaten and defeated, than all the universe besides, triumphing and crowned. I offer to you nothing but the alternative which every man sooner or later must place before himself. Shall he turn a deaf ear to the voice of reason, and lay himself open only to the light of faith? or shall he let human wisdom and human philosophy break up this light, as through a glass, and please himself with the varied colours upon the path of life? Every man must choose; and having chosen, it is futile to lament and regret; he must abide by his choice, and by the different fruit it brings. You wish this life's wisdom, and to walk with Christ as well; and you are your own witness that it cannot be. The two cannot walk together, as you have found. To you, especially, this is the great test and trial that Christ expects of you to the very full. We of this religious order have given ourselves to learning, as you know; nay, in former years, to that Pagan learning, which is so attractive to you, though of late years we devote ourselves to producing editions of the Fathers of the Church. But even this you must keep yourself from. To most men this study is no temptation: to you it is fatal. I put before you your life, with no false colouring, no tampering with the truth. Come with me to Douay; you shall enter our house according to the strictest rule; you shall engage in no study that is any delight or effort to the intellect; but you shall teach the smallest children in the schools, and visit the poorest people, and perform the duties of the household—and all for Christ. I promise you on the faith of a gentleman and a priest—I promise you, for I have no shade of doubt—that in this path you shall find the satisfaction of the heavenly walk; you shall walk with Jesus day by day, growing ever more and more like to Him; and your path, without the least fall or deviation, shall lead more and more into the light, until you come unto the perfect day; and on your death-bed—the death-bed of a saint—the vision of the smile of God shall sustain you, and Jesus Himself shall meet you at the gates of eternal life."

Every word that Cressy spoke went straight to Inglesant's conviction, and no single word jarred upon his taste. He implicitly believed that what the Benedictine offered him he should find. There was no doubt—could be no doubt—that it was by such choice as this that such men as Cressy gained for themselves a power in the heavenly warfare, and not only attained to the heavenly walk themselves, but moved the earth to its foundations, and drew thousands into the ranks of Christ. He saw the choice before him fairly, as Cressy had said, and indeed, it was not for the first time. Then his mind went back to his old master, and to that school where no such thing as this was required of him, and yet the heavenly light offered to him as freely as by this man. The sermon of the night before came into his mind again; surely where such doctrine as that was preached, might he not find rest? It was true that his coming there, and his confession, closed his lips before Cressy; but might he not have been too hasty? Life was not yet over with him; perchance he might yet find what he sought in some other way. He saw the path of perfect self-denial open before him,—renunciation, not of pleasure, nor even of the world, but of himself, of his intellect, of his very life,—and distinctly of his free choice he refused it. This only may be said for him:

he was convinced that every word the Benedictine had said to him was true,—that in the life he offered him he should follow and find the Lord; but he was not equally convinced that it was the will of Christ that he should accept this life, and should follow and find Him in this way, and in no other. Had he been as clear of this as of the truth of Cressy's words, then indeed would his turning away have been a clear denial of Jesus Christ; but it was the voice of Cressy that spoke to him, and not the voice of Christ; it came to him with a conviction and a power all but irresistible, but it failed to carry with it the absolute conviction of the heavenly call. How could it? The heavenly call itself must speak very loud before it silences and convinces the unwilling heart.

He rose from his seat before the monk, and looking sadly down upon him he said,—

"I believe all that you say and all that you promise, and that the heavenly walk lies before me in the road that you have pointed out; but I cannot follow it—it is too strait. I return your kindness and your plainness with words equally plain; and while you think of me as lost and unworthy, it may be some well-earned satisfaction to you to remember that none ever spoke truer, or nobler, or kinder words to any man than you have spoken to me."

"I do not look on you as lost, Mr. Inglesant,—far from it," said Cressy, rising as he spoke; "I expect you will yet witness a good confession for Christ in the world and in the Court; but I believe you have had to-day a more excellent way shown you, which, but for the trammels of your birth and training, you might have had grace to walk in, for your own exceeding blessedness and the greater glory of the Lord Christ. I wish you every benediction of this life and of the next; and I shall remember you at the altar as a young man who came to Jesus, and whom Jesus loves."

Inglesant took his leave of him, and left the monastery. He came away very sorrowful from Serenus de Cressy. Whether he also, at the same time, was turning away from Jesus Christ, who can tell?

The next day the Jesuit arrived in Paris.

CHAPTER XX.

INGLESANT was much struck with the change in the Jesuit's appearance. He was worn and thin, and looked discouraged and depressed. He was evidently extremely pleased to see his pupil again, and his manner was affectionate and even respectful. He appeared shaken and nervous, and Inglesant fancied that he was rather shy of meeting him; but if so, it soon passed off under the influence of the cordial greeting with which he was received.

To Inglesant's inquiry as to where he had been, the Jesuit answered that it did not matter; he had succeeded very imperfectly in his mission, whatever it had been. He asked Inglesant whether he had met with Sir Kenelm Digby, or heard anything of him. In reply to which Inglesant told him the reports which he had heard concerning him.

"He is mad," said the Jesuit, "and he is not the less dangerous. He was sent to Rome by the Queen, where he made great mischief, and offended the Pope by his insolence. He has sided with the Parliament in England, and is engaged on a scheme to persuade Cromwell to recall the King, and seat him on the throne as an elective monarch. The Queen does not wish to break with him altogether, both because he has great influence with some powerful Catholics, and because, if nothing better can be done, she would perforce accept the elective monarchy for her son. But the scheme is chimerical, and will come to nothing. Cromwell intends the crown for himself. You see, Johnny," continued St. Clare with a smile, "all our plans have failed. The English Church is destroyed, and those Catholics who always opposed it are thought much of at Rome now, and carry all before them. I have not altered my opinion, however, and I shall die in the same. But we must wait. I do not wish to influence you any more, nor to involve you any longer in any schemes of mine, but the Queen wants you to go as an agent to Rome in her behalf; and it would be of great service to me, and to any plans which I may in future have, if I had such a friend and correspondent as yourself in that city. If you have no other plans, I do not see that you could do much better than go. You shall have such introductions to my friends there —cardinals and great men—that you may live during your stay in the best company and luxury, and without expense. One of my friends is the Cardinal Rinuccini, brother of the Legate the Bishop of Fermo, whom you met in Ireland, and who, by the by, was much impressed with you. You cannot fail to make friends with many who will have it in their power to be of great use to you; and you may establish yourself in some lucrative post, either as a layman, or, if you choose to take orders, as a priest. You will believe me, also, when I say,—what I say to very few,—that I am under obligations to you which I can never repay, and nothing will give me greater pleasure than to see you rich and prosperous, and admired and powerful in the Roman Court. You have the qualities and the experience to command success. You will be backed by the whole power of my friends, with whom to make your fortune will be the work of an after-dinner's talk. You will see Italy, and delight yourself in the sight of all those places and antiquities of which we have so often talked; and with your cultivated and religious tastes you will enter, with the most perfect advantage, into that magic world of sight and sound which the churches and sacred services in Rome present to the devout. I cannot see that you can do better than go."

Inglesant sat looking at the Jesuit with a singular expression in his eyes, which the latter did not understand. Yes, surely it was a very different offer from that of Serenus de Cressy, yet Inglesant did not delay to answer from any indecision; from the moment the Jesuit began to speak he knew that he should go. But he took a kind of melancholy pleasure in contrasting the two paths, the two men, the different choice they offered him, and in reading a half sad, half sarcastic commentary on himself.

After a minute or two, he said,—

"I thank you much for your good-will and quite undeserved patronage. It is by far too good an offer to be refused, and I gladly accept it. You know, doubtless, what has happened to me, especially within these last few days, and that I have no friend left on earth save yourself; such a journey as that which you propose to me will, at the least, distract my thoughts from such a melancholy fate as mine."

"I knew of your brother's murder," said the Jesuit; "I have heard of the man before—one of those utterly lost and villainous natures which no country but Italy ever produced. Do you wish to seek him?"

Inglesant told him that one of his principal objects in staying in Paris was to seek his assistance for that purpose; and that he felt it a sacred duty, which he owed to his brother, that his murderer should not escape unpunished.

"I have no doubt I can learn where he is," said the other; "but I do not well see what you can do when you have found him, unless it happens to be in a place where you have powerful friends. It is true that he is so generally known and hated in Italy, that you might easily get help in punishing him should you meet him there: but he is hardly likely to return to his native country, except for some powerful reason."

"If I can do nothing else," said Inglesant bitterly, "I can tell him who I am and shoot him dead, or run him through the body. He murdered my brother, just as he had come back to me —to me in prison and alone, and was a loving friend and brother to me, and would have been through life. Do you suppose that I should spare him, or that any moment will be so delightful to me as the one in which I see him bleed to death at my feet, as I saw my poor brother, struck by his hand, as he shall be by mine?"

The Jesuit looked at Inglesant with surprise. The terrible earnestness of his manner, and the unrelenting and grim pleasure he seemed to take at the prospect of revenge, seemed so inconsistent with the refined and religious tone of his ordinary character, approaching almost to weakness; but the next moment he thought, "Why should I wonder at it! The man who has gone through what he did without flinching must have a strength of purpose about him far other than some might think."

He said aloud,—

"Well, I doubt not I can find him; he is well known in France, in Spain, and in Italy, and if he goes to Germany he can be traced. But what was the other sad misfortune you spoke of?—something within the last few days, you said."

Inglesant had been looking fixedly before him since he had last spoken, with a steady blank expression, which, since his imprisonment, his face sometimes wore,—part of a certain wildness in his look which bespoke a mind ill at ease and a confused brain. He was following up his prey to the death.

He started at the Jesuit's question, and seemed to recollect with an effort; then he said,—

"Mary Collet died at the convent of the Nuns of the —— last week. I only found her out the night before;" and as he spoke, the contrast arose in his mind of the death-bed of the saint-like girl, and the Italian's bleeding body struck down by his revenge. The footsteps of the Saviour he had promised his friend to follow, surely could not lead him to such a scene as that. If this were the first-fruits of his refusal to follow Serenus de Cressy, surely he must also have turned his back on Christ Himself.

He covered his face with his hands, and the Jesuit saw that he wept. He supposed it was simply from grief at the death of his friend, and he was surprised at the strength of his attachment. Like others, he had thought Inglesant's love a rather cool and Platonic passion.

"I always thought him one of those nice and coy lovers," he said to himself, "who always observe some defect in the thing they love, which weakens their passion, and shows them that the reality is so much inferior to their idea, that they easily desist from their enterprise, and vanish as if they had not so much intention to love as to vanish, and had more shame to have begun their courtship than purpose to continue it. He must be much shaken by his suffering and by his brother's death."

He waited a few moments, and then spoke to Inglesant about his health, of his brother's death, and of his imprisonment. He spoke to him of the late King, and of his distress at the necessity under which he lay of denying Inglesant's commission: and he said many other things calculated to cheer his friend and please his self-regard.

Inglesant listened to him not without pleasure, but he said little. An idea had taken possession of his mind, which he carried with him into Italy and for long afterwards. He was more than half convinced that, in rejecting Cressy's advice, he had turned his back on Christ; and he was the more confirmed in this belief because never had the image of the Italian, nor the desire of revenge, taken so strong a hold upon his imagination as now. It occurred to his excited imagination that Christ had deserted him, and the Fiend taken possession, and that the course and intention of the latter would be to lure him on, by such images, to some terrible and lonely place, where the Italian and he together should be involved in one common ghastly deed of crime, one common and eternal ruin. The sense of having had a great act of self-denial placed before him and having refused it, no doubt weighed down and blunted his conscience; and once placed, as he half thought, upon the downward path, nothing seemed before him but the gradual descent, adorned at first by some poor show of gaudy flowers, but ending speedily—for there was no self-delusion to such a nature as his, which had tasted of the heavenly food—in miserable and filthy mire, where, loathing himself and despised by others, nothing awaited him but eternal death. He answered the Jesuit almost mechanically, and on parting from him at night promised indifferently to accompany him on the morrow to an audience with the Queen.

CHAPTER XXI.

INGLESANT travelled to Marseilles, and by packet boat to Genoa. The beauty of the approach by sea to this city, and the lovely gardens and the country around, gave him the greatest delight. The magnificent streets of palaces, mostly of marble, and the thronged public places, the galleries of paintings, and the museums, filled his mind with astonishment; and the entrance into Italy, wonderful as he had expected it to be, surpassed his anticipation. He stayed some time in Genoa, to one or more of the Jesuit fathers in which city he had letters. Under the guidance of these cultivated men he commenced an education in art, such as in these days can be scarcely understood. From his coming into Italy a new life had dawned upon him in the music of that country. Fascinated as he had always been with the Church music at London and Oxford, for several years he had been cut off from all such enjoyment, and, at its best, it was but the prelude to what he heard now. For whole hours he would remain on his knees at mass, lost and wandering in that strange world of infinite variety, the mass music—so various in its phases, yet with a monotone of pathos through it all. The musical parties were also a great pleasure. He played the violin a little in England, and rapidly improved by the excellent tuition he met with here. He became, however, a proficient in what the Italians called the viola d'amore, a treble viol, strung with wire, which attracted him by its soft and sweet tone.

Amid a concord of sweet sounds, within hearing of the splash of fountains, and surrounded by the rich colours of an Italian interior, the young Englishman found himself in a new world of delight. As the very soul of music, at one moment merry and the next mad with passion and delightful pain, uttered itself in the long-continued tremor of the violins, it took possession in all its power of Inglesant's spirit. The whole of life is recited upon the plaintive strings, and by their mysterious effect upon the brain fibres, men are brought into sympathy with life in all its forms, from the gay promise of its morning sunrise to the silence of its gloomy night.

From Genoa he went to Sienna, where he stayed some time —the dialect here being held to be very pure, and fit for foreigners to accustom themselves to. He spoke Italian before with sufficient ease, and associating with several of the religious in this city he soon acquired the language perfectly. There can be nothing more delightful than the first few days of life in Italy in the company of polished and congenial men. Inglesant enjoyed life at Sienna very much; the beautiful clean town, all marble and polished brick, the shining walls and pavement softened and shaded by gardens and creeping vines, the piazza and fountains, the cool retired walks with distant prospects, the Duomo, within and without of polished marble inexpressibly beautiful, with its exceeding sweet music and well-tuned organs, the libraries full of objects of the greatest interest, the statues and antiquities everywhere interspersed.

The summer and winter passed over, and he was still in Sienna, and seemed loath to leave. He associated mostly with the ecclesiastics to whom he had brought letters of introduction, for he was more anxious at first to become acquainted with the country and its treasures of art and literature than to make many acquaintances. He kept himself so close and studious that he met with no adventures such as most travellers, especially those who abandon themselves to the dissolute courses of the country, meet with,—courses which were said at that time to be able to make a devil out of a saint. He saw nothing of the religious system but what was excellent and delightful, seeing everything through the medium of his friends. He read all the Italian literature that was considered necessary for a gentleman to be acquainted with; and though the learning of the Fathers was not what it had been a century ago, he still found several to whom he could talk of his favourite Lucretius and of the divine lessons of Plato.

When he had spent some time in this way in Italy, and considered himself fitted to associate with the inhabitants generally, the Benedictines took Inglesant to visit the family of Cardinal Chigi, who was afterwards Pope, and who was a native of Sienna. The Cardinal himself was in Rome, but his brother, Don Mario, received Inglesant politely, and introduced him to his son, Don Flavio, and to two of his nephews. With one of these, Don Agostino di Chigi, Inglesant became very intimate, and spent much of his time at his house. In this family he learnt much of the state of parties in Rome, and was advised in what way to comport himself when he should come there. The Cardinal Panzirollo, who with the Cardinal-Patron (Pamphilio) had lately been in great esteem, had just died, having weakened his health by his continued application to business, and the Pope had appointed Cardinal Chigi his successor as first Secretary of State. The Pope's sister-in-law, Donna Olympia Maldachini, was supposed to be banished, but many thought this was only a political retreat, and that she still directed the affairs of the Papacy. At any rate she soon returned to Rome and to power. This extraordinary woman, whose loves and intrigues were enacted on the stage in Protestant countries, was the sister-in-law of the Pope, and was said to live with him in criminal correspondence, and to have charmed him by some secret incantation—the incantation of a strong woman over a weak and criminal man. For a long time she had abused her authority in the most scandalous manner, and exerted her unbounded ascendency over the Pope to gratify her avarice and ambition, which were as unbounded as her power. She disposed of all benefices, which she kept vacant till she was fully informed of their value; she exacted a third of the entire value of all offices, receiving twelve years' value for an office for life. She gave audience upon public affairs, enacted new laws, abrogated those of former Popes, and sat in council with the Pope with bundles of memorials in her hands. Severe satires were daily pasted on the statue of Pasquin at Rome; yet it seemed so incredible that Cardinal Panzirollo, backed though he was by the Cardinal-Nephew, should be able to overthrow the power of this woman by a representation he was said to have made to the Pope, that when Innocent at length with great reluctance banished

Olympia, most persons supposed it was only a temporary piece of policy.

The Chigi were at this time living in Sienna, in great simplicity, at their house in the Strada Romana, and in one or two small villas in the neighbourhood; but they were of an ancient and noble family of this place, and were held in great esteem, and were all of them men of refinement and carefully educated. They had made considerable figure in Rome during the Pontificate of Julius II.; but afterwards meeting with misfortunes, were obliged to return to Sienna, where they had continued to reside ever since. At this time there was no idea that the Cardinal of this house would be the next Pope, and though well acquainted with the politics of Rome, the family occupied themselves mostly with other and more innocent amusements—in the arrangement of their gardens and estates, in the duties of hospitality, and in artistic, literary, and antiquarian pursuits. The University and College of Sienna had produced many excellent scholars and several Popes, and the city itself was full of remains of antique art, and was adorned with many modern works of great beauty—the productions of that school which takes its name from the town. Among such scenes as these, and with such companions, Inglesant's time passed so pleasantly that he was in no hurry to go on to Rome.

The country about the city was celebrated for hunting, and the wild boar and the stag afforded excellent and exciting, if sometimes dangerous sport. Amid the beautiful valleys, rich with vineyards, and overlooked by rocky hills and castled summits, were scenes fitted both for pleasure and sport; and the hunting gave place, often and in a moment, to *al fresco* banquets, and conversations and pleasant dalliance with the ladies, by the cool shade near some fountain, or under some over-arching rock. Under the influence of these occupations, so various and so attractive both to the mind and body, and thanks to so many novel objects and continual change of scene, Inglesant's health rapidly improved, and his mind recovered much of the calm and cheerfulness which were natural to it. He thought little of the Italian, and the terrible thoughts with which he had connected him were for the time almost forgotten, though, from time to time, when any accident recalled the circumstances to his recollection, they returned upon his spirits with a melancholy effect.

The first time that these gloomy thoughts overpowered him since his arrival at Sienna was on the following occasion. He had been hunting with a party of friends in the valley of Montalcino one day in early autumn. The weather previously had been wet, and the rising sun had drawn upward masses of white vapour, which wreathed the green foliage and the vine slopes, where the vintage was going on, and concealed from sight the hills on every side. A pale golden light pervaded every place, and gave mystery and beauty to the meanest cottages and farm-sheds. The party, having missed the stag, stopped at a small osteria at the foot of a sloping hill, and Inglesant and another gentleman wandered up into the vineyard that sloped upwards behind the house. As they went up, the vines became gradually visible out of the silvery mist, and figures of peasant men and women moved about—vague and half-hidden until they were close to them, pigeons and doves flew in and out. Inglesant's friend stopped to speak to some of the peasant girls, but Inglesant himself, tempted by the pleasing mystery that the mountain slope—apparently full of hidden and beautiful life—presented, wandered on, gradually climbing higher and higher, till he had left the vintage far below him, and heard no sound but that of the grasshoppers among the grass and the olive trees, and the distant laugh of the villagers, or now and then the music of a hunting horn which one of the party below was blowing for his own amusement. The mist was now so thick that he could see nothing, and it was by chance that he even kept the ascending path. The hill was rocky here and there, but for the most part was covered with short grass, cropped by the goats which Inglesant startled as he came unexpectedly upon them in the mist. Suddenly, after some quarter of an hour's climbing, he came out of the mist in a moment, and stood under a perfectly clear sky upon the summit of the hill. The blue vault stretched above him without a cloud, all alight with the morning sun; at his feet the grassy hill-top sparkling in dew, not yet dried up, and vocal with grasshoppers, not yet silenced by the heat. The hill-top rose like an island out of a sea of vapour, seething and rolling round in misty waves, and lighted with prismatic colours of every hue. Out of this sea, here and there, other hill-tops, on which goats were browsing, lay beneath the serene heaven; and rocky points and summits, far higher than these, reflected back the sun. He would have seemed to stand above all human conversation and walks of men if every now and then some break in the mist had not taken place, opening glimpses of landscapes and villages far below; and also the sound of bells, and the music of the horn, came up fitfully through the mist. Why, he did not know, but as he gazed on this, the most wonderful and beautiful sight he had ever seen, the recollection of Serenus de Cressy returned upon his mind with intense vividness; and the contrast between the life he was leading in Italy, amid every delight of mind and sense, and the life the Benedictine had offered him in vain, smote upon his conscience with terrible force. Upon the lonely mountain top, beneath the serene silence, he threw himself upon the turf, and, overwhelmed with a sudden passion, repented that he had been born. Amid the extraordinary loveliness, the most gloomy thoughts took possession of him, and the fiend seemed to stand upon the smiling mount and claim him for himself. So palpably did the consciousness of his choice, worldly as he thought it, cause the presence of evil to appear, that in that heavenly solitude he looked round for the murderer of his brother. The moment appeared to him, for the instant, to be the one appointed for the consummation of his guilt. The horn below sounding the recall drew his mind out of this terrible reverie, and he came down the hill, from which the mist was gradually clearing, as in a dream. He rejoined his company, who remarked the wild expression of his face.

His old disease, in fact, never entirely left him; he walked often as in a dream, and when the fit was upon him could never discern the real and the unreal. He knew that terrible feeling when the world and all its objects are slipping away, when the brain reels, and seems only to be kept fixed and steady by a violent exertion of the will; and the mind is confused and perplexed with thoughts which it cannot grasp, and is full of fancies of vague duties and acts which it cannot perform, though it is convinced that they are all important to be done.

The Chigi family knew of Inglesant's past life, and of his acquaintance with the Archbishop of Fermo, the Pope's Nuncio, and they advised him to make the acquaintance of his brother, the Cardinal Rinuccini, before going to Rome.

"If you go to Rome in his train, or have him for a patron on your arrival, you will start in a much better position than if you enter the city an entire stranger,—and the present is not a very favourable time for going to Rome. The Pope is not expected to live very long. Donna Olympia and the Pamphili, or pretended Pamphili (for the Cardinal-Nephew is not a Pamphili at all), are securing what they can, using every moment to enrich themselves while they have the power. The moment the Pope dies they fall, and with them all who have been connected with them It is therefore useless to go to Rome at present, except as a private person to see the city, and this you can do better in the suite of the Cardinal than in any other way. You may wonder that we do not offer to introduce you to our uncle the Cardinal Chigi; but we had rather that you should come to Rome at first under the patronage of another. You will understand more of our reasons before long; meanwhile, we will write to our uncle respecting you, and you may be sure that he will promote your interests as much as is in his power."

The Cardinal Rinuccini was at that time believed to be at his own villa, situated in a village some distance from Florence to the north, and Don Agostino offered to accompany Inglesant so far on his journey.

This ride, though a short one, was very pleasant, and endeared the two men to each other more than ever. They travelled simply, with a very small train, and did not hurry themselves on the route. Indeed, they travelled so leisurely that they were very nearly being too late for their purpose. On their arrival at the last stage before reaching Florence, they stopped for the night at a small osteria, and had no sooner taken up their quarters than a large train arrived at the inn, and on their inquiry they were informed it was the Cardinal Rinuccini himself on his way to Rome. They immediately sent their names to his Eminence, saying they had been coming to pay their respects to him, and offering to resign their apartment, which was the best in the house. The Cardinal, who travelled in great state, with his four-post bed and furniture of all kinds with him, returned a message that he could not disturb them in their room; that he remembered Mr. Inglesant's name in some letters from his brother; and that he should be honoured by their company to supper.

The best that the village could afford was placed on the Cardinal's table, and their host entertained the two young men with great courtesy.

He was descended from a noble family in Florence, which boasted among its members Octavio Rinuccini the poet, who came to Paris in the suite of Marie de Medicis, and is said by some to have been the inventor of the Opera. Besides the Pope's Legate another brother of the Cardinal's, Thomas Battista Rinuccini, was Great Chamberlain to the Grand Duke of Tuscany. All the brothers had been carefully educated, and were men of literary tastes; but while the Archbishop had devoted himself mostly to politics, the Cardinal had confined himself almost entirely to literary pursuits. He owed his Cardinal's hat to the Grand Duke, who was extremely partial to him and promoted his interests in every way. He was a man of profound learning, and an enthusiastic admirer of antiquity, but was also an acute logician and theologian, and perfectly well read in Church history, and in the controversy of the century, both in theology and philosophy. Before the end of supper Inglesant found that he was acquainted with the writings of Hobbes, whom he had met in Italy, and of whom he inquired with interest, as soon as he found Inglesant had been acquainted with him.

The following morning the Cardinal expressed his sorrow that the business which took him to Rome was of so important a nature that it obliged him to proceed without delay. He approved of the advice that Inglesant had already received, and recommended him to proceed to Florence, with Don Agostino, as he was so near; so that he might not have his journey for nothing, and might see the city under very favourable circumstances. Inglesant was the more ready to agree to this as he wished to see as much of Italy as he could, unshackled by the company of the great, which, in the uncertain state of health both of his body and mind, was inexpressibly burdensome to him. He had already seen in this last journey a great deal of the distress and bad government which prevailed everywhere; and he wished to make himself acquainted, in some measure, with the causes of this distress before going to Rome. As he rode through the beautiful plains he had been astonished at the few inhabitants, and at the wretchedness of the few. Italy had suffered greatly in her commerce by the introduction of Indian silks into Europe. Some of her most flourishing cities had been depopulated, their nobles ruined; and long streets of neglected palaces, deserted and left in magnificent decay, presented a melancholy though romantic spectacle. But bad government, and the oppression and waste caused by the accumulated wealth and idleness of the innumerable religious orders, had more to do in ruining the prosperity of the country than any commercial changes; and proofs of this fact met the traveller's eye on every hand.

It seemed to Inglesant that it was very necessary that he should satisfy himself upon some of these points before becoming involved in any political action in the country; and he shrank from entering Rome at present, and from attaching himself to any great man or any party. In a country where the least false step is fatal, and may plunge a man in irretrievable ruin, or consign him to the dungeons of the Holy Office, it is certainly prudent in a stranger to be wary of his first steps. Having communicated these resolutions to his friend, the two young men, on their arrival at Florence, took lodgings privately in the Piazza del Santo Spirito; and occupied their time for some days in viewing the city, and visiting the churches and museums, as though they had been simply travellers from curiosity.

Inglesant believed the Italian to be in Rome, which was a farther reason for delaying his journey there. He believed that he was going to engage in some terrible conflict, and he wished to prepare himself by an acquaintance with every form of life in this strange country. The singular scenes that strike a stranger in Italy—the religious processions, the character and habits of the poorer classes, their ideas of moral obligation, their ecclesiastical and legal government—all appeared to him of importance to his future fate.

As he was perfectly unacquainted with the person of his enemy, there was a sort of vague expectation—not to say dread—always present to his mind; for, though he fancied that it would be in Rome that he should find the Italian, yet it was not at all impossible that at any moment—it might be in Florence, or in the open country—he might be the object of a murderous attack. His person was doubtless known to the murderer of his brother, and he thus walked everywhere in the full light, while his enemy was hidden in the dark.

These ideas were seldom absent from his mind, and the image of the murderer was almost constantly before his eyes. Often, as some marked figure crossed his path, he started and watched the retreating form, wondering whether the object of his morbid dread was before him. Often, as the uncovered corpse was borne along the streets, the thought struck him that perhaps his fear and his search were alike needless, and that before him on the bier, harmless and strewn with flowers, lay his terrible foe. These thoughts naturally prevented his engaging unrestrainedly in the pursuits of his age and rank, and he often let Don Agostino go alone into the gay society which was open to them in Florence.

In pursuit of his intention Inglesant took every opportunity, without incurring remark, of associating with the lower orders, and learning their habits, traditions, and tone of thought. He chose streets which led through the poorer parts of the town in passing from one part to another, and in this way, and in the course of his visits to different churches and religious houses, he was able to converse with the common people without attracting attention. In excursions into the country, whether on parties of pleasure or for sport, he was also able to throw himself in the same way among the peasantry. Under the pretence of shooting quails he passed several days in more than one country village, and had become acquainted with several of the curés, from whom he gained much information respecting the habits of the people, and of their ideas of crime and of lawful revenge.

One of these curés—a man of penetration and intellect—strongly advised him to see Venice before he went to Rome.

"Venice," he said to him, "is the sink of all wickedness, and as such it is desirable that you should see the people there, and mix with them; besides, as such, it is not at all unlikely that the man you seek may be found there."

"What is the cause of this wickedness?" asked Inglesant.

"There are several causes," replied the priest. "One is that the Holy Office there is under the control of the State, and is therefore almost powerless. Wickedness and license of all kinds are therefore unrestrained."

Inglesant mentioned this advice to Don Agostino, and his desire to proceed to Venice; but as the other was unwilling to leave Florence till the termination of the Carnival, which was now approaching, he was obliged to postpone his intention for some weeks.

On one of the opening days of the Carnival, Inglesant had accompanied Don Agostino to a magnificent supper given by the

Grand Duke at his villa and gardens at the Poggio Imperiale some distance outside the Romana gate.

Inglesant had succeeded in throwing off for a time his gloomy thoughts, and had taken his share in the gaiety of the festival; but the effort and the excitement had produced a reaction, and towards morning he had succeeded in detaching himself from the company, many of whom—the banquet being over—were strolling in the lovely gardens in the cool air which preceded the dawn, and he returned alone to the city. As this was his frequent custom, his absence did not surprise Don Agostino, who scarcely noticed his friend's eccentricities.

When Inglesant reached Florence, the sun had scarcely risen, and in the miraculously clear and solemn light the countless pinnacles and marble fronts of the wonderful city rose with sharp colour and outline into the sky. It lay with the country round it studded with the lines of cypress and encompassed by the massy hills—silent as the grave, and lovely as paradise; and ever and anon, as it lay in the morning light, a breeze from the mountains passed over it, rustling against the marble façades and through the belfries of its towers, like the whisper of a God. Now and again, clear and sharp in the liquid air, the musical bells of the Campanile rang out the time. The cool expanse of the gardens, the country walk, the pure air, and the silent city, seemed to him to chide and reprove the license and gaiety of the night. Excited by the events of the Carnival, his mind and imagination were in that state in which, from the inward fancy, phantoms are projected upon the real stage of life, and, playing their fantastic parts, react upon the excited sense, producing conduct which in turn is real in its result.

As Inglesant entered the city and turned into one of the narrow streets leading up from the Arno, the market people were already entering by the gates, and thronging up with their wares to the Piazze and the markets. Carpenters were already at work on the scaffolds and other preparations for the concluding festivals of the Carnival; but all these people, and all their actions, and even the sounds that they produced, wore that unreal and unsubstantial aspect which the very early morning light casts upon everything.

As Inglesant ascended the narrow street, between the white stone houses which set off the brilliant blue above, several porters and countrywomen, carrying huge baskets and heaps of country produce, ascended with him, or passed him as he loitered along, and other more idle and equivocal persons, who were just awake, looked out upon him from doorways and corners as he passed. He had on a gala dress of silk, somewhat disordered by the night and by his walk, and must have appeared a suitable object for the lawless attempts of the ladroni of a great city; but his appearance was probably not sufficiently helpless to encourage attack.

Half-way up the street, at the corner of a house, stood an image of the Virgin, round which the villagers stopped for a moment, as much to rest as to pay their devotions. As Inglesant stopped also, he noticed an old man of a wretched and abject demeanour, leaning against the wall of the house, as though scarcely able to stand, and looking eagerly at some of the provisions which were carried past him. True to his custom, Inglesant—when he had given him some small coin as an alms—began to speak to him.

"You have carried many such loads as these, father, I doubt not, in your time, though it must be a light one now."

"I am past carrying even myself," said the other, in a weak and whining voice; "but I have not carried loads all my life. I have kept a shop on the Goldsmith's Bridge, and have lived at my ease. Now I have nothing left me but the sun—the sun and the cool shade."

"Yours is a hard fate."

"It is a hard and miserable world, and yet I love it. It has done me nothing but evil, and yet I watch it and seek out what it does, and listen to what goes on, just as if I thought to hear of any good fortune likely to come to me. Foolish old man that I am! What is it to me what people say or do, or who dies, or who is married? and why should I come out here to see the market people pass, and climb this street to hear of the murder that was done here last night, and look at the body that lies in the room above?"

"What murder?" said Inglesant. "Who was murdered, and by whom?"

"He is a foreigner; they say an Inglese—a traveller here merely. Who murdered him I know not, though they do say that too."

"Where is the body?" said Inglesant. "Let us go up." And he gave the old man another small coin.

The old man looked at him for a moment with a peculiar expression.

"Better not, Signore," he said, "better go home."

"Do not fear for me," said Inglesant; "I bear a charmed life; no steel can touch me, nor any bullet hurt me, till my hour comes; and my hour is not yet."

The old man led the way to an open door, carved with tracery and foliaged work, and they ascended a flight of stairs. It was one of those houses, so common in Italian towns, whose plain and massive exterior, pierced with few and narrow windows, gives no idea of the size and splendour of the rooms within. When they reached the top of the stairs, Inglesant saw that the house had once, and probably not long before, been the residence of some person of wealth. They passed through several rooms with carved chimney-pieces and cornices, and here and there even some massive piece of furniture still remained. From the windows that opened on the inner side Inglesant could see the tall cypresses of a garden, and hear the splash of fountains. But the house had fallen from its high estate, and was now evidently used for the vilest purposes. After passing two or three rooms, they reached an upper hall or dining-room of considerable length, and painted in fresco apparently of some merit. A row of windows on the left opened on the garden, from which the sound of voices and laughter came up.

The room was bare of furniture, except towards the upper end, where was a small and shattered table, upon which the body of the murdered man was laid. Inglesant went up and stood by its side.

There was no doubt whose countryman he had been. The fair English boy, scarcely bordering upon manhood—the heir, probably, of bright hopes—travelling with a careless or incompetent tutor, lay upon the small table, his long hair glistening in the sunlight, his face peaceful and smiling as in sleep. The fatal rapier thrust, marked by the stain upon the clothes, was the sole sign that his mother—waking up probably at that moment in distant England, with his image in her heart—was bereaved for ever of her boy. Inglesant stood silent a few moments, looking sadly down; that other terrible figure, upon the white hearthstone, was so constantly in his mind, that this one, so like it, scarcely could be said to recall the image of his murdered brother; but the whole scene certainly strengthened his morbid fancy, and it seemed to him that he was on the footsteps of the murderer, and that his fate was drawing near.

"His steps are still in blood," he said aloud; "and it is warm; he cannot be far off."

He turned, as he spoke, to look for the old man, but he was gone, and in his place a ghastly figure met Inglesant's glance.

Standing about three feet from the table, a little behind Inglesant, and also looking fixedly at the murdered boy, was the figure of a corpse. The face was thin and fearfully white, and the whole figure was wrapped and swathed in grave-clothes, somewhat disordered and loosened, so as to give play to the limbs. This form took no notice of the other's presence, but continued to gaze at the body with its pallid ghastly face.

Inglesant scarcely started. Nothing could seem more strange and unreal to him than what was passing on every side. That the dead should return and stand by him seemed to him not more fearful and unreal than all the rest.

Suddenly the corpse turned its eyes upon Inglesant, and regarded him with a fixed and piercing glance.

"You spoke of the author of this deed as though you knew him," it said.

"I am on the track of a murderer, and my fate is urging me on. It seems to me that I see his bloody steps."

"This was no murder," said the corpse, in an irritated and impatient voice. "It was a chance melée, and an unfortunate and unhappy thrust; we do not even know the name of the man who lies there. Are you the avenger of blood, that you see murder at every step?"

"I am in truth the avenger of blood," said Inglesant in a low and melancholy voice; "would I were not."

The corpse continued to look at Inglesant fixedly, and would have spoken, but the voices which had been heard in the garden now seemed to come nearer, and hurried steps approached the room. The laughter that Inglesant had heard was stilled, and deep and solemn voices strove together, and one above the rest said, "Bring up the murderer."

The corpse turned round impatiently, and the next moment from a small door, which opened on a covered balcony and outside staircase to the garden, there came hurriedly in a troop of the most strange and fantastic figures that the eye could rest upon. Angels and demons, and savage men in lions' skins, and men with the heads of beasts and birds, swarmed tumultuously in, dragging with them an unfortunate being in his night-clothes, and apparently just out of bed, whom they urged on with blows. This man, who was only half-awake, was evidently in the extremity of terror, and looked upon himself as already in the place of eternal torment. He addressed now one and now another of his tormentors, as well as he could find breath, in the most abject terms, endeavouring, in the most ludicrous manner, to choose the titles and epithets to address them most in accordance with the individual appearance that the spectre he entreated wore to his dazzled eyes—whether a demon or an angel, a savage or a man-beast. When he saw the murdered man, and the terrible figure that stood by Inglesant, he nearly fainted with terror; but, on many voices demanding loudly that he should be brought in contact with the body of his victim, he recovered a little, and recognizing in Inglesant, at least, a being of an earthly sphere, and by his dress a man of rank, he burst from his tormentors, and throwing himself at his feet, he entreated his protection, assuring him that he had been guilty of no murder, having just been dragged from a sound sleep, and being even ignorant that a murder had been committed.

Inglesant took little notice of him, but the corpse interposed between the man and the fantastic crew. It was still apparently in a very bad humour, especially with Inglesant, and said imperiously,—"We have enough and too much of this foolery. Have not some of you done enough mischief for one night? This gentleman says he is on the track of a murderer, and will have it that he sees his traces in this unfortunate affair."

At these words the masquers crowded round Inglesant with wild and threatening gestures, apparently half earnest and half the result of wine, and as many of them were armed with great clubs, the consequences might have seemed doubtful to one whose feelings were less excited than Inglesant's were.

He, however, as though the proceeding were a matter of course, merely took off his hat, and addressed the others in explanation.

"I am indeed in pursuit of a murderer, the murderer of my brother—a gallant and noble gentleman, who was slain foully in cold blood. The murderer was an Italian, his name Malvolti. Do any of you, signori, happen to have heard of such a man?"

There was a pause after this singular address, but the next moment a demon of terrific aspect forced his way to the front, saying in a tone of drunken consequence,—

"I knew him formerly at Lucca; he was well born and my friend."

"He was, and is, a scelerat and a coward," said Inglesant fiercely. "It would be well to be more careful of your company, sir."

"Have I not said he was my friend, sir?" cried the demon, furious with passion. "Who will lend me a rapier?"

A silent and melancholy person, with the head of an owl, who had several under his arm, immediately tendered him one with a low bow, and the masquers fell back in a circle, while the demon, drawing his weapon, threw himself into an attitude and attacked Inglesant, who, after looking at him for a moment, also drew his rapier and stood upon his guard. It soon appeared that the demon was a very moderate fencer; in less than a minute his guard was entered by Inglesant's irresistible tierce, and he would have been infallibly run through the body had he not saved himself by rolling ignominiously on the ground.

This incident appeared to restore the corpse to good humour; it laughed, and turning to the masquers said,—

"Gentlemen, let me beg of you to disperse as quickly as possible before the day is any farther advanced. . You know of the rendezvous at one o'clock. I will see the authorities as to this unhappy affair. Sir," he continued, turning to Inglesant, "you are, I believe, the friend of Don Agostino di Chigi, whom he has been introducing into Florentine society; if it will amuse you to see a frolic of the Carnival carried out, of which this is only the somewhat unfortunate rehearsal, and will meet me this afternoon at two o'clock, at the Great Church in the Via Larga, I shall be happy to do my best to entertain you; a simple domino will suffice. I am the Count Capece."

Inglesant gave his name in return. He apologized for not accepting the Count's courtesy, on the plea of ill-health, but assured him he would take advantage of his offer to cultivate his acquaintance. They left the house together, the Count covering himself with a cloak, and Inglesant accompanied him to the office of police, from whence he went to his lodging and to his bed.

He arose early in the afternoon, and remembering the

invitation he had received, he went out into the Via Larga. The streets formed a strange contrast to the stillness and calm of the cool morning. The afternoon was hot, and the city crowded with people of every class and rank. The balconies and windows of the principal streets were full of ladies and children; trophies and embroideries hung from the houses and crossed the street. Strings of carriages and country carts, dressed with flowers and branches of trees, paraded the streets. Every variety of fantastic and grotesque costume, and every shade of colour, filled and confused the eye. Music, laughter, and loud talking filled the ear. Inglesant, from his simple costume and grave demeanour, became the butt of several noisy parties; but used as he was to great crowds, and to the confused revelries of Courts, he was able to disentangle himself with mutual good-humour. He recognized his friends of the morning, who were performing a kind of comedy on a country cart, arched with boughs, in imitation of the oldest form of the itinerant theatre. He was recognized by them also, for, in a pause of the performance, as he was moving down a bye-street, he was accosted by one of the company, enveloped in a large cloak. He had no difficulty in recognizing beneath this concealment his antagonist of the morning, who still supported his character of demon.

"I offer you my apologies for the occurrences of this morning, signore," he said, "having been informed by my friends more closely concerning them than I can myself recollect. I am also deeply interested in the person of whom you spoke, who formerly was a friend of mine; and I must also have been acquainted with the signore, your brother, of which I am the more certain as your appearance every moment recalls him more and more to my mind. I should esteem it a great favour to be allowed to speak at large with you on these matters. If you will allow me to pay my respects at your lodgings, I will conduct you to my father's house, il Conte Pericon di Visalvo, where I can show you many things which may be of interest to you respecting the man whom I understand you seek."

Inglesant replied that he should gladly avail himself of his society, and offered to come to the Count's house early the next day.

He found the house, a sombre plain one, in a quiet street, with a tall front pierced with few windows. At the low door hung a wine-flask, as a sign that wine was sold within; for the sale of wine by retail was confined to the gentry, the common people being only allowed to sell wholesale. The Count was the fortunate possessor of a very fine vineyard, which made his wine much in request, and Inglesant found the whole ground-floor of his house devoted to this retail traffic. Having inquired for the Count, he was led up the staircase into a vestibule, and from thence into the Count's own room. This was a large apartment with windows looking on to the court, with a suite of rooms opening beyond it. It was handsomely furnished, with several cages full of singing birds in the windows. Outside, the walls of the houses forming the courtyard were covered with vines and creeping jessamine and other plants, and a fountain splashed in the centre of the court, which was covered with a coloured awning.

The old Count received Inglesant politely. He was a tall, spare old man, with a reserved and dignified manner, more like that of a Spaniard than of an Italian. Rather to Inglesant's surprise he introduced him to his daughter, on whom, as she sat near one of the windows, Inglesant's eyes had been fixed from the moment he had entered the room. The Italians were so careful of the ladies of their families, and it was so unusual to allow strangers to see them, that his surprise was not unnatural, especially as the young lady before him was remarkably beautiful. She was apparently very young, tall and dark-eyed, with a haughty and indifferent manner, which concentrated itself entirely upon her father.

The Count noticed Inglesant's surprise at the cordiality of his reception, and seemed to speak as if in explanation.

"You are no stranger to us, signore," he said; "my son has not only commended you to me, but your intimacy with Count Agostino has endeared you already to us who admire and love him."

As Agostino had told him the evening before that he knew little of these people, though he believed the old Count to be respectable, this rather increased Inglesant's surprise; but he merely said that he was fortunate in possessing a friend whose favour procured him such advantages.

"My son's affairs," continued the old man, "unavoidably took him abroad this morning, but I wait his return every moment."

Inglesant suspected that the Cavaliere, who appeared to him to be a complete debauchée, had not been at home at all that night; but if that were the case, when he entered the room a few moments afterwards, his manner was completely self-possessed and quiet, and showed no signs of a night of revelry.

As soon as they were seated the Cavaliere began to explain to Inglesant that both his father and himself were anxious to see him, to confer respecting the unfortunate circumstances which, as they imagined, had brought him to Italy upon a mission which they assured him was madly imprudent.

"Our nation, signore," said the Cavaliere, "is notorious for two passions—jealousy and revenge. Both of these, combined with self-interest, induced Malvolti to commit the foul deed which he perpetrated upon your brother. While in Italy your brother crossed him in some of his amours, and also resented some indiscretions, which the manners of our nation regard with tolerance, but which your discreeter countrymen resent with unappeasable disgust. Our people never forgive injuries; nay, they entail them on their posterity. We ourselves left our native city, Lucca, on account of one of these feuds, which made it unsafe for us to remain; and I could show you a gentleman's house in Lucca whose master has never set foot out of doors for nine years, nay, scarcely looked out of window, for fear of being shot by an antagonist who has several times planted ambushes to take away his life. It is considered a disgrace to a family that one of its members has forgiven an injury; and a mother will keep the bloody clothes of her murdered husband, to incite her young sons to acts of vengeance. You will see, signore, the evil which such ideas as these wind about our lives; and how unwise it must be in a stranger to involve himself needlessly in such an intrigue, in a foreign country, unknown and comparatively without friends. Italy swarms with bravoes hired to do the work of vengeance; merchants are assaulted in their warehouses in open day; in the public streets the highest personages in the land are not safe. What will be the fate then of a stranger whose death is necessary to the safety of an Italian?"

"I understand you, signore," said Inglesant, "and I thank you for your good-will, but you are somewhat mistaken. I am not seeking the man of whom we speak, though, I confess, I came to Italy partly with the expectation of meeting him, when it is the will of God, or the will of the Devil, whom He permits to influence the affairs of men, that this man and I should meet. I shall not attempt to avoid the interview; it would be useless if I did. The result of that meeting who can tell! But as I said yesterday to the Count Capece, till my hour comes I bear a charmed life that cannot be taken, and any result I regard with supreme indifference, if so be I may, by any means, escape in the end the snares of the Devil, who seeks to take me captive at his will."

The two gentlemen regarded Inglesant with profound astonishment as he uttered these words; and the young lady in the window raised her eyes towards him as he was speaking (he spoke very pure Italian) with some appearance of interest.

After a pause Inglesant went on, "I also venture to think, signore," he said, "that you are unaware of the position of this man, and of the condition to which his crimes have brought him. I am well informed from sure sources that he is without friends, and that his crimes have raised him more enemies in this country even than elsewhere; so that he is afraid to appear openly, lest he fall a victim to his own countrymen. He is also in abject poverty, and is therefore to a great extent powerless to do evil."

The Cavaliere smiled. "You do not altogether know this country, signore," he said; "there are always so many different factions and interests at work that a daring useful man is never without patrons, who will support and further his private interests in return for the service he may render them; and (though you may not be fully aware of it) it is because it is notorious that you are yourself supported and protected by a most powerful and widely spread faction, that your position in this country is as assured and safe as it is."

His words certainly struck Inglesant. The idea that he was already a known and marked man in this wonderful country, and playing an acknowledged part in its fantastic drama, was new to him, and he remained silent.

"From all ordinary antagonists," continued the Cavaliere, "this knowledge is sufficient to secure you; no man would wish, unless ruined and desperate, to draw on his head the swift and certain punishment which a hand raised against your life would be sure to invoke. But a reckless despairing man stops at nothing; and should you, by your presence even, endanger this man's standing in the favour of some new-found patron, or impede the success of some freshly planned scheme—perhaps the last hope of his ruined life—I would not buy your safety at an hour's rate."

While the Cavaliere was speaking it was evident that his sister was listening with great attention. The interest that she manifested, and the singular attraction that Inglesant felt towards her, so occupied his thoughts that he could scarcely attend to what the other was saying, though he continued speaking for some time. It is possible that the Cavaliere noticed this, for Inglesant was suddenly conscious that he was regarding him fixedly and with a peculiar expression. He apologized for his inattention on the ground of ill-health, and soon after took his leave, having invited the Cavaliere to visit him at his lodgings.

As Inglesant walked back through the streets of the city, he was perplexed at his own sensations, which appeared so different from any he had previously known. The attraction he experienced towards the lady he had just seen was quite different from the affection he had felt for Mary Collet. That was a sentiment which commended itself to his reason and his highest feelings. In her company he felt himself soothed, elevated above himself, safe from danger and from temptation. In this latter attraction he was conscious of a half-formed fear, of a sense of glamour and peril, and of an alluring force independent of his own free-will. The opinion he had formed of her brother's character may have had something to do with these feelings, and the sense of perpetual danger and insecurity with which he walked this land of mystery and intrigue no doubt increased it. He half resolved not to visit the old nobleman again; but even while forming the resolution he knew that he should break it.

The circumstances in which he was placed, indeed, almost precluded such a course. The very remarkable beauty of the young lady, and the extraordinary unreserve with which he had been introduced to her—unreserve so unusual in Italy—while it might increase the misgiving he felt, made it very difficult for him to decline the acquaintance. The girl's beauty was of a kind unusual in Italy, though not unknown there, her hair being of a light brown, contrasting with her magnificent eyes, which were of the true Italian splendour and brilliancy. She had doubtless been kept in the strictest seclusion, and Inglesant could only wonder what could have induced the old Count to depart from his usual caution.

The next day, being Ash Wednesday, Inglesant was present at the Duomo at the ceremony of the day, when the vast congregation received the emblematic ashes upon their foreheads. The Cavaliere was also present with his sister, whose name Inglesant discovered to be Lauretta. Don Agostino, to whom Inglesant had related the adventure, and the acquaintance to which it had led, was inclined to suspect these people of some evil purpose, and made what inquiries he could concerning them; but he could discover nothing to their discredit, further than that the Cavaliere was a well-known debauchée, and that he had been involved in some intrigue, in connection with some of the present Papal family, which had not proved successful. He was in consequence then in disgrace with Donna Olmypia and her faction,—a disappointment which it was said had rendered his fortunes very desperate, as he was very deeply involved in debts of all kinds. Don Agostino, the Carnival being over, was desirous of returning to Sienna, unless Inglesant made up his mind to go at once to Venice, in which case he offered to accompany him. His friend, however, did not appear at all desirous of quitting Florence, at any rate hastily, and Don Agostino left him and returned home, the two friends agreeing to meet again before proceeding to Venice.

His companion gone, Inglesant employed himself in frequenting all those Churches to which Lauretta was in the habit of resorting during the Holy Season; and as every facility appeared to be given him by her friends, he became very intimate with her, and she on her part testified no disinclination to his society. It will probably occur to the reader that this conduct was not consistent with the cautious demeanour which Inglesant had resolved upon; but such resolutions have before now proved ineffectual under similar circumstances, and doubtless the like will occur again. Lauretta looked round as a matter of course, as she came out of the particular Church she had that day chosen, for the handsome cavalier who was certain to be ready to offer the drop of holy water; and more than one rival whom the beautiful devotee had attracted to the service, noticed with envy the kindly look of the masked eyes which acknowledged the courtesy; and, indeed, it is not often that ladies' eyes have rested upon a lover more attractive to a girl of a refined nature than did Lauretta's when, in the dawn of the March mornings, she saw John Inglesant waiting for her on the marble steps. It is true that she thought the Cavaliere Inglese somewhat melancholy and sad, but her own disposition was reserved and pensive; and in her presence Inglesant's melancholy was so far charmed away that it became only an added grace of sweetness of manner, and of tender deference and protection. The servant of the polished King of England, the companion of Falkland and of Caernarvon, the French Princess's favourite page, trained in every art that makes life attractive, that makes life itself the finest art, with a memory and intellect stored with the poetry and learning of the antique world,—it would have been strange if, where once his fancy was touched, Inglesant had not made a finished and attractive lover.

The familiar streets of Florence, the bridges or the walks by the Arno, assumed a new charm to the young girl, when she saw them in company with her pleasant and courteous friend; and whether in the early morning it was a few spring flowers that he brought her, or a brilliant jewel that he placed upon her finger as he parted in the soft Italian night, it was the giver, and the grace with which the gift was made, that won the romantic fancy of the daughter of the South. Their talk was not of the kind that lovers often use. He would indeed begin with relating stories of the English Court, in the bright fleeting days before the war, of the courtly refined revels, of the stately dances and plays, and of the boating parties on the wooded Thames; but most often the narrative changed its tone instinctively, and went on to speak of sadder and higher things; of self-denial and devotion of ladies and children, who suffered for their King without complaint; of the Ferrars and their holy life; of the martyred Archbishop and of the King's death; and sometimes perhaps of some sight of battle and suffering the narrator himself had seen, as when the evening sun was shining upon the grassy slope of Newbury, and he knelt beside the dying Caernarvon, unmindful of the bullets that fell around.

"You have deserved well of the King," he said; "have you no request that I may make to him, nothing for your children, or your wife?"

And with his eyes fixed upon the western horizon the Earl replied,—

"No, I will go hence with no request upon my lips but to the King of kings."

How all this pleasant dalliance would have terminated, had it continued, we have no means of knowing, for a sudden and unexpected end was put to it, at any rate for a time.

Easter was over, and the Cavaliere had invited Inglesant to join in a small party to spend a day or two at his vineyard and country house among the Apennines, assuring him that at that time of the year the valleys and hill-slopes were very delightful.

The evening before the day on which the little company was to start, Inglesant had an engagement at one of the theatres in Florence, where a comedy or pantomime was being performed. The comedies in Italy at this time were paltry in character in everything except the music, which was very good. Inglesant accompanied a Signore Gabriotto, a violin player, who was engaged at the theatre, and of whom Inglesant had taken lessons, and with whom he had become intimate. This man was not only an admirable performer on the violin, but was a man of cultivation and taste. He had given much study to the music of the ancients, and especially to their musical instruments, as they are to be seen in the hands of the Apollos, muses, fauns, satyrs, bacchanals, and shepherds of the classic sculptors. As they walked through the streets in the evening sunlight, he favoured his companion, whom he greatly admired as an excellent listener, with a long discourse on this subject, showing how useful such an inquiry was, not only to obtain a right notion of the ancient music, but also to help us to obtain pleasanter instruments if possible than those at present in use.

"Not, signore," he said, "that I think we have much to learn from the ancients; for if we are to judge their instruments by the appearance they make in marble, there is not one that is comparable to our violins; for they seem, as far as I can make out, all to have been played on either by the bare fingers or the plectrum, so that they could not add length to their notes, nor could they vary them by that insensible swelling and dying away of sound upon the same string which gives so wonderful a sweetness to our modern music. And as far as I can see, their stringed instruments must have had very low and feeble voices from the small proportion of wood used (though it is difficult to judge of this, seeing that all our examples are represented in marble), which would prevent the instruments containing sufficient air to render the strokes full or sonorous. Now my violin," continued the Italian with enthusiasm, "does not speak only with the strings, it speaks all over, as though it were a living creature that was all voice, or, as is really the case, as though it were full of sound."

"You have a wonderful advantage," said Inglesant, "you Italians, that is, in the cultivation of the art of life; for you have the unbroken tradition, and habit and tone of mind, from the old world of pleasure and art—a world that took the pleasures of life boldly, and had no conscience to prevent its cultivating and enjoying them to the full. But I must say that you have not, to my mind, improved during the lapse of centuries, nor is the comedy we shall see to-night what might be expected of a people who are the descendants of the old Italians who applauded Terence."

"The comedy to-night," said the Italian, "would be nothing without the music, the acting is a mere pretence."

"The comedy itself," said Inglesant, "would be intolerable but for the buffoons, and the people show their sense in demanding that place shall be found in every piece for these worthies. The play itself is stilted and unreal, but there is always something of irony and wit in these characters, which men have found full of satire and humour; for four thousand years: Harlequin the reckless fantastic youth, Pantaleone the poor old worn-out 'Senex,' and Corviello the rogue. In their absurd impertinences, in their impossible combinations, in their mistakes and tumbles, in their falling over queens and running up against monarchs, men have always seemed to see some careless, light-hearted, half-indifferent sarcasm and satire upon their own existence."

When they reached the theatre, the slant rays of the setting sun were shining between the lofty houses, and many people were standing about the doors. Inglesant accompanied the violinist to the door of the play-house, and took his place near the orchestra, at either end of which were steps leading up on to the stage. The evening sunlight penetrated into the house through venetian blinds, lighting up the fittings and the audience with a sort of mystic haze. The sides of the stage were crowded with gentlemen, some standing, others sitting on small stools. Many of the audience were standing, the rest seated on benches. The part occupied in modern theatres by the boxes was furnished with raised seats, on which ladies and people of distinction were accommodated. There was no gallery.

As the first bars of the overture struck upon Inglesant's ear, with a long-drawn tremor of the bass viols and a shrill plaintive note of the treble violins, an irresistible sense of loneliness and desolation and a strange awe crept over him and weighed down his spirits. As the fantastic music continued, in which gaiety and sadness were mysteriously mingled, the reverberation seemed to excite each moment a clearer perception of those paths of intrigue and of danger in which he seemed to walk. The uneasy sentiment which accompanied, he knew not why, his attachment to Lauretta, and the insidious friendship of the Cavaliere, the sense of insecurity which followed his footsteps in this land of dark and sinful deeds, passed before his mind. It seemed to his excited fancy at that moment that the end was drawing very near, and amid the fascination of the lovely music he seemed to await the note of the huntsman's horn which would announce that the toils were set, and that the chase was up. From the kind of trance in which he stood he was aroused by hearing a voice, distinct to his ear and perfectly audible, though apparently at some considerable distance, say,—

"Who is that man by the curtain, in black satin, with the Point de Venice lace?"

And another voice, equally clear, answered, "His name is Inglesant, an agent of the Society of the Gesu."

Inglesant turned; but, amid the crowd of faces behind him, he could discern nothing that indicated the speakers, nor did any one else seem to have noticed anything unusual. The next moment the music ceased, and with a scream of laughter Harlequin bounded on the stage, followed by Pantaleone in an eager and tottering step, and after them a wild rout of figures, of all orders and classes, who flitted across the stage amid the applause of the people, and suddenly disappeared, while Harlequin and Pantaleone as suddenly reappearing, began a lively dialogue, accompanied by a quick movement of the violins. As Inglesant took his eyes off the stage for a moment, they fell on the figure of a man standing on the flight of steps at the farther end of the orchestra, who regarded him with a fixed and scrutinizing gaze. It was a tall and dark man, whose expression would have been concealed from Inglesant but for the fiery brilliancy of his eyes. Inglesant's glance met his as in a dream, and remained fixed as though fascinated, at which the gaze of the other became, if possible, more intense, as though he too were spell-bound and unable to turn away. At this moment the dialogue on the stage ceased, and a girl advanced to the footlights with a song, accompanied by the band in an air adapted from the overture, and containing a repetition of the opening bars. The association of sound broke the spell, and Inglesant turned his eyes upon the singer; when he looked again his strange examiner was gone.

The girl who was singing was a Roman, reputed the best treble singer then in Italy. The sun by this time was set, and the short twilight over. The theatre was sparsely lighted by candles, nearly the whole of the available light being concentrated upon the stage. This arrangement produced striking effects of light and shade, more pleasing than are the brilliantly lighted theatres of modern days. The figures on the stage came forward into full and clear view, and faded again into obscurity in a mysterious way very favourable to romantic illusion, and the theatrical arrangements were not seen too clearly. The house itself was shadowy and the audience unreal and unsubstantial; the whole scene wore an aspect of glamour and romance wanting at the present day.

When the girl's song was over there was a movement among the gentlemen on the stage, several coming down into the house. Inglesant took advantage of this, and went up on the stage, from which he might hope to see something of the stranger who had been watching him so closely, if he were still in the theatre.

Several of the actors who were waiting for their turn mingled with the gentlemen, talking to their acquaintance. The strange light thrown on the centre of the stage in which two or three figures were standing, the multitude of dark forms in the surrounding shadow, the dim recesses of the theatre itself full of figures, the exquisite music, now soft and plaintive, anon gay and dance-like, then solemn and melancholy, formed a singular and attractive whole. Lauretta had declined to come that night, but Inglesant thought it was not improbable that the Cavaliere would be there, and he was curious to see whether he could detect him in company with the mysterious stranger. From the moment that he had heard the distant voice inquiring his name the familiar idea had again occurred to his mind that this could be none other than the murderer of his brother, of whom he was in search; but this thought had occurred so often, and in connection with so many persons, that had it not been for the fixed and peculiar glance with which the stranger had regarded him, he would have thought little of it. He was, however, unable to distinguish either of the persons of whom he was in search from the crowd that filled the theatre; and his attention was so much diverted by the constantly changing scene before him that he soon ceased to attempt to do so. At that moment the opening movement of the overture was again repeated by the band, and was made the theme of an elaborate variation, in which the melancholy idea of the music was rendered in every variety of shade by the plaintive violins. Every phase of sorrow, every form and semblance of grief that Inglesant had ever known, seemed to float through his mind, in sympathy with the sounds which, inarticulate to the ear, possessed a power stronger than that of language to the mental sense. The anticipation of coming evil naturally connected itself with the person of Lauretta, and he seemed to see her lying dead before him upon the lighted stage, or standing in an attitude of grief, looking at him with wistful eyes. This last image was so strongly presented to his imagination that it partook almost of the character of an apparition; and before it the crowded theatre, the gaily dressed forms upon the stage, the fantastic actors, seemed to fade, and alone on the deserted boards the figure of Lauretta, as he had last seen it, slight and girl-like yet of noble bearing, stood gazing at him with wild and apprehensive eyes. Curiously too, as his fancy dwelt upon this figure, it saw in her hand a sealed letter fastened with a peculiarly twisted cord.

The burden of sorrow and of anticipated evil became at last too heavy to be borne, and Inglesant left the theatre and returned to his lodgings. But here he could not rest. Though he had no reason to visit the Count that night, and though it was scarcely seemly, indeed, that he should do so, yet, impelled by a restless discomfort which he sought to quiet, he wandered again into the streets, and found himself not unnaturally before the old nobleman's dwelling. Once here, the impulse was too strong to be denied, and he knocked at the low sunken door. The house seemed strangely quiet and deserted, and it was some time before an old servant who belonged to the lower part of the establishment, devoted to the sale of the wine, appeared at the wicket, and, on being assured whom it was who knocked at that unseasonable hour, opened the door.

The house was empty, he averred. The family had suddenly departed, whither he knew not. If the signore was pleased to go upstairs, he believed he would find some letters for him left by the Cavaliere.

Inglesant followed the old man, who carried a common brass lamp, which cast an uncertain and flickering glare, the sense of evil growing stronger at every step he took. His guide led him into the room in which he had first seen Lauretta, which appeared bare and deserted, but showed no sign of hasty departure. Upon a marble table inlaid with coloured stones were two letters, both directed to Inglesant. The one was from the Cavaliere, excusing their departure on the ground of sudden business of the highest political importance, the other from Lauretta, written in a hasty trembling hand. It contained but a few lines—"that she was obliged to follow her father;" but Inglesant hesitated a moment before he broke the seal, for it was tied round with a curiously twisted cord of blue and yellow silk, as he had seen in the vision his excited fancy had created.

CHAPTER XXII.

LAURETTA's letter had informed Inglesant that she would endeavour to let him know where she was; and with that hope he was obliged to be content, as by no effort he could make could he discover any trace of the fugitives' route. Florence, however, became distasteful to him, and he would have left it sooner but for an attack of fever which prostrated him for some time. Few foreigners were long in Italy, in those days, without suffering from the climate and the miasmas and unhealthy vapours, which, especially at night, were so hurtful even to those accustomed to the country. In his illness Inglesant was carefully nursed by some of the Jesuit fathers, and those whom they recommended; and it is possible that they took care that he should not be left too much to the care of the physicians, whose attentions, at that period at any rate, were so often fatal to their patients. In the course of a few weeks he was sufficiently recovered to think of leaving Florence, and he despatched a messenger to Don Agostino, begging him to meet him at Lucca, where they might decide either to visit Venice or go on straight to Rome. It was not without some lingering hope that he might find Lauretta in the town of her birth, that he set out for Lucca, but misfortune followed his path. It was reported that the plague had broken out in Florence, and travellers who were known to have come from thence were regarded with great suspicion. Inglesant's appearance, recently recovered from sickness, was not in his favour; and at Fucecchio, a small town on the road to Lucca, he was arrested by the authorities, and confined by them in the pest-house for forty days. It was a building which had formerly been a gentleman's house, and possessed a small garden surrounded by a high wall. In this dreary abode Inglesant passed many solitary days, the other inmates being three or four unfortunates like himself,— travellers on business through the country,—who, their affairs being injured by their detention, were melancholy and despondent. He was short of money, and for some time was unable to communicate with any of his friends either in Florence or Sienna. With nothing but his own misfortunes to brood upon, and with the apprehension of the future, which almost amounted to religious melancholy, frequently before his mind, it is surprising that he kept his reason. To add to his misfortunes, when the greater portion of the time fixed for his detention was expired, one of the inmates of the pest-house suddenly died; and although the physicians pronounced his disease not to be the plague, yet the authorities decreed that all should remain another forty days within its dreary walls. The death of this person greatly affected Inglesant, as he was the only one of the inmates with whom he had contracted any intimacy.

During the first part of his sojourn here, there was brought to the house, as an inmate, a wandering minstrel, who, the first evening of his stay, attracted the whole of the gloomy society around him by his playing. He played upon a small and curiously shaped instrument called a vielle, somewhat like a child's toy, with four strings, and a kind of small wheel instead of a bow. It was commonly used by blind men and beggars in the streets, and was considered a contemptible instrument, though some of these itinerant performers attained to such skill upon it that they could make their hearers laugh and dance, and it was said even weep, as they stood around them in the crowded streets. Inglesant soon perceived that the man was no contemptible musician, and after his performance was over he entered into conversation with him, asking him why he, who could play so well, was content with so poor an instrument. The man, who appeared to have a great deal of intelligence and humour, said that he was addicted to a wandering and unsettled life, among the poorer and disorderly classes in the low quarters of cities, in mountain villages, and in remote hostelries and forest inns; that the possession of a valuable viol, or other instrument, even if he should practise sufficient self-denial to enable him to save money to purchase such a one, would be a constant anxiety to him, and a source of danger among the wild companions with whom he often associated. "Besides, signore," he said, "I am attached to this poor little friend of mine, who will speak to me though to none else. I have learnt the secrets of its heart, and by what means it may be made to discourse eloquently of human life. You may despise my instrument, but I can assure you it is far superior to the guitar, though that is so high-bred and genteel a gentleman, found in all romances and ladies' bowers. For any music that depends upon the touch of a string, and is limited in the duration of the distinct sounds, is far inferior to this little fellow's voice."

"You seem trained to the profession of music," said Inglesant.

"I was serving-lad to an old musician in Rome, who not only played on several instruments, but gave a great deal of time to the study of the science of harmony, and of the mysteries of music. He was fond of me, and taught me the viol, as I was apt to learn."

"I have heard of musicians," said Inglesant, "who have written on the philosophy of sound. He was doubtless one of them."

"There are things concerning musical instruments," said the man, "very wonderful; such as the laws concerning the octaves of flutes, which, make them how you will, you can never alter, and which show how the principles of harmony prevail in the dead things of the world, which we think so blockish and stupid; and what is more wonderful still, the passions of men's souls, which are so wild and untamable, are all ruled and kept in a strict measure and mean, for they are all concerned in and wrought upon by music. And what can be more wonderful than that a maestro in the art can take delight in sound, though he does not hear it; and when he looks at some black marks upon paper, he hears intellectually, and by the power of the soul alone?"

"You speak so well of these things," said Inglesant, "that I wonder you are content to wander about the world at village fairs and country weddings, and do not rather establish yourself in some great town, where you might follow your genius and earn a competence and fame."

"I have already told you," replied the man, "that I am wedded to this kind of life; and if you could accompany me for some months, with your viol d'amore, across the mountains, and through the deep valleys, and into the old towns, where no travellers ever come, and where all stands still from century to century, you would never leave it, any more than I shall. I could tell you of many strange sights I have witnessed, and if we stay long in this place, perhaps you will be glad to hear some tales to while away the time."

"You spoke but now," said Inglesant, "of the power that music has over the passions of men. I should like to hear somewhat more of this."

"I will tell you a curious tale of that also," said the man.

THE VIELLE-PLAYER'S STORY.

"Some twenty-five years ago there lived in Rome two friends, who were both musicians, and greatly attached to each other. The elder, whose name was Giacomo Andrea, was maestro di capella of one of the Churches, the other was an accomplished lutinist and singer. The elder was a cavaliere and a man of rank; the younger of respectable parentage, of the name of Vanneo. The style of music in which each was engaged was sufficiently different to allow of much friendly contention; and many lively debates took place as to the respective merits of 'Sonate da Chiesa' and 'Sonate da Camera.' Their respective instruments also afforded ground for friendly dispute. Vanneo was very desirous that his friend should introduce viols and other instruments into the service, in concert with the voices, in the Church in which Vanneo himself sang in the choir; but the Cavaliere, who considered this a practice derived from the theatre, refused to avail himself of any instrument save the organ. Vanneo was more successful in inducing his friend to practise upon his favourite instrument the lute, though Andrea pretended at first to despise it as a ladies' toy, and liable to injure the shape of the performer. His friend, however, though devoted to secular music, brought to the performance and composition of it so much taste and correct feeling, that Andrea was ravished in spite of himself, and of his preference to the solemn music of the Church. Vanneo excelled in contrasting melancholy and pensive music with bright and lively chords, mingling weeping and laughter in some of the sweetest melodies that imagination ever suggested. He accompanied his own voice on the lute, or he composed pieces for a single voice with accompaniment for violins. In a word, he won his friend over to this grave chamber music, in some respects more pathetic and serious than the more monotonous masses and sonatas of the Church composers. Vanneo composed expressly for this purpose fantasies on the chamber organ, interposed, now and then, with stately and sweet dance music, such as Pavins (so named from the walk of a peacock), Almains, and other delightful airs, upon the violins and lute. In these fancies he blended, as it were, pathetic stories, gay festivities, and sublime and subtle ideas, all appealing to the secret and intellectual faculties, so that the music became not only an exponent of life but a divine influence. After these delightful meetings had continued for several years, circumstances obliged Vanneo to accompany a patron to France, and from thence he went over into England, to the great King of that nation, as one of his private musicians; for the Queen of England was a French Princess, and was fond of the lute. His departure was a great grief to the Cavaliere, who devoted himself more than ever to Church music and to the offices of religion. He was a man of very devout temper, and was distinguished for his benevolent disposition, and especially for his compassion for the poor, whom he daily relieved in crowds at his own door, and in the prisons of Rome, which he daily visited. From time to time he heard from his friend, to whom he continued strongly attached."

"I was brought up at the English Court," said Inglesant,

R

"and have been trying to recall such a man, but cannot recollect the name you mention, though I remember several lutinists and Italians."

"I tell the story as I heard it," replied the other. "The man may have changed his name in a foreign country. One day the Cavaliere had received a letter from his friend, brought to him by some English gentleman travelling to Rome. Having read it, and spent some time with the recollections that its perusal suggested to his mind, he set himself to the work in which he was engaged—the composition of a motet for some approaching festival of the Church; but although he attempted to fix his mind upon his occupation, and was very anxious to finish his work, he found himself unable to do so. The remembrance of his friend took complete possession of his mind; and his imagination, instead of dwelling on the solemn music of the motet, wandered perversely into the alluring world of phantasied melody which Vanneo had composed. Those sad and pensive adagios, passing imperceptibly into the light gaiety of a festival, never seemed so delightful as at that moment. He rose from time to time, and walked to and fro in his chamber, and as he did so he involuntarily took up a lute which Vanneo had left with him as a parting gift, and which always lay within reach. As he carelessly touched the strings, something of his friend's spirit seemed to have inspired him, and the lute breathed again with something of the old familiar charm. Each time that he took it up, the notes formed themselves again under his hand into the same melody, and at last he took up a sheet of paper, intended for the motet, and scored down the air he had involuntarily composed. His fancy being pleased with the occurrence, he elaborated it into a lesson, and showed it to several of his associates. He gave it the name of 'gli amici,' and it became very popular among the masters in Rome as a lesson for their pupils on the lute. Among those who thus learnt it was a youth who afterwards became page to a Florentine gentleman, one Bernard Guasconi, who went into England and took service under the King of that country, who, as you doubtless know better than I do, was at war with his people."

"I know the Cavaliere Guasconi," said Inglesant, "and saw him lately in Florence, where he is training running horses for the Grand Duke."

"This war," continued the man, "appears to have been the

ruin of Vanneo; for the English people, besides hating their King, took to hating all kinds of music, and all Churches and choristers. Vanneo lost his place as one of the King's musicians, and not being able to earn his living by teaching music where so few cared to learn, he was forced to enlist as a soldier in one of the King's armies, and was several times near losing his life. He escaped these dangers, however; but the army in which he served being defeated and dispersed, he wandered about the country, wounded, and suffering from sickness and want of food. He supported himself miserably, partly by charity, especially among the loyalist families, and partly by giving singing lessons to such as desired them. He was without friends, or any means of procuring money to enable him to return to Italy. As he was walking in this manner one day in the streets of London, without any hope, and with scarcely any life, he heard the sound of music. It was long since the melody of a lute, once so familiar, had fallen on his ear; and as he stopped to listen, the notes came to him through the thick moist air like an angelic and divine murmur from another world. The music seemed to come from a small room on the ground-floor of a poor inn, and Vanneo opened the door and went in. He found a young man, plainly dressed, playing on a double-necked theorbo-lute, which, from the number of its strings, enables, as you know, the skilful lutinist to play part music, with all the varieties of fugues and other graces and ornaments of the Italian manner. The piece which the young man was playing consisted of an allegro and yet sweet movement on the tenor strings, with a sustained harmony in thorough bass. The melody, being carefully distributed through the parts, spoke to Vanneo of gaiety and cheerfulness, as of his old Italian life, strangely combined at the same time with a soothing and pathetic melancholy, like a corpse carried through the streets of a gay city, strewn with flowers and accompanied with tapers and singing of boys. The whole piece finished with a pastorale, or strain of low and sweet notes. As Vanneo listened he was transported out of himself. It was not alone the beauty of the music which ravished him, but he was conscious that a mysterious presence, as of his friend the Cavaliere, was with him, and that at last the perfect sympathy which he had sought so long was established; and that in the music he had heard a common existence and sphere of life was at last created, in which they both lived, not any longer separate from each other, but enjoying as it were one common being of melody and ecstatic life of sound. When the music ceased Vanneo accosted the lutinist and inquired the name of the composer; but this the young man could not tell him. He only knew it was a favourite lesson for skilful pupils among the music-masters in Rome, and as such he had learnt it. Vanneo was confident the piece had been written by Andrea, and by none other, and told the young man so. By this time they had discovered that they were fellow-countrymen, and the lutinist sent for refreshments, of which Vanneo stood very much in need. He also told him that his name was Scacchi, and that he was page to the Signore Bernard Guasconi, who was then in arms for the King, and was besieged in some town of which I have forgotten the English name."

"It was Colchester," said Inglesant; "I was in prison at the time of the siege; but I know the history of it and its sad ending."

"Becoming very familiar with Vanneo, he advised him to accompany him to Colchester. His master, he said, would doubtless be set at liberty immediately as a foreigner and a friend of the Grand Duke's, and he could accompany him home to Italy as a domestic. As no better prospect was open to Vanneo of returning to his native country, he gladly accepted the page's offer, and agreed to accompany him next day. The besiegers of the town which you call Colchester were engaging persons from all parts of the country to work their trenches, and the town not being far from London, many persons went from that place to earn the wages offered. Many of the Loyalists also took advantage of this pretext, intending to join the besieged if a favourable opportunity offered. To one of these parties Vanneo and the page joined themselves. You may wonder that I know so much of these matters, but I have heard the story several times repeated by the page himself. The weather was very cold and wet, and the companions underwent much hardship on their march. They travelled through a flat and marshy country, full of woods and groves of trees, and crossed with dykes and streams. Vanneo, however, who had endured so much privation and suffering, began to sink under his fatigues. After travelling for more than two days they arrived at the leaguer. They were told that the besieged were expected every day to surrender at discretion; but they were sent into the trenches with several other volunteers to relieve those already there, many of whom were exhausted with the work, and were deserting. As they arrived at the extreme limit of the lines the besiegers had planted four great pieces of battering cannon against the town, and fired great shot all the forenoon, without, however, doing much damage. The Royalists mustered all their troops upon the line, intending, as it afterwards appeared, to break out at night and force their way through the leaguer. The lines were so close that the soldiers could throw stones at each other as they lay in the trenches; and Vanneo and the page could see the King's officers plainly upon the city walls. The Royalists did not fire, being short of ammunition, and in the night a mutiny took place among some of the foot-soldiers, which prevented the project of cutting their way out from taking effect. The soldiers of both armies were now already mixed on many places upon the line, and no fire was given on either side, as though the Royalists were already prisoners. The page left Vanneo, who was worn-out and ill, and easily made his way into the town, where he found his master. When he returned to the trenches he found Vanneo very ill, and a physician with him, a doctor of the town, named Gibson, as I remember, who told the page that he thought his companion was dying. Vanneo, in fact, appeared to be insensible, his eyes were closed, and he was perfectly pale. He lay in a small house, just within the lines, which had been deserted by its inhabitants, who were weavers. The gentlemen were under arrest in the town, and it was reported that several were to be immediately shot, of whom it was whispered the Signore Guasconi was to be one. About two in the afternoon the general of the besieging army entered the town, and a great rabble of the soldiers with him. The latter broke into many houses to search for plunder, and among them into that in which Vanneo was lying. As they came into the room and saw the dying man, they stopped and began to question the page as to who he was. Before he could reply Vanneo opened his eyes with a smile, raised himself suddenly from the straw on which he lay, and, stretching out his hand eagerly as one who welcomes a friend, exclaimed in Italian, 'Cavaliere, the consonance is complete;' and having said this he fell back upon the straw again, and, the smile still upon his face, he died."

The musician stopped a moment, and then glancing at Inglesant with a curious look said, "It is confidently said that about that very moment the Cavaliere Andrea died at Rome; at any rate, when the page returned to Italy and inquired for him at Rome, he was dead. He caught a fever in one of his visits to the prisons, and died in a few days."

"Did the page tell you of the two gentlemen who were shot at Colchester?" said Inglesant.

"Yes, he told me that Guasconi stood by with his doublet off expecting his turn; but when the others were shot he was taken back to his prison. They only found out he was an Italian by his asking leave to write to the Grand Duke."

"I have been told," he continued, "that this poor King was a great lover of music, and played the bass viol himself."

"He was a great admirer of Church music," said Inglesant; "I have often seen him appoint the service and anthems himself."

As the conversation of this man was a great entertainment to Inglesant, so his sudden and unexpected death was a great shock to him. The physician could give no clear explanation of his disease, and the general opinion was that he died of the plague, though it was, of course, the interest of every one in the pest-house that this should not be acknowledged.

A few days after the burial two of the Jesuit Fathers arrived from Florence, accompanied by Don Agostino, who, having in vain waited for his friend at Lucca, had sought him at Florence, and finally traced him to his dreary prison. By their influence Inglesant was allowed to depart; and actuated still by his desire to see Venice, set out, accompanied by Don Agostino, in the hope of reaching that city. They crossed the Apennines, and journeyed by Modena, Mantua, Verona, and Padua. These places, which at other times would have excited in Inglesant the liveliest interest, were passed by him now as in a dream. The listless indifference which grew day by day developed at Padua into absolute illness; and Agostino took lodgings for his friend in one of the deserted palaces of which the city was full. A few days' rest from travel, and from the excitement produced by novel scenes and by the scorching plains, had a soothing and beneficent effect; but Venice being reported to be at that time peculiarly unhealthy, and Inglesant becoming sensible that he was physically unable to prosecute any inquiries there, the friends resolved to abandon their journey in that direction, and to return towards Rome. At this juncture Don Agostino received letters which compelled him to return hastily to Sienna, and after spending a few days with his friend, he left, promising to return shortly and accompany Inglesant to Rome, when he was sufficiently recruited by a few weeks' repose.

The failure of the silk trade, owing to the importation of silk from India into Europe, had destroyed the prosperity of many parts of Italy; and in Padua long streets of deserted mansions attested by their beauty the wealth and taste of the nobility, whom the loss of the rents of their mulberry groves had reduced to ruin. Many houses being empty, rents were exceedingly cheap, and the country being very plentiful in produce, and the air very good, a little money went a long way in Padua. There was something about the quiet gloomy town, with its silent narrow streets and its winding dim arcades,—by which you might go from one end of the city to the other under a shady covert,—that soothed Inglesant's weary senses and excited brain.

His was that sad condition in which the body and the mind, being equally, like the several strings of an ill-kept lute, out of tune, jarred upon each other, the pains of the body causing phantasms and delusions of the mind. His disappointment and illness at Florence, his long confinement in the pest-house, and the sudden death of his friend the poor musician, preyed upon his spirits and followed him even in his dreams; and his body being weakened by suffering, and his mind depressed by these gloomy events and images, the old spiritual terrors returned with augmented force. Nature herself, in times of health and happiness so alluring and kind, turns against the wretch thus deprived of other comfort. The common sights and events of life, at one time so full of interest, became hateful to him; and amid the solemn twilights and gorgeous sunsets of Italy, his imagination was oppressed by an intolerable presentiment of coming evil. Finally, he despaired of himself, his past life became hateful to him, and nothing in the future promised a hope of greater success. He saw himself the mere tool of a political faction, and to his disordered fancy as little better than a hireling bravo and mercenary. The rustling of leaves, the falling of water, the summer breeze, uttered a pensive and melancholy voice, which was not soothing, but was like the distant moaning of sad spirits foreboding disaster and disgrace. On his first arrival in Padua Don Agostino had introduced him to two or three ecclesiastics, whose character and conversation he thought would please his friend; but Inglesant made little effort to cultivate their acquaintance. His principal associate was the Prior of the Benedictine monastery, a mile or two beyond the Ferrara Gate, who, becoming at last distressed at his condition, advised him to consult a famous physician named Signore Giovanni Zecca.

This man had the reputation of a wit, maintained chiefly by a constant study of Boccalini's "Parnassus," with quotations from which work he constantly adorned his discourse. He found Inglesant prostrate on a couch in his apartment, with the Prior by his side. The room had been the state reception-room of the former possessor, and the windows, which were open, looked upon the wide space within one of the gates. It was the most busy part of the city, and for that reason the rooms had been chosen by Don Agostino, as commanding the most agreeable and lively prospect.

The Prior having explained to the physician the nature of Inglesant's malady, as far as he was acquainted with it, inquired whether the situation of the rooms seemed suitable to the doctor, or whether it would be well to remove to some country house. The scene from the windows indeed was very lively, and might be considered too distracting for an invalid. The prospect commanded the greater part of the Piazza, or Place d'Armes, the gate and drawbridges and the glacis outside, with a stretch of country road beyond, lined with poplars. This extensive stage was occupied by ever-varying groups,—soldiers on guard in stiff and picturesque uniform, men carrying burdens, pack-horses, oxen, now and then a carriage with a string of horses and with running footmen, peasant women, priests, children, and beggars, with sometimes a puppet-show, or a conjuror with apes, and side by side with these last, in strange incongruity, the procession of the Host.

"From what I know of this gentleman's malady and disposition," said the physician, "I should suppose that these sights and sounds, though perhaps hurtful to his physical nature, are so dear to his moral nature that to speak against them were useless. These sounds, though physically unpleasant, contain to the philosophic mind such moral beauty as to be attractive in the highest degree, and to such a nature as this my patient possesses offer a fascination which it would be unwise to contend against."

"If," said the Prior to Inglesant with a smile, "your case requires philosophic treatment, you are fortunate in having secured the advice of Signore Zecca, who has the reputation of a philosopher and wit, as well as that of a most skilful physician."

"With respect to my calling as a physician, I may make some claim certainly," said the doctor, "if descent has any title to confer excellence, for my great-grandfather was that celebrated Giovanni Zecca, after whom I am named, the Physician of Bologna, whom you will find mentioned in the most witty 'Ragguagli' of Messere Trajano Boccalini; therefore, if I fail in my profession, it is not for want of generations of experience and precept; but as regards my proficiency as a philosopher, I have no one to depend upon but myself, and my proficiency is indeed but small."

"You are pleased to say so, Signore Fisico," said Inglesant languidly, "with the modesty usual with great minds; nevertheless the remark which you have just made shows you to be familiar with the deepest of all philosophy, that of human life. It is my misfortune that I am too deeply impressed already with the importance of this philosophy, and it is my inadequate following of its teaching which is killing me."

"It is a subject of curious study," said the physician, "for perplexity perhaps, certainly for much satire, but scarcely, I should think, for martyrdom. The noblest things in life are mixed with the most ignoble, great pretence with infinite substance, vain-glory with solidness. The fool of one moment, the martyr of the next: as in the case of that Spaniard mentioned by Messere Boccalini, whose work doubtless you know, signore, but if not, I should recommend its perusal as certain to do much to work your cure. This man—the Spaniard I mean—dying most gallantly upon the field of honour, entreated his friend to see him buried without unclothing him; and with these words died. His body being afterwards examined, it was found that he who was so sprucely dressed, and who had a ruff about his neck so curiously wrought as to be of great value, had never a shirt on his back. This discovery caused great laughter among the vulgar sort of mankind; but by order of Apollo, the great ruler of learning and philosophy, this Spaniard was given a public and splendid funeral, equal to a Roman triumph; and an oration was pronounced over him, who was so happy that, in his great calamity, he was careful of his reputation before his life. His noble funeral seems to me rather to proclaim the fact that our worst meannesses cannot deprive us of the dignity of that pity which is due to human nature standing by the brink of an open grave. A man has mistaken the secret of human life who does not look for greatness in the midst of folly, for sparks of nobility in the midst of meanness; and the well-poised mind distributes with impartiality the praise and the blame."

"It is my misfortune," replied Inglesant, "that my mind is incapable of this well-poised impartiality, but is worn out by the unworthy conflict which the spirit within us wages with the meannesses of life. As the Psalmist says, 'The very abjects make mouths at me, and cease not.'"

"You are like those people, signore," said the physician, "mentioned by Messere Boccalini, whom the greatest physicians failed to cure, but who were immediately restored to active health by the simple and common remedies of a quack. You seek for remedies among the stars and the eternal verities of creation, whereas your ailment of mind arises doubtless from some physical derangement, which perchance a learner in healing might overcome."

"The fatal confusion of human life," said Inglesant, "is surely too obvious a fact to be accounted for by the delusions of physical disease."

The physician looked at Inglesant for a moment, and said,—

"Some time, signore, I will tell you a story, not out of Boccalini, which perchance will convince you that, strange as it may seem, the realities of life and the delusions of disease are not so dissimilar as you think."

"If it be so," said Inglesant, "your prescription is more terrible than my complaint."

"I do not see that," replied the other. "I have said nothing but what should show you how unwise you will be, if you overlook the bodily ailment in searching into the diseases of the soul."

"I am well aware," replied Inglesant, "that my ailment is

one of the body as well as of the mind; but were my body made perfectly whole and sound, my cure could scarcely be said to be begun."

"I hold that most of the sorrows and perplexities of the mind are to be traced to a diseased body," replied the physician, not paying much attention to what his patient said; "the passion of the heart, heavy and dull spirits, vain imaginations, the vision of spectres and phantoms, grief and sorrow without manifest cause,—all these things may be cured by purging away melancholy humours from the body, especially as I conceive from the meseraic veins; and the heart will then be comforted, in the taking away the material cause of sorrow, which is not to be looked for in the world of spirits, nor in any providential government of God, nor even in outward circumstances and perplexities, but in the mechanism of the body itself."

"What cures do you propound that may be hoped to work such happy results?" said the Prior, for Inglesant did not speak.

"We have many such cures in physics—physics studied by the light of the heavenly science," said the physician; "such as the Saturica Sancti Juliani, which grows plentifully on the rough cliffs of the Tyrrhenian Sea, as the old Greek chronographers called it, called St. Julian's Rock; the Epithymum, or thyme, which is under Saturn, and therefore very fitted for melancholy men; the Febrifuga, or, in our Italian tongue, Artemisia Tenuifolia, good for such as be melancholy, sad, pensive, and without power of speech; the distilled water of the Fraga, or Strawberry, drunk with white wine reviveth the spirits, and as the holy Psalmist says, 'Lætificat cor hominis;' and the herb Panax, which grows on the top of the Apennine, and is cherished in all the gardens of Italy for its wonderful healing qualities; but the liquor of it, which you may buy in Venice, is not distilled in Italy, but is brought from Alexandria, a city of Egypt."

"You do not speak of the chemical medicines," said Inglesant, "which were much thought of in England when I was in Oxford; and many wonderful cures were worked by them, though I remember hearing that the young doctor who first introduced them, and wrought some great cures, died himself soon after."

"I have indeed no faith in the new doctrine of chemical

compositions and receipts," said the physician, "which from mere empirics must needs be very dangerous, but from a man that is well grounded in the old way may do strange things. The works of God are freely given to man. His medicines are common and cheap; it is the medicines of the new physicians that are so dear and scarce to find."

Signore Zecca soon after took his leave, promising to send Inglesant a cordial, the ingredients of which he said were gathered on "a Friday in the hour of Jupiter," and which would be sufficient to give sleep, pleasant dreams, and quiet rest to the most melancholy man in the world. For, as he sensibly observed, "waking is a symptom which much tortures melancholy men, and must therefore be speedily helped, and sleep by all means procured. To such as you especially, who have what I call the temperament of sensibility, are fearful of pain, covet music and sleep, and delight in poetry and romance, sleep alone is often a sufficient remedy."

The doctor frequently visited Inglesant, who found his humour and curious learning entertaining; and on one occasion, when they were alone together, he reminded him of his promise to relate a story which would prove his assertion that the ills of the soul were occasioned by those of the body.

* * * * *

Note.—The MSS. are here imperfect.

CHAPTER XXIII.

In spite, however, of the reasonings and prescriptions of the physician, the oppression upon Inglesant's brain became more intolerable. Every new object seemed burnt into it by the sultry outward heat, and by his own fiery thoughts. The livid scorched plains, with the dark foliage, the hot piazzas and highways, seemed to him thronged with ghastly phantoms, all occupied more or less in some evil or fruitless work. As to his physical sense all objects seemed distorted and awry, so to his mental perception the most ordinary events bore in them the germs, however slight, of that terrible act of murderous terror that had marred and ruined his own life. In some form or other, in the passionate look, in the gambler's gesture, in the lover's glance, in the juggler's grimace, in the passion of the little child, he saw the stealthy trail of the Italian murderer, before whose cowardly blow his brother fell. The cool, neglected courts of Padua afforded no relief to his racked brain, no solace to his fevered fancy. He frequented the shadowed churches and the solemn masses daily without comfort; for his conscience was once more weighted with the remembrance of Serenus de Cressy, and of his own rejection of the narrow path of the Holy Cross. A sense of oppression and confusion rested upon him mentally and physically, so that he could see no objects steadily and clearly; but without was a phantasmagoria of terrible bright colours, and within a mental chaos and disorder without a clue. A constant longing filled his mind to accept De Cressy's offer, and he would have returned to France but for the utter impossibility of making the journey in his condition of health. He withdrew himself more and more from society, and at last, without informing his friends of his intention, he retired to a small monastery without the city, about a mile from the Traviso Gate, and requested to be admitted as a novice. The result of this step at the outset was beneficial; for the perfect seclusion, and the dim light of the cells and shaded garden, relieved the brain, and restored the disordered sense of vision.

It was some time before Don Agostino received intelligence, through the Prior, of this step of his friend's. He immediately came to Padua, and had several interviews with Inglesant, but apparently failed to produce any impression upon him. He then returned to Florence, and induced the Cardinal Rinuccini, from whose influence upon Inglesant he hoped much, to accompany him to Padua.

The Cardinal was a striking-looking and singularly handsome man, his countenance resembling the reputed portraits of Molière, whose bust might be taken for that of a pagan god. There was the same open, free expression, as of a man who confined his actions by no bounds, who tasted freely of that tree of good and evil, which, it is reported, transforms a man into a god, and of that other tree which, since the flaming sword of the cherubim kept the way to the true, has passed in the world for the tree of life; who had no prejudices nor partialities, but included all mankind, and all the opinions of men, within the wide range of perfect tolerance and lofty indifference. He found Inglesant in his novice's dress walking in the small walled-in garden of the monastery, beneath the mulberry trees, his breviary in his hand. After the first greeting the Cardinal inquired touching his health.

"You are familiar with English, Eminence," replied Inglesant, "and remember Hamlet; and you will therefore understand the state of a man for whom the world is too strong."

"It is only the weak," replied the Cardinal, "for whom the world is too strong. You know what Terence says, 'Ita vita est hominum quasi cum ludas tesseris,' or, as we should rather say, 'Life is like a game of cards;' you cannot control the cards, but of such as turn up you must make the most."

"Illud quod cecidit forte, id arte ut corrigas."

"The freewill, the reason, and the power of self-command, struggle perpetually with an array of chance incidents, of mechanical forces, of material causes, beyond foresight or control, but not beyond skilful management. This gives a delicate zest and point to life, which it would surely want if we had the power to frame it as we would. We did not make the world, and are not responsible for its state; but we can make life a fine art, and, taking things as we find them, like wise men, mould them as may best serve our own ends."

"We are not all wise, your Eminence, and the ends that some of us make our aim are far beyond our reach."

"I was ever moderate in my desires," said the Cardinal with a smile; "I shoot at none of these high-flying game. I am content to live from day to day, and leave the future to the gods; in the meantime sweetening life as I can with some pleasing toys here and there, to relish it."

"You have read Don Quixote, Eminence," said Inglesant; "and no doubt hold him to have been mad."

"He was mad, doubtless," replied the Cardinal, smiling.

"I am mad, like him," replied the other.

"I understand you," said the Cardinal; "it is a noble madness, from which we inferior natures are free; nevertheless, it may be advisable for a time to consult some worldly physician, that by his help this nobleness may be preserved a little longer upon earth and among men."

"No worldly physician knows the disease, much less the cure," said Inglesant. "Don Quixote died in his bed at last, talked down by petty commonplace, acknowledging his madness, and calling his noble life a mistake; how much more shall I, whose life has been the more ignoble for some transient gleams of splendour which have crossed its path in vain! The world is too strong for me, and heaven and its solution of life's enigma too far off."

"There is no solution, believe me," said the Cardinal, "no solution of life's enigma worth the reading. But suppose there be, you are more likely to find it at Rome than here. Put off that monk's dress, and come with me to Rome. What solution can you hope to find, brooding on your own heart, on this narrow plot of grass, shut in by lofty walls? You, and natures like yours, make this great error; you are moralizing and speculating upon what life ought to be, instead of taking it as it is; and in the meantime it slips by you, and you are nothing, and life is gone. I have heard, and you doubtless, in a fine concert of viols, extemporary descant upon a thorough bass in the Italian manner, when each performer in turn plays such variety of descant, in concordance to the bass, as his skill and present invention may suggest to him. In this manner of play the consonances invariably fall true upon a given note, and every succeeding note of the ground is met, now in the unison or octave, now in the concords, preserving the melody throughout by the laws of motion and sound. I have thought that this is life. To a solemn bass of mystery and of the unseen, each man plays his own descant as his taste or fate suggests; but this manner of play is so governed and controlled by what seems a fatal necessity, that all melts into a species of harmony; and even the very discords and dissonances, the wild passions and deeds of men, are so attempered and adjusted that without them the entire piece would be incomplete. In this way I look upon life as a spectacle, 'in theatro ludus.' Have you sat so long that you are tired already of the play?"

"I have read in some book,"[1] said Inglesant, "that it is not the play—only the rehearsal. The play itself is not given till the next life. But for the rest your Eminence is but too right. There is no solution within my own heart, and no help within these walls."

There can be little doubt that had Inglesant remained much

---

[1] What this book is, I do not know. The remark was made by Jean Paul, in Hesperus, some hundred years after Inglesant's day.

longer in the monastery, he would have sunk into a settled melancholy. The quiet and calm, while it soothed his brain and relieved it of the phantoms that distracted it, allowed the mind to dwell exclusively upon those depressing thoughts and ideas which were exhausting his spirit and reducing him wellnigh to despair. However undesirable at other times the Cardinal's philosophic paganism might be, no doubt, at this moment, his society was highly beneficial to Inglesant, to whom, indeed, his conversation possessed a peculiar charm. It could, indeed, scarcely fail to attract one who himself sympathized with that philosophy of tolerance of, and attraction to, the multiform aspects of life which Paganism and the Cardinal equally followed. On the other hand, Rinuccini had from the first been personally strongly attracted towards Inglesant, and, as a matter of policy, attached just importance to securing his services, both on account of what he had learnt from his brother, and from the report of the Jesuits.

After some further conversation the Cardinal returned to Padua in triumph, bringing Inglesant with him, whom he loaded with kindness and attention. A suite of apartments was placed at his disposal, certain of the Cardinal's servants were ordered to attend him, and the finest horses were devoted to his use on the approaching journey. After waiting in Padua some days, to make preparations which were necessary in the neglected state of Inglesant's affairs, they set out for Rome. Don Agostino was still in Florence, the politics of his family not suffering him to visit the papal ctiy at present.

Their first day's journey took them, through the fertile and well-cultivated Venetian States, to Rovigo, where they crossed the Po, dividing the territory of the Republic from the Ferrarese, which State had lately been acquired by the Pope.

This country, which, while it possessed princes of its own, had been one of the happiest and most beautiful parts of Italy, was now abandoned and uncultivated to such an extent that the grass was left unmown on the meadows. At Ferrara, a vast city which appeared to Inglesant like a city of the dead as he walked through streets of stately houses without an inhabitant, the chief concourse of people was the crowd of beggars who thronged round the Cardinal's coach. After dinner Inglesant left his companion, who liked to linger over his wine, and walked out into the quiet streets. The long, deserted vistas of this vast city, sleeping in the light and shadow of the afternoon sun, disturbed now and then only by a solitary footstep, pleased his singular fancies as Padua had done. He entered several of the Churches, which were mean and poorly adorned, and spoke to several of the priests and loiterers. Everywhere he heard complaints of the poverty of the place, of the misery of the people, of the bad unwholesome air, caused by the dearth of inhabitants to cultivate the land. When he came to inquire into the causes of this, most held their peace; but one or two idlers, bolder or more reckless than the rest, seeing that he was a foreigner, and ignorant that he was riding in the train of the Cardinal, whispered to him something of the severity of the Papal government, and of the heavy taxes and frequent confiscations by which the nephews of several Popes had enriched themselves, and devoured many of the principal families of the city, and driven away many more. "They talk of the bad air," said one of these men to Inglesant; "the air was the same a century ago, when this city was flourishing under its own princes—princes of so eminent a virtue, and of so heroical a nobleness, that they were really the Fathers of their country. Nothing," he continued, with a mute gesture of the hands, "can be imagined more changed than this is now."

"But Bologna is under the Pope, also," said Inglesant, "and is flourishing enough."

"Bologna," he answered, "delivered itself up to the Popedom upon a capitulation, by which there are many privileges reserved to it. Crimes there are only punished in the persons of those who commit them. There are no confiscations of estates; and the good result of these privileges is evident, for, though Bologna is neither on a navigable river nor the centre of a sovereignty where a Court is kept, yet its happiness and wealth amaze a stranger; while we, once equally fortunate, are like a city in a dream."

Inglesant returned to the inn to the Cardinal, and related what he had heard; to all which dismal stories the Prelate only replied by significant gesture.

The next morning, however, as he was entering his carriage, followed by his friend, he seemed to take particular notice of the crowd of beggars that surrounded the inn. In Inglesant's eyes they only formed part (together with the strange, quiet streets, the shaded gardens, and the ever-changing scenes of their journey) in that shifting phantasm of form and colour, meaningless to him, except as it might suddenly, and in some unexpected way, become a part and scene of the fatal drama that had seized upon and crippled his life. But to the Cardinal, who had the training of a politician, though he subordinated politics to enjoyment, these swarms of beggars and these decaying States had at times a deeper interest.

"These people," he said, as the carriage moved on, "certainly seem very miserable, as you told me last night. To those whose tastes lay that way, it would not be a useless business to inquire into these matters, and to try to set them right. Some day, probably far distant, some of us, or those like us who clothe in scarlet and fine linen, will have to pay a reckoning for these things."

"They are less unhappy than I am," said Inglesant. "As to the luxurious persons of whom you speak, it has been my fate to be of their party all my life, and to serve them for very poor reward; and I doubt not that, when their damnation, of which your Eminence speaks, arrives, I shall share it with them. But it might seem to one who knows little of such things that some such attempt might be looked for from a sworn soldier and prince of the Church."

The Cardinal smiled. The freedom with which Inglesant's sarcastic humour showed itself at times, when the melancholy fit was upon him, was one of the sources of attraction which attached the young Englishman to his person.

"Life is short," he said, "and the future very uncertain; martyrs have died, nay, still harder fate, have lived long lives of such devotion as that which you wish me to attempt, and we see very little result. Christianity is not of much use apparently to many of the nations of the earth. Now, on my side, as I pass my life, I certainly enjoy this world, and I as certainly have cultivated my mind to sustain, as far as I can foresee the probable, the demand and strain that will be put upon it, both in the exit from this life, and in the entrance upon another. Why then should I renounce these two positive goods, and embrace a life of restless annoyance and discomfort, of antagonism to existing systems and order, of certain failure, disappointment, and the peevish protestation of a prophet to whom the world will not listen?"

"There is no reason why, certainly," said Inglesant, "for a

sane man like your Eminence. I see clearly, it must only have been madmen who in all ages have been driven into the fire and upon the sword's point in pursuit of an idea which they fancied was worth the pain, but which, as they never realized it, they could never put to the test."

"I perceive your irony," said the Cardinal, "and I recognize your wit. What astonishes me is the interest you take in these old myths and dreary services. The charm of novelty must have worn itself out by this time."

"Christ is real to many men," said Inglesant, "and the world seems to manifest within itself a remedial power such as may be supposed to be His."

"I do not dispute such a power," replied the Cardinal; "I only wonder at the attachment to these old myths which profess to expound it."

"The world has now been satisfied with them for some centuries," said Inglesant; "and for my own part, I cannot help thinking that, even in the blaze of a purer Mythos, some of us will look back with longing to 'one of the days of the Son of man.' I do not perceive either that your Eminence attempts to improve matters."

"I can afford to wait," replied the Cardinal, with lofty indifference; "the myths of the world are slow to change."

"This one certainly," replied Inglesant, with a smile, "has been slow to change, perhaps because men found in it something that reminded them of their daily life. It speaks of suffering and of sin. The cross of Christ is composed of many other crosses—is the centre, the type, the essence of all crosses. We must *suffer* with Christ whether we *believe* in Him or not. We must suffer for the sin of others as for our own; and in this suffering we find a healing and purifying power and element. This is what gives to Christianity, in its simplest and most unlettered form, its force and life. Sin and suffering for sin; a sacrifice, itself mysterious, offered mysteriously to the Divine Nemesis or Law of Sin,—dread, undefined, unknown, yet sure and irresistible, with the iron necessity of law. This the intellectual Christ, the Platonic-Socrates, did not offer: hence his failure, and the success of the Nazarene. Vicisti Galilæe."

CHAPTER XXIV.

AMONG the letters of introduction to persons in Rome which Inglesant carried with him, was one from Father St. Clare to the Rector of the English College, a Jesuit. The Cardinal had invited him to remain an inmate of his family, but there were several reasons which induced Inglesant to decline the offer. He was desirous of observing the situation and habits of the great city in a more unfettered way than he would probably be able to do if attached to the household of a great man. This reason alone would probably have decided him, but it was not the only one. In proportion as his mind recovered its natural tone, and was able to throw off the depression which had so long troubled him, another source of perplexity had taken its place. Most men, in those days, with the exception of very determined Puritans, approached Rome with feelings of veneration and awe. Inglesant's training and temperament inclined him to entertain these feelings as strongly perhaps as any man of the day; but since he had been in Italy, his eyes and ears had not been closed, and it had been impossible for him to resist a growing impression, scarcely perhaps amounting to conviction, that the nearer he approached the Papal capital the more wretched and worse governed did the country appear on every side. In the muttered complaints which reached his ear these evils were charged partly upon the abuses of the Papal chair itself, but principally upon the tyranny and oppression of the society of the Jesuits. Inglesant made these observations mostly in the taverns or cafés in the evenings, when those who were present, perceiving him to be a foreigner, were more disposed to be communicative than they otherwise would have been. But the Cardinal was known to associate rather with the Fathers of the Oratory than with the Jesuits; and men did not hesitate therefore to speak somewhat freely on these matters to his familiar companion. These accusations did not destroy Inglesant's faith in the Society, but they made him anxious to hear the other side, and to see, if possible from within, the working of this great and powerful organization, and to understand the motives which prompted those actions which were so much blamed, and which were apparently productive of such questionable fruits. If this were to be done, it must be done at once. He came to Rome recommended to the Jesuits' College, almost an accredited agent. He would be received without suspicion, and would probably be enabled to obtain an insight into much of their policy. But if at the outset he associated himself with persons and interests hostile, or at least indifferent, to those of the party to which he belonged, and which he wished to understand, this opportunity would doubtless soon be lost to him. Acting upon these considerations, he parted from the Cardinal, to whom he confided his motives, and made his way to the English College or house, which was situated in the street leading to St. Peter's and the Vatican, and not far from the Bridge and Castle of St. Angelo.

The College was a large and fair house, standing in several courts and gardens. Inglesant was received with courtesy by the rector, who said that he remembered seeing him in London, and that he had also been at his father's house in Wiltshire. He named to him several Priests who had also been there; but so many Papists had been constantly coming and going at Westacre, during the time that Father St. Clare had resided there, that Inglesant could not recall them to mind. The rector, however, mentioned one whom he remembered, the gentleman who had given him St. Theresa's Life. He advised Inglesant to remain some days at the College, as the usual and natural resort of all Englishmen connected in any way with the Court and Church of Rome, promising him pleasant rooms. He showed him his apartment, a small but handsome guest-chamber, looking upon a garden, with a sort of oratory or closet adjoining, with an altar and crucifix. The bell rang for supper, but the rector had that meal laid for himself and his guest in his private room. The students, and those who took their meals at the common table, had but one good meal in the day, that being a most excellent one. Their supper consisted of a glass of wine and a manchet of bread.

The rector and Inglesant had much talk together, and after the latter had satisfied his host, as best he could, upon all those points—and they were many—connected with the state of affairs in England upon which he desired information, the rector began in his turn to give his guest a description of affairs in

Rome, and of those things which he should see, and how best to see them.

"I will not trouble you now," he said, "with any policy or State affairs. You will no doubt wish to spend the next few days in seeing the wonderful sights of this place, and in becoming familiar with its situation, so that you may study them more closely afterwards. A man must indeed be ill-endowed by nature who does not find in Rome delight in every branch of learning and of art. The libraries are open, and the students have access to the rarest books; in the Churches the most exquisite voices are daily heard, the palaces are crowded with pictures and with statues, ancient and modern. You have, besides, the stately streets and noble buildings of every age, the presence of strangers from every part of the world, villas covered with 'bassi relievi,' and the enjoyment of nature in enchanting gardens. To a man who loves the practices of devotion I need not mention the life-long employment among the Churches, relics, and processions. It is this last that gives the unique completeness of the Roman life within itself. To the abundance of its earthly wealth, to the delights of its intellectual gratifications, is added a feeling of unequalled security and satisfaction, kept alive, in a pious mind, by the incessant contemplation of the objects of its reverence. I do not know if you are by taste more of a scholar than of a religious, but both tastes are worthy of cultivation, nor is all spiritual learning necessarily confined to the last. There is much that is very instructive in the lessons which the silent stones and shattered monuments of the fallen cities over which we walk teach us. It has been well observed that everything that has been dug out of the ruins of ancient Rome has been found mutilated, either by the barbarians, fanaticism, or time; and one of our poets, Janus Vitalis, seeing all the massive buildings mouldered or mouldering away, and the ever-changing Tiber only remaining the same, composed this ingenious and pleasing verse—

> 'Disce hinc quid possit fortuna; immota labascunt;
> Et quæ perpetuo sunt fluitura, manent.'

You will find that the Italian humour delights much in such thoughts as these, which make the French and other nations accuse us of melancholy. The Italian has a strong fancy, yet a strong judgment, and this makes him delight in such things as please the fancy, while at the same time they are in accordance with judgment and with reason. He delights in music, medals, statues, and pictures, as things which either divert his melancholy or humour it; and even the common people, such as shoemakers, have formed curious collections of medals of gold, silver, and brass, such as would have become the cabinet of a prince. Do you wish to begin with the Churches or with the antiquities?"

Inglesant said he wished to see the Churches first of all.

"You will, no doubt," said the rector, "find a great satisfaction in such a choice. You will be overcome with the beauty and solemnity of these sacred places, and the sweetness of the organs and of the singing will melt your heart. At the same time, I should wish to point out to you, to whom I wish to speak without the least reserve, that you will no doubt see some things which will surprise you, nay, which may even appear to you to be, to say the least, of questionable advantage. You must understand once for all, and constantly bear in mind, that this city is like none other, and that many things are natural and proper here which would be strange and ill-fitted elsewhere. Rome is the visible symbol and representation of the Christian truth, and we live here in a perpetual masque or holy interlude of the life of the Saviour. As in other countries and cities, outward representations are placed before the people of the awful facts and incidents on which their salvation rests, so here this is carried still farther, as indeed was natural and almost inevitable. It was a very small step from the representation of the flagellation of Christ, to the very pillar on which He leant. Indeed, where these representations were enacted, the simple country people readily and naturally conceived them to have taken place. Hence, when you are shown the three doors of Pilate's house in which Jesus passed and repassed to and from judgment, the steps up which He walked, the rock on which He promised to build His Church, the stone on which the cock stood and crowed when Peter denied Him, part of His coat and of His blood, and several of the nails of His cross,—more, possibly, than were originally used, over which the heretics have not failed to make themselves very merry;—when you see all these things, I say, and if you feel, as I do not say you will feel—but if you feel any hesitancy or even some repulsion, as though these miraculous things were to you matters more of doubt than worship, you will not fail at once to see the true nature and bearing of these things, nor to apply to them the solution which your philosophy has doubtless given already to many difficult questions of this life. These things are true to each of us according as we see them; they are, in fact, but shadows and likenesses of the absolute truth that reveals itself to men in different ways, but always imperfectly and as in a glass. To the simple-hearted peasant that pavement upon which in his mind's eye he sees Jesus walking, is verily and indeed pressed by the Divine feet; to him this pillar, the sight of which makes the stinging whips creep along his flesh, is the pillar to which the Lord was tied. Our people, both peasant and noble, are of the nature of children—children who are naughty one moment and sincerely penitent the next. They are now wildly dissolute, the next day prostrate before the cross; and as such, much that is true and beautiful in their lives seems otherwise to the cold and world-taught heart. But our Lord honoured the childlike heart, and will not send away our poor peasants when they come to Him with their little offerings, even though they lay them at the feet of a Bambino doll."

"But do you not find," said Inglesant, "that this devotion, which is so ephemeral, is rather given to the sensible object than to the unseen Christ?"

"It may be so," said the rector; "there is no good but what has its alloy; but it is a real devotion, and it reaches after Christ. Granted that it is dark; no doubt in the darkness it finds Him, though it cannot see His form."

"Doubtless," said Inglesant, who saw that the rector did not wish to dwell on this part of the subject, "as we say in our service in England, we are the sheep of His pasture, and we are all branded with the mark which He puts upon His sheep—the innate knowledge of God in the soul. I remember hearing of a man who believed that he had a guardian spirit who awoke him every morning with the audible words, 'Who gets up first to pray?' If this man was deluded, it could not have been by Satan."

In the morning, when Inglesant awoke, he saw from his window, over the city wall, the Monte Mario, with its pine woods, and the windows of its scattered houses lighted by the rising sun. The air was soft and balmy, and he remained at the open window, letting his mind grow certain of the fact that he was in Rome. In the clear atmosphere of the Papal city there was a strange shimmer of light upon the distant hills and on the green tufts and hillocks of the waste ground beyond the walls. The warm air fanned his temples, and in the stillness of the early morning a delicious sense of a wonderful and unknown land, into the mysteries of which he was about to enter, filled his mind.

It was indeed a strange world which lay before him, and resembled nothing so much as that to which the rector had aptly compared it the night before—a sacred interlude full of wild and fantastic sights; Churches more sublime than the dreams of fancy painted, across whose marble pavements saints and angels moved familiarly with men; pagan sepulchres and banqueting chambers, where the phantoms flickered as in Tartarus itself; vaults and Christian catacombs, where the cry of martyrs mingled with the chanting of masses sung beneath the sod, and where the torch-light flashed on passing forms of horror, quelled everywhere by the figure of the Crucified, that at every turn kept the place; midnight processions and singing, startling the darkness and scaring the doers of darkness, mortal and immortal, that lurked among the secret places, where the crimes of centuries stood like ghastly corpses at every step; and above all and through all the life of Jesus, enacted and re-enacted year after year and day by day continually, not in dumb show or memorial only, but in deed and fact before the eyes of men, as if, in that haunt of demons and possessed, in that sink of past and present crime, nothing but the eternal presence and power of Jesus could keep the fiends in check.

The rector took Inglesant over the College, and showed him the life and condition of the inmates under its most pleasing aspect. As he then saw it, it reminded him of a poem he had heard Mr. Crashaw read at Little Gidding, describing a religious house and condition of life, and he quoted part of it to the rector:—

> "No cruel guard of diligent cares, that keep
> Crowned woes awake, as things too wise for sleep:
> But reverend discipline, and religious fear,
> And soft obedience, find sweet biding here;
> Silence and sacred rest, peace and pure joys."

When they had seen the College the rector said,—

"We will go this morning to St. Peter's. It is better that you should see it at once, though the first sight is nothing. Then at three o'clock we will attend vespers at the Cappella del Coro, where there is fine music every day in the presence of a cardinal; afterwards, as Rome is very full, there will be a great confluence of carriages in the Piazza of the Farnese Palace, which is a favourite resort. There I can show you many of the great ones, whom it is well you should know by sight, and hear something of, before you are presented to them."

As they passed out into the street of the city the rector began a disquisition on the discovery of antiquities in Rome. He advised Inglesant to study the cabinets of medals which he would meet with in the museums and palaces, as they would throw great light upon the statues and other curiosities.

"A man takes a great deal more pleasure," he said, "in surveying the ancient statues who compares them with medals than it is possible for him to do without some such knowledge, for the two arts illustrate each other. The coins throw a great light upon many points of ancient history, and enable us to distinguish the kings and consuls, emperors and empresses, the deities and virtues, with their ensigns and trophies, and a thousand other attributes and images not to be learnt or understood in any other way. I have a few coins myself, which I shall be glad to show you, and a few gems, among which is an Antinöus cut in a carnelian which I value very highly. It represents him in the habit of a Mercury, and is the finest Intaglio I ever saw. I obtained it by accident from a peasant, who found it while digging in his vineyard."

Inglesant was too much occupied watching the passers-by in the thronged streets to pay much attention to what he said. The crowded pavements of Rome offered to his eyes a spectacle such as he had never seen, and to his imagination a fanciful pageant such as he had never pictured even in his dreams. The splendid equipages with their metal work of massive silver, the strange variety of the clerical costumes, the fantastic dresses of the attendants and papal soldiers, the peasants and pilgrims from all countries, even the most remote, crossed his vision in an entangled maze.

As they crossed the bridge of St. Angelo, the rector informed him of the invaluable treasures of antique art which were supposed to lie beneath the muddy waters of the river.

They passed beneath the castle, and a few moments more brought them to the piazza in front of the Church.

The Colonnade was not finished, one side of it being then in course of completion; but in all its brilliant freshness, with the innumerable statues, white from the sculptor's hand, it had an imposing and stately effect. The great obelisk, or Guglia, as the Italians called it, had been raised to its position some seventy years before, but only one of the great fountains was complete. Crossing the square, which was full of carriages, and of priests and laymen on foot, the rector and Inglesant ascended the marble stairs which had formed part of the old Basilica, and up which Charlemagne was said to have mounted on his knees, and passing through the gigantic porch, with its enormous pillars and gilt roof, the rector pushed back the canvas-lined curtain that closed the doorway, and they entered the Church.

The masons were at work completing the marble covering of the massive square pillars of the nave; but though the work was unfinished, it was sufficient to produce an effect of inexpressible richness and splendour. The vast extent of the pavement, prepared as for the heavenly host with inlaying of colours of polished stone, agate, serpentine, porphyry, and chalcedon; the shining walls, veined with the richest marbles, and studded with gems; the roof of the nave, carved with foliage and roses overlaid with gold; the distant walls and chambers of imagery, dim with incense, through which shone out, scarcely veiled, the statues and tombs, the paintings and crucifixes and altars, with their glimmering lights;—all settled down, so to speak, upon Inglesant's soul with a perception of subdued splendour, which hushed the spirit into a silent feeling which was partly rest and partly awe.

But when, having traversed the length of the nave without uttering a word, he passed from under the gilded roofs, and the spacious dome, lofty as a firmament, expanded itself above him in the sky, covered with tracery of the celestial glories and brilliant with mosaic and stars of gold; when, opening on all sides to the wide transepts, the limitless pavement stretched away beyond the reach of sense; when, beneath this vast work and finished effort of man's devotion, he saw the high altar, brilliant with lights, surmounted and enthroned by its panoply of clustering columns and towering cross; when, all around him, he was conscious of the hush and calmness of worship, and felt in his inmost being the sense of vastness, of splendour, and of awe ;—he may be pardoned if, kneeling upon the polished floor, he conceived for the moment that this was the house of God, and that the gate of heaven was here.

* * * * *

CHAPTER XXV.

"It is almost impossible for a man to form in his imagination," said the rector to Inglesant, as they left the Church, "such beautiful and glorious scenes as are to be met with in the Roman Churches and Chapels. The profusion of the ancient marble found within the city itself, and the many fine quarries in the neighbourhood, have made this result possible; and notwithstanding the incredible sums of money which have been already laid out in this way, the same work is still going forward in other parts of Rome; the last effort still endeavouring to outshine those that went before it."

Inglesant found this assertion to be true. As he entered Church after Church, during the first few days of his sojourn in Rome, he found the same marble walls, the same inlaid tombs, the same coloured pavements. In the sombre autumn afternoons this splendour was toned down and veiled, till it produced an effect which was inexpressibly noble,—a dim brilliance, a subdued and restrained glory, which accorded well with the enervating perfume and the strains of romantic music that stole along the aisles. In these Churches, and in the monasteries adjoining, Inglesant was introduced to many priests and ecclesiastics, among whom he might study most of the varieties of devout feeling, and of religious life in all its forms. To many of these he was not drawn by any feeling of sympathy; many were only priests and monks in outward form, being in reality men of the world, men of pleasure, or antiquarians and artists. But, introduced to the society of Rome in the first place as a "devoto" he became acquainted naturally with many who aspired to, and who were considered to possess, exceptional piety. Among these he was greatly attracted by report towards a man who was then beginning to attract attention in Rome, and to exert that influence over the highest and most religious natures, which, during a period of twenty years, became so overpowering as at one time to threaten to work a complete revolution in the system and policy of Rome. This was Michael de Molinos, a Spanish priest who, coming to Rome some years before, began to inculcate a method of mystical devotion which he had no doubt gathered from the followers of St. Theresa, who were regarded with great veneration in Spain, where the contemplative devotion which they taught was held in high esteem. On his first coming to Rome Molinos refused all ecclesiastical advancement, and declined to practise those austerities which were so much admired. He associated with men of the most powerful minds and of the most elevated thoughts, and being acknowledged at once to be a man of learning and of good sense, his influence soon became perceptible. To all who came to him for spiritual comfort and advice he insisted on the importance of mental devotion, of daily communion, and of an inward application of the soul to Jesus Christ and to His death. So attractive were his personal qualities, and so alluring his doctrine, to minds which had grown weary of the more formal ceremonies and acts of bodily penance and devotion, that thousands thronged his apartments, and " the method of Molinos " became not only a divine message to many, but even the fashionable religion of Rome.

It spoke to men of an act of devotion, which it called the contemplative state, in which the will is so united to God and overcome by that union that it adores and loves and resigns itself up to Him, and, not exposed to the wavering of the mere fancy, nor wearied by a succession of formal acts of a dry religion, it enters into the life of God, into the heavenly places of Jesus Christ, with an indescribable and secret joy. It taught that this rapture and acquiescence in the Divine Will, while it is the highest state and privilege of devotion, is within the reach of every man, being the fruit of nothing more than the silent and humble adoration of God that arises out of a pure and quiet mind; and it offered to every man the prospect of this communion—a prospect to which the very novelty and vagueness gave a hitherto unknown delight—in exchange for the common methods of devotion which long use and constant repetition had caused to appear to many but as dead and lifeless forms. Those who followed this method generally laid aside the use of the rosary, the daily repeating of the breviary, together with the common devotion of the saints, and applied themselves to preserve their minds in an inward calm and quiet, that they might in silence perform simple acts of faith, and feel those inward motions and directions which they believed would follow upon such acts.

To such a doctrine as this, taught by such a man, it is not surprising that Inglesant was soon attracted, and he visited Molinos's rooms several times. On one of these occasions he met in the anteroom a gentleman he had seen more than once before, but had never spoken to. He was therefore somewhat surprised when he accosted him, and seemed desirous of some private conference. Inglesant knew that he was the Count Vespiriani, and had heard him described as of a noble and refined nature, and a hearty follower of Molinos. They left the house together, and driving to the gardens of the Borghese Palace, they walked for some time.

The Count began by expressing his pleasure that at so early a period of his residence in Rome Inglesant had formed the acquaintance of Molinos.

"You are perhaps," he said, "not aware of the importance of the movement, nor of the extent to which some of us are not without hope that it may ultimately reach. Few persons are aware of the numbers already devoted to it, including men of every rank in the Church and among the nobility, and of every variety of opinion and of principle. It cannot be supposed that all these persons act thus under the influence of any extraordinary elevation of piety or devotion. To what then can their conduct be ascribed? It cannot have escaped your notice, since you have been in Italy, that there is much that is rotten in the state of government, and to be deplored in the condition of the people. I do not know in what way you may have accounted for this lamentable condition of affairs in your own mind; but among ourselves (those among us at any rate who are men of intelligence and of experience of the life of other countries, and especially Protestant ones) there is but one solution—the share that priests have in the government, not only in the Pope's territory, but in all the other courts of Italy where they have the rule. This does not so much arise from any individual errors or misdoing as from the necessary unfitness of ecclesiastics to interfere in civil affairs. They have not souls large enough nor tender enough for government; they are trained in an inflexible code of morals and of conduct from which they cannot swerve. To this code all human needs must bow. They are cut off from sympathy with their fellows on most points; and their natural inclinations, which cannot be wholly suppressed, are driven into unworthy and mean channels; and they acquire a narrowness of spirit and a sourness of mind, together with a bias to one side only of life, which does not agree with the principles of human society. All kinds of incidental evils arise from these sources, in stating which I do not wish to accuse those ecclesiastics of unusual moral turpitude. Among them is the fact that, having individually so short and uncertain a time for governing, they think only of the present, and of serving their own ends, or satisfying their own conceptions, regardless of the ultimate happiness or misery which must be the consequence of what they do. Whatever advances the present interests of the Church or of themselves, for no man is free altogether from selfish motives,—whatever enriches the Church or their own families, for no man can help interesting himself in those of his own house,—is preferred to all wise, great, or generous counsels. You will perhaps wonder what the mystic spiritual religion of Molinos has to do with all this, but a moment's explanation will, I think, make it very clear to you. The hold which the priests have upon the civil government is maintained solely by the tyranny which they exercise over the spiritual life of men. It is the opinion of Molinos that this function is misdirected, and that in the place of a tyrant there should appear a guide. He is about to publish a book called 'La Guida Spirituale,' which will appear with several approbations before it,—one by the general of the Franciscans, who is a Qualificator of the Inquisition, and another by a member of the Society to which you are attached, Father Martin de Esparsa, also one of the Qualificators. This book, so authorized and recommended, cannot fail not only to escape censure, but to exert a powerful influence, and will doubtless be highly esteemed. Now the importance of Molinos's doctrine lies in this, that he presses the point of frequent communion, and asserts that freedom from mortal sin is the only necessary qualification. At the same time he guards himself from the charge of innovation by the very title and the whole scope of his book, which is to insist upon the necessity of a spiritual director and guide. You will see at once what an important step is here gained; for the doctrine being once admitted that mortal sin only is a disqualification for receiving the sacrament, and the necessity of confession before communion being not expressed, the obligation of coming always to the priest, as the minister of the sacrament of penance, before every communion, cannot long be insisted upon. Indeed, it will become a rule by which all spiritual persons who adhere to Molinos's method will conduct their penitents, that they may come to the sacrament when they find themselves out of the state of mortal sin, without going at every time to confession; and it is beginning to be observed already in Rome that those who, under the influence of this method, are becoming more strict in their lives, more retired and serious in their mental devotions, are become less zealous in their whole deportment as to the exterior parts of religion. They are not so assiduous at mass, nor in procuring masses for their friends, nor are they so frequent at confession or processions. I cannot tell you what a blessing I anticipate for mankind should this method be once allowed; what a freedom, what a force, what a reality religion would obtain! The time is ripe for it, and the world is prepared. The best men are giving their adherence; I entreat you to lend your aid. The Jesuits are wavering; they have not yet decided whether the new method will prevail or not. The least matter will turn the scale. You may think that it is of little importance which side you take, but if so, you are mistaken. You are not perhaps aware of the high estimation in which the reports and letters which have preceded you have caused you to be held at the Jesuits' College. You are supposed to have great influence with the English Catholics and Protestant Episcopalians, and the idea of promoting Catholic progress in England is the dearest to the mind of the Roman Ecclesiastic."

Inglesant listened to the Count attentively, and did not immediately reply. At last he said,—

"What you have told me is of the greatest interest, and commends itself to my conscience more than you know. As to the present state and government of Italy I am not competent to speak. One of the things which I hoped to learn in Rome was the answer to some complaints which I have heard in other parts of Italy. I fear also that you may be too sanguine as to the result of such freedom as you desire. This age is witness of the state to which too much freedom has brought England, my own country, a land which, a few years ago, was the happiest and wealthiest of all countries, now utterly ruined and laid waste. The freedom which you desire, and the position of the clergy which you approve, is somewhat the same as that which existed in the Protestant Episcopal Church of England; but the influence they possessed was not sufficient to resist the innovations and wild excesses of the Sectaries. The freedom which I desire for myself I am willing to renounce when I see the evil which the possession of it works among others and in the State. What you attempt, however, is an experiment in which I am not unwilling to be interested; and I shall be very curious to observe the result. The main point of your method, the freedom of the blessed sacrament, is a taking piece of doctrine, for the holding of which I have always been attracted to the Episcopal Church of England. It is, as you say, a point of immense importance, upon which, in fact, the whole system of the Church depends. I have been long seeking for some solution of the mysterious difficulties of the religious life. It may be that I shall find it in your Society, which I perceive already to consist of men of the highest and most select natures, with whom, come what may, it is an honour to be allied. You may count on my adherence; and though I may seem a half-hearted follower, I shall not be found wanting when the time of action comes. I should wish to see more of Molinos."

"I am not at all surprised," said the Count, "that you do not at once perceive the full force of what I have said. It requires to be an Italian, and to have grown to manhood in Italy, to estimate justly the pernicious influence of the clergy upon all ranks of society. I have travelled abroad, and when I have seen such a country as Holland, a land divided between land and sea, upon which the sun rarely shines, with a cold and stagnant air, and liable to be destroyed by inundations: when I see this country rich and flourishing, full of people, happy and contented, with every mark of plenty, and none at all of want; when I see all this, and then think of my own beautiful land, its long and happy summers, its rich and fruitful soil, and see it ruined and depopulated, its few inhabitants miserable and in rags, the scorn and contempt instead of the envy of the world; when I think of what she was an age or two ago, and reflect upon the means by which such a fall, such a dispeopling, and

T

such a poverty, has befallen a nation and a climate like this,—I dare not trust myself to speak the words which arise to my lips. Those with whom you associate will doubtless endeavour to prevent these melancholy truths from being perceived by you, but they are too evident to be concealed. Before long you will have painful experience of their existence."

"You say," said Inglesant, "that one or two ages ago Italy was much more prosperous than at present; were not the priests as powerful then as now?"

"I do not deny," replied the Count, "that there have been other causes which have tended to impoverish the country, but under a different government many of these might have been averted or at any rate mitigated. When the commerce of the country was flourishing, the power of the wealthy merchants and the trading princes was equal or superior to that of the priests, especially in the leading States. As their influence and wealth declined, the authority of the clergy increased. A wiser policy might have discovered other sources of wealth and of occupation for the people; they only thought of establishing the authority of the Church, of adorning the altars, of filling the Papal coffers."

Inglesant may have thought that he perceived a weak point in this explanation, but he made no reply, and the Count supposed he was satisfied.

A few days afterwards he had the opportunity of a long and private conversation with Molinos.

The Spaniard was a man of tall and graceful exterior, with a smile and manner which were indescribably alluring and sweet. Inglesant confided to him something of his past history, and much of his mental troubles and perplexities. He spoke of De Cressy and of the remorse which had followed his rejection of the life of self-denial which the Benedictine had offered him. Molinos's counsel was gentle and kindly.

"It was said to me long ago," said Inglesant, "that 'there are some men born into the world with such happy dispositions that the cross for a long time seems very light, if not altogether unfelt. The strait path runs side by side with the broad and pleasant way of man's desires; so close are they that the two cannot be discerned apart. So the man goes on, the favourite seemingly both of God and his fellows; but let him not think that he shall always escape the common doom. God is preparing some great test for him, some great temptation, all the more terrible for being so long delayed. Let him beware lest his spiritual nature be enervated by so much sunshine, so that when the trial comes, he may be unable to meet it. His conscience is easier than other men's : what are sins to them are not so to him. But the trial that is prepared for him will be no common one : it will be so fitted to his condition that he cannot palter with it nor pass it by ; he must either deny his God or himself.' This was said to me by one who knew me not ; but it was said with something of a prophetic instinct, and I see in these words some traces of my own fate. For a long time it seemed to me that I could serve both the world and God, that I could be a courtier in kings' houses and in the house of God, that I could follow the earthly learning and at the same time the learning that is from above. But suddenly the chasm opened beneath my feet ; two ways lay before me, and I chose the broad and easy path ; the cross was offered to me, and I drew back my hand ; the winnowing fan passed over the floor, and I was swept away with the chaff."

"I should prefer to say," replied the Spaniard,—and as he spoke, his expression was wonderfully compassionate and urbane, —" I should prefer to say that there are some men whom God is determined to win by love. Terrors and chastisements are fit for others, but these are the select natures, or, as you have yourself termed them, the courtiers of the household of God. Believe me, God does not lay traps for any, nor is He mistaken in His estimate. If He lavishes favour upon any man, it is because he knows that that man's nature will respond to love. It is the habit of kings to assemble in their houses such men as will delight them by their conversation and companionship, 'amor ac deliciæ generis humani,' whose memory is fresh and sweet ages after, when they be dead. Something like this it seems to me God is wont to do, that He may win these natures for the good of mankind and for His own delight. It is true that such privilege calls for a return ; but what will ensure a return sooner than the consideration of such favour as this ? You say you have been unworthy of such favour, and have forfeited it for ever. You cannot have forfeited it, for it was never deserved. It is the kingly grace of God, bestowed on whom He will. If I am not mistaken in your case, God will win you, and He will win you by determined and uninterrupted acts of love. It may be that in some other place God would have found for you other work; you have failed in attaining to that place; serve Him where you are. If you fall still lower, or imagine that you fall lower, still serve Him in the lowest room of all. Wherever you may find yourself, in Courts or pleasure-houses or gardens of delight, still serve Him, and you will bid defiance to imaginations and powers of evil, that strive to work upon a sensitive and excited nature, and to urge it to despair. Many of these thoughts which we look upon as temptations of God are but the accidents of our bodily temperaments. How can you, nursed in Courts, delicately reared and bred, trained in pleasure, your ear and eye and sense habituated to music and soft sounds, to colour and to beauty of form, your brain developed by intellectual effort and made sensitive to the slightest touch —how can religious questions bear the same aspect to you as to a man brought up in want of the necessaries of life, hardened by toil and exposure, unenlightened by learning and the arts, unconscious of the existence even of what is agony or delight to you? Yet God is equally with both of these; in His different ways He will lead both of them, would they but follow, through that maze of accident and casualty in which they are involved, and out of the tumult of which coil they complain to the Deity of what is truly the result of their own temperaments, ancestry, and the besetments of life. I tell you this because I have no fear that it will exalt you, but to keep you from unduly depreciating yourself, and from that terrible blasphemy that represents God as laying snares for men in the guise of pretended kindness. God is with all, with the coarse and dull as with the refined and pure, but He draws them by different means,—those by terror, these by love."

Inglesant said little in answer to these words, but they made a deep impression upon him. They lifted a weight from his spirits, and enabled him henceforward to take some of the old pleasure in the light of heaven and the occurrences of life. He saw much of Molinos, and had long conferences with him upon the solution of the greatest of all problems, that of granting religious freedom, and at the same time maintaining religious truth. Molinos thought that his system solved this problem, and although Inglesant was not altogether convinced of this, yet he associated himself heartily, if not wholly, with the Quietists, as Molinos's followers were called, insomuch that he received some friendly cautions from the Jesuit College not to commit himself too far.

* * * * *

It must not be supposed, however, that he was altogether absorbed in such thoughts or such pursuits. To him, as to all the other inhabitants of Rome, each in his own degree and station, the twofold aspect of existence in the strange Papal city claimed his alternate regard, and divided his life and his intellect. The society of Rome, at one moment devout, the next philosophic, the next antiquarian, artistic, pleasure-seeking, imparted to all its members some tincture of its Protean character. The existence of all was coloured by the many-sided prism through which the light of every day's experience was seen. Inglesant's acquaintance with the Cardinal introduced him at once to all the different coteries, and procured him the advantage of a companion who exerted a strong and cultivated mind to exhibit each subject in its completest and most fascinating aspect. Accompanied by the Cardinal, and with one or other of the literati of Rome, each in his turn a master of the peculiar study to which the day was devoted, Inglesant wandered day after day through all the wonderful city, through the palaces, ruins, museums, and galleries. He stood among the throng of statues, that strange maze of antique life, which some enchanter's wand seems suddenly to have frozen into marble in the midst of its intricate dance, yet so frozen as to retain, by some mysterious art, the warm and breathing life. He saw the men of the old buried centuries, of the magic and romantic existence when the world was young. The beautiful gods with their white wands; the grave senators and stately kings; the fauns and satyrs that dwelt in the untrodden woods; the pastoral flute-players, whose airs yet linger within the peasant's reeds; the slaves and craftsmen of old Rome, with all their postures, dress, and bearing, as they walked those inlaid pavements, buried deep beneath the soil, whose mosaic figures every now and then are opened to the faded life of to-day. Nor less entrancing were those quaint fancies upon the classic tombs, which showed in what manner the old pagan looked out into the spacious ether and confronted death,—a child playing with a comic masque, bacchanals, and wreaths of flowers, hunting parties, and battles, images of life, of feasting and desire; and finally, the inverted torch, the fleeting seasons ended, and the actor's part laid down.

Still existing as a background to this phantom life was the stage on which it had walked; the ruined splendour of Rome, in its setting of blue sky and green foliage, of ivy and creeping plants, of laurels and ilex, enfolded in a soft ethereal radiance that created everywhere a garden of romance.

"Nothing delights and entertains me so much in this country," said Inglesant one day to a gentleman with whom he was walking, "as the contrasts which present themselves on every hand, the peasant's hut built in the ruins of a palace, the most exquisite carving supporting its tottering roof, cattle drinking out of an Emperor's tomb, a theatre built in a mausoleum, and pantomime airs and the 'plaudite' heard amid the awful silence of the grave; here a Christ, ghastly, naked, on a cross; there a charming god, a tender harmony of form and life; triumphal arches sunk in the ruins not of their own only, but of successive ages, monuments far more of decay and death than of glory or fame; Corinthian columns canopied with briers, ivy, and wild vine, the delicate acanthus wreaths stained by noisome weeds. The thoughts that arise from the sight of these contrasts are pleasing though melancholy, such ideas, sentiments, and feelings as arise in the mind and in the heart at the foot of antique columns, before triumphal arches, in the depths of ruined tombs, and on mossy banks of fountains; but there are other contrasts which bring no such soothing thoughts with them; nothing but what may almost be called despair; profusion of magnificence and wealth side by side with the utmost wretchedness; Christ's altar blazing with jewels and marble, misery indescribable around; luxury, and enjoyment, and fine clothes, almost hustled by rags, and sores, and filth. Amid the lesson of past ages, written on every ruined column and shattered wall, what a distance still exists between the poor and the rich! Should the poor man wish to overpass it, he is driven back at once into his original wretchedness, or condemned more mercifully to death, while every ruined column and obelisk cries aloud 'Let everything that creeps console itself, for everything that is elevated falls.'"

"We Romans," said the gentleman, "preserve our ruins as beggars keep open their sores. They are preserved not always from taste; nor from a respect of antiquity, but sometimes from mere avarice, for they attract from every corner of the world that crowd of strangers whose curiosity has long furnished a maintenance to three-fourths of Italy. But you were speaking of the charming gods of the ancients. We are not inferior to them. Have you seen the Apollo of Bernini pursuing Daphne, in the Borghese Palace? His hair waves in the wind, you hear the entreaties of the god."

"Yes, I have seen it," said Inglesant; "it is another of those wonderful contrasts with which Rome abounds. We are Catholic and Pagan at the same time."

"It is true," said the other; "nevertheless, in the centre of the blood-stained Coliseo stands a crucifix. The Galilean has triumphed."

Inglesant stopped. They were standing before the Apollo in the Belvedere gardens. Inglesant took from beneath his vest a crucifix in ivory, exquisitely carved, and held it beside the statue of the god. The one the noblest product of buoyant life, the proudest perfection of harmonious form, purified from all the dross of humanity, the head worthy of the god of day and of the lyre, of healing and of help, who bore in his day the selfsame name that the other bore, "the great physician;" the other, worn and emaciated, helpless, dying, apparently without power, forgotten by the world. "Has the Galilean triumphed? Do you prefer the Christ?" he said.

The gentleman smiled. "The benign god," he said, "has doubtless many votaries, even now."

It is probable that the life of Rome was working its effect upon Inglesant himself. Under its influence, and that of the Cardinal, his tone of thought became considerably modified. In a strange and unexpected way, in the midst of so much religion, his attention was diverted from the religious side of life, and his views of what was philosophically important underwent considerable change. He read Lucretius less, and Terence and Aristophanes more. Human life, as he saw it existing around him, became more interesting to him than theories and opinions. Life in all its forms, the Cardinal assured him, was the only study worthy of man; and though Inglesant saw that such a general assertion only encouraged the study of human thought, yet it seemed to him that it directed him to a truth which he had hitherto perhaps overlooked, and taught him to despise and condemn nothing in the common path of men in which he walked. If this were true, the more carefully he studied this common life, and the more narrowly he watched it, the more worthy it would appear of regard; the dull and narrow streets, the crowded dwellings, the base and vulgar life, the poverty and distress of the poorer classes, would assume an interest unknown to him before.

"This life and interest," the Cardinal would say, "finds its best exponent in the old pantomime and burlesque music of Italy. The real, everyday, commonplace, human life, which originates absolutely among the people themselves, speaks in their own music and street airs; but when these are touched by a master's hand, it becomes revealed to us in its essence, refined and idealized, with all its human features, which, from their very familiarity, escape our recognition as we walk the streets. In the peculiarity of this music, its graceful delicacy and lively frolic and grotesqueness, I think I find the most perfect presentment, to the ear and heart, of human life, especially as the slightest variation of time or setting reveals in the most lively of these airs depths of pathos and melodious sorrow, completing thus the analogy of life, beneath the gayest phases of which lie unnoticed the saddest realities."

"I have often felt," said Inglesant, "that old dance music has an inexpressible pathos; as I listen to it I seem to be present at long-past festivities, whose very haunts are swept away and forgotten; at evenings in the distant past, looked forward to as all important, upon whose short and fleeting hours the hopes and enjoyments of a lifetime were staked, now lost in an undistinguished oblivion and dust of death. The young and the beautiful who danced to these quaint measures, in a year or two had passed away, and other forms equally graceful took their place. Fancies and figures that live in sound, and pass before the eyes only when evoked by such melodies, float down the shadowy way and pass into the future, where other gay and brilliant hours await the young, to be followed as heretofore by pale and disappointed hopes and sad realities, and the grave."

"What do you mean," said the Cardinal, "by figures that live in sound?"

"It seems to me," said Inglesant, "that the explanation of the power of music upon the mind is, that many things are elements which are not reckoned so, and that sound is one of them. As the air and fire are said to be peopled by fairy inhabitants, as the spiritual man lives in the element of faith, so

I believe that there are creatures which live in sound. Every lovely fancy, every moment of delight, every thought and thrill of pleasure which music calls forth, or which, already existing, is beautified and hallowed by music, does not die. Such as these become fairy existences, spiritual creatures, shadowy but real, and of an inexpressibly delicate grace and beauty, which live in melody, and float and throng before the sense whenever the harmony that gave and maintains their life exists again in sound. They are children of the earth, and yet above it; they recall the human needs and hopes from which they sprang. They have shadowy sex and rank, and diversity of bearing, as of the different actors' parts that fill the stage of life. Poverty and want are there, but, as in an allegory or morality, purified and released from suffering. The pleasures and delights of past ages thus live again in sound, the sorrows and disappointments of other days and of other men mingle with our own, and soften and subdue our hearts. Apollo and Orpheus tamed the savage beasts; music will soften our rugged nature, and kindle in us a love of our kind and a tolerance of the petty failings and the shortcomings of men."

It was not only music that fostered and encouraged in Rome an easy tolerant philosophy. No society could be more adapted than that of the Papal city to such an end. A people whose physical wants were few and easily supplied (a single meal in such a climate, and that easily procured, sufficing for the day); a city full of strangers, festivals, and shows; a conscience absolutely at rest; a community entirely set apart from politics, absolutely at one with its government by habit, by interest, and by religion;—constituted a unique state and mental atmosphere, in which such philosophy naturally flourished. The early hours of the day were spent in such business as was necessary for all classes to engage in, and were followed by the dinner of fruit, vegetables, fish, and a little meat. From dinner all went to sleep, which lasted till six o'clock in the evening. Then came an hour's trifling over the toilette, all business was at an end, and all the shops were shut. Till three o'clock in the morning the hours were devoted to enjoyment. Men, women, and children repaired to the public walks, to the Corso and squares, to conversation in coteries, to assemblies in arcaded and lighted gardens, to collations in taverns. Even the gravest and most serious gave themselves up to relaxation and amusement till the next day. Every evening was a festival; every variety of character and conversation enlivened these delicious hours, these soft and starry nights.

Nothing pleased Inglesant's fancy so much, or soothed his senses so completely, as this second dawn of the day and rising to pleasure in the cool evening. Soothed and calmed by sleep, the irritated nerves were lulled into that delicious sense for which we have no name, but which we compare to flowing water, and to the moistening of a parched and dusty drought. All thoughts of trouble and of business were banished by the intervening hours of forgetfulness, from which the mind, half-aroused and fresh from dreamland, awoke to find itself in a world as strange and fantastic as the land of sleep which it had left; a land bathed in sunset light, overarched by rainbows; saluted by cool zephyrs, soothed by soft strains of music, delighted and amused by gay festivals, peopled by varied crowds of happy folk, many-coloured in dress, in green walks sparkling with fairy lamps, and seated at al fresco suppers, before cosy taverns famous for delicious wines, where the gossip of Europe, upon which Rome looked out as from a Belvedere, intrigue, and the promotions of the morning, were discussed.

Inglesant had taken lodgings in an antique villa on the Aventine, surrounded by an uncultivated garden and by vineyards. The house was partly deserted and partly occupied by a family of priests, and he slept here when he was not at the Cardinal's palace, or with other of his friends. The place was quiet and remote from the throng and noise of Rome; in the gardens were fountains in the cool shade; frescoes and paintings had been left on the walls and in the rooms by the owner of the villa; the tinkling of convent bells sounded from the slopes of the hills through the laurels and ilex and across the vines; every now and then the chanting of the priests might be heard from a small Chapel at the back of the house.

Inglesant awoke from his mid-day sleep one evening to the splash of the fountain, and the scent of the fresh-turned earth in the vineyard, and found his servant arranging his room for his toilette. He was to sup that evening at the Cardinal's with some of the Fathers of the Oratory, and he dressed, as was usual with him even in his most distracted moods, with scrupulous care. A sedan was waiting for him, and he set out for the Cardinal's palace.

It was a brilliant evening; upon the hill-sides the dark trees stood out against the golden sky, the domes and pinnacles of the Churches shone in the evening light. In the quiet lanes, in the neighbourhood of the Aventine, the perfume of odoriferous trees was wafted over lofty garden walls; quiet figures flitted to and fro, a distant hum of noisy streets scarcely reached the ear, mingled with the never-ceasing bells. That morning, before he went to sleep, Inglesant had been reading "The Birds" of Aristophanes, with a voluminous commentary by some old scholar, who had brought together a mass of various learning upon the subject of grotesque apologue, fable, and the fanciful representation of the facts and follies of human life under the characters of animals and of inanimate objects. A vast number of examples of curious pantomime and other stage characters were given, and the idea preserved throughout that, by such impersonations, the voices of man's existence were able to speak with clearness and pathos, and were more sure of being listened to than when they assumed the guise of a teacher or divine. Beneath a grotesque and unexpected form they conceal a gravity more sober than seriousness itself, as irony is more sincere than the solemnity which it parodies. Truth drops her stilted gait, and becomes natural and real, in the midst of ludicrous and familiar events. The broad types of life's players into which the race is divided, especially the meanest,—thieves, beggars, outcasts,—with whom life is a reality stripped of outward show, will carry a moral and a teaching more aptly than the privileged and affected classes. Mixed with these are animals and familiar objects of household life, to which everyday use has given a character of their own. These, not in the literal repulsiveness or dulness of their monotonous existence, but abstracted, as the types or emblems of the ideas associated with each one—not a literal beggar, in his dirt and loathsomeness, but poverty, freedom, helplessness, and amusing knavery, personified in the part of a beggar—not a mere article of household use in its inanimate stupidity, but every idea and association connected with the use of such articles by generations of men and women;—these and such as these, enlivened by the sparkle of genius, set forth in gay and exquisite music, and by brilliant repartee and witty dialogue, certainly cannot be far behind the very foremost delineation of human life.

Educated in the Court of King Charles to admire Shakespeare and the Elizabethan stage, Inglesant was better able to understand these things than the Italians were, suggestive as the Italian life itself was of such reflections. The taste for music and scenery had driven dialogue and character from the stage. Magnificent operas, performed by exquisite singers, and accompanied by mechanical effects of stupendous extent, were almost the only scenic performances fashionable in Italy; but this was of less consequence where every street was a stage, and every festival an elaborate play. The Italians were pantomimic and dramatic in the highest degree without perceiving it themselves. The man who delights in regarding this life as a stage cannot attach an overwhelming importance to any incident; he observes life as a spectator, and does not engage in it as an actor; but the Italian was too impetuous to do this—he took too violent an interest in the events themselves.

The narrow streets through which Inglesant's chair passed terminated at last in a wide square. It was full of confused figures, presenting to the eye a dazzling movement of form and colour, of which last, owing to the evening light, the prevailing tint was blue. A brilliant belt of sunset radiance, like molten gold along the distant horizon, threw up the white houses into strong relief. Dark cypress trees rose against the glare of the yellow sky, tinged with blue from the fathomless azure above. The white spray of fountains flashed high over the heads of the people in the four corners of the square, and long lance-like gleams of light shot from behind the cypresses and the white houses, refracting a thousand colours in the flashing water. A murmur of gay talk filled the air, and a constant change of varied form perplexed the eye.

Inglesant alighted from his chair, and, directing his servants to proceed at once to the Cardinal's, crossed the square on foot. Following so closely on his previous dreamy thoughts, he was intensely interested and touched by this living pantomime. Human life had never before seemed to him so worthy of regard, whether looked at as a whole, inspiring noble and serious reflections, or viewed in detail, when each separate atom appears pitiful and often ludicrous. The infinite distance between these two poles, between the aspirations and the exhortations of conscience, which have to do with humanity as a whole, and the actual circumstances and capacities of the individual, with which satirists and humourists have ever made free to jest,—this contrast, running through every individual life as well as through the mass of existence, seemed to him to be the true field of humour, and the real science of those "Humanities" which the schools pedantically professed to teach.

Nothing moved in the motley crowd before him but what illustrated this science,—the monk, the lover, the soldier, the improvisatore, the matron, the young girl; here the childish hand brandishing its toy, there the artisan, and the shop-girl, and the maid-servant, seeking such enjoyment as their confined life afforded; the young boyish companions with interlaced arms, the benignant priest, every now and then the stately carriage slowly passing by to its place on the Corso, or to the palace or garden to which its inmates were bound.

Wandering amid this brilliant phantasia of life, Inglesant's heart smote him for the luxurious sense of pleasure which he found himself taking in the present movement and aspect of things. Doubtless this human philosophy, if we may so call it, into which he was drifting, has a tendency, at least, very different from much of the teaching which is the same in every school of religious thought. Love of mankind is inculcated as a sense of duty by every such school; but by this is certainly not intended love of and acquiescence in mankind as it is. This study of human life, however, this love of human existence, is unconnected with any desire for the improvement either of the individual or of the race. It is man as he is, not man as he might be, or as he should be, which is a delightful subject of contemplation to this tolerant philosophy which human frailty finds so attractive. Man's failings, his self-inflicted miseries, his humours, the effect of his very crimes and vices, if not even those vices themselves, form a chief part in the changing drama upon which the student's eyes are so eagerly set, and without these it would lose its interest and attraction. A world of perfect beings would be to such a man of all things the most stale and unprofitable. Humour and pathos, the grotesque contrast between a man's aspirations and his actual condition, his dreams and his mean realities, would be altogether wanting in such a world. Indignation, sorrow, satire, doubt, and restlessness, allegory, the very soul and vital salt of life, would be wanting in such a world. But if a man does not desire a perfect world, what part can he have in the Christian warfare? It is true that an intimate study of a world of sin and of misfortune throws up the sinless character of the Saviour into strong relief; but the student accepts this Saviour's character and mission as part of the phenomena of existence, not as an irreconcilable crusade and battle-cry against the powers of the world on every hand. The study of life is indeed equally possible to both schools; but the pleased acquiescence in life as it is, with all its follies and fantastic pleasures, is surely incompatible with following the footsteps of the Divine Ascetic who trod the wine-press of the wrath of God. With all their errors, they who rejected the world and all its allurements, and taught the narrow life of painful self-denial, must be more nearly right than this.

Nevertheless, even before this last thought was completely formed in his mind, the sight of the moving people, and of the streets of the wonderful city opening out on every side, full of palaces and glittering shops and stalls, and crowded with life and gaiety, turned his halting choice back again in the opposite direction, and he thought something like this:—

"How useless and even pitiful is the continued complaint of moralists and divines, to whom none lend an ear, whilst they endeavour, age after age, to check youth and pleasure, and turn the current of life and nature backward on its course. For how many ages in this old Rome, as in every other city, since Terence gossiped of the city life, has this frail faulty humanity for a few hours sunned itself on warm afternoons in sheltered walks and streets, and comforted itself into life and pleasure, amid all its cares and toils and sins. Out of this shifting phantasmagoria comes the sound of music, always pathetic and sometimes gay: amid the roofs and belfries peers the foliage of the public walks, the stage upon which, in every city, life may be studied and taken to heart; not far from these walks is, in every city, the mimic stage, the glass in which, in every age and climate, human life has seen itself reflected, and has delighted, beyond all other pleasures, in pitying its own sorrows, in learning its own story, in watching its own fantastic developments, in foreshadowing its own fate, in smiling sadly for an hour over the still more fleeting representation of its own fleeting joys. For ever, without any change, the stream flows on, spite of moralist and divine, the same as when Phaedria and Thais loved each other in old Rome. We look back on these countless ages of city life, cooped in narrow streets and alleys and paved walks, breathing itself in fountained courts and shaded arcades, where youth and manhood and old age have sought their daily sustenance not only of bread but of happiness, and have with difficulty and toil enough found the one and caught fleeting glimpses of the other, between the dark thunder clouds, and under the weird, wintry sky of many a life. Within such a little space how much life is crowded, what high hopes, how much pain! From those high windows behind the flower-pots young girls have looked out upon life, which their instincts told them was made for pleasure, but which year after year convinced them was, somehow or other, given over to pain. How can we read this endless story of humanity with any thought of blame? How can we watch this restless quivering human life, this ceaseless effort of a finite creature to attain to those things which are agreeable to its created nature, alike in all countries, under all climates and skies, and whatever change of garb or semblance the long course of years may bring, with any other thought than that of tolerance and pity—tolerance of every sort of city existence, pity for every kind of toil and evil, year after year repeated, in every one of earth's cities, full of human life and handicraft, and thought and love and pleasure, as in the streets of that old Jerusalem over which the Saviour wept?"

* * * * *

The conversation that evening at the Cardinal's villa turned upon the antiquities of Rome. The chief delight of the Fathers of the Oratory was in music, but the Cardinal preferred conversation, especially upon Pagan literature and art. He was an enthusiast upon every subject connected with the Greeks,—art, poetry, philosophy, religion; upon all these he founded theories and deductions which showed not only an intimate acquaintance with Greek literature, but also a deep familiarity with the human heart. A lively imagination and eloquent and polished utterance enabled him to extract from the baldest and most obscure myths and fragments of antiquity much that was fascinating, and, being founded on a true insight into human nature, convincing also.

Inglesant especially sympathized with and understood the tone of thought and the line of reasoning with which the Cardinal regarded Pagan antiquity; and this appreciation pleased the Cardinal, and caused him to address much of his conversation directly to him.

The villa was full of objects by which thought and conversation were attracted to such channels. The garden was entered by a portico or door-case adorned with ancient statues, the volto or roof of which was painted with classic subjects, and the lofty doors themselves were covered with similar ones in relief. The walls of the house, towards the garden, were cased with bas-reliefs,—"antique incrustations of history" the Cardinal called them,—representing the Rape of Europa, of Leda, and other similar scenes. These antique stones and carvings were fitted into the walls between the rich pilasters and cornicing which adorned the front of the villa, and the whole was crossed with tendrils of citron and other flowering shrubs, trained with the utmost art and nicety, so as to soften and ornament without concealing the sculpture. The gardens were traversed by high hedges of myrtle, lemon, orange, and juniper, interspersed with mulberry trees and oleanders, and were planted with wide beds of brilliant flowers, according to the season, now full of anemones, ranunculuses, and crocuses. The whole was formed upon terraces, fringed with balustrades of marble, over which creeping plants were trained with the utmost skill, only leaving sufficient stone-work visible to relieve the foliage. The walks were full of statues and pieces of carving in relief. The rooms were ornamented in the same taste, and the chimney of the one in which the supper was laid was enriched with sculpture of wonderful grace and delicacy.

One of the Fathers of the Oratory asked Inglesant whether he had seen the Venus of the Medicean palace, and what he thought of it compared with the Venus of the Farnese; and when he had replied, the other turned to the Cardinal and inquired whether, in his opinion, the Greeks had any higher meaning or thought in these beautiful delineations of human form than mere admiration and pleasure.

"The higher minds among them assuredly," said the Cardinal; "but in another and more important sense every one of them, even the most unlettered peasant who gazed upon the work, and the most worldly artist buried in the mere outward conceptions of his art, were consciously or unconsciously following, and even worshipping, a divinity and a truth than which nothing can be higher or more universal. For the truth was too powerful for them, and so universal that they could not escape. Human life, in all the phases of its beauty and its deformity, is so instinct with the divine nature, that, in merely following its variety, you are learning the highest lessons, and teaching them to others."

"What may you understand by being instinct with the divine nature?" said the Priest, not unnaturally.

"I mean that general consensus and aggregate of truth in which human nature and all that is related to it is contained. That divine idea, indeed, in which all the facts of human life and experience are drawn together, and exalted to their utmost perfection and refinement, and are seen and felt to form a whole of surpassing beauty and nobleness, in which the divine image and plastic power in man is clearly discerned and intellectually received and appropriated."

The Priest did not seem altogether to understand this, and remained silent.

"But," said Inglesant, "much of this pursuit of the beautiful must have been associated, in the ideas of the majority of the people, with thoughts and actions the most unlovely and undesirable according to the intellectual reason, however delightful to the senses."

"Even in these orgies," replied the Cardinal, "in the most profligate and wild excesses of license, I see traces of this all-pervading truth; for the renouncing of all bound and limit is in itself a truth, when any particular good, though only sensual, is freed and perfected. This is, no doubt, what the higher natures saw, and it was this that reconciled them to the license of the people and of the unilluminated. In all these aberrations they saw ever fresh varieties and forms of that truth which, when it was intellectually conceived, it was their greatest enjoyment to contemplate, and which, no doubt, formed the material of the instructions which the initiated into the mysteries received. It is impossible that this could be otherwise, for there can be no philosophy if there be no human life from which to derive it. The intellectual existence and discourses of Socrates cannot be understood, except when viewed in connection with the sensual and common existence and carnal wisdom of Aristophanes, any more than the death of the one can be understood without we also understand the popular thought and feeling delineated to us by the other. And why should we be so ungrateful as to turn round on this 'beast within the man,' if you so choose to call it,—the human body and human delight to which we owe not only our own existence and all that makes life desirable, but also that very loftiness and refinement of soul, that elevated and sublime philosophy, which could not exist but for the contrast and antithesis which popular life presents? Surely it is more philosophical to take in the whole of life, in every possible form, than to shut yourself up in one doctrine, which, while you fondly dream you have created it, and that it is capable of self-existence, is dependent for its very being on that human life from which you have fled, and which you despise. This is the whole secret of the pagan doctrine, and the key to those profound views of life which were evolved in their religion. This is the worship of Priapus, of human life, in which nothing comes amiss or is to be staggered at, however voluptuous or sensual, for all things are but varied manifestations of life; of life, ruddy, delicious, full of fruits, basking in sunshine and plenty, dyed with the juice of grapes; of life in valleys cooled by snowy peaks, amid vineyards and shady fountains, among which, however, 'Sæpe Faunorum voces exauditæ, sæpe visæ formæ Deorum.'"

"This, Signore Inglesant," said the Priest, passing the wine across the table, with a smile, "is somewhat even beyond the teaching of your friends of the Society of the Gesu; and would make their doctrine even, excellently as it already suits that purpose, still more propitious towards the frailty of men."

Inglesant filled his glass, and drank it off before he replied. The wine was of the finest growth of the delicious Alban vineyards; and as the nectar coursed through his veins, a luxurious sense of acquiescence stole over him. The warm air, laden with perfume from the shaded windows, lulled his sense; a stray sunbeam lighted the piles of fruit and the deeply embossed gold of the service on the table before him, and the mellow paintings and decorated ceiling of the room. As he slowly drank his wine the memory of Serenus de Cressy, and of his doctrine of human life, rose before his mind, and his eyes were fixed upon the deep-coloured wine before him, as though he saw there, as in a magic goblet, the opposing powers that divide the world. It seemed to him that he had renounced his right to join in the conflict, and that he must remain as ever a mere spectator of the result; nevertheless he said,—

"Your doctrine is delightful to the philosopher and to the man of culture, who has his nature under the curb, and his glance firmly fixed upon the goal; but to the vulgar it is death; and indeed it was death until the voice of another God was heard, and the form of another God was seen, not in vineyards and rosy bowers, but in deserts and stony places, in dens and caves of the earth, and in prisons and on crosses of wood."

"It is treason to the idea of cultured life," said the Cardinal, "to evoke such gloomy images. My theory is at least free from such faults of taste."

"Do not fear me," said Inglesant; "I have no right to preach such a lofty religion. An asceticism I never practised it would ill become me to advocate."

"You spoke of the death of Socrates," said the Priest; "does this event fall within the all-embracing tolerance of your theory?"

"The death of Socrates," said the Cardinal, "appears to have been necessary to preserve the framework of ordinary everyday society from falling to pieces. At any rate men of good judgment in that day thought so, and they must have known best. You must remember that it was Socrates that was put to death, not Plato, and we must not judge by what the latter has left us of what the former taught. The doctrine of Socrates was purely negative, and undermined the principle of belief not only in the Gods but in everything else. His dialectic was excellent and noble, his purpose pure and exalted, the clearing of men's minds of false impressions; but to the common fabric of society his method was destruction. So he was put to death, unjustly of course, and contrary to the highest law, but according to the lower law of expediency, justly; for society must preserve itself even at the expense of its noblest thinkers. But," added the Cardinal with a smile, "we have only to look a little way for a parallel. It is not, however, a perfect one; for while the Athenians condemned Socrates to a death painless and dignified, the moderns have burnt Servetus, whose doctrine contained nothing dangerous to society, but turned on a mere point of the schools, at the stake."

"Why do they not burn you, Cardinal?" said one of the Oratorians, who had not yet spoken, a very intimate friend of the master of the house.

"They do not know whom to begin with in Rome," he

replied; "if they once commenced to burn, the holocaust would be enormous before the sacrifice was complete."

"I would they would burn Donna Olympia," said the same Priest; "is it true that she has returned?"

"Have patience," said the Cardinal; "from what I hear you will not have long to wait."

"I am glad you believe in purgatory," said the Priest who had spoken first. "I did not know that your Eminence was so orthodox."

"You mistake. I do not look so far. I am satisfied with the purgatory of this life. I merely meant that I fear we shall not long have his Holiness among us."

"The moderns have burnt others besides Servetus," said one of the guests—"Vaninus, for instance."

"I did not instance Vaninus," said the Cardinal, "because his punishment was more justifiable, and nearer to that of Socrates. Vaninus taught atheism, which is dangerous to society, and he courted his death. I suppose, Mr. Inglesant, that your bishops would burn Mr. Hobbes if they dared."

"I know little of the Anglican bishops, Eminence," replied Inglesant; "but from that little I should imagine that it is not impossible."

"What does Mr. Hobbes teach?" said one of the party.

The Cardinal looked at Inglesant, who shook his head.

"What he teaches would require more skill than I possess to explain. What they would say that they burnt him for would be for teaching atheism and the universality of matter. I fancy that it is at least doubtful whether even Vaninus meant to deny the existence of God. I have been told that he was merely an enthusiastic naturalist, who could see nothing but nature, which was his god. But as for Mr. Hobbes's opinions, he seems to me to have proclaimed a third authority in addition to the two which already claimed the allegiance of the world. We had first the authority of a Church, then of a book, now Mr. Hobbes asserts the authority of reason; and the supporters of the book, even more fiercely than those of the Church, raise a clamour against him. His doctrines are very insidiously and cautiously expressed, and it proves the acuteness of the Anglican divines that they have detected, under the plausible reasoning of Mr. Hobbes, the basis of a logical argument which would, if unconfuted, destroy the authority of Holy Scripture."

The Cardinal looked at Inglesant curiously, as though uncertain whether he was speaking in good faith or not, but the subject did not seem to possess great interest to the company at table, and the conversation took another turn.

CHAPTER XXVI.

SOME few days after the conversation at the Cardinal's villa, Inglesant received his first commission as an agent of the Society of the Gesu. He was invited to sup with the Superior of the English Jesuits, Father ———, at the college called St. Tommaso degli Inglesi. After the meal, over which nothing was spared to render it delicious, and during the course of which the Superior exerted himself to please, the latter said,—

"I am instructed to offer you a commission, which, if I mistake not, will both prove very interesting to you, and will also be of advantage to your interests. You are probably acquainted with the story of the old Duke of Umbria. You have heard that, wearied with age, and tired of the world, he resigned the dukedom to his son, his only child, the object of all his hopes and the fruit of careful training and instruction. This son, far from realizing the brilliant hopes of his father, indulged in every kind of riot and debauchery, and finally died young, worn out before his time. The old Duke, broken-hearted by this blow, has virtually made over the succession to the Holy Father, and lives now, alone and silent, in his magnificent palace, caring for no worldly thing, and devoting all his thoughts to religion and to his approaching end. He is unhappy in the prospect of his dissolution, and the only persons who are admitted to his presence are those who promise him any comfort in the anticipation, or any clearness in the vision, of the future life. Quacks and impostors of every kind, priests and monks and fanatics, are admitted freely, and trouble this miserable old man, and drive him into intolerable despair. To give to this old man, whose life of probity, of honour, of devotion to his people, of conscientious rectitude, is thus miserably rewarded— to give some comfort to this miserable victim of a jealousy which the superstitious miscall that of heaven, is a mission which the ethereal chivalry of the soul will eagerly embrace.

It is one, I may say without flattery, for which I hold you singularly fitted. A passionate religious fervour, such as yours, combined in the most singular manner with the freest speculative opinions, and commended by a courteous grace, will at once soothe and strengthen this old man's shattered intellect, distracted and tormented and rapidly sinking into imbecility and dotage."

Father —— paused and filled his glass; then passing the wine to Inglesant, he continued, half carelessly,—

"I said that the Duke had virtually made over the succession of his State to the Papal See; but this has not been formally ratified, and there has arisen some hesitation and difficulty respecting it. Some of the unsuitable advisers to whom the Duke in his mental weakness has unfortunately lent an ear, have endeavoured to persuade him that the interests of his people will be imperilled by their country being placed under the mild and beneficent rule of the Holy Father. We hear something of a Lutheran, who, by some unexplained means, has obtained considerable influence with this unhappy old man; and we are informed that there is great danger of the Duke's hesitating so long before he completes the act of succession, that his death may occur before it is complete. You will of course exert the influence which I hope and expect that you will soon gain at the ducal Court, to hasten this consummation, so desirable for the interests of the people, of the Papacy, and of the Duke himself."

Inglesant had listened to this communication with great interest. The prospect which the earlier part of it had opened before him was in many respects an attractive one, and the flattering words of the Superior were uttered in a tone of sincerity which made them very pleasant to hear. The description of the Duke's condition offered to him opportunities of mental study of absorbing interest, and the characters of those by whom he was surrounded would no doubt present combinations and varieties of singular and unusual curiosity. It must not be denied, moreover, that there entered into his estimate of the proposal made to him somewhat of the prospect of luxurious and courtly life— of that soft clothing, both of body and spirit, which they who live in kings' houses wear. It is difficult indeed for one who has been long accustomed to refined and dainty living, where every sense is trained and strengthened by the fruition it enjoys;

to regard the future altogether with indifference in respect to these things. The palace of the Duke was notorious throughout all Italy for the treasures of art which it contained, though its master in his old age was become indifferent to such delights. But though these thoughts passed through his mind as the Superior was speaking, Inglesant was too well versed in the ways of Courts and Ecclesiastics not to know that there was something more to come, and to attend carefully for its development. The latter part of the Superior's speech produced something even of a pleasurable amusement, as the skilfully executed tactics of an opponent are pleasing to a good player either at cards or chess. The part which he was now expected to play, the side which he was about to espouse, taken in connection with the difficulties and impressions which had perplexed him since he had arrived in Italy, and which had not been removed by what he had seen in Rome itself, corresponded so exactly with the scheme which, to his excited imagination, was being spiritually developed for his destruction—a morbid idea, possibly, which the lofty beneficence of Molinos's doctrine had only partially removed—that its appearance and recognition actually provoked a smile. But the smile, which the Superior noticed and entirely misunderstood, was succeeded by uneasiness and depression. There was, however, little hesitation and no apparent delay in Inglesant's manner of acceptance. The old habit of implicit obedience was far from obliterated or even weakened, and though Father St. Clare was not present the supreme motive of his influence was not unfelt. He had chosen his part when in Paris he had turned his back upon De Cressy, and accepted the Jesuit's offer of the mission to Rome. He had lived in Rome, had been received and countenanced and entertained as one who had accepted the service of those who had so courteously and hospitably treated him, and it was far too late now, when the first return was expected of him, to draw back or to refuse. To obey was not only a recognized duty, it was an instinct which not only long training but experience even served to strengthen. He assured the Superior that he was perfectly ready to set out. He assured himself indeed that it was not necessary to come to a decision at that moment, and that he should be much better able to decide upon his course of conduct when he had seen the Duke himself, and received more full instructions from Rome.

The Superior informed Inglesant that he would be expected to visit Umbria as a gentleman of station, and offered to provide the necessary means. Inglesant contented himself with declining this offer for the present. Since his arrival at Rome he had received considerable sums of money from England, the result of Lady Cardiff's bounty, and the Cardinal's purse was open to him in several indirect ways. He provided himself with the necessary number of servants, horses, and other conveniences, and some time, as would appear, after Easter, he arrived at Umbria.

On his journey, as he rode along in the wonderful clear morning light, in his "osteria" in the middle of the day, and when he resumed his journey in the cool of the evening, his thoughts had been very busy. He remembered his conversation with the Count Vespiriani, and was unable to reconcile his present mission with the pledge he had given to the Count. He was more than once inclined to turn back and refuse to undertake the duty demanded of him. Thoughts of Lauretta, and of the strange fate that had separated him from her, also occupied his mind; and with these conflicting emotions still unreconciled, he saw at last the white façade of the palace towering above the orange-groves, and the houses and pinnacles of the city.

The ducal palace at Umbria is a magnificent example of the Renaissance style. It is impossible to dwell in or near this wonderful house without the life becoming affected, and even diverted from its previous course, by its imperious influence. The cold and mysterious power of the classic architecture is wedded to the rich and libertine fancy of the Renaissance, treading unrestrained and unabashed the maze of nature and of phantasy, and covering the classic purity of outline with its exquisite tracery of fairy life. Over door and window and pilaster throng and cling the arabesque carvings of foliage and fruit, of graceful figures in fantastic forms and positions,—all of infinite variety; all full of originality, of life, of motion, and of character; all of exquisite beauty both of design and workmanship. The effect of the whole is lightness and joy, while the eye is charmed and the sense filled with a luxurious satisfaction at the abounding wealth of beauty and lavish imagination. But together with this delight to eye and sense there is present to the mind a feeling, not altogether painless, of oppressive luxury, and of the mating of incongruous forms, arousing as it were an uneasy conscience, and affecting the soul somewhat as the overpowering perfume of tropical vegetation affects the senses. To dwell in this palace was to breathe an enchanted air; and as the wandering prince of story loses his valour and strength in the magic castles into which he strays, so here the indweller, whose intellect was mastered by the genius of the architecture, found his simplicity impaired, his taste becoming more sensuous and less severely chaste, and his senses lulled and charmed, by the insidious and enervating spirit that pervaded the place.

At his first presentation Inglesant found the Duke seated in a small room fitted as an oratory or closet, and opening by a private door into the ducal pew in the Chapel. His person was bowed and withered by age and grief, but his eye was clear and piercing, and his intellect apparently unimpaired. He regarded his visitor with an intense and scrutinizing gaze, which lasted for several minutes, and seemed to indicate some suspicion. There was, however, about Inglesant's appearance and manner something so winning and attractive, that the old man's eyes gradually softened, and the expression of distrust that made his look almost that of a wild and hunted creature, changed to one of comparative satisfaction and repose. It is true that he regarded with pleasure and hope every new-comer, from whom he expected to derive consolation and advice.

Inglesant expected that he would inquire of the news of Rome, of the Pope's health, and such-like matters; but he seemed to have no curiosity concerning such things. After waiting for some time in silence he said,—

"Anthony Guevara tells us that we ought to address men who are under thirty with 'You are welcome,' or 'You come in a good hour,' because at that time of life they seem to be coming into the world; from thirty to fifty we ought to greet them with 'God keep you,' or 'Stand in a good hour;' and from fifty onwards, with 'God speed you,' or 'Go in a good hour,' for from thence they go taking their leave of the world. The first is easy to say, and the wish not unlikely to be fulfilled, but the last who shall ensure? You come in a good hour, graceful as an Apollo, to comfort a miserable old man; can you assure me that, when I pass out of this world, I shall depart likewise at a propitious time? I am an old man, and that unseen world which should be so familiar and near to me seems so far off and yet so terrible. A young man steps into life as into a dance, confident of his welcome, pleased himself and pleasing others; the stage to which he comes is bright with flowers, soft music sounds on every side. So ought the old man to enter into the new life, confident of his welcome, pleasing to his Maker and his God, the heavenly minstrelsy in his ears. But it is far otherwise with me. I may lay me down in the 'Angelica Vestis,' the monkish garment that ensures the prayers of holy men for the departing soul; but who will secure me the wedding garment that ensures admission to the banquet above?"

"Do you find no comfort in the Blessed Sacrament, Altezza?" said Inglesant.

"Sometimes I may fancy so; but I cannot see the figure of the Christ for the hell that lies between."

"Ah! Altezza," said Inglesant, his eyes full of pity, not only for the old Duke, but for himself and all mankind, "it is always thus. Something stands between us and the heavenly life. My temptation is other than yours. Communion after communion I find Christ, and He is gracious to me—gracious as the love of God Himself; but month after month and year after year I find not how to follow Him, and when the road is opened to me I am deaf, and refuse to answer to the heavenly call. You, Altezza, are in more hopeful case than I; for it seems to me that your Highness has but to throw off that blasphemous superstition which is found in all Christian creeds alike, which has not feared to blacken even the shining gates of heaven with the smoke of hell."

"All creeds are alike," said the Duke with a shudder, "but mostly your northern religions, harsh and bitter as your skies. I have heard from a Lutheran a system of religion that made my blood run cold, the more as it commends itself to my calmer reason."

"And that is, Altezza?" said Inglesant.

"This, that so far from the Sacrament of Absolution upon earth, or at the hour of death, availing anything, God Himself has no power to change the state of those who die without being entirely purified from every trace of earthly and sensual passion; to such as these, though otherwise sincere Christians, nothing awaits but a long course of suffering in the desolate regions of Hades, as the Lutheran calls it, until, if so may be, the earthly idea is annihilated and totally obliterated from the heart."

"This seems little different from the doctrine of the Church," said Inglesant.

"It is different in this most important part," replied the Duke, "that Holy Church purifies and pardons her penitent, though he feels the passions of earth strong within him till the last; but by this system you must eradicate these yourself. You must purify your heart, you must feel every carnal lust, every vindictive thought, every lofty and contemptuous notion, utterly dead within you before you can enjoy a moment's expectation of future peace. He that goes out of this world with an uncharitable thought against his neighbour does so with the chances against him that he is lost for ever, for his face is turned from the light, and he enters at once upon the devious and downward walks of the future life; and what ground has he to expect that he who could not keep his steps in this life will find any to turn him back, or will have power to turn himself back, from every growing evil in the world to come?"

As the Duke spoke it seemed to Inglesant that these words were addressed to him alone, and that he saw before him the snare of the Devil, baited with the murderer of his brother, stretched before his heedless feet for his eternal destruction.

The Duke took up a book that lay by him, and read,—

"The soul that cherishes the slightest animosity, and takes this feeling into eternity, cannot be happy, though in other respects pious and faithful. Bitterness is completely opposed to the nature and constitution of heaven. The blood of Christ, who on the cross, in the midst of the most excruciating torments, exercised love instead of bitterness, cleanses from this sin also, when it flows in our veins."

"I see nothing in this, Altezza," said Inglesant eagerly, "but what is in accordance with the doctrines of the Church. This is that idea of sacramental purification, that Christ's Body being assimilated to ours purifies and sanctifies. His Body, being exalted at that supreme moment and effort (the moment of His suffering death) to the highest purity of temper and of sweetness by the perfect love and holiness which pervaded His spirit, has been able ever since, in all ages, through the mystery of the Blessed Sacrament, to convert all its worthy recipients in some degree to the same pure and holy state. Many things which men consider misfortunes and painful experiences are in fact but the force of this divine influence, assimilating their hearts to His, and attempering their bodies to the lofty purity of His own. This is the master work of the Devil, that he should lure us into states of mind, as the book says, of bitterness and of violence, by which this divine sweetness is tainted, and this peace broken by suspicion, by hatred, and heat of blood."

"The book says somewhere," said the Duke, turning over the leaves, "that, as the penitent thief rose from the cross to Paradise, so we, if we long after Christ with all the powers of our souls, shall, at the hour of death, rapidly soar aloft from our mortal remains, and then all fear of returning to earth and earthly desires will be at an end."

"It must surely," said Inglesant after a pause, speaking more to himself than to the Duke, "be among the things most surprising to an angelic nature that observes mankind, that, shadows ourselves, standing upon the confines even of this shadowy land, and not knowing what, if aught, awaits us elsewhere, hatred or revenge or unkindness should be among the last passions that are overcome. When the veil is lifted, and we see things as they really are, nothing will so much amaze us as the blindness and perversity that marked our life among our fellow-men. Surely the lofty life is hard, as it seems hard to your Grace; but the very effort itself is gain."

Inglesant left the presence of the Duke after his first interview impressed and softened, but troubled in his mind more than ever at the nature of the mission on which he was sent. Now that he had seen the Duke, and had been touched by his eager questions, and by the earnest searching look in the worn face, his conscience smote him at the thought of abusing his confidence, and of persuading him to adopt a course which Inglesant's own heart warned him might not in the end be conducive either to his own peace or to the welfare of his people, whose happiness he sincerely sought. He found that, in the antechambers and reception rooms of the palace, and even at the Duke's own table, the principal subject of conversation was the expected cession of the dukedom to the Papal See; and that emissaries from Rome had preceded him, and had evidently received instructions announcing his arrival, and were prepared to welcome him as an important ally. On the other hand, there were not wanting those who openly or covertly opposed the cession, some of whom were said to be agents of the Grand Duke of Florence, who was heir to the Duchy of Umbria through his wife. These latter, whose opposition was more secret than open, sought every opportunity of winning Inglesant to their party, employing the usual arguments with which, since his coming into Italy, he had been so familiar. Many days passed in this manner, and Inglesant had repeated conferences with the Duke, during which he made great progress in his favour, and was himself won by his lofty, kindly, and trustful character.

He had resided at Umbria a little less than a month, when he received instructions by a courier from Rome, by which he was informed that at the approaching festival of the Ascension a determined effort was to be made by the agents and friends of the Pope to bring the business to a conclusion. The Duke had promised to keep this festival, which is celebrated at Venice and in other parts of Italy with great solemnity, with unusual magnificence; and it was hoped that while his feelings were influenced and his religious instincts excited by the solemn and tender thoughts and imaginations which gather round the figure of the ascending Son of man, he might be induced to sign the deed of cession. Hitherto the Duke had not mentioned the subject to Inglesant, having found his conversation upon questions of the spiritual life and practice sufficient to occupy the time; but it was not probable that this silence would continue much longer, and on the first day in Ascension week Inglesant was attending Vespers at one of the Churches in the town in considerable anxiety and trouble of mind.

The sun had hardly set, and the fête in the garden was not yet begun, when, Vespers being over, he came out upon the river-side lined with stately houses which fronted the palace gardens towering in terraced walks and trellises of green hedges on the opposite bank. The sun, setting behind the wooded slopes, flooded this green hillside with soft and dream-like light, and bathed the carved marble façade of the palace, rising above it, with a rosy glimmer, in which the statues on its roof, and the fretted work of its balustrades, rested against the darkening blue of the evening sky. A reflex light, ethereal and wonderful, coming from the sky behind him, and the marble buildings and towers on which the sun's rays rested more fully than they did upon the palace, brooded over the river and the bridge with its rows of angelic forms, and, climbing the leafy slopes, as if to contrast its softer splendour with the light above, transfigured with colour the wreaths of vapour which rose from the river and hung about its wharves.

The people were already crowding out of the city, and forcing their way across the bridge towards the palace, where the illuminations and the curious waterworks, upon which the young Duke had, during his short reign, expended much money, were to be exhibited as soon as the evening was sufficiently dark. The people were noisy and jostling, but as usual good-tempered and easily pleased. Few masques or masquerade dresses had appeared as yet, but almost every one was armed with a small trumpet, a drum, or a Samarcand cane from which to shoot peas or comfits. At the corner of the main street that opened on to the quay, however, some disturbing cause was evidently at work. The crowd was perplexed by two contending currents, the one consisting of those who were attempting to turn into the street from the wharf, in order to learn the cause of the confusion, the other, of those who were apparently being driven forcibly out of the street, towards the wharves and the bridge, by pressure from behind. Discordant cries and exclamations of anger and contempt rose above the struggling mass. Taking advantage of the current that swept him onward, Inglesant reached the steps of the Church of St. Felix, which stood at the corner of the two streets, immediately opposite the bridge and the ducal lions which flanked the approach. On reaching this commanding situation the cause of the tumult presented itself in the form of a small group of men, who were apparently dragging a prisoner with them, and had at this moment reached the corner of the wharf, not far from the steps of the Church, surrounded and urged on by a leaping, shouting, and excited crowd. Seen from the top of the broad marble bases that flanked the steps, the whole of the wide space, formed by the confluence of the streets, and over which the shadows were rapidly darkening, presented nothing but a sea of agitated and tossing heads, while, from the windows, the bridge, and even the distant marble terraced steps that led up to the palace, the crowd appeared curious, and conscious that something unusual was in progress.

From the cries and aspect of the crowd, and of the men who dragged their prisoner along, it was evident that it was the intention of the people to throw the wretched man over the parapets of the bridge into the river below, and that to frustrate this intention not a moment was to be lost. The pressure of the crowd, greater from the opposite direction than from the one in which Inglesant had come, fortunately swept the group almost to the foot of the steps. Near to Inglesant, and clinging to the carved bases of the half columns that supported the façade of the Church, were two or three priests who had come out of the interior, attracted by the tumult. Availing himself of their support, Inglesant shouted to the captors of the unhappy man, in the name of the Church and of the Duke, to bring their prisoner up the steps. They probably would not have obeyed him, though they hesitated for a moment; but the surrounding crowd, attracted towards the Church by Inglesant's gestures, began to press upon it from all sides, as he had indeed foreseen would be the case, and finally, by their unconscious and involuntary motion, swept the prisoner and his captors up the steps to the side of the priests and of Inglesant. It was a singular scene. The rapidly advancing night had changed the golden haze of sunset to a sombre gloom, but lights began to appear in the houses all around, and paper lanterns showed themselves among the crowd

The cause of all this confusion was dragged by his persecutors up the steps, and placed upon the last of the flight, confronting the priests. His hair was disordered, his clothes nearly torn from his limbs, and his face and dress streaked with blood. Past the curtain across the entrance of the Church, which was partly drawn back by those inside, a flash of light shot across the marble platform, and shone upon the faces of the foremost of the crowd. This light shone full upon Inglesant, who stood, in striking contrast to the dishevelled figure that confronted him, dressed in a suit of black satin and silver, with a deep collar of Point-de-Venice lace. The priests stood a little behind, apparently desirous to learn the nature of the prisoner's offence before they interfered; and the accusers therefore addressed themselves to Inglesant, who, indeed, was recognized by many as a friend of the Duke, and whom the priests especially had received instructions from Rome to support. The confusion in the crowd meanwhile increased rather than diminished; there seemed to be causes at work other than the slight one of the seizure by the mob of an unpopular man. The town was very full of strangers, and it struck Inglesant that the arrest of the man before him was merely an excuse, and was being used by some who had an object to gain by stirring up the people. He saw, at any rate, however this might be, a means of engaging the priests to assist him, should their aid be necessary in saving the man's life.

That there was a passionate attachment among the people to a separate and independent government of their city and state, an affection towards the family of their hereditary dukes, and a dread and jealous dislike of the Pope's government and of the priests, he had reason to believe. It seemed to him that the people were about to break forth into some demonstration of this antipathy, which, if allowed to take place, and if taken advantage of, as it would be, by the neighbouring princes, would be most displeasing to the policy of Rome, if not entirely subversive of it. With these thoughts in his mind, as he stood for a moment silent on the marble platform, and saw before him, what is perhaps the most impressive of all sights, a vast assemblage of people in a state of violent and excited opposition, and reflected on the causes which he imagined agitated them,—causes which in his heart he, though enlisted on the opposite side, had difficulty in persuading himself were not justifiable,—it came into his mind more powerfully than ever, that the moment foretold to him by Serenus de Cressy was at last indeed come. Surely it behoved him to look well to his steps, lest he should be found at last absolutely and unequivocally fighting against his conscience and his God; if, indeed, this looking well to their steps on such occasions, and not boldly choosing their side, had not been for many years the prevailing vice of his family, and to some extent the cause of his own spiritual failure.

The two men who held the apparent cause of all this uproar were two mechanics of jovial aspect, who appeared to look upon the affair more in the light of a brutal practical joke (no worse in their eyes for its brutality), than as a very serious matter. To Inglesant's question what the man had done they answered that he had refused to kneel to the Blessed Sacrament, as it was being carried through the streets to some poor, dying soul, and upon being remonstrated with, had reviled not only the

Sacrament itself, but the Virgin, the Holy Father, and the Italians generally, as Papistical asses, with no more sense than the Pantaleoni of their own comedies. The men gave this evidence in an insolent half-jesting manner, as though not sorry to utter such words safely in the presence of the priests.

Inglesant, who kept his eyes fixed upon the prisoner, and noticed that he was rapidly recovering from the breathless and exhausted condition the ill-treatment he had met with had reduced him to, and was assuming a determined and somewhat noble aspect, abstained from questioning him, lest he should make his own case only the more desperate; but, turning to the priests, he rapidly explained his fears to them, and urged that the man should be immediately secured from the people, that he might be examined by the Duke, and the result forwarded to Rome. The priests hesitated. Apart from the difficulty, they said, of taking the man out of the hands of his captors, such a course would be sure to exasperate the people still further, and bring on the very evil that he was desirous of averting. It would be better to let the mob work their will upon the man; it would at least occupy some time, and every moment was precious. In less than an hour the fireworks at the palace would begin, might indeed be hastened by a special messenger; and the fête once begun, they hoped all danger would be over. To this Inglesant answered that the man's arrest was evidently only an excuse for riot, and had probably already answered its purpose; that to confine the people's attention to it would be unfavourable to the intentions of those who were promoting a political tumult; and that the avowed cause of the man's seizure, and of the excitement of the mob, being disrespectful language towards the Holy Father, the tumult, if properly managed, might be made of service to the cause of Rome rather than the reverse.

Without waiting for the effect of this somewhat obscure argument on the priests, Inglesant directed the men who held their prisoner to bring him into the Church. They were unwilling to do so, but the crowd below was so confused and tumultuous, one shouting one thing and one another, that it seemed impossible that, if they descended into it again, they would be allowed to retain their prey, and would not rather be overwhelmed in a common destruction with him. On the other hand, by obeying Inglesant, they at least kept possession of their prisoner, and could therefore scarcely fail of receiving some reward from the authorities. They therefore consented, and by a sudden movement they entered the Church, the doors of which were immediately closed, after some few of the populace had managed to squeeze themselves in. A messenger was at once despatched to the palace to hasten the fireworks, and to request that a detachment of the Duke's guard should be sent into the Church by a back way.

The darkness had by this time so much increased that few of the people were aware of what had taken place, and the ignorance of the crowd as to the cause of the tumult was so general that little disturbance took place among those who were shut out of the Church. They remained howling and hooting, it is true, for some time, and some went so far as to beat against the closed doors; but a rumour being spread among the crowd that the fireworks were immediately to begin, they grew tired of this unproductive occupation, and flocked almost to a man out of the square and wharves, and crowded across the bridge into the gardens.

When the guard arrived, Inglesant claimed the man as the Duke's prisoner, to be examined before him in the morning. The curiosity of the Duke in all religious matters being well known, this seemed very reasonable to the officer of the guard, and the priests did not like to dispute it after the instructions they had received with regard to Inglesant's mission. The two artisans were propitiated by a considerable reward, and the prisoner was then transported by unfrequented ways to the palace, and shut up in a solitary apartment, whilst the rest of the world delighted itself at the palace fêtes.

The garden festivities passed away amid general rejoicing and applause. The finest effect was produced at the conclusion, when the whole mass of water at the command of the engines, being thrown into the air in thin fan-like jets, was illuminated by various coloured lights, producing the appearance of innumerable rainbows, through which the palace itself, the orangeries, the gardens, and terraces, and the crowds of delighted people, were seen illuminated and refracted in varied and ever-changing tints. Amid these sparkling colours strange birds passed to and fro, and angelic forms descended by unseen machinery and walked on the higher terraces, and as it were upon the flashing rainbows themselves. Delicious music from unseen instruments ravished the sense, and when the scene appeared complete and nothing farther was expected, an orange grove in the centre of the whole apparently burst open, and displayed the stage of a theatre, upon which antic characters performed a pantomime, and one of the finest voices in Italy sang an ode in honour of the day, of the Duke, and of the Pope.

CHAPTER XXVII.

The Duke had engaged the next morning to be present at a theatrical representation of a religious character, somewhat of the nature of a miracle play, to be given in the courtyard of the "Hospital of Death," which adjoined to the Campo Santo of the city.

Before accompanying his Highness, Inglesant had given orders to have the man, who had been the cause of so much excitement the evening before, brought into his apartment, that he might see whether or no his eccentricity made him sufficiently interesting to be presented to the Duke.

When the stranger was brought to the palace early in the morning, and having been found to be quite harmless, was entrusted by the guard to two servants to be brought into Inglesant's presence, he thought himself in a new world. Hitherto his acquaintance with Italian life had been that of a stranger and from the outside; he was now to see somewhat of the interior life of a people among whom the glories of the Renaissance still lingered, and to see it in one of the most wonderful of the Renaissance works, the ducal palace of Umbria. Born in the dull twilight of the north, and having spent most of his mature years amongst the green mezzotints of Germany, he was now transplanted into a land of light and colour, dazzling to a stranger so brought up. Reared in the sternest discipline, he found himself among a people to whom life was a fine art, and the cultivation of the present and its enjoyments the end of existence. From room to room, as he followed his guide, who pointed out from time to time such of the beauties of the place as he considered most worthy of notice, the stranger saw around what certainly might have intoxicated a less composed and determined brain.

The highest efforts of the genius of the Renaissance had been expended upon this magnificent house. The birth of a new instinct, differing in some respects from any instincts of art which had preceded it, produced in this and other similar efforts original and wonderful results. The old Greek art entered with unsurpassable intensity into sympathy with human life; but it was of necessity original and creative, looking always forward and not back, and lacked the pathos and depth of feeling that accompanied that new birth of art which sought much of its inspiration among the tombs and ruined grottoes, and most of its sympathetic power among the old well-springs of human feeling, read in the torn and faded memorials of past suffering and destruction. This new instinct of art abandoned itself without reserve to the pursuit of everything which mankind had ever beheld of the beautiful, or had felt of the pathetic or the sad, or had dreamed of the noble or the ideal. The genius of the Renaissance set itself to reproduce this enchanted world of form and colour, traversed by thoughts and spiritual existences mysterious and beautiful, and the home of beings who had found this form and colour and these mysterious thoughts blend into a human life delicious in its very sorrows, grotesque and incongruous in its beauty, alluring and attractive amid all its griefs and hardships; so much so indeed that, in the language of the old fables, the Gods themselves could not be restrained from throwing off their divine garments, and wandering up and down among the paths and the adventures of men. By grotesque and humorous delineation, by fanciful representation of human passion under strange and unexpected form, by the dumb ass speaking and grasshoppers playing upon flutes, was this world of intelligent life reproduced in the rooms and on the walls of the house through which the stranger walked for the first time.

He probably thought that he saw little of it, yet the bizarre effect was burning itself into his brain. From the overhanging chimney-pieces antique masques and figures such as he had never seen, even in dreams, leered out upon him from arabesque carvings of foliage, or skulked behind trophies of war, of music, or of the arts of peace. The door and window frames seemed bowers of fruit and flowers, and forests of carved leaves wreathed the pilasters and walls. But this was not all; with a perfection of design and an extraordinary power of fancy, this world of sylvan imagery was peopled by figures and stories of exquisite grace and sweetness, representing the most touching incidents of human life and history. Men and women; lovers and warriors in conflicts and dances and festivals, in sacrifices and games; children sporting among flowers; bereavement and death, husbandry and handicraft, hunters and beasts of chase. Again, among briony and jasmin and roses, or perched upon ears of corn and sheaves of maize, birds of every plumage confronted—so the grotesque genius willed—fish and sea monsters and shells and marine wonders of every kind.

Upon the walls, relieved by panelling of wood, were paintings of landscapes and the ruined buildings of antiquity overgrown with moss, or of modern active life in markets and theatres, of churches and cities in the course of erection, with the architects and scaffold poles, of the processions and marriages of princes, of the ruin of emperors and of kings. Below and beside these were credenzas and cabinets upon which luxury and art had lavished every costly device and material which the world conceived or yielded. Inlaid with precious woods, and glittering with costly jewels and marbles, they reproduced in these differing materials all those infinite designs which the carved walls had already wearied themselves to express. Plaques and vases from Castel Durante or Faience,—some of a strange pale colour, others brilliant with a grotesque combination of blue and yellow,—crowded the shelves.

Passing through this long succession of rooms, the stranger reached at last a library, a noble apartment of great size, furnished with books in brilliant antique binding of gold and white vellum, and otherwise ornamented with as much richness as the rest of the palace. Upon reading desks were open manuscripts and printed books richly illuminated. Connected with this apartment by open arches was an anteroom or corridor, which again opened on a loggia, beyond the shady arches of which lay the palace gardens, long vistas of green walks, and reaches of blue sky, flecked and crossed by the spray of fountains. The decorations of the anteroom and loggia were more profuse and extravagant than any that the stranger had yet seen. There was a tradition that this portion of the palace had been finished last, and that when the workmen arrived at it the time for the completion of the whole was very nearly run out. The attention of all the great artists, hitherto engaged upon different parts of the entire palace, was concentrated upon this unfinished portion, and all their workmen and assistants were called to labour upon it alone. The work went on by night and day, not ceasing even to allow of sleep. Unlimited supplies of Greek wine were furnished to the workmen; and stimulated by excitement and the love of art, emulating each other, and half-intoxicated by the delicious wine, the work exceeded all previous productions. For wild boldness and luxuriance of fancy these rooms were probably unequalled in the world.

In the anteroom facing the loggia the stranger found Inglesant conversing with an Italian who held rather a singular post in the ducal Court. He was standing before a cabinet of black oak, inlaid with representations of lutes and fifes, over which were strewn roses confined by coloured ribbons, and supporting vases of blue and yellow majolica, thrown into strong relief by the black wood. Above this cabinet was a painting representing some battle in which a former Duke had won great honour; while on a grassy knoll in the foreground the huntsmen of Ganymede were standing with their eyes turned upward towards the bird of Zeus, who is carrying the youth away to the skies, emblematical of the alleged apotheosis of the ducal hero. Richly dressed in a fantastic suit of striped silk, and leaning against the cabinet in an attitude of listless repose, Inglesant was contemplating an object which he held in his hand, and which both he and his companion appeared to regard with intense interest. This was an antique statuette of a faun, holding its tail in its left hand, and turning its head and body to look at it,—an occupation of which, if we may trust the monuments of antiquity, this singular creature appears to have been fond. The Italian was of a striking figure, and was dressed somewhat more gaily than was customary with his countrymen; and the whole group was fully in unison with the spirit of the place and with the wealth of beauty and luxury of human life that pervaded the whole.

The man who was standing by Inglesant's side, and who had the air of a connoisseur or virtuoso, was an Italian of some fifty years of age. His appearance, as has been said, was striking at first sight, but on longer acquaintance became very much more so. He was tall and had been dark, but his hair and beard were plentifully streaked with gray. His features were large and aquiline, and his face deeply furrowed and lined.

His appearance would have been painfully worn, almost to ghastliness, but for a mocking and humorous expression which laughed from his eyes, his mouth, his nostrils, and every line and feature of his face. Whenever this expression subsided, and his countenance sank into repose, a look of wan sadness and even terror took its place, and the large black eyes became fixed and intense in their gaze, as though some appalling object attracted their regard.

This man had been born of a good but poor family, and had been educated by his relations with the expectation of his becoming an ecclesiastic, and he had even passed some time as a novice of some religious order. The tendency of his mind not leading him to the further pursuit of a religious life, he left his monastery, and addressed himself to live by his wits, among the families and households of princes. He had made himself very useful in arranging comedies and pageantries, and he had at one time belonged to one of those dramatic companies called "Zanni," who went about the country reciting and acting comedies. Combined with this talent he discovered great aptitude in the management of serious affairs, and was more than once, while apparently engaged entirely on theatrical performances, employed in secret State negotiations which could not so well be entrusted to an acknowledged and conspicuous agent. In this manner of life he might have continued; but having become involved in one of the contests which disturbed Italy, he received a dangerous wound in the head, and on rising from his sick bed in the Albergo in which he had been nursed, he was merely removed to another as a singular if not dangerous lunatic. The symptoms of his disease first manifested themselves in a very unpleasant familiarity with the secrets of those around him, and it was probably this feature of his complaint which led to his detention. As he improved in health, however, he ceased to indulge in any conversation which might give offence, but, assuming a sedate and agreeable manner, he conversed with all who came to him, calling them, although strangers and such as he had never before seen, by their proper names, and talking to them pleasantly concerning their parents, relations, the coats-of-arms of their families, and such other harmless and agreeable matters.

What brought him prominently into notice was the strangely prophetic spirit he manifested before, or at the moment of the occurrence of, more than one public event. He was taken from the hospital and examined by the Pope, and afterwards at several of the sovereign Courts of Italy. Thus, not long before the time when Inglesant met him in the ducal palace at Umbria, he was at Chambery assisting at the preparation of some festivals which the young Duke of Savoy was engaged in celebrating. One day, as he was seated at dinner with several of the Duke's servants, he suddenly started up from his seat, exclaiming that he saw the Duke de Nemours fall dead from his horse, killed by a pistol shot. The Duke, who was uncle to the young monarch of Savoy, was then in France, where he was one of the leaders of the party of the Fronde. Before many days were passed, however, the news reached Chambery of the fatal duel between this nobleman and the Duke of Beaufort, which occurred at the moment the Italian had thus announced it.

These and other similar circumstances caused the man to be much talked of and sought after among the Courts of Italy, where a belief in manifestations of the supernatural was scarcely less universal than in the previous age, when, according to an eye-witness, "the Pope would decide no question, would take no journey, hold no sitting of the Consistory, without first consulting the stars; nay, very few cardinals would transact an affair of any kind, were it but to buy a load of wood, except after consultation duly held with some astrologer or wizard." The credit which the man gained, and the benefits he derived from this reputation, raised him many enemies, who did not scruple to assert that he was simply a clever knave, who was not even his own dupe. Setting on one side, however, the revelations of the distant and the unknown made by him, which seemed inexplicable except by supposing him possessed of some unusual spiritual faculty, there was in the man an amount of knowledge of the world and of men of all classes and ranks, combined with much learning and a humorous wit, which made his company well worth having for his conversation alone. It was not then surprising that he should be found at this juncture at the Court of Umbria, where the peculiar idiosyncrasies of the aged Duke, and the interest attached to the intrigue for the cession of the dukedom, had assembled a strange and heterogeneous company, and towards which at the moment all men's eyes in Italy were turned.

"Yes, doubtless, it is an antique," the Italian was saying, "though in the last age many artists produced masques and figures so admirable as to be mistaken for antiques; witness that masque which Messire Giorgio Vasari says he put in a chimney-piece of his house at Arezzo, which every one took to be an antique. I have seen such myself. This little fellow, however, I saw found in a vineyard near the Misericordia—a place which I take to have been at some time or other the scene of some terrible event, such as a conflict or struggle or massacre; for though now it is quiet and serene enough, with the sunlight and the rustling leaves, and the splash of a fountain about which there is some good carving, I think, of Fra Giovanni Agnolo,—for all this, I never walk there but I feel the presence of fatal events, and a sense of dim figures engaged in conflict, and of faint and distant cries and groans."

As he spoke these last words his eye rested upon the strange figure of the man so hardly rescued from death the night before, and he stopped. His manner changed, and his eyes assumed that expression of intense expectation of which we have spoken before. The appearance of the stranger, and the contrast it presented to the objects around, was indeed such as to make him almost seem an inhabitant of another world, and one of those phantasms of past conflict of which the Italian had just spoken. His clothes, which had originally been of the plainest texture, and most uncourtly make, were worn and ragged, and stained with damp and dirt. His form and features were gaunt and uncouth, and his gesture stiff and awkward; but, with all this, there was a certain steadiness and dignity about his manner, which threw an appearance of nobility over this rugged and unpleasing form. Contrasted with the dress and manner of the other men, he looked like some enthusiastic prophet, standing in the house of mirth and luxury, and predicting ruin and woe.

At this moment a servant entered the room, bringing a sottocoppa of silver, upon which were two or three stiff necked glasses, called caraffas, containing different sorts of wine, and also water, and one or two more empty drinking-glasses, so that the visitor could please himself as to the strength and nature of his beverage. Inglesant offered this refreshment to the Italian, who filled himself a glass and drank, pledging Inglesant as he did so. The latter did not drink, but offered wine and cakes to the stranger, who refused or rather took no heed of these offers of politeness; he remained silent, keeping his eyes fixed upon the face of the man who, but a few hours before, had saved him from a violent death.

"I have had some feelings of this kind myself, in certain places," said Inglesant, in answer to the Italian's speech, "and very frequently in all places the sense of something vanishing, which in another moment I should have seen; it has seemed to me that, could I once see this thing, matters would be very different with me. Whether I ever shall or not I do not know."

"Who can say?" replied the other. "We live and move amid a crowd of flitting objects unknown or dimly seen. The beings and powers of the unseen world throng around us. We call ourselves lords of our own actions and fate, but we are in reality the slaves of every atom of matter of which the world is made and we ourselves created. Among this phantasm of struggling forms and influences (like a man forcing his way through a crowd of masques who mock at him and retard his steps) we fight our way towards the light. Many of us are born with the seeds within us of that which makes such a fight hopeless from the first—the seeds of disease, of ignorance, of adverse circumstance, of stupidity; for even a dullard has had once or twice in his life glimpses of the light. So we go on. I was at Chambery once when a man came before the Duke in the palace garden to ask an alms. He was a worker in gold, a good artist, not unworthy of Cellini himself. His sight had failed him, and he could no longer work for bread to give to his children. He stood before the Prince and those who stood with him, among whom were a Cardinal and two or three nobles, with their pages and grooms, trying with his dim eyes to make out one from the other, which was noble and which was groom, and to see whether his suit was rejected or allowed. Behind him, beyond the garden shade the dazzling glitter stretched up to the white Alps. We are all the creatures of a day, and the puny afflictions of any man's life are not worth a serious thought: yet this man seemed to me so true an image of his kind, helpless and half-blind, yet struggling to work out some good for himself, that I felt a strange emotion of pity. They gave him alms—some more, some less. I was a fool, yet even now I think the man was no bad emblem of the life of each of us. We do not understand this enough. Will the time ever come when these things will be better known?"

As the Italian spoke the stranger took his eyes off Inglesant and fixed them on the speaker with a startled expression, as though the tone of his discourse was unexpected to him. He scarcely waited for the other to finish before he broke in upon the conversation, speaking slowly and with intense earnestness, as though above all things desirous of being understood. He spoke a strange and uncouth Italian, full of rough northern idioms, yet the earnestness and dignity of his manner ensured him an audience, especially with two such men as those who stood before him.

"Standing in a new world," he said, "and speaking as I speak, to men of another language, and of thoughts and habits distinct from mine, I see beneath the tinsel of earthly rank and splendour and a luxury of life and of beauty, the very meaning of which is unknown to me, something of a common feeling, which assures me that the voice I utter will not be entirely strange, coming as it does from the common Father. I see around me a land given over to idolatry and sensual crime, as if the old Pagans were returned again to earth: and here around me I see the symbols of the Pagan worship and of the Pagan sin, and I hear no other talk than that which would have befitted the Pagan revels and the Pagan darkness which overhung the world to come. Standing on the brink of a violent death, and able to utter few words that can be understood, I call, in these short moments which are given me, and in these few words which I have at command—I call upon all who will listen to me, that they leave those things which are behind, with all the filthy recollections of ages steeped in sin, and that they press forward towards the light—the light of God in Jesus Christ."

He stopped, probably for want of words to clothe his thoughts, and Inglesant replied,—

"You may be assured from the events of last night, signore, that you are in no danger of violent death in this house, and that every means will be taken to protect you, until you have been found guilty of some crime. You must, however, know that no country can allow its customs and its religion to be outraged by strangers and aliens, and you cannot be surprised if such conduct is resented both by the governors of the country and by the ignorant populace, though these act from different motives. As to what you have said respecting the ornaments and symbols of this house, and of the converse in which you have found us engaged, it would seem that to a wise man these things might serve as an allegory, or at least as an image and representation of human life, and be, therefore, not without their uses."

"I desire no representation nor image of a past world of iniquity," said the stranger, "I would I could say of a dead life, but the whole world lieth in wickedness until this day. This is why I travel through all lands, crying to all men that they repent and escape the most righteous judgment of God, if haply there be yet time. These are those latter days in which our Saviour and Redeemer Jesus Christ, the Son of God, predicted that iniquity 'should be increased;' wherein, instead of serving God, all serve their own humours and affections, being rocked to sleep with the false and deceitful lullaby of effeminate pleasures and delights of the flesh, and know not that an horrible mischief and overthrow is awaiting them, that the pit of Hell yawns beneath them, and that for them is reserved the inevitable rigour of the eternal fire. Is it a time for chambering and wantonness, for soft raiment and dainty living, for reading of old play-books such as the one I see on the table, for building houses of cedar, painted with vermilion, and decked with all the loose and fantastic devices which a disordered and debauched intellect could itself conceive, or could borrow from Pagan tombs and haunts of devils, full of uncleanness and dead sins?"

"You speak too harshly of these things," said Inglesant. "I see nothing in them but the instinct of humanity, differing in its outward aspect in different ages, but alike in its meaning and audible voice. This house is in itself a representation of the world of fancy and reality combined, of the material life of the animal mingled with those half-seen and fitful glimpses of the unknown life upon the verge of which we stand. This little fellow which I hold in my hand, speaks to me, in an indistinct and yet forcible voice, of that common sympathy—magical and hidden though it may be—by which the whole creation is linked together, and in which, as is taught in many an allegory and quaint device upon these walls, the Creator of us all has a kindly feeling for the basest and most inanimate. My imagination follows humanity through all the paths by which it has reached the present moment, and the more memorials I can gather of its devious footsteps the more enlarged my view becomes of what its trials, its struggles, and its virtues were. All things that ever delighted it were in themselves the good blessings of God—the painter's and the player's art—action, apparel, agility, music. Without these life would be a desert; and as it seems to me, these things softened manners so as to allow Religion to be heard, who otherwise would not have been listened to in a savage world, and among a brutal people destitute of civility. As I trace these things backward for centuries, I live far beyond my natural term, and my mind is delighted with the pleasures of nations who were dust ages before I was born."

"I am not concerned to dispute the vain pleasures of the children of this world," exclaimed the stranger with more warmth than he had hitherto shown. "Do you suppose that I myself am without the lusts and desires of life? Have I no eyes like other men, that I cannot take a carnal pleasure in that which is cunningly formed by the enemy to please the eye? Am not I warmed like other men? And is not soft clothing and dainty fare pleasing to me as to them? But I call on all men to rise above these things, which are transitory and visionary as a dream, and which you yourself have spoken of as magical and hidden, of which only fitful glimpses are obtained. You are pleasing yourself with fond and idle imaginations, the product of delicate living and unrestrained fancies; but in this the net of the devil is about your feet, and before you are aware you will find yourself ensnared for ever. These things are slowly but surely poisoning your spiritual life. I call upon you to leave these delusions, and come out into the clear atmosphere of God's truth; to tread the life of painful self-denial, leaving that of the powerful and great of this world, and following a despised Saviour, who knew none of these things, and spent His time not in kings' houses gorgeously tricked out, but knew not where to lay His head. You speak to me of pleasures of the mind, of music, of the painter's art; do you think that last night, when beaten, crushed, and almost breathless, in the midst of a bloodthirsty and howling crowd, I was dimly conscious of help, and looking up I saw you in the glare of the lanterns, in your courtier's dress of lace and silver, calm, beneficent, powerful for good, you did not seem to my weak human nature, and my low needs and instincts, beautiful as an angel of light? Truly you did; yet I tell you, speaking by a nature and in a voice that is more unerring than mine, that to the divine vision, of us two at that moment you were the one to be pitied, —you were the outcast, the tortured of demons, the bound hand and foot, whose portion is in this life, who, if this fleeting hour is left unheeded, will be tormented in the life to come."

The Italian turned away his head to conceal a smile, and even to Inglesant, who was much better able to understand the man's meaning, this result of his interference to save his life appeared somewhat ludicrous. The Italian, however, probably thinking that Inglesant would be glad to be relieved from his strange visitor, seemed desirous of terminating the interview.

"His Grace expects me," he said to Inglesant, "at the Casa di Morte this morning, and it is near the time for him to be there. I will therefore take my leave."

"Ah! the Casa di Morte; yes, he will expect me there also," said Inglesant, with some slight appearance of reluctance. "I will follow you anon."

He moved from the indolent attitude he had kept till this moment before the sideboard, and exchanged with the Italian those formal gestures of leave-taking and politeness in which his nation were precise. When the Italian was gone Inglesant summoned a servant, and directed him to provide the stranger with an apartment, and to see that he wanted for nothing. He then turned to the fanatic, and requested him as a favour not to attempt to leave the palace until he had returned from the Duke. The stranger hesitated, but finally consented.

"I owe you my life," he said,—"a life I value not at a straw's weight, but for which my Master may perchance have some use even yet. I am therefore in your debt, and I will give my word to remain quiet until you return; but this promise only extends to nightfall; should you be prevented by any chance from returning this day, I am free from my parole."

Inglesant bowed.

"I would," continued the man, looking upon his companion with a softened and even compassionate regard, "I would I could say more. I hear a secret voice, which tells me that you are even now walking in slippery places, and that your heart is not at ease."

He stopped, and seemed to seek earnestly for some phrases or arguments which he might suppose likely to influence a courtier placed as he imagined Inglesant to be; but before he resumed, the latter excused himself on the ground of his attendance on the Duke, and, promising to see him again on his return, left the room.

Inglesant found a carriage waiting to convey him to the "Hospital of Death," as the monastic house adjoining the public Campo Santo was called. The religious performance had already begun. Passing through several sombre corridors and across a courtyard, he was ushered into the Duke's presence, who sat, surrounded by his Court and by the principal ecclesiastics of the city, in an open balcony or loggia. As Inglesant entered by a small door in the back of the gallery a most extraordinary sight met his eyes. Beyond the loggia was a small yard or burial-ground, and beyond this the Campo Santo stretching out into the far country. The whole of the yard immediately before the spectators was thronged by a multitude of persons, of all ages and ranks, apparently just risen from the tomb. Many were utterly without clothing, others were attired as kings, bishops, and even popes. Their attitudes and conduct corresponded with the characters in which they appeared, the ecclesiastics collecting in calm and sedate attitudes, while many of the rest, among whom kings and great men were not wanting, appeared in an extremity of anguish and fear. Beyond the sheltering walls which enclosed the court the dazzling heat brooded over the Campo Santo to the distant hills, and the funereal trees stood, black and sombre, against the glare of the yellow sky. At the moment of Inglesant's entrance, it appeared that something had taken place of the nature of an excommunication, and the ecclesiastics in the gallery were, according to custom, casting candles and flaming torches, which the crowd of nude figures below were struggling and fighting to obtain. A wild yet solemn strain of music, that came apparently from the open graves, ascended through the fitful and half-stifled cries.

The first sight that struck upon Inglesant's sense, as he entered the gallery from the dark corridors, was the lurid yellow light beyond. The second was the wild confused crowd of leaping and struggling figures, in a strange and ghastly disarray, naked or decked as in mockery with the torn and disordered symbols of rank and wealth, rising as from the tomb, distracted and terror-stricken as at the last great assize. The third was the figure of the Duke turning to him, and the eyes of the priests and clergy fixed upon his face. The words that the fanatic had uttered had fallen upon a mind prepared to receive them, and upon a conscience already awakened to acknowledge their truth. A mysterious conviction laid hold upon his imagination that the moment had arrived in which he was bound to declare himself, and by every tie which the past had knotted round him to influence the Duke to pursue a line of conduct from which his conscience and his better judgment revolted. On the one hand, a half-aroused and uncertain conscience, on the other, circumstance, habit, interest, inclination, perplexed his thoughts. The conflict was uneven, the result hardly doubtful. The eyes of friends and enemies, of agents of the Holy See, of courtiers and priests, were upon him; the inquiring glance of the aged Duke seemed to penetrate into his soul. He advanced to the ducal chair, the solemn music, that streamed up as from the grave, wavered and faltered as if consciousness and idea were nearly lost. Something of the old confusion overpowered his senses, the figures that surrounded him became shadowy and unreal, and the power of decision seemed no longer his own.

Out of the haze of confused imagery and distracting thought which surrounded him, he heard with unspeakable amazement the Duke's words,—

"I have waited your coming, Mr. Inglesant, impatiently, for I have a commission to entrust you with; or rather my daughter, the Grand Duchess, has written urgently to me from Florence to request me to send you to her without a moment's delay. Family matters relating to some in whom she takes the greatest interest, and who are well known, she says, to yourself, are the causes which lead to this request."

Inglesant was too bewildered to speak. He had believed himself quite unknown to the Grand Duchess, whom he had never seen, but as he had passed before her in the ducal receptions at Florence. Who could these be in whom she took so great an interest, and who were known to him?

But the Duke went on, speaking with a certain melancholy in his tone.

"I have wished, Mr. Inglesant," he said, "to mark in some way the regard I have conceived for you, and the obligation under which I conceive myself to remain. It may be that, in the course that events are taking, it will no longer in a few weeks be in my power to bestow favours upon any man. I desire, therefore, to do what I have purposed before you leave the presence. I have caused the necessary deeds to be prepared which bestow upon you a small fief in the Apennines, consisting of some farms and of the Villa-Castle of San Giorgio, where I myself in former days have passed many happy hours." He stopped, and in a moment or two resumed abruptly, without finishing the sentence.

"The revenue of the fief is not large, but its possession gives the title of Cavaliere to its owner, and its situation and the character of its neighbourhood make it a desirable and delightful abode. The letters of naturalization which are necessary to enable you to hold this property have been made out, and nothing is wanting but your acceptance of the gift. I offer it you with no conditions and no request save that, as far as in you lies, you will be a faithful servant to the Grand Duchess when I am gone."

The Duke paused for a moment, and then, turning slightly to his chaplain he said, "The reverend fathers will tell you that this affair has not been decided upon without their knowledge, and that it has their full approval."

These last words convinced Inglesant of the fact that had occurred. Although the Duke had said nothing on the subject, he felt certain that the deed of cession had been signed, and that for some reason or other he himself was considered by the clerical party to have been instrumental in obtaining this result, and to be deserving of reward accordingly. He had never, as we have seen, spoken to the Duke concerning the succession, and his position at the moment was certainly a peculiar one. Nothing was expected of him but that he should express his grateful thanks for the Duke's favour, and leave the presence. Surely, at that moment, no law of heaven or earth could require him to break through the observances of civility and usage, to enter upon a subject upon which he was not addressed, and to refuse acts of favour offered to him with every grace and delicacy of manner. Whatever might be the case with other men, he certainly was not one to whom such a course was possible. He expressed his gratitude with all the grace of manner of which he was capable, he assured the Duke of his readiness to start immediately for Florence, and he left the ducal presence before many minutes had passed away.

Y

He found before long that all his conjectures were correct. The Duke had signed the deed of cession, and the report which was sent to Rome by the Papal agents stated that, in the opinion of the most competent judges, this result was due to Inglesant's influence. Before his arrival the Duke had leaned strongly towards the secular and anti-Papal interest, and had even encouraged heretical and Protestant emissaries. "Avoiding with great skill all positive allusion to the subject," the report went on to state, "Il Cavaliere Inglesant had thrown all his influence into the Catholic and religious scale, and had by the loftiness of his sentiment and the attraction of his manner entirely won over the vacillating nature of the Duke." Too much satisfaction, the Cardinal of Umbria and the heads of the Church in that city assured the Papal Court, could not be expressed at the manner in which the agent of the Society had fulfilled his mission.

Inglesant's departure from Umbria was so sudden that he had no opportunity of again seeing the stranger whom he had left in the palace, and he was afterwards at some trouble in obtaining any information respecting him. As far as could be ascertained, he waited in the palace, according to his promise, until the evening, when, finding that Inglesant did not return, he walked quietly forth, no man hindering him. What his subsequent fate was is involved in some obscurity; but it would appear that, having publicly insulted the Host in some cathedral in the south of Italy, he was arrested by the Holy Office, and thrown into prison, from which there is reason to believe he never emerged.

CHAPTER XXVIII.

NOT very long after Inglesant had left for Umbria, his friend, Don Agostino di Chigi, suddenly came to Rome. The Pope's health was rapidly failing, and the excitement concerning his successor was becoming intense. The choice was generally considered to lie between the Cardinals Barberini and di Chigi, though Cardinal Sacchetti was spoken of by some, probably however merely as a substitute, should both the other parties fail in electing their candidate.

It was the policy of the Chigi family to conduct their matters with great caution; none of the family, with the exception of the Cardinal, were openly in Rome; and when Don Agostino arrived he resided in one of the deserted villas hidden among vineyards and the gardens of solitary convents, which covered the Palatine and the Aventine in the southern portion of Rome within the walls. He remained within or with the Cardinal during the day, but at night he ventured out into the streets, and visited the adherents of his family and those who were working to secure his uncle's elevation.

One night the fathers of the Oratory gave a concert at which one of the best voices in Rome was to sing. It happened that Don Agostino passed the gate as the company were assembling, and as he did so the street was blocked by the train of some great personage who arrived in a sedan of blue velvet embroidered with silver, accompanied by several gentlemen and servants. Among the former, Agostino recognized the Cavaliere di Guardino, the brother of Lauretta, of whose acquaintance with Inglesant at Florence it may be remembered he was aware, and with him another man whose appearance seemed to recall some distant reminiscence to his mind. He could, however, see him but imperfectly in the flickering torchlight.

Apart from his desire to remain unrecognized in Rome, Agostino had no desire to associate with the Cavaliere, of whose character he had a very bad opinion. To his annoyance, therefore, as the sedan entered the courtyard, the two persons he had noticed, instead of following their patron, turned round, and in leaving the doorway met Agostino face to face. The Cavaliere recognized him immediately, and appeared to grasp eagerly the opportunity to accost him. He began by complimenting him on the near prospect of his uncle's elevation to the Papacy, professing to consider the chances of his election very good indeed, and added that he presumed business connected with these matters had brought him to Rome. To this Agostino replied that, so far as he knew, his uncle had no expectation of such an honour being at all likely to be offered him, and that private affairs of his own, of a very delicate nature,—of a kind indeed which a gentleman of the Cavaliere's known gallantry could well understand,—had brought him to Rome, as indeed he might see from the secrecy he maintained, and by his not being present at any of the entertainments which were going forward. He then inquired in his turn why the Cavaliere had not entered the college. The other made some evasive answer, but it appeared to Agostino that both the Cavaliere and his companion were not on the most familiar terms with the nobleman they had accompanied, although it might suit their purpose to appear in his train. Guardino indeed changed the subject hastily, and spoke of Inglesant, praising him highly. He inquired whether the Cardinal di Chigi was acquainted with him, and whether it was likely that either as an attendant upon him or upon Cardinal Rinuccini, Inglesant would be admitted into the conclave.

Don Agostino replied vaguely that Inglesant was then at Umbria, and that he could offer no opinion as to the probability of the latter part of his inquiry.

He thought that he could see from the expression on the other's face that the Cavaliere thought that he was deceiving him, and that he jumped at once to the conclusion that, as the attendant of one or other of the Cardinals, Inglesant would be present at the conclave.

Guardino went on to speak of Inglesant's character, regretting the craze of mind, as he called it, which his ill-health had produced, and which rendered him, as he said, unfit for business or for taking his part in the affairs of life. He went on to speak with unconcealed contempt of Inglesant's religious ideas and scruples, and of his association with Molinos; intimating, however, his opinion that it would not be impossible to overcome these scruples, could a suitable temptation be found. These fancies once removed, he continued, Inglesant's value as a trusted and secret agent would be greatly increased.

He seemed to be talking abstractedly and as a perfectly disinterested person, who was discussing an interesting topic of morals or mental peculiarity.

Agostino could not understand his drift. He answered him that the Jesuits did not need unscrupulous bravoes. If they did, they could be found at every street corner by the score. He added that he imagined that the services which Inglesant had already performed, and might perform again, were of a special and delicate character, for which his temperament and habit of mind, which were chiefly the result of the Society's training, especially fitted him.

They had by this time reached the Corso, and Agostino

took the opportunity of parting with his companions, excusing himself on the ground of his pretended assignation.

He was no sooner gone than the Cavaliere, according to the narrative which was afterwards related by Malvolti, began to explain more clearly than he had hitherto done what his expectations and intentions were. He was forced to confide in Malvolti more than he otherwise would have done, to prevent his ridding himself of Inglesant's presence by violent means.

When the Italian first saw Inglesant, whom he had never met in England, in the theatre in Florence, he was startled and terrified by his close resemblance to his murdered brother; and his first thought was that his victim had returned to earth, and, invisible to others, was permitted to avenge himself upon his murderer by haunting and terrifying his paths. When he discovered, however, that the Cavaliere not only saw the appearance which had so alarmed him, but could tell him who Inglesant was, and to a certain extent what the motives were which had brought him to Italy, his superstitious fears gave place to more material apprehensions and expedients. He at once resolved to assassinate Inglesant on leaving the theatre, in the first street through which he might pass—a purpose which he might easily have accomplished during Inglesant's careless and unguarded wanderings round the house of Lauretta's father that night. From this intention he was with difficulty diverted by the reasoning of the Cavaliere, who represented to him the rashness of such an action, protected as Inglesant was by the most powerful of Societies, which would not fail to punish any act which deprived it of a useful agent; the unnecessary character of the attempt, Inglesant being at present in complete ignorance that his enemy was near him; and above all, the folly of destroying a person who might otherwise be made the medium of great personal profit and advantage. He explained to Malvolti Inglesant's connection with the Chigi family, and the position of influence he would occupy should the Cardinal be elected to the Popedom; finally, he went so far as to hint at the possibility of an alliance between Malvolti and his sister, should Inglesant remain uninjured.

Malvolti had only arrived in Florence on the previous day, and the Cavaliere met him accidentally in the theatre; but Guardino's plans with relation to Inglesant and his sister were already so far matured, that he had arranged for the abrupt departure of his father and Lauretta from Florence. His object was to keep in his own hands a powerful magnet of attraction, which would bind, as he supposed, Inglesant to his interests; but he was by no means desirous that he should marry his sister immediately, if at all. The election for the Papacy was of very uncertain issue, and if the di Chigi faction failed, Inglesant's alliance would be of little value. He had two strings to his bow. Malvolti, between whom and the Cavaliere association in vice and even crime had riveted many a bond of interest and dependence, was closely connected with the Barberini faction, as an unscrupulous and useful tool. Should the Cardinal Barberini be elected Pope, or should Cardinal Sacchetti, who was in his interest, be chosen, his own connection with Malvolti might be of great value to the Cavaliere, and the greater service the latter could render to the Barberini faction in the approaching crisis the better. The weak point of his position on this side was the character of Malvolti, and the subordinate position he occupied among the adherents of the Barberini. On the other hand, if Cardinal Chigi were the future Pontiff, the prospects of any one connected with Inglesant would be most brilliant, as the latter, from his connection with the Jesuits, and as the favourite of the Pope's nephew, would at once become one of the most powerful men in Italy. The weak point on this side was that his hold on Inglesant was very slight, and that, even supposing it to be strengthened by marriage with Lauretta, Inglesant's character and temper were such as would probably make him useless and impracticable in the attempt to secure the glittering and often illicit advantages which would be within his reach. Between this perplexing choice the only wise course appeared to be to temporize with both parties, and to attempt, in the meantime, to secure an influence with either. The fortunes both of the Cavaliere and of Malvolti were at this moment pretty nearly desperate, and their means of influencing any one very small; indeed, having wasted what had once been considerable wealth and talent, there remained nothing to the Cavaliere but his sister, and of that last possession he was prepared to make unscrupulous use. It would be of small advantage to him to give his sister's hand to Inglesant unless he could first, by her means, corrupt and debase his conscience and that lofty standard of conduct which he appeared, to the Cavaliere at least, unswervingly to follow; and the Italian devil at his side suggested a means to this end as wild in conception as the result proved it impotent and badly planned.

This Italian devil was not Malvolti, though that person was one of his most successful followers and imitators. When the inspired writer has described the princes and angels which rule the different nations of the earth, he does not go on to enumerate the distinct powers of evil which, in different countries, pursue their divers malefic courses; yet it would seem that those existences are no less real than the others. That the character of the inhabitants of any country has much to do in forming a distinct devil for that country no man can doubt; or that in consequence the temptations which beset mankind in certain countries are of a distinct and peculiar kind. This fact is sometimes of considerable advantage to the object of the tempter's art, for if, acting upon his knowledge of the character of any people, this merely local devil lays snares in the path of a stranger, it is not impossible that the bait may fail. This was very much what happened to John Inglesant. Of the sins which were really his temptations the Cavaliere knew nothing; but he could conceive of certain acts which he concluded Inglesant would consider to be sins. These acts were of a gross and sensual nature; for the Italian devil, born of the fleshly lusts of the people, was unable to form temptations for the higher natures, and of course his pupils were equally impotent. The result was singular. Acting upon the design of ruining Inglesant's moral sense, of debasing the ideal of conduct at which he aimed, and of shattering and defiling what the Cavaliere considered the fantastic purity of his conscience, he formed a scheme which had the effect of removing Inglesant from a place where he was under the strongest temptation and in the greatest danger of violating his conscience, and of placing him in circumstances of trial which, though dangerous, he was still, from the peculiarity of his character, much better able to resist.

A marriage connection with Inglesant would at this juncture be of little avail; but a wild and illicit passion, which would involve him in a course of licentious and confused action, in which the barriers of morality and the scruples of conscience would be alike annihilated, and the whole previous nature of the victim of lawless desire altered, would, if any agent could produce so great a change, transform Inglesant into the worldly-minded and unscrupulous accomplice that the Cavaliere wished him to become. How great the fall would be he could of course in no way estimate; but he had sufficient insight to perceive that the shock of it would probably be sufficient (acting upon a consciousness so refined and delicate as that of Inglesant) to render recovery, if ever attained, very difficult and remote.

Upon this wild scheme he acted. He had removed his sister when he had thought that Inglesant had been sufficiently ensnared to make his after course certain and precipitate. Inglesant's character, which was so very imperfectly known to the Cavaliere, and circumstances, such as his confinement in the pest-house, had delayed the consummation of the plot. But the Cavaliere conceived that the time had now arrived for its completion. He brought his sister back to Florence, and placed her with the Grand Duchess, in some subordinate situation which his family and his sister's character enabled him to obtain. Having had some previous knowledge of her, the Duchess soon became attached to Lauretta, and obtained her confidence. From her she learnt Inglesant's story and character, and wished to see him at the Court. While the two ladies were planning schemes for future pleasure, the Cavaliere suddenly appeared at Florence, and informed his sister that he had concluded, with the approbation of his father, a marriage contract between herself and Malvolti.

Terrified by this threatened connection with a man whose person she loathed and whose character she detested, Lauretta flew to the Duchess and entreated her to send at once for Inglesant, who, they were both aware, was at that moment with the Duke of Umbria, the Grand Duchess's aged father. With the result we are acquainted.

CHAPTER XXIX.

On his arrival at Florence Inglesant found himself at once fêted and caressed, though the nature of his mission to Umbria, antagonistic as his supposed influence had been to the interests of the ducal party, might naturally have procured for him a far different reception. Trained as he had been in courts, the caprices of princes' favour did not seem strange to him, and were taken at their true worth. Unsuspicious, therefore, of any special danger, relieved from the intolerable strain which the position at Umbria had exerted upon his conscience, delighted with the society of his recovered mistress, and flattered by the attentions of the Duchess and of the whole Court, he gave himself up freely to the enjoyments of the hour. Plentifully supplied with money from his own resources, from the kindness of the aged Duke, and from the subsidies of his patrons at Rome, he engaged freely in the parties formed for the performance of masques and interludes, in which the Court delighted, and became conspicuous for the excellence of his acting and invention.

But it was not the purpose of the demon that followed on his footsteps to give him longer repose than might lull his senses, and weaken his powers of resisting evil. Day after day devoted to pleasure paved the way for the final catastrophe, until the night arrived when the plot was fully ripe. Supper was over, and the Court sat down again to play. Inglesant remembered afterwards, though at the time it did not attract his attention, that several gentlemen, all of them friends of Guardino, paid him particular attention, and insisted on drinking with him, calling for different kinds of wine, and recommending them to his notice. The saloons were crowded and very hot, and when Inglesant left the supper room and came into the brilliant marble hall lighted with great lustres, where the Court was at play, he was more excited than was his wont. The Court was gathered at different tables—a very large one in the centre of the hall, and other smaller ones around. The brilliant dresses, the jewels, the beautiful women, the reflections in the numberless mirrors, made a dazzling and mystifying impression on his brain. The play was very high, and at the table to which Inglesant sat down especially so. He lost heavily, and this did not tend to calm his nerves; he doubled his stake, with all the money he had with him, and lost again. As he rose from the table a page touched his elbow and handed him a small note carefully sealed and delicately perfumed. It was addressed to him by his new title, "Il Cavaliere di San Giorgio," and scarcely knowing what he did, he opened it. It was from Lauretta.

"Cavaliere,

"Will you come to me in the Duchess's lodgings before the Court rises from play? I need your help. L."

Inglesant turned to look for the boy, who, he expected, was waiting for him. He was not far off, and Inglesant followed him without a word. They passed through many corridors and rooms richly furnished until they reached the lodgings of the Grand Duchess. The night was sultry, and through the open windows above the gardens the strange odours that are born of darkness and of night entered the palace. In the dark arcades the nightingales were singing, preferring gloom and mystery to the light in which all other creatures rejoice; and in the stillness the murmur of brooks and the splash of the fountains oppressed the air with an unearthly and unaccustomed sound. Around the casements festoons of harmless and familiar flowers and leaves assumed wild and repulsive shapes, as if transformed into malicious demons who made men their sport. Inglesant thought involuntarily of those plants that are at enmity with man, which are used for enchantments and for poisoning, and whose very scent is death; such saturnine and fatal flowers seemed more at home in the lovely Italian night than the innocent plants which witness to lovers' vows, and upon which divines moralize and preach. The rooms of the Duchess were full of perfume of the kind that enervates and lulls the sense. It seemed to Inglesant as though he were treading the intricate pathways of a dream, careless as to what befell him, yet with a passionate longing which urged him forward, heedless of a restraining voice which he was even then half-conscious that at other times he should have heard. The part of the palace where he was seemed deserted, and the page led him through more than one anteroom without meeting any one, until they reached a curtained door, which the boy opened, and directed Inglesant to enter. He did so, and found himself at once in the presence of Lauretta, who was lying upon a low seat at the open window. The room was lighted by several small lamps in different positions, giving an ample, yet at the same time a soft and dreamy light. Lauretta was carelessly dressed, yet, in the soft light, and in her negligent attitude, there was something that made her beauty the more attractive, and her manner to Inglesant was unrestrained and clinging. Her growing affection, the urgency of her need, and the circumstances of the hour, caused her innocently to speak and act in a way the most fitted to promote her brother's atrocious purposes.

"Cavaliere," she said, "I have sent for you because I have no friend but you. I have sent for you to help me against my own family—my own brother—my father even, whom I love—whom I loved—more than all the world beside. They are determined to marry me to a man whom I hate; to the man whom you hate; to that Signore Malvolti, who, though they deny it, is, I am fully persuaded, the murderer of your brother; to that wretch whom Italy even refuses to receive; who, but for his useful crimes, would be condemned to a death of torment. My brother tells me that he will be here to-morrow to see me and demand my consent. He brings an authorization from my father, and insists upon the contract being made without delay. I would die rather than submit to such a fate, but it is not necessary to die. I must, however, leave the Court and escape from my brother's wardship. If I can reach some place of safety, where I can gain time to see my father, I am certain that I shall be able to move him. It cannot be that he will condemn me to such a fate,—me! the pride and pleasure of his life. He must be deceived and misled by some of these wicked intrigues and manœuvres which ruin the happiness and peace of men."

"I am wholly yours," said Inglesant; "whatever you desire shall be done. Have you spoken to the Duchess?"

"The Duchess advises me to fly," replied Lauretta; "she says the Duke will not interfere between a father and his child; especially now, when all Italy hangs in suspense concerning the Papacy, and men are careful whom they offend. She advises me to go to the convent of St. Catherine of Pistoia, where I lodged not many years ago while my father was in France. The Abbess is a cousin of my father's; she is a kind woman, and I can persuade her to keep me for a short time at least. I wish to go to-night. Will you take me?"

She had never looked so lovely in Inglesant's eyes as she did while she spoke. The pleading look of her dark eyes, and the excitement of her manner, usually so reserved and calm, added charms to her person of which he had previously been unconscious. In that country of formal restraint and suspicion, of hurried, furtive interviews, a zest was given to accidental freedom of intercourse such as the more unrestricted life of France and England knew little of. In spite of a suspicion of treachery, which in that country was never absent, Inglesant felt his frame aglow with devotion to this lovely creature, who thus threw herself unreservedly into his keeping. He threw himself upon a cushion at Lauretta's feet, and encircled her with his arms. She spoke of youth and life and pleasure,—of youth that was passing away so rapidly; of life that had been to her dreary and dull enough; of her jealously-guarded Italian home, of her convent cell, of her weak and helpless father, of her tyrannous brother; of pleasure, of which she had dreamed as a girl, but which seemed to fly before her as she advanced; finally of himself, whom, from the first day she had seen him in her father's room, she had loved, whom absence had only endeared, her first and only friend.

He spoke of love, of protection, of help and succour for the rest of life; of happy days to come at San Giorgio, when all these troubles should have passed away, when at last he should escape from intrigue and State policy, and they could make their home as joyous and free from care as that house of a Cardinal, on a little hilly bank near Velctri, whence you can see the sea, and which is called Monte Joiosa. He spoke of an Idyllic dream which could not long have satisfied either of them,—himself especially, but which pleased them at that moment, with an innocent and delicate fancy which calmed and purified their excited thoughts. Then, as the hour passed by, he rose from her embrace, promising to provide horses, and when the palace was quiet, to meet her at the end of one of the long avenues that crossed the park; for the Court was not at the Pitti Palace, but at the Poggio Imperiale without the walls of Florence.

The soft night air played upon Inglesant's forehead as he led his horses to the end of a long avenue, and waited for the lady to join him. He did not wait long; she came gliding past the fountains, by the long rows of orange and cypress hedges, and across the streaks of moonlight among the trees that closed the gardens and the park. As he lifted her into the saddle, her glance was partly scared and partly trustful: he felt as though he were moving in a delicious dream.

As they rode out of the park she told him that she had received a message from the Duchess, recommending her to stop at a pavilion on the borders of the great chase, beyond the Achaiano Palace, half-way to Pistoia, which the Duchess used sometimes when the Duke was diverting himself in the chase. She had sent a messenger to prepare the people who kept the pavilion for their coming. There was something strange in this message, Lauretta said, which was brought, not by one of the Duchess's usual pages, but by a boy who had not been long at the palace, and who scarcely waited to give his message, so great was his hurry. It seemed of little moment to Inglesant who brought the message, or whether any treachery were at work or no; he was only conscious of a delicious sense of coming pleasure which made him reckless of all beside. Along the first few miles of their road they passed nothing but the long lines of elms, planted between ridges of corn, upon which the vines were climbing in already luxuriant wreaths. Presently, however, after they had passed the Achaiano Palace, the country changed, and they came within the confines of the Duke's chase, thirty miles in compass, planted with cork trees and ilex, with underwood of myrtle thickets. Through these shades, lovely indeed by day, but weird and unhealthy by night, they rode silently, startled every now and then by strange sounds that issued from the forest depths. The ground was fenny and uneven, and moist exhalations rose out of the soil and floated across the path.

"The Duchess never sleeps at the pavilion," said Lauretta at last suddenly; "it is dangerous to sleep in the forest."

"It will be as well to stop an hour or so, however," said Inglesant, "else we shall be at Pistoia before they open the gates."

Presently, in the brilliant moonlight, they saw the pointed roofs of the pavilion on a little rising-ground, with the forest trees coming up closely to the walls. The moon was now high in the heavens, and it was as light as day. The upper windows of the pavilion were open, and within it lights were burning. The door was opened to them before they knocked, and the keeper of the pavilion came to meet them, accompanied by a boy who took the horses. The man showed no surprise at their coming, only saying some servants of the Duchess had been there a few hours previously, and had prepared a repast in the dining-room, forewarning him that he should expect visitors. He accompanied them upstairs, for they saw nothing of the other inmates of the place. The rooms were arranged with a sort of rustic luxury, and were evidently intended for repose during the heat of the day. A plentiful and delicate collation was spread on one of the tables, with abundance of fruit and wine. The place looked like the magic creation of an enchanter's wand, raised for purposes of evil from the unhealthy marsh, and ready to sink again, when that malefic purpose was fulfilled, into the weird depths from which it rose.

The old man showed them the other rooms of the apartment and left them. At the door he turned back and said,—

"I should not advise the lady to sleep here; the miasma from the forest is very fatal to such as are not used to it."

Inglesant looked at him, but could not perceive that he intended his words to have any deeper meaning than the obvious one. He said,—

"We shall stay only an hour or two; let the horses be ready to go on."

The man left them, and they sat down at the table.

The repast was served in Faience ware of a strange delicate blue, and consisted of most of the delicacies of the season, with a profusion of wine.

"This was not ordered by the Duchess," said Lauretta.

"We are safe from poison, Mignone," said Inglesant; "to destroy you as well as me would defeat all purposes. Not that I believe the Cavaliere would wish me dead. He rather hopes that I may be of use to him. Let us drink to him."

And he filled a glass for Lauretta of the Montepulciano, the "King of Wines," and drank himself.

Lauretta was evidently frightened, yet she followed his example and drank. The night air was heavy and close, not a breath of wind stirred the lights, though every window was thrown open, and the shutters that closed the loggia outside were drawn back. In the brilliant moonlight every leaf of the great forest shone with an unnatural distinctness, which, set in a perfect silence, became terrible to see. The sylvan arcades seemed like a painted scene-piece upon a Satanic stage supernaturally alight to further deeds of sin, and silent and unpeopled, lest the wrong should be interrupted or checked. To Inglesant's excited fancy evil beings thronged its shadowy paths, present to the spiritual sense, though concealed of set purpose from the feeble human sight. The two found their eyes drawn with a kind of fascination to this strange sight, and Inglesant arose and closed the shutters before the nearest casement.

They felt more at ease when the mysterious forest was shut out. But Lauretta was silent and troubled, and Inglesant's efforts to cheer and enliven her were not successful. The delicious wines to which he resorted to remove his own uneasiness and to cure his companion's melancholy, failed of their effect. At last she refused to drink, and rising up suddenly, she exclaimed,—

"Oh, it is terribly hot. I cannot bear it. I wish we had not come!"

She wandered from the room in which they sat, through the curtained doorway into the next, which was furnished with couches, and sank down on one of them. Inglesant followed her, and, as if the heat felt stifling also to him, went out upon the open verandah, and looked upon the forest once more.

Excited by the revels of the past few days, heated with wine, with the night ride, and with the overpowering closeness of the air, the temptation came upon him with a force which he had neither power nor desire to resist. He listened, but no sound met his ear, no breath stirred, no living being moved, no disturbance need be dreaded from any side. From the people in the pavilion he looked for no interference, from the object of his desires he had probably no need to anticipate any disinclination but what might easily be soothed away. The universal custom of the country in which he was now almost naturalized sanctioned such acts. The hour was admirably chosen, the place perfectly adapted in every way, as if the result not of happy chance but deeply concerted plan.

Why then did he hesitate? Did he still partly hope that some miracle would happen? or some equally miraculous change take place in his mind and will to save him from himself? It is true the place and the temptation were not of his own seeking—so far he was free from blame; but he had not come wholly unharmed out of the fiery trial at Umbria, and, by a careless walk since he came to Florence, he had prepared the way for the tempter, and this night even he had disregarded the warning voice and drifted recklessly onward. We walk of our own free will, heated and inflamed by wine, down the flowery path which we have ourselves decorated with garlands, and we murmur because we reach the fatal goal.

He gazed another moment over the illumined forest, which seemed transfigured in the moonlight and the stillness into an unreal landscape of the dead. The poisonous mists crept over the tops of the cork trees, and flitted across the long vistas in spectral forms, cowled and shrouded for the grave. Beneath the gloom indistinct figures seemed to glide,—the personation of the miasma that made the place so fatal to human life.

He turned to enter the room, but even as he turned a sudden change came over the scene. The deadly glamour of the moonlight faded suddenly, a calm pale solemn light settled over the forest, the distant line of hills shone out distinct and clear, the evil mystery of the place departed whence it came, a fresh and cooling breeze sprang up and passed through the rustling wood, breathing pureness and life. The dayspring was at hand in the eastern sky.

The rustling breeze was like a whisper from heaven that reminded him of his better self. It would seem that hell overdid it; the very stillness for miles around, the almost concerted plan, sent flashing through his brain the remembrance of another house, equally guarded for a like purpose—a house at Nuncham near Oxford, into which years ago he had himself forced his way to render help in such a case as this. Here was the same thing happening over again with the actors changed; was it possible that such a change had been wrought in him? The long past life of those days rushed into his mind: the sacramental Sundays, the repeated vows, the light of heaven in the soul, the kneeling forms in Little Gidding Chapel, the face of Mary Collet, the loveliness that blessed the earth where she walked, her death-bed, and her dying words. What so rarely happens happened here. The revulsion of feeling, the rush of recollection and association, was too powerful for the flesh. The reason and the affections rallied together, and, trained into efficiency by past discipline, regained the mastery by a supreme effort, even at the very moment of unsatisfied desire. But the struggle was fierce; he was torn like the demon-haunted child in the gospel story; but, as in that story, the demon was expelled.

He came back into the room. Lauretta lay upon a couch with rich drapery and cushions, her face buried in her hands. The cloak and hood in which she had ridden were removed, and the graceful outline of her figure was rendered more alluring by the attitude in which she lay. As he entered she raised her head from her hands, and looked at him with a strange, apprehensive, expectant gaze. He remained for a moment silent, his face very pale; then he said, slowly and uncertainly, like a man speaking in a dream,—

"The fatal miasma is rising from the plain. Lauretta, this place is safe for neither of us, we had better go on."

* * * * *

The morning was cloudy and chill. They had not ridden far before a splash of thunder-rain fell and the trees dripped dismally. A sense of discomfort and disappointment took possession of Inglesant, and so far from deriving consolation from his conquest, he seemed torn by the demon of discontent. He was half-conscious that his companion was regretting the evil and luxurious house they had left. The ride to Pistoia was silent and depressed. As they passed through the streets, early as it was, they were watched by two figures half concealed by projecting walls. One of them was the Cavaliere, the other was tall and dark. Whether it was the devil in the person of Malvolti, or Malvolti himself, is not of much consequence, nor would the difference be great. In either case the issue was the same,—the devil's plot had failed. It is not so easy to ruin him with whom the pressure of Christ's hand yet lingers in the palm.

When Inglesant presented himself again at the Convent grate, after a few hours' sleepless unrest at an inn, he was refused admittance; nor did repeated applications during that day and the next meet with a more favourable response. He became the prey of mortification and disgust that, having had the prize in his hand, he had of his own free will passed it into the keeping of another. On the evening of the third day, however, he received a note from Lauretta informing him that her brother had consented to postpone her betrothal to Malvolti indefinitely, and that she, on her part, had promised not to see Inglesant again until the Papal election had been decided. She entreated her lover not to attempt to disturb this compromise, as by so doing he would only injure her whom he had promised to help. She promised to be true, and did not doubt but that, having obtained the delay she sought, she should be able to gain her father's consent to their marriage, especially if the Papal election took the course they hoped it would.

There was something cold and formal about the wording of this note, which, however, might be explained by its contents having been dictated to the writer; but, unsatisfactory as it was, Inglesant was compelled to acquiesce in the request it contained. He was angry and disappointed, and it must be admitted that he had some cause. His mistress and his pleasant life at the ducal Court had vanished in the morning mist and rain, like the delusive pleasures of a dream, and the regret which a temptation yielded to would leave behind is not always counterbalanced by a corresponding elation when the trial is overcome. He departed for Rome, having sent orders to Florence for his servants and baggage to meet him on the road, and the same night on which he entered the city Pope Innocent the Tenth expired.

CHAPTER XXX.

THE portion of the Vatican Palace set apart for the election of the Pope, and called the Conclave, consisted of five halls or large marble rooms, two chapels, and a gallery seventy feet long. Each of these halls was divided temporarily into small apartments, running up both sides, with a broad alley between them, formed of wood, and covered with green or violet cloth. One of these apartments was assigned to each Cardinal with his attendants. The entrance to the whole of these rooms, halls, chapels, and gallery, was by a single door fastened by four locks and as many keys. As soon as the Cardinals had entered the Conclave this door was made fast, and the four keys were given to the four different orders of the city,—one to the Bishop of Rome, one to the Cardinals themselves, a third to the Roman Nobility, and the fourth to the Officer, a great noble, who kept the door. A wicket in the door, of which this Officer also kept the key, permitted the daily meals and other necessaries to be handed to the Cardinals' servants, every dish being carefully examined before it was allowed to pass in. Within the Conclave light and air were only obtained by sky-lights or windows opening upon interior courts, precluding communication from without. The gloom of the interior was so great, that candles were burnt throughout the Conclave at noon-day.

From the moment the Conclave was closed a silence of expectation and anxiety fell upon all Rome. The daily life of the city was hushed. The principal thoroughfares and fortresses were kept by strong detachments of armed troops, and the approaches to the mysterious door were jealously watched. Men spoke everywhere in whispers, and nothing but vague rumours of the proceedings within were listened to in the places of public resort, and in the coteries and gatherings of all ranks and conditions of the people.

In the interior of the Conclave, for those who were confined within its singular seclusion, the day passed with a wearisome monotony marked only by intrigue not less wearisome. Early in the morning a tolled bell called the whole of its inmates to mass in one of the small Chapels darkened with stained glass, and lighted dimly by the tapers of the altar, and by a few wax candles fixed in brass sockets suspended from the roof. The Cardinals sat· in stalls down either side of the Chapel, and at the lower end was a bar, kept by the master of the ceremonies and his assistants, behind which the attendants and servants were allowed to stand. Mass being over, a table was placed in front of the altar, upon which were a chalice and a silver bell. Upon six stools near the table are seated two Cardinal-Bishops, two Cardinal-Priests, and two Cardinal-Deacons. Every Cardinal in his turn, upon the ringing of the bell, leaves his seat, and having knelt before the altar in silent prayer for the guidance of Heaven in his choice, goes round to the front of the table and drops a paper, upon which he has written the name of a Cardinal, into the chalice, and returns in silence to his stall.

A solemn and awful stillness pervades the scene, broken only by the tinkling of the silver bell. The Cardinals, one by one, some of them stalwart and haughty men, with a firm step and imperious glance, others old and decrepit, scarcely able to totter from their places to the altar, or to rise from their knees without help, advance to their mysterious choice. To the eye alone it was in truth a solemn and impressive scene, and by a heart instructed by the sense of sight only, the awful presence of God the Paraclete might, in accordance with the popular belief, be felt to hover above the Sacred Host; but in the entire assembly to whom alone the sight was given there was probably not one single heart to which such an idea was present. The assembly was divided into different parties, each day by day intriguing and manœuvring, by every art of policy and every inducement of worldly interest, to add to the number of its adherents. "If perchance," says one well qualified to speak, "there entered into this Conclave any old Cardinal, worn by conflict with the Church's enemies 'in partibus infidelium,' amid constant danger of prison or of death, or perchance coming from amongst harmless peasants in country places, and by long absence from the centre of the Church's polity, ignorant of the manner in which her Princes trod the footsteps of the Apostles of old, and by the memory of such conflict and of such innocence, and because of such ignorance, was led to entertain dreams of Divine guidance, two or three days' experience caused such an one to renounce all such delusion, and to return to his distant battlefield, and so to see Rome no more."

When every Cardinal has deposited his paper, the Cardinal-Bishop takes them out of the chalice one by one, and hands them to the Cardinal-Deacon, who reads out the name of the elected, but not of the Cardinal who had placed the paper in the chalice (which is written on part of the paper so folded that even the reader does not see it); and as he reads the name, every Cardinal makes a mark upon the scroll of names he has before him. When all the names have been read, the Cardinal-Priest, from a paper which he has prepared, reads the name of him who has had the most voices and the number of the votes. If the number be more than two-thirds of the whole, the Cardinal who has received the votes is thereby elected Pope; but if not, the Cardinal-Priest rings the silver bell once more, and at the signal the master of the ceremonies, Monsignor Fabei, advances up the Chapel, followed by a groom carrying a brazier of lighted coals, into which, in the face of the whole assembly, the papers are dropped one by one till all are consumed.

At the beginning of the Conclave the Cardinals were always divided into two, if not more parties, of such relative strength as to make the attainment of such a majority by either of them impossible for many days. It was not until the persistent intrigues of a fortnight had increased the majority of any one Cardinal so much as to give a probability of his being ultimately elected, that the waverers of all sides, not willing to be known as the opponents of a new Pope, recorded their voices in his favour, and thus raised the majority to its necessary proportion. For this very delicate matter occurred at this period of the election, that, should the requisite majority of voices be obtained, the master of the ceremonies and his brazier were no longer called for, but the whole of the papers were opened to their full extent, and the names of the voters given to the world, whereby, as one conversant in these matters observes, "many mysteries and infidelities are brought to light." It is evident, therefore, that, as the majority of any one Cardinal increased or showed signs of increasing, morning and evening, as the suffrages were taken, the voting became a very exciting and delicate matter. No one could be certain but that at the next voting the majority from the cause mentioned would suddenly swell to the necessary size, and every man's name be made clear and plain on whose side he had been.

Upon entering the Conclave the friends of Cardinal Chigi adopted a quiet policy, and waited for the progress of events to work for them. The abuses of the late Pontificate, and the excitement and indignation of popular opinion, had made it clear to all parties that it was necessary to elect a Pope whose character and reputation would restore confidence. In these respects no one seemed more qualified than Cardinal Chigi, who was supposed to possess all the qualifications necessary to ensure the Romans from the apprehension of a revival of the past disorders, and to inspire the whole Christian world with the hopes of witnessing a worthy successor of St. Peter displaying the Christian virtues from the Papal Chair. The great reputation he had gained at Münster, the determination he was said to have manifested to reform all abuses, the authority and influence he derived from his post of Secretary of State, his attractive and gracious manner, the recommendation of the late Pope upon his death-bed,—all tended to bring his name prominently forward. He was supported by the Spanish Cardinals, chiefly on account of the enmity of the French Court and of his professed opposition to Cardinal Mazarin.

But, in spite of these advantages, the enmity of the French Court, and the opposition of the Barberini family, the relations and supporters of the late Pope, made it necessary for his friends to observe extreme caution. The French Cardinals were ordered to vote for Sacchetti, and Cardinal Barberini for the present supported him also, with all his party, chiefly because he had not yet made terms with the Spanish Court, which opposed Sacchetti; but also, as was supposed, because he himself had aspirations towards the Papal Chair, should he find the electors favourable to such a scheme.

Upon the entrance into the Conclave, therefore, Cardinal Sacchetti immediately obtained thirty-two or thirty-three votes. These were not quite so many as the Barberini expected, and indeed had a right to count upon, after the professions which the Cardinals of the party had made. This was owing to the defection of some members of what was called the Flying Squadron, composed chiefly of young Cardinals, who were supposed to be devoted to the Barberini, but of whom several were secretly favourable to Cardinal Chigi.

The Spanish faction, which was numerous enough to have secured the election of any Cardinal had it been united, but the members of which were agreed upon nothing but their determined opposition to Sacchetti, contented itself with voting negatively at every scrutiny, making use of the form "accedo nemini." This course was pursued for two entire months, during which time the scrutinies were taken regularly morning and evening, always with a slightly varying but indecisive result.

It would be difficult to realise the wearisomeness which reigned in the Conclave during so protracted a period. The crowding together of so large a number of persons in a few apartments, the closeness of the air, and the unbroken monotony of the hours that passed so slowly, made the confinement almost intolerable. One Cardinal was taken ill, and was obliged to be removed. The great gallery was generally used by the Cardinals themselves, for exercise and conversation, while their attendants were compelled to content themselves with their masters' apartments, or the corridors and passages. Those which opened on the interior courts, and thereby afforded some fresh air, were especially resorted to. Communication from without, though in theory absolutely prevented, was really frequent, all the chief among the Cardinals receiving advices from foreign Courts, and conveying intelligence thither themselves.

At intervals the whole of the inmates were assembled to listen to Father Quæchi, preacher to the Conclave, a Jesuit, and secretly in favour of Cardinal Chigi, as was the Society in general. The sermon was so contrived as to influence its hearers considerably by its evident application to the manners and conduct of the Cardinal.

The famous De Retz, then an exile from France and a supporter of Chigi, by whom he always sat in the Chapel, was the principal intriguer in his favour. He was in communication with the nominal supporters of Barberini, who sent him intelligence by Monsignor Fabei when to vote for Sacchetti, on occasions when it would be of no real service to him, and when to refrain. On one of these latter occasions Fabei entrusted his message to Inglesant, with whom he was intimate, and it afterwards appeared that Sacchetti, on that scrutiny, wanted but very few votes to have secured his election. This circumstance made a deep impression on De Retz, and he never recognized Inglesant afterwards without alluding to it.

The day after this scrutiny Cardinal Barberini appears to have thought that the time was come for his friends to make a demonstration in his behalf, and to the astonishment of the Conclave thirty-one votes appeared in his favour in the next scrutiny. This caused the friends of Cardinal Chigi to pay more attention to his conduct, and to the discourses of his Conclavists and other partizans, who neglected no opportunity of exalting his good qualities.

The exhaustion of the Conclave became extreme. Cardinal Caraffa, who, next to Sacchetti and Chigi, stood the greatest chance of election, became ill and died. Twelve other Cardinals were balloted for, one after another, without result. Cardinal San Clemente was then brought forward, and, but for the hostility of the Jesuits, might have been elected; but the Spanish Cardinals who supported him did not dare openly to offend the Society, and the election failed.

The Barberini began to despair of electing their candidate, and having received favourable advices from the Court of Spain, were willing, either with or without the concurrence of their leader, to negotiate with the friends of Cardinal Chigi. Sacchetti, finding his own chances hopeless, was not averse to be treated with. There remained only the Court of France.

*   *   *   *   *

The MSS. are here defective.

Be this as it may, Cardinal Sacchetti's letter had the desired effect upon Mazarin, who immediately sent the necessary letters to the French Cardinals, withdrawing the veto upon Chigi. Nothing remained now but to gain the concurrence of Cardinal Barberini. For a long time he refused to accede, but, the members of his party who had from the first secretly supported Chigi having now openly declared in his favour, Barberini at last consented to hold a conference. It took place immediately after the morning scrutiny, and lasted but a short time. But it sat long enough to arrange that the next morning Cardinal Chigi should be elected Pope.

This determination was so suddenly arrived at, and was concealed so carefully, that nothing certainly was known during the rest of the day, outside the number of those who had taken part in the conference. There were vague rumours, and many discontents, but the time was so short that many who would have declared in favour of Sacchetti, had longer time been given them, were not able to recover from their surprise.

Inglesant was of course informed by Cardinal Chigi of what had occurred immediately after the conference, and about midday he received a message from De Retz warning him to be upon his guard. During the afternoon, however, some further intelligence of the feeling within the Conclave came to the knowledge of that astute intriguer, and he sent Monsignor Fabei to Inglesant about five o'clock.

This man was a favourable specimen of the Italian servant of an Ecclesiastical Court. Belonging to a family which had been trained for generations in the service of the Curia, he was a man to whom the difficulties which perplexed others, and the anomalies which appeared to some men to exist between Christian polity as it might be conceived to be and Christian polity as it was practised in Rome, did not exist;—a man to whom the Divine, so far as it was manifested to him at all, took the form, without doubt or scruple, of that gorgeous though unwieldy, and, as it seemed to some, slightly questionable, economy of which he was the faithful servant. He was honest, yet he appeared—such was the peculiarity of his training and circumstances—to have solved the, on good authority, insoluble problem of serving two masters at the same time; for two opposing Cardinals, or two factions of Cardinals, alike commanded his reverence and service at the same moment. Much of this service was no doubt unthinking and unconscious, else the memoirs of such a man, composed by himself without reserve, would be perhaps as interesting a book as could be written.

"Something is going on within the Conclave, Cavaliere," he said, "of which I am not entirely cognizant. Of course I am aware of the communications which have been made from outside during this most protracted Conclave. The Princes of the Church must have every opportunity given them of arriving at a just conclusion in this most important matter, and I have never been backward in affording every assistance to their Eminences; but what we have to deal with to-night is of a very different kind. You have nothing to dread from the chiefs of the opposite party; they have accepted the situation, and will loyally carry out their engagements. But they have altered their policy without consulting or remembering their supporters, and among these, especially the inferior ones outside the Conclave, the disappointment is severe. They have not time, nor are they in a position to make terms with the successful party, and their expectations of advancement are annihilated. They are, many of them, absolutely unscrupulous, and would hazard everything to gain time. They have some means of communication between the outside world of Rome and their partizans within the Conclave, which they have not used till now, and with which, therefore, I am unacquainted. They are employing it now. What the exact effort will be I do not know, but should your Padrone, Cardinal Chigi, fall ill before to-morrow's scrutiny, it would delay his election, and delay is all they want. There are sufficient malcontents to prevent his election if they had only time; two or three days would give them all they want. I should advise you not to sleep to-night, but to watch with a wakefulness which starts at every sound."

The apartment assigned to Cardinal Chigi was subdivided into three smaller ones, the largest of which was appropriated to the bedchamber of the Cardinal, the two others to his attendants. These apartments communicated with each other, and only one opened upon the centre corridor running down the Hall. The Cardinal retired early to his own chamber, and most of the other Cardinals did the same. A profound silence reigned in the Conclave; if any of the attendants still stirred they were velvet-shod, and the floors and walls, lined with velvet, prevented the least sound from being heard.

Inglesant remained alone in the outermost of the three

apartments, and determined to keep his faculties on the alert For some reason, however, either the fatigue of the long confinement, or the deathlike stillness of the night, a profound drowsiness overpowered him, and he continually sank into a doze. He tried to read, but the page floated before his eyes, and it was only by continually rising and pacing the small chamber that he kept himself from sinking into a deep sleep.

A profound peace and repose seemed to reign in a place where so many scheming and excited brains, versed in every art of policy, were really at work.

Inglesant had sat down again, and had fallen once more into a slight doze, when suddenly, from no apparent cause, his drowsiness left him, and he became intensely and almost painfully awake. The silence around him was the same as before, but a violent agitation and excitement disturbed his mind, and an overpowering apprehension of some approaching existence, inimical to himself, aroused his faculties to an acute perception, and braced his nerves to a supreme effort. In another moment, this apprehension, at first merely mental, became perceptible to the sense, and he could hear a sound. It was, as it were, the echo of a low faint creeping movement, the very ghost of a sound. Whence it came Inglesant could not determine, but it was from without the apartment in which he sat. No longer able to remain passive, he rose, drew back the velvet curtain that screened the entrance from the corridor, opened the door silently, and went out.

The corridor was lighted here and there along its great length by oil lamps suspended before every third door of the Cardinals' rooms; but the dark and massive hangings, the loftiness of the hall overhead, and the dimness of the lamps themselves, caused the light to be misty and uncertain, as in a confused and troubled dream. One of these lamps was suspended immediately above the door at which Inglesant had appeared, and he stood in its full light, being himself much more distinctly seen than he was himself able to see anything. He was richly dressed in dark velvet, after the French fashion, and in the uncertain light his resemblance to his murdered brother was, in this dress, very great. He held a slight and jewelled dagger in his hand.

As he paused under the suspended lamp the sound he had before heard developed itself into low stealthy footsteps approaching down the corridor, apparently on the opposite side, and the next moment a figure, more like a phantom thrown on the opposite wall than a substantial being, glided into sight. It was shrouded in dark and flowing drapery, and kept so close to the heavy hangings that it seemed almost the waving of their folds stirred by some unknown breeze. Though it passed down the opposite side, it kept its attention turned in Inglesant's direction, and almost at the same moment at which he appeared through the opening door it saw him and instantly stopped. It lost its stealthy motion and assumed an attitude of intense and speechless terror, such as Inglesant had never seen depicted in a human being, and by this attitude revealed itself more completely to his gaze. The hood which shaded its face fell partly back, and displayed features pale as death, and lustrous eyes dilated with horror, and Inglesant could see that it held some nameless weapon in its hand. As it stood, arrested in its purpose, breathless and uncertain, it seemed to Inglesant a phantom murderer, or rather the phantom of murder itself, as though nothing short of the murderous principle sufficed any longer to dog his steps.

This strange figure confronted Inglesant for some seconds, during which neither stirred, each with his eyes riveted upon the other, each with his weapon in his hand. Then the phantom murmured in an inarticulate and broken voice, that faltered upon the air as though tremulous with horror, "It is himself! He has taken the dagger from his bleeding wound."

Then, as it had come, it glided backwards along the heavy drapery, becoming more and more lost in its folds, till, at first apparently but the shadow of a shade, it faded more and more into the hanging darkness, and vanished out of sight.

The next morning, at the scrutiny after early mass, Fabius Chigi, Cardinal and Secretary of State, was, by more than two-thirds of the whole Conclave, elected Pope.

CHAPTER XXXI.

THERE is, perhaps, no comparison so apposite, though it be a homely one, to the condition of affairs in Italy at this time—upon the election of a new Pope—as that of a change of trumps at a game of cards. All persons and matters remain the same as they were before, yet their values and relationships are all changed; the aspect of the entire scene is altered; those who before were in little esteem are exalted, and those who were in great power and estimation are abased. All the persons with whom Inglesant had been connected were more or less affected by it, except Cardinal Rinuccini, to whom it made little difference. To the Cavaliere and to Malvolti it was ruin. The former was so deeply involved in debt, in private feuds, and entanglements with the authorities, his character was so utterly lost with all parties, and his means of usefulness to any so small, that it is probable that even the elevation to power of the Barberini faction would not have been of much use to him. But, whatever might have been his prospects had the election resulted otherwise, his only chance now of safety from prison and even death was in Inglesant's connection with his sister, and in the protection he might hope to experience upon that account; his only hope depended upon the force of Inglesant's affection. The fear of private assassination kept him almost confined to his chamber. Malvolti's circumstances were still more hopeless; notorious for every species of vice and crime, and hateful even to the very bravoes and dregs of the Italian populace, he had now lost all hope of alliance or even assistance from his friend the Cavaliere, who discarded him the moment that he was of no further use. Maddened by this treatment and by despair, no way seemed open to him except that of desperate revenge. Towards Inglesant his hatred was peculiarly intense, being mixed with a certain kind of superstitious dread. He regarded him almost as the shade of his murdered brother, returned from the grave to dog his steps. It was his presence which had thwarted his last desperate attempt within the Conclave, his last hope of earning protection and rewards. He expected nothing but punishment and severe retribution at Inglesant's hands. Surrounded as he was by perils and enemies on every side, this peril and this dreaded enemy stood most prominently in his path; a blow struck here would be not only a measure of self-defence, but a sweet gratification of revenge, and a relief from an appalling supernatural terror. This terrible semblance of his murdered victim once out of his path, he might hope that the vision of a bloody hearthstone in England might not be so constantly before his eyes.

To Inglesant himself the bright prospects which seemed opening before him gave little satisfaction. He was exhausted in body by his long detention within the Conclave, and the tone of his spirit was impaired by the intrigue and hypocrisy of which he had been a witness and a partaker. It is impossible to kneel morning after morning before the Sacrament, in a spirit of worldliness and chicane, without being soiled and polluted in the secret places of the soul. The circumstances of his visit to Umbria and to Florence, howbeit in both he had been preserved almost by a miracle from actual sin, had left an evil mark upon his conscience. He felt little of the sweet calm and peace he had enjoyed for a season in the company of Molinos, during his first visit to Rome. Something of his old misery returned upon him, and he felt himself again the sport of the fiend, who was working out his destruction by some terrible crime, of which he was the agent, and the Italian murderer the cause.

"This man is at large in Rome," said Don Agostino to him one day; "I should advise you to have him assassinated. It is time the earth was rid of such a villain, and the Roman law is useless in such a case. All protection is withdrawn from him, and every man, high and low, within the city will rejoice at his death."

Inglesant shook his head.

"I do not value my life, God knows, at a straw's worth," he said. "Because he murdered my brother foully and treacherously, he and I shall too surely meet some day; but the time is not yet come. Surely if the devil can afford to wait, much more can I."

He spoke more to himself than to the other, and there is reason to suppose that Don Agostino made arrangements to have Malvolti assassinated on his own responsibility; but the Italian avoided his bravoes for a time.

Some short time after the Pope's election, in the height of the Carnival,[1] a masked ball was given in the Palace Doria, at which Don Agostino had arranged a set composed entirely of his own friends. It was composed in imitation of the old

---

[1] It is generally stated by historians that the election of Cardinal Chigi took place on April 7th, 1655, and as Easter that year fell on April 15th, there appears some discrepancy in this part of the narrative. The reader must decide between these contending authorities.

comedies of the Atellanæ, upon which the Punchinello and Harlequinade of all nations has been formed, and which being domestic dramas performed in masques by the Roman youth with an old-fashioned elegance and simplicity, were peculiarly fitted for performance at a modern masquerade. A primitive and rude form of pantomime, founded on caricature and burlesque, with a few characters boldly drawn, has none of the charm of the later comedy, which is a picture of real life with its variety of character and incident, and possesses that excellent art of showing men as they are, while representing them as they seem to be. But, though it fell short of this higher perfection, the broad farce and few characters of the older form of comedy are not wanting in much lively and yet serious painting of human life, which is all the more serious and pathetic from its broad and unconscious farce. The jester, the knave, the old man, the girl, the lover,—these types that are eternal and yet never old,—with the endless complication in which, both on the stage and real life, they are perpetually involved, are susceptible of infinite application and interest to the imagination. As the rehearsal progressed, Inglesant was struck and interested with these ideas, and as the night came on there seemed to him to be in the world nothing but play within play, scene within scene. Between the most incidental acts of an excited and boisterous crowd and the most solemn realities of life and death it seemed to him impossible to distinguish otherwise than in degree; all appeared part of that strange interlude which, between the Dramas of Eternity, is performed continually upon the stage of life.

The set was a large one, consisting of the ordinary pantomime types, supplemented by duplicates, peasants, priests, sbirri (always a favourite subject of satire and practical jokes), country girls, and others. Don Agostino, whose wit was ready and brilliant, took the part of clown or jester, and Inglesant that of the stage lover, a *rôle* requiring no great effort to sustain. The part of Columbine was sustained by a young girl, a mistress of Don Agostino, of considerable beauty and wit, and as yet unspoiled by the wicked life of Rome. She was dressed as a Contadina, or peasant girl, in holiday costume. Harlequin was played by a young Count, a boy of weak intellect, involved in every species of dissipation, and consigned to ruin by designing foes, of whom some were of his own family.

As the ball progressed the party attracted great notice by the clever interludes and acts they performed between the dances. In these the usual tricks and practical jokes were introduced sparingly, relieved by a higher style of wit, and by allusions to the topics of the day and to the foibles of the society of Rome. The parts were all well sustained, and Don Agostino exerted himself successfully to give brilliancy and life to the whole party. The young Harlequin-Count, who had at first seemed only to excel in lofty capers and somersaults, was the first who showed tokens of fatigue. He became gradually listless and careless, so that he changed his part, and became the butt of the rest, instead of their tormentor.

A dance in sets had just begun, and Inglesant could not help being struck with his disconsolate manner, which showed itself plainly, even through his mask and disguise. It seemed that others noticed it as well, for as Inglesant met the Contadina in one of the combinations of the figure, she said in the pause of the dance,—

"Do you see the Count, Cavaliere? He is on the brink of ruin, body and soul. His cousin, and one or two more who are in the set, are engaged with him in some desperate complication, and are working upon his feeble mind and his terror. Cannot you help him at all?"

When the dance ceased Inglesant went over to the Count, intending to speak to him, but his cousin and others of the set were talking earnestly to him, and Inglesant stepped back. He saw that the longer his treacherous friends spoke to him the more broken down and crushed in spirit did the poor Harlequin-Count become; and it was evident to Inglesant that here a play was being enacted within the play, and that, as often is the case, one of the deep tragedies of life was appearing in the fantastic dress of farce. As he stood dreamily watching what occurred, ·Don Agostino called him off to commence another comic act, and when at the first pause he turned to look for the Count, he could no longer see him. His cousin and the others were present, however, and soon after the set was again formed for another dance.

The stifling air of the crowded rooms, and the fatigue of the part he had to perform, wrought upon Inglesant's brain; the confused figures of the dance dazzled his sight, and the music sounded strange and grotesque. As the partners crossed each other, and he came again to the Contadina in his turn, she grasped his hand in hers, and said, hurriedly,—

"Do you see who is standing in the Count's place?"

Inglesant looked, and certainly, in the place of the dance which should have been occupied by the Count, was a tall figure in the dress of a white friar, over which was carelessly thrown a black domino, which allowed the dark fiery eyes of the wearer to be seen.

"The Count has gone," whispered the girl, trembling all over as she spoke, "no one knows whither; no one knows who this man is who has come in his place. He is gone to drown himself in the river; this is the devil who supports his part."

In spite of the girl's visible agitation and his own excitement, Inglesant laughed, and, taking her words as a jest, turned again to look at the strange masque, intending to make some ludicrous comment to reassure his friend. To his astonishment the words died upon his lips, and an icy chill seemed to strike through his blood and cause his heart to beat violently. A sensation of dread overpowered him, the dance-music sounded wild and despairing in his ears, and the ever-varying throng of figures, waving with a thousand colours, swam before his eyes. In the appearance of the stranger, which was simply that of a tall man, there was nothing to account for this; and except that he kept his piercing eyes steadily fixed upon Inglesant, there was nothing in his manner to attract attention. Inglesant went through the rest of the dance mechanically, and suddenly, as it seemed to him, the music stopped.

The dance being over, most of Don Agostino's party, tired with their exertions, withdrew to the buffet of an adjoining apartment for refreshment. Inglesant had taken off his masque, and standing by the buffet, a little apart from the rest, was fanning himself with it, and cooling his parched throat with iced wine, when he was aware that the strange figure had followed him. It was standing before him with a glass in its hand, which it seemed to fill from a bottle of peculiar shape, which Inglesant recognized as one only used to contain a rare Italian wine.

"Cavaliere," the strange masque said in a soft and polite voice, "this wine will do you more good than that which you are drinking; it cools and rests the brain. Will you drink with me?"

As he spoke he offered Inglesant the glass he held, and filled another, and at the same instant the Contadina came up to Inglesant and hung upon his arm.

Inglesant, who was unmasked, stood with the glass in his hand, waiting for the other to remove his domino before he bowed and drank; but the stranger did not do so.

After a moment's pause, amid the breathless silence of the whole group, who were looking on, the stranger said, speaking with a courteous speech and gesture, which if acted were perfectly well assumed,—

"Pardon me that I do not remove my masque; it is my misfortune that I am not able to do so."

Impressed by the other's manner, it struck Inglesant in a moment that this must be some great noble, perhaps a Prince of the Church, for whom it would be injudicious to appear unmasked, and bowing courteously, he raised the glass to his lips.

As he did so the black eyes of the disguised friar were fixed steadily upon him, and the Contadina said in his ear, in an eager, frightened whisper,—

"Do not drink."

The tremor of her voice, and of her figure on his arm, brought back in a moment the terror and distrust which the bearing and manner of the other had dispelled, and raising the cup, he let his lip rest for a moment in the liquor, but did not drink. Then replacing the glass upon the buffet he said coolly,—

"It is a good wine, but my English habit has spoiled my taste. I do not like the Italian Volcanic wines."

"I regret it," said the other, turning away; "they are a quietus for the fever of life."

The party breathed more freely as he left the room, and the Contadina, taking the glass which Inglesant had put down, emptied its contents upon the floor.

They followed the domino into the ball-room, where they saw him speaking to the Count's cousin, and to two or three others of the group, who had remained there or sought refreshment elsewhere.

As the last dance began, in the early daybreak which made the lamps burn faintly, and cast a pale and melancholy light over the gay dresses and the moving figures, over the gilding and marble, and the dim lovely paintings on the walls, Inglesant was conscious of a strange and death-like feeling that benumbed his frame. He was bitterly cold, and his sight became dim and uncertain. The music seemed to grow wilder and more fantastic, and the crowded dancers, grotesque and goblin-like to any eyes, became unreal as a dream to his.

Suddenly, as before, the music ceased, and not knowing what he did, Inglesant became separated from his friends, and was borne by the throng to the doors and down the staircase into the courtyard and the street.

The Piazza and the Corso beyond were crowded with carriages, and with servants carrying dim torches, and the morning air was rent with confused noise.

Nearly unconscious, Inglesant allowed himself to be carried onward by the crowd of persons leaving the palace on foot—a motley throng in every variety of costume, and he was soon borne out of the square into the Corso and down the street.

Suddenly he heard a voice behind, clear and distinct, to his ears at least, amid the confused noise,—

"There he is—now strike!"

Turning round quickly, he saw the masque within two yards of him, with something in the folds of his gown which shone in the light. In another moment he would have been close to him, when they were swept apart by a sudden movement of the crowd, and Don Agostino's carriage, surrounded by servants, passed close by the spot to which Inglesant had drifted. He was recognized, and Agostino welcomed him eagerly, saying,—

"I have been looking for you everywhere."

They proceeded along the Corso, Inglesant still like a man in a dream, and turned down towards the bridge of St. Angelo. At the corner of a street leading to the river, another pause occurred. The carriage of a great French noble and Prince of the Church—which had followed the Corso farther on—was passing when they turned into the street, and according to the formal étiquette of the day, even at that hour and in the crowded street, Don Agostino's coachman stopped his horses before the carriage of his master's superior, and the servants opened the door that one of the gentlemen at least might alight. At the same moment, there seemed to be some confusion in the crowd at the top of the short street leading to the river; and Inglesant, still hardly knowing what he did, alighted, with the double purpose of seeing what was the matter, and of saluting his patron. As he did so, one of the servants said to him,—

"They are bringing up a dead body, sir."

It was true. A body had just been drawn out of the river, and, placed on nets and benches of a boat, was being carried on the shoulders of fishermen up the street. As it passed, Inglesant could see the face, which hung drooping towards him over the edge of the nets. It was the face of the Harlequin-Count.

It had scarcely passed, when Inglesant heard—as a man hears over and over again repeated in a ghastly dream—the same voice that spoke before, saying,—

"There he is again. If you let him get back to the coach you will lose him. Go round by the horses' heads."

The restlessness of the impatient horses had made a little space clear of the crowd, and the same had happened in front of the horses of the Cardinal-Duke, so that the street between them was comparatively clear. Strangely frightened and distressed, Inglesant struggled back to Agostino's carriage, and had just reached the door when the masque, passing round the horses' heads, sprang upon him, and struck a violent blow with the shining steel. The state of his victim's brain saved him. The moment he reached the door he reeled against it, and the weapon glanced off his person, the hilt striking him a violent blow on the chest. He fell backwards into the coach, and Agostino caught a second blow in his sleeve. The startled servants threw themselves upon the murderer, but he slipped through their hands and escaped.

*   *   *   *   *

Two days after the ball, when the morning of Ash Wednesday broke with the lovely Italian dawn, a strange and sudden transformation had passed over Rome. Instead of a people wild with pleasure, laughing, screaming, joking like children, feasting, dancing, running about, from mere lightness of heart; in the place of fairs, theatres, and booths in the open streets, instead of the public gardens and walks crowded with particoloured masquers, full of sportive pranks, and decked out with every vagary and grotesque freak of costume, you saw a city quiet and silent as the grave, yet full of human forms; you heard nothing but the tolling of bells and the faint echo of solemn chants. The houses and churches were hung with black; the gay tapestries and silks, the theatres, the play-actors, and the gay dresses, had all vanished, and in their place the streets were full of cowled and silent penitents. They walked with downcast and pallid faces; if you spoke to them they did not answer, but gazed upon you with wondering eyes. Men and women alike wore the black gown and hood of penance, and from the proudest noble to the poorest peasant, thronged into the Churches and received alike the emblem of their common fate—the ashes and dust from whence they came, and to which they would return.

Before the masked ball, exhausted in health by the long confinement in the Conclave, and tormented in mind by disappointed desire and by accusing conscience, Inglesant had been sinking into almost as great misery as that which he had endured before he came to Rome. The perils and terror that had entered unbidden among the guests during that night of revelry had worked a marvellous change upon him, and he awoke from a species of trance, which had lasted two days, with his spirits cleared and strengthened. He was, in fact, like a man whom a violent fever has just left, languid in body, but with a mind at rest and in peace, with the wild dreams and visions of delirium gone. The earth seems, at least to him, calm and peaceful, full of voices of prayer and strains of penitential song. He looks out upon life languidly, it is true, but with a friendly, pleased countenance, as upon a well-known landscape recalling happy days. So it was with Inglesant, that, the wild riot of the Carnival being over, the peace of Lent began within his soul. The blow that had been struck at his life restored him to life, and took away the superstitious dread that was gradually consuming his reason. He had met his brother's murderer, not alone in some solitary place and picked time, planned before with diabolic purpose by the enemy of mankind, but in a crowd, and as it seemed by chance. He had himself been passive, and urged by no demoniac prompting to some terrible act of vengeance; still more, his enemy had failed, miraculously, as it seemed to him. Surely, then, his fears had been in vain; he was not delivered over to Satan, nay, probably the Lord Himself still regarded him with compassion, still watched over and defended his life. Some work was doubtless reserved for him to do; for him, living always on the verge of delirium, whom a little extra pressure upon the brain-nerve might at any moment estrange altogether from reason, and deprive of intellect and of intercourse with men. For such as he, nevertheless, under such protection, what might not yet be possible? The dews of the Divine Grace cool the fevered brain more surely than any cordial, and soften and water the parched and thirsty heart. The pleasant Italian March day was soft and balmy as the loveliest day of June in England. The scent of jasmin and Daphne flowers filled the air; soft showers fell at intervals over the garden slopes of that part of Rome; the breath of Zephyr swept sweetness into the weary sense. Let him join the hooded throng of penitents; let him, dust and ashes, snatched it may be "*e flamma*" from the very flames, yet still by the grace of God in his right mind, take his ashes with a grateful heart.

For the appearance, amid the chaos of his life, of a guiding Divine Hand, delightful as it is to any man, must be unspeakably so to him who, to the difficulties, sufficiently great, which ordinarily beset a man in his path through life, adds this overwhelming one—the imminent chance at any moment of losing consciousness altogether, with the power of thought and choice of seeing objects rightly, and of self-control and self-command. How eagerly one to whom life is complicated in such sort as this must welcome a Divine guidance may easily be seen—one who otherwise is wandering among a phantasmagoria of objects, among which he must, so far as his wavering consciousness allows him, and for the moment that consciousness may remain his own, shape his course so as to avoid ruin.

In the fresh morning air, full of delicious warmth and sweetness, and with this angelic messenger leading his soul, Inglesant went out. He had no sufficient motive to take him to any particular Church; but chance or some nobler power directed that he should turn his steps to the right in passing into the Via di S. Giovanni, and following the crowd of penitents, should arrive at the portico of the Church of the Lateran.

The space in front of the magnificent façade was crowded with draped forms, and the wail of the rare organ music reached the outer perfumed air. The marble pavement of the interior, precious beyond calculation, was thronged with the dark crowd, and the costly marble of the walls and tombs was streaked and veiled by the wreaths of incense which lingered in the building. The low chanting and the monotonous accompaniment of the organs filled the Church, and high over the altar, brilliant with a thousand lights, flashed the countless gems of the wonderful tabernacle, and the Cœna of plate of inestimable cost. On either side the gilded brass of the four columns of the Emperor Titus, brought from Jerusalem itself, reflected back the altar lights; and beset with precious stones where the body of the Lord once had hung, was evident to all beholders the very wood of the Holy Cross.

As Inglesant entered, the ashes had been sprinkled three times with holy water, and the clouds of incense gradually rose over the kneeling crowd, as the people began to receive the ashes upon their foreheads, thronging up in silence and order. At the same time the choir began to sing the Antiphons, accompanied by the heavenly music of the matchless organs, and penetrating by their distinct articulation the remotest corners of the Church.

"Immutemur habitu," they began, "let us change our garments; in ashes and sackcloth let us fast and lament before the Lord. Because," and the pealing anthem rose in ecstatic triumph to the emblazoned roof, "plenteous in mercy to forgive our sins is this God of ours."

"Ah! yes," thought Inglesant, "let us change our garments; these dark robes that seem ashes and sackcloth, may they not be the chosen garment of the marriage supper of the King? Clothed and in one's right mind, by the heavenly mercy we already walk the celestial pavement, and hear the pealing anthems of the angelic choir."

"Emendemus in melius," the anthem went on, "let us amend for the better in that in which we have ignorantly sinned—ne subito præoccupati die mortis, quæramus spatium pœnitentiæ, et invenire non possimus."

The mighty voice, as of God Himself, seemed to single out and speak to Inglesant alone, "Lest suddenly overtaken by the day of death." Ah! who so well as he knew what that meant, who so lately as he had stood face to face with the destroyer?

He covered his face with his hands.

As the chanting of the Antiphon continued, he reached the steps of the high altar, and in his turn knelt to receive the ashes upon his brow.

In a pause of the anthem the chanting ceased, and the organs played a slow movement in the interval. Nothing was heard but the monotonous undertone of the priests.

As Inglesant knelt upon the marble an overpowering sense

of helplessness filled his soul, so worthless and fragile he seemed to himself before the Eternal Existence, that the idea of punishment and penitence was lost in the sense of utter nothingness.

"Ah! Lord God," he thought, "shattered in mind and brain I throw myself on Thee; without Thee I am lost in the vortex of the Universe; my intellect is lost except it steadies itself upon the idea of Thee. Without Thee it has no existence. How canst Thou be angry with that which is not?"

He bowed his head in utter prostration of spirit to receive the ashes.

"Memento, homo," the priest began—ah! surely it must be easy to remember that, "quia pulvis es——"

Inglesant heard no more. A sudden thrill of earth, like the familiar scent of flowers to a dying man, passed through him, and he lifted up his eyes. Opposite to him across the corner of the altar steps knelt Lauretta, her lustrous eyes full of tears fixed upon him with an inexpressible tenderness and interest. His eyes met hers for an instant, then he dropped his head again before the priest; but the thought and presence of heaven was gone from him, and nothing but the roses and loves of earth remained.

He rose from his knees. The throng of penitents surrounded him, and he suffered himself to be swept onward, down the long nave, till he reached the door through which the crowd was pouring out. There, however, he stopped.

CHAPTER XXXII.

THE old Duke of Umbria was dying. He lay clothed, as he had once said to Inglesant, in the "Angelica Vestis," the sacred wafer in his mouth. Below in the Palace Chapel, in the great Duomo, in Rome itself, masses were being said day by day, and the ineffable Host raised to Heaven, in intercessory prayer for this man's soul. If any deserved an unruffled passage over the dark river, he did. He had sought long and earnestly to find a more excellent way, and had shrunk from no effort nor painful mortification if he might at last walk in it when found. He had resigned himself and all that he possessed in implicit obedience to the doctrine and the See of Rome. He had crowned a blameless and beneficent life by acts of unparalleled devotion and piety; nevertheless, an unruffled passage he did not have. The future was dark and full of dread, and he suffered all the terrors of the grave with a troubled mind. Lying thus in dull misery of body, and in mental apprehension and unrest, he bethought himself of Inglesant. Having surrendered himself, soul and body, into the hands of those who stood about his bed, he knew that it was useless to let his mind wander after any of those unauthorized teachers from whom in past days he had sought instruction; but in Inglesant he had, for the first time, met a man who, walking to all appearance in the straitest paths of the Catholic Church, seemed to possess a freedom of spirit greater than the Sectaries themselves could boast. Even when suffering the rebukes of an accusing conscience, and the bewilderment of a disordered brain, there was in Inglesant an unfettered possession of the things of this life, and even of the life to come, which had astonished the old man, who, unaccused by his own conscience, was yet so confined and hampered in this world, and in such continual dread of that other which was shortly to be revealed to him.

He expressed to his director a wish that Inglesant might be sent for. It was impossible to deny him this request, even had it been thought desirable. Inglesant was a trusted confidant of the dominant Society of Rome, a favourite of the new Pope, and had, besides, been influential, as was believed, in obtaining that crowning triumph—the cession of the Duchy to the Papal See. A messenger was therefore despatched to Rome requesting his immediate presence. The summons found him with Lauretta and her father, engaged in preparations for his speedy marriage.

This connection was regarded with great favour by Don Agostino and most of his friends; but was looked upon, as far as they condescended to notice it at all, with suspicion by the heads of the Jesuit Society.

They were beginning to dread the influence of Molinos, and Inglesant had already incurred some suspicion by his intimacy with the Spaniard. The Pope was supposed to be not altogether opposed to the new doctrine, and the Jesuits were unwilling to lose an obedient servant, who might be useful to them. There was, however, no sufficient reason in this why he should be forbidden to visit the old Duke, who was certainly dying, and therefore beyond the reach of dangerous influence; and Inglesant, remembering the interest he had felt in the Duke, and the favours which he had lavished upon him, hastened to set out.

When he arrived in Umbria he found the Duke had rallied a little, and he received him with the warmest expressions of delight. He was never content save when he was in the room, and his very presence seemed to restore strength and life to the exhausted old man. Those who watched about his bed in the interests of Rome, if they had felt any apprehensions of the result of Inglesant's visit, were speedily reassured, for the Duke did not seem desirous of conversing upon religious matters with him, and, indeed, rather avoided them. He seemed to cling to Inglesant as to the only remaining link to that world which he was so soon to leave, and to take a strange pleasure in furnishing him with those appliances of earthly enjoyment which had until now long ceased to be of interest to himself. Among other gifts he insisted on his accepting a suit of superb armour which had been made expressly for his idolized son. In this suit, in which he caused Inglesant to be arrayed, he declared that he well represented the patron saint of his nation, St. George of England, and pleased himself with the reflection that the fief with which he had endowed Inglesant bore the name of the same saint.

"You are il Cavaliere di San Giorgio," he said to his favourite, as he stood by his couch, sheathed in the superb but useless and fantastic armour of the seventeenth century, with cuirass, greaves, and cuisses of polished and jewelled metal, worn over the ordinary dress, and combined with the lace and velvet which ornamented the whole. It is true that the steel plates were covered with silver and gold chasing of arabesques not of the most Christian type, and the perfect sword-blade was engraved with hieroglyphics not of the most saintly kind; nevertheless Inglesant, as he stood, did certainly resemble somewhat closely a splendid renaissance St. George.

"You are il Cavaliere di San Giorgio," said the Duke, "and you must wear that armour when you go to meet your bride. I have arranged a train worthy of so illustrious a bridegroom."

Inglesant's marriage had taken a great hold in the imagination of the dying man, and his mind, to the surprise of those who had known him longest, seemed to dwell entirely upon nuptials and festivals. The strain and terror which his spirit had suffered for so long had probably done their work, and, like as on a harpsichord with a snapped string, the set purpose and composure was lost, and nothing but fragments of fantasias could be played. That magic influence of the wonderful ducal palace which Inglesant had been conscious of at his first visit, and of which the Duke had seemed hitherto altogether regardless, at the last moments of his life appeared to assert its power and force; and what to others seemed mere dotage appeared to Inglesant like a wintry gleam of mysterious light that might be the earnest of a happier time,—a return from the dark regions of superstitious fear to the simple delights of common human life. The sway of this strange house was as powerful over Inglesant himself as it had been before; but he now stood upon higher ground than he had done formerly. The events which had occurred in the meantime had not been entirely without effect. His triumph over the temptation of the flesh in the forest pavilion had secured to him a higher place in the spiritual walk, and the escape from the assassin's dagger had sobered his spirit and indescribably touched his heart. The "Kings' Courts," of which this house was but a type,— the Italian world in which he had lived so long,—had, therefore, now less power than ever to crush Inglesant's religious instinct; but it gave it a certain colour, a sort of renaissance Christianity, which bore a likeness to the character of the art-world in which it had grown up,—a Christianity of florid ornament and of somewhat fantastic issues.

As the Duke gradually became weaker, and seemed every day to be on the point of death, he became the more anxious that Inglesant's marriage should be completed, and at last insisted upon his delaying his return to Rome no longer. Inglesant, who expected almost hour by hour the Duke's decease, would have been content to wait; but the dying man would take no denial. He pleased himself with giving orders for Inglesant's train, and ordered his favourite page, an Austrian boy, to accompany him, and to return immediately when the marriage was celebrated, that he might receive the fullest description of the particulars of the event.

It was long before sunrise that Inglesant set out, accompanied by his train, hoping to cross the mountains before the heat began. His company consisted of several men-at-arms, with their grooms and horse boys, and the Austrian page. They ascended the mountains in the earlier part of the night, and towards dawn they reached a flat plain. The night had been too dark to allow them to see the steep and narrow defiles, full of oaks and beech; and as they passed over the dreary plain in the white mist, their figures seemed vast and indistinct in the dim light, but now, as the streaks of the dawn grew brighter in the east behind them, they could see the fir trees clothing the distant slopes, and here and there one of the higher summits still covered with white snow. The scene was cold and dead and dreary as the grave. A heavy mist hung over the mountain plain, and an icy lake lay black and cold beneath the morning sky. As they reached the crest of the hill the mist rose, stirred by a little breeze at sunrise, and the gorges of the descent lay clear before them. The sun arose behind them, gilding the mountain tops, and tracing streaks and shades of colour on the rising mist sparkling with glittering dew-drops; while dark and solemn beneath them lay the pine-clothed ravines and sloping valleys, with here and there a rocky peak; and farther down still the woods and hills gave place at last to the plain of the Tiber, at present dark and indistinguishable in the night.

As the sun arose behind them one by one the pine ravines became lighted, and the snowy summits, soft and pink with radiant light, stood out against the sky, which became every instant of a deeper blue. The sunlight, stealing down the defiles and calling forth into distinct shape and vision tree and rock and flashing stream, spread itself over the oak woods in the valleys, and shone at last upon the plain, embossed and radiant with wood and green meadow, and marble towers and glistering water—the waters of the Tiber running onwards towards Rome. Mysterious forms and waves of light, the creatures of the morning and of the mist, floated before the sight, and from the dark fir trees murmurs and mutterings of ethereal life fell upon the ear. Sudden and passionate flushes of colour tinted the pine woods and were gone, and beneath the branches and across the paths fairy lights played for a moment and passed away.

The party halted more than once, but it was necessary to make the long descent before the heat began, and they commenced carefully to pick their way down the stony mountain

road, which wound down the ravines in wild unequal paths
The track, now precipitous, now almost level, took them round
corners and masses of rock sometimes hanging above their heads,
revealing continually new reaches of valley and new defiles
clothed with fir and oak. Mountain flowers and trailing ivy
and creeping plants hung in festoons on every side, lizards ran
across the path, birds fluttered above them or darted into the
dark recesses where the mountain brooks were heard; everything sang the morning psalm of life, with which, from field
and mountain solitudes, the free children of nature salute the
day.

The Austrian boy felt the beauty of the scene, and broke
out into singing.

"When the northern gods," he said to Inglesant, "rode on
their chevisance they went down into the deep valleys singing
magic songs. Let us into this dark valley, singing magic songs,
also go down; who knows what strange and hidden deity, since
the old pagan times lost and forgotten, we may find among the
dark fir dingles and the laurel shades?"

And he began to sing some love ditty.

Inglesant did not hear him. The beauty of the scene,
ethereal and unreal in its loveliness, following upon the long
dark mountain ride, his sleepless nights and strange familiarity
with approaching death by the couch of the old Duke, confused
his senses, and a presentiment of impending fate filled his mind.
The recollection of his brother rose again in his remembrance,
distinct and present as in life; and more than once he fancied
that he heard his voice, as the cry of some mountain beast, or sound
of moaning trees, came up the pass. No other foreshadowing
than this very imperfect one warned him of the approaching
crisis of his life.

The sun was fully up, and the light already brilliant and
intense, when they approached a projecting point where the
slope of wood ended in a tower of rock jutting upon the road.
The path by which they approached it was narrow and ragged,
but beyond the rock the ground spread itself out, and the path
was carried inward towards the right, having the sloping hillside
on the one hand, covered with scattered oaks, while, on the
other, a slip of ground separated it from the ravine. At the
turning of the road, where the opening valley lay before them..
as they reached the corner, face to face with Inglesant as he

checked his horse, was the Italian, the inquisitive stranger of the theatre at Florence, the intruder into the Conclave, the masque of the Carnival ball, the assassin of the Corso—that Malvolti who had treacherously murdered his brother and sought his own life. Alone and weary, his clothes worn and threadbare, he came toiling up the pass. Inglesant reined in his horse suddenly, a strange and fierce light in his eyes and face. The Italian started back like some wild creature of the forest brought suddenly to bay, a terrified cry broke from him, and he looked wildly round as if intending flight. The nature of the ground caught him as in a trap; on the one hand the sloping hillside steep and open, on the other tangled rugged ground, slightly rising between the road and the precipice, cut off all hope of sudden flight. He looked wildly round for a moment, then, when the horsemen came round the rocky wall and halted behind their leader, his eyes came back to Inglesant's face, and he marked the smile upon his lips and in his eyes, and saw his hand steal downwards to the hunting piece he carried at the saddle; then with a terrible cry, he threw himself on his knees before the horse's head, and begged for pity,—pity and life.

Inglesant took his hand from his weapon, and turning slightly to the page and to the others behind him, he said,—

"This man, messeri, is a murderer and a villain, steeped in every crime; a cruel secret midnight cut-throat and assassin; a lurker in secret corners to murder the innocent. He took my brother, a noble gentleman whom I was proud to follow, treacherously at an advantage, and slew him. I see him now before me lying in his blood. He tried to take my life,—I, who scarcely even knew him,—in the streets of Rome. Now he begs for mercy, what say you, gentlemen? what is his due?"

"Shoot the dog through the head. Hang him on the nearest tree. Carry him into Rome and torture him to death."

The Italian still continued on his knees, his hands clasped before him, his face working with terror and agony that could not be disguised.

"Mercy, monsignore," he cried. "Mercy. I cannot, I dare not, I am not fit to die. For the blessed Host, monsignore, have mercy—for the love of Jesu—for the sake of Jesu."

As he said these last words Inglesant's attitude altered, and the cruel light faded out of his eyes. His hand ceased to finger the carabine at his saddle, and he sat still upon his horse, looking down upon the abject wretch before him, while a man might count fifty. The Italian saw, or thought he saw, that his judge was inclining to mercy, and he renewed his appeals for pity.

"For the love of the crucifix, monsignore; for the blessed Virgin's sake."

But Inglesant did not seem to hear him. He turned to the horsemen behind him, and said,—

"Take him up, one of you, on the crupper. Search him first for arms. Another keep his eye on him, and if he moves or attempts to escape, shoot him dead. You had better come quietly;" he continued, "it is your only chance for life."

Two of the men-at-arms dismounted and searched the prisoner, but found no arms upon him. He seemed indeed to be in the greatest distress from hunger and want, and his clothes were ragged and thin. He was mounted behind one of the soldiers and closely watched, but he made no attempt to escape, and indeed appeared to have no strength or energy for such an effort.

They went on down the pass for about an Italian league. The country became more thickly wooded, and here and there on the hillsides patches of corn appeared, and once or twice in a sheltered spot a few vines. At length, on the broad shoulder of the hill round which the path wound, they saw before them a few cottages, and above them, on the hillside, in a position that commanded the distant pass till it opened on the plain, was a Chapel, the bell of which had just ceased ringing for mass.

Inglesant turned his horse's head up the narrow stony path, and when the gate was reached, he dismounted and entered the Chapel, followed by his train. The Cappella had apparently been built of the remains of some temple or old Roman house, for many of the stones of the front were carved in bold relief. It was a small narrow building, and possessed no furniture save the altar and a rude pulpit built of stones; but behind the altar, painted on the plaster of the wall, was the rood or crucifix, the size of life. Who the artist had been cannot now be told; it might have been the pupil of some great master, who had caught something of the master's skill, or, perhaps, in the old time, some artist had come up the pass from Borgo san Sepolcro, and had painted it for the love of his art and of the Blessed

Virgin; but, whoever had done it, it was well done, and it gave a sanctity to the little Chapel, and possessed an influence of which the villagers were not unconscious, and of which they were even proud.

The mass had commenced some short time as the train entered, and such few women and peasants as were present turned in surprise.

Inglesant knelt upon the steps before the altar, and the men-at-arms upon the floor of the Chapel, the two who guarded the prisoner keeping close behind their leader.

The priest, who was an old and simple-looking countryman, continued his office without stopping; but when he had received the sacred elements himself, he turned, and, influenced probably by his appearance and by his position at the altar, he offered Inglesant the Sacrament. He took it, and the priest, turning again to the altar, finished the mass.

Then Inglesant rose, and when the priest turned again he was standing before the altar with his drawn sword held lengthwise across his hands.

"My Father," he said, "I am the Cavaliere di San Giorgio, and as I came across the mountains this morning on my way to Rome, I met my mortal foe, the murderer of my brother, a wretch whose life is forfeit by every law, either of earth or heaven, a guilty monster steeped in every crime. Him, as soon as I had met him,—sent by this lonely and untrodden way as it seems to me by the Lord's hand,—I thought to crush at once, as I would a venomous beast, though he is worse than any beast. But, my Father, he has appealed from me to the adorable Name of Jesus, and I cannot touch him. But he will not escape. I give him over to the Lord. I give up my sword into the Lord's hands, that He may work my vengeance upon him as it seems to Him good. Henceforth he is safe from earthly retribution, but the Divine Powers are just. Take this sword, reverend Father, and let it lie upon the altar beneath the Christ Himself; and I will make an offering for daily masses for my brother's soul."

The priest took the sword, and kneeling before the altar, placed it thereon like a man acting in a dream.

He was one of those child-like peasant-priests to whom the great world was unknown, and to whom his mountain solitudes were peopled as much by the saints and angels of his breviary as by the peasants who shared with him the solitudes and the legends that gave to these mountain fastnesses a mysterious awe. To such a man as this it seemed nothing strange that the blessed St. George himself, in jewelled armour, should stand before the altar in the mystic morning light, his shining sword in his hand.

He turned again to Inglesant, who had knelt down once more.

"It is well done, monsignore," he said, "as all that thou doest doubtless is most well. The sword shall remain here as thou sayest, and the Lord doubtless will work His blessed will. But I entreat, monsignore, thy intercession for me, a poor sinful man; and when thou returnest to thy place, and seest again the Lord Jesus, that thou wilt remind Him of His unworthy priest. Amen."

Inglesant scarcely heard what he said, and certainly did not understand it. His sense was confused by what had happened, and by the sudden overmastering impulse upon which he had acted. He moved as in a dream; nothing seemed to come strange to him, nothing startled him, and he took slight heed of what passed. He placed his embroidered purse, heavy with gold, in the priest's hand, and in his excitement totally forgot to name his brother, for whose repose masses were to be said.

He signed to his men to release the prisoner, and, his trumpets sounding to horse before the Chapel gate, he mounted and rode on down the pass.

But his visit was not forgotten, and long afterwards, perhaps even to the present day, popular tradition took the story up, and related that once, when the priest of the mountain Chapel was a very holy man, the blessed St. George himself, in shining armour, came across the mountains one morning very early, and himself partook of the Sacrament and all his train; and appealed triumphantly to the magic sword—set with gold and precious stones—that lay upon the altar from that morning, by virtue of which no harm can befall the village, no storm strike it, and, above all, no pillage of armed men or any violence can occur.

The Austrian boy returned to Umbria with his story of the marriage; but the old Duke never heard it. No sooner had Inglesant left him than his depression and despair returned; he loathed the sight of the day, and of the costly palace in which he lived; the gay arts and the devised fancies by which men have sought to lure happiness became intolerable to him; and, ill as he was, he caused himself to be removed to the Castel Durante, amid the lonely mountain ravines, to abide his end. As Inglesant bowed beneath the care-cloth—the fine linen cloth laid over the newly-married in the Church,—kneeling till mass was ended, with his heart full of love and brightness and peace, the last of the house of Revere—"worn out," says the chronicler, with a burst of unusual candour, "by priestly torments"—breathed his last, and went to another world, where, it may be hoped, sacrifice and devotion are better rewarded than they are here, and superstitious terrors are unknown.

CHAPTER XXXIII.

THE Castello di San Giorgio, or, as it might more properly have been called, the "Casa" or Villa di San Giorgio, was built upon the summit of a small conical hill, amid the sloping bases of the Apennines, at a part of their long range where the summits were low and green. In that delightful region, the cultivation and richness of the plain is united to the wildness and beauty of the hills. The heat is tempered in the shady valleys and under the thick woods. A delicious moisture and soft haze hangs about these dewy, grassy places, which the sun has power to warm and gladden, but not to parch. Flowers of every hue cover the ground beneath the oaks and elms. Nightingales sing in the thickets of wild rose and clematis, and the groves of laurel and of the long-leaved olives are crowded with small creatures in the full enjoyment of life and warmth. Little brooks and rippling streams, half hidden by the tangled thickets, and turned from their courses by the mossy rocks, flow down from the hill ravines, as joyful and clear as in that old time when each was the care of some protecting nymph or rural god. In the waters of the placid lake are reflected the shadows of the hills, and the tremulous shimmer of waving woods.

In this favoured region, the Villa di San Giorgio stood upon its leafy hill-top, set in the background of the mountains. The steep slope was terraced here and there in patches of ground planted with fruit-trees, and at the foot, towards the south, a large lake slept beneath the blue sky, its shores lined with brushwood, interspersed here and there with grassy slopes, where the orchis and hyacinth and narcissus sprang up from the green rich turf.

Through this pastoral land, at all seasons of the year, wandering shepherds with their flocks, peasants with their cattle and dogs, ladies and cavaliers from the neighbouring villas, woodmen, vine-dressers, fishermen from the lake, traversed the leafy stage, and diversified the scene; but when the grape was fully ripe, and the long year was crowned at last with the fatness of the vintage, a joyous age of rural wealth and jollity seemed for a time to fill the mellow, golden-tinted land. Then, indeed, wandering amid the woods and rocks interspersed with vineyards and patches of yellow wheat, as you met the loaded wain, or came upon the wine-press, trodden by laughing girls and boys, you seemed to understand the stories of the rural wanderings of the gods, for you met with many a scene to which it might well be fancied that they might still be allured, as to that garden at the foot of Mount Bermion where the roses grew. The gracious gods of plenty still filled the luscious vats; rustling Zephyr still whispered love among the flowers, still came laden with the ripening odours of the fruit. The little cherub Loves peeped out from behind oak stems and ruined plinth and sculptured frieze, half hidden among roots and leaves.

The Castello was a modern building, although there were ruins in one of the courtyards of a very antique date. It consisted of three or four lofty blocks of buildings, at right angles to each other, covered with low, red-tiled roofs. The principal windows were in the upper stories, and gave light to large and handsome rooms, from which on all sides the most enchanting landscapes satisfied the eye.

The weeks that succeeded Inglesant's marriage grew into months, and the months into years, in this delightful scene. The old Count spent some months in peaceful satisfaction with his daughter and her husband, delighted with the company of his one grandchild, a little boy. In the spacious dining-saloon, with its cool polished floor, it was a pretty sight to see the old, courteous nobleman tempting the child with the ripest fruit.

The shaded light fell upon the plate and yellow ware on the table, and upon the old cabinets of Italian marqueterie against the walls; whilst by the carved mantelpiece sat the pleased parents, of whom it is recorded that in Rome they passed for the handsomest pair in Italy. In this way, the days of some three sunny summers passed away, while the winters were spent in the Papal city,

But this Arcadian life was not lasting. The old Count was not long content if absent from city life, and the time at the Castello hung somewhat heavily upon the spirits of both Inglesant and his wife. They were neither of them fitted by previous habits and education for a retired country life; but the circumstance which outwardly appeared to weigh upon Lauretta's mind was uncertainty concerning her brother's fate. From the time of the marriage the Cavaliere had disappeared, and from that day no word of tidings had been received respecting him. It was known that his circumstances were desperate, and the danger he lay under from secret enemies imminent. The account which her husband had given her of the condition in which he had seen Malvolti dwelt in her imagination, and she brooded over the idea of her brother in a similar state of destitution and misery. It seemed probable that, had he been assassinated, tidings of the event would have reached his family; and if alive, it was strange that he had made no application for assistance to those who were so well able and so willing to render it. This suspense and mystery were more insupportable than certainty of evil would have been.

The characters of Inglesant and his wife were of such a nature as most effectively to produce and aggravate this sleepless uneasiness. Upon Lauretta's lenient and gracious, if somewhat pleasure-loving disposition, the impression of the unkindness she had experienced from her brother faded without leaving a trace, and she thought only of some pleasant, long-past incidents, when she had been a pretty, engaging child; whilst the life of romance and excitement, combined with a certain spiritual Quixotism, which Inglesant had so long followed, had rendered any other uncongenial to him, and it required little persuasion to induce him to re-enter upon it.

But there were other causes at work which led to the same result. For many weeks a sultry wind had, without variation, passed over the south of Italy, laden with putrid exhalations from the earth, and by its sullen steadiness causing stagnation in the air. It would be difficult to describe the terrible effect upon the mind and system of the long continuance of such a state of the atmosphere. A restless fear and depression of spirits prepared the body for the seeds of disease, and the contagion, which was not perhaps generated in the atmosphere, was carried by it with fearful rapidity. The plague struck down its victims at once in city and in country, and spared no rank nor condition of life. Then all bond of fellowship and of society was loosened, strange crimes and suspicions,—strange even to that land of crime and treachery,—influenced the lives and thoughts of all men. Innocent persons were hunted to death, as poisoners and spreaders of infection; the terrors of the grave broke through the forms of artificial life, and the depravity of the heart was exposed in ghastly nakedness, as the bodies of the dead lay unburied by the waysides.

The Castello di San Giorgio, standing on the summit of a breezy hill, in a thinly-peopled district, was as safe a refuge as could perhaps be found, and, if uneasiness of mind could have been banished, might have been a happy one. Three hundred years before, in the child-like unconsciousness of spiritual conflict which the unquestioned rule of Rome for so long produced, it had been possible, in the days of Boccaccio, for cultivated and refined society to shut itself up in some earthly paradise, and, surrounded by horrors and by death, to spend its days in light wit and anecdote, undisturbed in mind, and kept in bodily health by cheerful enjoyment; but the time for such possibilities as these had long gone by. A mental trouble and uneasiness, which pervaded the whole of human life at the most quiet times, gave place, at such periods of dread and fear, to an intolerable restlessness, which altogether precluded the placid enjoyment of the present, however guarded and apparently secure.

The apprehension which most weighed upon Lauretta's mind, was that her brother, flying from some city where the pestilence raged, might be refused succour and assistance, and might even be murdered, in the village to which he might flee. Such incidents were of daily occurrence, nor can it be wondered at that human precaution and terror became cruel and merciless, when it is an authenticated fact that the very birds themselves forsook the country places, and disappeared from their native groves, at the approach of the plague. Nor were inanimate things, even, indifferent to the scourge; patches and blotches of infection broke out upon the walls and houses, and when scraped off would reappear until the house itself was burnt down.

It was in the midst of this ghastly existence, this life in death, that a wandering mendicant, driven from Rome by the pestilence and craving alms at the Castello, asserted that he knew the Cavaliere di Guardino, and that he was ill in Rome, doubtless by this time dead. The man probably lied, or if it were true that he had known the Cavaliere, as he had passed him on the steps of the Trinità, the latter part of his story was certainly imaginary. It caused Lauretta, however, so much distress, that her husband, to comfort her, proposed to ride to Rome, and endeavour to discover the truth. The plague was not so virulent in Rome as it was in the south of Italy, and especially in Naples, and to a man using proper precautions the danger might not be very great. Lauretta was distracted. The restless anxiety, which gave her no peace until her brother's fate was known, urged her to let her husband go. How, then, should she be more at ease when, in addition to one vision of dread and apprehension, she would be haunted by another? The new anxiety seemed a relief from the old; anyhow the old was intolerable,—any change offered hope.

Upon his arrival at Rome Inglesant went hither and thither, from place to place, as one false report and another led him. Every beggar in the city seemed to have known the Cavaliere. The contagion was sufficiently virulent to stop all amusements, and to drive every one from the city who was not compelled to remain. The streets were almost deserted, and those who passed along them walked apart, avoiding each other, and seldom spoke. The most frequented places were the Churches, and even there the services were short and hurried, and divested of everything that could attract the eye. In the unusual silence the incessant tolling of the bells was more marked than ever. White processions carrying the Host glided over the hushed pavements.

Once Inglesant thought he had discovered the man of whom he was in search. The Cavaliere, the story now ran, had arrived in Rome a few days ago from Naples, where the plague had the mastery, so that the living could not bury the dead. He had come, flying towards the healthy north before the pestilence, which had overtaken him as he entered the Giovanni gate, and had taken refuge in a pest-house, which had been established in the courtyard of a little church, "S. Salvatoris in Laterano ad scalas sanctas." Thither Inglesant repaired, in the full glare of an afternoon in the late summer. In a sort of cloister, round a little courtyard, the beds were laid out side by side, on which lay the dying and the dead. Between the worn stones of the courtyard, sprinkled with water, bright flowers were springing up. The monks were flitting about; two or three of these also were dead already. Inglesant inquired for the stranger who had arrived from Naples. He was dead, the monks told him, but not yet taken away for burial; he lay there still upon his couch. They took Inglesant to a corner of the courtyard, where, looking down upon the dead body, he saw at once it was not that of the Cavaliere. It was the body of a man in the very prime of life, of a singularly noble and lofty look. He lay with his hands clasped over a little bit of crossed wood the monks had made, his eyes closed, something like a smile upon his lips.

"The Cavaliere will not look like that," thought Inglesant to himself.

Who was he? In some part of Italy, doubtless, there were at this moment those who waited for him, and wondered, just as he and Lauretta were doing. Perhaps in some distant lazaretto some one might be standing over the body of the Cavaliere, at just such a loss for a name and clue. It did not seem strange to Inglesant; he had wandered through these cross ways and tangled paths of life from a child.

He went out into the hot sunshine and down the long straight street, by the great church of the Santa Maria, into the Via Felix, scarcely knowing where he went. Across the whole breadth of Rome the few persons he met regarded him with suspicion, and crossed over to the other side. He himself carried a pomander of silver in the shape of an apple, stuffed with spices, which sent out a curious faint perfume through small holes. He wandered down the steps of the Trinità, where even the beggars were few and quiet, and seeking unconsciously the cooler air of the river, passed the desolate Corso, and came down to the Ripetta, to the steps.

The sun was sinking now, and the western sky was all ablaze with a strange light. All through the streets the image of the dead man had haunted Inglesant, and the silent city seemed full of such pale and mystic forms. The great dome of St. Peter's stood out dark and clear against the yellow light, which shone through the casements below the dome till the whole seemed faint and ethereal as the air itself. In the foreground, across the river, were low meadows, and the bare branches of trees the leaves of which had already withered and fallen. In the distance the pollard firs upon the ramparts stood out distinctly in fantastic forms; to the left the pinnacles and vanes of the city shone in the light; in front flowed the dark river, still and slow. The large steps by the water's edge, usually so crowded and heaped with market produce, were bare and deserted; a wild superstitious terror took possession of Inglesant's mind.

In this solitude and loneliness, amid the busiest haunts of life, with the image of death on every hand, he felt as though the unseen world might at any moment manifest itself; the lurid sky seemed ready to part asunder, and amid the silent courts and pavements the dead would scarcely seem strangers were they to appear. He stood waiting, as though expecting a message from beyond the grave.

And indeed it seemed to come. As he stood upon the steps a gray form came along the pathway on the farther side beneath the leafless trees and down the sloping bank. It entered the small boat that lay moored beneath the alders, and guided itself across the stream. It stood erect and motionless, propelling the skiff doubtless by an oar at the stern, but from the place where Inglesant stood the boat seemed to move of its own accord, like the magic bark in some romance of chivalry. In its left hand the figure held something which shone in the light; the yellow glamour of the sunset, dazzling to Inglesant's eyes, fluttered upon its vestment of whitish gray, and clothed in transparent radiance this shadowy revenant from the tomb. It made no stay at the landing-place, but, as though on an errand of life and death, it came straight up the wide curved steps, holding forward in its left hand a crucifix of brass. It passed within a step of Inglesant, who was standing, wonder-struck, at the summit of the steps, his silver pomander in his hand. As it passed him he could see the face, pale and steadfast, with a bright lustre in the eyes, and looking full upon him without pausing, the friar, if it were a friar, said,—

"He is in Naples. In that city, or near it, you will find the man you seek. Ay! and far more than you seek. Let there be no delay on your part."

Then, still holding the crucifix forward at arm's length, as though to cleave the poisoned air before him as he went, the figure passed up the street, turning neither to the right nor to the left, and, taking no notice of any of the few loiterers in his way, passed quickly out of sight.

Inglesant turned to two fishermen who were coming slowly down towards the ferry.

"Did you see that Servite friar?" he said.

The men gazed at him uneasily. "He is light-headed," one of them muttered; "he has the plague upon him, and does not know what he says."

Though he said this, they might have seen the friar all the same, for Inglesant's manner was excited, and those were perilous times in which to speak to strangers in the streets. The two men got into the boat, and passed over hastily to the other side.

Naples! It was walking straight into the jaws of death. The dead were lying in the streets in heaps, sprinkled hastily with lime; and lavish gifts of freedom and of gold could scarcely keep the galley slaves from breaking out of the city, though they knew that poverty and probably destruction awaited them elsewhere. But this strange message from another world, which bore such an impress of a higher knowledge, how could he disobey it? "Far more than he sought." These words haunted him. He made inquiries at the monastery of the Jesuits in the Corso, but could hear nothing of such a man. Most of those to whom he spoke were of opinion that he had seen a vision. He himself sometimes thought it an illusion of the brain, conjured up by the story of the man who came from Naples, by the afternoon heat, and by the sight of the dead; but in all this the divine wisdom might be working; by these strange means the divine hand might guide. "Let there be no delay on your part." These words sounded like a far-off echo of Father St. Clare's voice; once again the old habit of obedience stirred within him. Wife and child and home stood in the path, but the training which first love had been powerless to oppose was not likely to fail now. Once again his station seemed to be given him. Before—upon the scaffold, at the traitor's dock, in prison—he had been found at the appointed post; would it be worth while now, when life was so much farther run out, to falter and turn back? The higher walks of the holy life had indeed proved too difficult and steep, but to this running-footman's sort of business he had before proved himself equal;—should he now be found untrustworthy even in this?

He resolved to go. If he returned at all, he would be back at the Castello before any increased apprehension would be felt; if it were the will of God that he should never return, the Jesuit fathers would undertake the care of Lauretta and his child.

He confessed and received the Sacrament at the Church of the Gesu, in the Chapel of St. Ignatio, in the clear morning light, kneeling upon the cold brilliant marble floor. It was the last day of July, very early, and the Church was swept and garnished for the great festival of the Saint. Inglesant did not wait for the saddened festival, but left Rome immediately that the early mass was done.

CHAPTER XXXIV.

WHEN Inglesant had passed the Pontine Marshes, and had come into the flowery and wooded country about Mola, where the traveller begins to rejoice and to delight his eyes, he found this beautiful land little less oppressive than the dreary marshes he had left. The vineyards covered the slopes, and hung their festoons on every side. The citron and jasmin and orange bloomed around him; and in the cooler and more shady walks flowers yet covered the ground, in spite of the heat. The sober tints of the oaks and beeches contrasted with the brilliant orange groves and vineyards, and, with the palms and aloes, offered that variety which usually charms the traveller; and the distant sea, calm and blue, with the long headlands covered with battlements and gay villas, with plantations and terraces, carried the eye onward into the dim unknown distance, with what is usually a sense of delightful desire.

But as Inglesant rode along, an overpowering sense of oppression and heaviness hung over this beautiful land. The heat was intense; no rain nor dew had fallen for many weeks. The ground in most places was scored and hard, and the leaves were withered. The brooks were nearly dry, and the plantations near the roads were white with dust. An overpowering perfume, sickly and penetrating, filled the air, and seemed to choke the breath; a deadly stillness pervaded the land; and scarcely a human form, either of wayfarer or peasant, was to be seen.

At the small towns near to Naples every form of life was silent and inert. Inglesant was received without difficulty, as he was going towards Naples; but he was regarded with wonder, and remonstrated with as courting certain death. He halted at Aversa, and waited till the mid-day heat was past. Here, at last, there seemed some little activity and life. A sort of market even appeared to be held, and Inglesant asked the host what it meant.

"When the plague first began in Naples, signore," he said, "a market was established here to supply the city with bread, fresh meat, and other provisions. Officers appointed by the city came out hither, and conveyed it back. But, as the plague became more deadly, most of those thus sent out never returned to the city, in spite of the penalties to which such conduct exposed them. Since the plague spread into the country places, the peasants have mostly ceased to bring their produce; but what little is brought you see here, and one of the magistrates is generally obliged to come out from Naples to receive it."

"Is the city suffering from famine then?" asked Inglesant.

"The city is like hell itself, Signore il Cavaliere," replied the host. "They tell me that he who looks upon it will never be able to sleep peacefully again. They lie heaped together in the streets, the dying and the dead. The hospitals are choked with dead bodies, so that none dare go in. They are blowing up masses of houses, so as to bury the bodies under the ruins with lime and water and earth. Twenty thousand persons have died in a single day. Those who have been induced to touch the dead to cart them away never live more than two days."

"The religious, and the physicians, and the magistrates, then, remain at their posts?" said Inglesant.

The host shrugged his shoulders.

"There is not more to be said of one class than another," he said; "there are cowards in all. Many of the physicians fled; but, on the other hand, two strange physicians came forward of their own accord, and offered to be shut up in the Santa Casa Hospital. They never came out alive. Many of the religious fled; but the Capuchins and the Jesuits, they say, are all dead. Most of the Franciscan Friars are dead, and all the great Carmelites. They run to all houses that are most infected, and to those streets that are the most thronged with putrefied bodies, and into those hospitals where the plague is hottest; and confess the sick and attend them to their last gasp; and receive their poisonous breath as though it were the scent of a rose."

"But is no attempt made to bury the dead?"

"They are letting out the galley slaves by a hundred at a time," replied the host; "they offer freedom and a pension for life to the survivors, but none do survive. Fathers and mothers desert their own children; children their parents; nay, they throw them out into the streets to die. What would you have?"

The host paused, and looked at Inglesant curiously, as he sat drinking some wine.

"Have you a lady-love in Naples, signore?" he said at last; "or are you heir to a rich man, and wish to save his gold?"

"I am leaving wife and child," replied Inglesant, bitterly, "to seek a man whom I hate, whom I shall never find under the heaps of dead. You had better say at once that I am mad. That is nearest to the truth."

The host looked at him compassionately, and left the room.

In the cool of the evening Inglesant rode through the deserted vineyards, and approached the barriers. On the way he met some few foot-passengers, pale and emaciated, trudging doggedly onwards. They were leaving death behind them, but they saw nothing but misery and death elsewhere. They took no notice of Inglesant as they passed. Many of them, exhausted and smitten with the disease, sank down and died by the wayside. When he arrived at the barriers, he found them deserted, and no guard whatever kept. He left his horse at a little osteria without the gate, which also seemed deserted. There was hay in the stable, and the animal might shift for himself if so inclined. Inglesant left him loose. As he entered the city, and passed through the Largo into the Strada Toledo, the sight that met his eyes was one never to be forgotten.

The streets were full of people,—more so, indeed, than is usual even in Naples; for business was at a stand, the houses were full of infection, and a terrible restlessness drove every one here and there. The stately rows of houses and palaces, and the lofty churches, looked down on a changing, fleeting, restless crowd,—unoccupied, speaking little, walking hither and thither with no aim, every few minutes turning back and retracing their steps. Every quarter of an hour or thereabouts a confused procession of priests and laymen, singing doleful and despairing misereres, and bearing the sacred Host with canopy and crosses, came from one of the side streets, or out of one of the Churches, and proceeded along the Strada. As these processions passed, every one prostrated themselves, with an excess and desperate earnestness of devotion, and many followed the Host; but in a moment or two those who knelt or those who followed rose or turned away with gestures of despair or distraction, as though incapable of sustained action, or of confidence in any remedy. And at this there could be no wonder, since this crowd of people were picking their way amid a mass of dead corruption on every side of them under their feet. On the stone pavement of the stately Strada, on the palace stairs, on the steps before the Churches, lay corpses in every variety of contortion at which death can arrive. Sick people upon beds and heaps of linen— some delicate and costly, some filthy and decayed—lay mingled with the dead; they had been turned out of the houses, or had deserted them to avoid being left to die alone; and every now and then some one of those who walked apparently in health would lie down, stricken by the heat or by the plague, and join this prostrate throng, for whom there was no longer in this world any hope of revival.

This sight, which would have been terrible anywhere, was unutterably distressing and ghastly in Naples, the city of thoughtless pleasure and of reckless mirth,—a city lying under a blue and cloudless sky, by an azure sea, glowing in the unsurpassable brilliancy and splendour of the sun. As this dazzling blue and gold, before which all colours pale, made the scene the most ghastly that could have been chosen as the theatre for such an appalling spectacle, so, among a people child-like and grotesque, seducing the stranger into sympathy with its delight —a people crowned with flowers, and clothed in colours of every shade, full of high and gay spirits, and possessed of a conscience that gives no pain—this masque and dance of death assumed an aspect of intolerable horror. Naples was given over to pantomime and festival, leading dances and processions with Thyrsis and garlands, and trailing branches of fruit. The old Fabulæ and farce lingered yet beneath the delicious sky and in the lovely spots of earth that lured the Pagan to dream that earth was heaven. The poles and scaffolds and dead flowers of the last festival still lingered in the streets.

In this city, turned at once into a charnel-house—nay, into a hell and place of torment,—the mighty, unseen hand suddenly struck down its prey, and without warning seized upon the wretched conscience, all unprepared for such a blow. The cast of a pantomime is a strange sight beneath the glare and light of mid-day; but here were quacks and nobles, jugglers and soldiers, comic actors and "filosofi," pleasure-seekers and monks, gentry and beggars, all surprised as it were, suddenly, by the light and glare of the death angel's torch, and crowded upon one level stage of misery and despair.

Sick and dizzy with horror, and choked with the deadly smell and malaria, Inglesant turned into several osteria, but could find no host in any. In several he saw sights which chilled his blood. At last he gave up the search, and, weary as he was, sought the hospitals. The approaches to some of these were so blocked up by the dead and the dying who had vainly sought admission, that entrance was impossible. In others the galley slaves were at work. In every open spot of ground where the earth could be disturbed without cutting off the water pipes which ran through the city, trenches had been dug, and the bodies which were collected from the streets and hospitals were thrown hastily into them, and covered with lime and earth. Inglesant strayed into the "Monte della Misericordia" which had recently been cleared of the dead. A few sick persons lay in the beds; but the house seemed wonderfully clean and sweet, and the rooms cool and fresh. The floors were soaked with vinegar, and the place was full of the scent of juniper, bay berries, and rosemary, which were burning in every room. It seemed to Inglesant like a little heaven, and he sank exhausted upon one of the beds. They brought him some wine, and presently the Signore di Mauro, one of the physicians appointed by the city, who still remained bravely at his post, came and spoke to him.

"I perceive that you are a stranger in Naples and untouched by the disease," he said. "I am at a loss to account for your presence here. This house is indeed cleared for a moment, but it is the last time that we can expect help. The supply of galley slaves is failing, and when it stops entirely, which it must in a few days, I see nothing in the future but the general extirpation of all the inhabitants of this fated city, and that its vast circumference, filled with putrefaction and venom, will afterwards be uninhabitable to the rest of mankind."

This doleful foreboding made little impression upon Inglesant, who was, indeed, too much exhausted both in mind and body to pay much attention to anything.

"I am come to Naples," he said faintly, "in search of another; will you let me stay in this house to-night? I can find no one in the inns."

"I will do better for you than that," said the good physician; "you shall come to my own house, which is free from infection. I have but one inmate, an old servant, who, I think, is too dry and withered a morsel even for the plague. I am going at once."

Something in Inglesant's manner probably attracted him, otherwise it is difficult to account for his kindness to a stranger under such circumstances.

They went out together. Inglesant by chance seemed to be about to turn into another and smaller street—the physician pulled him back hurriedly with a shudder.

"Whatever you do," he said in a whisper, "keep to the principal thoroughfares. I dare not recollect—the most heated imagination would shrink from conceiving—the unutterable horrors of the bye-streets."

Picking their way among the dead bodies, which the slaves, with handkerchiefs steeped in vinegar over their faces, were piling into carts, the two proceeded down the Strada.

Inglesant asked the physician how the plague first began in Naples.

"It is the terrible enemy of mankind," replied the other—he was rather a pompous man, with all his kindness and devotion, and used long words—"that walks stained with slaughter by night. We know not whence it comes. Before it are beautiful gardens, crowded habitations, and populous cities; behind it unfruitful emptiness and howling desolation. Before it the guards and armies of mighty princes are as dead men, and physicians are no protection either to the sick or to themselves. Some imagine that it comes from the cities of the East; some that it arises from poverty and famine, and from the tainted and perishing flesh, and unripe fruits and hurtful herbs, which, in times of scarcity and dearth, the starving people greedily devour to satisfy their craving hunger. Others contend that it is inflicted immediately by the hand of God. These are mostly the priests. When we have puzzled our reason, and are at our wit's end through ignorance, we come to that. I have read something in a play, written by one of your countrymen—for I perceive you are an Englishman—where all mistakes are laid upon the King."

They were arrived by this time at the physician's house, and were received by an old woman whose appearance fully justified her master's description. She provided for Inglesant's wants, and prepared a bed for him, and he sank into an uneasy and restless sleep. The night was stiflingly hot, suppressed cries and groans broke the stillness, and the distant chanting of monks was heard at intervals. Soon after midnight the Churches were again crowded; mass was said, and thousands received the Sacrament with despairing faith. The physician came into Inglesant's room early in the morning.

"I am going out," he said; "keep as much as possible out of the Churches; they spread the contagion. The magistrates wished to close them, but the superstitious people would not hear of it. I will make inquiries, and if any of the religious, or any one else, has heard your friend's name, I will send you word. I may not return."

Shortly after he was gone, the crowd thronging in one direction before Inglesant's window caused him to rise and follow. He came to one of the slopes of the hill of Santo Martino, above the city. Here a crowd, composed of every class, from a noble down to the lowest lazzaroni, were engaged, in the clear morning light, in building a small house. Some were making bricks, some drawing along stones, some carrying timber. A nun had dreamed that were a hermitage erected for her order the plague would cease, and the people set to work, with desperate earnestness, to finish the building. By the wayside up the ascent were set empty barrels, into which the wealthier citizens dropped gold and jewels to assist the work. As Inglesant was standing by, watching the work, he was accosted by a dignified, highly bred old gentleman, in a velvet coat and Venice lace, who seemed less absorbed in the general panic than the rest.

"This is a strange sight," he said; "what the tyranny of the Spaniards was not able to do, the plague has done. When the Spaniard was storming the gates the gentlemen of the Borgo Santa Maria and the lazzaroni fought each other in the streets, and the gentlemen avowed that they preferred any degree of foreign tyranny to acknowledging or associating with the common people. With this deadly enemy not only at the gates but in the very midst of us, gentlemen and lazzaroni toil together without a thought of suspicion or contempt. The plague has made us all equal. I perceive that you are a stranger. May I ask what has brought you into this ill-fated city at such a time?"

"I am in search of my relation, il Cavaliere di Guardino," replied Inglesant; "do you know such a name?"

"It seems familiar to me," replied the old gentleman. "Have you reason to suppose that he is in Naples?"

Inglesant said that he had.

"The persons most likely to give you information would be the Signori, the officers of the galleys. They would doubtless be acquainted with the Cavaliere before the plague became so violent, and would know, at any rate, whether it was his intention to leave Naples or not. The galleys lie, as you know, moored together there in the bay, and many other ships lie near them, upon which persons have taken refuge who believe that the plague cannot touch them on the water—an expectation in which, I believe, many have been fatally deceived."

Inglesant thanked the gentleman, and inquired how it was that he remained so calm and unconcerned amidst the general consternation.

"I am too old for the plague," he replied; "nothing can touch me but death itself. I am also," he continued with a peculiar smile, "the fortunate possessor of a true piece of the holy Cross; so that you see I am doubly safe."

Inglesant went at once to the harbour, musing on the way on these last words, and wondering whether they were spoken in good faith or irony.

The scenes on the streets seemed more terrible even than on the preceding day. The slaves were engaged here and there in removing the bodies, but the task was far beyond their strength. Cries of pain and terror were heard on all sides, and every now and then a maddened wretch would throw himself from a window, or would rush, naked perhaps, from a house, and, stumbling and leaping over the corpses and the dying, like the demoniac among the tombs, would fling himself in desperation into the water of the harbour, or over the walls into the moats. One of these maniacs, passing close to Inglesant, attempted to embrace a passer-by, who coolly ran him through the body with his sword, the bystanders applauding the act.

In the harbour corpses were floating, which a few slaves in boats were feebly attempting to drag together with hooks. They escaped their efforts, and rose and sank with a ghastly resemblance to life. Upon the quay Inglesant fortunately found the physician, Signore Mauro, who was himself going on board the galleys to endeavour to procure the loan of more slaves. He offered to take Inglesant with him.

As they went the physician told him he had not discovered any trace of the Cavaliere; but what was very curious, he said, many other persons appeared to be engaged in the same search. It might be that all these people were in fact but one, multiplied by the forgetfulness, and by the excited imaginations of those from whom Signore Mauro had obtained his information; but, if these persons were to be believed, monks, friars, physicians, soldiers, and even ladies, were engaged in this singular search in a city where all ties of friendship were forgotten, for a man whom no one knew.

As they shot over the silent water, and by the shadowy hulks of ships lying idle and untended, with the cry of the city of the dead behind them and the floating corpses around, Inglesant listened to the physician as a man listens in a dream. Long shadows stretched across the harbour, which sparkled beneath the rays of the newly-risen sun; a sudden swoon stole over Inglesant's spirits, through which the voice of the physician sounded distant and faint. He gave himself up for lost, yet he felt a kind of dim expectation that something was about to happen which these unknown inquirers foretold.

The galleys lay moored near together, with several other ships of large size in company. Signore Mauro climbed to the quarter-deck of the largest galley, on which the commodore was, and Inglesant followed him, still hardly knowing what he did.

The oars were shipped, but the slaves were chained to their benches, as though the galleys were at sea. They were singing and playing at cards. Upon the quarter-deck, pointing to the long files of slaves, were two loaded howitzers, behind each of which stood a gunner with a lighted match. Soldiers heavily armed, and with long whips, paraded the raised gangway or passage which ran the whole length of the ship between the rows of benches upon which the slaves were placed. The officers were mostly on the quarter-deck; they looked pale and excited, though it was singular that few or no cases of the plague had occurred among the slaves who remained on board. The decks were washed with vinegar, and the galleys and slaves were much cleaner than usual.

The physician stated his request to the commander, who ordered ten slaves from every galley to be sent on shore. Some were wanted to act as bakers, some as butchers, most of the artizans in the city having fled or perished. A boatswain was ordered to make the selection. He chose one or two, and then called upon the rest to volunteer. Inglesant was standing by him on the gangway, looking down the files of slaves. There were men of every age, of every rank, and almost of every country. As the boatswain gave the word, every hand was held up; to all these men death was welcome at the end of two or three days' change of life, abundance of food, and comparative freedom. The boatswain selected ten by chance.

Signore Mauro inquired among the officers concerning the Cavaliere, but could obtain no positive information. Most had heard the name, some professed to have known him intimately; all united in saying he had left Naples. Inglesant and the physician visited two or three other galleys, but with no greater success. They returned on shore as the heat was becoming intense; the Churches were crowded, and the Holy Sacrament was exhibited every few moments. The physician refused to enter any of them.

Then Inglesant determined to try the hospitals again. He went to the "Santa Casa degli Incurabili," which the day before he had not been able to approach for the dying and the dead. The slaves had worked hard all night, and hundreds of corpses had been removed and buried in a vast trench without the wall of the hospital. Inglesant passed through many of the rooms, and spoke to several of the religious persons who were tending the sick, but could learn nothing of the object of his search. At last one of the monks conducted him into the strange room called the "Anticamera di Morte," to which, in more orderly times, the patients whose cases were hopeless were removed.

There, at the last extremity of life, before they were hurried into the great pit outside the walls, lay the plague-stricken. Some unconscious, yet with fearful throes and gasps awaiting their release; some in an agony of pain and death, crying upon God and the Saints. Kneeling by the bedsides were several monks; but at the farther end of the room, bending over a sick man, was a figure in a friar's gown that made Inglesant stop suddenly, and his heart beat quicker as he caught his companion's arm.

"Who is that friar, Father?" he said, "the one at the end, bending over the bed?"

"Ah! that," said the priest, "that is Father Grazia of the Capuchins; a very holy man, and devoted to mortification and good works. He is blind, though he moves about so cleverly. He says that, to within the last few years, his life was passed in every species of sin; and he relates that he was solemnly given over to the vengeance of the blessed Gesu by his mortal enemy, the minion of a Cardinal, and that the Lord has afflicted him with untold sorrows and sufferings to bring him to Himself and to a life of holy mortification and charity, which he leads unceasingly—night and day. He is but now come in hither, knowing that the sick man by whose bed he is, is dying of the plague in its most fearful form,—a man whom none willingly will approach. Mostly he is in the vilest dens of the city, reeking with pestilence, where to go, to all save him, is certain death. His holiness and the Lord's will keep him, so that the plague cannot touch him. Ah! he is coming this way."

It was true. The friar had suddenly started from his recumbent position, conscious that the man before him was no more. At the same moment, his mind, released from the attention which had riveted it before, seemed to become aware of a presence in the chamber of death which was of the intensest interest. He came down the passage in the centre of the room with an eager unfaltering step, as though able to see, and coming to within a few feet of the two men, he stopped, and looked towards them with an excited glance, as though he saw their faces. Inglesant was embarrassed, and hesitated whether to recognize him or not. At last, pitying the look in the blind man's face, he said,—

"This holy Father is not unknown to me, though I know not that he would desire to meet me again. I am 'the minion of a Cardinal' of whom you spoke."

The friar stretched out his hands before him, with an eager, delighted gesture.

"I knew it," he said; "I felt your presence long before you spoke. It signifies little whether I am glad to find you or no. It is part of the Lord's purpose that we should meet."

"This is a strange and sanctified meeting," said the priest, "in the room of death, and by the beds of the dead. Doubtless you have much to say that can only be said to yourselves alone."

"I cannot stay," said the friar, wildly. "I came in here but for a moment; for this wretched man who is gone to his account needed one as wretched and as wicked as himself. But they are dying now in the streets and alleys, calling upon the God whom they know not; they need the vilest sinner to whom the Lord has been gracious, to kneel by their side; they need the vilest sinner; therefore I must go."

He stopped for a moment, then he said more calmly, "Meet me in the Santa Chiara, behind the altar, by the tomb of the wise King, this evening at sunset. By that time, though the need will be as pressing, yet the frail body will need a little rest, and I will speak with you for an hour. Fail not to come. You will learn how your sword was the sword, and your breath was the breath, of the Lord."

"I will surely be there," said Inglesant.

The friar departed, leaving the priest and Inglesant alone. They went out into the garden of the hospital, a plot of ground planted with fruit trees, and with vines trailing over the high stone walls. Walking up and down in the shade, with the intense blue of the sky overhead, one might for a time forget the carnival of death that was crowding every street and lane around. Inglesant inquired of his companion more particularly concerning the friar.

"He is a very holy man," said the priest, with a significant gesture; "but he is not right in his head. His sufferings have touched his brain. He believes that he has seen the Lord in a vision, and not only so, but that all Rome was likewise a witness of the miracle. It is a wonderful story, which doubtless he wishes to relate to you this evening."

CHAPTER XXXV.

In the vast Church of the Santa Chiara, with its open nave which spread itself on every side like a magic hall of romance, the wide floor and the altars of the side Chapels had been crowded all day by prostrate worshippers; but when Inglesant entered it about sunset, it was comparatively empty. A strange unearthly perfume filled the Church, and clouds of incense yet hovered beneath the painted ceiling, and obscured the figure of the Saint chasing his enemies. Streaks of light, transfigured through the coloured prism of the prophets and martyrs that stood in the painted glass, lighted up the wreaths of smoke, and coloured the marbles and frescoes of the walls and altars. The mystic glimmer of the sacred tapers in the shaded chapels, and the concluding strains of the chanting before the side altars, which had followed the vesper service and benediction, filled the Church with half light and half shadow, half silence and half sound, very pleasing and soothing to the sense.

Inglesant passed up the Church towards the high altar, before which he knelt; and as he did so, a procession, carrying the Sacrament, entered by another door, and advanced to the altar, upon which it was again deposited. The low, melancholy miserere—half entreating, half desponding—spoke to the heart of man a language like its own; and as the theme was taken up by one of the organs, the builder's art and the musician's melted into one—in tier after tier of carved imagery, wave after wave of mystic sound. All conscious thought and striving seemed to fade from the heart, and before the altar and amid the swell of sound the soul lost itself, and lay silent and passive on the Eternal Love.

Behind the high altar Inglesant found the friar by the grave of the wise King. Upon the slabs of the Gothic tomb, covered with carving and bas-relief, the King is seated and dressed in royal robes; but upon the sarcophagus he lies in death bereft of all his state, and clothed in no garment but a Franciscan's gown. Beside him lies his son in his royal robes, covered with fleurs-de-lis; and other tombs of the kingly race of Anjou surround him, all emblazoned with coat armour and device of rank.

Between the tombs of the two kings stood the friar, his head bowed upon his hands. The light grew every moment less and less bright, and the shadows stretched ever longer and longer across the marble floor. The lamps before the shrines, and the altar tapers in the funeral chapels, shone out clearer and more distinct. The organs had ceased, but the dolorous chanting of the miserere from beyond the high altar still came to them with a remote and wailing tone.

Inglesant advanced towards the friar, who appeared to be aware of his presence by instinct, and raised his head as he drew near. He returned no answer to Inglesant's greeting, but seated himself upon a bench near one of the tombs, and began at once, like a man who has little time to spend.

"I am desirous," he said, "of telling you at once of what has occurred to me. Who can tell what may happen at any moment to hinder unless I do? It is a strange and wonderful story, in which you and I and all men would be but puppets in the Divine Hand were not the Divine Love such that we are rather children led onward by their Father's hand—welcomed home by their Mother's smile."

It was indeed a strange story that the friar told Inglesant in the darkening Church. In places it was incoherent and obscure. The first part of his narrative, as it relates to others besides himself, is told here in a different form, so that, if possible, what really happened might be known. The latter part, being untranslatable into any other language and inexplicable upon any basis of fact, must be told in his own words.

"When you left me at the mountain chapel," said the friar, "I thought of nothing but that I had escaped with life. I thought I had met with a Fantastic, whose brain was turned with monkish fancies, and I blessed my fortunate stars that such had been the case. I thought little of the Divine vengeance that dogged my steps."

When Inglesant met Malvolti upon the mountain pass (as he gathered from the friar's narrative), the latter, utterly penniless and undone, having exhausted every shift and art of policy, and being so well known in all the cities of Italy that he was safe in none of them, had bethought himself of his native place. It was, indeed, almost the only place where his character was unknown, and his person comparatively safe. But it had other attractions for the hunted and desperate man. Malvolti's father had died when his son was a boy, and his mother in a year or two married again. His step-father was harsh and unkind to the fatherless child, and the seeds of evil were sown in the boy's heart by the treatment he received; but a year after this marriage a little girl was born, who won her way at once into the heart of the forlorn and unhappy lad. He was her constant playmate, protector, and instructor. For several years the only happy moments of his life were passed when he could steal away with her to the woods and hills, wandering for hours together alone or with the wood-cutters and charcoal-burners; and when, after a few years, the unkindness of his parents and his own restless and passionate nature sent him out into the world in which he played so evil a part, the image of the innocent child followed him into scenes of vice, and was never obliterated from his memory. The murmur of the leaves above the fowling-floor where they lay together during the mid-day heat, the splash of the fountains where they watched the flocks of sheep drinking, followed him into strange places and foreign countries, and arose to his recollection in moments of danger, and even of passion and crime.

The home of Malvolti's parents had been in the suburb of a small town of the Bolognese. Here, at some little height above the town on the slope of the wooded hills, a monastery and chapel had been erected, and in course of time some few houses had grouped themselves around, among which that of Malvolti's father had been the most considerable. The sun was setting behind the hills when Malvolti, weary, dispirited, and dying of hunger, came along the winding road from the south, which skirted the projecting spurs of the mountains. The slanting rays penetrated the woods, and shone between the openings of the hills, lighting up the grass-grown buildings of the monastery, and the belfry of the little Chapel, where the bell was ringing for vespers. Below, the plain stretched itself peacefully; a murmur of running water blended with the tolling of the bell. A waft of peace and calm, like a breeze from paradise, fell upon Malvolti's heart, and he seemed to hear soft voices welcoming him home. He pictured to himself his mother's kind greeting, his sister's delight; even his stern step-father's figure was softened in the universal evening glow. It was a fairy vision, in which the passing years had found no place, where the avenging footsteps that follow sin did not come, and which had no reality in actual existence. He turned the angle of the wood, and stood before his home. It lay in ruins and desolate.

The sun sank below the hills, the bell went on tolling monotonously through the deepening gloom. Dazed and faint, Malvolti followed its tones into the Chapel, where the vesper service began. When it was ended the miserable man spoke to one of the monks, and craved some food. Deprived of his last hope, his senses faint and dull with weariness and hunger, and lulled by the soft strains of devout sound—his life confessed at last to have been completely a failure, and the wages of sin to have turned to withered leaves in his hand—his heart was more disposed than perhaps it had ever been to listen to the soft accents of penitence, and to hear the whispering murmur that haunts the shadowy walks of mortified repentance. Comforted by food, the kindly words of pity and exhortation stole upon his senses, and he almost fancied that he might find a home and peace without further wandering and punishment. He was much deceived.

He inquired concerning the fate of those whom, debased and selfish as he was, he still loved, especially now, when the sight of long-forgotten but still familiar places recalled the past, and seemed to obliterate the intervening years. The monks told him a story of sorrow and of sin, such as he himself often had participated in, and would have heard at another time with a smile of indifference. His step-father was dead, killed in a feud which his own insolent temper had provoked. His mother and sister had continued for some time to live in the same house, and there perhaps he might have found them, had not a gentleman, whose convenience had led him to claim the hospitality of the monastery for a night's rest, chanced to see his sister in the morning as he mounted his horse. The sight of a face, whose beauty combined a haughty clearness of outline with a certain coy softness of expression, and a figure of perfect form, detained him from his intended journey, and he obtained admittance into the widow's house. What wizard arts he practised the monks did not know, but when he departed he left anxiety and remorse where he had found content and a certain peace. In due time the two women, despairing of his return, had followed him, and the younger, the monks had heard (and they believed the report)—ill-treated and spurned—was now living in Florence a life of sin. The softened expression of rest and penitence which had begun to show itself in Malvolti's face left it, and the more habitual one of cruel and hungry sin returned as he inquired,—

"Did the Reverend Fathers remember the name of this man?"

The good monks hesitated as they saw the look in the inquirer's face; but it was not their duty to conceal the truth from one who undoubtedly had a right to be informed of it.

"It is our duty to practise forgiveness, even of the greatest injuries, my son," one of them replied; "our blessed Lord has enjoined it, and left us this as an example, that He has forgiven us. The man was called il Cavaliere di Guardino."

The monks were relieved when they saw that their guest showed no emotion upon hearing this name; only he said that he must go to Florence and endeavour to find his sister.

But in truth there was in the man's mind, under a calm exterior, a crisis of feeling not easy to describe. That the Cavaliere, his familiar accomplice, in whose company and by whose aid he had himself so often committed ravages upon the innocent, should, in the chance medley of life, be selected to inflict this blow, affected him in a strange and unaccustomed way, with the sense of a hitherto unrecognized justice at work among the affairs of men. He was so utterly at the end of all his hopes, life was so completely closed to him, and his soul was so sorely stricken, in return for all his sins, in the only holy and sacred spot that remained in his fallen nature,—his love and remembrance of his sister,—that it seemed as if a revulsion of feeling might take place, and that, in this depth and slough, there might appear, though dimly, the possibility of an entrance into a higher life. He was better known in Florence than in any city of Italy, except Rome; and if he went there his violent death was almost certain, yet he determined to go. He assured Inglesant afterwards, in relating the story, that his object was not revenge, but that his desire was to seek out and rescue his sister. Revenge doubtless brooded in his mind; but it was not the motive which urged him onward.

He told Inglesant a strange story of his weary journey to Florence, subsisting on charity from convent to convent; of his wandering up and down in the beautiful city, worn out with hunger and fatigue, unknown, and hiding himself from recognition. Amid the grim forms of vice that haunted the shadowy recesses of the older parts of the city, in the vaulted halls of deserted palaces and the massive fastnesses of patrician strife, he flitted like a ghost, pale and despairing, urged on by a restless desire that knew no respite. In these dens of a reckless life, which had thrown off all restraint and decorum, he recognized many whom he had known in other days, and in far different places. In these gloomy halls, which had once been bright with youth and gaiety, but were now hideous with poverty and crime,—in which the windows were darkened, and the coloured ceilings and frescoed walls were blurred with smoke and damp, and which were surrounded by narrow alleys which shut out the light, and cut them off from all connection with the outer world,—he at last heard of the Cavaliere. He was told that, flying from Rome after his sister's marriage, he had been arrested for some offence in the south of Italy, and those into whose hands he fell being old enemies, and bearing him some grudge, he was thrown into prison, and even condemned to the galleys, for, since the Papal election, he was no longer able to claim even a shadow of protection from any of the great families who had once been his patrons. After a short imprisonment he was deputed, among others, to perform some such office as Inglesant had seen undertaken by the slaves in Naples, for the plague had raged for some summers past, with more or less intensity, in southern Italy. While engaged in this work he had managed to make his escape, and had not long since arrived in Florence, where he had kept himself closely concealed. Malvolti was told the secret lurking-place where he might probably be found.

"It was a brilliantly hot afternoon," continued Malvolti, speaking very slowly; "you will wonder that I tell you this; but it was the last time that I ever saw the sun. I remember the bright and burning pavements even in the narrow alleys out of which I turned into the long and dark entries and vaulted rooms. I followed some persons who entered before me, and some voices which led me onward, into a long and lofty room in the upper stories, at the farther end of which, before a high window partially boarded up, some men were at play. As I came up the room, all the other parts of which lay in deep shadow, the light fell strongly upon a corner of the table, and upon the man who was casting the dice. He had just thrown his chance, and he turned his head as I came up. He appeared to be naked except his slippers and a cloak or blanket of white cloth, with pale yellow stripes. His hair was closely cropped; his face, which was pale and aquiline, was scarred and seamed with deep lines of guilt and misery, especially around the eyes, from which flashed a lurid light, and his lips were parted with a mocking and Satanic laugh. His dark and massive throat and chest and his long and sinewy arms forced their way out of the cloth with which he was wrapped, and the lean fingers of both hands, which crossed each other convulsively, were pointed exultantly to the deuce of ace which he had thrown. The last sight I ever saw, the last sight my eyes will ever behold until they open before the throne of God, was this demon-like figure, standing out clear and distinct against the shadowy gloom in which dim figures seemed to move, and the dice upon the table by his side.

"He burst out into a wild and mocking laugh. 'Ah, Malvolti,' he said, 'you were ever unlucky at the dice. Come and take your chances in the next main.'

"I know not what fury possessed me, nor why, at that moment especially, this man's mocking villainy inspired me with such headlong rage. I remembered nothing but the crimes and wrongs which he had perpetrated. I drew the dagger I carried beneath my clothes, and sprang upon him with a cry as wild as his own. What happened I cannot tell. I seemed to hear the laughter of fiends, and to feel the tortures of hell on every side. Then all was darkness and the grave."

Overpowered as it seemed by the recollection of his sufferings, the friar paused and sank upon his knees upon the pavement. The miserere had died away, and a profound gloom, broken only by the flicker of tapers, filled the Church. Inglesant was deeply moved,—less, however, by sympathy with the man's story than by the consciousness of the emotions which he himself experienced. It was scarcely possible to believe that he was the same man who, some short years before, had longed for this meeting with a bloodthirsty desire that he might take some terrible vengeance upon his brother's murderer. Now he stood before the same murderer, who not so long before had attempted to take his life also with perhaps the very dagger of which he now spoke; and as he looked down upon him, no feeling but that of pity was in his heart. In the presence of the awful visitant who at that moment was filling the city which lay around them with death and corruption, and before whose eternal power the strife and enmity of man shrank away appalled and silenced, it was not wonderful that inordinate hate should cease; but, as he gazed upon the prostrate man before him, an awe-inspiring feeling took possession of Inglesant's mind, which still more effectually crushed every sentiment of anger or revenge. The significance of his own half-conceived action was revealed to him, and he recognized, with something approaching to terror, that the cause was no longer his, that another hand had interposed to strike, and that his sword had spared the murderer of his brother only that he might become the victim of that divine vengeance which has said, "I will repay."

The friar rose from his knees. "I found myself in the monastery of the Cappuccini on the bank of the river, blind, and holding life by the faintest thread. That I lived was a miracle. I had been struck with some twenty wounds, and in mere wantonness my eyes had been pierced as I lay apparently dead. I was thrown into the river which flowed by gloomy vaults beneath the houses, and had been carried down by the stream to the garden of a monastery where I was found. As I recovered strength the monks thought that my reason would not survive. For days and nights I lay bound a raving madman. At last, when my pains subsided, and my mind was a little calmed and subdued, I was sent out into the world and begged my way from village to village, not caring where I went, my mind an utter blank, filled only now and then with horrible sights and dreams. I had no sense of God or Christ; no feeling but a blind senseless despair and confusion. Thus I wandered on. I got at last a boy to lead me and buy me food. I know not why I did not rather lie down and die. Sometimes I did fling myself down, resolving not to move again; but some love of life or some divine prompting caused me to rise and wander on in my miserable path. At last, towards the end of the year,

I came to Rome, and wandered about the city seeking alms. The boy who led me, and who had attached himself to me, God knows why, told me all he saw and all that passed; and I, who knew every phase and incident of Roman life, explained to him such things in a languid and indifferent way, for I found no pleasure nor relief in anything. I grew more and more miserable; our life was hard, and we were ill fed, and the terrors of my memory haunted my spirits, weakened and depressed for want of food. The forms of those whom I had wronged, nay, murdered, lay before me. They rose and looked upon me from every side. My misery was greater than I could bear. I desired death and tried to accomplish it, but my hand always failed. I bought poison, but my boy watched me and changed the drink. I did not know this, and expected death. It did not come. Then suddenly, as I lay in a kind of trance, that morning in the mountain pass came into my remembrance, and it flashed suddenly into my mind that I was not my own; that no poison could hurt me, no sword slay me; that the sword of vengeance was in the Lord's hand, and would work His will alone. What greater punishment could be in store for me I knew not, but stunned by this idea I ceased to strive and cry any more. I waited in silence for the final blow; it came. The year had come nearly to an end, and it was Christmas Eve. All day long, in the Churches in Rome, had the services, the processions, the religious shows, gone on. My boy and I had followed them one by one, and he had, in his boyish way, told me all that he saw. The new Pope went in procession to S. Giovanni in Laterano, with all the Cardinals, Patriarchs, Archbishops, and Bishops, all the nobility and courtiers, and an interminable length of attendants, Switzers, soldiers, led horses, servants, pages, rich coaches, litters, and people of every class, under triumphal arches, with all excess of joy and triumph. As midnight drew on the streets were as light as day. Every pageant became more gorgeous, every service more sweet and ravishing, every sermon more passionate. I saw it all in my mind's eye,—all, and much besides. I saw in every Church, lighted by sacred tapers before the crucifix, the pageants and ceremonies that, in every form and to every sense, present the story of the mystic birth, of that divine fact that alone can stay the longing which, since men walked the earth, they have uttered in every tongue, that the Deity would come down and dwell with man. We had wandered through all the Churches, and at last, wearied out, we reached the Capitol, and sank down beneath the balusters at the top of the marble stairs. Close by, in the Ara Cœli, the simple country people and the faithful whose hearts were as those of little children, kneeling as the shepherds knelt upon the plains of Bethlehem, saw the Christ-Child lying in a manger, marked out from common childhood by a mystic light which shone from His face and form; while the organ harmonies which filled the Church resigned their wonted splendours, and bent for once to pastoral melodies, which, born amid the rustling of sedges by the river brink, have wandered down through the reed-music and festivals of the country people, till they grew to be the most fitting tones of a religion which takes its aptest similes from the vineyard and the flock. All over Rome the flicker of the bonfires mingled with the starlight. I was blind, yet I saw much that would have been hidden from me had I been able to see. I saw across the roofs before me, the dome of the Pantheon and St. Peter's, and the long line of the Vatican, and the round outline of St. Angelo in the light of the waning moon. This I should have seen had I had my sight; but I saw behind me now what otherwise I should not have seen—the Forum, and the lines of arches and ruins, and beyond these the walks of the Aventine and of the Cœlian, with their vineyards and white convents, and tall poplar and cypress trees. I saw beyond them the great Churches of the Lateran and Santa Croce in Gerusalemme, standing out from the green country, pale and spectral in the light. To the left I saw Santa Maria Maggiore, stately and gorgeous, facing the long streets of palaces and courts, and the gardens and terraces of the Quirinale, all distinct and clear in the mystic light. The white light covered the earth like a shroud, and over the vault of the sky were traced, by the pale stars, strange and obscure forms, as over the dome of St. Peter's at evening when the Church is dim. A confused sound filled my ears, a sound of chanting and of praise for that advent that brought peace to men, a sound of innumerable passing feet, and in all the Churches and Basilicas I saw the dead Christs over the altars and the kneeling crowds around. Suddenly it seemed to me that I was conscious of a general movement and rush of feet, and that a strange and wild excitement prevailed in every region of Rome. The Churches became emptied, the people pouring out into the streets; the dead Christs above the altars faded from their crosses, and the sacred tapers went out of their own accord; for it spread through Rome, as in a moment, that a miracle had happened at the Ara Cœli, and that the living Christ was come. From where I stood I could see the throngs of people pouring through every street and lane, and thronging up to the Campidoglio and the stairs; and from the distance and the pale Campagna, and San Paolo without the walls, and from subterranean Rome, where the martyrs and confessors lie, I could see strange and mystic shapes come sweeping in through the brilliant light.

"He came down the steps of the Ara Cœli, and the sky was full of starlike forms, wonderful and gracious; and all the steps of the Capitol were full of people down to the square of the Ara Cœli, and up to the statue of Aurelius on horseback above; and the summit of the Capitol among the statues, and the leads of the palace Caffarelli, were full of eager forms, for the starlight was so clear that all might see; and the dead gods, and the fauns, and the satyrs, and the old pagans, that lurked in the secret hiding-places of the ruins of the Cæsars, crowded up the steps out of the Forum, and came round the outskirts of the crowd, and stood on the fallen pillars that they might see; and Castor and Pollux, that stood by their unsaddled horses at the top of the stairs, left them unheeded and came to see; and the Marsyas who stood bound broke his bonds and came to see; and spectral forms swept in from the distance in the light, and the air was full of Powers and Existences, and the earth rocked as at the Judgment Day.

"He came down the steps into the Campidoglio, and He came to me. He was not at all like the pictures of the saints; for He was pale, and worn, and thin, as though the fight was not yet half over—ah no!—but through this pale and worn look shone infinite power, and undying love, and unquenchable resolve. The crowd fell back on every side, but when He came to me He stopped. 'Ah!' he said, 'is it thou? What doest thou here? Knowest thou not that thou art mine? Thrice mine—mine centuries ago when I hung upon the cross on Calvary for such as thou—mine years ago, when thou camest a little child to the font—mine once again, when, forfeit by every law, thou wast given over to me by one who is a servant and friend of mine. Surely, I will repay.' As He spoke, a shudder and a trembling ran through the crowd, as if stirred by the breath of His voice. Nature seemed to rally and to grow beneath Him, and heaven to bend down to touch the earth. A healing sense of help and comfort, like the gentle dew, visited the weary heart. A great cry and shout rose from the crowd, and He passed on; but among ten thousand times ten thousand I should know Him, and amid the tumult of a universe I should hear the faintest whisper of His voice."

The friar stopped and looked at Inglesant with his darkened eyeballs, as though he could read his looks. Inglesant gazed at him in silence. That the man was crazed he had no doubt; but that his madness should have taken this particular form appeared to his listener scarcely less miraculous than if every word of his wonderful story had been true.

"Heard you nothing else?" he said at last.

An expression of something like trouble passed over the other's face.

"No," he said in a quieter voice; "by this time it was morning. The artillery of St. Angelo went off. His Holiness sang mass, and all day long was exposed the cradle of the Lord."

There was another pause which Inglesant scarcely knew how to break. Then he said,—

"And have you heard nothing since of the Cavaliere?"

"He is in this neighbourhood," said Malvolti, "but I have not found him. I wondered and was impatient, ignorant and foolish as I am; now I know the reason. The Lord waited till you came. How could he be found except by us both? We must lose no time, or it will be too late. How did you know that he was here?"

Inglesant told him.

"It was the Lord's doing," said the friar, a light breaking over his darkened face. "It was Capece. You remember, at Florence, the leader of that extravagant frolic of the Carnival, who was dressed as a corpse?"

"I remember," said Inglesant, "and the poor English lad who was killed."

"He is one of the Lord's servants," continued the friar, "whom He called very late. I do not know that he was guilty of any particular sins, but he was the heir of a poor family, and lived for many years in luxury and excess. He was brought under the influence of Molinos's party, and shortly after I had seen the Lord, he came to me to know whether he should become a religious. I told him I thought there was a time of trial and of sifting for the Lord's people at hand, and that I thought the strongholds were the safest spots. He joined the order de Servi. Not three weeks ago I was with him at Frascati, at the house of the Cappuccini, when I heard that the Cavaliere was here. You must have seen him three or four days afterwards."

CHAPTER XXXVI.

THE night after Inglesant had met the friar in Naples there was "the sound of abundance of rain," and the "plague was stayed." As constantly happened in the cities desolated by this mysterious pestilence, no adequate reason could be perceived for its cessation. Some change in the state of the atmosphere took place, and the sick did not die, at least in the same proportion as formerly. This was the only indication that the most acute observer could detect; but the change was marvellously rapid. The moment that contact with the dead bodies became less fatally infectious, help offered on all sides, tempted by the large rewards. The dead rapidly disappeared from sight, and the city began to resume something of its ordinary appearance. The terrors of the grave vanished into air, and gloomy resolutions faded from the mind. The few survivors of the devoted men who, throughout the heat of the conflict, had remained at their posts, were, many of them at least, forgotten and overlooked; for their presence was an unpleasing reminder to those whose conduct had been of a far more prudent and selfish sort. Those who had fled returned into the city to look after their deserted homes, and to re-open their shops. The streets and markets were once more gay with wares. The friar was now as eager to leave Naples as he had before been determined to remain. His sole object was to find the Cavaliere, and he constantly insisted that no time was to be lost if they wished to see him alive. They left Naples together; the friar mounted upon a mule which Inglesant purchased for him.

Notwithstanding the friar's eagerness, their journey was

slow, for he was not able to resist the impulse to turn aside to help when any appearance of distress or poverty called upon them for aid. Inglesant was not impatient at this delay, nor at the erratic and apparently meaningless course of their singular journey. The country was delightful after the heavy rains, and seemed to rejoice, together with its inhabitants, at the abatement of the plague. People who had remained shut up in their houses in fear now appeared freely in the once deserted roads. Doors were thrown open, and the voice of the lute and of singing was heard again in the land. As for those who had passed away, it was wonderful how soon their name was forgotten, as of " a dead man out of mind;" and those who had come into comfortable inheritance of fruit-closes, and olive-grounds and vineyards, and of houses of pleasure in the fields, which, but for the pestilence, had never been theirs, soon found it possible to reconcile themselves to the absence of the dead.

For some time after leaving Naples the road lay through a richly cultivated land, with long straight ditches on either side. Rows of forest trees crossed the country, and shaded the small closes of fruit-trees and vines. Here and there a wine tavern, or a few cottages, or a village church, stopped them. At all of these the friar alighted from his mule, and made inquiries for any who were ill or in distress. In this way they came across a number of people of the peasant class, and heard the story of their lives; and now and then a religious, or a country signore, riding by on his mule or palfrey, stopped to speak with them.

They had proceeded for many days through this cultivated country, and had at last, after many turnings, reached that part of the road which approaches the slopes of the Apennines about Frosinone. The path wound among the hills, the slopes covered with chestnut trees, and the crags crowned with the remains of Gothic castles. Fields of maize filled the valleys, and lines of lofty poplars crossed the yellow corn. As the road ascended, distant reaches of forest and campagna lay in bright sunlight between the craggy rocks, and down the wooded glens cascades fell into rapid streams spanned here and there by a half-ruined bridge. At last they entered a deep ravine of volcanic tufa, much of which cropped out from the surface, cold and bare. Between these sterile rocks laurels forced their way, and spread out their broad and brilliant leaves. Creeping plants hung in long and waving festoons, and pines and forest trees of great size crowned the summits. Here and there sepulchral excavations were cut in the rock, and more than one sarcophagus, carved with figures in relief, stood by the wayside.

The air in these ravines was close and hot, and sulphurous streams emitted an unpleasant odour as they rode along. Inglesant felt oppressed and ill. The valley of the Shadow of Death, out of which he had come into the cool pastures and olive-yards, had left upon the mind an exaltation of feeling rather than terror: and in the history of the friar, through the course of which traces of a devised plan penetrated the confusion of a disordered brain, the gracious prediction of Molinos seemed to promise fulfilment. The supreme effort of Divine mercy surely is that which shapes the faltering and unconscious actions of man into a beneficent and everlasting work.

But the very clearness and calm of this transcendental air produced a wavering of the spiritual sense; and the companionship of a blind enthusiast, who, from the lowest depth of reckless sin, had suddenly attained a height of religious fervour, did not tend to reduce the fever of his thoughts. The scenes and forms of death with which he had been familiar in Naples returned again and again before his eyes, and his old disease again tormented him; so that once more he saw strange figures and shapes walking by the wayside. These images of a disordered fancy jostled and confused his spiritual perceptions. He felt wearied by those thoughts and desires which had formerly been dear to him, and the ceaseless reiteration of the friar's enthusiastic conceptions jarred and irritated him more than he liked to confess. The brain of the blind man, unoccupied by the sights of this world, was full of visions of a mystic existence, blended and confused with such incidents and stories of earth as he had heard along the way. With such phantasmal imaginations he filled Inglesant's ears.

Proceeding in this manner, they came to a place where the ravine, opening out a little, exposed a distant view of the Campagna, with its aqueducts and ruined tombs. At the opening of the valley stood one of those isolated rocks so strange to English eyes, yet so frequently seen in the paintings of the old masters, crowned with the ruins of a Temple, and fringed with trees of delicate foliage, poplars and pines. At the foot of the rock an arch of ruined brickwork, covered with waving grass and creepers, spanned the road with a wide sweep, and on the opposite side a black sulphurous pool exhaled a constant vapour. Masses of strange, nameless masonry, of an antiquity dateless and undefined, bedded themselves in the rocks, or overhung the clefts of the hills; and out of a great tomb by the wayside, near the arch, a forest of laurel forced its way, amid delicate and graceful frieze-work, moss-covered and stained with age.

In this strangely desolate and ruinous spot, where the fantastic shapes of nature seem to mourn in weird fellowship with the shattered strength and beauty of the old Pagan artlife, there appeared unexpectedly signs of modern dwelling. The base of the precipitous rock for some distance above the road was concealed by a steep bank of earth, the crumbling ruin and dust of man and of his work. At the top of this bank was one of those squalid erections, so common in Italy, where, upon a massive wall of old brickwork, embedded in the soil, a roof of straw affords some kind of miserable shelter. Some attempt had been made to wall in the space covered by this roof, and a small cross, reared from the gable, and a bell beneath a penthouse of wood, seemed to show that the shed had been used for some ecclesiastical purpose. At the bottom of the slope upon which this structure was placed, and on the other side of the ruined arch and of the road, there stood, near to the tomb, a very small hut, also thatched, and declared to be a tavern by its wine-bush. At the door of this hut, as Inglesant and the friar rode up, stood a man in a peasant's dress, in an attitude of perplexity and nervous dread. A long streak of light from the western sun penetrated the ruined arch, and shone upon the winding road, and, against the blaze of light, rock and arch and hanging woods stood out dark and lowering in the delicate air.

The dazzling light, the close atmosphere of the valley, and the fumes of the sulphurous lake, affected Inglesant's brain so much that he could scarcely see; but they did not appear to disturb the friar. He addressed the man as they came up, and understanding more from his own instinct than from the few words that Inglesant spoke that the man was in trouble, he said,—

"You seem in some perplexity, my son. Confide in me, that I may help you."

As the man hesitated to reply, Inglesant said, "What is that building on the hill?"

"It is a house for lepers," said the peasant.

"Are you the master of this tavern?" said Inglesant.

"No, Santa Madre," replied the man. "The mistress of the inn has fled. This is the case, Padre," he continued, turning to the friar. "I was hired a week or so ago at Ariano to bring a diseased man here, who was a leper; but I did not know that he was a leper who was stricken with the plague. I brought him in my cart, and a terrible journey I had with him. When I had brought him here, and the plague manifestly appeared upon him, all the lepers fled, and forsook the place. The Padrona, who kept this tavern upon such custom as the peasants who brought food to sell to the lepers brought her, also fled. I stayed a day or two to help the wretched man— they told me that he was a gentleman—till I could stay no longer, such was his condition, and I fled. But, my Father, I have a tender heart, and I came back to-day, thinking that the holy Virgin would never help me if I left a wretched man to die alone—I, who only know where and in what state he is. I spoke to one or two friars to come and help me, but they excused themselves. I came alone. But when I arrived here my courage failed me, and I dared not go up. I know the state he was in two days ago; he must be much more terrible to look at now. Signore," concluded the man, turning to Inglesant with an imploring gesture, "I dare not go up."

"Do you know this man's name?" said Inglesant.

"Yes; they told me his name."

"What is it?"

"Il Cavaliere di Guardino."

At the name of his wife's brother, Inglesant started, and would have dismounted, but checked himself in the stirrup, struck by the action of the friar. He had thrown his arms above his head with a gesture of violent excitement, his sightless eyeballs extended, his face lighted with an expression of rapturous astonishment and delight.

"Who?" he exclaimed. "Who sayest thou? Guardino a leper, and stricken with the plague! Deserted and helpless, is he? too terribly disfigured to be looked upon? The lepers flee him, sayest thou? Holy and blessed Lord Jesus, this is Thy work! He is my mortal foe—the ravisher of my sister—

the destroyer of my own sight! Let me go to him! I will minister to him—I will tend him! Let me go!"

He dismounted from his mule, and, with the wonderful instinct he seemed to possess, turned towards the rock, and began to scramble up the hill, blindly and with difficulty, it is true, but still with sufficient correctness to have reached the ruin without help. There was, to Inglesant, something inexpressibly touching and pitiful in his hurried and excited action, and his struggling determination to accomplish the ascent.

The peasant would have overtaken him to prevent his going up, probably misdoubting his intention. Inglesant checked him.

"Do not stop him," he said. "He is a holy man, and will do what he says. I will go with him. Stay here with my horse."

"You do not know to what you are going, signore," said the peasant, looking at Inglesant with a shudder; "let him go alone. *He cannot see.*"

Inglesant shook his head, and, his brain still slightly dizzy and confused, hastened after the friar, and assisted him to climb the rocky bank. When they had reached the entrance to the hut the friar went hastily in, Inglesant following him to the doorway.

It was a miserable place, and nearly empty, the lepers having carried off most of their possessions with them. On a bed of straw on the farther side, beneath the rock, lay what Inglesant *felt* to be the man of whom he was in search. What he *saw* it is impossible to describe here. The leprosy and the plague combined had produced a spectacle of inexpressible loathing and horror, such as nothing but absolute duty would justify the description of. The corruption of disease made it scarcely possible to recognize even the human form. The poisoned air of the shed was such that a man could scarcely breathe it and live.

The wretched man was rolling on his couch, crying out at intervals, groaning and uttering oaths and curses. Without the slightest faltering the friar crossed the room (it is true he could not see), and kneeling by the bedside, which he found at once, he began, in low and hurried accents, to pour into the ear of the dying man the consoling sound of that Name, which alone, uttered under heaven, has power to reach the departing soul, distracted to all beside. Startled by the sound of a voice close to his ear, for his sight also was gone, the sick man ceased his outcries and lay still.

Never ceasing for a moment, the friar continued, in a rapid and fervent whisper, to pour into his ear the tenderness of Jesus to the vilest sinner, the eternal love that will reign hereafter, the sweetness and peace of the heavenly life. The wretched man lay perfectly still, probably not knowing whether this wonderful voice was of earth or heaven; and Inglesant, his senses confused by the horrors of the room, knelt in prayer in the entrance of the hut.

The fatal atmosphere of the room became more and more dense. The voice of the friar died slowly away; his form, bending lower over the bed, faded out of sight: and there passed across Inglesant's bewildered brain the vision of Another who stood beside the dying man. The halo round His head lighted all the hovel, so that the seamless coat He wore, and the marks upon His hands and feet, were plainly seen, and the pale alluring face was turned not so much upon the bed and upon the monk as upon Inglesant himself, and the unspeakable glance of the Divine eyes met his.

A thrill of ecstasy, terrible to the weakened system as the sharpest pain, together with the fatal miasma of the place, made a final rush and grasp upon his already reeling faculties, and he lost all consciousness, and fell senseless within the threshold of the room.

When he came to himself he had been dragged out of the hut by the peasant, who had ventured at last to ascend the hill. The place was silent; the Cavaliere was dead, and the friar lay across the body in a sort of trance. They brought him out and laid him on the grass, thinking for some time that he was dead also. By and by he opened his sightless eyes, and asked where he was; but he still moved as in a trance. He seemed to have forgotten what had happened; and, with the death of the Cavaliere, the great motive which had influenced him, and which, while it lasted, seemed to have kept his reason from utterly losing its balance, appeared to be taken away. He had lived only to meet and bless his enemy, and this having been accomplished, all reason for living was gone.

Inglesant and the peasant dug a grave with some implements they found in the tavern, and hastily buried the body, the friar pronouncing a benediction. The latter performed this office mechanically, and seemed almost unconscious as to what was passing. His very figure and shape appeared changed, and presented but the shadow of his former self; his speech was broken and unintelligible. Inglesant gave the peasant money, which seemed to him to be wealth, and they mounted and rode silently away.

At Venafro, where they found a monastery of the Cappuccini, they stayed some days, Inglesant expecting that his companion would recover something of his former state of health. But it soon became apparent that this would not be the case; the friar sank rapidly into a condition of mental unconsciousness, and the physicians told Inglesant that although he might linger for weeks, they believed that a disease of the brain was hastening him towards the grave. Inglesant was impatient to return to the Castello; and, leaving the friar to the care of the brothers of his own order, he resumed his journey.

Was it a strange coincidence, or the omniscient rule and will of God, that, at the moment Inglesant lay insensible before the hut, the plague had done its work in the home that he had left? The old Count died first, then some half of the servants, finally, in the deserted house, a little child lay dead upon its couch, and beside it, on the marble floor, lay Lauretta—dead —uncared for.

It was the opinion of Martin Luther that vision of the Saviour, which he himself had seen, were delusions of Satan for the bewildering of the Papists; and there is a story of a monk who left the Beatific Vision that he might take his service in the choir.

Malvolti died at Venafro a short time after Inglesant had left him.

CHAPTER XXXVII.

AFTER the narration of the events just detailed the papers from which the life of Mr. Inglesant has hitherto been compiled become much less minute and personal in character; and when the narrative is resumed, a considerable period of time has evidently elapsed. It is stated that some time after the death of his wife Mr. Inglesant returned to Rome, and assumed a novice's gown in some religious order, but to which of the religious bodies he attached himself is doubtful. It might be thought that he would naturally become a member of the Society of Jesus; but there is reason to conclude that the rule which he intended to embrace was either that of the Benedictines or the Carmelites. As will soon appear, he proceeded no farther than the noviciate, and this uncertainty therefore is of little consequence.

It must be supposed that the distress caused by the death of his wife and child, and by his absence from them at the last, was one motive which caused Inglesant to seek in Rome spiritual comfort and companionship from the Spanish priest Molinos, in whose society he had before found so much support and relief. It was thought, indeed, by many beside Inglesant, amid the excitement which the spread of the method of devotion taught by this man had caused, that a dawn of purer light was breaking over spiritual Rome. God seemed to have revealed Himself to thousands in such a fashion as to make their past lives and worship seem profitless and unfruitful before the brightness and peace that was revealed; and the lords of His heritage seemed for a time to be willing that this light should shine. It appeared for a moment as if Christendom were about to throw off its shackles, its infant swaddling clothes, in which it had been so long wrapped, and, acknowledging that the childhood of the Church was past, stand forth before God with her children around her, no longer distrusted and enslaved, but each individually complete, fellow-citizens with their mother of the household of God. The unsatisfactory rotation of formal penitence and sinful lapse, of wearisome devotion and stale pleasures, had given place to an enthusiasm which believed that, instead of ceremonies and bowing in outer courts, the soul was introduced into heavenly places, and saw God face to face. A wonderful experience, in exchange for lifeless formality and rule, of communion with the Lord, with nothing before the believer, as he knelt at the altar, save the Lord Himself, day by day, unshackled by penance and confession as heretofore. Thousands of the best natures in Rome attached themselves to this method; it was approved by a Jesuit Father, the Pope was known to countenance it, and his nephews were among its followers. The bishops were mostly in favour of it, and in the nunneries of Rome the directors and confessors were preaching it; and the nuns, instead of passing their time over their beads and "Hours," were much alone, engaged in the exercise of mental prayer.

It would indeed be difficult to estimate the change that would have passed over Europe if this one rule of necessary confession before every communion had been relaxed; and in the hope that some increased freedom of religious thought would be secured, many adopted the new method who had no great attachment to the doctrine, nor to the undoubted extravagances which the Quietists, in common with other mystics, were occasionally guilty of, both in word and deed. It cannot be denied, and it is the plea that will be urged in defence of the action of the Jesuits, that freedom of thought as well as of devotion was the motive of numbers who followed the teaching of Molinos. That free speculation and individual growth could be combined with loyalty to acts and ceremonies, hallowed by centuries of recollection and of past devotion, was a prospect sufficiently attractive to many select natures. Some, no doubt, entered into this cause from less exalted motives—a love of fame, and a desire to form a party, and to be at the head of a number of followers; but even among those whose intentions were not so lofty and spiritual as those of Molinos probably were, by far the greater number were actuated by a desire to promote freedom of thought and of worship among Churchmen.

But it was only for a moment that this bright prospect opened to the Church.

The Jesuits and Benedictines began to be alarmed. Molinos had endeavoured to allay the suspicion attached to his teaching, and diminish the aversion that the Jesuits felt towards him, by calling his book "The Spiritual Guide," and by constantly enjoining the necessity of being in all things under the direction of a religious person; but this was felt to point more at the submission to general council than to coming always to the priest, as to the minister of the sacrament of penance, before every communion; especially as Molinos taught that the only necessary qualification for receiving was the being free from mortal sin.

Suddenly, when the reputation of this new society appeared to be at its height, Molinos was arrested, and Father Esparsa, the Jesuit whose approbation had appeared before "The Spiritual Guide," disappeared. What became of the latter was not known, but it was generally supposed that he was "shut up between four walls;" and at any rate he appeared no more in Rome. In the midst of the excitement consequent on these events seventy more persons, all of the highest rank,—Count Vespiriani and his lady, the Confessor of Prince Borghese, Father Appiani of the Jesuits, and others equally well known, —were arrested in one day, and before the month was over more than two hundred persons crowded the prisons of the Inquisition.

The consternation was excessive, when a method of devotion which had been extolled throughout Italy for the highest sanctity to which mortals could aspire was suddenly found to be heretical, and the chief promoters of it hurried from their homes and from their friends, shut up in prison, and in peril of perpetual confinement, if not death. The arrest of Father Appiani was the most surprising. He was accounted the most learned priest in the Roman College, and was arrested on a Sunday in April as he came from preaching. After this no one could guess on whom the blow would fall next. The Pope himself, it was reported, had been examined by the Jesuits. The imminence of the peril brought strength with it. The prisoners, it was whispered, were steady and resolute, and showed more learning than their examiners. Their friends who were still at large, recovering from their first panic, assumed a bold front. Many letters were written to the Inquisitors, advising them to consider well what they did to their prisoners, and assuring them that their interests would be maintained even at the cost of life. Nor did these protests end here. As soon as possible after the arrests a meeting was held at Don Agostino's palace in the Piazza Colonna, to which ladies were summoned as well as men. There, in a magnificent saloon, amid gilding and painting and tapestry, whose splendour was subdued by softened colour and shaded light, were met the élite of Rome. There were ladies in rich attire, yet in whose countenances was seen that refinement of beauty which only religion and a holy life can give—ladies, who, while appearing in public in the rank which belonged to them, were capable in private of every self-denial, trained in the practice of devotion and acts of mercy. There were nuns of the Conception and of the Palestrina, distressed and mortified at being compelled to return to their beads and to their other abandoned forms.

There were present Cereri, Cardinal-Bishop of Como; Cardinals Carpegna and Cigolini, and Cardinal Howard of England (the noblest and most spiritually-minded of the Sacred College), Absolini and Coloredi, Cardinals and Fathers of the Oratory, and Cardinal D'Estrées. Petrucci himself, the most prominent advocate of the Quietist doctrine, was in the room, though incognito, it not being generally known that he was in Rome. There were present many Fathers of the Oratory, men of intellect, refinement, and blameless lives; Don Livio, Duke di Ceri, the Pope's nephew, was there, and the Prince Savelli, many of the highest nobility, and above a hundred gentlemen, all of whom, by their presence, might be supposed to prove their attachment to the teaching of Molinos, their superiority to the sordid motives of worldly prudence and pleasure, and their devotion to spiritual instincts and desires. It would be difficult to imagine scenes more unlike each other; yet, strange as it may appear, it was nevertheless true that this brilliant company, attired in the height of the existing mode, sparkling with jewels and enriched with chastened colour, might not unfitly be considered the successor of those hidden meetings of a few slaves in Nero's household, who first, in that wonderful city, believed in the crucified Nazarene.

The addresses were commenced by the Duke di Ceri, who spoke of the grief caused by the arrest of their friends, and of the exertions that had been made on their behalf. He was followed by other of the great nobles and cardinals, who all spoke in the same strain. All these speeches were delivered in somewhat vague and guarded terms, and as one after another of the speakers sat down, a sense of incompleteness and dissatisfaction seemed to steal over the assembly, as though it were disappointed of something it most longed to hear. The meeting was assured, over and over again, that extreme measures would not be taken against those in prison; that their high rank and powerful connections would save them; the Duke di Ceri had expressly said that he believed his relation and servant, Count Vespiriani, and his lady, would soon be released. The fact was, though the Duke did not choose to state it publicly, that they had been proscribed solely from information gained at the confessional; and this having been much talked of, the Jesuits had resolved, rather than bring any further odium on the sacrament of confession, to discharge both the lady and her husband at once. But, though all this might be true, there was something that remained unsaid—something that was filling all hearts.

What was to be the spiritual future of those assembled? Was this gate of Paradise and the Divine life to be for ever closed, and was earth and all its littleness once more to be pressed upon them without denial, and hypocrisy and the petty details of a formal service once more to be the only spiritual food of their souls? Must they, if they resolved to escape this spiritual death, quit this land and this glorious Church, and seek, in cold and distant lands, and alien Churches, the freedom denied by the tyranny of the leaders of their own? These thoughts filled all minds, and yet none had given them utterance, nor was it surprising that it should be so. Select and splendid as that assembly was, no one knew for certain that his neighbour was not a spy. As was known soon after, Cardinal D'Estrées, who sat there so calm and lofty-looking, furnished the principal evidence against Molinos, swearing that, being his intimate friend, he knew that the real meaning of his friend's printed words was that heretical one of which, in fact, Molinos had never dreamt. It was no wonder that the speeches were cautious and vague.

At last Don Agostino rose, and in a quiet and unaffected tone requested a hearing for his very dear friend, the Cavaliere di San Giorgio, one well known to most of them, whose character was known to all.

A murmur of satisfaction ran through the room, and the audience settled itself down to listen, as though they knew that the real business of the day was about to begin. Inglesant rose in his seat immediately behind his host. He was evidently dressed carefully, with a view to the effect to be produced upon a fastidious and ultra-refined assembly. He wore a cassock of silk, and the gown of a Benedictine made of the finest cloth. His head was tonsured and his hair cut short. He had round his neck a band of fine cambric, and at his wrists ruffles of rich lace; and he wore on his hand a diamond of great value. He had, indeed, to one who saw his dress and not his face, entirely the look of a petit-maître, and even—what is more contemptible still—of a petit-maître priest; yet, as he rose in his seat, there was not a man in all that assembly who would have given a silver scudo for the chances of his life.

His romantic and melancholy story, the death of his wife and child, his assumption of the religious life, and above all, his friendship with Molinos, were known to all; it seemed to many a fitting close to a life of such vicissitude, that at this crisis he should sacrifice himself in the spiritual cause that was dear to all.

He had his speech written before him, every word carefully considered and arranged by himself and some of the first masters of style then in Rome. He began deliberately and distinctly, so that every word was heard, though he spoke in a low voice.

After deprecating the judgment of the assembly upon the artless and unpolished words he was about to address to it, and excusing his rashness in consenting to speak in such an assembly at all, he said,—

"The words of the noble and august personages who have already spoken have left me little to say. Nothing is necessary to be added to their wise and reverend advice. All that remains for us to do is to attempt to carry out in action what they have so well counselled. Our first object, our first duty, is the safety of our friends. But, when this is happily accomplished—as, under such leaders and protected by such names, how can we doubt that it will be?—there are many among us who, with sinking hearts and hushed voices, are inquiring, 'What will come next?'"

He paused, and looked up for a moment, and a murmur of encouragement ran through the room.

"I am not mistaken when I say that in this room, and also in Rome, are many hearts which, within the last few years, and by the teaching of him for whom night and day the prayers of the Church ascend to heaven, have found a peace and a blessedness before unknown; many who have breathed celestial air, and walked the streets of God. Nor am I mistaken—my heart and your presence tell me I am not mistaken—when I say that many are asking themselves, 'How can they renounce this heavenly birthright? How can they live without this Divine intercourse which they have found so sweet—which the purest saints have hallowed with their approval? How can they live without God who have seen Him face to face?' And many are asking themselves, 'Must we leave the walks of men, and the Churches where the saints repose, and wander into the wilderness—into byways among the wild places of heresy, since the

Church seems to close the gates upon this way which is their life?' I risk the deserved censure of this august assembly when I venture to advise—yet even this I am willing to do, if I may serve any—and I venture to advise, No. I myself was born in another country, amid contending forms of faith. I believe that, in the sacrificial worship of our most Holy Church, room is amply given for the perfection of the Contemplative State; and that such lofty devotion can find no fitter scene than the altar of the Lord. As we may hope that, at some future time, the whole Church may come to this holy state, and be raised above many things which, though now perhaps necessary, may in a higher condition fall away; so, if by our continuing in this posture we may hasten such a happy time, this doubtless will be the path Heaven wishes us to walk in. But"—he paused, and the whole assembly listened with breathless attention—"if such is to be our course, it is evident that an understanding is necessary of adjustment between ourselves and the Fathers of the Holy Office and of the Society of Jesus—an adjustment by which a silence must be allowed our Faith—a silence which, for the sake of those amongst us whose consciences are the most refined and heaven-taught, must be understood to imply dissent to much that has lately been acted and taught. We must understand that this exertion of authority is aimed only at the *open* teaching of doctrines in which we still believe, and which are still dear to us; and that liberty is allowed our faith so long as we observe a discreet silence—a liberty which shall extend as far as to admission to the Sacrament without previous confession. On this point surely it is necessary that we have a clearer understanding."

Inglesant stopped, and applause, sufficiently loud and unmistakably sincere, showed that a large proportion of the assembly approved of what had been said.

He spoke a word to Don Agostino, and then went on,—

"I am willing to confess, and this august assembly will be willing to confess, that to the rulers of Christ's ark—those who have to answer for the guidance of the peoples of the world, and who know far better than we can the difficulties and dangers which environ such a task—this allowance to the lower masses of the people, so prone to run to extremes and to err in excess, would seem unwise; and I am not unwilling also to admit that we may have erred in making this way too public, before the world was sufficiently prepared for it. Both for this, and for any other fault, we are willing to suffer penance, and to submit to the Holy Church in silence; but, this acknowledged and performed, we must be allowed, within certain limits, to retain the freedom we have enjoyed, and some manifest token must be given us that such will be the case."

A singular murmur again filled the room—a murmur compounded of intense sympathy and of admiration at the boldness of the speaker.

Inglesant went on.

"But you will ask me, how is this to be obtained? I am allowed to say that I have not undertaken the mission save at the request of others whom it well becomes to direct my service in all things. They consider that for some reason I am fitted for the task. I am—and I speak with all gratitude—a pupil of the reverend and holy Society of Jesus, and whatever I possess I owe to its nursing care. I am besides, though I have never acted in such capacity, still an accredited agent of the Queen Mother of England, that most faithful daughter—I had almost said Martyr—of the Church. I will see the General of the Order, and if this assembly will allow me to speak in its name, I will offer to him our dutiful submission if he, on his part, will give us some public sign that we are allowed our private interpretation upon the late events, and our liberty upon the point which I have named."

When Inglesant sat down Cardinal Howard spoke. He was followed by several others, all of whom complimented the Cavaliere upon his devotion to so good a cause, but abstained from expressing any decided opinion on the expediency of his proposal. But when two or three speeches had been made, the mixed character of the assembly began to show itself. It is true that it had been carefully selected, yet, in order to give it importance and influence, it had been necessary to include in the invitations as many as possible, and the result was soon apparent. There were many present who had joined the ranks of the Quietists more from a weariness of the existing order than from sincere devotion. There were many present who had joined them sincerely, but who, from timidity and caution, were desirous to escape the anger of the Inquisition by submission and silence, and who deprecated any risk of exciting a still more harsh exertion of authority. Both these parties, increased by waverers from the more devoted portion of the company, united in advising that no action should be taken, farther than that which had been already used, and which, it might be hoped, had secured the principal object of their wishes, the release of their friends.

They argued that confession before each communion could not be burdensome to those who were in a state of grace, and therefore had nothing to confess; and even if it were, as the Fathers of the Church judged it necessary for the suppression of error, and for the good of the ignorant and unenlightened, it ought to be submitted to most willingly by those farthest advanced in the spiritual life. These speakers also argued that many things which were held by the Quietists harmlessly to themselves were liable to be misunderstood, and that anything which tended to draw off the mind from the mystery of the Sacrifice of the Mass, or from the examples of the saints, tended to divert the vulgar from devotion to the Saviour, and savoured of Deism.

They argued that although perhaps many things were unnecessary to those whose religious life was far advanced, such as the breviary, beads, images, many prayers, etc., yet it was not so to others, and that no doubt, where it was suitable, relaxation would be easily obtained from one's director. No one had insisted more upon the necessity of a spiritual guide than had Molinos, and it was now the time to prove the reality of our obedience to the voice of the Church.

It was argued that many things in Molinos's writings seemed to tend towards Calvinism, and the doctrine of Efficacious Grace, which no one present—no true child of the Church—could defend,—a doctrine which limited the Grace of God, and turned the free and wide pastures of Catholicism into the narrow bounds of a restricted sect; and it was finally hinted that there was some reason to believe that the promoters of the meeting were acting with a farther intention than at first appeared, and that they desired to introduce changes into the Catholic faith and discipline, under cover of this discussion.

This last insinuation was a home thrust, and was so felt by the meeting. The subject of Efficacious Grace had also been introduced very skilfully by a young priest, a pupil of the Jesuits himself.

After a brief consultation with his party Inglesant replied that a great deal of what had been advanced was unanswerable; that he himself, a pupil of the Jesuits, was as much opposed to the doctrine of Efficacious Grace as any one could be; that it was the intention of no one present to urge any course of action unless the meeting unanimously approved of it; and that, as it appeared that the majority of those present were prepared to submit to the Holy Office, and did not desire any negotiation, nothing farther would be attempted.

There weighed, in truth, upon the hearts of all, and had probably oppressed Inglesant as he spoke, a sense of hopelessness and of contention with an irresistible power. In spite of this feeling, however, the decision of the chiefs drew forth expressions of impatience and regret from the more enthusiastic partizans; but as these were mostly women, who could not address the assembly, or such as were not prepared to make themselves prominent in face of almost certain arrest, the discussion became desultory and ineffectual, and the meeting finally broke up without any decision having been arrived at.

The Piazza was full of carriages and servants, and the Duke di Ceri had an enormous train of equipages following his carriage to escort him beyond the gate, on the way to his villa near Civita Vecchia, whither he returned immediately, not choosing to stay in Rome.

The meeting being over, Don Agostino urged Inglesant to leave Rome; indeed, the Duke had already pressed him to accompany him to Civita Vecchia, but Inglesant declined.

The motives which influenced him were of a mixed nature. He was prompted by the most sincere desire to find out a way both for himself and for others, in which the highest spiritual walk, and the purest condition of spiritual worship, might be possible within the Church of Rome. There was probably nothing in this world which he desired more than this, for in this was included that still more important freedom, the liberty of the reason; for if it were possible for the spirit to be free, while fulfilling the outward observances, and participating in the outward ordinances of the Church, so also it must be possible for the reason to be free too.

It had been this very desire, singular as it may seem, which had attached him to the Society of the Jesuits. Not only were their tenets—notably that of sufficient grace given to all men —of wider and more catholic nature than the Augustinian doctrines held by most bodies both of Churchmen and Protestants, but the Society had always, in all its dealings with men, shown a notable leaning to tolerance, even, so its enemies asserted, of sin and vice.

But besides these motives which had something of a refined and noble character, Inglesant had others. A life of intrigue and policy had, from training and severe practice, become a passion and necessity of his life. To leave the field where such a fight was going on, to remain in Rome, even, an inactive spectator, allowed to pursue his own path merely from the ignoble fact that he was not worth arrest—both these courses of action were intolerable to him. He had promised Molinos that he would not be wanting in the hour of trial, and he would keep his word. He was utterly powerless, as the events of the last few moments would have shown him had he not known it before. The most powerful, the noblest confederacy fell away impotently before an invisible yet well-understood power, and a sense of vague irresistible force oppressed him, and showed him the uselessness of resistance.

Nevertheless he requested the loan of Don Agostino's carriage that he might go at once to the General of the Society. He was shown at once into a small cabinet, where he was kept waiting a few moments, the General in fact being engaged at that moment in listening to a detailed account of the meeting, and of the speeches delivered at it. He however entered the room in a few minutes, and the two men saluted each other with the appearance of cordial friendship. Inglesant had not changed his dress, and the General ran his eyes over it with somewhat of an amused expression, doubtless comparing the account he had just received with the appearance of his visitor, the purpose of which he was fully alive to.

Inglesant began the conversation.

"Your reverence is probably acquainted already with the meeting in the Piazza Colonna, and with its objects and results. I, however, have come to relate what passed as far as you may be disposed to listen, and to give any information, in a perfectly open and sincere manner, which you may wish to receive. In return for this I wish to ask your reverence two or three questions which I hope will not be unpleasant, and which you will of course answer or not as it pleases you."

"As I understand the meeting, Signore Cavaliere," said the General with a slight smile, "it rejected your mediation, in spite of the elaborate care with which the proposal was brought before it, a care extending to the minutest particulars, and the chastened eloquence and perfect style in which it was offered."

This sarcasm fell comparatively harmlessly upon Inglesant, preoccupied as his thoughts were. He therefore bowed, saying,—

"The meeting rejected my mediation, or rather it thought that no mediation was necessary, and trusted itself implicitly to the fatherly care of the Society of Jesus."

"What does the meeting representing this new heresy demand?"

"It demands nothing but the deliverance of its friends now in prison."

"And nothing else?"

"Nothing else from the meeting. I am here to demand something else."

"On your own behalf alone?"

"On my own responsibility solely; but if my request is granted, many will be benefited by my work."

"Have you no abettors? You came here in Don Agostino's coach."

"I am Don Agostino's dear and intimate friend, and it is not much that he should lend me his coach. I have many friends in Rome."

"I know it," said the Jesuit cordially, "and among them the Order of Jesus is not the least sincere."

Inglesant bowed, and there was a slight pause. Then the General said,—

"What do you demand?"

"I demand spiritual freedom—the freedom of silence."

"Freedom will be abused."

"Not by me nor by my friends. We pledge ourselves to unbroken silence. All we demand is freedom to worship God in private as He Himself shall lead us. We ask for no change in public doctrine. We seek no proselytes. In fact, we confine ourselves to one desire, the sacrament without confession."

The Jesuit made no reply, but continued to look fixedly into Inglesant's face.

"It seems to me, Father," Inglesant went on, with a touch of bitterness in his tone, "that the Society is changing its policy, or rather that it has a different policy for different classes of men. So far as I have known it, it has pursued a course of compromise with all men, and especially with the weak and frail. It has always appeared to me a trait much to be admired, that in which it is likest to the divine charity itself; but the world has been very severe upon it. And when the world says, 'You have pandered to vice in every form; you have rendered the confessional easy of approach, and the path of penitence smooth to the impenitent; you have been lenient, nay more than lenient, to the loose liver, to the adulterers and menslayers,—surely you might be mild to the devout; surely you might extend a little of this infinite pity to the submissive and obedient, to the pure in life and soul who seek after God; 'Difficile est satiram non scribere. Nam quis iniquae tam patiens urbis, tam ferreus, ut teneat se?'' If the world says this, what am I to answer? For, if it be so necessary to confine the soul to narrow dogmas lest she go astray, it must be also necessary to deal freely and sharply with these sins of the flesh, lest they bring men to sensuality and to hell. By thus acting, as it seems to me, and not by making the righteous sad, you would follow the teaching of those beautiful words of one of your Fathers, who says, 'that the main design of our Society is to endeavour the establishment of virtue, to carry on the war against vice, and to cultivate an infinite number of souls.'"

"You are a bold man, Signore Cavaliere. For far less words than you have spoken men have grown old in the dungeons of Saint Angelo, where the light of day never comes."

Inglesant, who rather wished to be imprisoned, and flattered himself that he should soon be released, was not alarmed at this menace, and remained silent.

A pause ensued, during which something like this ran through the Jesuit's mind :—

"Shall I have this man arrested at once, or wait? He came to us well recommended—the favourite pupil of an important member of the Society, who assured us that he was an instrument perfectly trained, ready at all points for use, and of a temper and spirit far above the average, not to be lost to the Order on any account. He has proved all that was said of him, and much more. The Papal throne itself is under obligation to him. But do we want such a man so much? I have scores of agents, of instruments ready to my hand, with whom I need use no caution—no finesse; why waste any on *one*, however highly finished and trained? But, on the other hand, I speak this in Rome, where everything is our own, and where the sense of power may have unfitted me from properly understanding this man's value. In the rough regions *in partibus,* such a tool as this, fine and true as steel, tried in the fire as steel, doubtless is not lightly to be thrown away; at all events, nothing is to be done hastily. So long as he is in Rome he is safe, and may be clapped up at any moment. I almost wish he would leave, and go back to his teacher."

All this occupied but a few seconds, and, as the Jesuit made no answer, Inglesant, who scarcely expected any definite reply, took his leave. To his surprise, however, the General insisted on accompanying him to his coach. They crossed the courtyard to where the equipage of Don Agostino stood in the street. In the excited imagination of Rome at that moment, the sight of Don Agostino's carriage before the Jesuits' College had attracted a crowd. When Inglesant appeared, accompanied by the General, the excitement became intense. As they reached the carriage door, Inglesant knelt upon the pavement, and requested the Jesuit's blessing; the foremost of the crowd, impressed by this action, knelt too. Inglesant rose, entered the carriage, and was driven off; and two different rumours spread through Rome— one, that the Society had come to terms with the Quietists through the mediation of the Cavaliere; the other, that the Cavaliere di San Giorgio had betrayed the Quietists, and made his peace with the Order; and this last report received the greatest amount of credit.

CHAPTER XXXVIII.

The Inquisitors and the Jesuits continued to adopt a policy of great leniency to those who were in prison. The majority, after one examination, were released, merely going through the form of abjuring heresies and errors of which they had never dreamed. Owing to this politic course of action, assisted by the dislike and contempt which the people felt towards the then Pope, who was supposed to be a favourer of Molinos, and of whose dull reign the Romans were weary, a great change took place in the opinions of the populace. The credit of the Jesuits rose exceedingly, and they became celebrated for their excessive mildness, who before had been blamed for their rigour. To such an extent did they gain in popular estimation, that the chiefs of the defeated party were unable to keep back great numbers of the followers of Molinos from coming in to the Inquisitors every day, to accuse themselves of heresy, and to offer themselves to penance. These being very gently treated, and dismissed in peace, testified everywhere to the clemency of the Holy Office and of the Jesuits. The excitement, which before had set in one direction, was now turned with equal impetuosity in another; and many who had before, doubtless in perfect sincerity, found—or fancied they found—spiritual satisfaction in the "method of contemplation," now discovered an equal benefit in an excessive orthodoxy. The Quietist party was utterly crushed, and put to ignominious silence; and Molinos himself became an object of hatred and contempt; while, all the time, with extraordinary inconsistency, it was publicly reported that the reason of this surprising clemency was the great support which his doctrine received from the mystical Divinity, which had been authorized by so many canonizations, and approved by so many Councils and Fathers of the Church.

The leaders of the defeated party lived as in a desert. Their saloons, which only a few days before had been crowded, were now empty, and Cardinal Petrucci himself was visited by no one; while the Jesuits were everywhere received with enthusiasm, so true to the character that the Satirist gave fifteen hundred years before did the Roman populace remain—

"Sequitur fortunam, ut semper, et odit
"Damnatos."

Some slight portion of this popular applause fell to Inglesant's lot, whichever report was believed—whether as the agent of the Society he had betrayed his friends, or had used his influence to procure this unexpected policy of mercy—either supposition procured him notoriety and even approbation. It now only remained to watch the fate of Molinos, and the inmates of Don Agostino's palace waited in silence the policy of their triumphant opponents. The Jesuits began by circulating reports of his hypocrisy and lewd course of life—facts of which they said they had convincing evidence. They said that these scandals had been proved before the Pope, who then, and not till then, had renounced his cause. The Romans replied to this story that they believed it, for the Pope was a good judge of such matters, but none at all of the questions of theology on which the quarrel had previously turned. There was not at the time, and there never has been since, the slightest evidence offered publicly that these stories had the least foundation; but they amply served their turn, insomuch that when Molinos was brought out to the Minerva on the day of his condemnation, he was saluted by the people with cries of "Fire! Fire!" and, but that his coach was resolutely defended by the Sbirri and guards, he would have been massacred by the furious mob.

When the morning rose upon the day on which his condemnation was to take place, the tribunal of the Minerva, and all the avenues and corridors leading to it, were thronged with an excited crowd. For days before, all the efforts both of money and favour had been exerted to procure good places in the court itself, and those who were unable to gain these coveted seats lined the corridors and staircases, while the populace outside thronged the streets leading from the prison of the Inquisition. The windows and house-tops were crowded; scarcely an inhabitant of Rome but was to be found somewhere on the line of route; the rest of the city was a desert.

The vine-clad wastes of the Aventine, the green expanse of the Campo Vaccino, and the leafy walls of the Colosseum and of the arches, were lying under the morning sunlight, calm and quiet as in the midst of a happy and peaceful world. As Inglesant came across from the lonely convent where he still occasionally lodged, and turned out of the square of the Ara Cœli, the silent tenantless houses and palaces looked down with dim eyes like a city of the dead; and as he came into the Via del Gesu the distant hum and murmur of the crowd first broke upon his ear. Here and there a belated spectator like himself turned out of some bye-street or doorway, and hastened towards the Piazza della Minerva.

Inglesant turned off by a side street, and, following the narrow winding lanes with which he was well acquainted, came out into the Via di Coronari at some midway distance between the prison of the Inquisition and the Minerva. He was just in time. As he stationed himself against the wall of the Church of St. Maria de Anima and the German Hospital, he knew, by the excitement and frantic cries of the crowd, that

Molinos was not far off. He was brought along the street in a large coach with glass windows, a Dominican friar seated at his side. On each side of the carriage and at the horses' heads the Sbirri and Swiss guards exerted themselves manfully to keep back the people and to clear the way. A deafening shout and cry rose unceasingly, and every few moments the crowd, pressing upon the carriage and the guards, caused them to come to a dead stop. Clinging to the horses' heads, to the carriage itself, to the halberds of the Swiss, climbing on the steps and on the back of the coach, had the crowd desired a rescue, Inglesant thought one bold and decided leader might have accomplished it in a few desperate moments. But the mob desired nothing less. This man—who but a few weeks ago had been followed by admiring crowds, who had been idolized in courtly saloons, whose steps and walks had been watched with the tender and holy devotion with which a people watches the man whose life it takes to be hid in God; whom loving modest women had pointed out to their children as the holy priest whom they must love and remember all their lives; whom passionate women, on whose souls the light of God had broken, had followed trembling, that they might throw themselves at his feet, and, clinging to his gown, hear the words of gospel from his lips; to whom desperate men had listened whom no other voice had ever moved;—this man was now the execration of the mob of Rome. Amidst the roar and din around no word was distinguishable but that terrible one of "Fire!" that pointed to a heretic's death at the stake; and, but for the determined resistance of the guards, Molinos would have been dragged from the coach and butchered in the streets.

When the carriage arrived opposite the spot upon which Inglesant had posted himself, he could see Molinos's face as he sat in the coach. He was carefully dressed in his priestly habit, and looked about him with a cheerful serene countenance. "He looks well," said a man, not far from Inglesant, who had been very bitter against the prisoner; "the secret of his success is not far to seek, for his face possesses all the charms that are able to captivate, especially the fair sex."

When the coach was close to Inglesant the crowd made another and most determined attack, and the horses came to a stand. The cries of "Fire! Fire!" rose louder and more fiercely, and the guards were for a moment beaten from one of the doors. It seemed that nothing could prevent the people from dragging their victim into the street; Inglesant felt his blood turn cold, fully expecting to see the massacre performed before his eyes; but before the people could open the door, which seemed fastened on the inside, the guard rallied, and by the free use of their halberds and short swords recovered the coach, and drove back the mob.

Through all this scene Molinos had preserved his perfectly unconcerned expression, and his eyes, wandering calmly over the people, at last rested upon the spot where Inglesant stood. Whether he recognized him or not Inglesant did not know, for he involuntarily drew back and shrank from his eye. He learned afterwards that Molinos did recognize him, and also noticed his recoil. "He fears I should compromise him with the furious crowd," he thought; "he need not fear."

Inglesant's movement was caused, however, by a thought very different from this one, which indeed never occurred to him. He was ashamed to meet Molinos's eye. In the daylight and sunshine they had walked together, but when the trial came, the one was taken, and all the rest escaped. It was impossible but that some at least of the fortunate many should feel some pangs of uneasiness and doubt. Inglesant especially, the agent and confidant of the Jesuits, was open to such thoughts, and before the single-hearted uncompromising priest and confessor could not but feel in some sort condemned. The carriage passed on amid the unabated fury of the people, and, turning aside down a narrow winding lane, he entered the Dominicans' Church, to the reserved part of which he had a ticket of admission, to be ready for the final scene.

Molinos was taken to one of the corridors of the Minerva, where he stood for some time looking about him very calmly, and returning all the salutes which were made him by those who had formerly been of his acquaintance. To all inquiries he returned but one answer; that they saw a man who was defamed, but who was penitent (infamato ma penitente). After he had stood here some time he was conducted into a small apartment, where a sumptuous repast was spread before him, and he was invited to partake as of his last luxurious indulgence before being shut up in a little cell for life. A strange banquet! and a strange taste such delicacies must have to a man at such a time.

After dinner he was carried into the Church, as in a triumph, in an open chair upon the shoulders of the Sbirri. The tapers upon the altar shrines showed more clearly than did the dim and sober daylight that penetrated beneath the darkened roofs the three mystic aisles of the strange Church, which were filled with a brilliant company of cardinals, nobles, innumerable ladies, gentlemen of every rank, ecclesiastics without end. The dark marble walls, the sumptuous crowd, the rich colours of the stained glass, gave a kind of lurid splendour to the scene; while on every side the sculptured forms upon the monuments, with stolid changeless features, stood out pale amidst the surrounding gloom; and here and there, where free space was kept, the polished marble floor reflected the sombre brilliancy of the whole.

As Molinos was brought up to his place he made a low and devout reverence to the Cardinals, and his manner was perfectly possessed and without a show of fear or shame. He was made to stand up before the altar, a chain was bound round him and fastened to his wrists, and a wax taper was placed in his hand. Then with a loud voice a friar read his Process, so as to be heard by all in the Church; and as some of the articles were read, there were loud cries from the reverend and polite assembly of "Fire! Fire!"

In a few moments the sight was over, and Molinos was led back to the street, to be placed this time in a close carriage, and taken back to the prison, where his cell was prepared. As Inglesant stepped back into the aisle of the Church he felt some one pull him by his Benedictine gown, and, turning round, he saw a lady in a velvet masque. She appeared excited, and, as far as he could see, was weeping, and her voice, which he thought he recognized, was broken and indistinct.

"Cavaliere," she said, "he will stop a moment in the vestibule before they put him in the coach. I want him to have this—he must have it—it will be a relief and consolation to him unspeakable. They will stop all of us, and will let no one come to him; but they will let you. You are a Jesuit, and their friend. For the love of Gesu, Cavaliere, do him and me and all of us this favour. He will bless you and pray for you. He will intercede for you. For the love of God, Cavaliere!"

She was pleading with such eager tearfulness and such

hurried speech and gesture, that he could not doubt her truth, yet he paused a moment.

"Surely I know your voice?" he said.

"Ah! you know me," replied the masque, "but that is of no consequence. Another moment, and it will be too late. Cavaliere! for the love of Gesu!"

Inglesant took the small paper packet, which seemed to contain a casket, and went down the fast emptying Church. As he reached the entrance he turned and looked back for the velvet masque, but she was nowhere to be seen. His mind was full of suspicion, yet he was not unwilling to fulfil his mission. He should, at any rate, speak to Molinos, and perhaps grasp his hand.

In the vestibule Molinos stood alone, a circle being kept at some distance round him by the guard. His manner was unchanged and calm. The select crowd stood around gazing at him with eager curiosity; outside might be heard again the shouting of the mob, and the cry of "Fire!" Inglesant advanced towards the Captain of the Sbirri; but to his surprise, before he could speak, the latter made a sign, and the guards fell back to let him pass. A murmur ran through the crowd, and every one pressed forward with intense eagerness. Molinos looked up, and an expression of grateful pleasure lighted up his face as he extended his hand. Inglesant grasped it with emotion, and looking him in the face, said,—

"Adieu, Father; you are more to be envied than we. You are clothed in the heavenly garment and sit down at the supper of the King; we wander in the outer darkness, with an aching conscience that cannot rest."

The expression of the other's face was compassionate and beautiful, and he said,—

"Adieu, Cavaliere; we shall meet again one day, when the veil shall be taken from the face of God, and we shall see Him as He is.".

As Inglesant grasped his hand he slipped the casket into it, and as he did so dropped on one knee. The hand of the priest rested on his head for a moment, and in the next he had risen and stepped back, and the guards closed in for the last time round Molinos, and the crowd pressed after, following them to the coach.

When the carriage had driven off, and the crowd somewhat

dispersed, Inglesant came down the steps, and was turning to the right into the Corso when he was surprised to see that the Captain of the Sbirri had not followed his prisoner, but was standing on the causeway with two or three of his men, near a plain carriage which was waiting. As Inglesant came up he turned to him, and said politely,—

"Pardon, Signore Cavaliere, I must ask you to come with me. You have conveyed a packet to a condemned prisoner— a grave offence—a packet which contains poison. You will come quietly, no doubt."

"I will come quietly, certainly," said Inglesant. "Where are we going? to the Inquisition?"

"No, no," said the other, as he followed the new prisoner into the coach; "yours is a civil offence; we are going to the St. Angelo."

"The General must have a taste for theatricals," thought Inglesant as the coach rolled off, "or he never could have planned such a melodrama."

On their arrival at the Castle he was conducted into a good room, not in the tower, which commanded an extensive view of St. Peter's. Great liberty was allowed him, everything he liked to pay for was procured for him, and at certain hours he was allowed to walk on the glacis and fortifications.

The second day of his confinement was drawing to a close when he was visited by the Dominican who had attended Molinos. This monk, who seemed a superior person, had evidently been impressed by the conversation and character of his prisoner. After the first greeting he said,—

"That unhappy man requested me to bring you a message. It was to the effect that he had done you wrong. He saw you among the crowd as he was being brought to the Minerva, and noticed that you shrank back. He accused you in his mind of fearing to be compromised; he knows now that, on the contrary, you were watching for an opportunity to do him a service. It was but the thought of a moment, but he could not rest until he had acknowledged it, and begged your forgiveness. He bade me also to tell you that 'the bruised reed is not broken, nor the smoking flax quenched.'"

"Where did you leave him?" said Inglesant.

"At the door of his cell, which he calls his cabinet."

"'The smoking flax is not quenched,'" said Inglesant; "I

hear that one of his followers, a day or two ago, before the tribunal told the examiners to their faces that they 'were a company of unjust, cruel, and heretical men, and that the measure which they dealt to others was the same that Christ Himself had received from His persecutors.'"

"It is true," said the Dominican, "and it is true also that he is released; such, on the contrary, is the clemency of the Church."

After an imprisonment of about a fortnight, as Inglesant was one day taking his usual walk upon the fortifications, he was informed that the General of the Order was in his room, and desired to see him. He went to him immediately, and was received with great appearance of friendliness.

"You will pardon my little plot, Cavaliere," said the General, "especially as I gave orders that you should be made very comfortable here. I wished to see in what manner and how far you were our servant, and I have succeeded admirably. I find, as I imagined, that you are invaluable; but it must be on your own terms, and at your own time. You are faithful and unflinching when you have undertaken anything, but each mission must be entered upon or renounced at your own pleasure. I hope you have not been nourishing bitter thoughts of me during your incarceration here."

"Far from it," replied Inglesant; "I have nothing to complain of. I have all I want, and the view from these windows is, as you see, unrivalled in Rome. If it consists with your policy, I should take it as a great favour were you to inform me whether the velvet masque was a mere tool or not. I could have sworn that her accent and manner were those of a person speaking the truth; still, when the captain of the Sbirri made way for me I thought I was in the toils."

"Your penetration did not err. The lady was the Countess of ——. She conceived the idea of communicating with Molinos herself, and confided it to her director—not in confession, observe. He consulted me, and we advised what took place; and, what may console you still farther, we did the lady no wrong. We have reason to know that, besides the poison, some writing was conveyed to Molinos together with the casket, by which he obtained information which he was very desirous of receiving. You will forgive me now, since your 'amour propre' is not touched, and your friend's purpose is served."

There was a pause, after which the General said,—

"You have deserved well of the Order—few better; and whatever their enemies may say, the Companions of Jesus are not unmindful of their children, nor ungrateful, unless the highest necessities of the general good require it. You look upon the prosecution of Molinos as an act of intolerable tyranny, and you are yourself eager to enter upon a crusade on behalf of religious freedom and of the rights of private devotion and judgment. You are ready to engage almost single-handed against the whole strength of the Society of Jesus, of the Curia, and of the existing powers. I say nothing of the Quixotic nature of the enterprise; that would not deter you. Nor of its utter hopelessness; how hopeless you may judge from the sudden collapse of the party of Molinos—a party so favoured in high places, so fashionable, patronized, as has been said, even by the Pope himself. You may also judge of this from the fact, of which you are probably aware, that every detail of your late meeting was communicated to us by the President of that meeting, and by many of those who attended it. But in speaking of these matters to you, whose welfare I sincerely seek, I address myself to another argument which I imagine will have more weight. You have only considered this coveted spiritual freedom as the right of the favoured few, of the educated and refined. You have no desire and no intention that it should be extended to the populace. But you do not consider, as those who have the guidance of the Church polity are bound to consider, that to grant it to the one and deny it to the other is impossible; that these principles are sure to spread; that in England and in other countries where they have spread they have been the occasion of incalculable mischiefs. You are standing at this moment, thanks chiefly to the nurture and clemency of the much-abused Society of Jesus, at a point where you may choose one of two roads, which, joining here, will never meet again. The question is between individual license and obedience to authority; and upon the choice, though you may not think it, depends the very existence of Christianity in the world. Between unquestioning obedience to authority and absolute unbelief there is not a single permanent resting-place, though many temporary halts may be made. You will scarcely dispute this when you remember that every heretical sect admits it. They only differ as to what the authority is to which obedience is due. We, in Rome at least, cannot be expected to allow any authority save that of the Catholic Church, and indeed what other can you place instead of it— a Book? Do you think that those who have entered upon the path of inquiry will long submit to be fettered by the pages of dead languages? You know more of this probably than I do, from your acquaintance with the sceptics of other lands."

He paused as if waiting for a reply, but Inglesant did not speak; perhaps the logic of the Jesuit seemed to him unanswerable—especially in the St. Angelo at Rome.

After a few seconds the latter went on,—

"Ah! I fear you still bear me some malice. If so, I regret it very much. As I said before, you have no truer friend in Rome than the Order and its unworthy General. I am convinced, both by my own experience and by the reports of others, that you are an invaluable friend and agent of the Society in countries where men like you, gentlemen of honour, bold, unflinching, and of spotless name, are wanted at every turn,— men who have the confidence of both parties, of enemies as well as friends. But long ere this you will have seen that here in Rome we do things differently; here we strike openly and at once, and we require agents of a far lower type, not so much agents, indeed, as hammers ready to our hand. Your refined nature is altogether out of place. As a friend I recommend your return to England. Father St. Clare is there, and no doubt requires you, and I am very certain that the climate of Rome will not suit your health. You have passed some years very pleasantly in Italy, as I believe, in spite of your share in those great sorrows to which we all are heir; and though I am grieved to separate you from your friends, the noblest in Rome, yet it is better that you should be parted in this manner than by sharper and more sudden means. Every facility shall be given you for transferring your property to England, and I hope you will take with you no unpleasant recollections of this city and of the poor Fathers of Jesus, who wish you well."

He pronounced these last words with so much feeling that Inglesant could only reply,—

"I have nothing to say of the Society but what is good. It has ever been most tender and parental to me. I shall go away with nothing but sadness and affection in my heart; with nothing but gratitude towards you, Father, with nothing but reverence towards this city—the mother of the World."

CHAPTER XXXIX.

For a long time nothing was found among the papers from which these memoirs have been compiled relative to Mr. Inglesant's life subsequent to his return to England; but at last the following imperfect letter was found, which is here given as containing all the information on the subject which at present is known to exist.

The date, with the first part of the letter, is torn off. The first perfect line is given. The spelling has been modernized throughout. The superscription is as follows:—

>   Mr. Anthony Paschall,
>   Physician,
>   London.
> from his friend,
>   Mr. Valentine Lee,
>   Chirurgeon,
>   Of Reading.

From a certain tone in parts of the letter it would seem that the writer was one of those who gave cause for the accusation of scepticism brought in those days against the medical profession generally.

* * * * * that vine, laden with grapes worked in gold and precious stones, after the manner of Phrygian work, which, according to Josephus, Tacitus, and other writers, adorned the Temple at Jerusalem, and was seen of many when that Temple was destroyed; a manifest continuance of the old Eastern worship of Bacchus, so dear to the human frailty. As says the poet Anacreon, " Make me, good Vulcan, a deep bowl, and carve on it neither Charles's Wain, nor the sad Orion, but carve me out a vine with its swelling grapes, and Cupid, Bacchus, and Bathillus pressing them together." For it is a gallant philosophy, and the deepest wisdom, which, under the shadow of talismans and austere emblems, wears the colours of enjoyment and of life.

Methinks if the Puritans of the last age had known that the same word in Latin means both worship and the culture of polite life, they would not have condemned both themselves and us to so many years of shadowy gloom and of a morose antipathy to all delight. And though they will perchance retort upon me that the same word in the Greek meaneth both worship and bondage, yet I shall reply that it was a service of love and pleasure—a service in which all the beauties of earth were called upon to aid, and in which the Deity was best pleased by the happiness of His creatures, whose every faculty of delight had been fully husbanded and trained. In these last happy days, since his gracious Majesty's return, we have seen a restoration of a cheerful gaiety, and adorning of men's lives, when painting and poetry, and, beyond all, music, have smoothed the rough ways and softened the hard manners of men.

I came to Oxford, travelling in the Flying Coach with a Quaker who inveighed greatly against the iniquity of the age. At Oxford I saw more than I have space to tell you of; amongst others, Francis Tatton, who, you will recollect, left his religion since the King's return, and sheltered himself amongst the Jesuits. He was but lately come to Oxford, and lodged at Francis Alder's against the Fleur-de-lis. I dined with him there along with some others, and it being a Friday, they had a good fish dinner with white wine. Among the guests was one Father Lovel, a Jesuit. He has lived in Oxford many years to supply service for the Catholics, so bold and free are the Papists now.

I conversed with another of the guests, a physician, who after dinner took me to his house in Bear Lane, and showed me his study, in a pleasant room to the south, overlooking some of Christ Church gardens. Here he began to complain of the Royal Society, and the Virtuosi, and I soon saw that he was a follower of Dr. Gideon Harvey and Mr. Stubbes. "The country owes much," he said, "to such men as Burleigh, Walsingham, Jewel, Abbot, Usher, Casaubon; but if this new-fangled philosophy and mechanical education is to bear the bell, I foresee that we shall look in vain in England for such men again. In these deep and subtle inquiries into natural philosophy and the intricate mechanisms by which this world is said to be governed.

neither physic will be unconcerned nor will religion remain unshaken amidst the writings of these Virtuosi. That art of reasoning by which the prudent are discriminated from fools, which methodizes and facilitates our discourse, which informs us of the validity of consequences and the probability of arguments—that art which gives life to solid eloquence, and which renders statesmen, divines, physicians, and lawyers accomplished —how is this cried down and vilified by the ignoramuses of these days!"

I pleased myself with inspecting this man's books, with which his study was well stored, and with the view from his window; but I let his tongue run on uncontradicted, seeing that he was of the old Protestant and scholastic learning, which is never open to let in new light. He entertained me, besides, with a long discourse to prove that Geber the chemist was not an Indian King, and informed me with great glee that the Royal Society, among other new-fangled propositions, had conceived the idea of working silk into hats, which project, though the hatters laughed at it, yet to satisfy them trial was made, and for twenty shillings they had a hat made, but it proved so bad that any one might have bought a better one for eighteenpence.

He was entering upon a long argument against Descartes, to refute whom he was obliged to contradict much that he had said before, but at this time I excused myself and left him.

When I came out from this man's house the college bells were going for Chapel, as they used to do in the old time; methought it was the prettiest music I had heard for many a day. I went to see an old man I remembered in Jesus Lane. I found him in the same little house, dressed in his gown tied round the middle, the sleeves pinned behind, and his dudgeon with a knife and bodkin; it was the fashion for grave people to wear such gowns in the latter end of Queen Elizabeth's days. He says he is 104. When I was a boy at Oxon I used to be always inquiring of him of the old time, the rood lofts, the ceremonies in the College Chapels; and his talk is still of Queen Bess her days, and of the old people who remembered the host and the wafer bread and the roods in the Churches. In my time, at Oxford, crucifixes were common in the glass in the study windows, and in the chamber windows pictures of saints. This was "before the wars." What a different world it was before the wars! What strange old-world customs and thoughts and stories vanished like phantoms when the war trumpets sounded, and great houses and proud names, and dominions and manors, and stately woods, crumbled into dust, and every man did as seemed good to himself, and thought as he liked.

On the Sunday I went to St. Mary's, and heard a preacher and herbalist, who spoke of the virtues of plants and of the Christian life in one breath. He told us that Homer writ sublimely and called them χειρες θεων, the hands of the Gods, and that we ought to reach to them religiously with praise and thanksgiving. "God Almighty," he said, "hath furnished us with plants to cure us within a few miles of our own abodes, and we know it not."

The next day I came to Worcester by the post, to the house of my old friend Nathaniel Tomkins, who is now one of the Prebends and Receptor. He lives in the close, or College Green, as they call it here. He comes of a family of musicians. His grandfather was chanter of the Choir of Gloucester; his father organist to the same Cathedral of Worcester, and one of his uncles organist of St. Paul's and gentleman of the Chapel Royal, and another, of whom more anon, gentleman of the Privy Chamber to His Majesty Charles the First, and well skilled in the practical part of music, and was happily translated to the celestial choir of angels before the troubles.

I was pleased to see the faithful city recovered from the ashes in which she sat when I was here last, and the daily service of song again restored to the Cathedral Church, though the latter is much out of repair and dimmed as to its splendour. I like that religion the best which gives us sweet anthems and solemn organ music and lively parts of melody.

I had not been here long when my friend the Receptor told me that if I should stay two or three days longer, I should hear as good a concert of violins as any in England, and also hear a gentleman lately come from Italy, whose skill as a lutinist and player on the violin had preceded him. When I asked for the name of this gentleman, he told me it was that Mr. John Inglesant who was servant to the late King, and of whom so much was spoken in the time of the Irish Rebellion. When I heard this I resolved to stay, as you may suppose, considering that we have more than once spoken together of this person and desired to see him, especially since it had been reported that he was returned to England.

I therefore willingly promised to remain, and spent my time in practising on the violin, and in the city and cathedral. I walked upon the river bank, and up and down the fine broad streets leading from the bridge to the cathedral. From the gates of the chancel down the stone steps the strange light streamed on to the paved floor of the nave, chill and silent as the grave until the strains of the organs awoke. Mr. Tomkins told me that the loyal gentry of the surrounding counties had, during the usurpation, made it a point of honour to purchase and trade in Worcester, for the relief and encouragement of the citizens, who were reduced to so low an ebb by the battle and taking of the city.

Thursday was the day appointed for the music meeting, and on that day I accompanied Mr. Tomkins to the house of Mr. Barnabas Oley, another of the Prebends, who, you may remember, wrote a preface, a year or two ago, to Mr. Herbert's "Country Parson." He also lives in the College Green, and we found the company assembling in an oak parlour, which looked upon an orchard where the trees were in full blossom. There were present several of the clergy, and two or three physicians and other gentlemen, who practised upon the violin.

As we entered the room, Mr. Oley was speaking of Mr. Inglesant, who was expected to come presently with the Dean.

"I remember him well," he was saying, "when I was in poverty and sequestration in the late troubles. He was supposed to be in all the King's secrets, and was constantly employed in private messages and errands. Some said that he was a concealed Papist, but I have known him to attend the Church service very devoutly. I recollect when I was in the garrison at Pontefract Castle, and used to preach there as long as it held out for his Majesty, that this Mr. Inglesant suddenly appeared amongst us, though the leaguer was very close, and I know he attended service there once or twice. I was often at that time in want of bread, during my hidings and wanderings, and obliged to change my habit, and did constantly appear in a cloak and gray clothes. On one of these occasions, when I was in great distress and was diligently and particularly sought for by the rebels, who would willingly have gratified those that would have discovered me, I fell in with this Mr. Inglesant at an inn in Buckinghamshire. He was then in company with one whom I knew to be a Popish Priest, but they both exerted themselves very kindly in my behalf, and conducted me to the house of a Catholic gentleman in those parts by whom I was entertained several days. Before this, I now recollect, at the beginning of the wars, I met Mr. Inglesant at Oxford. I was in the shop of a bookseller named Forrest, against All Souls' College. I remember that I took up Plato's select dialogues, 'De rebus divinis,' in Greek and Latin, and excepted against some things as superfluous and cabalistical, and that Mr. Inglesant, who was then a very young man, defended the author in a way that showed his scholarship. It was summer weather and very warm, and the enemy's cannon were playing upon the city as we could hear as we talked in the shop."

While Mr. Oley was thus recollecting his past troubles, Mr. Dean was announced, and entered the room accompanied by Mr. Inglesant and by a servant who carried their violins. You are, I know, acquainted with the Dean, who is also Bishop of St. David's, and who, they say, will be Bishop of Worcester also before long, so I need not describe him. The first sight of Mr. Inglesant pleased me very much. He wore his own hair long, after the fashion of the last age, but in other respects he was dressed in the mode, in a French suit of black satin, with cravat and ruffles of Mechlin lace. His expression was lofty and abstracted, his features pale and somewhat thin, and his carriage gave me the idea of a man who had seen the world, and in whom few things were capable of exciting any extreme interest or attention. His eyes were light blue, of that peculiar shade which gives a dreamy and indifferent expression to the face. His manner was courteous and polite, almost to excess, yet he seemed to me to be a man who was habitually superior to his company, and I felt in his presence almost as I should do in that of a prince. Something of this doubtless was due to the sense I had of the part he had played in the great events of the late troubles, and of the nearness of intercourse and of the confidence he had enjoyed with his late Majesty of blessed memory. It was impossible not to look with interest upon a man who had been so familiar with the secret history of those times, and who had been taken into the confidence both of Papists and Churchmen.

When he had been introduced to the company, Mr. Oley reminded him of the incidents he had been relating before his arrival. When he mentioned the meeting in the inn in Buckinghamshire, Mr. Inglesant seemed affected.

"I remember it well," he said. "I was with Father St. Clare, whose deathbed I attended not two months after my return to England. Do you remember, Mr. Oley," he went on to say, "the sermons at St. Martin's in Oxford, where Mr. Giles Widdowes preached? I remember seeing you there, sir, and indeed his high and loyal sermons were much frequented by the royal party and soldiers of the garrison; and I have heard that he was most benevolent to many of the most needy in their distress. I remember that poor Whitford played the organs there often, before he was killed in the trenches."

"Ah," said Mr. Oley, "we have heard strange music in our day. I was in York when it was besieged by three very notable and great armies—the Scotch, the Northern under Lord Fairfax, and the Southern under the Earl of Manchester and Oliver. At that time the service at the Cathedral every Sunday morning was attended by more than a thousand ladies, knights, and gentlemen, besides soldiers and citizens; when the booming of cannon broke in upon the singing of the psalms, and more than once a cannon bullet burst into the Minster amongst the people, like a furious fiend or evil spirit, yet no one hurt."

After some talk of this nature we settled ourselves to our music and to tune our instruments. Mr. Inglesant's violin was inscribed "Jacobus Stainer in Absam propé Œnipontem 1647;" Œnipons is the Latin name of Inspruck in Germany, the chief city of the Tyrol, where this maker lived. As soon as Mr. Inglesant drew his bow across the strings I was astonished at the full and piercing tone, which seemed to me to exceed even that of the Cremonas.

We played a concert or two, with a double bass part for the violone, which had a noble effect; and Mr. Inglesant being pressed to oblige the company, played a descant upon a ground bass in the Italian manner. I should fail were I to attempt to describe to you what I felt during the performance of this piece. It seemed to me as though thoughts, which I had long sought and seemed ever and anon on the point of realizing, were at last given me, as I listened to chords of plaintive sweetness broken now and again by cruel and bitter discords—a theme into which were wrought street and tavern music and people's songs, which lively airs and catches, upon the mere pressure of the string, trembled into pathetic and melancholy cadences. In these dying falls and closes all the several parts were gathered up and brought together, yet so that what before was joy was now translated into sorrow, and the sorrowful transfigured to peace, as indeed the many shifting scenes of life vary upon the stage of men's affairs.

The concert being over, Mr. Dean informed us that it was his intention to attend the afternoon service in the Cathedral, and Mr. Inglesant accompanying him, the physicians departed to visit their patients, and my host and some of the clergy and myself went to the Cathedral also, entering rather late.

After the service, in which was sung an anthem by Dr. Nathaniel Giles, Mr. Dean retired to the vestry, and Mr. Inglesant coming down the Church, I found myself close to him at the west door. We stopped opposite to the monument of Bishop Gauden, who is depicted in his effigy holding a book, presumably the "*Icôn Basilikè*," in his hand. I inquired of Mr. Inglesant what his opinions were concerning the authorship of that work, and finding that he was disposed to converse, we went down to the river side, the evening being remarkably fine, and crossing by the ferry, walked for some time in the chapter meadows upon the farther bank. The evening sun was setting towards the range of the Malvern Hills, and the towers and spires of the city were shining in its glow, and were reflected in the water at our feet.

I said to Mr. Inglesant that I was greatly interested in the events of the last age, in which he had been so trusted and prominent an actor, and that I hoped to learn from him many interesting particulars, but he informed me that he knew but little except what the world was already possessed of. He said that he very deeply regretted that, during the last two years of the life of the late King, he himself was a close prisoner in the Tower; and was therefore prevented from assisting in any way, or being useful to His Majesty. He said that there was something peculiarly affecting in the position of the King in those days, as he was isolated from his friends, and entirely dependent upon three or four faithful and subordinate servants. He said that, since his return to England, he had made it his business to seek out several of these, and had received much interesting information from them, which, as he hoped it would soon be made public, he was not at present at liberty to communicate. Mr. Inglesant, however, told me one incident relating to the last days of the King of so affecting a character, that, as it is too long to be repeated here, I shall hope to inform you of when we meet together. He said, moreover, that the fatal mistake the King made was consenting to the death of Lord Strafford; that on many occasions he had yielded when he should have been firm; but that most of his misfortunes, such as reverses and indecisions in the field, were caused by circumstances entirely beyond his control. There is nothing new in these opinions, but I give them just as Mr. Inglesant stated them, lest you should think I had not taken advantage of the opportunity presented to me. It appeared to me that he was not very willing to discourse upon these bygone matters of State intrigue.

Seeing this I changed the topic, and said that as Mr. Inglesant had had much experience in the working of the Romish system, I should be glad to know his opinion of it, and whether he preferred it to that of the English Church. Here I found I was on different ground. I saw at once beneath the veil of polite manner, which was this man's second nature, that his whole life and being was in this question.

"This is the supreme quarrel of all," he said. "This is not a dispute between sects and kingdoms; it is a conflict within a man's own nature—nay, between the noblest parts of man's nature arrayed against each other. On the one side obedience and faith, on the other, freedom and the reason. What can come of such a conflict as this but throes and agony? I was not brought up by the Papists in England, nor, indeed, did I receive my book learning from them. I was trained for a special purpose by one of the Jesuits, but the course he took with me was different from that which he would have taken with other pupils whom he did not design for such work. I derived my training from various sources, and especially, instead of Aristotle, and the schoolmen, I was fed upon Plato. The difference is immense. I was trained to obedience and devotion; but the reason in my mind for this conduct was that obedience and devotion and gratitude were ideal virtues, not that they benefited the order to which I belonged, nor the world in which I lived. This I take to be the difference between the Papists and myself. The Jesuits do not like Plato, as lately they do not like Lord Bacon. Aristotle, as interpreted by the schoolmen, is more to their mind. According to their reading of Aristotle, all his Ethics are subordinated to an end, and in such a system they see a weapon which they can turn to their own purpose of maintaining dogma, no matter at what sacrifice of the individual conscience or reason. This is what the Church of Rome has ever done. She has traded upon the highest instincts of humanity, upon its faith and love, its passionate remorse, its self-abegnation and denial, its imagination and yearning after the unseen. It has based its system upon the profoundest truths, and upon this platform it has raised a power which has, whether foreseen by its authors or not, played the part of human tyranny, greed, and cruelty. To support this system it has habitually set itself to suppress knowledge and freedom of thought, before thought had taught itself to grapple with religious subjects, because it foresaw that this would follow. It has, therefore, for the sake of preserving intact its dogma, risked the growth and welfare of humanity, and has, in the eyes of all except those who value this dogma above all other things, constituted itself the enemy of the human race. I have perhaps occupied a position which enables me to judge somewhat advantageously between the Churches, and my earnest advice is this. You will do wrong—mankind will do wrong—if it allows to drop out of existence, merely because the position on which it stands seems to be illogical, an agency by which the devotional instincts of human nature are enabled to exist side by side with the rational. The English Church, as established by the law of England, offers the supernatural to all who choose to come. It is like the Divine Being Himself, whose sun shines alike on the evil and on the good. Upon the altars of the Church the divine presence hovers as surely, to those who believe it, as it does upon the splendid altars of Rome. Thanks to circumstances which the founders of our Church did not contemplate, the way is open; it is barred by no confession, no human priest. Shall we throw this aside? It has been won for us by the death and torture of men like ourselves in bodily frame, infinitely superior to some of us in self-denial and endurance. God knows—those who know my life know too well—that I am not worthy to be named with such men; nevertheless, though we cannot endure as they did—at least do not let us needlessly throw away what they have won. It is not even a question of religious freedom only; it is a question of learning and culture in every form. I am not blind to the peculiar dangers that beset the English Church. I fear that its position, standing, as it does, a mean between two extremes, will engender indifference and sloth; and that its freedom will prevent its preserving a discipline and organizing power, without which any community will suffer grievous damage; nevertheless, as a Church it is unique: if suffered to drop out of existence, nothing like it can ever take its place."

"The Church of England," I said, seeing that Mr. Inglesant paused, "is no doubt a compromise, and is powerless to exert its discipline, as the events of the late troubles have shown. It speaks with bated assurance, while the Church of Rome never falters in its utterance, and I confess seems to me to have a logical position. If there be absolute truth revealed, there must be an inspired exponent of it, else from age to age it could not get itself revealed to mankind."

"This is the Papist argument," said Mr. Inglesant; "there is only one answer to it—Absolute truth is not revealed. There were certain dangers which Christianity could not, as it would seem, escape. As it brought down the sublimest teaching of Platonism to the humblest understanding, so it was compelled, by this very action, to reduce spiritual and abstract truth to hard and inadequate dogma. As it inculcated a sublime indifference to the things of this life, and a steadfast gaze upon the future, so, by this very means, it encouraged the growth of a wild unreasoning superstition. It is easy to draw pictures of martyrs suffering the torture unmoved in the face of a glorious hereafter; but we must acknowledge, unless we choose to call these men absolute fiends, that it was these selfsame ideas of the future, and its relation to this life, that actuated their tormentors. If these things are true,—if the future of mankind is parcelled out between happiness and eternal torture,—then, to ensure the safety of mankind at large, the death and torment for a few moments of comparatively few need excite but little regret. From the instant that the founder of Christianity left the earth, perhaps even before, this ghastly spectre of superstition ranged itself side by side with the advancing faith. It is confined to no Church or sect; it exists in all. Faith in the noble, the unseen, the unselfish, by its very nature encourages this fatal growth; and it is nourished even by those who have sufficient strength to live above it; because, forsooth, its removal may be dangerous to the well-being of society at large, as though anything could be more fatal than falsehood against the Divine Truth."

"But if absolute truth is not revealed," I said, "how can we know the truth at all?"

"We cannot say how we know it," replied Mr. Inglesant, "but this very ignorance proves that we can know. We are the creatures of this ignorance against which we rebel. From the earliest dawn of existence we have known nothing. How then could we question for a moment? What thought should we have other than this ignorance which we had imbibed from our growth, but for the existence of some divine principle, 'Fons veri lucidus,' within us? The Founder of Christianity said, 'the kingdom of God is within you.' We may not only know the truth, but we may live even in this life in the very household and court of God. We are the creatures of birth, of ancestry, of circumstance; we are surrounded by law, physical and psychical, and the physical very often dominates and rules the soul. As the chemist, the navigator, the naturalist, attain their ends by means of law, which is beyond their power to alter, which they cannot change, but with which they can work in harmony, and by so doing produce definite results, so may we. We find ourselves immersed in physical and psychical laws, in accordance with which we act, or from which we diverge. Whether we are free to act or not, we can at least fancy that we resolve. Let us cheat ourselves, if it be a cheat, with this fancy, for we shall find that by so doing we actually attain the end we seek. Virtue, truth, love, are not mere names; they stand for actual qualities which are well known and recognized among men. These qualities are the elements of an ideal life, of that absolute and perfect life of which our highest culture can catch but a glimpse. As Mr. Hobbes has traced the individual man up to the perfect state, or Civitas, let us work still lower, and trace the individual man from small origins to the position he at present fills. We shall find that he has attained any position of vantage he may occupy by following the laws which our instinct and conscience tell us are Divine. Terror and superstition are the invariable enemies of culture and progress. They are used as rods and bogies to frighten the ignorant and the base, but they depress all mankind to the same level of abject slavery. The ways are dark and foul, and the gray years bring a mysterious future which we cannot see. We are like children, or men in a tennis court, and before our conquest is half won the dim twilight comes and stops the game; nevertheless, let us keep our places, and above all things hold fast by the law of life we feel within. This was the method which Christ followed, and He won the world by placing Himself in harmony with that law of gradual development which the Divine Wisdom has planned. Let us follow in His steps and we shall attain to the ideal life; and, without waiting for our 'mortal passage,' tread the free and spacious streets of that Jerusalem which is above."

He spoke more to himself than to me. The sun, which was just setting behind the distant hills, shone with dazzling splendour for a moment upon the towers and spires of the city across the placid water. Behind this fair vision were dark rain clouds, before which gloomy background it stood in fairy radiance and light. For a moment it seemed a glorious city, bathed in life and hope, full of happy people who thronged its streets and bridge, and the margin of its gentle stream. But it was "breve gaudium." Then the sunset faded, and the ethereal vision vanished, and the landscape lay dark and chill.

"The sun is set," Mr. Inglesant said cheerfully, "but it will rise again. Let us go home."

I have writ much more largely in this letter than I intended, but I have been led onward by the interest which I deny not I feel in this man. When we meet I will tell you more.

Your ever true friend,
VALENTINE LEE.

THE END.

Printed by R. & R. CLARK, *Edinburgh.*

Macmillan's Popular 6s. Novels.

By CHARLES KINGSLEY.

WESTWARD HO!
HEREWARD THE WAKE.
TWO YEARS AGO.
ALTON LOCKE. With Portrait.
HYPATIA.
YEAST.

By WILLIAM BLACK.

A PRINCESS OF THULE.
MADCAP VIOLET.
STRANGE ADVENTURES OF A PHAETON. Illustrated.
THE MAID OF KILLEENA, and Other Tales.
GREEN PASTURES AND PICCADILLY.
MACLEOD OF DARE. Illustrated.
WHITE WINGS. A Yachting Romance.
THE BEAUTIFUL WRETCH: THE FOUR MacNICOLS: THE PUPIL OF AURELIUS.

By CHARLOTTE M. YONGE.

With Illustrations by KATE GREENAWAY, HERBERT GANDY, ADRIAN STOKES, J. P. ATKINSON, MARIAN HUXLEY, W. J. HENNESSY, and JANE E. COOK.

THE HEIR OF REDCLYFFE.
HEARTSEASE.
HOPES AND FEARS.
DYNEVOR TERRACE.
THE DAISY CHAIN.
THE TRIAL.
PILLARS OF THE HOUSE. 2 Vols.
CLEVER WOMAN OF THE FAMILY.
THE YOUNG STEPMOTHER.
THE THREE BRIDES.
MY YOUNG ALCIDES.
THE CAGED LION.
THE DOVE IN THE EAGLE'S NEST.
THE CHAPLET OF PEARLS.

By CHARLOTTE M. YONGE

(*Continued.*)

LADY HESTER, and the DANVERS PAPERS.
MAGNUM BONUM.
LOVE AND LIFE.

By HENRY JAMES Jun.

THE AMERICAN.
THE EUROPEANS.
DAISY MILLER: an International Episode: Four Meetings.
RODERICK HUDSON.
THE MADONNA OF THE FUTURE; and Other Tales.
WASHINGTON SQUARE: THE PENSION BEAUREPAS: A BUNDLE OF LETTERS.
THE PORTRAIT OF A LADY.

By the AUTHOR of "JOHN HALIFAX, GENTLEMAN."

THE OGILVIES. Illustrated by J. M. M'RALSTON.
THE HEAD OF THE FAMILY. Illustrated by WALTER CRANE.
OLIVE. Illustrated by G. BOWERS.
AGATHA'S HUSBAND. Illustrated by WALTER CRANE.
MY MOTHER AND I. Illustrated by J. M. M'RALSTON.

By ANNIE KEARY.

CASTLE DALY.
OLDBURY.
A YORK AND A LANCASTER ROSE.
A DOUBTING HEART.
CLEMENCY FRANKLIN.
JANET'S HOME.

MACMILLAN & CO., LONDON, W.C.

Macmillan's Popular 6s. Novels,
(CONTINUED.)

By Mrs. MACQUOID.
THE BERKSHIRE LADY.
PATTY.

By FRANCES H. BURNETT.
HAWORTH'S.
LOUISIANA; and THAT LASS O' LOWRIE'S.

By LADY AUGUSTA NOEL.
FROM GENERATION TO GENERATION.
OWEN GWYNNE'S GREAT WORK.

By GEORGE FLEMING.
A NILE NOVEL.
MIRAGE.

CHRISTINA NORTH. By E. M. ARCHER.
UNDER THE LIMES. By E. M. ARCHER.
BENGAL PEASANT LIFE. By LAL BEHARI DAY.
VIRGIN SOIL. By TOURGÉNIEF.
VIDA. The Study of a Girl. By AMY DUNSMUIR.

By the AUTHOR of "HOGAN, M.P."
THE HON. MISS FERRARD.
HOGAN, M.P.
FLITTERS, TATTERS, AND THE COUNSELLOR: THE GAME HEN: BAUBIE CLARK: WEEDS.
CHRISTY CAREW.

TOM BROWN'S SCHOOLDAYS.
TOM BROWN AT OXFORD.
A BELEAGUERED CITY. By Mrs. OLIPHANT.
THE FOOL OF QUALITY. By H. BROOKE. Edited by CHARLES KINGSLEY.
REALMAH. By the Author of "Friends in Council."
HUGH CRICHTON'S ROMANCE. By C. R. COLERIDGE.
MY TIME AND WHAT I'VE DONE WITH IT. By F. C. BURNAND.
ROSE TURQUAND. By ELLICE HOPKINS.
ESTELLE RUSSELL.
OLD SIR DOUGLAS. By the Hon. Mrs. NORTON.
SEBASTIAN. By KATHARINE COOPER.
THE LAUGHING MILL, and Other Tales. By JULIAN HAWTHORNE.
THE HARBOUR BAR.

Macmillan's 2s. Novels.
In Cloth Binding, Crown 8vo, 2s. each.

By the AUTHOR of "JOHN HALIFAX, Gentleman."
THE OGILVIES.
TWO MARRIAGES. OLIVE.
AGATHA'S HUSBAND.
THE HEAD OF THE FAMILY.

By Mrs. OLIPHANT.
THE CURATE IN CHARGE.
A SON OF THE SOIL.
YOUNG MUSGRAVE.
HE THAT WILL NOT WHEN HE MAY.

Macmillan's Shilling Series.
Crown 8vo, Paper Wrapper.

DEMOCRACY: An American Novel. | LOUISIANA. By FRANCES H. BURNETT.
HINTS TO HOUSEWIVES ON SEVERAL POINTS; PARTICULARLY ON THE PREPARATION OF ECONOMICAL AND TASTEFUL DISHES. By Mrs. FREDERICK.

MACMILLAN & CO., LONDON, W.C.

Macmillan & Co.'s New Series.

Price 4s. 6d. each Volume.

DEMOCRACY: An American Novel. Crown 8vo. 4s. 6d.
Popular Edition. Paper Covers, 1s.

A NEW NOVEL BY AN AMERICAN WRITER.

MR. ISAACS: A Tale of Modern India. By F. MARION CRAWFORD. Crown 8vo. 4s. 6d.

MISS YONGE'S NEW NOVELS.

STRAY PEARLS FROM THE MEMOIRS OF MARGARET DE RIBAUMONT, VICOMTESSE DE BELLAISE. By CHARLOTTE M. YONGE, Author of "The Heir of Redclyffe," etc. 2 Vols. Crown 8vo. 9s.

UNKNOWN TO HISTORY. By CHARLOTTE M. YONGE, Author of "The Heir of Redclyffe." 2 Vols. Crown 8vo. 9s.

"A charming story. . . . She has written an interesting and delightful story. . . . A clever and attractive novel."—*Pall Mall Gazette.*

DR. GEORG EBERS' NEW NOVEL.

ONLY A WORD. By Dr. GEORG EBERS, Author of "The Egyptian Princess," etc. Translated by CLARA BELL. Crown 8vo. 4s. 6d.

THE BURGOMASTER'S WIFE. A Tale of the Siege of Leyden. By Dr. GEORG EBERS, Author of "The Egyptian Princess," etc. Translated by CLARA BELL. Crown 8vo. 4s. 6d.

A MEMOIR OF DANIEL MACMILLAN. By THOMAS HUGHES, Q.C. With a Portrait engraved on Steel by C. H. JEENS, from a Painting by LOWES DICKINSON. Fourth Thousand. Crown 8vo. 4s. 6d.

THE BURMAN; His Life and Notions. By SHWAY YOE. 2 Vols. Crown 8vo. 9s.

LECTURES ON ART. Delivered in support of the Society for Protection of Ancient Buildings. By REGD. STUART POOLE, Professor W. B. RICHMOND, E. J. POYNTER, R.A., J. T. MICKLETHWAITE, and WILLIAM MORRIS. Crown 8vo. 4s. 6d.

THE STORY OF MELICENT. By FAYR MADOC. Crown 8vo. 4s. 6d.

THE EXPANSION OF ENGLAND. By Professor J. R. SEELEY. Crown 8vo. 4s. 6d. [*In the Press.*

*** *Other Volumes to follow.*

MACMILLAN & CO., LONDON, W.C.

Macmillan & Co.'s Publications.

A NEW NOVEL. 2 Vols. Crown 8vo, 12s.

MRS. LORIMER: A Study in Black and White. By LUCAS MALET. 2 vols. Crown 8vo. 12s.

"One of the cleverest first books we ever read. It has merit, and great merit, as a study of characters, of manners, and of emotion; it is fortunate and elegant in style; it abounds in delicate touches of observation and in kindly and searching criticism; it has the quality of completeness, and commands attention, not as a sheaf of brilliant pages, or a string of taking scenes, but as a finished work of art."—*The Academy.*

A LITTLE PILGRIM: In the Unseen. Crown 8vo. 2s. 6d.

"This little prose poem."—*Academy.*
"No writing of the kind has been more talked about since the publication of 'The Gates Ajar.'"—*Literary World, Boston, U.S.A.*

DANTE GABRIEL ROSSETTI: A Record and a Study. By WILLIAM SHARP. With an Illustration after D. G. ROSSETTI. Crown 8vo. 10s. 6d.

"Mr. Sharp has brought to his allotted labour the truest enthusiasm, and a perseverance which nothing can daunt; and he has produced what may be regarded as, for all practical purposes, a complete account of the life-work of Rossetti in art and literature. . . . The volume will always remain as good an introduction and primer to the art and poetry of Rossetti as need be desired."—*Edinburgh Daily Courant.*

THROUGH THE RANKS TO A COMMISSION. New and Popular Edition. Crown 8vo. 2s. 6d.

Macmillan's Biographical Series.

Crown 8vo. Uniformly bound. Price 6s. each.

Spinoza Study. By Rev. Dr. JAMES MARTINEAU.

Catherine and Craufurd Tait. Wife and son of ARCHIBALD CAMPBELL, Archbishop of Canterbury: a Memoir. Edited, at the request of the Archbishop, by the Rev. W. BENHAM, B.D. With two portraits engraved by JEENS. New and Cheaper Edition.

The Life and Work of Mary Carpenter. By J. ESTLIN CARPENTER, M.A. With Steel Portrait.

Bernard (St.) The Life and Times of ST. BERNARD, Abbot of Clairvaux. By J. C. MORISON, M.A. New Edition.

Charlotte Brontë: A Monograph. By T. WEMYSS REID. Third Edition.

St. Anselm. By the Very Rev. R. W. CHURCH, M.A., Dean of St. Paul's. New Edition.

Great Christians of France: St. Louis and Calvin. By M. GUIZOT, Member of the Institute of France.

Alfred the Great. By THOMAS HUGHES, Q.C.

Biographical Sketches, 1852-75. By HARRIET MARTINEAU. With Four Additional Sketches, and Autobiographical Sketch. Fifth Edition.

Francis of Assisi. By Mrs. OLIPHANT. New Edition.

Victor Emmanuel II., First King of Italy. By G. S. GODKIN. New Edition.

MACMILLAN & CO., LONDON, W.C.

Macmillan & Co.'s Publications.

PRICE ONE GUINEA. NEW ISSUE, WITH A PREFACE.

THE LITERARY HISTORY OF ENGLAND IN THE END OF THE EIGHTEENTH AND BEGINNING OF THE NINETEENTH CENTURY. By Mrs. OLIPHANT. 3 Vols. Demy 8vo. 21s.

"Her three volumes abound with passages of eloquence and insight, and to the young student of English literature will be of the utmost value as suggesting new points of view, and stimulating interest and enthusiasm for the subject."—*British Quarterly Review.*

THE ENGLISH POETS. Selections, with Critical Introductions by various Writers, and a General Introduction by MATTHEW ARNOLD. Edited by T. H. WARD, M.A. 4 Vols.

Vol. I. CHAUCER to DONNE.—Vol. II. BEN JONSON to DRYDEN.—Vol. III. ADDISON to BLAKE.—Vol. IV. WORDSWORTH to SYDNEY DOBELL. Crown 8vo. Each 7s. 6d.

"Mr. Ward is to be congratulated in having published an excellently well selected collection that is not only a pleasant resource for leisure hours, but a methodical handbook to a poetical education."—*Times.*

ESSAYS. By the late GEORGE BRIMLEY, M.A., Librarian of Trinity College, Cambridge. Edited by W. G. CLARK, M.A., Fellow and Tutor of Trinity College, Cambridge. A New Edition. Globe 8vo. 5s.

CONTENTS :—Tennyson's Poems.—Wordsworth's Poems.—Poetry and Criticism.—Carlyle's Life of Sterling. — "Esmond." — "Westward Ho!" — Wilson's "Noctes Ambrosianæ."—Comte's "Positive Philosophy," etc.

NOW READY, PARTS XV., XVI. (DOUBLE NUMBER), SCHOBERLECHNER TO SKETCHES, PRICE 7s.

A DICTIONARY OF MUSIC AND MUSICIANS, by Eminent Writers, English and Foreign. Edited by GEORGE GROVE, D.C.L. Vols. I. and II. A to Plain Song. Price 21s. each. Demy 8vo, cloth, with Illustrations in Music Type and Woodcut. Also published in Quarterly Parts. Parts I. to XIV., price 3s. 6d. each. Parts XV., XVI., price 7s.

"Dr. Grove's Dictionary will be a boon to every intelligent lover of music."—*Saturday Review.*

SERMONS OUT OF CHURCH. By the Author of "John Halifax, Gentleman." New Edition. Crown 8vo. 6s.

ANNALS OF OUR TIME. A Journal of Events, Social and Political, Home and Foreign, from the Accession of Queen Victoria to the Peace of Versailles, 28th February 1871. By JOSEPH IRVING. New Edition, revised. 8vo, half-bound. 18s. Supplement. From February 1871 to March 1874. 4s. 6d. Supplement. From March 1874 to July 1878. 8vo. 4s. 6d.

MACMILLAN & CO., LONDON, W.C.

Macmillan & Co.'s Publications.

Now Publishing, in Crown 8vo, Price 2s. 6d. each.

ENGLISH MEN OF LETTERS.
Edited by JOHN MORLEY.

"This admirable series."—*British Quarterly Review.*
"Enjoyable and excellent little books."—*Academy.*

JOHNSON. By LESLIE STEPHEN.
SCOTT. By R. H. HUTTON.
GIBBON. By J. C. MORISON.
SHELLEY. By J. A. SYMONDS.
HUME. By Prof. HUXLEY, F.R.S.
GOLDSMITH. By WILLIAM BLACK.
DEFOE. By W. MINTO.
BURNS. By Principal SHAIRP.
SPENSER. By the Very Rev. the DEAN of ST. PAUL'S.
THACKERAY. By ANTHONY TROLLOPE.
BURKE. By JOHN MORLEY.
DE QUINCEY. By Prof. MASSON.
MILTON. By MARK PATTISON.
HAWTHORNE. By HENRY JAMES Jun.
SOUTHEY. By Prof. DOWDEN.
CHAUCER. By Prof. A. W. WARD.
BUNYAN. By JAMES A. FROUDE.

POPE. By LESLIE STEPHEN.
BYRON. By Prof. NICHOL.
COWPER. By GOLDWIN SMITH.
LOCKE. By Prof. FOWLER.
WORDSWORTH. By F. W. H. MYERS.
DRYDEN. By G. SAINTSBURY.
LANDOR. By Prof. SYDNEY COLVIN.
CHARLES LAMB. By Rev. A. AINGER.
BENTLEY. By Prof. R. C. JEBB.
DICKENS. By A. W. WARD.
GRAY. By E. W. GOSSE.
STERNE. By H. D. TRAILL.
MACAULAY. By J. C. MORISON.
FIELDING. By AUSTIN DOBSON.
 [*Just Ready.*
SHERIDAN. By Mrs. OLIPHANT.
 [*In the Press*

*** *Other Volumes to follow.*

Now Publishing, in Crown 8vo, Price 3s. 6d. each.

The English Citizen:
A SERIES OF SHORT BOOKS ON
HIS RIGHTS AND RESPONSIBILITIES.

THIS series is intended to meet the demand for accessible information on the ordinary conditions, and the current terms, of our political life. The series will deal with the details of the machinery whereby our Constitution works, and the broad lines upon which it has been constructed.

The following are the titles of the Volumes:—

CENTRAL GOVERNMENT. H. D. TRAILL, D.C.L., late Fellow of St. John's College, Oxford. [*Ready.*
THE ELECTORATE AND THE LEGISLATURE. SPENCER WALPOLE, Author of "The History of England from 1815." [*Ready.*
LOCAL GOVERNMENT. M. D. CHALMERS. [*In the press.*
JUSTICE AND POLICE. F. POLLOCK, late Fellow of Trinity College, Cambridge, etc.
THE NATIONAL BUDGET: THE NATIONAL DEBT, TAXES, AND RATES. A. J. WILSON. [*Ready.*
THE STATE AND EDUCATION. HENRY CRAIK, M.A.
THE POOR LAW. Rev. T. W. FOWLE, M.A. [*Ready.*

THE STATE IN ITS RELATION TO TRADE. T. H. FARRER. [*Ready.*
THE STATE IN RELATION TO LABOUR. W. STANLEY JEVONS, LL.D., M.A., F.R.S. [*Ready.*
THE STATE AND THE LAND. F. POLLOCK, late Fellow of Trinity College, Cambridge. [*In the Press.*
THE STATE AND THE CHURCH. Hon. A. D. ELLIOTT, M.P. [*Ready.*
FOREIGN RELATIONS. SPENCER WALPOLE, Author of "The History of England from 1815." [*Ready.*
INDIA. J. S. COTTON, late Fellow of Queen's College, Oxford. [*In the Press.*
(2) COLONIES & DEPENDENCIES. E. J. PAYNE, Fellow of University College, Oxford. [*In the Press.*

MACMILLAN & CO., LONDON, W.C.

BEDFORD STREET, STRAND, LONDON, W.C.
March, 1883.

MACMILLAN & Co.'s CATALOGUE of Works in the Departments of History, Biography, Travels, Critical and Literary Essays, Politics, Political and Social Economy, Law, etc.; and Works connected with Language.

HISTORY, BIOGRAPHY, TRAVELS, &c.

ADDISON.—ESSAYS OF JOSEPH ADDISON. Chosen and edited by JOHN RICHARD GREEN, M.A., LL.D., Honorary Fellow of Jesus College, Oxford. 18mo. 4s. 6d. (Golden Treasury Series.)

ALBEMARLE.—FIFTY YEARS OF MY LIFE. By GEORGE THOMAS, Earl of Albemarle. With Steel Portrait of the First Earl of Albemarle, engraved by JEENS. Third and Cheaper Edition. Crown 8vo. 7s. 6d.

ALFRED THE GREAT.—By THOMAS HUGHES, Q.C. Crown 8vo. 6s. (Biographical Series.)

ANDERSON.—MANDALAY TO MOMIEN; a Narrative of the Two Expeditions to Western China, of 1868 and 1875, under Colonel E. B. Sladen and Colonel Horace Browne. By Dr. ANDERSON, F.R.S.E., Medical and Scientific Officer to the Expeditions. With numerous Maps and Illustrations. 8vo. 21s.

APPLETON.—Works by T. G. APPLETON:—
A NILE JOURNAL. Illustrated by EUGENE BENSON. Crown 8vo. 6s.
SYRIAN SUNSHINE. Crown 8vo. 6s.

ARNOLD (MATTHEW.)—Works by MATTHEW ARNOLD, D.C.L.
ESSAYS IN CRITICISM. By MATTHEW ARNOLD. New Edition, Revised and Enlarged. Crown 8vo. 9s.
HIGHER SCHOOLS AND UNIVERSITIES IN GERMANY. Second Edition. Crown 8vo. 6s.

ARNOLD (W. T.)—THE ROMAN SYSTEM OF PROVINCIAL ADMINISTRATION TO THE ACCESSION OF CONSTANTINE THE GREAT. Being the Arnold Prize Essay for 1879. By W. T. ARNOLD, B.A. Crown 8vo. 6s.

ART.—THE YEAR'S ART: A concise Epitome of all Matters relating to the Arts of Painting, Sculpture, and Architecture, which have occurred during the Year 1880, together with Information respecting the Events of the Year 1881. Compiled by MARCUS B. HUISH. Crown 8vo. 2s. 6d.
THE SAME, 1879—1880. Crown 8vo. 2s. 6d.

ATKINSON.—AN ART TOUR TO NORTHERN CAPITALS OF EUROPE, including Descriptions of the Towns, the Museums, and other Art Treasures of Copenhagen, Christiana, Stockholm, Abo, Helsingfors, Wiborg, St. Petersburg, Moscow, and Kief. By J. BEAVINGTON ATKINSON. 8vo. 12s.

BAILEY.—THE SUCCESSION TO THE ENGLISH CROWN. A Historical Sketch. By A. BAILEY, M.A., Barrister-at-Law. Crown 8vo. 7s. 6d.

CARSTARES.—WILLIAM CARSTARES: a Character and Career of the Revolutionary Epoch (1649—1715). By ROBERT STORY, Minister of Rosneath. 8vo. 12s.

CHALLENGER.—REPORT ON THE SCIENTIFIC RESULTS OF THE VOYAGE OF H.M.S. "CHALLENGER," DURING THE YEARS 1873-76. Under the command of Captain Sir GEORGE NARES, R.N., F.R.S., and Captain FRANK TURLE THOMSON, R.N. Prepared under the Superintendence of Sir C. WYVILLE THOMSON, Knt., F.R.S., &c., and now of JOHN MURRAY, F.R.S.E., one of the Naturalists of the Expedition. With Illustrations. *Published by order of Her Majesty's Government.*

Volume I. Zoology. Royal, 37s. 6d. Or
Part I. Report on the Brachiopoda, 2s. 6d.
II. Report on the Pennatulida, 4s.
III. Report on the Ostracoda, 15s.
IV. Report on the Bones of Cetacea, 2s.
V. The Development of the Green Turtle, 4s. 6d.
VI. Report on the Shore Fishes, 10s.

Volume II. Zoology. 50s. Or
Part VII. Report on the Corals, 15s.
VIII. Report on the Birds, 35s.

Volume III. Zoology. 50s. Or
Part IX. Report on the Echinoidea, 36s.
X. Report on the Pycnogonida, 14s.

Volume IV. Zoology. 50s. Or
Part XI. Report on the Anatomy of the Tubinares, 6s.
XII. Report on the Deep-sea Medusæ, 20s.
XIII. Report on the Holdthurioidea (Part I.), 24s.

Volume V. Zoology. 50s. Or
Part XIV. Report on the Ophiuroidea.
XV. Some points in the Anatomy of the Thylasine, Cuscus, and Phascogale, with an account of the Comparative Anatomy of the Intrinsic Muscles and Nerves of the Mammalian Pes.

Volume VI. Zoology. 30s.
Part XVI. Report on the Actiniaria, 12s.
XVII. Report on the Tunicata, 30s.

NARRATIVE, Volume II. Royal. 30s. Or
Magnetical and Meteorological Observations. 25s.

Appendix A. Report on the Pressure Errors of the "Challenger" Thermometers 2s. 6d.

Appendix B. Report on the Petrology of St. Paul's Rocks. 2s. 6d.

CHATTERTON: A BIOGRAPHICAL STUDY. By DANIEL WILSON, LL.D., Professor of History and English Literature in University College Toronto. Crown 8vo. 6s. 6d.

CHATTERTON: A STORY OF THE YEAR 1770. By Professor MASSON, LL.D. Crown 8vo. 5s.

CICERO.—THE LIFE AND LETTERS OF MARCUS TULLIUS CICERO: being a New Translation of the Letters included in Mr. Watson's Selection. With Historical and Critical Notes, by Rev. G. E. JEANS, M.A., Fellow of Hertford College, Oxford, Assistant-Master in Haileybury College, 8vo. 10s. 6d.

CLARK.—MEMORIALS FROM JOURNALS AND LETTERS OF SAMUEL CLARK, M.A., formerly Principal of the National Society's Training College, Battersea. Edited with Introduction by his WIFE. With Portrait. Crown 8vo. 7s. 6d.

HISTORY, BIOGRAPHY, TRAVELS, ETC.

CLASSICAL WRITERS.—Edited by JOHN RICHARD GREEN. Fcap. 8vo. Price 1s. 6d. each.
EURIPIDES. By Professor MAHAFFY.
MILTON. By the Rev. STOPFORD A. BROOKE.
LIVY. By the Rev. W. W. CAPES, M.A.
VERGIL. By Professor NETTLESHIP, M.A.
SOPHOCLES. By Professor L. CAMPBELL, M.A.
DEMOSTHENES. By Professor S. H. BUTCHER, M.A.
TACITUS. By Rev. A. J. CHURCH, M.A., and W. J. BRODRIBB, M.A.
Other Volumes to follow.

CLIFFORD (W. K.)—LECTURES AND ESSAYS. Edited by LESLIE STEPHEN and FREDERICK POLLOCK, with Introduction by F. POLLOCK. Two Portraits. 2 vols. 8vo. 25s.

COMBE.—THE LIFE OF GEORGE COMBE, Author of "The Constitution of Man." By CHARLES GIBBON. With Three Portraits engraved by JEENS. Two Vols. 8vo. 32s.

COOPER.—ATHENÆ CANTABRIGIENSES. By CHARLES HENRY COOPER, F.S.A., and THOMPSON COOPER, F.S.A. Vol. I. 8vo., 1500—1585, 18s.; Vol. II., 1586—1609, 18s.

CORREGIO.—ANTONIO ALLEGRI DA CORREGIO. From the German of Dr. JULIUS MEYER, Director of the Royal Gallery, Berlin. Edited, with an Introduction, by Mrs. HEATON. Containing Twenty Woodbury-type Illustrations. Royal 8vo. Cloth elegant. 31s. 6d.

COX (G. V.)—RECOLLECTIONS OF OXFORD. By G. V. Cox, M.A., New College, late Esquire Bedel and Coroner in the University of Oxford. Cheaper Edition. Crown 8vo. 6s.

CUNYNGHAME (SIR A. T.)—MY COMMAND IN SOUTH AFRICA, 1874—1878. Comprising Experiences of Travel in the Colonies of South Africa and the Independent States. By Sir ARTHUR THURLOW CUNYNGHAME, G.C.B., then Lieutenant-Governor and Commander of the Forces in South Africa. Third Edition. 8vo. 12s. 6d.

"DAILY NEWS."—THE DAILY NEWS' CORRESPONDENCE of the War between Russia and Turkey, to the fall of Kars. Including the letters of Mr. Archibald Forbes, Mr. J. E. McGahan, and other Special Correspondents in Europe and Asia. Second Edition, Enlarged. Cheaper Edition. Crown 8vo. 6s.

FROM THE FALL OF KARS TO THE CONCLUSION OF PEACE. Cheaper Edition. Crown 8vo. 6s.

DARWIN.—CHARLES DARWIN: MEMORIAL NOTICES REPRINTED FROM "NATURE." By Professor HUXLEY, F.R.S.; G. J. ROMANES, F.R.S.; ARCHIBALD GEIKIE, F.R.S; and W. T. THISELTON DYER, F.R.S. With a Portrait engraved by C. H. JEENS. Crown 8vo. 2s. 6d. *Nature Series.*

DAVIDSON.—THE LIFE OF A SCOTTISH PROBATIONER; being a Memoir of Thomas Davidson, with his Poems and Letters. By JAMES BROWN, Minister of St. James's Street Church, Paisley. Second Edition, revised and enlarged, with Portrait. Crown 8vo. 7s. 6d.

DAWSON.—AUSTRALIAN ABORIGINES. The Language and Customs of Several Tribes of Aborigines in the Western District of Victoria, Australia. By JAMES DAWSON. Small 4to. 14s.

DEAK.—FRANCIS DEAK, HUNGARIAN STATESMAN: A Memoir. With a Preface, by the Right Hon. M. E. GRANT DUFF, M.P. With Portrait. 8vo. 12s. 6d.

DEAS.—THE RIVER CLYDE. An Historical Description of the Rise and Progress of the Harbour of Glasgow, and of the Improvement of the River from Glasgow to Port Glasgow. By J. DEAS, M. Inst. C.E. 8vo. 10s. 6d.

DELANE.—LIFE AND LETTERS OF JOHN T. DELANE, late Editor of the *Times*. By Sir GEORGE W. DASENT, D.C.L. 8vo. [*In the Press.*

DENISON.—A HISTORY OF CAVALRY FROM THE EARLIEST TIMES. With Lessons for the Future. By Lieut.-Colonel GEORGE DENISON, Commanding the Governor-General's Body Guard, Canada, Author of "Modern Cavalry." With Maps and Plans. 8vo. 18s.

DICKENS'S DICTIONARY OF PARIS, 1882.—An Unconventional Handbook. With Maps, Plans, &c. 18mo. Paper Cover, 1s. Cloth, 1s. 6d.

DICKENS'S DICTIONARY OF LONDON, 1882.—(Fourth Year.) An Unconventional Handbook. With Maps, Plans, &c. 18mo. Paper Cover, 1s. Cloth, 1s. 6d.

DICKENS'S DICTIONARY OF THE THAMES, 1882.—An Unconventional Handbook. With Maps, Plans, &c. Paper Cover, 1s. Cloth, 1s. 6d.

DICKENS'S CONTINENTAL A.B.C. RAILWAY GUIDE. Published on the 1st of each Month. 18mo. 1s.

DILKE.—GREATER BRITAIN. A Record of Travel in English-speaking Countries during 1866—67. (America, Australia, India.) By the Right Hon. Sir CHARLES WENTWORTH DILKE, M.P. Sixth Edition. Crown 8vo. 6s.

DILETTANTI SOCIETY'S PUBLICATIONS. ANTIQUITIES OF IONIA. Part IV. Folio, half-morocco. £3 13s. 6d.

DOLET.—ETIENNE DOLET: the Martyr of the Renaissance. A Biography. With a Biographical Appendix, containing a Descriptive Catalogue of the Books written, printed, or edited by Dolet. By RICHARD COPLEY CHRISTIE, Lincoln College, Oxford, Chancellor of the Diocese of Manchester. With Illustrations. 8vo. 18s.

DOYLE.—HISTORY OF AMERICA. By J. A. DOYLE. With Maps. 18mo. 4s. 6d. [*Historical Course.*

DRUMMOND OF HAWTHORNDEN: THE STORY OF HIS LIFE AND WRITINGS. By Professor MASSON. With Portrait and Vignette engraved by C. H. JEENS. Crown 8vo. 10s. 6d.

DUFF.—Works by the Right Hon. M. E. GRANT DUFF.
NOTES OF AN INDIAN JOURNEY. With Map. 8vo. 10s. 6d.
MISCELLANIES, POLITICAL AND LITERARY. 8vo. 10s. 6d.

EADIE.—LIFE OF JOHN EADIE, D.D., LL.D. By JAMES BROWN, D.D., Author of "The Life of a Scottish Probationer." With Portrait. Second Edition. Crown 8vo. 7s. 6d.

ELLIOTT.—LIFE OF HENRY VENN ELLIOTT, of Brighton. By JOSIAH BATEMAN, M.A. With Portrait, engraved by JEENS. Third and Cheaper Edition. Extra fcap. 8vo. 6s.

ELZE.—ESSAYS ON SHAKESPEARE. By Dr. KARL ELZE. Translated with the Author's sanction by L. DORA SCHMITZ. 8vo. 12s.

HISTORY, BIOGRAPHY, TRAVELS, ETC.

ENGLISH MEN OF LETTERS.—Edited by JOHN MORLEY, M.P. A Series of Short Books to tell people what is best worth knowing as to the Life, Character, and Works of some of the great English Writers. In Crown 8vo. price 2s. 6d. each.

I. DR. JOHNSON. By LESLIE STEPHEN.
II. SIR WALTER SCOTT. By R. H. HUTTON.
III. GIBBON. By J. COTTER MORISON.
IV. SHELLEY. By J. A. SYMONDS.
V. HUME. By Professor HUXLEY.
VI. GOLDSMITH. By WILLIAM BLACK.
VII. DEFOE. By W. MINTO.
VIII. BURNS. By Principal SHAIRP.
IX. SPENSER. By the Very Rev. the DEAN OF ST. PAUL'S.
X. THACKERAY. By ANTHONY TROLLOPE.
XI. BURKE. By JOHN MORLEY.
XII. MILTON. By MARK PATTISON.
XIII. HAWTHORNE. By HENRY JAMES, Jun.
XIV. SOUTHEY. By Professor DOWDEN.
XV. BUNYAN. By J. A. FROUDE.
XVI. CHAUCER. By Professor A. W. WARD.
XVII. COWPER. By GOLDWIN SMITH.
XVIII. POPE. By LESLIE STEPHEN.
XIX. BYRON. By Professor NICHOL.
XX. LOCKE. By Professor FOWLER.
XXI. WORDSWORTH. By F. W. H. MYERS.
XXII. DRYDEN. By G. SAINTSBURY.
XXIII. LANDOR. By Professor SIDNEY COLVIN.
XXIV. DE QUINCEY. By Professor MASSON.
XXV. CHARLES LAMB. By Rev. ALFRED AINGER.
XXVI. BENTLEY. By Professor R. C. JEBB.
XXVII. DICKENS. By Professor A. W. WARD.
XXVIII. GRAY. By EDMUND W. GOSSE.
XXIX. SWIFT. By LESLIE STEPHEN.
XXX. STERNE. By H. D. TRAILL.
XXXI. MACAULAY. By J. COTTER MORISON.
XXXII. FIELDING. By AUSTIN DOBSON.
XXXIII. SHERIDAN. By Mrs. OLIPHANT. [*In the Press.*]

In Preparation :—
ADAM SMITH. By LEONARD H. COURTNEY, M.P.
BERKELEY. By Professor HUXLEY.
SIR PHILIP SIDNEY. By J. A. SYMONDS.
Other Volumes to follow.

ENGLISH POETS: SELECTIONS, with Critical Introductions by various Writers, and a General Introduction by MATTHEW ARNOLD, Edited by T. H. WARD, M.A., late Fellow of Brasenose College, Oxford. 4 vols. Crown 8vo. 7s. 6d. each.

Vol. I. CHAUCER to DONNE.
Vol. II. BEN JONSON to DRYDEN.
Vol. III. ADDISON to BLAKE.
Vol. IV. WORDSWORTH to SYDNEY DOBELL.

ETON COLLEGE, HISTORY OF. By H. C. MAXWELL LYTE, M.A. With numerous Illustrations by Professor DELAMOTTE, Coloured Plates, and a Steel Portrait of the Founder, engraved by C. H. JEENS. New and Cheaper Issue, with Corrections. Medium 8vo. Cloth elegant. 21s.

EUROPEAN HISTORY, Narrated in a Series of Historical Selections from the best Authorities. Edited and arranged by E. M. SEWELL, and C. M. YONGE. First Series, crown 8vo. 6s.; Second Series, 1088-1228, crown 8vo. 6s. Third Edition.

FARADAY.—MICHAEL FARADAY. By J. H. GLADSTONE, Ph.D., F.R.S. Second Edition, with Portrait engraved by JEENS from a photograph by J. WATKINS. Crown 8vo. 4s. 6d.
    PORTRAIT. Artist's Proof. 5s.

FISON AND HOWITT.—KAMILAROI AND KURNAI GROUP. Marriage and Relationship, and Marriage by Elopement, drawn chiefly from the usage of the Australian Aborigines. Also THE KURNAI TRIBE, their Customs in Peace and War. By LORIMER FISON, M.A., and A. W. HOWITT, F.G.S., with an Introduction by LEWIS H. MORGAN, LL.D., Author of "System of Consanguinity," "Ancient Society," &c. Demy 8vo. 15s.

FORBES.—LIFE AND LETTERS OF JAMES DAVID FORBES, F.R.S., late Principal of the United College in the University of St. Andrews. By J. C. SHAIRP, LL.D., Principal of the United College in the University of St. Andrews; P. G. TAIT, M.A., Professor of Natural Philosophy in the University of Edinburgh; and A. ADAMS-REILLY, F.R.G.S. With Portraits, Map, and Illustrations. 8vo. 16s.

FRANCIS OF ASSISI. By Mrs. OLIPHANT. New Edition. Crown 8vo 6s. (Biographical Series.)

FREEMAN.—Works by EDWARD A. FREEMAN, D.C.L., LL.D.:—HISTORICAL ESSAYS. Third Edition. 8vo. 10s. 6d.
    "CONTENTS:—I. "The Mythical and Romantic Elements in Early English History;" II. "The Continuity of English History;" III. "The Relations between the Crowns of England and Scotland;" IV. "St. Thomas of Canterbury and his Biographers;" V. "The Reign of Edward the Third;" VI. "The Holy Roman Empire;" VII. "The Franks and the Gauls;" VIII. "The Early Sieges of Paris;" IX. "Frederick the First, King of Italy;" X. "The Emperor Frederick the Second;" XI. "Charles the Bold;" XII. "Presidential Government."
    HISTORICAL ESSAYS. Second Series. Second Edition, Enlarged. 8vo 10s. 6d.
    The principal Essays are:—"Ancient Greece and Mediæval Italy:" "Mr. Gladstone's Homer and the Homeric Ages:" "The Historians of Athens:" "The Athenian Democracy:" "Alexander the Great:" "Greece during the Macedonian Period:" "Mommsen's History of Rome:" "Lucius Cornelius Sulla:" "The Flavian Cæsars."
    HISTORICAL ESSAYS. Third Series. 8vo. 12s.
    CONTENTS:—"First Impressions of Rome." "The Illyrian Emperors and their Land." "Augusta Treverorum." "The Goths of Ravenna." "Race and Language." "The Byzantine Empire." "First Impressions of Athens." "Mediæval and Modern Greece." "The Southern Slaves." "Sicilian Cycles." "The Normans at Palermo."
    COMPARATIVE POLITICS.—Lectures at the Royal Institution. To which is added the "Unity of History," the Rede Lecture at Cambridge, 1872. 8vo. 14s.
    THE HISTORY AND CONQUESTS OF THE SARACENS. Six Lectures. Third Edition, with New Preface. Crown 8vo. 3s. 6d.
    HISTORICAL AND ARCHITECTURAL SKETCHES: chiefly Italian. With Illustrations by the Author. Crown 8vo. 10s. 6d.
    SUBJECT AND NEIGHBOUR LANDS OF VENICE. Being a Companion Volume to "Historical and Architectural Sketches." With Illustrations. Crown 8vo. 10s. 6d.
    HISTORY OF FEDERAL GOVERNMENT, from the Foundation of the Achaian League on the Disruption of the United States. Vol I, General Introduction. History of the Greek Federations. 8vo. 21s.
    OLD ENGLISH HISTORY. With Five Coloured Maps. New Edition. Half-bound. Extra fcap. 8vo. 6s.

HISTORY, BIOGRAPHY, TRAVELS, ETC. 9

FREEMAN—*continued.*

HISTORY OF THE CATHEDRAL CHURCH OF WELLS, as illustrating the History of the Cathedral Churches of the Old Foundation. Crown 8vo. 3s. 6d.

THE GROWTH OF THE ENGLISH CONSTITUTION FROM THE EARLIEST TIMES. Third Edition, revised. Crown 8vo. 5s.

GENERAL SKETCH OF EUROPEAN HISTORY. Being Vol. I. of a Historical Course for Schools, edited by E. A. FREEMAN. New Edition, enlarged with Maps, Chronological Table, Index, &c. 18mo. 3s. 6d.

THE OTTOMAN POWER IN EUROPE: its Nature, its Growth, and its Decline. With Coloured Maps. Crown 8vo. 7s. 6d.

GALILEO.—THE PRIVATE LIFE OF GALILEO. Compiled principally from his Correspondence and that of his eldest daughter, Sister Maria Celeste, Nun in the Franciscan Convent of S. Matthew in Arcetri. With Portrait. Crown 8vo. 7s. 6d.

GALLOWAY.—Works by ROBERT L. GALLOWAY, Mining Engineer.

THE STEAM-ENGINE AND ITS INVENTORS: a Historical Sketch. With numerous Illustrations. Crown 8vo. 10s. 6d.

A HISTORY OF COAL MINING IN GREAT BRITAIN. Crown 8vo. 7s. 6d.

GEIKIE.—GEOLOGICAL SKETCHES AT HOME AND ABROAD. By ARCHIBALD GEIKIE, LL.D., F.R.S., Director General of the Geological Surveys of the United Kingdom. With illustrations. 8vo. 10s. 6d.

GARDNER.—SAMOS AND SAMIAN COINS. By PERCY GARDNER, M.A., F.S.A. British Museum, Disnay Professor of Archæology in the University of Cambridge, and Hon. Foreign Secretary of the Numismatic Society. Demy 8vo. 7s. 6d.

GEDDES.—THE PROBLEM OF THE HOMERIC POEMS. By W. D. GEDDES, LL.D., Professor of Greek in the University of Aberdeen. 8vo. 14s.

GLADSTONE.—Works by the Right Hon. W. E. GLADSTONE, M.P.:—

JUVENTUS MUNDI. The Gods and Men of the Heroic Age. With Map. Second Edition. Crown 8vo. cloth. 10s. 6d.

HOMERIC SYNCHRONISM. An inquiry into the Time and Place of Homer. Crown 8vo. 6s.

GOETHE AND MENDELSSOHN (1821—1831). Translated from the German of Dr. KARL MENDELSSOHN, Son of the Composer, by M. E. VON GLEHN. From the Private Diaries and Home Letters of Mendelssohn, with Poems and Letters of Goethe never before printed. Also with two New and Original Portraits, Fac-similes, and Appendix of Twenty Letters hitherto unpublished. Second Edition, enlarged. Crown 8vo. 5s.

GOLDSMID.—TELEGRAPH AND TRAVEL. A Narrative of the Formation and Development of Telegraphic Communication between England and India, under the orders of Her Majesty's Government, with incidental Notices of the Countries traversed by the Lines. By Colonel SIR FREDERICK GOLDSMID, C.B., K.C.S.I., late Director of the Government Indo-European Telegraph. With numerous Illustrations and Maps. 8vo. 21s.

GORDON.—LAST LETTERS FROM EGYPT, to which are added Letters from the Cape. By LADY DUFF GORDON. With a Memoir by her Daughter, Mrs. Ross, and Portrait engraved by JEENS. Second Edition. Crown 8vo. 9s.

GRAY.—CHINA. A History of the Laws, Manners, and Customs of the People. By the VENERABLE JOHN HENRY GRAY, LL.D., Archdeacon of Hong Kong, formerly H.B.M. Consular Chaplain at Canton. Edited by W. Gow Gregor. With 150 Full-page Illustrations, being Fac-similes of Drawings by a Chinese Artist. 2 vols. Demy 8vo. 32s.

GRAY (MRS.)—FOURTEEN MONTHS IN CANTON. By Mrs. GRAY. With Illustrations. Crown 8vo. 9s.

GREAT CHRISTIANS OF FRANCE: ST. LOUIS and CALVIN. By M. GUIZOT, Member of the Institute of France. Crown 8vo. 6s. (Biographical Series.)

GREEN.—Works by JOHN RICHARD GREEN, M.A., LL.D. :—

HISTORY OF THE ENGLISH PEOPLE. Vol. I.—Early England—Foreign Kings—The Charter—The Parliament. With 8 Coloured Maps. 8vo. 16s. Vol. II.—The Monarchy, 1461—1540: The Restoration, 1540—1603. 8vo. 16s. Vol. III.—Puritan England, 1603—1660; The Revolution, 1660—1688. With 4 Maps. 8vo. 16s. Vol. IV.—The Revolution, 1683—1760; Modern England, 1760—1815. With Maps and Index. 8vo. 16s.

A SHORT HISTORY OF THE ENGLISH PEOPLE. With Coloured Maps, Genealogical Tables, and Chronological Annals. Crown 8vo. 8s. 6d. Eighty-eighth Thousand.

STRAY STUDIES FROM ENGLAND AND ITALY. Crown 8vo. 8s. 6d. Containing: Lambeth and the Archbishops—The Florence of Dante—Venice and Rome—Early History of Oxford—The District Visitor—Capri—Hotels in the Clouds—Sketches in Sunshine, &c.

READINGS FROM ENGLISH HISTORY. Selected and Edited by JOHN RICHARD GREEN. In Three Parts. Fcap. 8vo. 1s. 6d. each. Part I.—From Hengest to Cressy. Part II.—From Cressy to Cromwell. Part III.—From Cromwell to Balaklava.

THE MAKING OF ENGLAND. With Maps. Demy 8vo. 16s.

GUEST.—LECTURES ON THE HISTORY OF ENGLAND. By M. J. GUEST. With Maps. Crown 8vo. 6s.

HAMERTON.—Works by P. G. HAMERTON :—

ETCHINGS AND ETCHERS. Third Edition, revised, with Forty-eight new Plates. Columbier 8vo.

THE INTELLECTUAL LIFE. With a Portrait of Leonardo da Vinci, etched by LEOPOLD FLAMENG. Second Edition. Crown 8vo. 10s. 6d.

THOUGHTS ABOUT ART. New Edition, revised, with an Introduction, Crown 8vo. 8s. 6d.

HEINE.—A TRIP TO THE BROCKEN. By HEINRICH HEINE. Translated by R. MCLINTOCK. Crown 8vo. 3s. 6d.

HELLENIC STUDIES—JOURNAL OF. 8vo. Parts I. and II., constituting Vol. I. with 4to. Atlas of Illustrations, 30s. Vol. II., with 4to. Atlas of Illustrations, 30s., or in Two Parts, 15s. each. Vol. III., Part I., with 4to. Atlas of Illustrations, 15s.

The Journal will be sold at a reduced price to Libraries wishing to subscribe, but official application must in each case be made to the Council. Information on this point, and upon the conditions of Membership, may be obtained on application to the Hon. Secretary, Mr. George Macmillan, 29, Bedford Street, Covent Garden.

HILL.—THE RECORDER OF BIRMINGHAM. A Memoir of Matthew Davenport-Hill, with Selections from his Correspondence. By his daughters ROSAMOND and FLORENCE DAVENPORT-HILL. With Portrait engraved by C. H. JEENS. 8vo. 16s.

HILL.—WHAT WE SAW IN AUSTRALIA. By ROSAMOND and FLORENCE HILL. Crown 8vo. 10s. 6d.

HODGSON.—MEMOIR OF REV. FRANCIS HODGSON, B.D., Scholar, Poet, and Divine. By his son, the Rev. JAMES T. HODGSON, M.A. Containing numerous Letters from Lord Byron and others. With Portrait engraved by JEENS. Two vols. Crown 8vo. 18s.

HISTORY, BIOGRAPHY, TRAVELS, ETC.

HOLE.—A GENEALOGICAL STEMMA OF THE KINGS OF ENGLAND AND FRANCE. By the Rev. C. HOLE, M.A., Trinity College, Cambridge. On Sheet, 1s.

A BRIEF BIOGRAPHICAL DICTIONARY. Compiled and Arranged by the Rev. CHARLES HOLE, M.A. Second Edition. 18mo. 4s. 6d.

HOLIDAY RAMBLES BY A WIFE WITH HER HUSBAND.—Republished from the *Spectator*. New and Cheaper Edition. Crown 8vo. 6s.

HOOKER AND BALL.—MOROCCO AND THE GREAT ATLAS: Journal of a Tour in. By Sir JOSEPH D. HOOKER, K.C.S.I., C.B., F.R.S., &c., and JOHN BALL, F.R.S. With an Appendix, including a Sketch of the Geology of Morocco, by G. MAW, F.L.S., F.G.S. With Illustrations and Map. 8vo. 21s.

HOUSE OF LORDS.—FIFTY YEARS OF THE HOUSE OF LORDS. Reprinted from *The Pall Mall Gazette*. Crown 8vo. 2s. 6d.

HOZIER (H. M.)—Works by CAPTAIN HENRY M. HOZIER, late Assistant Military Secretary to Lord Napier of Magdala:—

THE SEVEN WEEKS' WAR; Its Antecedents and Incidents. New and Cheaper Edition. With New Preface, Maps, and Plans. Crown 8vo. 6s.

THE INVASIONS OF ENGLAND: a History of the Past, with Lessons for the Future. Two Vols. 8vo. 28s.

HÜBNER.—A RAMBLE ROUND THE WORLD IN 1871. By M. LE BARON HÜBNER, formerly Ambassador and Minister. Translated by LADY HERBERT. New and Cheaper Edition. With numerous Illustrations. Crown 8vo. 6s.

HUGHES.—Works by THOMAS HUGHES, Q.C., Author of "Tom Brown's School Days."

MEMOIR OF A BROTHER. With Portrait of GEORGE HUGHES, after WATTS, Engraved by JEENS. Sixth Edition. Crown 8vo. 5s.

ALFRED THE GREAT. Crown 8vo. 6s.

MEMOIR OF DANIEL MACMILLAN. With Portrait after LOWES DICKINSON, Engraved by JEENS. Fourth Thousand. Crown 8vo. 4s. 6d.

RUGBY, TENNESSE. Being some account of the Settlement founded on the Cumberland Plateau by the Board of Aid to Land Ownership. With a report on the Soils of the Plateau by the Hon. F. W. KILLEBREW, A.M., Ph.D., Commissioner for Agriculture for the State of Tenessee. Crown 8vo. 4s. 6d.

HUNT.—HISTORY OF ITALY. By the Rev. W. HUNT, M.A. Being the Fourth Volume of the Historical Course for Schools. Edited by EDWARD A. FREEMAN, D.C.L. 18mo. 3s.

HUTTON.—ESSAYS THEOLOGICAL AND LITERARY. By R. H. HUTTON, M.A. Cheaper issue. 2 vols. 8vo. 18s.

CONTENTS OF VOL. I.:—The moral significance of Atheism—The Atheistic Explanation of Religion—Science and Theism—Popular Pantheism—What is Revelation?—Christian Evidences, Popular and Critical—The Historical Problems of the Fourth Gospel—The Incarnation and Principles of Evidence—M. Renan's "Christ"—M. Renan's "St. Paul"—The Hard Church—Romanism, Protestantism, and Anglicanism.

CONTENTS OF VOL. II.:—Goethe and his Influence—Wordsworth and his Genius—Shelley's Poetical Mysticism—Mr. Browning—The Poetry of the Old Testament—Arthur Hugh Clough—The Poetry of Matthew Arnold—Tennyson—Nathaniel Hawthorne.

INGLIS (JAMES) ("MAORI").—Works by JAMES INGLIS ("Maori"):—
OUR AUSTRLIAN COUSINS. 8vo. 14s.
SPORT AND WORK ON THE NEPAUL FRONTIER; or, Twelve Years' Sporting Reminiscences of an Indigo Planter. By "MAORI." With Illustrations. 8vo. 14s.

IONIA.—THE ANTIQUITIES OF IONIA, see under Dilettanti Society's Publications.

IRVING.—THE ANNALS OF OUR TIME. A Diurnal of Events, Social and Political, Home and Foreign, from the Accession of Queen Victoria to the Peace of Versailles. By JOSEPH IRVING. New Edition, revised. 8vo. half-bound. 18s.
ANNALS OF OUR TIME. Supplement. From Feb. 28, 1871, to March 19, 1874. 8vo. 4s. 6d. ANNALS OF OUR TIME. Second Supplement. From March, 1874, to the Occupation of Cyprus. 8vo. 4s. 6d.

JAMES (Sir. W. M.).—THE BRITISH IN INDIA. By the late Right Hon. Sir WILLIAM MILBOURNE JAMES, Lord Justice of Appeal. Edited by his Daughter, MARY J. SALIS SCHWABE. Demy 8vo. 12s. 6d.

JAMES.—FRENCH POETS AND NOVELISTS. By HENRY JAMES, Jun. Crown 8vo. 8s. 6d.
CONTENTS:—Alfred de Musset; Théophile Gautier; Baudelaire; Honoré de Balzac; George Sand; The Two Ampères; Turgénieff, &c.

JEBB.—MODERN GREECE. Two Lectures delivered before the Philosophical Institution of Edinburgh. With papers on "The Progress of Greece," and "Byron in Greece." By R. C. JEBB, M.A., LL.D. Edin. Professor of Greek in the University of Glasgow. Crown 8vo. 5s.

JOHNSON'S LIVES OF THE POETS.—The Six Chief Lives —Milton, Dryden, Swift, Addison, Pope, Gray. With Macaulay's "Life of Johnson." Edited, with Preface, by MATTHEW ARNOLD. Crown 8vo. 6s.

JONES.—THE LIFE'S WORK IN IRELAND OF A LANDLORD WHO TRIED TO DO HIS DUTY. By W. BENCE JONES, of Lisselan. Crown 8vo. 6s.

KANT.—THE LIFE OF IMMANUEL KANT. By J. H. STUCKENBERG, D.D., late Professor in Wittenburg College, Ohio. With Portrait. 8vo. 14s.

KANT—MAX MÜLLER.—CRITIQUE OF PURE REASON BY IMMANUEL KANT. In commemoration of the Centenary of its first Publication. Translated into English by F. MAX MÜLLER. With an Historical Introduction by LUDWIG NOIRÉ. 2 vols. Demy 8vo. 32s.

KEARY.—ANNIE KEARY: a Memoir. By ELIZA KEARY. With a Portrait. Second Thousand. Crown 8vo. 6s.

KILLEN.—ECCLESIASTICAL HISTORY OF IRELAND, from the Earliest Date to the Present Time. By W. D. KILLEN, D.D., President of Assembly's College, Belfast, and Professor of Ecclesiastical History. Two Vols. 8vo. 25s.

KINGSLEY (CHARLES).—Works by the Rev. CHARLES KINGSLEY, M.A., Rector of Eversley and Canon of Westminster. (For other Works by the same Author, see THEOLOGICAL and BELLES LETTRES CATALOGUES.)
AT LAST: A CHRISTMAS in the WEST INDIES. With nearly Fifty Illustrations. New Edition. Crown 8vo. 6s.
THE ROMAN AND THE TEUTON. A Series of Lectures delivered before the University of Cambridge. New and Cheaper Edition, with Preface by Professor MAX MÜLLER. Crown 8vo. 6s.

HISTORY, BIOGRAPHY, TRAVELS, ETC. 13

KINGSLEY (CHARLES)—*Continued.*
PLAYS AND PURITANS, and other Historical Essays. With Portrait of Sir WALTER RALEIGH. New Edition. Crown 8vo. 6s.
In addition to the Essay mentioned in the title, this volume contains other two—one on "Sir Walter Raleigh and his Time," and one on Froude's "History of England."
HISTORICAL LECTURES AND ESSAYS. Crown 8vo. 6s.
SANITARY AND SOCIAL LECTURES AND ESSAYS. Crown 8vo. 6s.
SCIENTIFIC LECTURES AND ESSAYS. Crown 8vo. 6s
LITERARY AND GENERAL LECTURES. Crown 8vo. 6s.

KINGSLEY (HENRY).—TALES OF OLD TRAVEL. Re-narrated by HENRY KINGSLEY, F.R.G.S. With Eight Illustrations by HUARD. Fifth Edition. Crown 8vo. 5s.

LANG.—CYPRUS: Its History, its Present Resources and Future Prospects. By R. HAMILTON LANG, late H.M. Consul for the Island of Cyprus. With Two Illustrations and Four Maps. 8vo. 14s.

LAOCOON.—Translated from the Text of Lessing, with Preface and Notes by the Right Hon. Sir ROBERT J. PHILLIMORE, D.C.L. With Photographs. 8vo. 12s.

LECTURES ON ART.—Delivered in support of the Society for Protection of Ancient Buildings. By REGD. STUART POOLE, Professor W. B. RICHMOND, E. J. POYNTER, R.A., J. T. MICKLETHWAITE, and WILLIAM MORRIS. Crown 8vo. 4s. 6d.

LEONARDO DA VINCI AND HIS WORKS.—Consisting of a Life of Leonardo da Vinci, by Mrs. CHARLES W. HEATON, Author of "Albrecht Dürer of Nürnberg," &c., an Essay on his Scientific and Literary Works, by CHARLES CHRISTOPHER BLACK, M.A., and an account of his more important Paintings and Drawings. Illustrated with Permanent Photographs. Royal 8vo., cloth, extra gilt. 31s. 6d.

LETHBRIDGE.—A SHORT MANUAL OF THE HISTORY OF INDIA, with an account of INDIA AS IT IS. The Soil, Climate, and Productions; the People—their Races, Religions, Public Works, and Industries; the Civil Services and System of Administration. By ROPER LETHBRIDGE, M.A., C.I.E., Press Commissioner with the Government of India, late Scholar of Exeter College, &c. &c. With Maps. Crown 8vo. 5s.

LIECHTENSTEIN.—HOLLAND HOUSE. By Princess MARIE LEICHTENSTEIN. With Five Steel Engravings by C. H. JEENS, after paintings by WATTS and other celebrated Artists, and numerous Illustrations drawn by Professor P. H. DELAMOTTE, and engraved on Wood by J. D. COOPER, W. PALMER, and JEWITT & Co., about 40 Illustrations by the Woodbury-type process, and India Proofs of the Steel Engravings. Two vols. Medium 4to., half morocco elegant. 4l. 4s.

LLOYD.—THE AGE OF PERICLES. A History of the Arts and Politics of Greece from the Persian to the Peloponnesian War. By W. WATKISS LLOYD. Two Vols. 8vo. 21s.

LOCH ETIVE AND THE SONS OF UISNACH.—With Illustrations. 8vo. 14s.

LOFTIE.—A RIDE IN EGYPT FROM SIOOT TO LUXOR, IN 1879; with Notes on the Present State and Ancient History of the Nile Valley, and some account of the various ways of making the voyage out and home. By the Rev. W. J. LOFTIE, B.A. With Illustrations. Crown 8vo. 10s. 6d.

LUBBOCK.—Works by Sir JOHN LUBBOCK, Bart., M.P., D.C.L., F.R.S.
ADDRESSES, POLITICAL AND EDUCATIONAL. 8vo. 8s. 6d.
FIFTY YEARS OF SCIENCE. Being the address delivered at York to the British Association, August, 1881. 8vo. 2s. 6d.

MACDONELL.—FRANCE SINCE THE FIRST EMPIRE. By JAMES MACDONELL. Edited with Preface by his Wife. Crown 8vo. 6s.

MACARTHUR.—HISTORY OF SCOTLAND. By MARGARET MACARTHUR. Being the Third Volume of the Historical Course for Schools, Edited by EDWARD A. FREEMAN, D.C.L. Second Edition. 18mo. 2s.

MACMILLAN (REV. HUGH).—For other Works by same Author, see THEOLOGICAL and SCIENTIFIC CATALOGUES.
HOLIDAYS ON HIGH LANDS; or, Rambles and Incidents in search of Alpine Plants. Second Edition, revised and enlarged. Globe 8vo. 6s.

MACMILLAN (DANIEL).—MEMOIR OF DANIEL MACMILLAN. By THOMAS HUGHES, Q.C., Author of "Tom Brown's Schooldays," etc. With Portrait engraved on Steel by C. H. JEENS, from a Painting by LOWES DICKINSON. Fourth Thousand. Crown 8vo. 4s. 6d.

MACREADY.—MACREADY'S REMINISCENCES AND SELECTIONS FROM HIS DIARIES AND LETTERS. Edited by Sir F. POLLOCK, Bart., one of his Executors. With Four Portraits engraved by JEENS. New and Cheaper Edition. Crown 8vo. 7s. 6d.

MAHAFFY.—Works by the Rev. J. P. MAHAFFY, M.A., Fellow of Trinity College, Dublin:—
SOCIAL LIFE IN GREECE FROM HOMER TO MENANDER. Fourth Edition, revised and enlarged, with a new chapter on Greek Art. Crown 8vo. 9s.
RAMBLES AND STUDIES IN GREECE. With Illustrations. New and enlarged Edition, with Map and Illustrations. Crown 8vo. 10s. 6d.

MARGARY.—THE JOURNEY OF AUGUSTUS RAYMOND MARGARY FROM SHANGHAE TO BHAMO AND BACK TO MANWYNE. From his Journals and Letters, with a brief Biographical Preface, a concluding chapter by Sir RUTHERFORD ALCOCK, K.C.B., and a Steel Portrait engraved by JEENS, and Map. 8vo. 10s. 6d.

MARKHAM.—NORTHWARD HO! By Captain ALBERT H. MARKHAM, R.N., Author of "The Great Frozen Sea," &c. Including a narrative of Captain Phipps's Expedition, by a Midshipman. With Illustrations. Crown 8vo. 10s. 6d.

MARTIN.—THE HISTORY OF LLOYD'S, AND OF MARINE INSURANCE IN GREAT BRITAIN. With an Appendix containing Statistics relating to Marine Insurance. By FREDERICK MARTIN, Author of "The Statesman's Year Book." 8vo. 14s.

MARTINEAU.—BIOGRAPHICAL SKETCHES, 1852-75. By HARRIET MARTINEAU. With Four Additional Sketches, and Autobiographical Sketch. Fifth Edition. Crown 8vo. 6s. (Biographical Series.)

MASSON (DAVID).—For other Works by same Author, see PHILOSOPHICAL and BELLES LETTRES CATALOGUE.
CHATTERTON: A Story of the Year 1770. By DAVID MASSON, LL.D., Professor of Rhetoric and English Literature in the University of Edinburgh. Crown 8vo. 5s.
THE THREE DEVILS: Luther's, Goethe's, and Milton's; and other Essays. Crown 8vo. 5s.
WORDSWORTH, SHELLEY, AND KEATS; and other Essays. Crown 8vo. 5s.

MATHEWS.—LIFE OF CHARLES J. MATHEWS, Chiefly Autobiographical. With Selections from his Correspondence and Speeches. Edited by CHARLES DICKENS. Two Vols. 8vo. 25s.

MAURICE.—THE FRIENDSHIP OF BOOKS; AND OTHER LECTURES. By the Rev. F. D. MAURICE. Edited with Preface, by THOMAS HUGHES, Q.C. Crown 8vo. 10s. 6d.

MAXWELL.—PROFESSOR CLERK MAXWELL, A LIFE OF. With a Selection from his Correspondence and Occasional Writings, and a Sketch of his Contributions to Science. By LEWIS CAMPBELL, M.A., LL.D., Professor of Greek in the University of St. Andrews, and Professor WILLIAM GARNETT, M.A., late Fellow of St. John's College, Cambridge, &c. With Three Portraits engraved on Steel, Coloured Plates, Illustrations, &c. 8vo. 18s.

MAYOR (J. E. B.)—WORKS edited by JOHN E. B. MAYOR, M.A., Kennedy Professor of Latin at Cambridge:—

CAMBRIDGE IN THE SEVENTEENTH CENTURY. Part II. Autobiography of Matthew Robinson. Fcap. 8vo. 5s. 6d.

LIFE OF BISHOP BEDELL. By his SON. Fcap. 8vo. 3s. 6d.

MELBOURNE.—MEMOIRS OF THE RT. HON. WILLIAM, SECOND VISCOUNT MELBOURNE. By W. M. TORRENS, M.P. With Portrait after Sir T. Lawrence. Second Edition. Two Vols. 8vo. 32s.

MENDELSSOHN.—LETTERS AND RECOLLECTIONS. By FERDINAND HILLER. Translated by M. E. VON GLEHN. With Portrait from a Drawing by KARL MÜLLER, never before published. Second Edition. Crown 8vo. 7s. 6d.

MEREWETHER.—BY SEA AND BY LAND. Being a Trip through Egypt, India, Ceylon, Australia, New Zealand, and America—All Round the World. By HENRY ALWORTH MEREWETHER, one of Her Majesty's Counsel. Crown 8vo. 8s. 6d.

MICHAEL ANGELO BUONAROTTI; Sculptor, Painter, Architect. The Story of his Life and Labours. By C. C. BLACK, M.A. Illustrated by 20 Permanent Photographs. Royal 8vo. cloth elegant. 31s. 6d.

MICHELET.—A SUMMARY OF MODERN HISTORY. Translated from the French of M. MICHELET, and continued to the present time by M. C. M. SIMPSON. Globe 8vo. 4s. 6d.

MILLET.—JEAN FRANÇOIS MILLET; Peasant and Painter. Translated from the French of ALFRED SENSIER. With numerous Illustrations Globe 4to. 16s.

MILTON.—LIFE OF JOHN MILTON. Narrated in connection with the Political, Ecclesiastical, and Literary History of his Time. By DAVID MASSON, M.A., LL.D., Professor of Rhetoric and English Literature in the University of Edinburgh. With Portraits. Vol. I. 1608—1639. New and Revised Edition. 8vo. 21s. Vol. II. 1638—1643. 8vo. 16s. Vol. III. 1643—1649. 8vo. 18s. Vols. IV. and V. 1649—1660. 32s. Vol. VI. 1660—1674. With Portrait. 21s.

[*Index Volume in preparation.*]

This work is not only a Biography, but also a continuous Political, Ecclesiastical, and Literary History of England through Milton's whole time.

MITFORD (A. B.)—TALES OF OLD JAPAN. By A. B. MITFORD, Second Secretary to the British Legation in Japan. With upwards of 30 Illustrations, drawn and cut on Wood by Japanese Artists. New and Cheaper Edition. Crown 8vo. 6s.

MONTEIRO.—ANGOLA AND THE RIVER CONGO. By JOACHIM MONTEIRO. With numerous Illustrations from Sketches taken on the spot, and a Map. Two Vols. Crown 8vo. 21s.

MOSELEY.—NOTES BY A NATURALIST ON THE *CHALLENGER*; being an Account of various Observations made during the Voyage of H.M.S. *Challenger* Round the World in 1872—76. By H. N. MOSELEY, F.R.S., Member of the Scientific Staff of the *Challenger*. With Maps, Coloured Plates, and Woodcuts. 8vo. 21s.

MURRAY.—ROUND ABOUT FRANCE. By E. C. GRENVILLE MURRAY. Crown 8vo. 7s. 6d.

MUSIC.—DICTIONARY OF MUSIC AND MUSICIANS (A.D. 1450—1881). By Eminent Writers, English and Foreign. Edited by GEORGE GROVE, D.C.L. Three Vols. 8vo. With Illustrations and Woodcuts. Parts I. to XIV., 3s. 6d. each. Parts XV. and XVI., 7s. Vols. I. and II. 8vo. 21s. each.

Vol. I.—A to Impromptu. Vol. II.—Improperia to Plain Song.

NAPIER.—MACVEY NAPIER'S SELECTED CORRESPONDENCE. Edited by his Son, MACVEY NAPIER. 8vo. 14s.

NAPOLEON.—THE HISTORY OF NAPOLEON I. By P. LANFREY. A Translation with the sanction of the Author. Four Vols. 8vo. Vols. I. II. and III. price 12s. each. Vol. IV. With Index. 6s.

NEWTON.—ESSAYS ON ART AND ARCHÆOLOGY. By CHARLES THOMAS NEWTON, C.B., Ph.D., D.C.L., LL.D., Keeper of Greek and Roman Antiquities at the British Museum, &c. 8vo. 12s. 6d.

NICHOL.—TABLES OF EUROPEAN LITERATURE AND HISTORY, A.D. 200—1876. By J. NICHOL, LL.D., Professor of English Language and Literature, Glasgow. 4to. 6s. 6d.
TABLES OF ANCIENT LITERATURE AND HISTORY, B.C. 1500—A.D. 200. By the same Author. 4to. 4s. 6d.

NORDENSKIÖLD'S ARCTIC VOYAGES, 1858-79.—With Maps and numerous Illustrations. 8vo. 16s.
VOYAGE OF THE *VEGA*. By ADOLF ERIK NORDENSKIÖLD. Translated by ALEXANDER LESLIE. With numerous Illustrations, Maps, Plans, Steel Plates, &c. 2 vols. Medium 8vo. 45s.

OLIPHANT (MRS.).—Works by Mrs. OLIPHANT.
THE MAKERS OF FLORENCE: Dante, Giotto, Savonarola, and their City. With numerous Illustrations from drawings by Professor DELAMOTTE, and portrait of Savonarola, engraved by JEENS. New and Cheaper Edition. Crown 8vo. 10s. 6d.
THE LITERARY HISTORY OF ENGLAND IN THE END OF THE EIGHTEENTH AND BEGINNING OF THE NINETEENTH CENTURY. New Issue, with a Preface. 3 vols. Demy 8vo. 21s.

OLIPHANT.—THE DUKE AND THE SCHOLAR; and other Essays By T. L. KINGTON OLIPHANT. 8vo. 7s. 6d.

OTTE.—SCANDINAVIAN HISTORY. By E. C. OTTE. With Maps. Extra fcap. 8vo. 6s.

OWENS COLLEGE ESSAYS AND ADDRESSES.—By PROFESSORS AND LECTURERS OF OWENS COLLEGE, MANCHESTER. Published in Commemoration of the Opening of the New College Buildings, October 7th, 1873. 8vo. 14s.

PALGRAVE (R. F. D.)—THE HOUSE OF COMMONS; Illustrations of its History and Practice. By REGINALD F. D. PALGRAVE, Clerk Assistant of the House of Commons. New and Revised Edition. Crown 8vo. 2s. 6d.

HISTORY, BIOGRAPHY, TRAVELS, ETC.

PALGRAVE (SIR F.)—HISTORY OF NORMANDY AND OF ENGLAND. By Sir FRANCIS PALGRAVE, Deputy Keeper of Her Majesty's Public Records. Completing the History to the Death of William Rufus. 4 Vols. 8vo. 4*l.* 4*s.*

PALGRAVE (W. G.)—A NARRATIVE OF A YEAR'S JOURNEY THROUGH CENTRAL AND EASTERN ARABIA, 1862–3. By WILLIAM GIFFORD PALGRAVE, late of the Eighth Regiment Bombay N.I. Sixth Edition. With Maps, Plans, and Portrait of Author, engraved on steel by JEENS. Crown 8vo. 6*s.*

ESSAYS ON EASTERN QUESTIONS. By W. GIFFORD PALGRAVE. 8vo. 10*s.* 6*d.*

DUTCH GUIANA. With Maps and Plans. 8vo. 9*s.*

PATTESON.—LIFE AND LETTERS OF JOHN COLERIDGE PATTESON, D.D., Missionary Bishop of the Melanesian Islands. By CHARLOTTE M. YONGE, Author of "The Heir of Redclyffe." With Portraits after RICHMOND and from Photograph, engraved by JEENS. With Map. Fifth Edition. Two Vols. Crown 8vo. 12*s.*

PAULI.—PICTURES OF OLD ENGLAND. By Dr. REINHOLD PAULI. Translated with the approval of the Author, by E. C. OTTE, Cheaper Edition. Crown 8vo. 6*s.*

PAYNE.—A HISTORY OF EUROPEAN COLONIES. By E. J. PAYNE, M.A. With Maps. 18mo. 4*s.* 6*d.* [*Historical Course for Schools.*

PERSIA.—EASTERN PERSIA. An Account of the Journeys of the Persian Boundary Commission, 1870-1-2.—Vol. I. The Geography, with Narratives by Majors ST. JOHN, LOVETT, and EUAN SMITH, and an Introduction by Major-General Sir FREDERIC GOLDSMID, C.B., K.C.S.I., British Commissioner and Arbitrator. With Maps and Illustrations.—Vol. II. The Zoology and Geology. By W. T. BLANDFORD, A.R.S.M., F R.S. With Coloured Illustrations. Two Vols. 8vo. 42*s.*

PHEAR.—THE ARYAN VILLAGE IN INDIA AND CEYLON. By Sir JOHN B. PHEAR. Crown 8vo. 7*s.* 6*d.*

POOLE.—A HISTORY OF THE HUGUENOTS OF THE DISPERSION AT THE RECALL OF THE EDICT OF NANTES. By REGINALD LANE POOLE. Crown 8vo. 6*s.*

PRICHARD.—THE ADMINISTRATION OF INDIA. From 1859 to 1868. The First Ten Years of Administration under the Crown. By I. T. PRICHARD, Barrister-at-Law. Two Vols. Demy 8vo. With Map. 21*s.*

RAPHAEL.—RAPHAEL OF URBINO AND HIS FATHER GIOVANNI SANTI. By J. D. PASSAVANT, formerly Director of the Museum at Frankfort. With Twenty Permanent Photographs. Royal 8vo. Handsomely bound. 31*s.* 6*d.*

REED (SIR CHAS.).—SIR CHARLES REED. A Memoir by CHARLES E. B. REED, M.A. Crown 8vo. [*Just ready.*

REMBRANDT.—THE ETCHED WORK OF REMBRANDT. A MONOGRAPH. By FRANCIS SEYMOUR HADEN. With three Plates. 8vo. 7*s.* 6*d.*

ROGERS (JAMES E. THOROLD).—HISTORICAL GLEANINGS:—A Series of Sketches. Montague, Walpole, Adam Smith, Cobbett. By Prof. ROGERS, M.P. Crown 8vo. 4*s.* 6*d.* Second Series. Wiklif, Laud, Wilkes, and Horne Tooke. Crown 8vo. 6*s.*

ROSSETTI.—DANTE GABRIEL ROSSETTI: a Record and a Study. By WILLIAM SHARP. With an Illustration after Dante Gabriel Rossetti. Crown 8vo. 10*s.* 6*d.*

b

ROUTLEDGE.—CHAPTERS IN THE HISTORY OF POPULAR PROGRESS IN ENGLAND, chiefly in Relation to the Freedom of the Press and Trial by Jury, 1660—1820. With application to later years. By J. ROUTLEDGE. 8vo. 16s.

RUMFORD.—COUNT RUMFORD'S COMPLETE WORKS, with Memoir, and Notices of his Daughter. By GEORGE ELLIS. Five Vols. 8vo. 4l. 14s. 6d.

RUSSELL.—NEW VIEWS ON IRELAND, OR IRISH LAND GRIEVANCES AND REMEDIES. By CHARLES RUSSELL, Q.C., M.P. Third Edition. Crown 8vo. 2s. 6d.

SCHILLER.—A LIFE OF SCHILLER. By Professor DÜNTZER. Translated by P. E. PINKERTON. With Illustrations. Crown 8vo. [Just ready.

SEELEY (PROFESSOR).—LECTURES AND ESSAYS. By J. R. SEELEY, M.A., Professor of Modern History in the University of Cambridge. 8vo. 10s. 6d.
CONTENTS:—Roman Imperialism: 1. The Great Roman Revolution; 2. The Proximate Cause of the Fall of the Roman Empire; The Later Empire.—Milton's Political Opinions—Milton's Poetry—Elementary Principles in Art—Liberal Education in Universities—English in Schools—The Church as a Teacher of Morality—The Teaching of Politics: an Inaugural Lecture delivered at Cambridge.

SHELBURNE.—LIFE OF WILLIAM, EARL OF SHELBURNE, AFTERWARDS FIRST MARQUIS OF LANDSDOWNE. With Extracts from his Papers and Correspondence. By Lord EDMOND FITZMAURICE. In Three Vols. 8vo. Vol. I. 1737—1766, 12s.; Vol. II. 1766—1776, 12s.; Vol. III. 1776—1805. 16s.

SIBSON.—COLLECTED WORKS OF FRANCIS SIBSON, M.D., Lond., Fellow of the Royal Society, Honorary M.D. Trinity College, Dublin, and D.C.L. Durham, Fellow of the Royal College of Physicians, &c. Edited by WILLIAM M. ORD, M.D. With Illustrations. Four Volumes. 8vo. 3l. 3s.

SIME.—HISTORY OF GERMANY. By JAMES SIME, M.A. 18mo. 3s. Being Vol. V. of the Historical Course for Schools. Edited by EDWARD A. FREEMAN, D.C.L.

SMITH (GOLDWIN).—THREE ENGLISH STATESMEN. A Course of Lectures on the Political History of England. By GOLDWIN SMITH, M.A., D.C.L. New Edition. Crown 8vo. 5s.

SPINOZA.—SPINOZA: a Study of. By JAMES MARTINEAU, LL.D., D.D., Principal of Manchester New College, London. With Portrait. Crown 8vo. 6s.

SQUIER.—PERU: INCIDENTS OF TRAVEL AND EXPLORATION IN THE LAND OF THE INCAS. By E. G. SQUIER, M.A., F.S.A., late U.S. Commissioner to Peru. With 300 Illustrations. Second Edition. 8vo. 21s.

ST. ANSELM.—By the Very Rev. R. W. CHURCH, M.A., Dean of St. Paul's. New Edition. Crown 8vo. 6s. (Biographical Series.)

STATHAM.—BLACKS, BOERS, AND BRITISH: A Three-Cornered Problem. By F. R. STATHAM. Crown 8vo. 6s.

STEVENSON.—HOUSE ARCHITECTURE. By J. J. STEVENSON, Fellow of the Royal Institution of British Architects. With numerous Illustrations. Royal 8vo. 2 Vols. 18s. each. Vol. I. Architecture. Vol. II. House Planning.

STRANGFORD.—EGYPTIAN SHRINES AND SYRIAN SEPULCHRES, including a Visit to Palmyra. By EMILY A. BEAUFORT (Viscountess Strangford), Author of "The Eastern Shores of the Adriatic." New Edition. Crown 8vo. 7s. 6d.

HISTORY, BIOGRAPHY, TRAVELS, ETC. 19

TAIT.—AN ANALYSIS OF ENGLISH HISTORY, based upon Green's "Short History of the English People." By C. W. A. TAIT, M.A., Assistant Master, Clifton College. Crown 8vo. 3s. 6d.

TAIT.—CATHARINE AND CRAUFURD TAIT, WIFE AND SON OF ARCHIBALD CAMPBELL, ARCHBISHOP OF CANTERBURY: a Memoir, Edited, at the request of the Archbishop, by the Rev. W. BENHAM, B.D., Rector of St. Edmund-the-King and St. Nicholas Acons, One of the Six Preachers of Canterbury Cathedral. With Two Portraits engraved by JEENS. New and Cheaper Edition. Crown 8vo. 6s. (Biographical Series.) Abridged Edition. Crown 8vo. 2s. 6d.

TERESA.—THE LIFE OF ST. TERESA. By MARIA TRENCH. With Portrait engraved by JEENS. Crown 8vo, cloth extra. 8s. 6d.

THOMAS.—THE LIFE OF JOHN THOMAS, Surgeon of the "Earl of Oxford" East Indiaman, and First Baptist Missionary to Bengal. By C. B. LEWIS, Baptist Missionary. 8vo. 10s. 6d.

THOMPSON.—A HANDBOOK TO THE PUBLIC PICTURE GALLERIES OF EUROPE. With a Brief Sketch of the History of the various Schools of painting. From the Thirteenth Century to the Eighteenth inclusive. By KATE THOMPSON. Third Edition. With Illustrations. Crown 8vo. 7s. 6d.

THOMPSON.—HISTORY OF ENGLAND. By EDITH THOMPSON. Being Vol. II. of the Historical Course for Schools, Edited by EDWARD A. FREEMAN, D.C.L. New Edition, revised and enlarged, with Coloured Maps. 18mo. 2s. 6d.

THROUGH THE RANKS TO A COMMISSION.—New and Popular Edition. Crown 8vo. 2s. 6d.

TODHUNTER.—THE CONFLICT OF STUDIES; AND OTHER ESSAYS ON SUBJECTS CONECTED WITH EDUCATION. By ISAAC TODHUNTER, M.A., F.R.S., late Fellow and Principal Mathematical Lecturer of St. John's College, Cambridge. 8vo. 10s. 6d.

TRENCH (ARCHBISHOP).—For other Works by the same Author, see THEOLOGICAL and BELLES LETTRES CATALOGUES, and page 28 of this Catalogue.

GUSTAVUS ADOLPHUS IN GERMANY, and other Lectures on the Thirty Years' War. Second Edition, revised and enlarged. Fcap. 8vo. 4s.

PLUTARCH, HIS LIFE, HIS LIVES, AND HIS MORALS. Five Lectures. Second Edition, enlarged. Fcap. 8vo. 3s. 6d.

LECTURES ON MEDIEVAL CHURCH HISTORY. Being the substance of Lectures delivered in Queen's College, London. Second Edition, revised. 8vo. 12s.

AN ESSAY ON THE LIFE AND GENIUS OF CALDERON. With Translations from his "Life's a Dream" and "Great Theatre of the World." Second Edition, revised and improved. Fcap. 8vo. 5s.

TRENCH (MRS. R.).—REMAINS OF THE LATE MRS. RICHARD TRENCH. Being Selections from her Journals, Letters, and other Papers. Edited by ARCHBISHOP TRENCH. New and Cheaper Issue, with Portrait. 8vo. 6s.

TREVELYAN.—THE IRISH CRISIS. Being a Narrative of the Measures for the Relief of the Distress caused by the Great Irish Famine of 1846-7. By Sir CHARLES TREVELYAN, Bart., K.C.B. 8vo. 2s. 6d.

TROLLOPE.—A HISTORY OF THE COMMONWEALTH OF FLORENCE FROM THE EARLIEST INDEPENDENCE OF THE COMMUNE TO THE FALL OF THE REPUBLIC IN 1831. By T. ADOLPHUS TROLLOPE. 4 Vols. 8vo. Cloth, 21s.

TYLOR.—ANTHROPOLOGY: an Introduction to the Study of Man and Civilisation. By E. B. TYLOR, D.C.L., F.R.S. With Illustrations. Crown 8vo. 7s. 6d.

UPPINGHAM BY THE SEA.—A NARRATIVE OF THE YEAR AT BORTH. By J. H. S. Crown 8vo. 3s. 6d.

VICTOR EMMANUEL II., FIRST KING OF ITALY. By G. S. GODKIN. New Edition. Crown 8vo. 6s. (Biographical Series.)

WALLACE.—THE MALAY ARCHIPELAGO: the Land of the Orang Utan and the Bird of Paradise. By ALFRED RUSSEL WALLACE. A Narrative of Travel with Studies of Man and Nature. With Maps and numerous Illustrations. Sixth Edition. Crown 8vo. 7s. 6d.

WARD.—A HISTORY OF ENGLISH DRAMATIC LITERATURE TO THE DEATH OF QUEEN ANNE. By A. W. WARD, M.A., Professor of History and English Literature in Owens College, Manchester. Two Vols. 8vo. 32s.

WARD (J.)—EXPERIENCES OF A DIPLOMATIST. Being recollections of Germany founded on Diaries kept during the years 1840—1870. By JOHN WARD, C.B., late H.M. Minister-Resident to the Hanse Towns. 8vo. 10s. 6d.

WARD.—ENGLISH POETS. Selections, with Critical Introductions by various writers, and a General Introduction by MATTHEW ARNOLD. Edited by T. H. WARD, M.A. 4 vols. Crown 8vo. 7s. 6d. each.
Vol. I. CHAUCER to DONNE.
Vol. II. BEN JONSON to DRYDEN.
Vol. III. ADDISON to BLAKE.
Vol. IV. WORDSWORTH to SYDNEY DOBELL.

WATERTON (C.)—WANDERINGS IN SOUTH AMERICA, THE NORTH-WEST OF THE UNITED STATES, AND THE ANTILLES IN 1812, 1816, 1820, and 1824. With Original Instructions for the perfect Preservation of Birds, etc., for Cabinets of Natural History. By CHARLES WATERTON. New Edition, edited with Biographical Introduction and Explanatory Index by the Rev. J. G. WOOD. M.A. With 100 Illustrations. Cheaper Edition. Crown 8vo. 6s.

WATSON.—A VISIT TO WAZAN, THE SACRED CITY OF MOROCCO. By ROBERT SPENCE WATSON. With Illustrations. 8vo. 10s. 6d.

WESLEY.—JOHN WESLEY AND THE EVANGELICAL REACTION of the Eighteenth Century. By JULIA WEDGWOOD. Crown 8vo. 8s. 6d.

WHEELER.—A SHORT HISTORY OF INDIA, AND OF THE FRONTIER STATES OF AFGHANISTAN, NEPAUL, AND BURMA. By J. TALBOYS WHEELER, late Assistant-Secretary to the Government of India, Foreign Department, and late Secretary to the Government of British Burma. With Maps and Tables. Crown 8vo. 12s.

WHEWELL.—WILLIAM WHEWELL, D.D., late Master of Trinity College, Cambridge. An account of his Writings, with Selections from his Literary and Scientific correspondence. By I. TODHUNTER, M.A., F.R.S. Two Vols. 8vo. 25s.

WHITE.—THE NATURAL HISTORY AND ANTIQUITIES OF SELBORNE. By GILBERT WHITE. Edited, with Memoir and Notes, by FRANK BUCKLAND, A Chapter on Antiquities by LORD SELBORNE, and numerous Illustrations by P. H. DELAMOTTE. New and Cheaper Edition. Crown 8vo. 6s.

Also a Large Paper Edition, containing, in addition to the above, upwards of Thirty Woodburytype Illustrations from Drawings by Prof. DELAMOTTE. Two Vols. 4to. Half morocco, elegant. 4l. 4s.

HISTORY, BIOGRAPHY, TRAVELS, ETC.

WILSON.—A MEMOIR OF GEORGE WILSON, M.D., F.R.S.E., Regius Professor of Technology in the University of Edinburgh. By his SISTER. New Edition. Crown 8vo. 6s.

WILSON (DANIEL, LL.D.)—Works by DANIEL WILSON, LL.D., Professor of History and English Literature in University College, Toronto :—

PREHISTORIC ANNALS OF SCOTLAND. New Edition, with numerous Illustrations. Two Vols. Demy 8vo. 36s.

PREHISTORIC MAN : Researches into the Origin of Civilization in the Old and New World. New Edition, revised and enlarged throughout, with numerous Illustrations and Two Coloured Plates. Two Vols. 8vo. 36s.

CHATTERTON : A Biographical Study. Crown 8vo. 6s. 6d.

YOE.—THE BURMAN : His Life and Notions. By SHWAY YOE. Two Vols. Crown 8vo. 9s.

YONGE (CHARLOTTE M.)—Works by CHARLOTTE M. YONGE, Author of the "Heir of Redclyffe," &c. &c. :—

A PARALLEL HISTORY OF FRANCE AND ENGLAND: Consisting of Outlines and Dates. Oblong 4to. 3s. 6d.

CAMEOS FROM ENGLISH HISTORY. From Rollo to Edward II. Extra Fcap. 8vo. Third Edition. 5s.

SECOND SERIES, THE WARS IN FRANCE. Extra fcap. 8vo. Third Edition. 5s.

THIRD SERIES, THE WARS OF THE ROSES. Extra fcap. 8vo. 5s.

FOURTH SERIES, REFORMATION TIMES. Extra fcap. 8vo. 5s.

HISTORY OF FRANCE. Maps. 18mo. 3s. 6d.
[*Historical Course for Schools*

POLITICS, POLITICAL AND SOCIAL ECONOMY, LAW, AND KINDRED SUBJECTS.

ANGLO-SAXON LAW.—ESSAYS IN. Contents: Law Courts—Land and Family Laws and Legal Procedure generally. With Select cases. Medium 8vo. 18*s*.

ARNOLD.—THE ROMAN SYSTEM OF PROVINCIAL ADMINISTRATION TO THE ACCESSION OF CONSTANTINE THE GREAT. Being the Arnold Prize Essay for 1879. By W. T. ARNOLD, B.A. Crown 8vo. 6*s*.

BALL.—THE STUDENT'S GUIDE TO THE BAR. By WALTER W. BALL, M.A., of the Inner Temple, Barrister-at-Law. Crown 8vo. 2*s*. 6*d*.

BERNARD.—FOUR LECTURES ON SUBJECTS CONNECTED WITH DIPLOMACY. By MONTAGUE BERNARD, M. A., Chichele Professor of International Law and Diplomacy, Oxford. 8vo. 9*s*.

BIGELOW.—HISTORY OF PROCEDURE IN ENGLAND, FROM THE NORMAN CONQUEST. The Norman Period, 1066-1204. By MELVILLE MADISON BIGELOW, Ph.D., Harvard University. 8vo. 16*s*.

BRIGHT (JOHN, M.P.).—Works by the Right Hon. JOHN BRIGHT, M.P.

SPEECHES ON QUESTIONS OF PUBLIC POLICY. Edited by Professor THOROLD ROGERS, M.P. Author's Popular Edition. Globe 8vo. 3*s*. 6*d*.

LIBRARY EDITION. Two Vols. 8vo. With Portrait. 25*s*.

PUBLIC ADDRESSES. Edited by J. THOROLD ROGERS, M.P. 8vo. 14*s*.

BUCKNILL.—Works by J. C. BUCKNILL, M.D., F.R.S., late Lord Chancellor's Visitor of Lunatics:—

HABITUAL DRUNKENNESS AND INSANE DRUNKARDS. Crown 8vo. 2*s*. 6*d*.

THE CARE OF THE INSANE, AND THEIR LEGAL CONTROL. Crown 8vo. 3*s*. 6*d*.

CAIRNES.—Works by J. E. CAIRNES, M.A., Emeritus Professor of Political Economy in University College, London:—

POLITICAL ESSAYS. 8vo. 10*s*. 6*d*.

THE CHARACTER AND LOGICAL METHOD OF POLITICAL ECONOMY. New Edition, enlarged. 8vo. 7*s*. 6*d*.

COBDEN (RICHARD).—SPEECHES ON QUESTIONS OF PUBLIC POLICY. By RICHARD COBDEN. Edited by the Right Hon John Bright, M.P., and J. E. Thorold Rogers, M.P. Popular Edition. 8vo. 3*s*. 6*d*.

COSSA.—GUIDE TO THE STUDY OF POLITICAL ECONOMY. By Dr. LUIGI COSSA, Professor of Political Economy in the University of Pavia. Translated from the Second Italian Edition. With a Preface by W. STANLEY JEVONS, F.R.S. Crown 8vo. 4*s*. 6*d*.

FAWCETT.—Works by Right Hon. HENRY FAWCETT, M.A., M.P., F.R.S., Fellow of Trinity Hall, and Professor of Political Economy in the University of Cambridge:—

THE ECONOMIC POSITION OF THE BRITISH LABOURER. Extra fcap. 8vo. 5*s*.

FAWCETT—*continued.*
MANUAL OF POLITICAL ECONOMY. Fifth Edition, with New Chapters on the Depreciation of Silver, etc. Crown 8vo. 12s.

PAUPERISM: ITS CAUSES AND REMEDIES. Crown 8vo. 5s. 6d.

SPEECHES ON SOME CURRENT POLITICAL QUESTIONS. 8vo. 10s. 6d.

FREE TRADE AND PROTECTION: and Inquiry into the Causes which have retarded the general adoption of Free Trade since its introduction into England. Fourth and Cheaper Edition. Crown 8vo. 3s. 6d.

INDIAN FINANCE. Three Essays, with Introduction and Appendix. 8vo. 7s. 6d.

ESSAYS ON POLITICAL AND SOCIAL SUBJECTS. By Right Hon. HENRY FAWCETT, M.P., and MILLICENT GARRETT FAWCETT. 8vo. 10s. 6d.

FAWCETT (MRS.)—Works by MILLICENT GARRETT FAWCETT:—
POLITICAL ECONOMY FOR BEGINNERS. WITH QUESTIONS. New Edition. 18mo. 2s. 6d.

TALES IN POLITICAL ECONOMY. Crown 8vo. 3s.

GOSCHEN.—REPORTS AND SPEECHES ON LOCAL TAXATION. By GEORGE J. GOSCHEN, M.P. Royal 8vo. 5s.

GUIDE TO THE UNPROTECTED, in Every Day Matters Relating to Property and Income. By a BANKER'S DAUGHTER. Fifth Edition, Revised. Extra fcap. 8vo. 3s. 6d.

HAMILTON.—MONEY AND VALUE: an Inquiry into the Means and Ends of Economic Production, with an Appendix on the Depreciation of Silver and Indian Currency. By ROWLAND HAMILTON. 8vo. 12s.

HARWOOD.—Works by GEORGE HARWOOD, M.A.
DISESTABLISHMENT: a Defence of the Principle of a National Church. 8vo. 12s.

THE COMING DEMOCRACY. Crown 8vo. 6s.

HILL.—OUR COMMON LAND; and other Short Essays. By OCTAVIA HILL. Extra fcap. 8vo. 3s. 6d.

CONTENTS:—Our Common Land. District Visiting. A more Excellent Way of Charity. A Word on Good Citizenship. Open Spaces. Effectual Charity. The Future of our Commons.

HOLLAND.—THE TREATY RELATIONS OF RUSSIA AND TURKEY FROM 1774 TO 1853. A Lecture delivered at Oxford, April 1877. By T. E. HOLLAND, D.C.L., Professor of International Law and Diplomacy, Oxford. Crown 8vo. 2s.

HOLMES.—THE COMMON LAW. By O. W. HOLMES, JR. 8vo. 12s.

HUGHES (THOS.)—THE OLD CHURCH: WHAT SHALL WE DO WITH IT? By THOMAS HUGHES, Q.C. Crown 8vo. 6s.

JEVONS.—Works by W. STANLEY JEVONS, LL.D., M.A., F.R.S. (For other Works by the same Author, *see* EDUCATIONAL and PHILOSOPHICAL CATALOGUES.):—

THE THEORY OF POLITICAL ECONOMY. Second Edition, revised, with new Preface and Appendices. 8vo. 10s. 6d.

PRIMER OF POLITICAL ECONOMY. 18mo. 1s.

LAVELEYE.—PRIMITIVE PROPERTY. By EMILE DE LAVELEYE. Translated by G. R. L. MARRIOTT, LL.B., with an Introduction by T. E. CLIFFE LESLIE. LL.B. 8vo. 12s.

LEADING CASES DONE INTO ENGLISH.—By an APPRENTICE OF LINCOLN'S INN. Third Edition. Crown 8vo. 2s. 6d.

LUBBOCK.—ADDRESSES, POLITICAL AND EDUCATIONAL. By Sir JOHN LUBBOCK, Bart., M.P., &c., &c. 8vo. 8s. 6d.

MACDONELL.—THE LAND QUESTION, WITH SPECIAL REFERENCE TO ENGLAND AND SCOTLAND. By JOHN MACDONEL, Barrister-at-Law. 8vo. 10s. 6d.

MARSHALL.—THE ECONOMICS OF INDUSTRY. By A. MARSHALL, M.A., late Principal of University College Bristol, and MARY PALEY MARSHALL. late Lecturer at Newnham Hall, Cambridge. Extra fcap. 8vo. 2s. 6d.

MONAHAN.—THE METHOD OF LAW: an Essay on the Statement and Arrangement of the Legal Standard of Conduct. By J. H. MONAHAN, Q.C. Crown 8vo. 6s.

PATERSON.—Works by JAMES PATERSON, M.A., Barrister-at-Law, sometime Commissioner for English and Irish Fisheries, &c.

THE LIBERTY OF THE SUBJECT AND THE LAWS OF ENGLAND RELATING TO THE SECURITY OF THE PERSON. Commentaries on. Cheaper issue. Crown 8vo. 21s.

THE LIBERTY OF THE PRESS, OF SPEECH, AND OF PUBLIC WORSHIP. Being Commentaries on the Liberty of the Subject and the Laws of England. Crown 8vo. 12s.

PHEAR.—INTERNATIONAL TRADE, AND THE RELATION BETWEEN EXPORTS AND IMPORTS. A Paper read before the Exmouth Liberal Association, on July 22, 1881. By Sir JOHN B. PHEAR. Crown 8vo. 2s. 6d.

PHILLIMORE.—PRIVATE LAW AMONG THE ROMANS, from the Pandects. By JOHN GEORGE PHILLIMORE, Q.C. 8vo. 16s.

POLLOCK (F.).—ESSAYS IN JURISPRUDENCE AND ETHICS. By FREDERICK POLLOCK, M.A., LL.D., late Fellow of Trinity College, Cambridge. 8vo. 10s. 6d.

PRACTICAL POLITICS.—ISSUED BY THE NATIONAL LIBERAL FEDERATION. Complete in one volume. 8vo. 6s. Or :—

I. THE TENANT FARMER: Land Laws and Landlords. By JAMES HOWARD. 8vo. 1s.
II. FOREIGN POLICY. By Right Hon. M. E. GRANT DUFF, M.P. 8vo. 1s.
III. FREEDOM OF LAND. By G. SHAW LEFEVRE, M.P. 8vo. 2s. 6d.
IV. BRITISH COLONIAL POLICY. By Sir DAVID WEDDERBURN, Bart., M.P. Demy 8vo. 1s.

RICHEY.—THE IRISH LAND LAWS. By ALEXANDER G. RICHEY, Q.C., LL.D., Deputy Regius Professor of Feudal and English Law in the University of Dublin. Crown 8vo. 3s. 6d.

STATESMAN'S YEAR BOOK, THE: A STATISTICAL AND HISTORICAL ANNUAL OF THE STATES OF THE CIVILIZED WORLD, FOR THE YEAR 1883. Twentieth Annual Publication. Revised after Official Returns. Crown 8vo. 10s. 6d.

STEPHEN (C. E.)—THE SERVICE OF THE POOR; Being an Inquiry into the Reasons for and against the Establishment of Religious Sisterhoods for Charitable Purposes. By CAROLINE EMILIA STEPHEN. Crown 8vo. 6s. 6d.

STEPHEN.—Works by Sir JAMES FITZJAMES STEPHEN, K.C.S.I., D.C.L. A Judge of the High Court of Justice, Queen's Bench Division.

A DIGEST OF THE LAW OF EVIDENCE. Fourth Edition, with new Preface. Crown 8vo. 6s.

A HISTORY OF THE CRIMINAL LAW OF ENGLAND. Three Vols. Demy 8vo. 48s.

A DIGEST OF THE CRIMINAL LAW. (Crimes and Punishments.) 8vo. 16s.

A DIGEST OF THE LAW OF CRIMINAL PROCEDURE IN INDICTABLE OFFENCES. By Sir JAMES F. STEPHEN, K.C.S.I., a Judge of the High Court of Justice, Queen's Bench Division, and HERBERT STEPHEN, LL.M , of the Middle Temple, Barrister-at-Law. 8vo. 12s. 6d.

STUBBS.—VILLAGE POLITICS. Addresses and Sermons on the Labour Question. By C. W. STUBBS, M.A., Vicar of Granborough, Bucks. Extra fcap. 8vo. 3s. 6d.

THORNTON.—Works by W. T. THORNTON, C.B., Secretary for Public Works in the India Office:—

A PLEA FOR PEASANT PROPRIETORS: With the Outlines of a Plan for their Establishment in Ireland. New Edition, revised. Crown 8vo. 7s. 6d.

INDIAN PUBLIC WORKS AND COGNATE INDIAN TOPICS. With Map of Indian Railways. Crown 8vo. 8s. 6d.

WALKER.—Works by F. A. WALKER, M.A., Ph.D., Professor of Political Economy and History, Yale College:—

THE WAGES QUESTION. A Treatise on Wages and the Wages Class. 8vo. 14s.

MONEY. 8vo. 16s.

MONEY IN ITS RELATIONS TO TRADE AND INDUSTRY. Crown 8vo. 7s. 6d.

WILSON.—RECIPROCITY, BI-METALLISM, AND LAND-TENURE REFORM. By A. J. WILSON, Author of "The Resources of Modern Countries." 8vo. 7s. 6d.

WORKS CONNECTED WITH THE SCIENCE OR THE HISTORY OF LANGUAGE.

ABBOTT.—A SHAKESPERIAN GRAMMAR: An Attempt to illustrate some of the Differences between Elizabethan and Modern English. By the Rev. E. A. ABBOTT, D.D., Head Master of the City of London School. New and Enlarged Edition. Extra fcap. 8vo. 6s.

BREYMANN.—A FRENCH GRAMMAR BASED ON PHILOLOGICAL PRINCIPLES. By HERMANN BREYMANN, Ph.D., Professor of Philology in the University of Munich, late Lecturer on French Language and Literature at Owens College, Manchester. Extra fcap. 8vo. 4s. 6d.

ELLIS.—PRACTICAL HINTS ON THE QUANTITATIVE PRONUNCIATION OF LATIN, FOR THE USE OF CLASSICAL TEACHERS AND LINGUISTS. By A. J. ELLIS, B.A., F.R.S., &c. Extra fcap. 8vo. 4s. 6d.

FASNACHT.—Works by G. EUGENE FASNACHT, Author of "Macmillan's Progressive French Course," Editor of "Macmillan's Foreign School Classics," &c.

THE ORGANIC METHOD OF STUDYING LANGUAGES. I. French. Crown 8vo. 3s. 6d.

A SYNTHETIC FRENCH GRAMMAR FOR SCHOOLS. Crown 8vo. 3s. 6d.

FLEAY.—A SHAKESPEARE MANUAL. By the Rev. F. G. FLEAY. M.A., Head Master of Skipton Grammar School. Extra fcap. 8vo. 4s. 6d.

GOODWIN.—Works by W. W. GOODWIN, Professor of Greek Literature in Harvard University:—

SYNTAX OF THE GREEK MOODS AND TENSES. New Edition. Crown 8vo. 6s. 6d.

A SCHOOL GREEK GRAMMAR. Crown 8vo. 3s. 6d.

A GREEK GRAMMAR. Crown 8vo. 6s.

HADLEY.—ESSAYS PHILOLOGICAL AND CRITICAL. Selected from the Papers of JAMES HADLEY, LL.D., Professor of Greek in Yale College, &c. 8vo. 16s.

HALES.—LONGER ENGLISH POEMS. With Notes, Philological and Explanatory, and an Introduction on the Teaching of English. Chiefly for use in Schools. Edited by J. W. HALES, M.A., Professor of English Literature at King's College, London, &c. &c. Fifth Edition. Extra fcap. 8vo. 4s. 6d.

HELFENSTEIN (JAMES).—A COMPARATIVE GRAMMAR OF THE TEUTONIC LANGUAGES: Being at the same time a Historical Grammar of the English Language, and comprising Gothic, Anglo-Saxon, Early English, Modern English, Icelandic (Old Norse), Danish, Swedish, Old High German, Middle High German, Modern German, Old Saxon, Old Frisian, and Dutch. By JAMES HELFENSTEIN, Ph.D. 8vo. 18s.

WORKS ON LANGUAGE. 27

MASSON (GUSTAVE).—A COMPENDIOUS DICTIONARY OF THE FRENCH LANGUAGE (French-English and English-French). Adapted from the Dictionaries of Professor ALFRED ELWALL. Followed by a List of the Principal Diverging Derivations, and preceded by Chronological and Historical Tables. By GUSTAVE MASSON, Assistant-Master and Librarian, Harrow School. Fourth Edition. Crown 8vo. 6s.

MAYOR.—A BIBLIOGRAPHICAL CLUE TO LATIN LITERATURE. Edited after Dr. E. HUBNER. With large Additions by JOHN E. B. MAYOR, M.A., Professor of Latin in the University of Cambridge. Crown 8vo. 10s. 6d.

MORRIS.—Works by the Rev. RICHARD MORRIS, LL.D., President of the Philological Society, Editor of "Specimens of Early English," &c., &c.:—

HISTORICAL OUTLINES OF ENGLISH ACCIDENCE, comprising Chapters on the History and Development of the Language, and on Word-formation. New Edition. Fcap. 8vo. 6s.

ELEMENTARY LESSONS IN HISTORICAL ENGLISH GRAMMAR, containing Accidence and Wood-formation. Third Edition. 18mo. 2s. 6d.

OLIPHANT.—THE OLD AND MIDDLE ENGLISH. By T. L. KINGTON OLIPHANT, M.A., of Balliol College, Oxford. A New Edition, revised and greatly enlarged, of "The Sources of Standard English." Extra fcap. 8vo. 9s.

PEILE (JOHN, M.A.)—AN INTRODUCTION TO GREEK AND LATIN ETYMOLOGY. By JOHN PEILE, M.A., Fellow and Tutor of Christ's College, Cambridge. Third and revised Edition. Crown 8vo. 10s. 6d.

PHILOLOGY.—THE JOURNAL OF SACRED AND CLASSICAL PHILOLOGY. Four Vols. 8vo. 12s. 6d. each.

THE JOURNAL OF PHILOLOGY. New Series. Edited by JOHN E. B. MAYOR, M.A., and W. ALDIS WRIGHT, M.A. 4s. 6d. (Half-yearly.)

THE AMERICAN JOURNAL OF PHILOLOGY. Edited by BASIL L. GILDERSLEEVE, Professor of Greek in the John Hopkins University. 8vo. 4s. 6d. (Quarterly.)

PHRYNICHUS.—THE NEW PHRYNICHUS. Being a Revised Text of *The Ecloga* of the Grammarian *Phrynichus*. With Introductions and Commentary. By W. GUNION RUTHERFORD, M.A., of Balliol College, Oxford, Assistant-Master at St. Paul's. 8vo. 18s.

ROBY (H. J.)—Works by HENRY JOHN ROBY, M.A., late Fellow of St. John's College, Cambridge.

A GRAMMAR OF THE LATIN LANGUAGE, FROM PLAUTUS TO SUETONIUS. In Two Parts. Second Edition. Part I. containing:—Book I. Sounds. Book II. Inflexions. Book III. Word Formation. Appendices. Crown 8vo. 8s. 6d. Part II.—Syntax. Prepositions, &c. Crown 8vo. 10s. 6d.

A LATIN GRAMMAR FOR SCHOOLS. Crown 8vo. 5s.

SCHMIDT.—THE RYTHMIC AND METRIC OF THE CLASSICAL LANGUAGES. To which are added, the Lyric Parts of the "Medea" of Euripides and the "Antigone" of Sophocles; with Rhythmical Scheme and Commentary. By Dr. J. H. SCHMIDT. Translated from the German by J. W. WHITE, D.D. 8vo. 10s. 6d.

TAYLOR.—Works by the Rev. ISAAC TAYLOR, M.A.:—
 ETRUSCAN RESEARCHES. With Woodcuts. 8vo. 14s.
 WORDS AND PLACES; or, Etymological Illustrations of History, Ethnology, and Geography. By the Rev. ISAAC TAYLOR. Third Edition, revised and compressed. With Maps. Globe 8vo. 6s.
 GREEKS AND GOTHS: a Study on the Runes. 8vo. 9s.

TRENCH.—Works by R. CHENEVIX TRENCH, D.D., Archbishop of Dublin. (For other Works by the same Author, see THEOLOGICAL CATALOGUE.)
 SYNONYMS OF THE NEW TESTAMENT. Ninth Edition, enlarged. 8vo. cloth. 12s.
 ON THE STUDY OF WORDS. Lectures Addressed (originally) to the Pupils at the Diocesan Training School, Winchester. Eighteenth Edition, enlarged. Fcap. 8vo. 5s.
 ENGLISH PAST AND PRESENT. Eleventh Edition, revised and improved. Fcap. 8vo. 5s.
 A SELECT GLOSSARY OF ENGLISH WORDS USED FORMERLY IN SENSES DIFFERENT FROM THEIR PRESENT. Fifth Edition, enlarged. Fcap. 8vo. 5s.

VINCENT AND DICKSON.—A HANDBOOK TO MODERN GREEK. By EDGAR VINCENT, M.A., and T. G. DICKSON. Second Edition, revised and enlarged. With an Appendix on the Relation of Modern Greek to Classical Greek. By Professor R. C. JEBB. Crown 8vo. 6s.

WHITNEY.—A COMPENDIOUS GERMAN GRAMMAR. By W. D. WHITNEY, Professor of Sanskrit and Instructor in Modern Languages in Yale College. Crown 8vo. 6s.

WHITNEY AND EDGREN.—A COMPENDIOUS GERMAN AND ENGLISH DICTIONARY, with Notation of Correspondences and Brief Etymologies. By Professor W. D. WHITNEY, assisted by A. H. EDGREN. Crown 8vo. 7s. 6d.
 The GERMAN-ENGLISH Part may be had separately. Price 5s.

ZECHARIAH.—THE HEBREW STUDENT'S COMMENTARY ON HEBREW AND LXX. With Excursus on Several Grammatical Subjects. By W. H. LOWE, M.A., Hebrew Lecturer at Christ's College, Cambridge. Demy 8vo. 10s. 6d.

THE GOLDEN TREASURY SERIES.

Uniformly printed in 18mo, with Vignette Titles by J. E. MILLAIS, T. WOOLNER, W. HOLMAN HUNT, SIR NOEL PATON, ARTHUR HUGHES, &c. Engraved on Steel by JEENS. Bound in extra cloth, 4s. 6d. each volume. Also kept in morocco and calf bindings.

"Messrs. Macmillan have, in their Golden Treasury Series, especially provided editions of standard works, volumes of selected poetry, and original compositions, which entitle this series to be called classical. Nothing can be better than the literary execution, nothing more elegant than the material workmanship."—BRITISH QUARTERLY REVIEW.

THE GOLDEN TREASURY OF THE BEST SONGS AND LYRICAL POEMS IN THE ENGLISH LANGUAGE. Selected and arranged, with Notes, by FRANCIS TURNER PALGRAVE.

THE CHILDREN'S GARLAND FROM THE BEST POETS. Selected and arranged by COVENTRY PATMORE.

THE BOOK OF PRAISE. From the best English Hymn Writers. Selected and arranged by LORD SELBORNE. *A New and Enlarged Edition.*

THE FAIRY BOOK; the Best Popular Fairy Stories. Selected and rendered anew by the Author of "JOHN HALIFAX, GENTLEMAN."

"A delightful selection, in a delightful external form; full of the physical splendour and vast opulence of proper fairy tales."—SPECTATOR.

THE BALLAD BOOK. A Selection of the Choicest British Ballads. Edited by WILLIAM ALLINGHAM.

THE JEST BOOK. The Choicest Anecdotes and Sayings. Selected and arranged by MARK LEMON.

"The fullest and best jest book that has yet appeared."—SATURDAY REVIEW.

BACON'S ESSAYS AND COLOURS OF GOOD AND EVIL. With Notes and Glossarial Index. By W. ALDIS WRIGHT, M.A.

"The beautiful little edition of Bacon's Essays, now before us, does credit to the taste and scholarship of Mr. Aldis Wright."—SPECTATOR.

THE PILGRIM'S PROGRESS from this World to that which is to come. By JOHN BUNYAN.

"A beautiful and scholarly reprint."—SPECTATOR.

THE SUNDAY BOOK OF POETRY FOR THE YOUNG. Selected and arranged by C. F. ALEXANDER.

"A well-selected volume of sacred poetry."—SPECTATOR.

A BOOK OF GOLDEN DEEDS of All Times and All Countries. Gathered and Narrated Anew. By the Author of "THE HEIR OF REDCLYFFE."

"... To the young, for whom it is especially intended, as a most interesting collection of thrilling tales well told; and to their elders as a useful handbook of reference, and a pleasant one to take up when their wish is to while away a weary half-hour. We have seen no prettier gift-book for a long time."—ATHENÆUM.

THE ADVENTURES OF ROBINSON CRUSOE. Edited, from the Original Edition, by J. W. CLARK, M.A, Fellow of Trinity College, Cambridge.

THE REPUBLIC OF PLATO, Translated into English, with Notes by J. Ll. Davies, M.A., and D. J. Vaughan, M.A.

"A dainty and cheap little edition."—Examiner.

THE SONG BOOK. Words and tunes from the best Poets and Musicians. Selected and arranged by John Hullah, Professor of Vocal Music in King's College, London.

"A choice collection of the sterling songs of England, Scotland, and Ireland, with the music of each prefixed to the words. How much true wholesome pleasure such a book can diffuse, and will diffuse, we trust, through many thousand families."—Examiner.

LA LYRE FRANÇAISE. Selected and arranged, with Notes, by Gustave Masson, French Master in Harrow School.

"We doubt whether even in France itself so interesting and complete a repertory of the best French Lyrics could be found."—Notes and Queries.

TOM BROWN'S SCHOOL DAYS. By an Old Boy.

"A perfect gem of a book. The best and most healthy book about boys for boys that ever was written."—Illustrated Times.

A BOOK OF WORTHIES. Gathered from the Old Histories and written anew by the Author of "The Heir of Redclyffe."

"An admirable addition to an admirable series."—Westminster Review.

GUESSES AT TRUTH. By Two Brothers. *New Edition.*

THE CAVALIER AND HIS LADY. Selections from the Works of the First Duke and Duchess of Newcastle. With an Introductory Essay by Edward Jenkins, Author of "Ginx's Baby," &c.

"A charming little volume."—Standard.

SCOTCH SONG. A Selection of the Choicest Lyrics of Scotland Compiled and arranged, with brief Notes, by Mary Carlyle Aitkin.

"The book is one that should find a place in every library, we had almost said in every pocket."—Spectator.

DEUTSCHE LYRIK: The Golden Treasury of the best German Lyrical Poems. Selected and arranged, with Notes and Literary Introduction, by Dr. Buchheim.

"A book which all lovers of German poetry will welcome."—Westminster Review.

HERRICK: Selections from the Lyrical Poems. Arranged, with Notes, by F. T. Palgrave.

"For the first time the sweetest of English pastoral poets is placed within the range of the great world of readers."—Academy.

POEMS OF PLACES. Edited by H. W. Longfellow. England and Wales. Two Vols.

"A very happy idea, thoroughly worked out by an editor who possesses every qualification for the task."—Spectator.

MATTHEW ARNOLD'S SELECTED POEMS.
(Also a Large Paper Edition. Crown 8vo. 12s. 6d.)

"A volume which is a thing of beauty in itself."—Pall Mall Gazette.

THE GOLDEN TREASURY SERIES.

THE STORY OF THE CHRISTIANS AND MOORS IN SPAIN. By C. M. Yonge, Author of the "Heir of Redclyffe." With Vignette by Holman Hunt.

CHARLES LAMB'S TALES FROM SHAKESPEARE. Edited by the Rev. A. Ainger, M.A., Reader at the Temple.

POEMS OF WORDSWORTH. Chosen and Edited, with Preface by Matthew Arnold. (Also a Large Paper Edition. Crown 8vo. 9s.)

"A volume, every page of which is weighted with the golden fruit of poetry."—Pall Mall Gazette.

SHAKESPEARE'S SONNETS. Edited by F. T. Palgrave.

POEMS FROM SHELLEY. Selected and arranged by Stopford A. Brooke, M.A. (Also a Large Paper Edition. Crown 8vo. 12s. 6d.)

"Full of power and true appreciation of Shelley."—Spectator.

ESSAYS OF JOSEPH ADDISON. Chosen and Edited by John Richard Green, M.A., LL.D.

"This is a most welcome addition to a most excellent series."—Examiner.

POETRY OF BYRON. Chosen and arranged by Matthew Arnold. (Also a Large Paper Edition, Crown 8vo.) 9s.

"It is written in Mr. Arnold's neatest vein, and in Mr. Arnold's most pellucid manner."—Athenæum.

SELECTIONS FROM THE WRITINGS OF WALTER SAVAGE LANDOR.—Arranged and Edited by Professor Sidney Colvin.

SIR THOMAS BROWNE'S RELIGIO MEDICI; Letter to a Friend, &c., and Christian Morals. Edited by W. A. Greenhill, M.D.

"Dr. Greenhill's annotations display care and research to a degree rare among English editors. The bibliographical details furnished leave nothing to be desired."—Athenæum.

THE SPEECHES AND TABLE-TALK OF THE PROPHET MOHAMMAD.—Chosen and Translated, with an Introduction and Notes, by Stanley Lane-Poole.

SELECTIONS FROM COWPER'S POEMS.—Chosen and arranged by Mrs. Oliphant. [*In the press.*

Now Publishing, in Crown 8vo. Price 3s. 6d. each.

The English Citizen.

A SERIES OF SHORT BOOKS ON HIS RIGHTS AND RESPONSIBILITIES.

This series is intended to meet the demand for accessible information on the ordinary conditions, and the current terms, of our political life. Ignorance of these not only takes from the study of history the interest which comes from a contact with practical politics, but, still worse, it unfits men for their place as intelligent citizens. The series will deal with the details of the machinery whereby our Constitution works, and the broad lines upon which it has been constructed.

The following Volumes are ready:—

CENTRAL GOVERNMENT. By H. D. TRAILL, D.C.L., late Fellow of St. John's College, Oxford.

THE ELECTORATE AND THE LEGISLATURE. By SPENCER WALPOLE, Author of "The History of England from 1815."

THE NATIONAL BUDGET; THE NATIONAL DEBT; TAXES AND RATES. By A. J. WILSON.

THE POOR LAW. By Rev. T. W. FOWLE, M.A.

THE STATE AND ITS RELATION TO TRADE. By T. H. FARRER.

THE STATE IN RELATION TO LABOUR. By W. STANLEY JEVONS, LL.D., F.R.S.

THE STATE AND THE CHURCH. By the Hon. A. ARTHUR ELLIOT, M.P.

FOREIGN RELATIONS. By SPENCER WALPOLE, Author of "The History of England from 1815."

LOCAL GOVERNMENT. By M. D. CHALMERS.

In Preparation:—

THE STATE AND EDUCATION. By HENRY CRAIK, M.A.

JUSTICE AND POLICE. By FREDERICK POLLOCK, late Fellow of Trinity College, Cambridge.

THE STATE AND THE LAND. By F. POLLOCK, late Fellow of Trinity College, Cambridge. [*In the press.*

INDIA. By J. S. COTTON, late Fellow of Queen's College, Oxford. *In the press.*

COLONIES AND DEPENDENCIES. By E. J. PAYNE, Fellow of University College, Oxford. [*In the press.*

LONDON: R. CLAY, SONS, AND TAYLOR, PRINTERS.

www.ingramcontent.com/pod-product-compliance
Lightning Source LLC
Chambersburg PA
CBHW021425300426
44114CB00010B/649